W9-DCY-559

WITHDRAWN

THE
UNKNOWN
LEONARDO

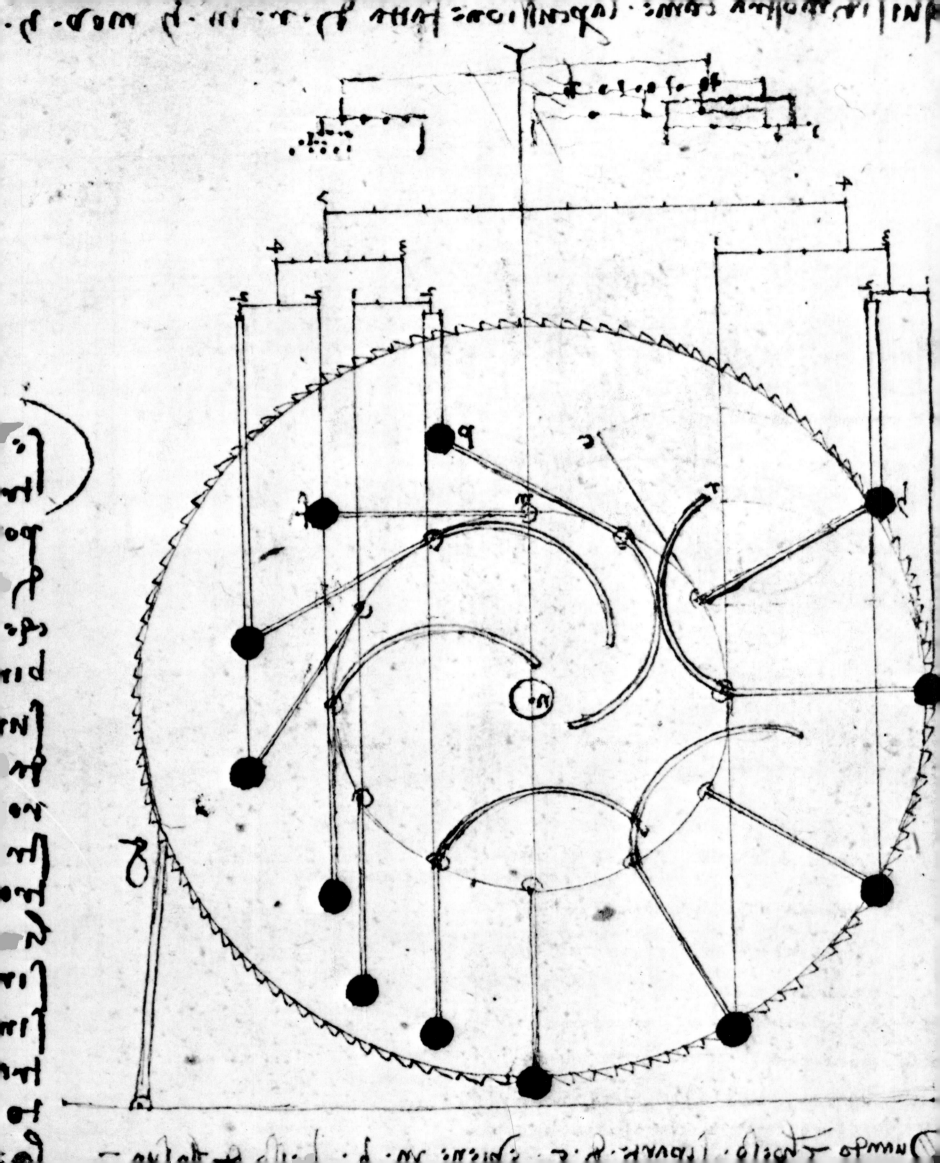

THE UNKNOWN LEONARDO

EDITED BY

LADISLAO RETI

DESIGNED BY

EMIL M. BÜHRER

McGRAW-HILL BOOK COMPANY

NEW YORK   ST. LOUIS   SAN FRANCISCO   TORONTO

THIS BOOK IS DEDICATED TO
DR. ELMER BELT
FOR HIS MANY CONTRIBUTIONS TO THE ADVANCEMENT
OF VINCIAN SCHOLARSHIP.

Library of Congress Cataloging in Publication Data
Reti, Ladislao. The unknown Leonardo.
1. Leonardo da Vinci, 1452–1519.
2. Madrid. Biblioteca Nacional. MSS. (8936–8937).
I. Title.

ND623.L5R45   759.5   73-15962
ISBN 0-07-037196-2

Phototypeset in 'Linofilm' Garamond by Jolly & Barber Ltd.,
Rugby, England
Printed in Switzerland by Polygraphische Gesellschaft, Laupen
Bound by Grossbuchbinderei H. & J. Schuhmacher, Berne

THE AUTHORS

SILVIO A. BEDINI
DEPUTY DIRECTOR, NATIONAL MUSEUM OF HISTORY & TECHNOLOGY
WASHINGTON, D.C.

ANNA MARIA BRIZIO
PROFESSOR OF ART HISTORY
UNIVERSITÀ STATALE OF MILAN
MEMBER OF THE "COMMISSIONE VINCIANA"

MARIA VITTORIA BRUGNOLI
SUPERINTENDENT OF THE MUSEUMS OF MANTUA
LIBERO DOCENTE OF ART HISTORY
UNIVERSITY OF ROME

ANDRÉ CHASTEL
PROFESSOR AT THE COLLÈGE DE FRANCE
PARIS

BERN DIBNER
DIRECTOR, BURNDY LIBRARY
NORWALK, CONNECTICUT

LUDWIG H. HEYDENREICH
HONORARY PROFESSOR, UNIVERSITY OF MUNICH
FORMER DIRECTOR, ZENTRALINSTITUT FÜR KUNSTGESCHICHTE

AUGUSTO MARINONI
PROFESSOR OF FILOLOGIA ROMANZA, UNIVERSITÀ CATTOLICA OF MILAN
MEMBER OF THE "COMMISSIONE VINCIANA"
MEMBER OF THE ACCADEMIA DEI LINGEI

LADISLAO RETI
PROFESSOR EMERITUS, UNIVERSITY OF CALIFORNIA
LOS ANGELES

EMANUEL WINTERNITZ
CURATOR OF MUSICAL INSTRUMENTS, METROPOLITAN MUSEUM OF ART
VISITING PROFESSOR OF MUSIC, CITY UNIVERSITY OF NEW YORK

CARLO ZAMMATTIO
ENGINEER, TRIESTE

TABLE OF CONTENTS

CAPTIONS THROUGHOUT BY RON BAILEY

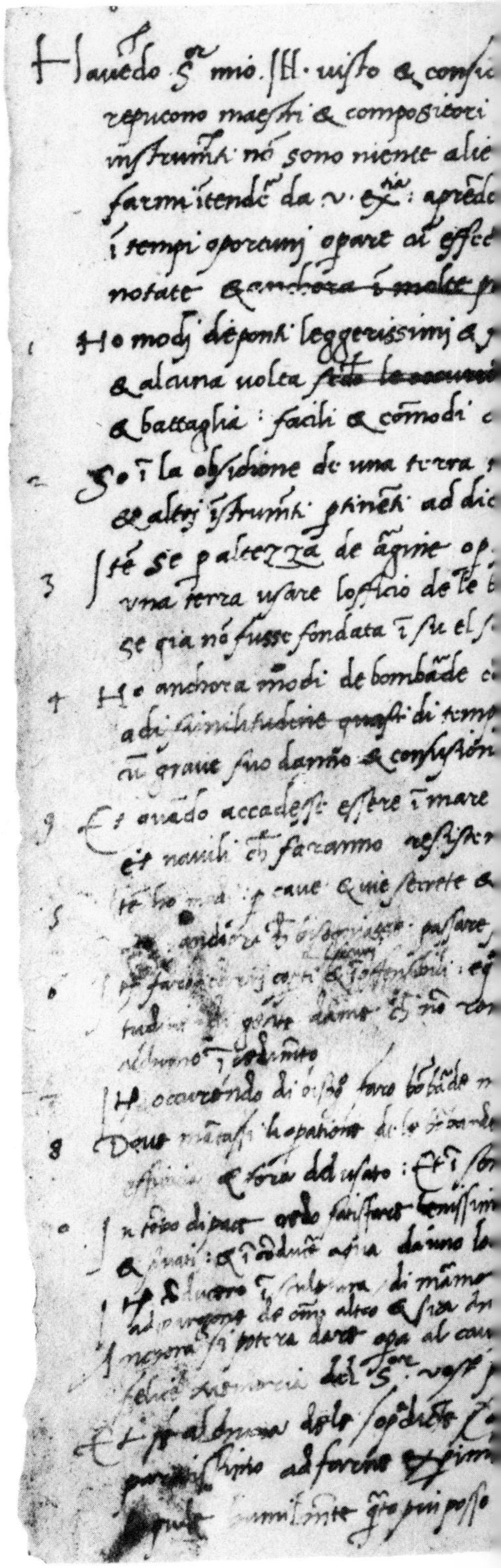

INTRODUCTION

"He was like a man who awoke too early in the darkness, while the others were all still asleep," wrote Sigmund Freud. Many of Leonardo's notebooks, folios, writings, and drawings disappeared into that darkness, and it is their rediscovery and reassemblage that is gradually illuminating the enigma of his genius, gradually extending our knowledge of the unknown Leonardo.

Leonardo's notebooks reveal a man whose curiosity seemed boundless, who could explore

Most Illustrious Lord, Having now sufficiently considered the specimens of all those who proclaim themselves skilled contrivers of instruments of war, and that the invention and operation of the said instruments are nothing different from those in common use: I shall endeavour, without prejudice to any one else, to explain myself to your Excellency, showing your Lordship my secrets, and then offering them to your best pleasure and approbation to work with effect at opportune moments on all those things which, in part, shall be briefly noted below.

1 I have a sort of extremely light and strong bridges, adapted to be most easily carried, and with them you may pursue, and at any time flee from the enemy: and others, secure and indestructible by fire and battle, easy and convenient to lift and place. Also methods of burning and destroying those of the enemy.

2 I know how, when a place is besieged, to take the water out of the trenches, and make endless variety of bridges, and covered ways and ladders, and other machines pertaining to such expeditions.

3 Item. If, by reason of the height of the banks, or the strength of the place and its position, it is impossible, when besieging a place, to avail oneself of the plan of bombardment, I have methods for destroying every rock or other fortress, even if it were founded on a rock, &c.

4 Again, I have kinds of mortars; most convenient and easy to carry; and with these I can fling small stones almost resembling a storm; and with the smoke of these cause great terror to the enemy, to his great detriment and confusion.

9 And if the fight should be at sea I have kinds of many machines most efficient for offence and defence; and vessels which will resist the attack of the largest guns and powder and fumes.

5 Item. I have means by secret and tortuous mines and ways, made without noise, to reach a designated [spot], even if it were needed to pass under a trench or a river.

6 Item. I will make covered chariots, safe and unattackable, which, entering among the enemy with their artillery, there is no body of men so great but they would break them. And behind these, infantry could follow quite unhurt and without any hindrance.

7 Item. In case of need I will make big guns, mortars, and light ordnance of fine and useful forms, out of the common type.

8 Where the operation of bombardment might fail, I would contrive catapults, mangonels, trabocchi, and other machines of marvellous efficacy and not in common use. And in short, according to the variety of cases, I can contrive various and endless means of offence and defence.

10 In time of peace I believe I can give perfect satisfaction and to the equal of any other in architecture and the composition of buildings public and private; and in guiding water from one place to another.

Item. I can carry out sculpture in marble, bronze, or clay, and also I can do in painting whatever may be done, as well as any other, be he who he may.

Again, the bronze horse may be taken in hand, which is to be to the immortal glory and eternal honour of the prince your father of happy memory, and of the illustrious house of Sforza.

And if any of the above-named things seem to any one to be impossible or not feasible, I am most ready to make the experiment in your park, or in whatever place may please your Excellency — to whom I commend myself with the utmost humility, &c.

This is the famous letter of self-recommendation from Leonardo da Vinci to the Duke of Milan, Lodovico Sforza. Though the surviving document is not in Leonardo's handwriting, its authenticity is unquestioned. ATLANTICUS 391a

painting techniques as well as hydraulic engineering, comparative anatomy and musical instruments, massive sculpture and machines of all kinds. Many of his designs and concepts were too advanced for his contemporaries; interestingly, many of the projects he worked on became more widely understood approximately 200 years after his death. This book, *The Unknown Leonardo,* developed from the rediscovery of two manuscripts in Madrid in 1965.

The two notebooks found in Madrid had been the cause of speculation in the world of letters since Leonardo's death, when many of his notebooks had become widely dispersed. By the early 18th century the two volumes known today as Codex Madrid I and II were in the palace library of Philip V of Spain, where they remained until about 1830. At that time, they were transferred to what is now the Biblioteca Nacional. Although the manuscripts previously had been identified with the call numbers Aa. 119 and Aa. 120, in the transfer they were instead catalogued as Aa. 19 and Aa. 20. For 135 years, the notebooks were officially lost, until a new search was undertaken at the urging of Vincian scholars, and in early 1965 the two manuscripts were found in the place corresponding exactly to their correct call numbers. The notebooks were exhibited, and shortly thereafter, the Spanish Ministry of Education authorized McGraw-Hill and Taurus Ediciones to publish a five-volume facsimile edition of the codices, with accompanying transcription, translation, and commentary by the distinguished Vincian scholar Ladislao Reti. *The Unknown Leonardo,* also edited by Reti, presents for the general reader new evidence gathered from the two codices. Codex Madrid

I, a well-organized notebook dealing with applied mechanics and mechanical theory, confirms Leonardo's position as the first systematic technologist in history. Codex Madrid II is much more typical of Leonardo's writings. Loosely organized, it is a fascinating mixture of rough notes and sketches about canal building, geometry, fortifications, painting, perspective, optics, casting, and other subjects. It contains maps and topographic sketches, and the designs of an enormous bronze statue for the Sforza family, his long-time patrons.

The essays in *The Unknown Leonardo,* written by 10 of the world's foremost Leonardo scholars, clarify the contents of these two "new" codices, using better-known Vincian writings to place the information in a clear perspective.

The first chapter, by Anna Maria Brizio, concerns Leonardo's thoughts about painting, which he considered as "really science and the legitimate daughter of nature." Science and painting were directly connected for Leonardo, as Brizio discusses in terms of the *Last Supper.* His studies on physics and mechanics and his knowledge of perspective and painting merge there to produce a timelessly beautiful work of art. The Madrid Codices also establish time and technical references for the destroyed masterpiece, the *Battle of Anghiari.* Beyond all this, however, the codices are in themselves works of art, with their quick sketches, detailed studies and mechanical designs.

Augusto Marinoni's chapter on Leonardo's writing traces the history and dispersal of the various manuscripts, especially the Madrid Codices, placing them in relation to the other known writings. This chapter also reviews the style and content of the various codices, showing the reader the difficulty of following Leonardo's tumultuous and often-disorganized thought processes.

However, some sections of the codices are very clear, such as the folios in Codex Madrid II dealing with the Sforza monument described in Maria Vittoria Brugnoli's chapter. This monument, a 23-foot-high bronze equestrian statue, was an ongoing project for Leonardo throughout the 20 years he remained in Milan at the court of Lodovico; political vicissitudes prevented its realization. Leonardo formulated for the monument a new and sophisticated casting process, designed to eliminate the problems of the centuries-old lost-wax process. The new process was not to be tried out for almost 200 years, but it seems clear that later sculptors must have been aware of Leonardo's writings and that the new process that he invented here revolutionized casting methods. Again, Brugnoli clarifies the link between art and science.

The chapter by Emanuel Winternitz on music treats systematically Leonardo's profound occupation with music, which he considered the highest of arts, after painting. In the Madrid Codices Leonardo's sketches include a bell with two hammers and multiple dampers, a unique type of three-tone bagpipe, and a portable organ. In creating these ideas for new musical instruments, Leonardo applied what he knew about one instrument to another.

The chapter by Ludwig Heydenreich on military architecture deals with the information in Codex Madrid II regarding Leonardo's plans to divert the Arno as part of the ongoing war between Florence and Pisa, and also to fortify the town of Piombino. Again, as Heydenreich points out, the scientific notes for the fortifications are mingled with musings on the natural beauty of this coastal town, and again the multiple facets of Leonardo's mind can be seen at work in his notes.

The chapters by Bern Dibner on machines and weaponry and Carlo Zammattio on hydraulics and structures are more technical in scope. Dibner discusses in detail Leonardo's ballistic concerns and sketches, such as those of the paraboloid curve of a trajectory that is deformed by air resistance, which was developed into mathematical ballistics years later by Newton. Leonardo also designed experimentally a handgun matchlock, a multiple-barrel light cannon, and even a steam cannon similar to a type used in the American Civil War.

Zammattio's chapter also mentions specific structural and hydraulic discoveries that were hypothesized by Daniel Bernoulli in the 18th century. For example, through his study of water flow connected with the plans to alter the course of the Arno discussed in Codex Madrid II, Leonardo worked out what was to become the basic theorem of hydrodynamics. It is in Codex Madrid I that he noted energy was a function of position and motion, thus differentiating potential from kinetic energy. He also worked on stress distribution, especially in regard to arch construction, again combining visual and structural elements, synthesizing his capacities of engineer and artist.

The chapter by André Chastel on the treatise on painting discusses the notes in Codex Madrid II that would later be elaborated in Libro A, with his principles of painting and notes on anatomy, visual perception, color range, perspective, and light reflections, or *lustro.* Chastel's chapter indicates Leonardo's broad view of the entire field of painting.

Further technical discoveries are explicated in

the chapter on time measurement by Silvio Bedini and Ladislao Reti, where Leonardo's designs incorporating pendulums are discussed. Although Leonardo did not specifically design a pendulum clock, Codex Madrid I provides substantial evidence of his grasp of the relationship between the length of the pendulum and the period of its swing which, combined with his general interest in time measurement, points out another area where later inventions were foreshadowed.

Finally, Reti's chapter on the elements of machines discusses in detail the mechanical devices of Codex Madrid I, showing that Leonardo had adopted a true scientific mode of thought: that a general principle can be derived through specific examples. This attitude is as novel as were some of the specifics Leonardo studied – screws, gears, bearings, rollers, axles – the entire range and variety of mechanics. Again, many of his sketches were years ahead of application, including a sketch for a ball-bearing design identical to one made as late as the 1920s for blind-flying instruments used in airplane navigation.

In each chapter, sketches and text re-emphasize the complexity of Leonardo's mind, his unrestrained curiosity, the congruence of art and science. The studies hint, too, at Leonardo the man – persistent, incredibly imaginative, fascinated by minute detail. The reader gains a sense of the isolation and frustration of a mind working in situations where he could receive encouragement but rarely the challenge of cooperative work with his peers. Although he worked with the brilliant leaders of his time – Verrocchio, Machiavelli, Luca Pacioli, Lodovico Sforza – none of these were fully his peer, and in the end he was alone with his curiosity.

On some levels, one can only speculate about Leonardo, "the most relentlessly curious man in history," as Kenneth Clark describes him. The more one learns, the more one desires to learn and the more challenging Leonardo's mystery becomes. Perhaps this is best expressed by Leonardo himself in Codex Madrid I, in a declaration addressed to the reader which indicates his awareness of his own isolation in time, and challenges people through the years to join him in examining the mystery of being alive:
"Peruse me O reader, if you find delight in my work, since this profession very seldom returns to this world, and the perseverance to pursue it and to invent such things anew is found in few people. And come men, to see the wonders which may be discovered in nature by such studies."   MADRID I 6r

Opposite page. Self-portrait of Leonardo from Windsor 12579 recto.

HIS LIFE
HIS WORK
HIS TIME

The 67 years that made up the life of Leonardo da Vinci embraced one of the most tumultuous and creative eras in human history. Events during that period helped set the stage for the modern world. His lifetime saw the development of the printing press, the discovery of the New World and the sea lanes to the Orient, and a burst of creativity including the works of a most complex genius – Leonardo himself. On the opposite page is a description of the great rebirth of the human spirit, the Renaissance, which was reaching its peak as Leonardo came into the world. On the following pages are a brief account of his boyhood and an illustrated chronology of his adult life, his works, and the cultural and political events that helped shape Leonardo's world.

THE RENAISSANCE
WAS THE REBIRTH
OF MAN OUT OF THE DARK YEARS
OF MEDIEVAL SUPERSTITION
AND BELIEF
AND A RETURN TO THE LIGHT
OF HUMAN REASON

THE RENAISSANCE

The Renaissance was the rebirth of man out of the dark years of medieval superstition and belief and a return to the light of human reason. Italy and particularly Florence were at the heart of this reawakening of the human spirit – what more promising time or place could have existed as Leonardo's milieu? At the time of his birth in 1452, Italy had been rapidly moving away from the medieval era. This movement had begun on a scholarly level, with the humanist writers, but was clearly linked with scientific developments, ecclesiastical change, and the growth of capitalistic rather than feudal economic structures.

Florence, scarcely 20 miles away from Vinci, Leonardo's birthplace, was at this time the richest city in Europe. Bankers and wool merchants had produced a stable economic basis upon which healthy merchant and craftsmen classes could be built. In addition, Florence, a republic for thirty years when Leonardo was born, had been governed by humanist leaders who believed in the dignity of man and the possibility of achieving happiness through the application of intelligence, and who initiated interest in the classical age of ancient Rome and Greece. This in turn influenced the poet scholars like Boccaccio, Petrarch, and Dante in that revival of classical learning, literature, architecture, and art called humanism because it centered on man.

Scientific developments were also connected with the changes in Leonardo's world. For example, the improvement and increased use of cannon and gunpowder drastically altered the concepts of feudal knighthood and armored battle. Later, the invention of the mariner's compass made possible the voyages of Columbus and Vasco da Gama, which literally expanded European medieval horizons. Similarly, Copernican astronomy changed man's perspective of himself and his world in relation to the universe. Gutenberg's invention of the printing press and the concurrent development of inexpensive paper were perhaps the most devastating blow to feudal hierarchies, opening up literature, science, art, philosophy – anything that could be written – to the common man.

These scientific and economic changes were to profoundly affect the church. The growth of national identities and languages gave people a view now broader than parish limits. In the medieval world, final authority for both temporal and religious matters had been the church. However, ecclesiastical battles over scientific discoveries further weakened the church, whose authority was finally challenged by the Protestant Reformation. Martin Luther, born only 30 years after Leonardo, symbolizes this challenge to ecclesiastical power.

Luther is, however, also a representative of the "giants" who changed the medieval world: international financiers like the Fuggers; writers like Shakespeare, Montaigne, Rabelais, Cervantes; philosophers like Calvin and Erasmus; scientists like Copernicus and Galileo; political leaders like the Medici, the Borgias, and Machiavelli. Throughout Europe, the limitations of the medieval world were being transformed into the open challenges of the Renaissance. In Italy, the visual arts dominated, and Leonardo, who studied with the great master Verrocchio, had as his contemporaries artists such as Bramante, Botticelli, Donatello, Michelangelo, and Raphael.

By the late fifteenth century, the Renaissance was poised between the humanist links to antiquity and the challenges of new social, political, economic, scientific, and ecclesiastical developments. The world was ready for an artist who could go beyond art, a scientist whose curiosity accepted no limitations, a man who could go from the ancient world to a modern one. Leonardo was both the product of his times, artist, scientist, inventor, sculptor, engineer, musician, writer, technologist – and more – and the shaper of his times as well as our own. From the Renaissance to the twentieth century, the work of Leonardo transcends time.

FROM
THE RENAISSANCE
TO THE
TWENTIETH CENTURY
THE WORK
OF
LEONARDO
TRANSCENDS TIME

This stone house in the village of Anchiano
near Vinci was the childhood home
of Leonardo da Vinci.
It may also have been the house where he was born.

"A grandson of mine was born,
son of Ser Piero my son, on April 15,
Saturday at three o'clock in the night.
His name was Lionardo."

Thus the grandfather, following the notary's custom of writing down noteworthy events in his family, recorded the birth of Leonardo da Vinci. The boyhood home and perhaps his birthplace was the stone house above, which still stands near the little town of Vinci, about 20 miles west of Florence. The house belonged to the family of his father, who, like four generations before him, was a notary, an interpreter of deeds and other documents in trading transactions. The family had lived around Vinci since the 13th century and had become members of the local gentry, upper-middle-class landholders. Leonardo's mother Caterina was of a lower class, and she and Ser Piero were not married. Tax records of the time refer to "Lionardo, son of Ser Piero, illegitimate," but bastardy carried little stigma at a time when even the Pope sired children and recognized them as his own. Before he was five, records show, Leonardo was living in his father's house and had a new mother, the first of Ser Piero's lawful wives. In all Leonardo's voluminous writings there is scarcely any mention of his father or his mother. Ser Piero had 12 children and lived to the age of 77. When he died Leonardo made a rather impersonal note of the fact in a notebook – and got the age wrong.

AN ILLUSTRATED CHRONOLOGY OF LEONARDO

At right begins an illustrated chronology in capsule form of the life, works, and turbulent era of Leonardo da Vinci. Section I is a biography underscored by a band of various colors denoting the lifetime itinerary that took him from his birthplace Vinci to retirement and death in France – at Cloux, near Amboise – 67 years later. Section II presents a sampling of paintings, drawings, and other works by Leonardo for which some documentation exists. Section III describes the cultural events that were occurring in Italy and the rest of Europe even as Leonardo was shaking the very foundations of art and science. Section IV tells of the political context in which he lived: a time of intrigue and constantly shifting alliances that made warfare the most important of the arts. A portion of the chronology, beginning on page 15, is shaded green to indicate the 15-year period covered by the newly rediscovered Madrid Codices.

■ = Illustration
✳ = Date of birth
† = Date of death

I HIS LIFE

Of his youth Leonardo says virtually nothing in the many notebooks he left. His formal education most likely consisted of reading, writing, and basic mathematics. Later he would bemoan his lack of a scholar's education and would struggle to master Latin and geometry. Perhaps more of significance in shaping the artist was the breathtaking landscape over which he roamed as a boy – with its vineyards, pines, and tumbling streams still one of the most beautiful in Italy. Art was regarded by many as a low calling, and ordinarily the boy would have been destined to follow his forebears as a notary. One explanation for his father's willingness to let him become a painter is presented below.

VINCI

II HIS WORK

There exists no documentary evidence of works executed by Leonardo during his first 20 years. But a story has been handed down of an early painting that foreshadowed both the mature artist and the ingenious creator of court amusements. A peasant is said to have asked Leonardo's father Ser Piero to get a wooden shield decorated for him in Florence. Ser Piero gave it instead to his son. Leonardo painted on the shield – from his own collection of lizards, bats, and other animals – a monster so artfully fearsome that it startled his father. Ser Piero bought another decorated shield for the peasant and sold Leonardo's for a handsome profit. Thus convinced there was a market for Leonardo's talent, so the story goes, he decided to apprentice his son to the noted Florentine artist Andrea del Verrocchio.

III HIS TIME   Cultural Events

About the time of Leonardo's birth an event took place in Germany that would profoundly effect the Renaissance: the perfection by Gutenberg of the first printing press and the reproduction of the Gutenberg Bible (right). Printing spread rapidly through Italy, intensifying the revived interest in learning and opening up an era of wider communication. It was to be one of the many ironies of Leonardo's life that his extraordinary ideas and inventions would remain buried in his notebooks for nearly 150 years before any of them reached the world through the medium of print.

IV HIS TIME   Political Events

Not far from Leonardo's birthplace and about the same time was born another major figure of the Renaissance who would have a vastly different influence. He was Girolamo Savonarola, the Dominican friar who sparked a fiery revival of religion and became the scourge of Florence. He attacked the worldliness of the Pope and the self-indulgence of Florence. He encouraged the burning of all "vanities" – cosmetics, jewelry, even some major works of art. Having driven the Medicis from power, he ruled the city for 3 years; at one time he even had Botticelli ready to burn some of his "worldly" paintings. Savonarola was excommunicated by the Pope and burned at the stake as an alleged heretic and a martyr.

1469	1470	1471	1472	1473	1474	1475	1476

Leonardo's father lives in Palazzo del Podestrè in Florence ; Leonardo begins apprentice-ship in Verrocchio's ■ workshop with Botticelli, Perugino, Lorenzo di Credi.

Under Lorenzo de' Medici (the Magni-ficent), ■ Florence is the center of the Renaissance and humanism in Italy.

Leonardo's name is listed in the register of Florentine painters, *The Guild of St. Luke.* ■

1473–1475: Leonardo collaborates on the *Baptism of Christ* commissioned to Ver-rocchio; contributes the kneeling angel ■ and some landscape in the background. Florence, Uffizi.

Leonardo with all the pupils of Verrocchio is accused anony-mously of sodomy. The accusation is not proved and all are declared not guilty. He remains in Verrocchio's workshop.

FLORENCE

No work by Leonardo known from this period.

Aug. 5, 1473: Pen drawing of the Arno valley, ■ Florence, Uffizi; first dated work known to be by Leonardo.
1473–1475: *Annunciation*, Florence, Uffizi.
1473–1475: *Madonna with the Flower*, Munich, Alte Pinakothek.

✳ Vasco da Gama, Port. seafarer and viceroy in India; dis-coverer of sea route to East India (†1524). Venice develops to be-come the most impor-tant printing and pub-lishing place under Aldus Manutius, founder of the Aldine Press.
†Fra Filippo Lippi, Ital. painter.

Pollaiuolo engraves *Battle of Nude Men*. ■
✳ Pietro Bembo, who fostered the use of the Tuscan language as Ital. written word (†1547).
Facade S. Maria No-vella (designed by Alberti) completed.

Piero della Francesca paints the portrait of the Duke of Urbino. ■
First printing of Dante's *Divine Come-dy*.
✳ Fra Bartolommeo, Ital. painter (†1517).
✳ Lucas Cranach the Elder, Germ. painter (†1553).

✳ Albrecht Dürer, Germ. painter, copper-plate engraver, wood-cutter in Nuremberg (†1528). First Euro-pean observatory is founded in Nuremberg. Oldest map printing in Germany. Commines writes *Mé-moires sur le règne de Louis XI*.

Printing of musical notes introduced. ■

✳ Copernicus, in Thorn; Polish astron-omer. Creator of the heliocentric world picture (†1543). Rise of oil painting in Italy.

Caxton publishes first book printed in English, *The Game and*

Playe of the Chess. ■
Syrlin the Elder com-pletes choir stalls in Ulm Cathedral (Germ.)

Pope Sixtus IV opens the Vatican Library to the public.
✳ Michelangelo Buonarroti, Ital. sculptor, painter, architect, and poet (†1564).
†Paolo Uccello. The use of the rosary spreads.
Botticelli, *Mars and Venus* (portraits of Giuliano de' Medici and Simonetta).

Verrocchio's sculpture *David*. ■
Botticelli paints *Adoration of the Kings*.

The Platonic Academy rises under Lorenzo's patronage.

✳ Niccolò Machia-velli, ■ Ital. statesman, philosopher, poet (†1527).
†Piero de' Medici.

After fruitless attempt of Florentine families to oust Medicis, Loren-zo de' Medici rules in Florence (until †1492).

✳ Charles VIII, King of France from 1483 until 1498 (†). Turks chase Venetians out of Negropont. Henry VI (Lancaster) temporarily (until 1471) pushes Edward IV (York) off the English throne (War of the Roses).

†Pope Paul II. Francesco della Rove-re is elected Pope Sixtus IV (†1484); ■ under him extensive nepotism and simony. Ferrara becomes duke-dom under the house of Este.

Concordat with Louis XI. Crimea comes under Turkish supreme authority.

Charles the Bold ■ conquers Geldern and Zutphen. Venice tries to con-solidate its protec-torate in Cyprus.

Louis XI ■ forms league with Swiss against Charles the Bold. Isabella I (the Cath-olic), Queen of Castile and Aragon as wife of Ferdinand V. Date of union of both countries to govern the kingdom of Spain.

Celebration in Piazza Santa Croce of re-newed league between Venice and Florence.
✳ Cesare Borgia, son of the Spanish cardi-nal Rodrigo Borja who will be Pope Alexan-der VI.
✳ Condottiere Barto-lommeo Colleoni. Under Huaina Capac the Inca empire reach-es its highest level.
✳ Francisco Pizarro, Span. conqueror of Inca empire (†1541, assassinated).

Assassination of Galeazzo Maria Sforza, ■ Duke of Mi-lan; succeeded by Gian Galeazzo II (†1494). The Swiss defeated Charles the Bold.

| 1477 | 1478 | 1479 | 1480 | 1481 | 1482 | 1483 | 1484 |

1478
January: Commission to Leonardo for the altarpiece of the chapel in the Palazzo della Signoria. Later executed by Filippino Lippi.
Jan. 10: Receives commission for altarpiece in the Palazzo Vecchio.
Mar. 14: Leonardo receives first payment for altarpiece in Palazzo Vecchio.

1479
View of Florence ■ during the time of Leonardo.

1481
Monastery of S. Donato a Scopeto commissions the *Adoration of the Magi,* ■ Florence, Uffizi.
Sept. 28: Monks of S. Donato make last payment for *Adoration of the Magi.*

1482

Leonardo goes to Milan without having completed the *Adoration,* and will stay there until the fall of Lodovico il Moro ■ in 1499.

1483
Apr. 25: The Brethren of the Immaculate Conception commission Leonardo (and the De Predis brothers) to paint the altarpiece in their Chapel of San Francesco il Grande. The painting is to be the *Virgin of the Rocks.*

MILAN

1476–1478: *Annunciation,* ■ Paris, Louvre. Originally commissioned to Verrocchio.

1478
1478–1518: Codex Atlanticus.
1478–1518: Windsor Collection.
Last third of 1478: Pen drawing of two heads and mechanical devices, Florence, Uffizi. The folio is torn; at the bottom one can read, "...ber 1478 I started the two Virgins Mary."
Benois Madonna, Leningrad, Hermitage.
1478–1480: *Portrait of Ginevra Benci,* Washington, National Gallery of Art.

Dec. 28: Drawing of Bernardo Bandini Baroncelli, ■ murderer of Giuliano de' Medici, Bayonne, Musée Bonnat.

1481
1481: *Adoration of the Magi,* ■ Florence, Uffizi.
1480–1518: Codex Arundel.
1480: Leonardo paints *St. Jerome,* Rome, Vatican Picture Gallery.

1483
1483–1486: Leonardo paints the *Virgin of the Rocks,* ■ Paris, Louvre.

1484
This drawing ■ can be dated among the first studies for the bronze statue dedicated to Lodovico il Moro's father, Francesco Sforza. Windsor 12358r.

1477
Botticelli paints the *Primavera.* ■
✳ Titian, Ital. painter (†1576).
Universities of Upsala, Tübingen, and Mainz founded.

1478
Reuchlin, ■ Germ. humanist, starts to teach the Greek language in Germany.
✳ Thomas More, Engl. statesman and philosopher (†1535, decapitated).

1479
†Antonello da Messina, Ital. painter (✳1430).
Church of the Assumption in Moscow by Fioravante, Ital. architect (1415–1486).
University of Copenhagen founded.
Verrocchio *Decapitation of St. John the Baptist,* relief.

1480
Albrecht Altdorfer, Germ. painter and copperplate engraver (†1538).
Schongauer's *Death of Mary,* engraving.
Memling portrait of Barbara Morel.
†Jean Fouquet, French painter (✳1420).
Benedetto da Maiano paints *Filippo Strozzi.*

1481
Michael Pacher does altarpiece of St. Wolfgang, ■ Austria.

1482
†Luca della Robbia, Florentine sculptor (†1482).
Hans Memling's *Annunciation.*
Botticelli, Ghirlandaio, Perugino, Piero di Cosimo, and Cosimo Roselli are summoned to Rome by Sixtus IV to decorate the Sistine Chapel.

1483

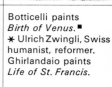

★ Luther, ■ Germ. religious reformer (†1546).
★ Raphael, Ital. painter and architect (†1520).
✳ William Tindale, Engl. reformer and Bible translator (†1536, assassinated).

1484
Botticelli paints *Birth of Venus.* ■
✳ Ulrich Zwingli, Swiss humanist, reformer.
Ghirlandaio paints *Life of St. Francis.*

1477
†Charles the Bold, slain in Battle of Nancy. ■
Maximilian I marries Mary of Burgundy (†1482) and wins the Netherlands for Hapsburg.

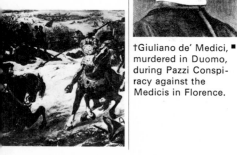

1478

†Giuliano de' Medici, ■ murdered in Duomo, during Pazzi Conspiracy against the Medicis in Florence.

1479
The Sforza Castle, ■ residence of Lodovico Sforza (il Moro), who seized power during the revolt in Milan.

1480

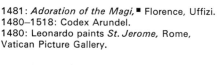

King Louis XI of France unites Anjou, Maine, and Provence with the crown. Turks driven from Otranto. Reintroduction of Inquisition in Spain.

Ivan III (the Great), ■ grandfather of Ivan IV (the Terrible), frees Russia from the Tatar yoke.
Beginning of "Age of the Fighting Empires" in Japan (until 1600).

1483

†Louis XI, King of France since 1461. Charles VIII, ■ king until 1498.
Richard III kills Edward V and succeeds as King of England (until †1485).

1484
†Pope Sixtus IV. Innocent VIII, ■ Pope until 1492, greatly increased witch persecution.

1485	1486	1487	1488	1489	1490	1491	1492

Apr. 23: Leonardo receives a commission to do a Nativity for Matthias Corvinus, King of Hungary.

July, until January 1488: Payment for a model of a section of the dome of Milan Cathedral.

Studies by Francesco di Giorgio Martini, and note by Leonardo. ■ July 22: The 10-year-old Salai (Jacopo dei Caprotti) comes to live with Leonardo.

Jan. 26 and following days: Tournament to celebrate the marriage of Lodovico Sforza with Beatrice d'Este. ■ (Painting by Leonardo, Milan, Ambrosiana).

1484–1488: Leonardo paints the portrait of Cecilia Gallerani, ■ mistress of Il Moro, the *Lady with an Ermine*, Cracow, Czartoryski Gallery.

Ca. 1487: Grotesque heads, ■ Windsor 12495r.
1487–1490: Codex Forster I₂ (folios 41–55).
1487–1488: Ms. B.

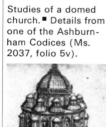

Studies of a domed church. ■ Details from one of the Ashburnham Codices (Ms. 2037, folio 5v).

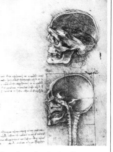

Anatomical studies of skulls, ■ Windsor 19057r. "April 2": date written by Leonardo on folio 42 of Anatomy Ms. B (Windsor 19059r).

Leonardo paints the *Portrait of a Musician*, ■ Milan, Ambrosiana. Ms. C, folio 15v, "On April 23, 1490, I started this book and restarted on the horse."

May 17: Preparing to cast *Il Cavallo*, ■ Codex Madrid II 157r.
1491–1493: Codex Madrid II folios 141–157.

Ms. A.
1492–1497: Codex Madrid I.

Alberti's book on architecture published. Mantegna's *Madonna with Singing Angels*.
✴ Adrian Willaert, Dutch composer, head of Venetian school (†1562).
†Rudolf Agricola, leading Germ. humanist at University of Tübingen.
Giovanni Bellini paints *Santa Conversazione*.

Savonarola begins his preaching. ■ Pico della Mirandola invites the "world of letters" to discuss his 900 theses.
✴ Andrea del Sarto, Florentine painter (†1531).

Filippino Lippi ■ paints *Vision of St. Bernard*. Memling paints *Portrait of Martin Nieuwenhoven*.
Main mosque, El Haram, built in Medina with tombs of Mohammed, Fatima, and the first caliphs.

†Verrocchio, Ital. sculptor and painter in Florence and Venice, before casting of his monument of Colleoni (✴ 1436). The sacristy of S. Satiro, Milan, is completed; one of Bramante's most original designs.
✴ Vittoria Colonna, Ital. poet; wife of Pescara and friend of Michelangelo (†1547).

Veit Stoss carves the Cracow altar.
✴ Antonio Allegri da Correggio, Ital. painter (†1534). Palazzo Strozzi in Florence begun by Benedetto da Maiano.
✴ Thomas Craumer, Engl. reformer (†1556).
✴ Thomas Münzer, Germ. reformer (†1525). *Hexenhammer*, book on witch persecution, printed 29 times up to 1669.

Vittore Carpaccio paints *Legend of St. Ursula*. ■ Hieronymus Bosch paints *Adoration of the Kings*.

Symbolic ornament from an incunabulum of Nuremberg. ■ Botticelli: 92 pen drawings for Dante's *Divine Comedy*.

Columbus ■ discovers Cuba and Haiti with flagship *Santa Maria*; also discovers "mispointing" of magnetic needle.

After victory over King Richard III, Henry VII ■ (Tudor) is King of England (until †1509).
Matthias Corvinus, King of Hungary, conquers Vienna.

During the Renaissance the use of mercenaries is widespread. ■ Maximilian I elected King of Germany.

The Spaniards conquer Malaga (from Muslims).

King Maximilian I imprisoned by the citizens of Bruges. Crusade against the Waldensians in the Alps. Foundation of Swabian confederation.

Beginning of Reichstag in Frankfurt. ■ Venice occupies Cyprus.

†Matthias Corvinus, King of Hungary since 1458. He furthered Ital. Renaissance at his court.
Start of Serbish war congress in Rome; Pope Innocent VIII captures Prince Dschem.

Peasants revolt in the Netherlands. ■
✴ Henry VIII, King of England between 1509 and 1547 (†). Wedding of Charles VIII with Anne of Brittany.

†Pope Innocent VIII; succeeded by Alexander VI, ■ father of Cesare and Lucrezia Borgia.
†Lorenzo de' Medici; succeeded by son Pietro the Unfortunate.
Expulsion of Jews from Spain.

1493

July 16: "Caterina" (Leonardo's mother?) is living in Leonardo's house.

November to Dec. 20: Exhibition of a full-scale model of

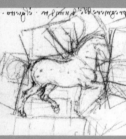

the horse. Casting discussed in Codex Madrid II 151v. ▪
1493–1495: Codex Forster II₁, II₂, III.
1493–1499: Ms. H.

Albrecht Dürer paints *Self-Portrait*. ▪
✻ Paracelsus, Germ. doctor and philosopher (†1541).
Second journey of Columbus to the West.

†Frederick III; succeeded by Maximilian I, ▪ Holy Roman emperor until 1519 (†).
Pope Alexander VI divides the New World between Spain and Portugal.

1494

Leonardo compares the strengths of various arches, ▪ Codex Forster II₂ 92r.

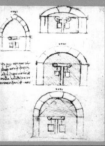

Luca Pacioli writes first book on arithmethic.
Brant's *Ship of Fools*, collection of sermons against human weakness; illustrated with 100 woodcuts by Dürer.
✻ Hans Sachs, Germ. poet and Meistersinger (†1567).
✻ François Rabelais, French poet (†1553).
†Hans Memling, Dutch religious painter (✻1433).
†Pico della Mirandola, Ital. humanist (✻1463).

Pietro de' Medici ▪ chased out of Florence, Savonarola rules (until 1498).
✻ Francis I, King of France (†1547).
France enters Florence.

1495

Leonardo visits Florence to see the new great hall of the governing council.

1495–1497: Decoration of the *Sala delle Asse* (detail ▪), Milan, Sforza Castle.
Ca.1495–1497: Ms. M.
1495–1499: Ms. I.

Hieronymus Bosch paints *Garden of Earthly Delights*. ▪
Dürer's first journey to Italy.

Charles VIII takes possession of Naples. ▪
Lodovico Sforza (il Moro) is Duke of Milan.

1496

Friendship and collaboration with Luca Pacioli. ▪
Jan. 31: The *Danaë* play is presented at Gian Francesco Sanseverino's home.

1495–1498: Leonardo paints the *Last Supper*, ▪ Milan, S.

Maria delle Grazie. Leonardo's drawings of the "regular bodies" for Pacioli's *De divina proportione*.

Adam Kraft completes tabernacle of St. Lorenz in Nuremberg; self-portrait. ▪
First stay of Michelangelo in Rome (until 1501).
Perugino completes *Crucifixion*.

Wedding of Philip the Handsome, son of Maximilian I, with Joanna of Castile brings Spanish crown to house of Hapsburg.

1497

Matteo Bandello in his *Novelle* writes that he saw Leonardo painting from dawn to sunset.

Ms. L (also 1502–1503).
June: The *Last Supper* is nearly done.

✻ Philipp Melanchthon, ▪ Germ. humanist and religious reformer (†1560).
✻ Hans Holbein the Younger, Germ. painter (†1543).
First news of "intoxicating" tobacco plant reaches Europe.

Pope Alexander VI creates Ferdinand of Aragon and Isabella of Castile "Catholic Majesties."
Expulsion of Jews from Portugal.
Savonarola is excommunicated.
†Beatrice d'Este, the influential wife of Lodovico il Moro.
Severe famine in Florence.

1498

Feb. 9: The "laudable and scientific duel" at the Sforza Castle, supervised by Lodovico il Moro. Participants: Leonardo, Pacioli, and theologians, teachers, and physicians.
Oct. 2: Leonardo receives a vineyard from Lodovico il Moro. Pacioli writes that Leonardo has just finished a book on painting and is finishing a treatise on "forces and weights."

1498–1499: Draws cartoon for the *Virgin and Child with St. Anne*, ▪ London, National Gallery.

Vasco da Gama ▪ discovers sea route to India; Columbus on third voyage of exploration.
Dürer's *Apocalypse*, 15 woodcuts.

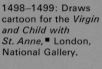

Savonarola declared heretic by the Pope and burned in Florence. ▪
†Charles VIII (✻1470); succeeded by Louis XII, King of France until 1515 (†).

1499

Apr. 26: Donation of vineyard is registered.
Dec. 14: Leonardo leaves Milan after having sent 600 gold florins to be deposited to his account in Florence.

Albrecht Dürer paints *Portrait of Oswolt Krel*.
Giorgione paints *Young Man*.
Amerigo Vespucci discovers with Alonso de Ojeda the Amazon River.

Alliance of Louis XII ▪ with Venice and Florence against Milan which France wins.
Nov. 27: Cesare Borgia conquers Imola. Switzerland secedes from the Germ. empire.

1500

February: In Mantua with Pacioli.
March: In Venice. Leonardo travels over all the Venetian state.
Apr. 24: Back in Florence, still with Pacioli.

MANTUA VENICE FLOREN

In Mantua, draws cartoon for *Portrait of Isabella d'Este*, ▪ Paris, Louvre.
Plans a dam in the Isonzo valley in order to flood the country to prevent Turkish invasion.

Oldest illustration of a printing press in a "dance of death" ▪.

Il Moro defeated by French; made prisoner in Novara. ▪
✻ Charles V; Holy Roman emperor, 1519–1556.

16

1501	1502	1503	1504	1505	1506	1507	1508

pr. 3: In a letter to [Is]abella d'Este, [N]ovellara writes [a]bout the cartoon [L]eonardo has done [fo]r a Virgin and [S]t. Anne.

Aug. 18: Cesare Borgia ■ sends letter hiring Leonardo as his chief architect and military engineer. Travels with Borgia and Machiavelli in Romagna.

March: Back in Florence. Draws money from his account.

Jan. 25: Asked about the most desirable place to display Michelangelo's *David*. Receives monthly sums of money for painting the *Battle of Anghiari*.
July 9: †Ser Piero da Vinci, Leonardo's father.
Nov. 1 to 30: At Piombino (Codex Madrid II, folio 15 recto and others).

Receives more money for the *Battle of Anghiari*.

May 30: Leonardo leaves Florence for temporary return to Milan.
Aug. 18: Governor of Milan requests three-month extension of Leonardo's leave from Florence governing council.
Aug. 28: Council grants final extension for Leonardo to remain in Milan until the end of September.

Leonardo meets Melzi.
Jan. 12: Still in Milan. Louis XII wants Leonardo in his service.
Mar. 5: Leonardo in Florence.
July 26: Leonardo in Milan in the service of King Louis XII; is referred to as "our dear and well-loved Leonardo da Vinci, our regular painter and engineer."
Sept. 18: Back in Florence.

July: In Milan.
October: Leonardo receives money and lends part of it to Salai.

	ROMAGNA	FLORENCE		◀PIOMBINO	MILAN	FL.	FLORENCE	MILAN

pr. 4: Letter from [N]ovellara mentions [th]at Leonardo is [w]orking on the [M]adonna with the [Ya]rnwinder.

Map of Imola (Windsor 12284) ■ and topographic studies executed in the service of the Duke Valentino, Cesare Borgia.   Ms. L.

1503–1506: Cartoon and mural painting of the *Battle of Anghiari* (detail of a sketch, ■ Windsor 12326r).
1503–1505: Codex Madrid II folios 1–140. Invents relief etching.

1504–1505: *Mona Lisa* ■ (portrait of Mona Lisa del Giocondo), Paris, Louvre.

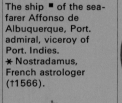

Drawing from the Codex on the Flight of Birds, folio 8 recto. ■ Codex Forster I₁.

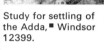

Study for the *Leda*, ■ Windsor 12518.
Ca. 1506: Codex Leicester.
Works on Trivulzio's monument.

Study for settling of the Adda, ■ Windsor 12399.

Several booklets of Codex Arundel "started in the house of

Piero di Baccio Mortelli on March 2, 1508."
Ca. 1508: Ms. D.
Ca. 1508–1509: Ms. F.

[M]ichelangelo ordered [by] the city council [to] sculpt *David*. ■

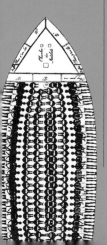

Giovanni Bellini's *Portrait of the Doge Loredan*. ■ Pocket watches by Henlein (one called "Egg of Nuremberg"). *Titian's Gypsy Madonna*.

The ship ■ of the seafarer Affonso de Albuquerque, Port. admiral, viceroy of Port. Indies.
✱ Nostradamus, French astrologer (†1566).

Raphael, who has moved from Perugia to Florence, paints some 15 Madonnas in the following years; *Madonna della Sedia*. ■
†Filippino Lippi, Ital. painter (✱1457).

Cranach paints series of Venus ■ (Louvre). Second stay of Dürer in Venice.
Pope Julius II calls Michelangelo to Rome.

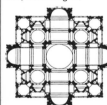

Bramante starts to build St. Peter's in Rome. ■
†Christopher Columbus, believing he found waterway to India.
†Andrea Mantegna, Ital. painter (✱1431).

Luther is ordained priest.
Raphael paints *Holy Family with a Palm*. Altdorfer paints *St. Francis and St. Hieronymus*. Public Vienna-Brussels "Riderpost" (postal service—monopoly of princely Thurn and Taxis family).

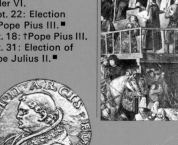

Michelangelo begins to paint the ceiling of the Sistine Chapel. ■ Giorgione paints *Sleeping Venus*, completed by Titian.

[B]eginning of slave [tr]ade to America. ■ [C]esare Borgia, Duke [of] Romagna. [Lu]crezia Borgia [m]arried for third time [Al]fonso d'Este).

Rash of "little wars" between France and Spain over Italy. Peasant revolts in Germany. Expulsion of non-Christian Jews from Spain.

Aug. 18: †Pope Alexander VI.
Sept. 22: Election of Pope Pius III. ■
Oct. 18: †Pope Pius III.
Oct. 31: Election of Pope Julius II. ■

Kingdom of Naples and Sicily under Spanish rule (until 1713).
Inquisition trial ■ in Spain.

†Ivan III, first emperor of entire Russia (✱1440).
†Ercole I, Duke of Ferrara; succeeded by Alfonso I.

Jan. 21: Foundation of Swiss guards. ■ Pope Julius II begins series of Italian wars. Machiavelli forms the Florentine militia.

For the first time the term South America is used (after Amerigo Vespucci). ■
†Cesare Borgia, in whom Machiavelli saw the personification of his "prince."

Without the Pope crowning him, Maximilian I takes on the title "Chosen Roman Emperor." The financier Jakob Fugger finances the war against Venice for Maximilian I; the emperor creates him a "Knight of the Holy Roman Empire." League of Cambrai against Venice.
†Lodovico Sforza (il Moro), still a prisoner of Louis XII.

17

1509	1510	1511	1512	1513	1514	1515	1516

1510 Leonardo works with Marcantonio della Torre,▪ professor of anatomy. Oct. 21: At Milan Cathedral to do the stalls of the choir.

1511 February: †Charles d'Amboise,▪ Leonardo's patron preceding his services for Louis XII in 1507. 1510–1511: Stipend from Louis XII.

1513 Mar. 25: The administration of the Milan Cathedral asks Leonardo for advice. Sept. 24: Leonardo leaves Milan with friends and pupils. Oct. 10: In Florence. Dec. 1: Goes to Rome; has a studio in the Belvedere of the Vatican.

1514 1514–1516: Living in Rome but travels often. Spring: In Civitavecchia. Sept. 25: In Parma. Dec. 14: In Rome.

1515 Mar. 17: †Giuliano de' Medici, patron of Leonardo. Leonardo in Florence. Dec. 9: Leonardo in Milan. Letter to his steward in Florence. Trip to Tivoli looking for ancient ruins.

1516 Leonardo in Rome, leaves for France in the winter with Salai and Melzi,▪ who will later take most of Leonardo's inheritance.

FL. ROME

1509–1510: Paints *St. Anne,*▪ Paris, Louvre. 1509–1512: Ms. K₃. Apr. 30: Leonardo solves a problem in geometry (Windsor 12658, 19145).

Winter: Anatomy Ms. A; on folio A 17▪ (Windsor 19016) one can read "this winter of 1510 I think I will finish all this anatomy." 1510–1516: Ms. G.

Ca. 1512: Self-portrait,▪ Biblioteca Reale, Turin.

1513–1514: Ms. E. Two paintings now lost, for G. B. Branconi. 1513–1516: Leonardo paints *St. John the Baptist,* Paris, Louvre.

Ca. 1514: *The Deluge,*▪ Windsor 12380.

Sends a mechanical lion to Lyon for the coronation procession of King Francis I (July 12). Projects for the stable of Giuliano de' Medici and for the reclamation of Pontine Marshes.

Ca. 1516: A young man on horseback wearing a masquerade costume,▪ Windsor 12574. Notes on the dimensions of St. Paul's, Rome, in Codex Atlanticus 172v.

✶ Calvin, theologian, reformer (†1564).▪ Erasmus of Rotterdam writes *Praise of Folly,* dedicated to Thomas More.

Riemenschneider carves Mary Altar in Creglingen, Germany, including self-portrait. ▪ Altdorfer paints *Flight to Egypt.*

The financier Jakob Fugger (the Rich) ▪ takes over the family estates in Augsburg. ✶ Giorgio Vasari, Ital. sculptor, painter, writer (†1574).

Fifth Lateran Council pronounces immortality of the soul as a dogma of the church. Raphael's *Madonna in Foligno, Madonna with Fish,* and *Julius II.* Copernicus *Commentariolus* (the earth spins, with the other planets, around the sun). Andrea del Sarto paints the *Annunciation.*

Michelangelo's *Moses.* ▪ Dürer engraves *Knight, Death, and Devil.*

Symbolic representation of the indulgence trade. ▪ †Donato Bramante, Ital. architect (✶1444). Titian's *Sacred and Profane Love.*

Grünewald completes Isenheim Altar (begun 1511). Doge's Palace completed in Venice.

Ariosto ▪ (portrait by Titian) writes *Orlando Furioso,* Ital. epic in stanzas. Erasmus of Rotterdam first edition of New Testament in Greek.

†King Henry VII; succeeded by Henry VIII,▪ who marries Catherine of Aragon. Pope Julius II joins the League of Cambrai.

Luther in Rome, received by Cardinal Gaetani. ▪ Hamburg becomes free imperial city.

Pope Julius II forms with Venice and Ferdinand II a "Holy League" against France (after having formed in 1509, with France and the emperor, a league against Venice).

Giuliano de' Medici ▪ (Duke of Nemours) rules in Florence. Defeat of French in Italy (Pavia). Massimiliano Sforza, son of Lodovico il Moro, reigns in Milan.

†Pope Julius II. Giovanni de' Medici elected Pope Leo X.▪ Lorenzo de' Medici, son of Pietro the Unfortunate, rules in Florence.

Ulrich Württemberg crushes "Poor Konrad" peasant revolt. ▪

†Louis XII; succeeded by Francis I as King of France (†1547). He begins reconquest of Italy, wins at Marignano ▪ over Massimiliano Sforza, and recaptures Milan.

Concordat between the Pope and Francis I, ▪ King of France. †Ferdinand II; succeeded by Charles I, the future Emperor Charles V.

1517	1518	1519
Jan. 17: Leonardo Romorantin with Francis I; plans a castle for the Queen Mother. Ascension Day: Leonardo at Cloux near Amboise.	June 19: Plans festival at Amboise for the wedding of Lorenzo di Pietro de' Medici and Madeleine de La Tour d'Auvergne.	The Castle of Amboise. ■ Apr. 23: Last will. May 2: Death. Buried in Amboise.

AMBOISE

Geometric and architectonic studies.

Ca. 1518: One of Leonardo's last drawings, ■ Windsor 12670v.

Leonardo was buried at the Church of St. Florentin in Amboise, France.

Ulrich von Hutten, ■ Germ. poet, created "poeta laureatus" by Maximilian I.
Cardinal Ximenes creates polyglot Bible edition.

Thomas More's *Utopia* published; woodcut by Ambrosius Holbein. ■
＊Tintoretto, Ital. painter (†1594).

†Lucrezia Borgia. ■
Dürer paints *Maximilian I.*
Magellan begins first circumnavigation of the globe.

Beginning of Reformation in Germany; Luther posts his 95 theses in Wittenberg. ■
The Portuguese reach Canton by seaway.

Francis I obliges the Parliament to ratify the Concordat of 1516.

†Maximilian I; succeeded by Charles V, ■ emperor until 1556.
Luther condemned by the Pope.

Excerpts from Leonardo's Testament

The said Testator desires
to be buried within the church of Saint Florentin at Amboise,
and that his body shall be borne thither by the chaplains of the church.
He desires that at his funeral
sixty tapers shall be carried which shall be borne by sixty poor men,
to whom shall be given money for carrying them. . . .
The same Testator
gives and bequeaths henceforth forever to
Battista de Vilanis his servant
one half . . . of his garden which is outside the walls of Milan,
and the other half of the same garden
to Salai his servant. . . .
The said Testator
gives to Maturina his waiting-woman
a cloak of good black cloth lined with fur. . . .
The aforesaid Testator
gives and bequeaths to Messer Francesco da Melzi,
nobleman, of Milan,
in remuneration for services and favors
done to him in the past,
each and all of the books the Testator is at present possessed of,
and the instruments and portraits
appertaining to his art and calling as a painter.
Given on the 23rd day of April, 1519,
before Easter.

"... where nature finishes
producing its shapes, there man begins
with natural things and with the help
of nature itself, to create infinite
varieties of shapes."

THE PAINTER

ANNA MARIA BRIZIO

20/1
*This head is a detail from the kneeling angel
painted by the young Leonardo in Andrea
Verrocchio's* Baptism of Christ. *He was then an
apprentice in the famed workshop of Verrocchio in
Florence. The angel's head, in its luminous modeling and emotional intensity, differs markedly from
the figures of Verrocchio.* UFFIZI, FLORENCE

*On the opposite page are reproduced the most famous
paintings by Leonardo that show the various successive stages of his artistic development. The period
of the* Battle of Anghiari – *lost* – *is indicated by the
drawing 21/3, which is, however, not accepted by
all scholars to be by Leonardo.*

The extraordinary economic and cultural expansion of Florence throughout the 14th and 15th centuries had resulted in such an accumulation of artistic potential in the city, in so many *botteghe* of art, and in such widespread fame for the artists of Florence that for some time Florentine artists had been called upon everywhere to present their work. Beginning in the 1480s, however, the succession of exoduses took on an impressive rhythm: a veritable diaspora spread throughout Italy. It is my belief that in these years a specific policy of Lorenzo de' Medici was developed to foster a purposeful exportation of artistic labor. By sending Florentine artists to the various Italian courts, Lorenzo the Magnificent gained both an opportunity for exchanges and a source of prestige.

In 1482 Botticelli, Ghirlandaio, Perugino, Piero di Cosimo, and Cosimo Rosselli were summoned to Rome by Sixtus IV to decorate the Sistine Chapel. The work completed, they went back to Florence. But in the meantime Verrocchio too had received commissions from both Rome and Venice. Leaving Lorenzo di Credi in charge of his *bottega* in Florence, Verrocchio moved to Venice in order to carry out on the spot the equestrian monument to Bartolommeo Colleoni, and it was there that he died in 1488. The *botteghe* of Verrocchio and Antonio Pollaiuolo were the most important in Florence at that time. Pollaiuolo also moved away from Florence with his brother Piero in 1489, summoned by Innocent VIII to Rome, where he remained until his death. During the same years, approximately from 1488 to 1493, Filippino Lippi was also in Rome, working on the frescoes for the Carafa Chapel in the Church of Santa Maria sopra Minerva – and the list could go on.

The transfer of Leonardo from Florence to Milan in 1482 takes place at precisely this historical moment and in this climate. The information given by the Anonimo Gaddiano and later taken up by Vasari, that Leonardo was sent to Lodovico il Moro in Milan by Lorenzo the Magnificent – bringing with him a silver *lira* in the form of a horse's skull – is usually thought to savor an episode of a novel. Yet it can be better seen as a significant indication of the role played by Lorenzo the Magnificent in promoting a great exportation of works of art and Florentine artists all over Italy.

The consequences for the artistic future of Florence were serious and irreversible; the city never again regained the role of artistic capital which it had held for 200 years. But the effects of this diffusion upon the development of Italian art were extraordinary. Until then the regional schools of art had greatly differed among themselves, but with the exodus of the 1480s a process began that was to lead, in the space of less than half a century, to the formation of an art that could thenceforth claim without reservations to be "Italian." Where politicians had failed to create the Italian nation, the artists succeeded – and so completely as to place the stamp of the Italian Renaissance on all European art for more than two centuries.

I am convinced that the first act of this grand process took place in Milan, in the period of almost 20 years that Bramante and Leonardo remained in continuous contact with one another at the court of Lodovico il Moro. Both came from central Italy, from two centers of very high culture, related by common roots and a similar direction: Bramante from Urbino in the Marches, Leonardo from the most important Florentine *bottega* of the time. In Milan, both Leonardo and Bramante found themselves plunged into a milieu that, by its language, its social and political system, and its customs and mentality, was very different from their places of origin. Judging by the consequences, this change must have provided them with a strong stimulus that led to a profound renewal of interests, to new problems, new solutions, and a new course for their artistic activity. In Leonardo's case, the activity was not only artistic: for we cannot speak of Leonardo as a painter and ignore, or even pass lightly over, the fundamental question of the relationship between art and science in his work.

Italian Renaissance art enjoyed a prestige that cannot be matched by any other artistic epoch, because in that period Italian artists, for a favored moment,

21/1
Virgin of the Rocks, *1483–1486.*
LOUVRE, PARIS

21/2
Last Supper, *1495–1498.*
SANTA MARIA DELLE GRAZIE, MILAN

21/3
Drawing for the
Battle of Anghiari,
1503–1506.
WINDSOR 12339r

21/4 *below*
Cartoon for St.
Anne, *1498–1499.*
NATIONAL GALLERY,
LONDON

21/5 *Above right*
Detail from the
Sala delle Asse,
1495–1497.
SFORZA CASTLE, MILAN

21/6
Mona Lisa
("La Gioconda"),
1504–1505.
LOUVRE, PARIS

In Perugino's fresco Consignment of the Keys to St. Peter, *painted in the Sistine Chapel of the Vatican, the perspective method is not merely a demonstration, but is used to represent the scene more naturally and narratively more efficient. The characters are placed in the immediate foreground; the buildings in the background recede into the distance, and have a geometric regularity and a symmetrical arrangement. The young Perugino was an apprentice with Leonardo in Verrocchio's workshop.*

The precise proportions of this drawing of a chalice reflect the two complementary leading themes of Florentine art of the first half of the Quattrocento: *linear perspective, which gives a new rational definition of*

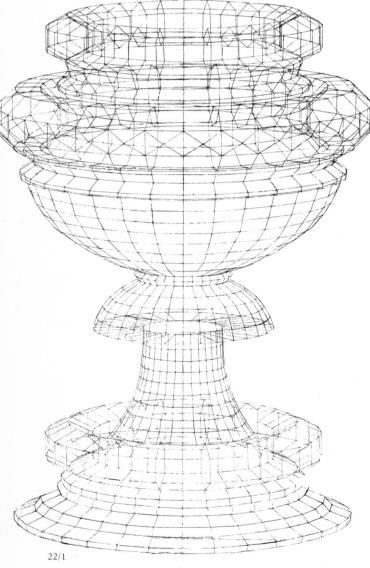

22/1

space according to the constant ratios of proportional measurements; and the construction of solid bodies, the volumes of which become regular geometrical bodies complementary to the geometrical and proportional dividing of the empty spaces. The drawing is attributed to Paolo Uccello (recently also to Piero della Francesca) and is kept in the Gallery of the Uffizi in Florence.

not only were very great as artists but also represented the spearhead of the culture of their day. In a 1938 essay, which has not had the echo it deserved among the historians of art, W. M. Ivins unreservedly declares that "the most important thing that happened during the Renaissance was the emergence of ideas which led to the rationalization of sight." [1] Not the fall of Constantinople, not the discovery of America, neither the Reformation nor the Counter Reformation, insists Ivins, but the rationalization of sight was the most significant event of the Renaissance. And the rationalization of sight was the work, first and foremost, of the Florentine artists, through the invention of perspective [22/1–2].

By a long academic tradition we have become accustomed to consider perspective as a device for the correct formal representation of the proportions of figures and as a measure of space. But this is only the fossilized sediment of what perspective originally was. The Florentine artists of the Renaissance cast away all the interminable case studies of medieval optics and retained only the basic data of visual angles. To the angulation of the visual rays, with its vertex in the eye, the Euclidean principle of proportional triangles was applied. By cutting the visual angle at any point whatsoever with a perpendicular line it became possible to measure with a constant rule any image that fell at any given distance from the vertex.

This system was perfected by the Florentine artists Brunelleschi and Alberti and was applied at first to painting. It made possible a composition that was calculable in constant terms of proportions and measures and was thus delivered

22/2

from traditional empiricism: it was precisely the rationalization of sight. But with perspective the artists created an instrument that was to acquire great value even in the scientific field, because it made possible the measurement of dimensions and distances in exact and constant terms. The perspective of the Renaissance was the first link in the chain that, as Ivins affirms, was to lead to Kepler and Desargues, and on to the projective geometry of Monge and Poncelet. It is at this point that art and science in the Renaissance meet. And on this path, art leads the way.

Along with perspective the other great concept that dominated Renaissance art was that of the imitation of nature. This is not to be interpreted in the petty 19th-century sense of the reproduction of the external, epidermic appearances of nature. For the Florentine artists of the 15th century the imitation of nature was a "subtle speculation": they felt an injunction to investigate

the laws of nature and according to these same laws to create, reproducing the creative process of nature itself [24/1–2]. "The artist disputes and competes with nature," Leonardo wrote. It is understandable how such an attitude brought with it the inclination to look with fresh interest into all natural phenomena, an inclination that became one of the most revolutionary and innovative factors in all the culture of the time. Placed at the center of this process is Leonardo, who pushed it so far forward as to provoke the separation of the two fields, "art" and "science."

In our own times, dominated as they are by scientific and technological interests, the whole of Leonardo's scientific and technical activity, so brilliant and so extraordinarily precursory, is increasingly attracting the attention of scholars. The rediscovery of the Madrid Codices – especially the extraordinary Codex Madrid I, with its splendid series of drawings of machines of exceptional demon-

In contrast to the previous figures, this red-chalk drawing emphasizes the different way Leonardo has of looking at nature. He had detached himself from the Florentine school and around 1505 arrived at this vision, much more animated and organic. Emerging from the abstract geometrical space of the Florentine perspective, Leonardo takes into consideration all the atmospheric and optical effects of the physical space. This shoot of blackberry, lush with fruit and leaves, is not isolated from its environment to receive a more accurate formal definition, but acquires intense vitality directly from its immersion in the atmospheric environment which surrounds it, by the use of irregular and mobile effects of light and shadow. WINDSOR 12419

This drawing of a locust tree (Windsor 12431 verso), also datable around 1505, is another example of Leonardo's organic vision of nature. The variations of light and shade depend on the thickness of the tree's

strative clarity – provides new subject matter that reinforces the tendency for Leonardo's scientific interests to overshadow his concerns as an artist. For these reasons, in this volume which is intended to accompany the publication of the Madrid Codices, it seems all the more appropriate to establish clearly that the starting point for Leonardo was painting.

Let us discard every academic interpretation of painting and bring it back more to its essence: the force of image, the power of expression through images, of creating the image most pertinent and meaningful of that which the mind "dictates within and formulates." There is no doubt that Leonardo expresses himself prevalently by images and figures, that for him drawing is the fundamental instrument of analysis and of representation; but that also, his investigations predominantly begin with visual data. "If you look down on painting," he wrote, "which is the only imitator of all the works manifest in nature, you will certainly be looking down on a subtle invention, which with philosophic and subtle speculation considers all the qualities of forms. . . . This is really science and the legitimate daughter of nature." Leonardo does not see painting as the repetition of the forms of nature, but considers man himself as a force of nature continuing its work and creation. "Where nature finishes producing its shapes, there man begins, with natural things and with the help of nature itself, to create infinite varieties of shapes." For Leonardo,

foliage. From the beginning Leonardo had a very lively taste for landscape. The detail above, taken from the Uffizi Annunciation, *painted when he was young, shows the opening into the distant landscape which this dark curtain of trees tends to repel even further in the clearness of the extreme horizon.*

25/1

During the years of the Battle of Anghiari *Leonardo painted the* Mona Lisa, *one of the most famous paintings of the world. "Caught Leonardo painting for Francesco del Giocondo," writes Vasari, "the portrait of Mona Lisa, his wife . . . , work which is today with King Francis of France." A new direction that departed from the lucid certainty of the foregoing Florentine humanism is seen in the famous "smile of the Mona Lisa," which has mysterious and ambiguous psychological depths. One can also feel this new awareness of Leonardo in the background landscape. It is not a real landscape, but a kind of geological composition in which, in the stratification of the rocks, in the shape of the waters, the temporal stratification of centuries past is reflected.* LOUVRE, PARIS

painting – and drawing, which is the fastest kind of painting – is the most direct and effective means of "mental discourse" in every field.

In Leonardo himself this aspect becomes more evident and acquires increasing development and urgency as the years go by. It begins to assert itself a few years after his arrival in Milan.

When he came to Milan, Leonardo must have been deeply struck by the difference of atmosphere in Lombardy, where medieval guild systems were still in force and where painters, sculptors, and architects were still regarded as craftsmen. At the same time, he must have become fully aware of the new and extraordinary instruments with which his Florentine education had provided him, and of the possibilities of applications in every field that they opened to him. From the time of his arrival in Milan his interests and his experiments tended to branch out in every direction. But the admirable advances in technical and scientific pursuits did not distract him from the art of painting. Scientific attitude and artistic vision are never in antithesis in Leonardo; on the contrary, the one springs incessantly from the other.

The period to which the Madrid Codices date – from 1491 to 1505, to stick literally to the extreme dates that are written there – corresponds to the central and most fertile period of Leonardo's activity. During that time he developed

25/1

his studies on force, motion, and weight, on the "mechanical elements," on the motion of water and air, on hydraulics, on the flight of birds, and on anatomy, along with a succession of discoveries and inventions extraordinarily ingenious and anticipatory. And during that time he executed his main works of art in painting: the *Last Supper*, the *Cartoon of St. Anne*, the *Gioconda*, the *Battle of Anghiari* – works that, to take up again Vasari's famous phrase concerning the frescoes of Masaccio at the Carmine church, "changed the face of painting."

The first important commission that Leonardo received in Milan was the task entrusted to him and to the De Predis brothers by the Brethren of the Conception on April 25, 1483, of painting the altarpiece for the Chapel of San Francesco il Grande. And it is useful to remember the Louvre *Virgin of the Rocks* – which is all that remains of Leonardo's work on the altarpiece – in establishing a limit of comparison in order to measure the distance that separates the *Last Supper* from Leonardo's previous artistic production.

The *Virgin of the Rocks* [27/1] still bears so strongly the stamp of the Florentine style that Vincian scholars of authority have been able to subscribe to the opinion that it was carried out in Florence and that Leonardo brought it with him when he moved to Milan and then thought of using it for the altarpiece for the Brethren of the Conception. The supposition is unsustainable, and difficult to believe for anyone who knows how slow and unreliable Leonardo was in carrying out a work, even when bound by a contract. We can imagine what the situation would be like when no obligations existed! But above all we already see in the *Virgin of the Rocks*, in spite of its Florentine stylistic features, a sum of new thoughts. Its iconography is linked with the theme of the Conception, which was the object of a special cult in Milan.

The big wooden altar (commissioned by the Brethren of the Conception to Giacomo del Maino, on April 18, 1480, for their chapel in San Francesco il Grande) for which Leonardo and the De Predis brothers should have successively executed paintings, is now lost. The altar represented below, however, still in existence in the Church of the Virgin Mary in San Lorenzo at Morbegno in Valtellina, can give an idea of it. It is also a large wooden construction: the sculptures, which prevail, alternate with paintings. The top is in the shape of a small half-dome on which stands a statue of the Virgin. Below her, around the cornice, we see the apostles, turned upwards, and in between her and the apostles a garland of cherubs. On the panels, left empty and flat, the Virgin with the Child on the throne and other figures were painted by Gaudenzio Ferrari and Fermo Stella, exactly as Leonardo and

26/1

the De Predis brothers contributed paintings to the altarpiece of San Francesco. Both groups of painters also had the duty of coloring and gilding all the carved parts.

26/2 and 3 and 27/1

This is the first version of the Virgin of the Rocks, *entirely by Leonardo's own hand, painted for the altarpiece of the Brethren of the Conception in San Francesco il Grande in Milan. The contract was made on April 25, 1483. It is uncertain whether this first (Louvre) version has ever been placed in the wooden altar. The second version (National Gallery, London) comes directly from the altar of San Francesco; it is a work executed with the collaboration of helpers. One should notice here the novelty of such a composition at that time: in the great mountain of carved wood that was Giacomo del Maino's archaic altar, Leonardo boldly put a composition full of shadows and imbued with depth. It must have seemed to actually deepen into a mysteriously complex grotto, foreshadowed in the semi-obscurity. At right are two details from the* Virgin of the Rocks.
LOUVRE, PARIS

27/1

26/2

26/3

It is too often forgotten – accustomed as we are to seeing the *Virgin of the Rocks* on the wall of a museum and to contemplating it for its own sake – that this painting was only a small part of the whole. The altar of the Chapel of San Francesco il Grande was a monumental sculptured altar. According to the custom in Lombardy at that time, the contract charged Leonardo and the De Predis brothers first of all to color and to gild the sculptured wooden part; and then to fill in the panels left free of carvings with a larger scene dedicated to the Virgin, flanked on each side by four angels playing instruments and singing. To think of Leonardo working like a simple artisan on the gilding

and coloring of these frames, columns, and reliefs fits in badly with the image that has been built up of him over the centuries. It is still more difficult to think of the *Virgin of the Rocks* forming part of that great complex swarming with reliefs and glittering with gold. It sounds like a challenge for Leonardo; and it reveals an unshakable determination not to withdraw from his own artistic intention that he carried out for an altarpiece of this kind a painting so overflowing with shadows, so subtle and mysterious, as the *Virgin of the Rocks*. It must surely have seemed like a dark cave submerged in that brilliant golden mass of frames, columns, and reliefs.

While Leonardo was painting the Last Supper *in the refectory of Santa Maria delle Grazie, Bramante was building the large tribune for it. The church is composed of two parts easily distinguishable from each other in structure and style: the first part was built by Giuniforte Solari, in the*

28/1

dominant style in Lombardy, still full of the Romanesque tradition. It was done between 1464 and 1482. A few years later, on Il Moro's request, Solari's choir was demolished and in its place Bramante built the sumptuous and monumentally conceived tribune, with central ground plan, covered with a cupola.

Now the first day of the feast of unleavened bread the disciples came to Jesus, saying unto him, Where wilt thou that we prepare for thee to eat the passover?
And he said, Go into the city to such a man, and say unto him, The Master saith, My time is at hand; I will keep the passover at thy house with my disciples.
And the disciples did as Jesus had appointed them; and they made ready the passover.
Now when the even was come, he sat down with the twelve.
And as they did eat, he said, Verily I say unto you, that one of you shall betray me.
And they were exceeding sorrowful, and began every one of them to say unto him, Lord, is it I?   MATTHEW 26:17-22

The composition of the painting is perspectively outlined in depth. The figures are slightly drawn back from the foreground towards the rear; the open arms of the Virgin forming a pyramid and the angel's finger pointing to St. John seem to explore and scan space in various directions; and everything is surrounded by shade and light – a very sparing light that is used to draw from the shade, with soft gradations, the relief of the forms.

Just over 10 years later, the relationship between figures and space in the *Last Supper* [29/1] is profoundly changed; the growth of the figures is striking. Table and apostles are placed in front, at the forelimit of the room where the scene takes place, which rapidly shrinks behind them; the figures are dominating and seem to come forth into the *real* space of the refectory. Leonardo has carried out a profound change in the lucid perspective of the Brunelleschi–Alberti tradition by means of a minimal but fundamental shift. Instead of considering the eye as an abstract point, simply the apex of the visual pyramid, he has made it coincide with the real eye of the spectator,

The Last Supper *and the tribune conceived by Bramante for the church are the two works that from Milan initiated the new course of Italian art in the 1500s. A little more than 10 years after the* Virgin of the Rocks, *the relation between space and figures is profoundly changed. The persons*

represented dominate the foreground. Their gestures and attitudes not only show physical motions but also express their emotional reactions, each one individually characterized, to the words of Christ, "One of you will betray me."

29/1

creating the illusion that painted space and real space interpenetrate and continue in each other. In this way the spectator finds himself taken illusorily inside pictorial fiction, and a new, far more dynamic and dramatic relationship is established between him and the persons represented, resulting in a much stronger effect of reality and participation. At the other end of the long room of the refectory, the *Crucifixion* of Montorfano, executed in fresco in exactly the same years (it bears the date 1495) and facing the *Last Supper,* seems like a tapestry stuck to the wall.

The studies on physics and mechanics that Leonardo had pursued to an ever-widening extent since his arrival in Milan overflowed into his pictorial vision and shook the foundations of Florentine 15th-century figurative art. This is a very important turning point in painting; it is brought about by Leonardo, and the first great accomplishment to come from it is the *Last Supper.*

"Another lays his hand on the table and is looking."
"Another with his hands spread open shows the palms. . . ."
"Another . . . holds a knife in one hand."
"Another who has turned, holding a knife in his hand, upset with his hand a glass on the table."

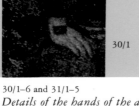

30/1   *Bartholomew.*

30/2
Both hands from James the Lesser and Andrew; Peter's hand holding a knife.

30/4   *Peter.*

30/6   *Christ.*

30/3   *Judas.*   30/5   *Judas and John.*

30/1–6 and 31/1–5
Details of the hands of the apostles and of Christ in the Last Supper. *The gestures and movements are particularly expressive of each individual's state of mind and emotional reaction. The hands are placed so that they serve as an element of the composition, linking each group of three apostles.*

Every element of the pictorial composition is involved in this profound transformation. The attitudes and gestures not only represent physical motions but also are the expression of the emotional reactions, each one individually characterized, of the apostles to the words of Christ: "One of you will betray me." The motions of the hands, so carefully studied and expressed, are worthy of note. This most dramatic moment of the Supper had been represented in the traditional way in the previous Florentine versions of the 15th century. But the traditional gesture of Christ offering the bread to Judas, a gesture of denunciation and accusation, has been omitted by Leonardo; and the meaning and resonance of Christ's words are grasped only in the reactions of the apostles, which spread like a chain from one end of the table to the other. One apostle quickly rises from his seat, another leans forward towards Christ, another draws back. The apostles draw closer together in lively groups which, as the figures

Bartholomew, James the Lesser, and Andrew.

"Another shrugs his shoulders up to his ears, making a mouth of astonishment." "Another speaks into his neighbor's ear and the listener turns to him . . . ."
Judas, Peter, and John.

30/7   30/8

separate and join up, leave irregular intervals among them. The traditional symmetrical arrangement of the apostles on the sides of Christ, sitting motionless along the table, is dramatically stirred up and brought to life in Leonardo's version. It is a new way of composing, much more complex in articulations and connections.

The only one who remains outside the wave of emotional turmoil, immersed in the liberating depths of meditation and acceptance, is the Christ, who lowers his glance and gently opens his arms, brushing the tablecloth lightly with his hands. His gesture creates space and a pause around him; it isolates him and makes him the center of the scene. The triple window that opens behind him onto a distant scene accentuates further his central position.

But the light which illuminates the scene as a whole does not come from the triple window in the background; it comes transversely from the left; Leonardo has intentionally made it coincide with the actual lighting of the room, coming from the row of open windows on the wall to the left. This

31/1 *Thomas and James the Greater.*

31/3 *Philip and Matthew.*

31/4 *Matthew.*

31/5 *Simon and Thaddaeus.*

31/2 *Christ.*

coincidence of source of light, together with the artifice of perspective, leads to a fusion of fiction and reality.

The *Last Supper,* as soon as it appeared, struck contemporaries as a powerful revelation of reality. The traditional way of painting was suddenly a thing of the past; from here begins a new trend in painting. All contemporary sources speak of the *Last Supper* in admiring terms. The King of France would have liked to have it taken down from the wall and transported to France, and only the difficulty of the task, according to what Vasari writes, "saw to it that His Majesty took his desire with him, and it [the painting] was left to the Milanese." In the course of the two or three following decades the copies of it multiplied in France, in Italy, and in Flanders. When the future King Henry II of France married Caterina de' Medici in 1533, Pope Clement VII,

30/7 and 8 and 31/6 and 7
Like the hands, but in a more open and direct manner, the apostles' heads are all masterpieces of psychological and physiognomical investigation. The details reproduced here, in the traditional grouping by

Thomas, James the Greater, and Philip. "Another . . . turns with stern brows to his companion." "Another leans forward to see the speaker. . . ."

Matthew, Simon, and Thaddaeus.

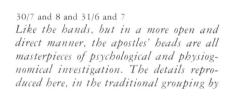

31/6

31/7

himself one of the Medici, sent to the newlyweds as a wedding gift a unicorn magnificently and preciously worked, a masterpiece of jewelry; and King Francis I returned the compliment with a piece of tapestry reproducing Leonardo's *Last Supper,* which has recently been put on view in the Vatican Picture Gallery. Woven into the rich edge that frames it are the monogram and the royal devices of France. The alterations that Leonardo's composition underwent in the tapestry show how difficult it was to grasp the noble, very lofty essence of the Leonardesque conception. The tapestry is far more ornate and flaunts in the background a very complicated "modern" French architecture.

three, clearly demonstrate the mode of composition of the Last Supper, *which seems to arise naturally from the gestures and impetuous movements caused by the words of Christ. These various dynamic groupings enhance the interaction within each group and cause the strongest energy to surge towards the center of the fresco.*

All the subtle hidden correspondences between the groups of apostles and the simple but monumental relation between figures and space that exist in Leonardo's Last Supper are blatantly ignored in this faded and torn copy by an unknown artist of the 16th century. Also omitted are the windows, which in Leonardo's original open the enclosed space towards a vast, luminous distance behind Christ.

During the years he devoted to the *Last Supper*, Leonardo was working for Lodovico il Moro at the Sforza Castle. Of his paintings in the *camerini* and the *saletta negra*, of which the sources speak, nothing remains. Only the famous decoration of the *Sala delle Asse* [37/1–41/2] survives. Although repainted, indeed largely remade, during the restorations made by Luca Beltrami in 1901 and 1902, it still produces a grandiose and engaging effect. Basing his work on the few remaining traces of the original, Beltrami completed the decoration's motifs by repeating them until he had covered the whole vault. The hall is situated in the tower on the northeast corner of the castle and on account

32/1

32/2

The setting of the Last Supper, *in the refectory of Santa Maria delle Grazie, was conceived by Leonardo so as to seem to be an extension of the real space of the room itself; and the light in the painting has been made to coincide with the real light that comes*

from the windows on the left. Leonardo here combined fiction and reality to create a unique effect. The crescent-shaped lunettes above the fresco correspond to a Vincian conception, but they are too badly preserved for us to judge whether he actually painted them.

32/3

This pen-and-ink drawing is an early study for the Last Supper, *in which Judas still sits with his back to the viewer, opposite Christ, according to the traditional*

32/2

32/3

of its position must have been used especially in the summer season. This circumstance was, I think, of some importance in suggesting to Leonardo the choice of the decorative arboreal motif. It must also have been suggested to him by the persistence in Lombardy of this kind of motif, typically Gothic in its origin but still widely used throughout the north in the late 15th century. Gothic art had always favored a varied, intricate, and fantastic wealth of plants, leaves, flowers, hedges, and espaliers as a background for tapestries and murals of large dimensions, as well as for short illuminated pages. In Leonardo's day frescoes such as those of Bembo and of Michelino da Besozzo and their circles,

33/1

This large tapestry, representing the Last Supper *and now exhibited in the Picture Gallery of the Vatican, was given by King Francis I of France to Pope Clement VII in 1533 in exchange for a gift from the Pope on the occasion of the dauphin's wedding, the future Henry II, to the niece of Clement VII, Caterina de' Medici. The tapestry had been woven in Flanders on the king's order. The powerful simplicity of Leonardo's* Last Supper *is replaced by a richer set-*

33/1

disposition. The sketch at the lower right shows Christ with John and Judas, who is briskly standing up from his stool, stooping forward towards Christ. WINDSOR 12542r

33/2 and 3

Study in black chalk, "morbidissimo and sfumato," for the head of the apostle Philip. WINDSOR 12551
Detail of the same head painted in the Last Supper *in the refectory of Santa Maria delle Grazie.*

33/2

ting, ignoring the great significance of Leonardo's composition entirely impregnated by the dramatic action of the persons represented. The sumptuous architecture, however, in which this Last Supper *takes place documents the strongly italianized style prevalent at the Court of Francis I.*

33/3

which still exist in the Milanese palace and in the Rocca d'Angera of the Borromei, must have been quite usual in the mansions and castles of the duchy of Milan. Thus, to choose that motif for the *Sala delle Asse* was an affirmation of the community of origins and traditions that linked the duke to the duchy. The linkage was made explicit in the great tablets that hang from the ropes twisted around the branches and display coats of arms and inscriptions celebrating Lodovico il Moro.

But the Gothic muralists had drawn up their vegetal backgrounds, their espaliers of greenery along the walls, like tapestry or cloth, on the surface. Leonardo

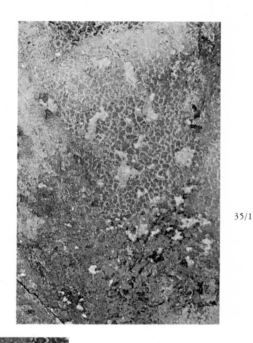

35/1

35/2

34/1 *On the opposite page, in a detail from the* Last Supper, *the central figure of the Christ sits alone against the luminous background of the window that opens on a distant landscape. It is immediately apparent that he is the protagonist. The axial position of his bust, in contrast to the accentuated displacement of the busts of the apostles, the wide gesture of the arms, his eyes looking down and inward, all indicate the infinite distance between Christ and his supreme acceptance, and the wave of emotions, so much more passionately human, which strikes and agitates the groups of apostles.*

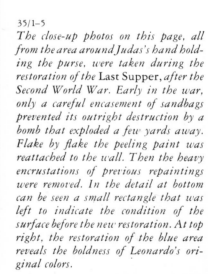

35/3

35/4

35/1–5
The close-up photos on this page, all from the area around Judas's hand holding the purse, were taken during the restoration of the Last Supper, *after the Second World War. Early in the war, only a careful encasement of sandbags prevented its outright destruction by a bomb that exploded a few yards away. Flake by flake the peeling paint was reattached to the wall. Then the heavy encrustations of previous repaintings were removed. In the detail at bottom can be seen a small rectangle that was left to indicate the condition of the surface before the new restoration. At top right, the restoration of the blue area reveals the boldness of Leonardo's original colors.*

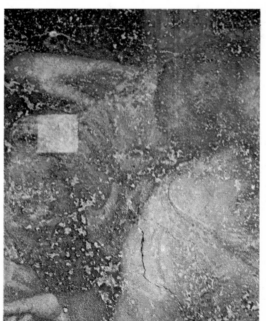

35/5

imagines an arboreal cap curved like a vault, which illusorily substitutes itself for the true vault, opening the space of the room, and uncovering it by simulating the open sky beyond the entanglement of the branches.

Huge branches bent by force intertwine, describing a plurality of acute intersecting arches which compose designs very similar to those that cornices and fretwork make at the top of large Gothic windows. Leonardo must have observed and studied them with keen interest, attracted by their complexity and their ornate magnificence. In the *Sala delle Asse*, to the already complicated interlacings of branches are added those of a rope – a single continuous rope – which

Although the Sforza Castle in Milan has, on occasions, been greatly remodeled, the ancient ground plans and the large proportions of the apartments around the ducal courtyard and the courtyard of the Rocchetta remain. Some interior rooms,

36/1

including, at the northeast corner, the famous Sala delle Asse where Leonardo executed the great arboreal decoration, also remain unaltered.

36/2-5

These four drawings were all, except perhaps the first one, done after the decoration of the Sala delle Asse. They show that Leonardo's interest in and study of plants, grass, flowers, and foliage existed throughout his life.

36/2

The stalk of a lily (Lilium candidum). *The authenticity of this drawing has been doubted by some scholars; but despite a certain ponderousness of the outline and of the light tones, I attribute it to Leonardo, dated around 1498.* WINDSOR 12418

36/2

36/3

Pen drawing of two small flowering plants of similar kind yet slightly different. This drawing and the two following ones are part of a series, although executed in different techniques. They most probably date from around 1505–1506. WINDSOR 12423

36/4

36/4

A cluster of Star of Bethlehem (Ornithogalum umbellatum) *in red chalk. Beautiful volutes are traced by the revolving movement of the long leaves.*

36/5

All these drawings give an intense sense of organic growth to the flowers, which are immersed in their environment. WINDSOR 12424

36/4

Red-chalk drawing of a spray of oak leaves with cluster of acorns. To be noted is the mastery with which the weight and the density of the spray are rendered. WINDSOR 12422

twines and untwines in recurrent knots and meanders, insinuating itself and re-emerging among the foliage. Leonardo's innate taste for labyrinthine complications finds in the vault of the *Sala delle Asse* a monumental development. Yet everything has been architecturally structured. In the spaces between the branches appears the blue of the sky. Originally the effect of opening and of brightness must have been much stronger and far more illusory. An example of what it must have been like, although worn out and discolored, is glimpsed in the zone above the window of the east side, where during restorations in 1954 a thorough cleaning was done. The restorers did not dare to remove completely all the reconstructions of Beltrami; they limited themselves to relieving the heaviness of the repaintings. But in the zone indicated they went so far as nearly to bring out the original. In that area the interstices of the foliage leave a greater opening to the brightness of the sky; the leaves and branches are lighter and more wavy, studied in a much more naturalistic way, and rendered in their morphological details. The vegetal motif, although used for a decorative purpose, is animated by a charge of organic life and a naturalistic significance which is completely new.

The patron intended the work to be highly decorative; Leonardo lavished upon it the results of his studies on nature, which he pursued relentlessly in those years, and transformed into something of new, more complex implications even the traditional cultural motifs he received from the past.

The restorations of 1954 have also brought back to view a large monochrome fragment on the east wall of large roots that insinuate themselves between stratifications of rocks and swell up into a big, broad, solid base of a tree trunk, full of protuberances, from which the stem begins to grow. This fragment

leads one to suppose that initially Leonardo not only thought of decorating the vault but also imagined a single complex which would stretch across the whole hall, rising more organically from the earth. At the bottom, all around on the walls, as far as the impost of the vault, were to be big tree trunks, with their roots splitting and lifting the stratified rocks. Branches were meant to grow upwards and then bend to form an arbor, substituting for the enclosure of the stonework an arboreal construction in the open air. It was all conceived as the much more grandiose naturalistic poem that the surviving fragments show today.

37/1

This detail of the first lunette and vault from the northeast corner of the Sala delle Asse *is from the area where recent restorations have achieved their finest result in removing the heavy repaintings. The intersections of the branches form complicated pointed arches like the tops of Gothic windows. Through the entire vault runs a single unbroken strand of rope, looped and interlaced, whose patterns resemble the intricate workings of Leonardo's mind.*

37/2 and 3

Upper part of the trunk, nearly a large arboreal console, which is immediately below the second corbel, from the northeast corner of the Sala delle Asse. *All around the walls, placed below each corbel, are tree trunks with large branching boughs, rich with twigs and foliage, that simulate a*

37/4

The knotwork pattern employed on such a monumental scale in the Sala delle Asse *corresponds rather well to the red-chalk drawing of interwoven ribbons below. Use of these interlacings in the complicated pattern of knots and loops in the decoration*

enhances the work of nature and reflects the intricacy of Leonardo's mind.

WINDSOR 12351v

37/2

37/5

The coat of arms of the Sforza family, emblazoned with falcons and serpents, was painted at the very center of the decoration as a kind of keystone for the Sala delle Asse.

huge pergola in the open air on the entire ceiling of the Sala. *Isolated from its context, this detail of a tree with its first short branches beginning to have leaves reveals the interest and care with which each morphological detail has been represented and the wonderful organic aliveness that has been infused into it by Leonardo. The detail at right shows clusters of leaves and fruit so vigorous and thick that they virtually obscure the branches.*

37/3

38/1

Overleaf: A large detail from the Sala delle Asse *demonstrates how Leonardo's trees, growing up the walls and then arching with the vaulted ceiling, follow and emphasize the structure of the ceiling. The large branches bend out from the trunks and intersect, forming patterns resembling Gothic arches.*

40/1

On the opposite page is the view looking straight up at the ceiling of the Sala delle Asse. *In the middle is the Sforza coat of arms, towards which rise the strong branches from tree trunks placed all around the hall. The painted tablets at the top and bottom honor Leonardo's patron, Lodovico Sforza (il Moro). The ample and arbitrary repairs executed by Beltrami on the basis of scattered fragments of the original decoration do not allow us to judge whether the intersections of the tree trunks were indeed so close and regular: certainly they were not so monotonous and persistent. The foliage, besides the fact that it has been inserted in areas originally left blank, appears heavy and stiff because of the thick and dull repaintings. In the places where the repaintings have been removed, the foliage is less dense, allowing sky to penetrate and lending an airy openness that must have permeated the work originally [38/1].*

41/1

41/2

In 1954 restoration brought to light large fragments of Leonardo's work on the east wall of the Sala delle Asse. *In the two details of the fragment shown here, roots can be seen insinuating their way through stratified rock and swelling into the base of a tree trunk. The roots, twisted and contorted like animals trying to free themselves from the rocks, have a dynamic quality typical of Leonardo's work. The fragment had been covered over by Beltrami who thought it the work of a later artist. It suggests that Leonardo originally may have envisioned trees around the entire hall, breaking through rocks and bursting forth to create his "pergola." The detail at left is a continuation of the extreme ramification to the left of the main fragment.*

42/2

The famous painting of St. Anne, *now in the Louvre, was executed by Leonardo in a rather advanced period of his activity, around 1509–1510. For about a decade he had been meditating on this theme: he aimed at placing the four figures in a compact group, in which the reciprocal positions, gestures, and even looks would flow from one to the other, and from the top to the bottom by successive interlacings, torsions, and flexions, widening towards the base like a pyramid. This pyramidal scheme became an example for Italian painting of the first decades of the 16th century.*

Beltrami had covered over the big monochrome fragment, considering it as "work carried out during the Spanish domination"; it was rediscovered in the restorations of 1954 by Constantino Baroni, who judged it to be from Leonardo's own hand. I do not doubt that it belongs to Leonardo; and it amazes me that a piece of this grandeur has so little aroused the attention of scholars. Joseph Gantner, after the presentation of Baroni, dedicated admiring and penetrating comments to it in his book on "Leonardo's visions,"[2] perhaps insisting even too much on its visionary character. The great contorted roots and the rising of the trunk swollen with protuberances do suggest strange forms; but I have never succeeded in seeing the human skull that Gantner discerns there.

43/1

Due to the extraordinary structural and stylistic importance assumed by "pyramidal composition" in 16th-century Italian art, the comments about the various Vincian versions of the group of the St. Anne *tend to polarize on this particular aspect. But such an exegesis would be defrauding the* Cartoon for St. Anne *(now in the National Gallery in London), one of the greatest works of Leonardo, which belongs to the creative and stylistic phase of the* Last Supper. *It is true that the cartoon marks the beginning of a research series for the pyramidal composition, which ends with the painting in the Louvre; but in the long process many things have changed in Leonardo's thought, and the new realisations have not come about without discarding other elements. The version in London has the same emotional and psychological density, the same force and "naturalness" of execution as found in the* Last Supper. *The clash of the glance of St. Anne, coming from the shade, full of the awareness of the world, with the much more youthful and unaware face of the Virgin would have been impossible in the perfect pyramidal composition in the Louvre.*

Kenneth Clark comments on this drawing (Windsor 12533) for the head of St. Anne: "This . . . shows how much Leonardo regularized features in his pictures to attain his ideal of beauty, and perfection, losing thereby something of freshness and humanity. The drawing has human mystery, the painting artificial." The drawing is from the same period as the painting at right, about 1509–1510. In the earlier sketch at bottom (Galleria dell'Accademia 230, Venice), one can catch compositional research in the act: Leonardo sketches twice the head of St. Anne.

42/1

42/2

Would they not be the famous spots on the walls of which Leonardo speaks and which stimulate the imagination to see there innumerable strange forms? The way in which the roots insinuate themselves between the joints and the stratifications of the rocks – upsetting them, breaking them, and making them rise – expresses a dynamic, almost animal vitality, bearing a stamp that is purely Leonardesque. When he carries out thoroughly the structural and representative analysis of the things in nature, Leonardo is eminently capable of extracting from it at the same time the maximum suggestion of compressed powers that may be enclosed there and are about to free themselves, overturning the difficult and precarious equilibrium of forces in tension. The result is an extraordinary metamorphic fantasy, a vision of the world – forces and forms – in perpetual action and transmutation left us by one with a formidable capacity for formulating them: "such a terrible demonstration," as Vasari called it.

42/3

Hundreds of drawings – survivors of who knows what mass dispersed and lost – illustrate Leonardo's vision of the world. I choose one in which this metamorphic vision materializes in a particularly striking way, a precise transition from a horse's head with fiercely upcurled nostrils to the heads of a roaring lion and of a screaming man, such a swift and yet securely interrelated transition as to suggest in the flashing rapidity of the image the whole sequence of the "photograms" implied. It is 12326 recto of Windsor, containing a series

43/1

of sketches for the *Battle of Anghiari* [44/1], which follows the works in the *Sala delle Asse* by roughly seven years. A mighty horse rears up to the right; another very small horse doubles up and launches into the fray like a meteor at the upper left; a whole series of beautiful horses' heads of a wild ferocity are scattered over the folio; and finally comes the unleashing of the threefold sequence of heads: horse, lion, screaming man – the three blending into one another from top to bottom, halfway up the folio. *Pazzia bestialissima* ("beastly

44/1

This folio must be related to "a book of horses sketched for the cartoon" of the Battle of Anghiari, *mentioned in the long list of books that spreads over folios 2 verso and 3 recto of Codex Madrid II. At the left, going from top to bottom, are drawn the head of a horse with its nostrils ferociously opened followed by the head of a roaring lion and then the head of a screaming man in a series of events so fast and connected that they give rise to the suggestion of a metamorphosis from one to the other image. Pazzia bestialissima, "beastly madness," Leonardo calls war, and this thought is here set down in a vision of lightning speed.*

madness"), Leonardo calls war, and this thought is here set down in a vision with lightning speed. How disengaged from the dull reality of the apparent fact this staunch representer of nature can be! From the image he arrives simultaneously at metaphor, mental discourse, and fantastic suggestion.

The style of the *Cartoon of St. Anne* [43/1] recently transferred to the Royal Academy at the National Gallery of London belongs to the period of the *Last Supper*. The presence of the great figures in the foreground, gravitating towards the real space from which the spectator looks at them, is once more felt. The painting shows the same plasticity in its fullness, and there are analogies of gestures, attitudes, and groupings. The *Last Supper* and the *Cartoon of St. Anne* were developed along the same lines of thought leading to an intense affirmation of naturalness, but on a monumental scale and involving a sum of ideas with universal significance.

A recent dating seeks to place the *Cartoon of St. Anne* two or three years after the *Battle of Anghiari.* Such a dating is unsustainable in my opinion, as it does not fit in with internal developments of Leonardo's art or even

– indeed, much less so – with the developments of that crucial decade in Italian art, 1500–1510. Too many Florentine drawings, as well as paintings and sculptures, in the first years of the 16th century re-echo that very new motif and make it the theme of variations and developments – not excluding Michelangelo, Raphael, and Andrea del Sarto. The style of the *St. Anne* does not deviate much from that of the *Last Supper;* it still belongs to that phase. The following phase is that of the *Battle of Anghiari.*

45/1
This ferocious horse is another of Leonardo's sketches for the Battle of Anghiari.
WINDSOR 12327r

A di 6 di giugno 1505 in venerdì al tocco delle ore 13 cominciai a colorire in palazzo; nel qual punto di posare il pennello si guastò il tempo e sonò a banco, chiamando l'omini a ragione. Il cartone si straccio, l'acqua si versò e ruppesi il vaso dell'acqua che si portava; e subito si guastò il tempo e piovve insino a sera acqua grandissima e stette il tempo come notte.

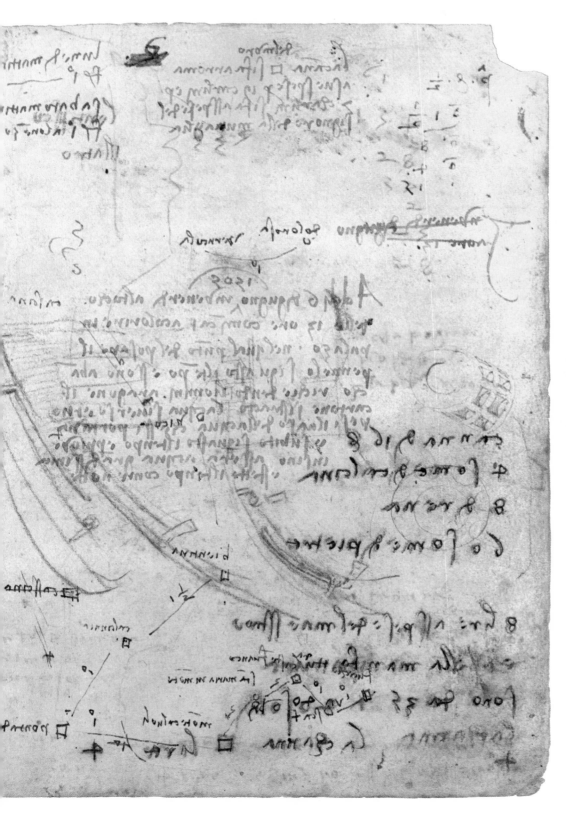

45/2   This folio from the newly rediscovered Codex Madrid II immediately became famous for the explicit mention of the Battle of Anghiari. The passage referring to it is written in the middle of the folio (and transcribed above): "Friday the 6th of June, 1505, at the stroke of the 13th hour, I started to paint in the Palace. And just as I lowered the brush, the weather changed for the worse and the bell started to toll, calling the men to their duty. The cartoon was torn, water poured down and the vessel of the water that was carried broke. Suddenly the weather became even worse and it rained very heavily till nightfall and the day was as night." The note has been interpreted by some as the solemn autobiographical mention of the day when Leonardo started his painting on the wall of the Hall of the Great Council in the Palazzo Vecchio. I believe however that, as in other cases, Leonardo is fascinated by a meteorological phenomenon, exceptional and spectacular, and mentions the exact day, hour, and moment: "At the moment I put the brush down the weather deteriorated...."

MADRID II 1r

The Battle of Anghiari belongs to a totally different cycle of experiences and concepts. A new dynamism breaks into it with shattering vehemence. Here again the protagonist is man, but a savage ferocity is present. The figures whirl around in a vortex of motions, as if the forces dominant in nature were unleashing the elements in an attempt to absorb man himself. An abyss separates

Leonardo's conception from the battles of Paolo Uccello, for example, of just 50 years before, in which every gesture and attitude is frozen in posture and every single part surrealistically composed and fixed within the network of the abstract and unchangeable relationships of specular perspective. With the *Battle of Anghiari* there is a violent break away from the perspective syntax of the 15th century; the group turns and rushes forward like a hurricane unleashed. Leonardo's mind becomes increasingly more removed from humanism and passes on to consider in an ever wider and more cosmic sense the forces, motions, and elements "of heaven and earth."

46/1

Up to now this essay on Leonardo's painting has followed the Madrid Codices chronologically, making reference, not to the manuscripts themselves, but to Leonardo's artistic work corresponding to the period which they span. This period runs from 1491 (which is the earliest date written on folio 157 verso of Codex Madrid II, in the notebook dealing with the casting of "the great horse of Milan") to 1505 (on folio 2 recto of the same codex, where the record of the *Battle of Anghiari* is found). The other codex, Codex Madrid I, more unitary and homogeneous, contains the two extreme dates of 1493 and 1497.

At this point it is time that the essay concentrated on the Madrid Codices. The passage of folio 2 recto [45/2] of Codex Madrid II which is illustrated and transcribed above became immediately famous for its reference to such a well-known work as the *Battle of Anghiari*. It has been published several

47/1 and 2

Two preparatory drawings for the heads of the second screaming warrior – on the left – and of the last horseman on the extreme right of the group in the Struggle around the Standard. *Full of dynamism, caught in the act of screaming, these horsemen in the* Battle of Anghiari *are neverthe-*

47/1   47/2

47/3

less strongly individualized, physically and psychologically. The same fullness of definition that characterizes the methods of drawing the heads of the apostles in the Last Supper *can still be noticed here.*

MUSEUM OF FINE ARTS 343, 344, BUDAPEST

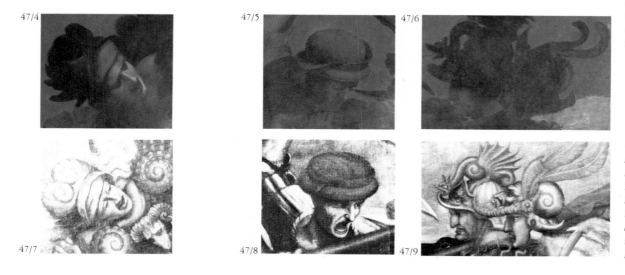

47/4   47/5   47/6

47/7   47/8   47/9

47/4–9

A comparison of the details of warriors' heads at left with the copies above and Leonardo's drawings at the top indicates the changes they underwent at the hands of the copiers. The top row at left is from the copy in the Uffizi in Florence; the bottom row is from the copy in the Casa Horne in Florence.

All the drawings reproduced on these two pages refer to the Battle of Anghiari.

In the drawing at right, a fight between horsemen and foot soldiers is represented with an overwhelming violence of line.

GALLERIA DELL'ACCADEMIA 215 A, VENICE

48/2

48/1

Figures of walking soldiers are studied in order to investigate fully the play of muscles in various movements and attitudes of attacking and striking. These serpentine movements became, like the pyramidal scheme of the St. Anne, a dominant means of composition in the following decades of the 16th century.

GALLERIA DELL'ACCADEMIA 215, VENICE

The drawing at right, with its angry and roughly defined swirl of horses and men, seems to be a study of the central drama, the struggle around the standard. Vasari wrote of the horses: "Rage, hatred, and revenge are seen in them no less than in the men."

GALLERIA DELL'ACCADEMIA 215, VENICE

48/3

49/1

49/1
Another sketch for the Battle of Anghiari
*(below) pits nude warriors against horse-
men.*
GALLERIA DELL'ACCADEMIA 215 A, VENICE

49/2
*The rough sketch below, at center, shows a
galloping horse and rider, his cloak flying
out behind him in the fury of the run; to the
left the outlines of foot soldiers.*
WINDSOR 12340

49/2

49/3
*Of the three studies for the same group of
fighters sketched on this folio, this one is the
closest to the wall painting [46/1].*
GALLERIA DELL'ACCADEMIA 214, VENICE

The previous drawings by Leonardo referred or led to paintings; the following drawings were made for demonstrations of theories and principles in optics; photometry; and mechanics – force, motion, weight, and impact. They illustrate the beautiful Vincian phrase: "a mental discourse."

times already, and differing opinions have arisen as to its precise meaning. By some the passage has been taken as a solemn – and superstitious – autobiographical record of the day on which Leonardo began the *Battle of Anghiari*, recalling the first stroke of his brush on the wall of the Palazzo Vecchio in Florence. It has been underlined at some length how Leonardo emphasizes that June 6, 1505, fell on a Friday, a day considered by popular superstition to be unlucky, and notes the breaking out of a terrible storm, an event likewise popularly interpreted as an ill omen. But if Leonardo too was superstitious, why on earth would he have chosen precisely a Friday to begin "to paint in the Palace"? Unfortunately, these inauspicious premonitory signs seem to

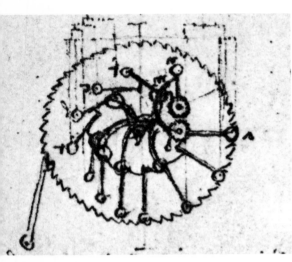 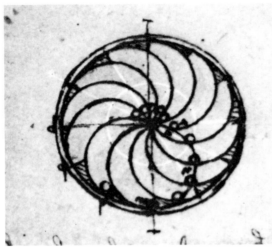 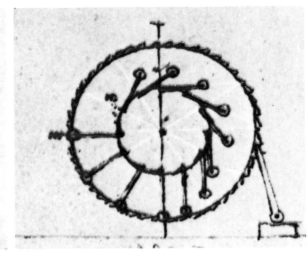

50/1   50/1–3 and 51/1   50/2   50/3   51/1

For Leonardo, drawing was a kind of language, in images that were more immediate and telling than the word itself. Often, in his notebooks, he switched from the written word to sketches to make his point graphic or even as a means of debating with others or himself. He made the beautiful drawings on these two pages to demonstrate the impossibility of perpetual motion – a chimera that had intrigued many thinkers over the ages and a notion that Leonardo himself may have had interest in as a young man. The pinwheel-like drawings on this page, from Codex Forster II, folios 90 recto, 91 verso and 90 verso, show with what forcefulness Leonardo suggests with a stroke of the pen the energy of movement. The drawing on the opposite page is from Codex Madrid II, folio 145 recto, where Leonardo made repeated notes on gravity, trying to define that then elusive force. In Forster II he is scornful of the seekers after perpetual motion, likening them to the alchemists who tried to convert base metals into gold:

Oh speculators on perpetual motion, how many vain projects in this search you have created! Go and be the companions of the searchers for gold.

be confirmed *a posteriori* by the fact that the *Battle of Anghiari* was left unfinished following a series of accidents and contretemps. Nevertheless this interpretation does not seem to me to have solid bases, and I consider the meaning of the passage to be quite different. In its excited crescendo, it sounds like the record of an exceptional meteorological phenomenon ("Suddenly, the weather became even worse and it rained very heavily till nightfall and the day turned to night"); and the punctual reminders of the day ("Friday the 6th of June") and the time ("at the stroke of the 13th hour") and even of the action ("As I took up the brush") take on the meaning and the value of a conscientious chronological note and document of the extraordinary happening. However interesting the passage may be for its reference to the famous *Battle of Anghiari*, it is still nothing more than a note and a document, viewing Leonardo's artistic work from the outside.

The wonderful series of drawings that illustrate almost every page of the Madrid Codices constitutes in itself the subject and substance of a work of art. Indeed so great is the many-sided variety of aspects presented by this great mass of drawings, so multiple the meanings and implications contained in it that even the definition "work of art" seems to be an understatement. In the centuries after Leonardo, cultural processes took place which brought about a specification of the concept of art. Art – and consequently drawing – became more and more emphatically stylistic and aesthetic, with the end result being discriminative and restrictive.

In Leonardo's day and in his hands, drawing still had a polyvalence, a high inventive and creative quality. Its rules were flexible and it possessed such a wealth of meaning and communicative force as to enable it to be truly associated with the word. This is language expressed through images, but more direct and more readily intelligible than the word itself, because "painting does not have need of interpreters for different languages as does literature," as Leonardo declares in the *Treatise on Painting* in the *Paragone*, where he compares the arts. Later in the *Paragone* he continues:

"By means of her basic principle, that is design, she [painting] teaches the architect to make his edifice so that it will be agreeable to the eye, and teaches

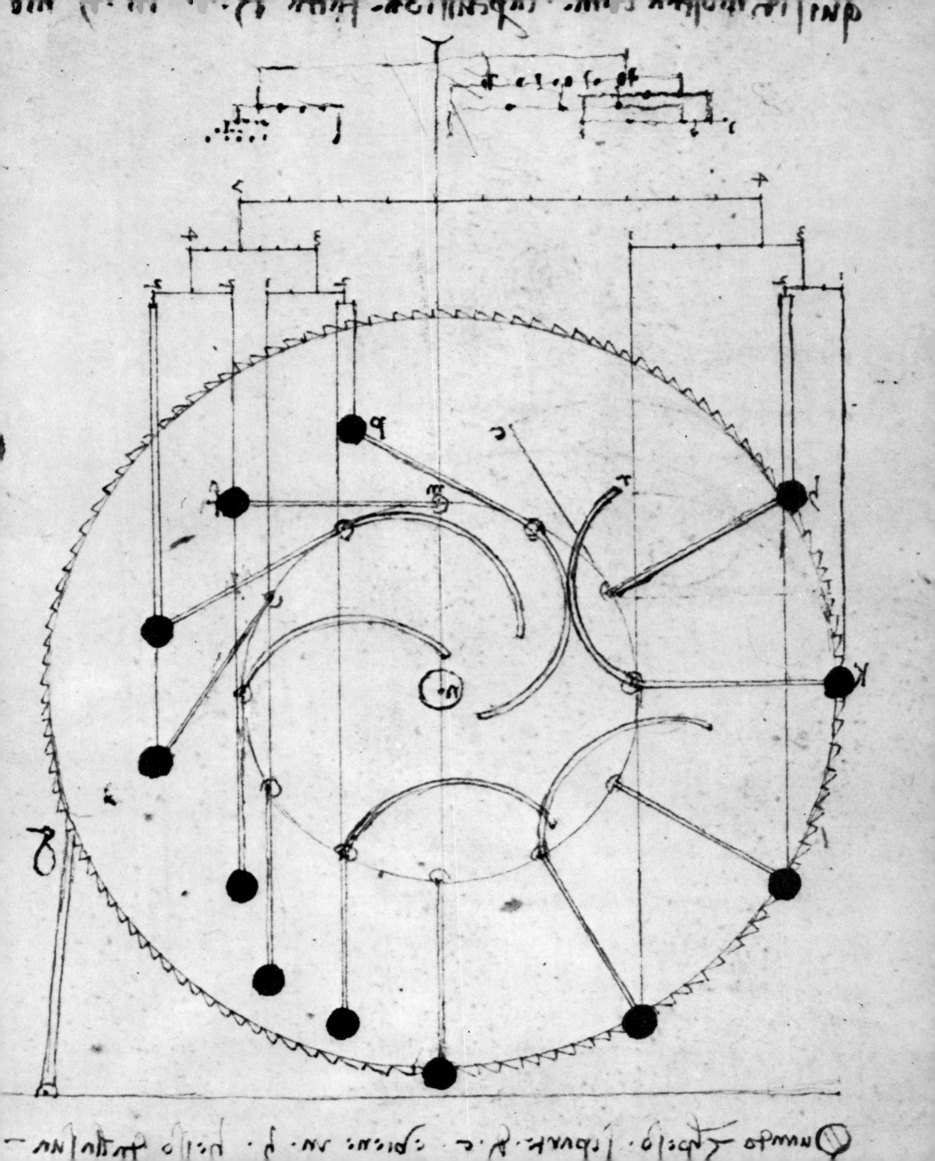

52/1–7

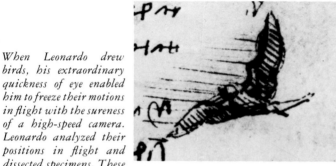

When Leonardo drew birds, his extraordinary quickness of eye enabled him to freeze their motions in flight with the sureness of a high-speed camera. Leonardo analyzed their positions in flight and dissected specimens. These drawings demonstrate this progression from art to the abstractions of science. In the top sketches his birds in flight are naturalistic; then the figures become simple outlines, and in the bottom sketch they are reduced to two elements essential to flight – the shape of the body and the wing configuration. In this manner he has gone from depicting the flight of birds to depicting the mechanics of flight. The details are taken from (top to bottom): Madrid II 102 recto, Codex on the Flight of Birds 6 recto (two drawings) and 8 recto, Madrid II 101 verso, Codex on the Flight of Birds 14 recto, and Madrid II 101 verso.

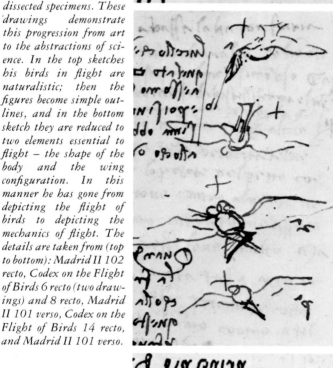

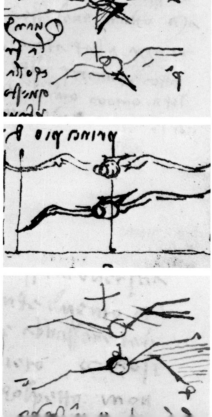

the composers of variously shaped vases, as well as goldsmiths, weavers and embroiderers. She has discovered the characters by which different languages are expressed, has given numerals to the arithmetician, has taught us how to represent the figures of geometry; she teaches masters of perspective and astronomy, machinists and engineers."[3]

The very last words of this passage can stand as the most pertinent introduction to the wonderful series of drawings of machines, devices, and mechanisms [55/1] which fill Codex Madrid I. Exquisitely clear, these become the instrument of research and analysis. Even as they are in progress, the drawings become a means of testing and checking the device which they are intended to represent; successive versions are tried out, and improvements are proposed and discussed through the illustrations: a true mental discourse, a creative process which, evolving and developing, finds in the drawing its clarifying and communicating instrument. Leonardo's drawing of machines is so straightforward and demonstrative that it even succeeds in charging the representation with a dynamic suggestion which makes clear not only their structure but also their function.

In the sketches where the idea is more rapidly committed to paper, this power of suggestion is conveyed especially by the unfinished, barely outlined aspect of the diagram, by the fleeting character of the tracing, and by its interruptions, which serve to illuminate improvements of the modeling of the form; or by the deep impressions in pen-point. The most typical examples of this rough and hasty type of sketch in the Madrid Codices are found in Codex Madrid II, which is much less homogeneous than Codex I and whose prevalent character is that of a notebook. On folio 76 recto, for example, on musical instruments, the tracing is thrown in various directions, sometimes making such a deep impression as to finish in pen-point, sometimes light and swift, seeming to suggest not only the form of the musical instruments but even the bursting forth from these of the sound and the musical notes.

Another example in the same manuscript is found on the pages he dedicated to the flight of birds[4] [52/1, 5, and 7]. In the margin beside the text they contain a row, running from top to bottom, of figures of birds drawn synthetically: a few strokes for the spindle-shaped body, a few strokes for the open wings in a succession of various positions and motions of flight. The progressive simplification of the form succeeds in the last figure in representing the tapered body of the bird, in a foreshortened frontal view, like a circle, and the wings in the form of two articulated arms which make it move – a wonderfully illustrated conclusion in synthesis of the mental process by which Leonardo interpreted the flight of birds in terms of elementary mechanics.

In the other codex, Codex Madrid I, which on account of its homogeneousness and coherent succession of arguments could be called a book of the elements of machines, even the drawing has a more analytic and finite character. The various machines and their "elements" are described with precision and objective evidence of details, in their form and structure. But here too Leonardo finds a way of getting across most effectively the image of their motion and function by other means. He makes his drawing technique conform to the different processes of his "mental discourse." It is enough for him to mark with a light stroke around the pivot – the "pole" as he calls it – a circle over the regular shadings which give body to the drawing of the machine, so that this circle, all the more immaterial because of the lightness of the stroke, suggests the rotating motion which takes place around the pivot.[5]

On other occasions, the diagrams of motions are freed from any reference to a given device and are studied abstractly for their own sakes, and their courses are noted and related to variations of force and weight. The concepts are illustrated according to the direction of the motions, with intersections and points of reference. Sometimes very complicated abstract compositions of great harmonic beauty result from this, as on folio 148 recto; sometimes we see instead an open succession, as it were, of single diagrams placed in

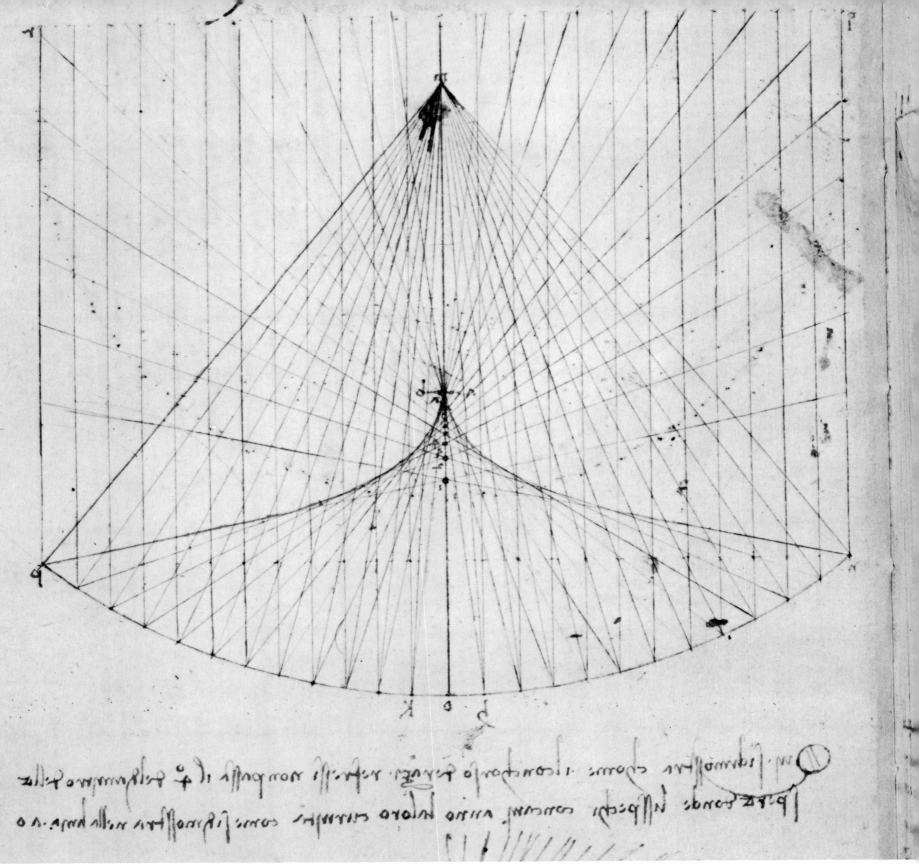

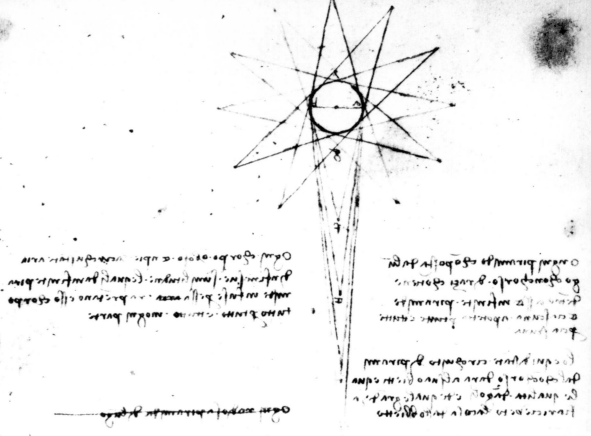

54/1

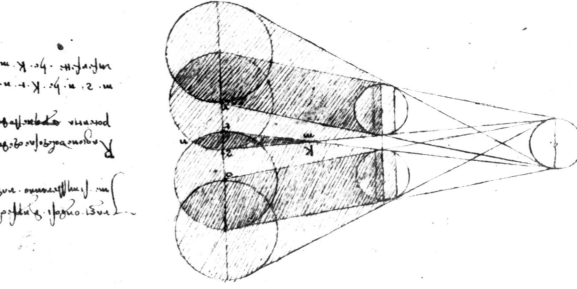

54/2

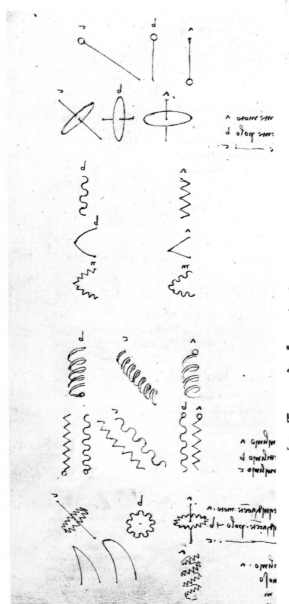

54/3

54/1 and 2   *The study of rays, their angles and paths and the countless figures they compose was for Leonardo the vehicle in studying optics, perspective, photometry and in general all the phenomena of impact. In the drawing at right, from Ms. A, folio 86 verso, the crown of pyramids sketched around a spherical body is to demonstrate that its image spreads out in a circular manner. The most elongated pyramid below shows that the smaller the image appears, the more acute the angle is, and the more distant from the object the apex is – conventionally identified with the eye receiving the image.*
The drawing below at right, from Ms. C, folio 14 recto, is a study of photometry: the spherical body on the right represents the source of light; the spheres of growing dimensions that follow each other on their path represent opaque bodies – "ombroso" – which intercept the luminous rays. The drawing demonstrates graphically the number of intercepted rays and as a consequence the greater or lesser density of the shade behind the intercepting bodies.

The graphic inventions of Leonardo are inexhaustible. This folio shows a series of diagrams on motion that communicate demonstratively and immediately. They depict movements of wheels around a pivot, springs and spirals.   MADRID I 131v

a row one behind the other like numbers in an addition; but even in this case the tracing is so evident and pertinent to the concept as to constitute its most direct and effective demonstration. In such cases the drawing becomes the equivalent of the word, equally capable of conveying abstract mental pro-

cesses. On folio 131 verso [54/3], on one side the text lists a whole series of "simple" motions, and opposite this a series of diagrams alive in its sequence of lines, circles, zig-zags, and spirals visualizes and makes immediately evident – and dynamic – the definitions of the written words. And while we are on the subject of these two pages, it ought to be pointed out what a magnificent page-setter Leonardo can be when, instead of amassing his notes in such a disorderly fashion that they often overlap one another, he takes pride in setting his page as in these last two folios.

In the drawings of machines in Codex Madrid I we can also trace the formation of a method of drawing which, side by side with the evolving method of architectural drawing, tries to perfect representation in plan and in elevation. A typical example is folio 44 verso. And in elevation, it is interesting how Leonardo seeks to obtain a variety of views – front, side – as if aiming at presenting successive orthogonal projections without optical deformation.[6] Architectural design and, as it is known today, industrial design reveal even in the Renaissance a researching of analogous methods of representation, and Leonardo participates directly in this process in both fields. His own words reveal how aware he was of the creative quality of drawing in it: "Drawing is of such excellence that it not only searches the works of nature, but infinitely more than what nature does."[7]

The discussion has dwelt upon these particular aspects of Leonardo's drawing because the very characteristics of the greater part of the drawings that illustrate the Madrid Codices required that it be so. The discussion would seem to risk being incomplete, however, were it to pass over the other more generally known and more properly artistic aspects: the drawing of figures and landscapes. As usual, Leonardo interpreted and rendered these in a way which was very original in comparison with the tradition of the Florentine school and which showed that he was ahead of his time.

In the Madrid manuscripts drawings of human figures are hardly present but there are magnificent examples of landscape drawings [146/1, 2,and 4] on folios 7 verso, 4 recto, and 17 recto of Codex Madrid II: crests of mountain chains, light, aerial, yet so individualized in their depressions and profiles as to be immediately recognizable even though unmarked by little names. For example the mountains of Monte Pisano. To draw them, Leonardo used red chalk, supple so as to make it possible to avoid every harshness of profiling, crumbling softly

55/2

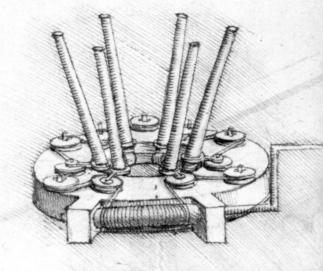

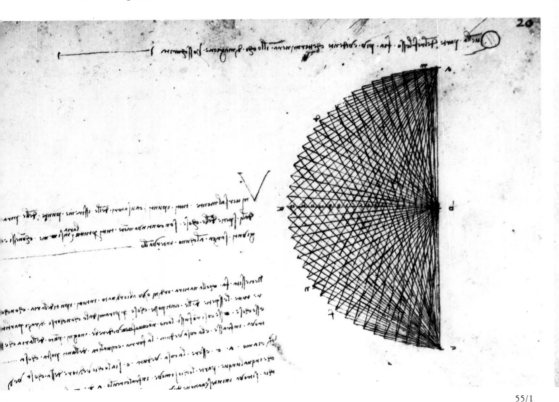

55/1

on the sheet to render the luminous richness of the whirling air. Here he indeed "searches the works of nature," and one cannot but recall, while admiring the aerial beauty of the drawings, the intelligence and openness of the phrase. He did not write "imitates," but "searches." His phrase welds these landscape drawings, although intended to express quite different interests and sensibilities, to the spirit of research, of contemplation, and of investigation, and to the extraordinary open-mindedness and organicity that characterize everything Leonardo did.

The expression "literary legacy" refers to that relatively small part of the mass of Leonardo's writings that has come down to us. J. P. Richter, who wanted to gather in a single work as many of the writings as possible, entitled his collection *The Literary Works of Leonardo da Vinci.*

THE WRITER

LEONARDO'S LITERARY LEGACY

AUGUSTO MARINONI

However, the term "literary" has a particular meaning, since, for the most part, the Vincian manuscripts that have come down to us are more or less provisional, generally unrelated, often repetitive, and intermingled with extracts transcribed from the books of others, personal notes, arithmetical calculations, etc., so that we are unable to identify even one organically completed chapter, let alone a book. Edward MacCurdy for this reason entitled his collection of writings by Leonardo *The Notebooks of Leonardo da Vinci.* But not even this work reflects faithfully the precise character of Vincian writings, because it disregards the drawings that have a prominent part in them. Leonardo was in fact convinced that he could communicate more by the drawing than by the word, and often the verbal text served to illustrate a drawing or vice versa. And a distinction must be made between the purely artistic drawings and those whose purpose is only to clarify a scientific concept or to present a technical project.

"... a splendor that can only shine briefly in a word, in a sentence, or in the space of a few lines, and yet leaves a profound impression on the reader."

The most substantial Vincian manuscripts are today in Italy, France, England, and Spain. Isolated leaves are located in Germany, Austria, Switzerland, Holland, Hungary, and the United States.

In the Biblioteca Ambrosiana of Milan in Italy is the large collection of over 1,200 folios of various sizes that the art collector Pompeo Leoni in the 16th century pasted on about 400 large folios of an album to create the Codex Atlanticus. (In recent years Leonardo's drawings and writings have been detached from the album of Leoni and have been restored and remounted in 12 splendid volumes.) In Milan too, at the Biblioteca Trivulziana, the Codex Trivulzianus is kept; the Biblioteca Reale of Turin has the small Codex on the Flight of Birds; and in the Galleria dell'Accademia of Venice there is a group of drawings.

57/1

57/3

57/2

Besides the very rich collection of drawings in Windsor Castle, England possesses the Codex Leicester, the Codex Arundel of the British Museum, and the 3 Forster Codices of the Victoria and Albert Museum of London.

The French holding, in Paris, consists of 12 of 13 manuscripts that Napoleon removed from the Biblioteca Ambrosiana. They bear the marks A, B, C, D, E, F, G, H, I, K, L, and M (the two Ashburnham Codices are part of Manuscripts A and B, from which they were torn out in the past century).

We have known only for a few years that the Biblioteca Nacional of Madrid is the home of the two important manuscripts Codex Madrid I and Codex Madrid II.

Unfortunately, with the passing of the centuries, the traces of many other manuscripts have been lost. How many we can only guess. Leonardo himself several times records books and treatises composed by him that we are unable to identify among the surviving manuscripts. What became of the "book on painting and

57/1–3

Leonardo wrote, sketched, and painted with his left hand, and most of the entries in his notebooks – even his own signature, "Io, Lionardo" – run right to left in the seemingly mysterious mirror writing. A signature intended for the eyes of others was written in the conventional manner (top right). The portrait of his own left hand at work appears in Codex Atlanticus, folio 283 verso-b, on a page that Leonardo had cluttered, as was his habit, with unrelated matter – a nude figure, a drawing of human hair, an architectural sketch.

human movements" which, according to Luca Pacioli, Leonardo had already composed in 1498, while he was coming to the end of the "invaluable" work "on local movement"? Some of Leonardo's writings undoubtedly ended up in the hands of others while he was alive.

But Codex Madrid II will perhaps enable us to establish how many of his own notebooks Leonardo had in his possession in 1504. In the important and already famous list [58/1] of 116 books that Leonardo was leaving "at the monastery"[1] at least two items name his own work: the "book of my words" and the "book

58/1 and 2

58/1

58/2

The rediscovery of the Madrid Codices reveals the contents of Leonardo's library and yields a clue to the number of his own notebooks. On these two pages from Codex Madrid II, folios 2 verso and 3 recto, he listed the titles of 116 books that he left in Florence when he went to Piombino in 1504. Despite Leonardo's attempts to depict himself as unlettered, the list suggests a well-read person with wide-ranging interests in medicine, mathematics, Latin

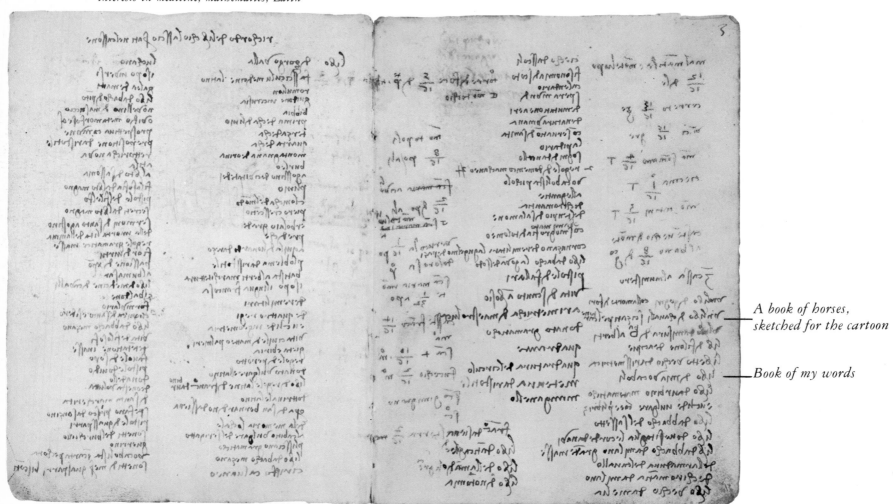

A book of horses, sketched for the cartoon

Book of my words

grammar, and even the Fables of Aesop. *In several instances he carefully has noted books lent to friends. Two books in his library, one of "my words" and one of "horses, sketched," probably were by his own hand. But on the following page of Madrid II, folio 3 verso, is a second, more tantalizing list (below) – untitled but arranged by physical format, leading to the belief that it may be an accounting of Leonardo's own notebooks. Though the list adds up to 50, Leonardo, the avid mathematician, made a simple error in arithmetic and got 48.*

25 small books
2 larger books
16 still larger books
6 books bound in vellum
1 book with green chamois cover

of horses, sketched for the cartoon." After this list Leonardo inventories[2] a mass of books of which he gives us neither the titles nor the characteristics apart from the number and, roughly, the dimensions. There are 25 "small" books, 2 "larger" books, 16 "still larger" books, 6 "bound in vellum," and 1 "with green chamois cover" [58/2]. Later, too, it was to be the custom of collectors of Vincian manuscripts to arrange them according to size – this is what Leoni, Melzi, and Arconati did – and as the 50 large and small books that are included in Leonardo's inventory are not part of the 116 whose titles are listed in the two preceding pages, we seem right in thinking that we have here works originated by Leonardo.[3]

The manuscripts that Leonardo still possessed when he died were inherited and carried to Italy by his faithful disciple Francesco Melzi [59/1], who preserved them with great care in his villa at Vaprio. He put them in order and distinguished them sometimes with alphabetical letters, sometimes with strange code marks, and added to them some notes on the number of folios present or missing. In addition he tried to do what Leonardo had wanted to do but in fact never did. He carefully read all the manuscripts, marked with an *o* passages related to painting, then copied them into the Codex Urbinas and thus compiled Leonardo's *Treatise on Painting*. Folio 231, recto and verso, contains the list of Vincian manuscripts from which the *Treatise* was taken

– 18 in all, of which 3 are defined as "booklets," that is, in sextodecimo. Only 7 of these 18 manuscripts are known today.[4] The various comparisons that have been made between the original writings of Leonardo and the *Treatise* show the accuracy of the copy and lead to the disturbing discovery that about three-quarters of the material found in the *Treatise* cannot be traced in the known Vincian manuscripts. This gives a measure of the losses suffered by Leonardo's writings, even admitting that the pages dealing with painting were the most sought after by the artists of the 16th century and consequently more subject to plunder than those related to other subjects.

On the death of Francesco Melzi around 1570 his heirs, especially his son Orazio, ignorant of the value of Leonardo's papers, relegated them to the attic, so that the tutor of the house, Lelio Gavardi, observing this indifference, thought he committed no crime by removing 13 manuscripts that he tried in vain to sell to the Duke of Florence. Remorse for the improper act was stirred up in his soul by his fellow student at Pisa, G. A. Mazenta, who himself undertook to return to Milan the ill-gotten property and restore it to Orazio Melzi. The latter merely reconfirmed his own lack of interest in the booklets and told Mazenta to keep them. Thus it is that the 13 manuscripts were divided between Mazenta's two brothers: Guido, who kept 6, and Alessandro.

It is here that the figure of Pompeo Leoni comes into the story. He was court sculptor to the King of Spain, Philip II, and a great collector of works of art. Promising Orazio Melzi the favors of the king and a place in the Senato, he obtained Alessandro Mazenta's 7 manuscripts, but only after 15 years did he succeed in recovering 3 of the 6 in the possession of Guido. The other 3 had already been given to Cardinal Borromeo (the present Manuscript C), to the Duke of Savoy, and to A. Figgini. Just as Melzi had done, Leoni meticulously set about cataloguing the vast material. Having arranged the manuscripts according to format, from the largest to the smallest, he first marked each with a progressive number, placed at the beginning or at the end of every volume. The highest number among those which have come down to us is 46. Then he wrote, or had an assistant write, an alphabetical mark as well. Of the manuscripts marked by Leoni only 19 remain, which again gives us some idea of how many of the manuscripts have been lost.[5]

But Leoni did not stop at distinguishing each manuscript with a number and an alphabetical mark. What Melzi had done in some cases – note the number of folios contained in the manuscript – Leoni did systematically, adding beside the alphabetical marks numbers corresponding to those of the leaves making up the volume: for example, A 190, O 140, BB 14, LL 48. This is invaluable indication that allows us to establish how many folios constituted a given manuscript in Leoni's time, how many were afterwards removed, and how many had already been taken away.[6]

In the case of the Madrid manuscripts we observe that Leoni wrote the mark A 190 on folio 191 verso of Codex Madrid I. The manuscript had been made up of two volumes of 96 folios each, numbered on the recto in Leonardo's own hand from 1 to 95 with the omission of the first folio, which was at first left blank as a flyleaf, as a temporary cover, or because it was destined to be pasted on the back of the cover during binding. The fact that the two series of numbers 1 to 95 proceed in opposite directions from the beginning and from the end, meeting in the middle, makes us suppose that Leonardo, although distinguishing the two volumes, intended to consider them as two parts of the same work. The fact is that when they came into Leoni's hands they already formed a single volume; and Leoni himself, or one of his assistants or others before him (Melzi?), took care to unify the numeration from folio 95 to the end. It can also be taken for granted that the folios now missing and once numbered from 37 to 42 and from 55 to 56 were lost after the operations carried out by Leoni.[7]

Besides the bound manuscripts, Leoni gathered together a large mass of loose papers of various sizes that Leonardo had written or drawn upon. The latter – in the interests of economy, we can say – used every piece of paper that

59/1 and 2
Leonardo bequeathed his manuscripts to his disciple and pupil, Francesco Melzi (left), who had remained with the master until his death at Cloux in 1519. Melzi took the works back to Milan, treasured them, and undertook the kind of extensive cataloguing Leonardo always had put off. After Melzi's

59/1
Francesco Melzi

59/2
Cardinal Borromeo

death around 1570, the dispersal of the manuscripts began and avarice took over – many of the unpublished notebooks passed through the hands of thieves and dealers as well as scholars. One of the manuscripts wound up with Cardinal Federigo Borromeo (right), founder of the Biblioteca Ambrosiana in Milan, and he donated it to the library in 1609. Eventually, the library's collection included 13 manuscripts, but on Napoleon's instructions they were carted off to Paris in 1796. After the Napoleonic wars, only the Codex Atlanticus was returned to Milan. The rest remained in Paris.

happened to come into his hands provided it still had a blank face: leaves from registers, letters, the writings of others. The paper was often of such poor quality that Leonardo could write on one side only, as the ink went through the whole thickness of the paper. Even these isolated sheets have in great part been classified with a progressive number generally placed at the center of the page. However, the fact that many numbers are repeated several times on different sheets makes us think that they came from diverse collections and that they were not then reordered systematically. In order to save such papers from dispersion and to give them physical unity, Leoni

60/1

thought of pasting them onto large folios of two big albums: one the present Windsor Collection, with the original title of *Designs of Leonardo da Vinci Restored by Pompeo Leoni*, and the other the Codex Atlanticus, entitled *Designs of Machines and of Secret Arts and Other Things of Leonardo da Vinci Gathered by Pompeo Leoni*. When both sides of the paper were written on, Leoni made a hole or a window in the supporting folio of the album and pasted the edges of the paper so that both sides remained visible.

The discussion of the most startling discovery made as a consequence of the recent restoration of the Codex Atlanticus is contained in the Appendix, on page 288.

For a long time it was considered that Leoni had taken apart and mutilated a certain number of Vincian notebooks in order to make up the Codex Atlanticus. This, it was thought, would explain the disappearance of many notebooks and lead to the reassuring conclusion that these were still present in the Codex Atlanticus and in the Windsor Collection, although mixed up and mutilated. But we were mistaken, or we had exaggerated. André Corbeau rightly pointed out that if Leoni had in fact taken apart actual manuscripts, many sheets of the Codex Atlanticus would still show the holes of the stitches and the fold in the middle. But there are no holes, and folds in the middle are not very frequent. The recent restoration of the Codex Atlanticus freed the folios from the superimpositions and foldings to which, in the interests of economy of space, Leoni had subjected them, thus making a more accurate examination of the individual pages possible and leading to fresh conclusions. Leoni certainly permitted himself many arbitrary procedures, such as separating into two different albums two types of drawings and subjects; to do this, he cut out from the interior of various pages of the Codex Atlanticus figures which he arranged in the Windsor Collection, and then patched up the holes he had made. Again, he distributed and spaced out over different pages several folios that probably constituted little quires that were still loose but dealt with the same subject matter. Nevertheless it cannot be said that he dismembered original volumes; on the contrary, we ought to praise him for having saved so many unbound sheets from probable dispersion.

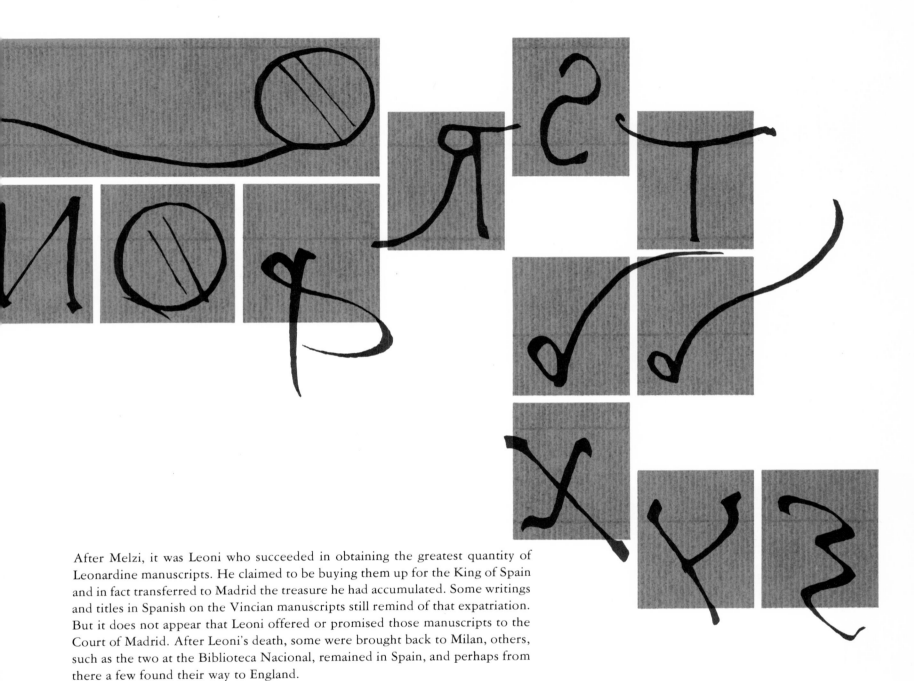

After Melzi, it was Leoni who succeeded in obtaining the greatest quantity of Leonardine manuscripts. He claimed to be buying them up for the King of Spain and in fact transferred to Madrid the treasure he had accumulated. Some writings and titles in Spanish on the Vincian manuscripts still remind of that expatriation. But it does not appear that Leoni offered or promised those manuscripts to the Court of Madrid. After Leoni's death, some were brought back to Milan, others, such as the two at the Biblioteca Nacional, remained in Spain, and perhaps from there a few found their way to England.

Leoni died in Madrid in 1608. Shortly after, another keen collector of Vincian manuscripts asserts himself: Count Galeazzo Arconati, whose son, Luigi Arconati, clearly taking advantage of his father's library, compiled from the Vincian manuscripts a book to which he gave the title *Treatise on the Motion and the Measure of Water* (1634). In 1637, Count Galeazzo Arconati donated to the Biblioteca Ambrosiana 11 Vincian manuscripts which are well enough described in the deed of donation to be identifiable as the Codex Atlanticus, the Codex Trivulzianus, the little Codex on the Flight of Birds, and the present Manuscripts A, B, E, G, H, I, L, and M. The number of folios of each manuscript is registered, and so we know, for example, that the Codex Trivulzianus, originally made up of 92 folios but reduced at the time of Pompeo Leoni to 55, was further cut down to 54 at the time of Arconati; today it contains only 51 folios. Arconati did not immediately

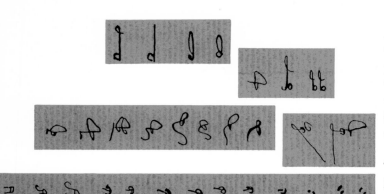

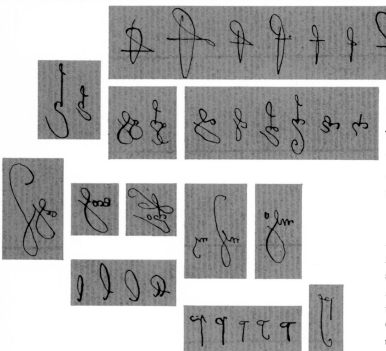

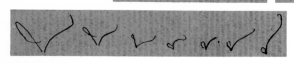

62/1
This montage of Leonardo's handwriting shows examples of his small alphabet taken from various manuscripts. In the clusters of individual letters can be traced the evolution of his style of penmanship. The differences are so pronounced that scholars sometimes can date a manuscript to the precise years by studying the forms of the letters. As a young man Leonardo's hand was influenced by the world of merchants and notaries – his own father was a notary – and was therefore ornamental, slow, full of flourishes. From about age 38 to 63 his writing displayed increasing simplicity and speed to keep up with his impatient mind. In the final years before his death it grew heavy and labored.

hand manuscripts over to the Ambrosiana, however, because he had reserved the right to keep them with him as long as he lived; and when they were at last presented to the library, Manuscript D had taken the place of the Trivulzianus, which in 1770 was sold to Prince Trivulzio by Gaetano Caccia. Manuscript C was given by Cardinal Federigo Borromeo [59/2] to the Biblioteca Ambrosiana in 1609 and Manuscript K was given to that library by Count Orazio Archinti in 1674.

The vicissitudes that took the folios of the precious Windsor Collection to England are not so clear. The early history of the Forster Codices is also obscure; they were in Vienna when Lord Lytton purchased them before giving them to John Forster [81/1], who presented them to the Victoria and Albert Museum in 1876. We know that Lord Arundel [81/3] carried out a prolonged search for Vincian papers; those at the British Museum have been put together in a rather disorderly way into the codex that is named after him. Finally, the codex that bears the name of Lord Leicester [81/2] we know to have been purchased in Rome in the 18th century.

A further displacement was caused by the Napoleonic wars, when all the Vincian manuscripts of the Ambrosiana were gathered up in the vast seizure of works of art and precious books carried out by Napoleon. After his fall only the Codex Atlanticus returned to Milan; the others remained in Paris. It must be added that the last quires of Manuscripts A and B, torn out criminally in the 19th century by Count Libri and sold in England, became two autonomous little codices that took the name of their owner, Lord Ashburnham [81/4], who sent them back to Paris when he learned of their illegal provenance.

The early collectors of Vincian manuscripts such as Melzi, Leoni, and Arconati used to list the manuscripts and then regroup them according to size from the largest to the smallest. Chronological classification would have been far more scientific, but its drawback becomes immediately evident when we take into account the uncertainty of many dates and the fact that Leonardo wrote in the same manuscripts, and even on the same page, at different times.[8]

Another way of classifying Leonardo's manuscripts is to distinguish between those composed with great care and those of the "miscellaneous" type. The first category consists of those that are well written and well drawn and contain homogeneous subject matter probably ready for a reader or at least elaborated to a point that only just precedes the final draft.[9] In these, Leonardo's original intention seems evidently directed towards a homogeneous treatment, but afterwards he often adds other subjects, a date, a drawing, completely unrelated to the original theme of the volume. Only 28 of the 36 pages of the Codex on the Flight of Birds are actually related to the subject.

In the second category we put the "miscellaneous" little books whose pages receive at different times the most varied notes, sometimes in pen, sometimes in pencil or red chalk, which are often placed in the spaces left free by the previous notes. In this type of manuscript, which we can consider a "rough-book" or even "scribbling pad," we also find pages that Leonardo transcribed verbatim or summarily from the books of others for his personal study requirements. We come across both kinds of writing even in the loose leaves that Pompeo Leoni gathered together in the Codex Atlanticus: ordered, unitary, elegant pages and pages hastily sketched and without any order whatever.

The two Madrid manuscripts provide clear examples of both types of composition. Madrid I, with its very elegant handwriting, splendid drawings, harmonious pagination, and complex unity of subject matter, belongs to the first category. The first 140 folios of Codex Madrid II, on the other hand, comprise a typical rough-book which is worth studying at least summarily in order to examine the intricate network of interests and problems tackled by Leonardo.[10] It is certain that the notes and drawings were not written in orderly fashion one after the other, one page after the other. Occasionally, when it came to different subjects and different periods, Leonardo began his notes or drawings at different points in the manuscript, leaving frequent intervals of blank pages, which became fewer and fewer as time went on.[11]

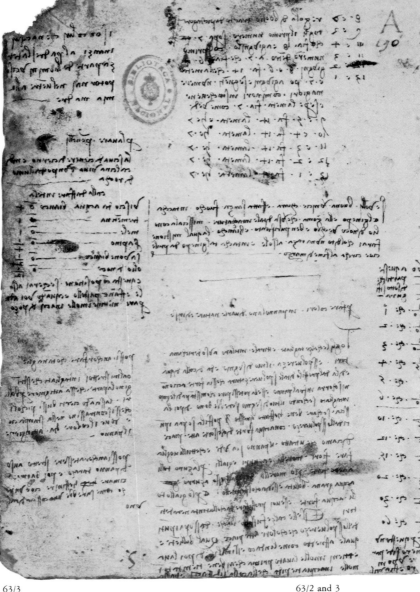

63/1
Leonardo's notebooks were a librarian's nightmare as they passed through the hands of heirs legitimate and otherwise – a priceless but randomly put-together mass. Francesco Melzi, his pupil and heir, compiled the Treatise on Painting *by painstakingly copying all the passages related to painting into the Codex Urbinas. At the end he listed the 18 Leonardo manuscripts that were his sources and gave each a distinguishing mark (above). Only 7 of these manuscripts survive today.*

63/2   63/3

63/2 and 3
Later, Pompeo Leoni, court sculptor to the King of Spain, acquired some 50 Leonardo notebooks and set about arranging them by size, from largest to smallest. He numbered each notebook, then added an alphabetical mark and the number of folios or sheets in each. The last page of Codex Madrid I, folio 191 verso (above), bears the mark A 190. The original last page of Madrid II, folio 140 verso (above, left), is marked O 140 (17 more folios were bound on later).

64/1 and 65/1
Overleaf: Two pages from Leonardo's notebooks illustrate his powerful impulse towards graphic harmony. On page 64, a perplexing exercise in geometry creates pleasing rosette patterns in Codex Atlanticus, folio 168 recto-a. On page 65, the words, wheels, and gears of Codex Madrid I, folio 5 recto, mesh in symmetrical design.

On July 22, 1503, "the day of the Magdalene," Leonardo started some cartographic surveys of the valley of the Arno from Florence to the sea. On the first three pages of Madrid II[12] he made some topographic sketches showing the course of the Arno and giving the names of places and the distances represented. On other sheets[13] the profiles of the Monte Pisano hills are beautifully outlined. Two magnificent geographic maps[14] bear testimony to this activity. Intermingled with these pages, or even superimposed on them, are other notes, drawings, and arithmetical calculations, made at Piombino in the last months of 1504, that deal with the project for the fortifications requested by the lord of that city and include estimates of the costs involved in the operation.

To the tens of pages devoted to the fortifications of Piombino [156/1–159/6] must be added those inspired by the observation of the sea, which cannot have failed to arouse Leonardo's curiosity during his stay. There are observations on the motion of waves[15] [66/2]; on quite a few folios can be seen drawings

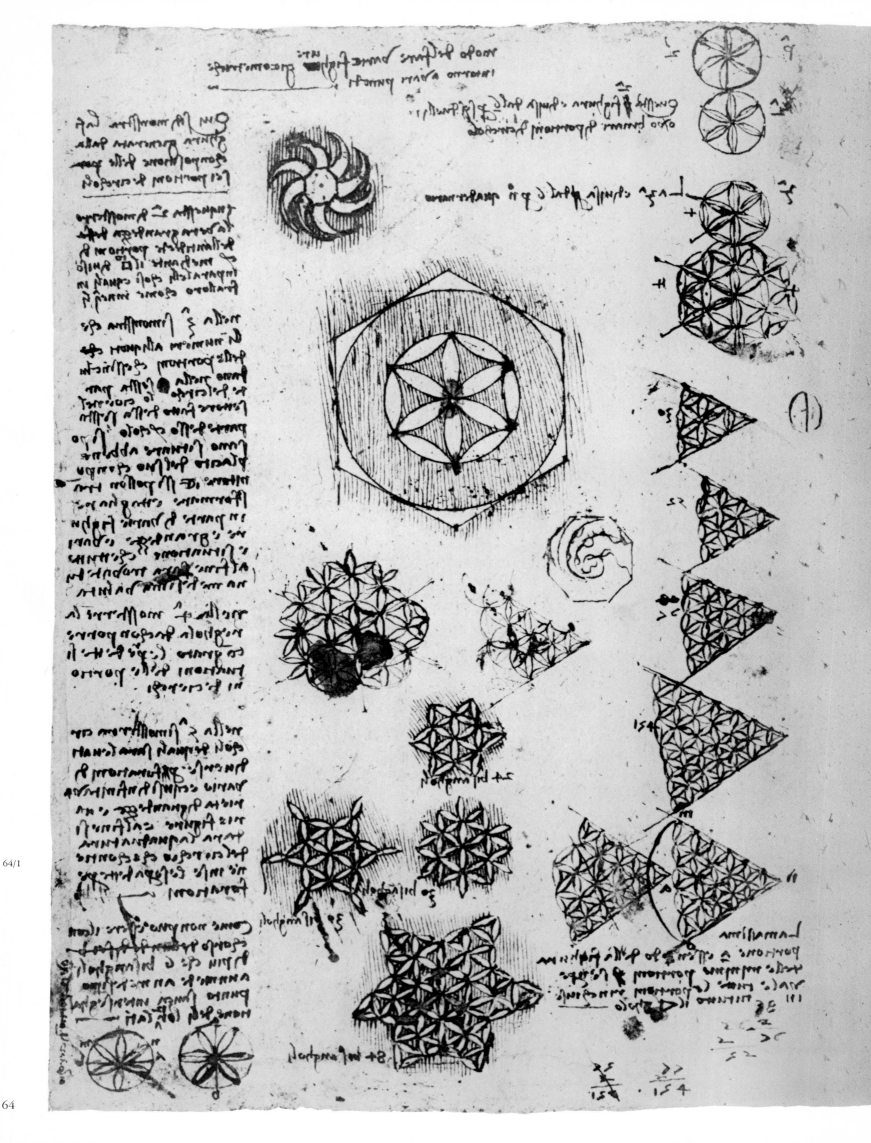

64/1

and notes on the direction of winds and on sailing ships and sailing [66/1].

No element in the natural world so beguiled Leonardo as water and the endless beauty of its form. His notebooks abound with sketches of waves rising, unfurling, or whirling in rapid vortices. He sketched human hair and flowers in their likeness and arrived by analogy at wave theories of light and sound that foreshadowed modern physics. In his later years he even described and drew an apocalyptic vision of the world destroyed by deluge. Leonardo seldom had the opportunity to observe the oceans firsthand. In 1504 he went to Piombino, on the west coast of the Italian peninsula, to undertake a study of military fortifications. He made notes in Codex Madrid II, on the handling of sailboats, on folio 35 recto (below), and the swirling action of waves pounding upon the shore, on folio 24 recto (right). His writings often liken the earth to man's body, and water to his blood: "As man has in him a pool of blood in which the lungs rise and fall in breathing, so the body of the earth has its ocean tide which likewise rises and falls every six hours, as if the world breathed."

66/1

and notes on the direction of winds and on sailing ships and sailing [66/1].

Although it seems as if the book was opened at random and the various notes added here and there haphazardly, one still has the impression that in the first part of the manuscript Leonardo was following the direction of the present numeration as he wrote. This impression is strengthened by the

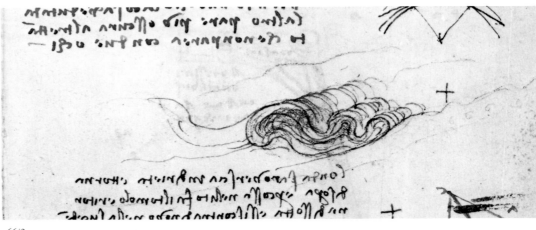

66/2

notes that he took from the *Summa de arithmetica* of Pacioli – to be exact, from the treatise on proportions [67/1–2]. Similarly, if we move to the other end of the manuscript,[16] we see that there he begins to write in a very neat hand a fair copy in the vernacular of the text of the *Elements* of Euclid.[17] The transcription of Euclid's text is then interrupted, but the pages dedicated to geometry continue through almost the whole of the final section with a significant deterioration in quality: from the simple but ordered transcription of a famous text he passes to disorderly personal research into particular problems that are grouped under the title "Science of equiparation."[18] Leonardo has something of his own to say in the field of geometric studies. In the next year, 1505, he was to write Codex Forster I, which is the treatise on the transformation of plane figures and geometric solids into equivalents. He is now evidently preparing the material for that treatise, and so geometry has a predominant part in Codex Madrid II.[19] The prevailing problem in this "Science of equiparation" is that of the equivalence between curvilinear and rectilinear figures, which includes the squaring of the circle. Codex Madrid II has the merit of revealing to us an elated moment in Leonardo's life: the moment at which he thought he had discovered the solution to the famous problem.

The manuscript is thus a mixture where the most various notes (not excluding two "jokes") alternate with pages copied from other books: Pacioli, Euclid, extracts from Francesco di Giorgio Martini's treatise on the construction of a fortress that are certainly connected with the works projected for Piombino. Perhaps it was prior to his departure for Piombino that Leonardo made out the lists of books and clothes that he was leaving in Florence.[20] The last note may be that appended on the first page of the manuscript recording the violent storm on June 6, 1505, during the work on the great painting that was to represent the Battle of Anghiari.

We have cast a glance at the literary legacy of Leonardo. We must add that the reading of Leonardo's writings presents great difficulties and can cause disappointments. Although he planned several treatises, he almost always wrote tentative notes, often a few lines, hardly ever more than a page. The same note is repeated many times in different manuscripts with slight modifications. A great many notes are not written for a reader, but are mere memoranda for his own use. Moreover, he alternates his original ideas with the transcriptions from the pages of various books. All this makes the reading of the text, its comprehension, and its relationship with other texts scattered in different manuscripts difficult for a nonspecialist. In addition, the transcriptions of his writings

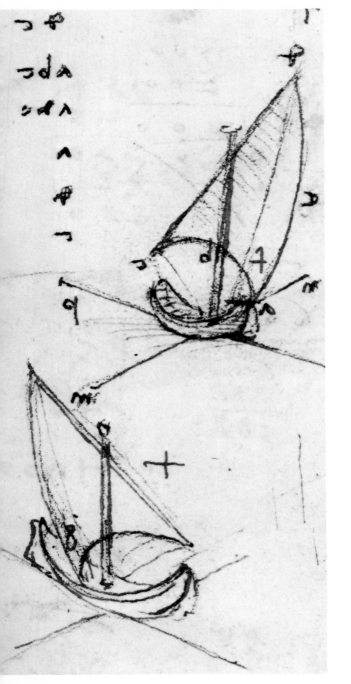

available today contain a certain number of errors, which are obviously reflected in the translation.[21]

Naturally, in these conditions, the persons who have read Leonardo's writings in full are few.[22] And naturally, fragmentary reading has made it possible for the great legend of Leonardo as a superhuman being, the genius who embraced

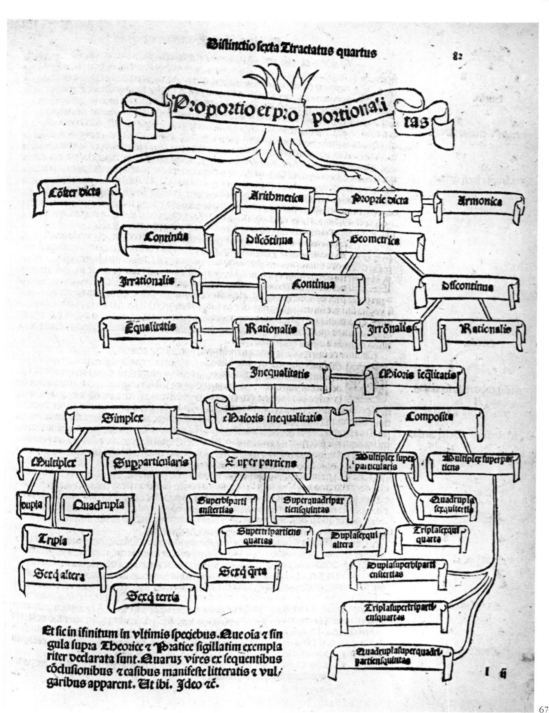

67/2

67/1

Through the notebooks flow countless images of flight – the caged birds that Leonardo bought, set free, and sketched lovingly, and his fantasy of man flying. The note above, from Codex Madrid II, folio 83 verso, is entitled "Of flying creatures." He inserts a sketch of a bird in the text to make his thought easier to follow.

67/2 and 3   67/3

In his early forties a new obsession overtook Leonardo – mathematics – and his notebooks began to fill up with geometrical sketches and calculations. As a painter, he long had been interested in the study of proportions, but his meeting with Luca Pacioli in Milan about 1496 seemed to have a decisive impact on his future involvement. Pacioli, one of the leading mathematicians of the day, asked Leonardo to provide the illustrations for his book De divina proportione. *Leonardo studied Pacioli's* Summa de arithmetica *and copied from it the family tree of proportions at left. The chart includes 40 denominations distributed in a vast ramification of types and subtypes. A page from Codex Madrid II, folio 78 recto (above), shows that Leonardo became distracted or tired of the task and copied down only 20 of the 40 names.*

all the knowledge of his time and anticipated that of the future, to survive and grow. This legend has some truth in it, but there are several false elements that must be removed.

The fact that Leonardo's earliest manuscripts go back to the last years of the penultimate decade of the 15th century[23] means that up until about the age of 35 he had not yet decided to write books or keep a record of his ideas. Among these very early manuscripts, Manuscript B is not meant to be a treatise, but is only a miscellany devoid of literary and stylistic pretensions, containing notes on books read,[24] many rules, memoranda, and various observations in great disorder. But the very early Codex Trivulzianus, documents one of Leonardo's main concerns when he decided to become a writer. As Leonardo himself admitted, he was "without letters"; that is, he had no knowledge of Latin and was unable to read and

quote "the authors." He realized that his native language, the Florentine dialect and the technical jargon of the artisan *botteghe*, provided him with a terminology capable of naming all the objects of the visible and tangible world, but that it was rather poor in abstract nouns, adjectives, adverbs, and verbs that only men of letters knew or made up via Latin derivations. Leonardo sought to remedy this fundamental and primary defect by collecting words of this kind either from

68/1
His letter I, like a fishhook.

68/2
Ornamental variations on the letter E.

68/3
Above: A sentence in which the letter l loops above the line like unfurled flags.

68/4
Below: The loop of a simple I and of an l, building the article "il."

68/5
Left and above: The letter Q with a long tail.

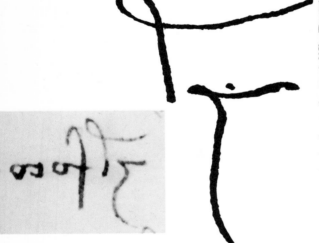
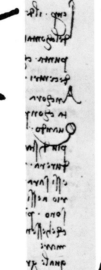

68/6
Left: His shorthand for the syllable per.

68/7
Right: A study of equilibrium in the arms of a balance.

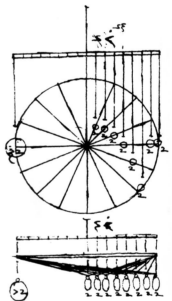

68/8
Below: A demonstration in geometry.

68/9
Above: Decorative flourishes on the tails of small letters.

68/10
Left: Three variations on the shorthand syllable di.

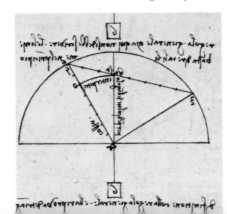

68/11
Left: A demonstration of numerical proportion.

grammars and dictionaries[25] or from the very books he was reading. This took place when he was 40 years old. Later he decided to confront the study of Latin directly.[26] He had all the books necessary, but there is no evidence that he was able to take full advantage of them.

The preparation he had received in the field of mathematical sciences in his youth

was also very inadequate. He was never very good at calculation, and even in terms of the knowledge of concepts the gaps in his education were far from insignificant. For a while he shared the doubt of many inexperienced persons as to the validity of some basic rules.[27]

Pacioli [70/1] claims to have been Leonardo's colleague in the pay of Lodovico il Moro from 1496 to 1499 and to have been his companion in the following years. He further states that in 1498 Leonardo had written or was writing some books and had sketched the "wonderful drawings for the five regular bodies." To carry out such a task, Leonardo must have been acquainted with the problems involved in the construction of regular polygons and in general with the theory of proportions. It is significant that from 1496 on Leonardo's manuscripts devote more space to geometry. Manuscripts M and I, datable between 1496 and 1499, dedicate a hundred pages to the study of the very first books and some parts of Book X of Euclid's *Elements,* something that was almost certainly conditioned by the mere presence of Pacioli and by Leonardo's commitment to illustrate *De divina proportione* [70/2–71/5]. The

69/2

his ongoing self-education, especially in language and mathematics. Above, in Codex Madrid II, folio 48 verso, he copies down the multiplication table from Pacioli's Summa de arithmetica (top). Next to the table Leonardo summarizes part of his mentor's written discourse by linking with lines the numbers that form a class and labeling each class – the first is "multiples."

On the opposite page are samples from the Madrid Codices of Leonardo's meticulous hand. The beautifully wrought letters, the shorthand symbols that stand for syllables, even a mechanical drawing and two geometric demonstrations – all illustrate the success with which he sought to recreate the harmony and proportion he found in nature.

The Franciscan monk and mathematician Luca Pacioli (below left) not only influenced Leonardo's interest in geometry and proportions but was the first man of letters to proclaim him publicly as a writer. In his

70/1

introduction to De divina proportione, for which Leonardo drew the illustrations. Pacioli praises both these drawings and "a worthy book on painting and human movements" – a work since lost.

Leonardo's illustrations for De divina proportione – complex three-dimensional designs in solid geometry (right) – were extolled by Pacioli as "extraordinary and most beautiful figures." Among the drawings were the so-called "Platonic regular bodies;" five polyhedra that Plato had said defined the forms of the five natural elements: the pyramid – fire; the cube – earth; the 8-sided octahedron – air; the 20-sided icosahedron – water; the 12-sided dodecahedron – heaven. Leonardo drew these in all of their variants; he already had been exposed to the geometry of perspective in his early days in Florence, and the abstract perfection of these intricate forms must have pleased and intrigued him. In 1501 he was so obsessed with mathematics that he neglected his painting and, writes an observer, "the sight of a brush puts him out of temper." A new interest, however, always took him back to old familiar ones, enriching his painting and helping him penetrate engineering theory and practice. In Manuscript K he writes, "Let proportion be found not only in numbers and measures, but also in sounds, weights, times, and positions, and whatever force there is."

70/2

SEPTVAGINTA DVARVM
BASIVM VACVVM

LXXXXIIII

TETRACEDRON ELEVA TVS VACVVS.

DVODECEDRON ELEVA TVS VACVVS.

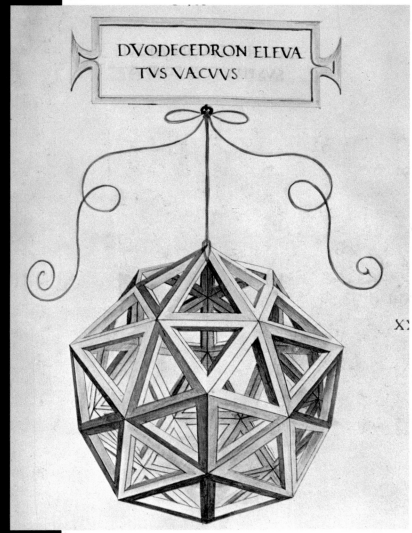

LXXXXVI

EXACEDRON ABSCISVS VACVVS.

.C.

OCTOCEDRON ABSCISVS VACVVS.

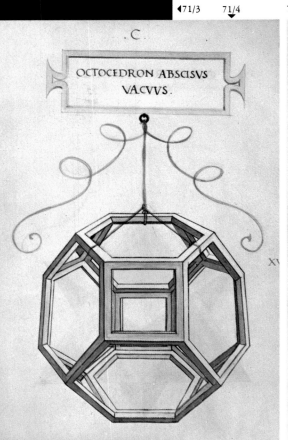

.CIII.

VCOCEDRON ABSCISVS VACVVS.

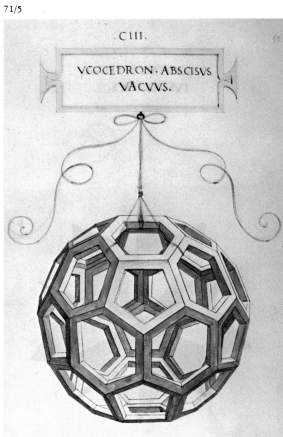

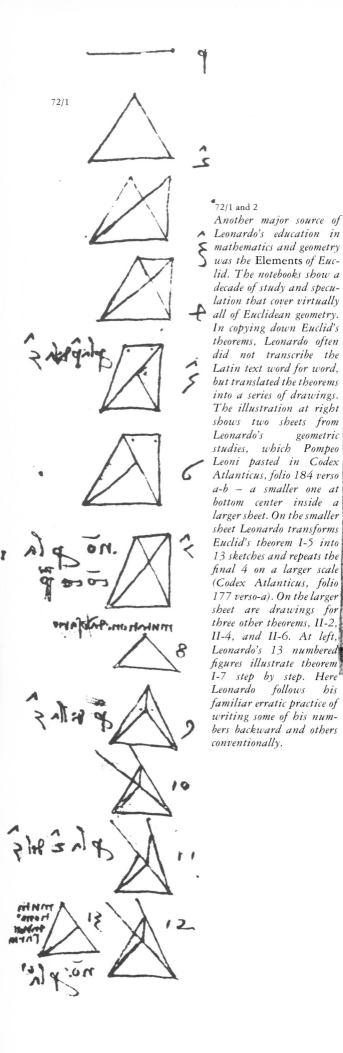

notes of Manuscripts M and I have a particular form; Leonardo never transcribes anywhere from the Latin text, which nevertheless he has at hand, but just traces some geometric figures, often adding in the upper margin or beside the drawing the number of the corresponding Euclidean proposition, or even a few words representing a fragment of the discourse which is taking place in his mind. This shows us clearly that he is writing only for himself. Since in Manuscript I we also find notes that Leonardo made for an elementary study of Latin, we ask ourselves how he was able to read and understand the difficult

72/1 and 2

Another major source of Leonardo's education in mathematics and geometry was the Elements of Euclid. *The notebooks show a decade of study and speculation that cover virtually all of Euclidean geometry. In copying down Euclid's theorems, Leonardo often did not transcribe the Latin text word for word, but translated the theorems into a series of drawings. The illustration at right shows two sheets from Leonardo's geometric studies, which Pompeo Leoni pasted in Codex Atlanticus, folio 184 verso a-b – a smaller one at bottom center inside a larger sheet. On the smaller sheet Leonardo transforms Euclid's theorem I-5 into 13 sketches and repeats the final 4 on a larger scale (Codex Atlanticus, folio 177 verso-a). On the larger sheet are drawings for three other theorems, II-2, II-4, and II-6. At left, Leonardo's 13 numbered figures illustrate theorem I-7 step by step. Here Leonardo follows his familiar erratic practice of writing some of his numbers backward and others conventionally.*

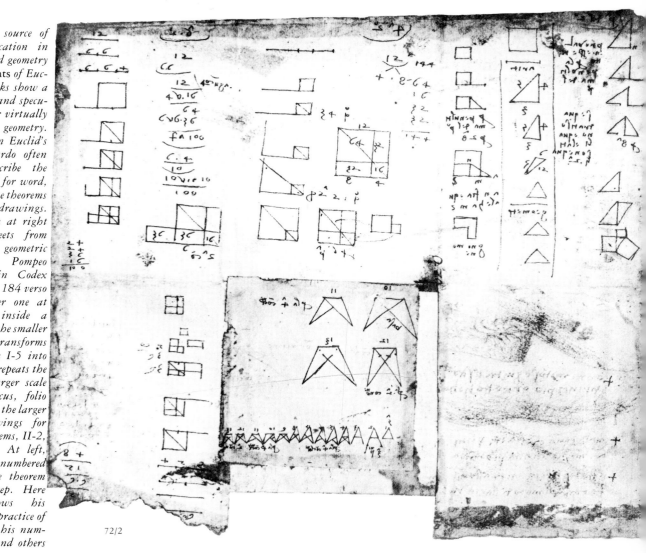

72/2

Latin of Campano, who translated and wrote a commentary on Euclid. That Leonardo is using the Campano Latin edition is confirmed by the exact correspondence of the drawings and by the occasional tell-tale Latin word, such as *conclusio* or *propositum*.[28] The presence of an expert would have been indispensable in overcoming the linguistic barrier, and it seems likely that it was his friend, inspirer, and master, Luca Pacioli. The latter must have made a précis for him of the Euclidean page, which he condensed in a few lines. In the first two parts of Manuscript K, of 1504, many pages are given over to the study of other books of the *Elements,* and a group of folios of the Codex Atlanticus [72/1–73/2] seems to be intended as a résumé of them in a more organic and complete form.[29]

We thus reach the very important conclusion that only between 1496 and 1504 did Leonardo come to know and study Euclid's book; in other words, at the age of 50 or thereabouts Leonardo was still a student as far as Latin and mathematics were concerned.

While there is no proof that he continued to study Latin, geometry became a real passion for the rest of his life. He worked intensely on the problem of the duplication of the cube, trying out various solutions which were clearly absurd. In Madrid II[30] appears a drawing, unaccompanied by a text, of the solution given by the ancients and referred to by Giorgio Valla.[31] Leonardo severely criticized several times this old solution until he succeeded in perfecting it by means of a little but authentic discovery,[32] which has passed unnoticed until today, and of which he declared himself to be very proud.

He is not so justified in his pride at having surpassed Archimedes in the problem of the quadrature of the circle. The solution which came to him in a flash on St. Andrew's night, 1504, consists of comparing two circles whose

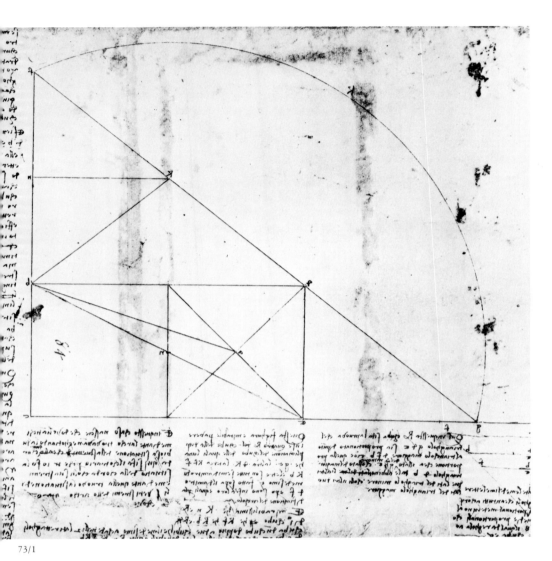

73/1

73/2

areas are in the ratio 1:1,000,000. The smaller circle is therefore equivalent to a sector of the larger circle and equal to one-millionth of it. Such a sector would practically be equal to a triangle, as the arc which closes it, being very short, would be – says Leonardo – "almost flat." In other words, whereas Archimedes divided the circumference into 96 parts, Leonardo divides it into a million parts, as if constructing a polygon with a million sides. However, while Archimedes by his demonstration arrived at the ratio 22:7, very useful for the actual measuring of the circle, Leonardo goes no further than to affirm the equivalence of a circle to a sector of another circle, without calculating any measure. According to Leonardo, Archimedes' quadrature was "well said and badly presented," but his own is only described and not presented at all.

It is clear that after studying Euclid and Archimedes for roughly eight years Leonardo follows his own direction. In 1505 he composes Codex Forster I, which is dedicated to the transformation of one area into another or one solid into another equivalent one; and he fills up part of Codex Madrid II and hundreds of folios of the Codex Atlanticus [74/1–75/1 and 78/1] with studies of the transformation of curvilinear surfaces into an equal number of rectilinear ones. The first are triangles with three curved sides or "falcates" with one or two curved sides; they are circular segments, or "portions," which lie between the sides of a polygon inscribed in a circle and the circle's circumference. Several times he shows the intention of putting together the conclusions of his studies into one or more treatises, for which he proposes the titles: "The Science of Equiparation," "Book on Equation," and "Geometric Play."[33] The results, when considered from a strictly scientific point of view, are not significant, but it cannot be thought that Leonardo dedicated so much time in the last 15 years of his life to a banal work.

To the end, the figures to which he comes back most often are curvilinear stars inscribed in a circle, often forming complex and harmonious drawings. The

The problem in geometry that engrossed Leonardo interminably was the squaring of the circle. From 1504 on, he devoted hundreds of pages in his notebooks to this question of quadrature – finding a square equal in area to a curved figure – that so fasci-

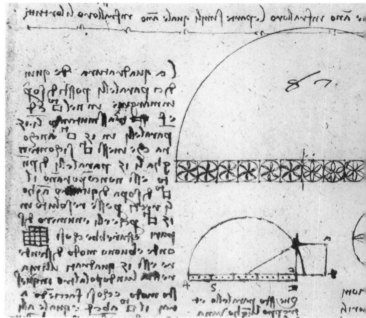

74/1

In the drawing at left Leonardo demonstrates how to subdivide a part of a circle into 14 equal segments. With one of the sides of a hexagon, inscribed in a circle, he constructs a square and then divides it into 14 rectangles. Leonardo continues his demonstration by indicating that one of these rectangles is now transformed into a square into which in turn a circle is inscribed and inside it another hexagon. This new circle, the hexagon, and the portions made from it are now in the ratio 1:14 to the original circle, its hexagon, and the corresponding portions.

On the right Leonardo recommends avoiding a subdivision into an odd number of proportional parts.

74/2

nated his mentor Pacioli. In his later years he indulged in a kind of intellectual game involving the problem. The game produced no appreciable gain for the science of mathematics, but – as indicated in these drawings from Codex Atlanticus – it did create a multiplicity of complex and pleasing designs. He begins by inscribing in a circle a regular polygon such as a hexagon (above), thus forming leaflike patterns in the portions between the straight lines and the circumference. These are then subdivided into increasingly complex designs resembling rosettes. Through all the infinite variations, the relative proportions of the white and dark areas always remain equal – and in proportion to the polygon and the original leaflike portions. Leonardo must have sensed in his intricate doodling more than a game or even a problem of geometry. He came to envision the entire universe as subject to similar mathematical laws, through which nature, employing always the same quantity of matter, varies her wondrous forms endlessly.

ATLANTICUS 111v-a, 106r-b, 110v-a

construction of these figures is regulated by a constant mathematical norm, which serves to "vary ad infinitum" one or more surfaces but at the same time maintain the same quantity.[34] The principle of proportion dominated Vincian thought. In the study of Pacioli or Euclid the theory of proportions always had an important place. Now Leonardo delights in constructing infinite geometric "equations," deriving the same pleasure that a mathematician gets from developing algebraic equations. Let us imagine a square inscribed in a circle. The straight sides of the four circular segments, or "portions," that remain outside the square are then joined up in twos. They will form two "double angles" with curved sides (Leonardo calls them *bisangoli*), similar to olive leaves, which can be placed inside the circle dividing its area into two parts: one situated between the circle's circumference and the contours of the two *bisangoli* which is no longer a square but is still equivalent to it, and the other comprising the two "leaves" which correspond to the four original segments.

He sees in the structure of the natural world the sovereignty of "Necessity, bridle and eternal rule" which is of a mathematical nature and subjects everything to the law of proportion.

What does nature do if not vary infinitely its forms with a limited and unchangeable quantity of material? Playing with the mathematical laws of proportion and proportionality Leonardo practices infinite variations on the forms of a quantitatively unchangeable area. This is the meaning of the title *Book of Equation;* even the inexhaustible forms of nature are only the infinite variations of a basic equation. This is form seen as function, one of the conquests of Renaissance science; and to its realization the artists and those who studied natural philosophy, the inventors of perspective and the experimenter-engineers, Luca Pacioli and Leonardo, all contributed. It is the final result of geometric research begun with the collaboration of the two on the treatise on divine proportion, research pursued for many years by the artist Leonardo alone

Having inscribed a section of a hexagon in a circle, Leonardo wants to divide the portions outside the hexagon into a certain number of submultiple portions. He recommends that such a number always be a multiple of 6. Therefore he makes a table with two columns (sketched horizontally): one of them with the numbers from 1 to 50 (which we would call the "independent variable," or x), the other with

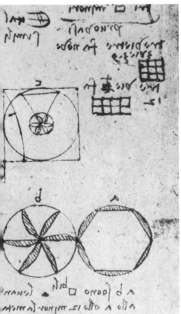

the corresponding multiples of 6 (the "dependent variable," or y), hence it is clear that y is a function of x.

However, the table contains a strange oversight. After number 198 (33 × 6), instead of 204 (34 × 6), Leonardo mistakenly writes 104 and continues writing the following numbers with 1 instead of 2 so that the last number is (50 × 6 =) 200! Below the drawing (at the bottom) Leonardo says he has divided or he will divide the large circle into seven smaller circles, each of them containing 84 portions, in all 588 portions. "Tell me the number of the portions and I shall tell you their size."

75/1

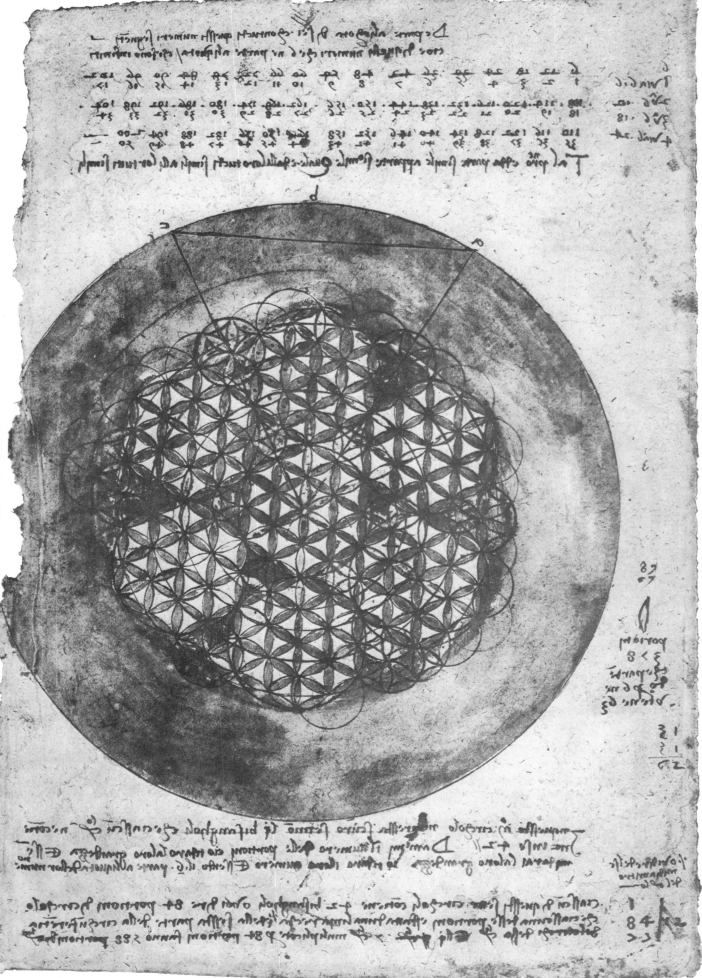

with limited means and concluded, not with the definition of a scientific law, but with a series of illustrations showing it applied.

This new vision of the activity of Leonardo in the study of Latin and the mathematical sciences makes it easier to answer certain questions which in

In the pages of Codex Madrid I, Leonardo's concern for proportion and harmony keeps breaking through and transforming ordinary blocks of words into works of intricate visual beauty. Here, to emphasize the extraordinary graphic qualities, folio 1 verso is

76/1

reproduced twice at right, positive and negative, and rendered schematically above. In the schematic, Leonardo's potpourri of mundane jottings takes on an abstract and subtle harmony suggestive of a painting by Mondrian. The contents of the page seem random. The top line announces the date, New Year's Day 1493. Below it are three blocks of writing. The first muses on the problem of making a perfectly round large circle; the two others, each with a one-line title, relate to the use of geared wheels. The tall block of writing at the lower left of the page is one of those items of practical advice, like household hints, that pepper the notebooks – this one tells how "to make burnished iron appear as if it were painted with blue spots." Most interesting to scholars, however, is the list of words written at the top left of the page (see detail on opposite page).

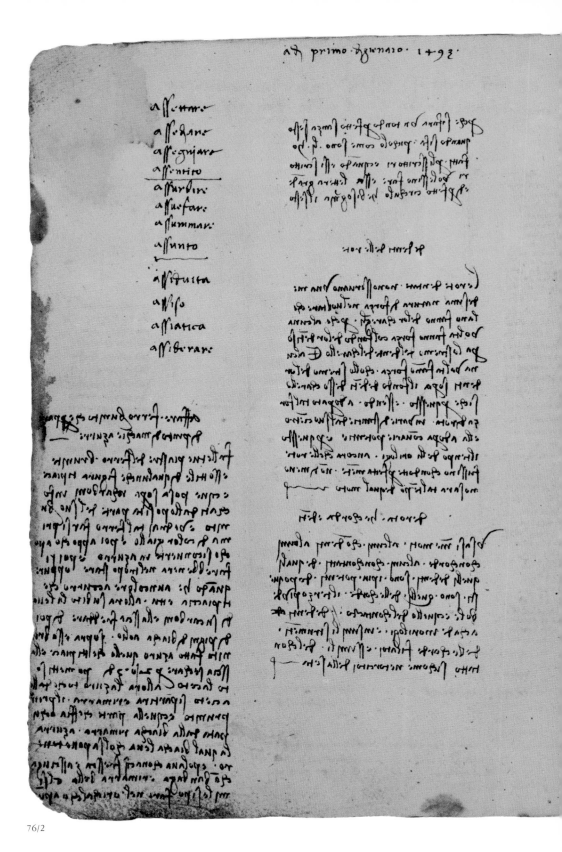

76/2

the past have aroused considerable perplexity. Was Leonardo an artist or a scientist? Did he discover experimental method? Did he really create Italian scientific prose?

Leonardo was certainly a great artist, and the artists of the Renaissance made a great contribution to science. With the discovery of perspective, with the conception of space divided and unified by the geometric projections of rays of light, with the use of the drawing as the perfect instrument for scientific demonstrations, with the conception of art and of beauty as mathematical proportion and harmonious unity of the parts, scientific thought took a new direction. It was a decisive turning point. Artists were not completely isolated from the official world of science. Between the masters of the liberal arts and those of the mechanical arts, between abstract thought and the practical applications in the world of manual work, there was no lack of contact. Toscanelli and

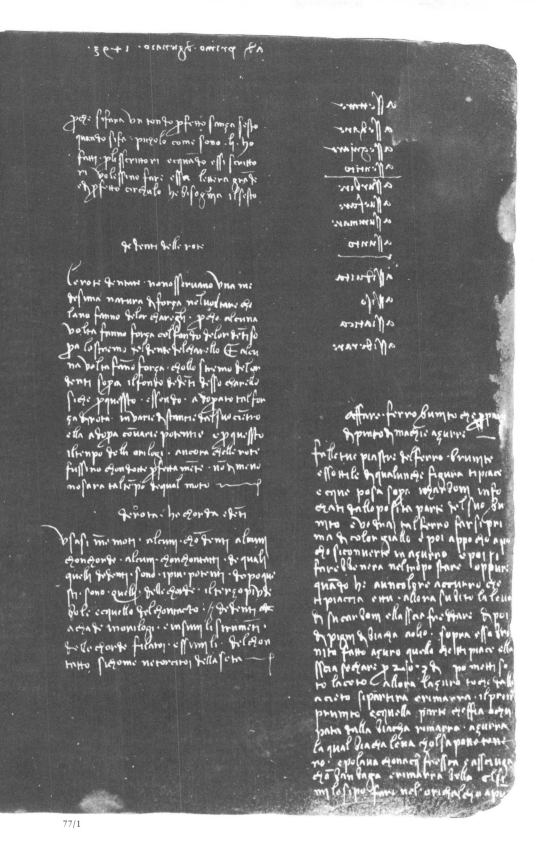

77/1

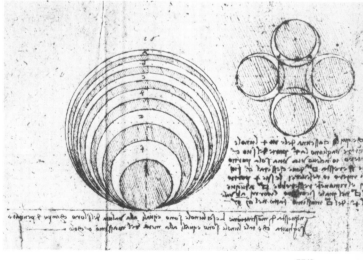

assettare	assettare
assediare	assediare
assegniare	assegniare
assentito	assentito
assurbire	assurbire
assuefare	assuefare
assummare	assummare
assunto	assunto
assiduità	assiduità
assiso	assiso
assiatica	assiatica
assiderare	assiderare

77/2

This list of Italian words, taken from the page reproduced at left, was part of Leonardo's course in self-improvement. Lists of the same sort – abstract nouns, adjectives, and verbs known to scholars but not ordinary people – fill 54 pages in the earlier Codex Trivulzianus. He began collecting such words from grammars, dictionaries, and other books when he was about 40, labeling them vocabuli Latini *because they sounded like Latin. Later he decided to study Latin itself. Forever fretting about his scholarly critics, he wrote "They will say that, being without letters, I cannot say properly what I want to treat of."*

77/3

Below, Leonardo's 12 concentric circles create mathematical proportion – the six white crescents together have an area equal

77/3

to half that of the largest circle – and a maze of receding crescent moons.

ATLANTICUS 221v-b

78/1

Overleaf: The abstract game of squaring portions of a circle comes to life under Leonardo's pen in rows of crescents, paired leaves, pinwheels, and rosettes.

ATLANTICUS 167r-ab

Manetti influenced Brunelleschi, Alberti combined the double experience of literary and artisan activities; Leonardo and Luca Pacioli worked together for many years, and as we have seen, the intervention of Master Luca was decisive. Nevertheless there existed between the two categories a social and hierarchical conflict, even if no one had ever placed in doubt the supremacy of the liberal arts as the only depositories of true science. And the one who rose up resolutely against the exclusion of the mechanical arts from the sphere of science, or as it was then known, "philosophy," was Leonardo.

Perhaps the very idea of writing a treatise on painting was born out of a dispute with men of letters and philosophers over the supremacy of the arts. By placing the polemical discussion of Leonardo on the supremacy of painting at the beginning of the *Treatise,* Francesco Melzi shows that he understood that this was really a beginning and a revolutionary turning point. The first

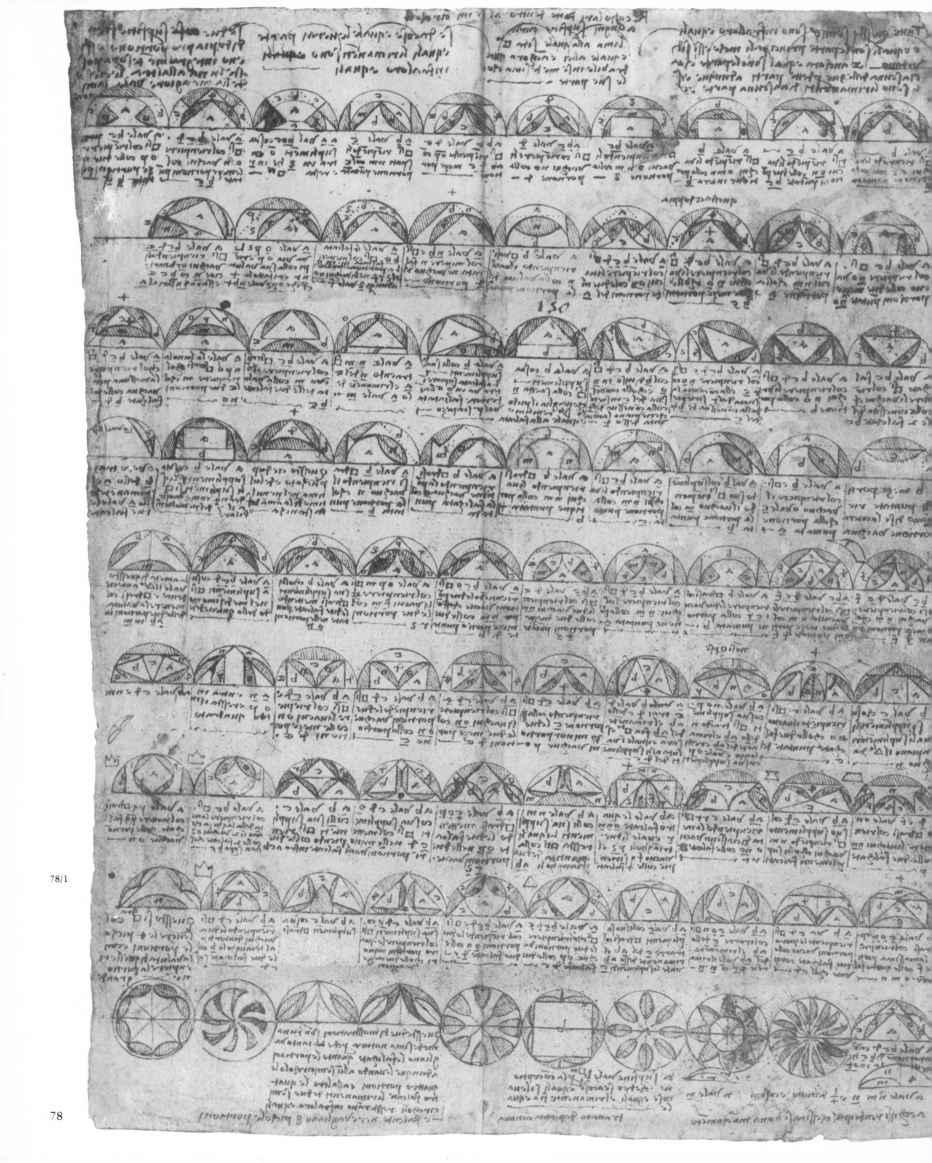

79

At the beginning of the Treatise on Painting *– as Francesco Melzi later arranged it – Leonardo argues at great length the supremacy of painting over the other arts. He takes on poetry first and tells the following story:*

"On King Matthias's birthday a poet brought him a poem composed in praise of the event which he said was for the benefit of the world, and a painter presented him with a portrait of his beloved. The king quickly closed the book of the poet and turning to the picture fixed his eyes on it with great admiration. Then the poet very indignantly said, 'Oh king, read, but read, and you will learn matter of far weightier substance than a mute picture.' Then the king, resenting the reproach that he was admiring mute things, said, 'Silence, oh poet, you do not know what you are saying; this picture serves a nobler sense than your work which might be for the blind. Give me something that I can see and touch and not only hear, and I do not blame my choice when I put your book under my arm and am holding the painting with both hands for my eyes to enjoy; because my hands chose of their own accord to serve the nobler sense and not the sense of hearing.'"

Leonardo's tale of King Matthias may have been based on an actual occurrence. King Matthias of Hungary was known as a great patron of the arts. He got on well with Lodovico Sforza, and there is evidence that Sforza asked Leonardo to paint a picture of the Madonna for the king.

objective of Leonardo's polemic is poetry, the literature that he places under accusation. By accusing he defends himself, because he admits his deficiencies. The painter is a man "without letters" who does not possess to the full the contemporary linguistic instruments, knows that "he cannot express himself well," and so is unable to read and quote the great books of humanity. But the painter reads and studies every day the divine book of nature, interpreting and reproducing directly the words of the supreme master and author without having recourse to other interpreters. No poet can surpass the painter in representing the "works of nature" and the "beauty of the whole world." The poet may surpass the painter in the capacity to reproduce human discourse. But "how much more difficult it is to understand the works of nature than the book of a poet!"[35]

The second objective is music. This is considered a mental science and therefore included in the nonmechanical, or liberal, arts, because it is founded on the numbers of harmonic proportions. But painting too is a mental science, because just as "music and geometry consider the proportions of continuous quantities and arithmetic those of discontinuous quantities," painting "considers all the continuous qualities and the qualities of the proportions of shade and light in its perspective."[36] The redemption of painting and its transformation into a mental science became possible thanks to the invention of perspective, which introduced number into the artist's technique.

All this is not enough to define the excellence of painting. The life of men and things is not fixed in the synchronous unity of immobile space; it flows on in the river of time, continually varying the lines, the surfaces, and the forms of things. Herein could be found the weak point of painting, "which encompasses the surface, colors and forms," while "philosophy penetrates within those same bodies, examining their properties."[37] So the painter's perspective "spreads in the increasing and decreasing of bodies and their colors. . . . Therefore painting is philosophy." But Leonardo feels that the pyramids of the rays of light in which the painter arranges the objects, graduating their dimensions in proportion to their distance, have a character of rigid immobility; they envelop the bodies from the outside, while science penetrates into them in order to discover their internal properties. Life flows in them like a wave and from their heart irradiates the heat of internal energy. Ficino, of whose teaching Leonardo had received at least an echo during the youthful period of his Florentine formation, had criticized the definition of beauty as harmony or proportion of parts and had defined it as "vividness of action and a certain agreeable quality shining brightly in movement itself." Leonardo has this in mind when, using Ficino's words, he "proves that painting is a philosophy because it deals with the movements of the bodies in the *vividness of their actions*."[38] A careful observation of many of Leonardo's paintings and drawings will enable us to discover that their beauty is a "certain agreeable quality shining brightly in movement itself."

Leonardo combines the legacy of the inventors of perspective, of those who favored light as the principle of vision and then of knowledge, and that of the investigators of the "spiritual virtues" (that is, the physical energies inherent in the world – heat, force, gravity) as the principle of movement and of life. For him space is not a simple receptacle, but a field traveled over by visible and invisible forces; surfaces do not merely reflect light, but betray the internal tensions of sensitive and insensitive beings. Before reading Euclid Leonardo had studied *De ponderibus,* where it is stated that a heavy body "desires to be under what is light, and what is light to rest above what is heavy." From there derives a jargon dear to Leonardo in which "every body *desires* to fall," "force always *desires* to become weak and use itself up," and "when the weight comes to a halt there it *rests*."

Leonardo goes further than to place painting as a mental science in the sphere of liberal arts. His polemic broadens so far as to deny traditional science a real validity and to propose a new kind of science. The opposition between the poetry of the men of letters and the painting of the men without letters ends by dividing science into two distinct fields: "poetry extends into moral philosophy" and "painting into natural philosophy";[39] "literature represents with greater truth the words," "painting represents for the senses the works of nature with greater truth and certainty."[40] There is thus opposition between moral philosophy and natural philosophy, divided by diverse methodology. The painter who comes out of the schools of mechanical arts possesses the method of practical experience which checks the validity of the rules imparted. Moral philosophy "begins and ends in the mind," but "in such mental discourses experience is absent and without this, there is no certainty."[41] On the other hand, experience alone is not sufficient. "No certainty exists where none of the mathematical sciences can be applied."[42] Only the mathematical sciences with their geometric demonstrations and numerical calculus make it possible to frame experience in a mental discourse which forms real science, or rather the new science as conceived by Leonardo. This leaves to the men of letters the study of metaphysical problems and the essence of things, very noble objects but unattainable by experience and consequently the source of interminable disputes. "Where there is shouting, true science is not to be found, because truth has only one term, and once this is made public, controversy is destroyed once and for all."[43] Forced to give up a source of certainty like experimental examination, the traditional philosophers take refuge in the authority of the ancients and often are reduced to repeating their words without adding anything of their own – mouth-pieces and reciters of the works of others.[44] Leonardo rejects the principle of authority, gives up metaphysical problems, announces the birth of a new science born of the union of mathematics and experimental activity. Even if he does not succeed in formulating with precision and applying the correct rules of the experimental method, he has clearly realized and affirmed that science could not progress without taking over the method of the mechanical arts which were looked down upon. Manual work, once reserved for slaves, and direct contact with the material, considered an obstacle to the purity of ideal contemplation, are now fully redeemed as necessary elements for the attainment of scientific truth.

From what has been said it clearly appears that Leonardo cannot be compared with the traditional types of scientist and writer and that it is useless to ask whether he was more an artist or more a scientist, and whether he founded Italian scientific prose. The very famous notion of his universality must also be freshly defined within precise limits. The artists of the 15th century were scientists as well, up to a point, but no one was more conscious than Leonardo of the revolutionary character of the contribution made by the pupils of the artisan *botteghe* to the progress of science. And even if Ghiberti had written his modest *Commentaries,* if Francesco di Giorgio Martini, Piero della Francesca, and above all Leon Battista Alberti had composed various detailed treatises on perspective, painting, architecture, and other subjects, Leonardo, although having an inferior literary and scientific preparation to that of Piero and of Leon Battista, imagined a much vaster treatment that included – in addition to painting – mechanics, engineering, anatomy, and hydraulics and touched on problems of geology, cosmology, astronomy (the greatness of the sun and the distance of the stars), and botany. It does not matter if the means of solving these problems were not always adequate and the results not always happy; what does matter is that Leonardo wanted to create a rational theory for all the practical activities of engineers and proposed with great certainty a new vision of scientific progress, liberated from the authority of the past, that would search for the criteria of truth and certainty only with proper logical coherence and with experimental proof.

From the literary and stylistic point of view, too, Leonardo's writings present varying degrees of care, depending on the particular moment at which they were drawn up. But they all have one common characteristic. In spite of Leonardo's impressive affirmations about the many books projected by him and the titles he placed at the top of various pages, we are unable to trace even a partial draft of any book whatsoever that is organically continued over a substantial number of pages.

81/1–4
A large number of Leonardo's manuscripts and drawings now reside in England, though the precise routes by which they reached there are murky. In the 19th century the three Forster Codices – two of them small pocket notebooks – were purchased in Vienna by Lord Lytton. He gave them to John Forster, who in turn donated them to the Victoria and Albert Museum. Sometime between 1713 and

81/1
John Forster.

81/2
Lord Leicester.

81/3
Lord Arundel.

81/4
Lord Ashburnham.

1717, Thomas Coke, later Lord Leicester, purchased from a painter in Rome the codex named after him, which deals only with the subject of water. In the 19th century, the fourth Lord Ashburnham gave his name to two codices that actually had been torn out of Manuscripts A and B by Count Guglielmo Libri. Libri brazenly sold the ill-gotten manuscripts to Ashburnham, who later returned them to Paris. The most successful English collector was Lord Arundel, a 17th-century seeker of Vinciana. He owned the codex that bears his name and most likely was responsible for taking to England the big collection of drawings now at Windsor Castle. The evidence also indicates that he tried unsuccessfully to obtain one of the Madrid Codices.

82/1

> *The wave of the sea bursts open and crashes before its base and that part of the crest will be lowest which formerly was highest.*

82/1

Francesco's treatise was one of the most important early Renaissance works on civil and military architecture. In his own notebooks Leonardo borrowed freely from the book by his older contemporary. Such a treatise also may have inspired Leonardo to arrange his own writings in more systematic form, as in Codex Madrid I.

The artisan environment in which he received his early formation certainly influenced his literary style. It was an environment that expressed itself not by means of organic and complete treatments of problems, but by series of rules, more or less fragmentary formulas, and directly by means of the manual operation, which dismisses words and provides an immediate and clear demonstration.

Rarely does Leonardo's discourse cover more than a page and very often a single page contains many propositions, made at different times, of different or analogous subject matter but always clearly separated from one another. The art of elaborating a question in a dense texture of inductions and logical deduction until it becomes an architectural development is unknown to Leonardo. Neither is he capable of passing gradually from one thought to another, gathering together a vast complex of considerations and at the same time pleasantly entertaining the reader. His style is certain, decisive, and sometimes aggressive.

The fragmentary character is therefore a constant feature of Leonardo's writings. It corresponds to his habit of rapidly committing to paper an unexpected idea, a simple memorandum, a temporary note to be taken up and developed later. He concentrates for a short time only on his effort to achieve good expression. The world of artist-engineers is accustomed to expressing itself more by means of the drawing and practical demonstration than by means of ample discourses. For Leonardo the drawing is a scientific and demonstrative instrument far superior to the word. "O writer, what letters will you use to write the whole figuration with such perfection as the drawing achieves here?"[45] This is not valid for all the sciences, but it strongly influenced the general arrangement of ideas throughout all Leonardo's work, where figurative discourse alternates with oral discourse. The subordination and underestimation of the latter is one of the main causes of the fragmentation of this thought into thousands of disconnected and unrelated notes.

But this is not enough to suffocate the fascination of Leonardo's writing: a beauty that cannot emerge evenly from all the notes he made in his manuscripts in circumstances greatly varying from one to the next; a splendor that can only shine briefly in a word, in a sentence, or in the space of a few lines, and yet leaves a profound impression on the reader: "Sea, universal lowness and sole resting-place of the roaming waters of the rivers."[46]

The famous description of the Flood in Windsor 12665 is a page where the dramatic details that the painter must gather together into the grandiose representation of the universal cataclysm are amassed in disorderly fashion. There is an evident contrast between the profound unitary sentiment (that would be fully expressed only in the real pictorial representation) and the desultory general texture of the narration. It therefore arouses no wonder that from a stylistic point of view the summary of this description, placed by Leonardo under the title "Divisions" and almost reduced to a mere list of words, appears as freed from rhetorical encumbrances, from tiring grammatical connections, from every attempt to achieve a careful architectural construction, and relies solely upon the rhythm of a genuine interior scansion: "Darkness, wind, sea-storm, bolts from heaven, earthquakes and ruin of mountains, leveling of cities. . . ."

In this changeable musical rhythm that binds and exalts Leonardo's phrasing in its better moments we can recognize the lyrical component of his temperament. Although his phrasing tends through habit towards a linear and concise development, the scheme of which can be abstractly illustrated in a sequence of rectilinear and almost equal segments, there are moments when such segments tend to overlap one another as if bound together by reverberations of rhythm and of sound into stanzas: "If the loved thing is vile, the lover becomes vile. . . . When the lover is joined to the loved thing, there he rests. – When the weight reaches the ground, there it rests." Here the breaking up of the grammatical texture is only apparent, as the brevity of the phrases represents only the concentration of an energy that links them all together in a single rhythm; it is a means by which truth is announced and stressed intensely, solemnly.

But there is a great variety of rhythms, from a gentle, timorous, and light flow – as in "Pay attention to the faces of the men and women in the streets as evening falls, when the weather is bad. What grace and gentleness they reveal!" – to the violent and flashing rhythm of these definitions of force: "It lives by violence and dies by freedom." "It transforms every body and obliges it to change situation and shape." "Great power gives it the desire of death." "With fury it drives away anything that obstructs its path of destruction." In these extracts the exact scientific thought is not well formulated; rather it is replaced by the contemplation of images and operations that constitute the concrete effects of a scientific principle not yet clearly specified. This means that at these moments the poet, the artist, the wonderstruck spectator of the amazing effects of nature prevails over the man of science.

It is no easy matter to find beautiful passages in Codex Madrid II, where care as to form is very rare. Neither does Codex Madrid I distinguish itself from a literary standpoint by special stylistic merits. The writing is more careful than usual, and the haste that characterizes other manuscripts is not present, but the subjects are very technical: the description of devices and parts of machines, from which only a few notes deviate. The flyleaf had been used up for some outbursts, such as the one against the seeker after perpetual motion, and some confidences, such as the doubt that seems to torment Leonardo concerning the realization of the great equestrian statue dedicated to Francesco Sforza. The creation of a great bronze horse could, in the event of a war, arouse the cupidity of the enemies, who would take it away to their own cities. Rome in fact was full of grand monuments plundered from conquered cities. If he were to make it in marble with dimensions and weight so great as to render it untransportable, it would be destroyed to make "walls and mortar." The point is, however, that destiny is inevitable. "Do as you will, everything has its death." This sounds like a foreboding of the end of his masterpiece, destroyed by enemy soldiers not through cupidity or for utility, but as a game, thus rendering vain even the last doubt that closes the extract: is it fair that the work of art brings more honor to the artist than to the person who commissions it? It is normal, replies Leonardo, but the glory of his horse could be appreciated neither by posterity nor by his contemporaries.

Another parenthesis of great interest is the following declaration addressed by Leonardo to the reader: "Peruse me O reader, if you find delight in my work, since this profession very seldom returns to this world, and the perseverance to pursue it and to invent such things anew is found in few people. And come men, to see the wonders which may be discovered in nature by such studies."[47] It is unlikely that these words refer directly to the astronomical drawing that is beneath them, but they certainly have to do with the study of nature and its laws that Leonardo had been pursuing for so many years in so many different fields.

Now compare this page with that very well-known one[48] on which Leonardo modestly compares himself to "the man who arrives last at the fair because of his poverty" with "merchandise that is looked down upon and rejected" as not of "great usefulness and pleasure," and note the reversal of the situation. The profession practiced by Leonardo has appeared only on very rare occasions in the world, as it demands a patience reserved to few, but it is the cause of great pleasure, because it reveals to men the wonders of nature. Nature is the center of Leonardo's basic interests, the spectacle he examines with unexhausted wonder. Against those who look down on the study of natural phenomena and prefer the description of "miracles and . . . those things that the human mind is not capable of demonstrating and that cannot be demonstrated by any human example,"[49] Leonardo, with a radical inversion, sets another type of miracle, that of which "the mathematical sciences" succeed in giving a rational explanation. This miracle gives rise to amazement, but an amazement produced by the discovery of the reason infused in things – that is, by the dissolution of the mystery that enshrouds them.

This is a delicate point. The rationality that constitutes the intimate structure

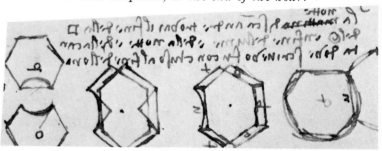

83/1

83/2

of the universe is a law, which Leonardo calls "Necessity," restraint, a rein imposed by God upon the free expansion of the cosmic energies. On the essence of these energies that animate the world nothing can be said; science, which shuns metaphysical discourses, devotes itself only to their effects, that is, the rhythms and the formalities of their operations. The true miracle, which can be known and admired as the revelation of an immeasurable wisdom, is the law, or necessity, to which the elements of matter and the forces that move them are subjected. Herein lies the metaphysical residue that Leonardo does not want to investigate; he is satisfied with the spectacle offered to his

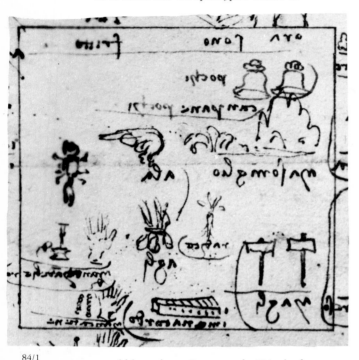

84/1

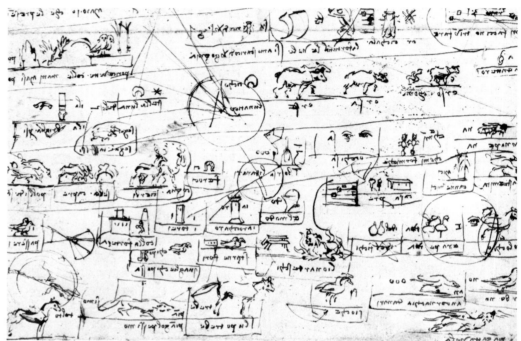

84/2

eyes and with the harmonious motions whose rhythms and mathematical proportions his mind measures; but it cannot be denied that Leonardo's soul is stirred by this metaphysical residue that is preserved from intellectual investigation. We only have to remember the splendid definitions of force already cited, where the changeable behaviors of an energy are felt and presented as an invisible, mighty, individualized protagonist. Of this eternal and unchangeable substance the only knowledge, the only discourse conceded to man, consists of the description of its effects, of the definitions of its functions. Here too – as said earlier about Leonardo's geometry – we are witnessing the shift of the focal point of scientific discourse: from the substance to the function.

Even the concept that Leonardo has of beauty feels the effect of these two poles of his thought: beauty is rationality, harmony of mathematical proportions, but it is also, as Ficino said, "vividness of the actions," the manifestation of a vital impetus, and therefore the revelation of a substance or invisible essence. The passing from medieval to Renaissance concepts thus takes place gradually, without violent contrasts. The rationality and the beauty of the universe are the stamp of the divine mind in the world. God is still thought of as creator – though called author and master – in the sense that this word had in the artisan *botteghe:* the artist who imagines the form and causes it to materialize. The world is the masterpiece of the supreme artist. The study of nature leads to the revelation of the divine mind; the imitation of nature confers on the mind of the painter the creative character of the divine mind. Here we can discover the unifying center of all Leonardo's activities. He studies nature like a pupil who wants to discover the secrets of the master so as to compete with him in inventing and painting pictures that pulsate with life, in making machines and devices that make inert material seem to come alive.

85/1

85/3

Però se la Fortuna mi fa felice, tal viso asponerò.
Thus if Fortune makes me happy, I will show such a face.

85/4

Felice sarei, se dell'amore ch'i'ti porto restaorata fossi.
I should be happy, if my love for you were reciprocated.

85/2

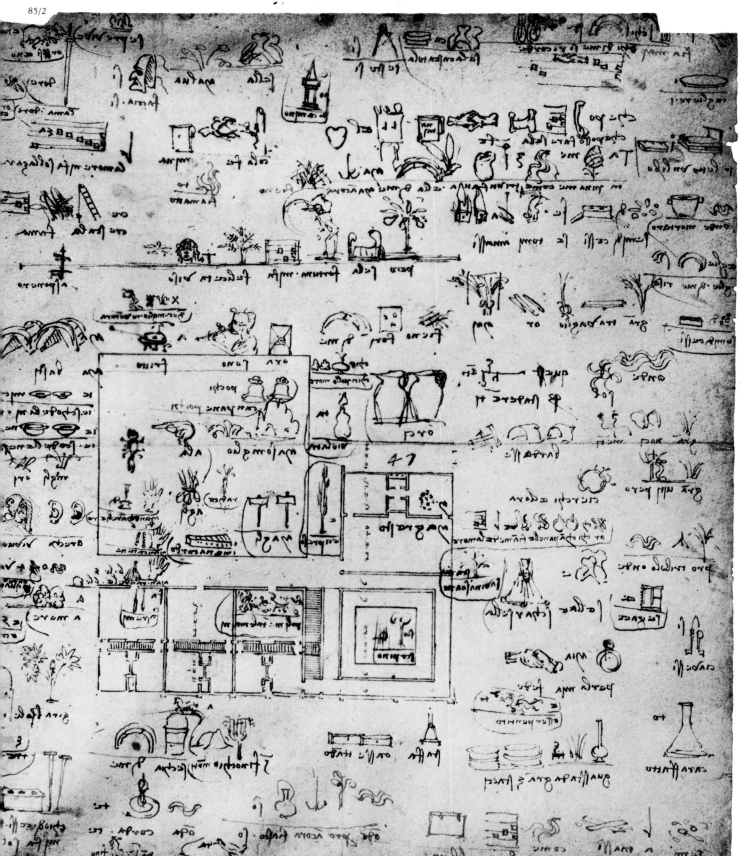

85/5

Però tribolo, onde . . .
But I suffer, therefore . . .

85/6

Po[n] l'occhio.
Be careful.

85/7

Lionardeschi
Leonardesque

85/8

Cogli acierbi
With the bitter ones

86/1

Leonardo made the note above on folio 157 verso of Codex Madrid II, which brought to light 17 sheets of important new drawings and notes about his most ambitious project – the great bronze horse, Il Cavallo, that he was creating for the Duke of Milan.

In the evening, May 17, 1491.

Here a record shall be kept of everything related to the bronze horse presently under execution.

IL CAVALLO

MARIA VITTORIA BRUGNOLI

86/2

Il Cavallo – "The Horse" – was a colossal equestrian statue commissioned by the Duke of Milan, Lodovico Sforza, in honor of his father, Francesco (left). The monument was to be the largest such sculpture ever built – Leonardo designed the horse alone to be more than 23 feet high – and would require the development of a radical new casting method. Astride it would be Francesco Sforza, a onetime free-lance general who had overthrown the Visconti rulers and established himself as Duke of Milan.

"In the evening, May 17, 1491. Here a record shall be kept of everything related to the bronze horse presently under execution." These words, from Codex Madrid II, folio 157 verso, are the starting point of Leonardo's notes on a project which could well symbolize both the times – the tumultuous changes of Renaissance Italy – and the man – artist, scientist, innovator.

The "bronze horse" was to be a monument to Francesco Sforza, father of Lodovico il Moro, who was Leonardo's patron in Milan for many years. *Il Cavallo* – "The Horse" – was actually to be a horse and rider as envisioned by Galeazzo Maria Sforza, Francesco's older son who commissioned the creation of a life-size equestrian monument. However, when Lodovico succeeded Galeazzo Maria and established his court as one of Italy's most glittering, the plans for *Il Cavallo* developed to a statue that would measure over 23 feet high, weighing some 158,000 pounds. Lodovico's political maneuvering was unfortunately not adept enough to establish a permanent reign, and his political difficulties were reflected in the monument's erratic progress during the 16 years that Leonardo worked on it. The ultimate fall of the house of Sforza was parallel to the fate of *Il Cavallo*, which was never realized in bronze. Folios 141 to 157 of Codex Madrid II, the record of Leonardo's work on the enormous bronze monument, are thus a unique source commenting on the passage of a grandiose Renaissance concept through the political upheaval so much a part of that time.

This series of folios is important not only for its political and historical contributions but also for what it reveals about Leonardo. The sketches here confirm what is known from the rest of Codex Madrid II and the other notebooks about the beauty of Leonardo's drawings, his perfectionist attempts to understand fully the musculature and bone structure of a living subject, his attention to the most minute detail of a mechanical device. The writings confirm the image of Leonardo as scientist: experimenting with different combinations of materials for molds, advising in instance after instance that his assistants try out all kinds of different materials to see which would best suit the purposes and circumstances of a particular problem, considering and weighing everything relevant to the problem, and explaining in precise scientific detail his reasoning and methodology for every step.

Leonardo the innovator – this is perhaps the greatest significance of the Codex Madrid II folios on *Il Cavallo*. The problem that Il Moro presented to Leonardo, to cast a bronze horse four times greater than life size, could not be solved to the satisfaction of a perfectionist like Leonardo with the then existing methods of casting bronze. In this codex he clearly outlines a new method of casting bronze in a single operation. Once again Leonardo the innovator proved himself to be years ahead of his contemporaries: in fact we find the first reference to his new method of casting in the treatise on "Pyrotechny" written between 1530 and 1535 by Vannoccio Biringucci, an expert cannon founder. Giorgio Vasari and Benvenuto Cellini give a detailed description of it around the mid-16th century, but they recommend its use only for life-size or slightly larger figures. Only two centuries after this new method was developed by Leonardo was it to be used for a large-size monument like the one planned for Francesco Sforza: the equestrian statue of Louis XIV of France, the Sun King.[1]

To read and understand the Codex Madrid II story of *Il Cavallo* gives one a better knowledge of Leonardo and also provides a fascinating parallel to the political history of the Italian Renaissance. For the story revealed in Leonardo's notes is also that of the Sforza family, who serve as a symbol of their time. The Sforzas rose to power in Milan in a style that could perhaps typify the political mood of 15th-century Italy. Francesco Sforza [86/2] was a *condottiere*, a free-lance general hired by Milan to fight against Venice. Claiming that his wife was the illegitimate daughter of the previous Duke of Milan, Francesco took Milan for himself. His son Galeazzo Maria [90/2], who came to power at Francesco's death, suggested that a monument be built to his father's memory. This monument was to be life-size and "placed in the open somewhere in our castle of Milan." In November 1473 he instructed Bartolomeo Gadio, an architect, to seek out a "master capable of realizing" the monument. Gadio was authorized to search beyond Milan – to

Leonardo's patron, Lodovico Sforza, was known as Il Moro – the black – probably because of his swarthy complexion. He is shown here in a detail from the Sforza Altarpiece, which represents Lodovico being introduced to the Virgin and Child. The

87/1

prayerful attitude contrasts with his real-life attitudes of cunning, caution, and vanity. He gathered to his court a colorful mélange of beautiful women, entertainers, and brilliant personages like Leonardo, whom he hired in 1482. Though he often employed Leonardo as an entertainer and ignored his inventions, he shared with the artist the dream and the destiny of the equestrian monument to his father, Francesco Sforza.

The duchy over which Lodovico Sforza presided covered much of the Lombardy area. The city of Milan with its 100,000 residents and rich textile and arms factories

88/1

was the administrative and cultural capital, but the duchy also took in the important towns of Pavia and Parma to the south.

Opposite page: The downfall of Lodovico Sforza – and the horse – became imminent late in 1499 when the French invaded Milan. Il Moro fought on for a few months but he was defeated in a battle at Novara and led off to a French prison. This illustration from an old Swiss chronicle – the Diebold Schilling chronicle, kept in Lucerne – shows Sforza, disguised as a Swiss civilian, being arrested by one of his Swiss mercenaries who had betrayed him. Lodovico's serpent-and-falcon flag is shown at left. At right are Swiss flags and the fleur-de-lis of the French troops.

88/2 88/3

The king of the French troops who took Milan and threw out Lodovico Sforza was Louis XII (above, right). His commander at Milan was himself a Milanese – Marshal Gian Giacomo Trivulzio, a noted condottiere, or mercenary leader. Later he asked Leonardo to create an equestrian statue as his own burial monument.

inquire anywhere that "this master so excellent as to be able to carry out his work was to be found."[2]

Three years later, in 1476, Galeazzo Maria was murdered, and his son Gian Galeazzo inherited the dukedom. At this point Lodovico [87/1], Galeazzo Maria's brother, took the throne away from his nephew; he claimed that his status as Francesco's younger son was a more direct link to the dukedom than Gian Galeazzo's. Lodovico revived the idea of the monument and renewed the search for a master.

Leonardo, in Florence, must have been following the changing events in Milan with some interest. In 1482 he wrote to Lodovico introducing himself to the Sforza court in a manner that suggests he was somehow selecting the winner in the struggle for Milan. He offered designs for bridges to be used in sieges, mortars and big guns, covered chariots, catapults; architectural designs for public and private buildings for times of peace; and, at the end of the letter, referred to the "bronze horse" – "to the immortal glory and eternal honor of the prince your father of happy memory, and of the illustrious house of Sforza."[3]

The court of Il Moro to which Leonardo came was one of the most brilliant in Europe. Lodovico lived in a grand manner – filling the court with poets, beautiful women, musicians, dwarfs, astrologers, and, of course, Leonardo.

He came to the court prepared to work on the bronze monument to Francesco, and there are some drawings from this period of a rearing horse.[4] [91/1] He was already posing for himself the problem of casting a bronze model of such a horse.[5] Although Lodovico aroused great public enthusiasm for the horse, work progressed gradually during the artist's stay in Milan, since Leonardo was also occupied with painting the Last Supper and other works such as portraits and was involved in a variety of civic and military improvements: he designed a new city plan and safe sewage system after the plague killed thousands in the 1480s; he also designed dozens of new weapons and an improved defense system for the castle. But Lodovico ignored these designs and preferred to employ Leonardo on such projects as managing opulent wedding festivities, or composing rhymes and puzzles for the ladies of the court. Not only did Il Moro utilize Leonardo's talents on trivial matters while ignoring the more serious ones, he was sometimes also stingy with Leonardo, who once wrote to Il Moro complaining: "It vexes me greatly that having to earn my living has forced me to interrupt my work and to attend to small matters, instead of following up the work which your Lordship entrusted to me . . . if your Lordship thought I had money, your Lordship was deceived."

For the 16 years that Leonardo remained at the Sforza court, Il Cavallo was the project that united him with Lodovico, but even here the encouragement was uneven. When Leonardo's work was still at a preparatory stage, Lodovico decided to impose far more spectacular proportions on the monument, probably to symbolize his own increased political power. Leonardo's early studies had been of a rearing horse which would be feasible, although difficult, to execute life-size in bronze. A sketch in Codex Atlanticus folio 148 recto-a of a high and ornate base [98/2] confirms that this statue would have been life-size and placed, probably, in front of the main entrance of the castle.[6] However, Lodovico's changed demand for a horse and rider four times larger than life-size presented enormous technical problems. Leonardo may have felt dubious about such a large-scale project, and it is evident that Il Moro questioned Leonardo's ability to complete the project. On July 20, 1489, a letter was sent to Lorenzo de' Medici in Florence from Il Moro. (This letter was the first document relating to the Sforza monument that describes it as enormous.)[7] Il Moro asked Lorenzo for the names of one or two masters capable of realizing "a worthy funeral monument to my father . . . that is a very big bronze horse carrying the Duke Francesco in armor." Although the mold of the monument had already been commissioned from Leonardo, this letter reveals Lodovico's lack of confidence in his ability to finish. It was difficult, however, for Lorenzo to find a master on the level of Leonardo, particularly since Verrocchio, Leonardo's teacher, had since died. Thus on April 23, 1490, Leonardo wrote, "I resumed work on the horse."[8] In the drawings of the early 1490s, including

those of Codex Madrid II, the equestrian monument shifts from a rearing to a pacing horse, the first sign that Leonardo was now working seriously on the tremendous monument. And it was approximately a year later, in May 1491, that Leonardo began the record in Codex Madrid II, that was lost for so many years, from which the modern reader gains his knowledge not only of the completely innovative techniques derived for casting and molding the Sforza horse but also of the design and final model of the monument.

A rearing horse of such magnitude presented great problems. The other option with which Leonardo must have been familiar was a pacing horse cast in a frozen position with both fore and hind legs on the same side moving simultaneously, as seen in Verrocchio's Colleoni monument in Venice [95/2], as well as the equestrian statues of San Marco in Venice [95/3] and the Gattamelata of Donatello in Padua [95/1]. Although practical to cast and more stable than the rearing horse of Leonardo's drawings, the horses of those monuments have an unnatural and restrained appearance to a keen observer such as Leonardo.

Leonardo's problem was thus to find a way of rendering the pacing horse more realistically. His drawings from the Windsor Collection include a sketch of the Regisole monument of Pavia [94/2] and in Codex Atlanticus we find a description which shows his regard for the successful resolution of the problem in that monument: "What is admired above all else in the Pavia horse is the movement. . . . The trot is almost of the same quality as the trot of a free horse."[9] Interestingly, Petrarch's description of the Regisole monument – "the statue of a horse almost running to the top of a hill"[10] – is very similar to the description of the model of the Sforza horse – "impetuous and panting in appearance" – which was made by Paolo Giovio.[11] It is thus most likely that the Regisole exerted a greater influence than any other monument on Leonardo's choice of design and model for the Sforza monument.

this horse in his early studies for the Sforza monument and later for the Battle of Anghiari.　　　　UFFIZI, FLORENCE

It is probable that Leonardo devoted a greater proportion of his time, especially at these early stages, to the study of horses than to the study of monuments. Again, the Windsor notes contain his sketches and observations made in Il Moro's stables, where he drew the horses repeatedly, measuring their proportions, the bone and muscle structure, the movement of their limbs[12] [96/1 and 2]. Although Codex Madrid II contains primarily diagrams and sketches that explain the technical notes, there are also beautiful freehand drawings, as on folios 147 recto [97/3] and 151 verso [97/4] of December 20, 1493. These drawings represent the model at a more advanced stage and show a horse in a brisk pacing rhythm between the walk and the trot, with left hind leg raised from the ground and right foreleg bent at almost a 90-degree angle.[13] This is a very slight exaggeration of the natural pace and is somewhat like the parade step of the classical monument to Marcus Aurelius [94/3].

It is difficult to say, however, which of the two drawings mentioned above represents the final choice adapted by Leonardo for his model. The hasty black-pencil drawing of folio 147 recto appears more spirited and seems better fitted to Paolo Giovio's description of the actual model. The red-chalk drawing of folio 151 verso is, however, more contained and perhaps more elegant. It is quite similar to the "caged" drawing on folio 216 verso-a of the Codex Atlanticus [105/2], which uses the motif of an overturned pitcher to prop the flexed foreleg.[14] There is no further trace of this motif in the drawings of Codex Madrid II, and it is probable that Leonardo discarded it because it made the horse's pace appear less natural. Unfortunately, the drawings cannot demonstrate conclusively the exact posture and movement of the horse in the final position. Even after the substantial contribution Codex Madrid II makes to knowledge of the Sforza monument, this question remains unanswerable.

There is also some confusion concerning the design for the base of the statue. Earlier monuments, such as those to Gattamelata or Colleoni, had marble bases, to which they were anchored by means of the pivot of the plinth. On folios 147 recto and 146 verso Leonardo introduces the problem of casting the base in bronze, and Codex Madrid II does not offer any answers as to why he posed this additional problem for himself. It is possible that he wished to avoid the imperfections of sutures between bronze plinths and marble. A reasonable answer could be found if the base of the monument had been planned in a limited elevation, as this would leave more or less within eye level the surface upon which the horse was to rest, thus revealing the unavoidable imperfections of the sutures between the bronze plinths and the marble. The hypothesis advanced here is not so farfetched if it is considered that a base projecting vertically like those of the Gattamelata and Colleoni monuments, if related in scale to the proportions of the Sforza monu-

91/1

In his early studies for the Sforza monument Leonardo repeated the motif of a rearing horse that he had painted so successfully in the Adoration. *No one could rival him at rendering this form from nature, but from a sculptural standpoint it was a highly impractical design. In the drawing at left, Windsor Collection 12358 recto, the rearing horse carries a nude rider with a*

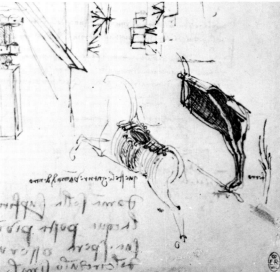

91/2

baton in his right hand. The horse's left foreleg rests upon a trampled enemy warrior, who serves as a base for the weight of the horse. Leonardo must have thought this was a solution to the problem of the horse's balance. At that time, in the 1480s, the commission apparently still called for the life-size monument originally envisioned by Lodovico's brother, Galeazzo Maria Sforza. In the drawing at right, Windsor 12349 recto, Leonardo still has the horse rearing and it appears he was ready to cast it that way. The diagram at the right of the sheet shows the placement of a metal framework inside the mold to reinforce the bronze skin after the casting of the metal.

ment, would have reached such abnormal dimensions as to be very difficult to insert into the environmental and urbanistic spaces of the time.

Similarly, Codex Madrid II does not reveal any clear answer regarding the actual placement of the monument. Galeazzo Maria's original idea had been for a monument placed in the open outside of the palace. Old Milanese chronicles suggest the possibility of placing the monument near Francesco's burial mound;[15] a 1491 manuscript of Bartolomeo Gambagnola containing a miniature with an equestrian statue very similar to the sketches of *Il Cavallo* suggests the placement of the statue in the vestibule of a temple.[16] It is likely that Leonardo favored neither of these alternatives and preferred a large open courtyard, but the codex offers no further clues on this problem.

The Codex Madrid II section on *Il Cavallo* is almost entirely concerned with the problems of casting and molding the enormous bronze statue of the horse and provides very explicit explanations of the processes of model building, preparation of the molds, casting the countermodel, preparing the casting pits and

92/1

ovens, and finally casting the actual statue. Leonardo's system was revolutionary in terms of pre-existing techniques, and a close review of the material revealed in Codex Madrid II demonstrates the advantages of this system while also providing another context in which Leonardo's brilliance of conception and thoroughness of attention to detail can be seen.

Leonardo had resumed work on the monument in April 1490, and by May 1491 he had completed an earthen model for the great horse, as he writes in Codex Madrid II [17] concerning the relationship between the mold and the initial model of "the earthen horse." This mention in the codex is the first direct confirmation by Leonardo of the descriptions written by his contemporaries. Luca Pacioli confirms the enormity of the horse: it was 12 braccia, or over 23 feet high.[18] Others mention the substance of the horse. Paolo Cortese mentions a "clayey horse," Paolo Giovio a colossus in "clay," and Matteo Bandello an "earthen horse."[19] The codex does not clarify precisely what earthy substance the model was composed of. The Codex Atlanticus [20] does mention a "molding stucco" in an entry datable to about 1490, which may be the same mixture used for this model of *Il Cavallo*. This earthen model was unveiled in the old yard of the ducal residence in November

After 1489, when Sforza apparently decided to increase vastly the size of the monument, Leonardo changes its positioning. In the sketch above he draws a more conventional walking gait with the bent right foreleg raised. WINDSOR 12346

The chart below – comparing the metric height of the Sforza horse with that of four equestrian statues – illustrates the challenge facing Leonardo after his patron ordered a horse four times larger than life-size.

92/2

Marcus Aurelius
Roman emperor and philosopher; Rome; dated from antiquity; horse and rider 4.24 meters (14 feet) high.

Gattamelata
Famed mercenary general; Padua; 1453; horse and rider 3.20 meters (10½ feet) high.

Colleoni
Famed mercenary general; Venice; 1488; horse and rider 4 meters (13 feet) high.

Sforza
Duke of Milan; Milan; never cast; horse (only) 7.20 meters (24 feet) high.

Louis XIV
King of France; Paris; 1699 (destroyed in French Revolution); horse and rider 6.82 meters (22⅔ feet) high.

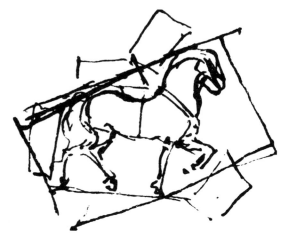

92/3

In 1492 Leonardo was laying plans for casting the new enlarged horse. This sketch portrays a walking horse mold enclosed by three braces. WINDSOR 12350r

1493, as the climax of celebrations of the betrothal of Bianca Maria Sforza to the Holy Roman Emperor Maximilian. It is not difficult to imagine the multiple prestigious effects of so prominent a marriage and so enormous a monument.

Even the mention of this earthen model reveals important information concerning Leonardo's decisions about the final casting. To make an earthen or stucco model meant rejection of the "lost-wax" process that was the universally used method of casting sculpture in the Renaissance. This process, of ancient tradition, was used in the classical age, and is clearly described in the *Schedula* of the monk Theophilus.[21] To cast a statue using the lost-wax method, models of the projected work are fashioned in wax over a core of refractory clay; an outer mold is then applied over the wax and the whole is heated in a casting pit so that the wax runs out (hence, lost wax). Molten bronze is then poured into the cavity left by the wax. This system accompanied the practice of casting the work, even of medium proportions, in several pieces, which were soldered together, trimmed, and integrated when casting was complete.

At the beginning of the 16th century, soon after Leonardo's work on the Sforza horse, Pomponio Gaurico (or, in Latin, Pomponius Gauricus) discussed the

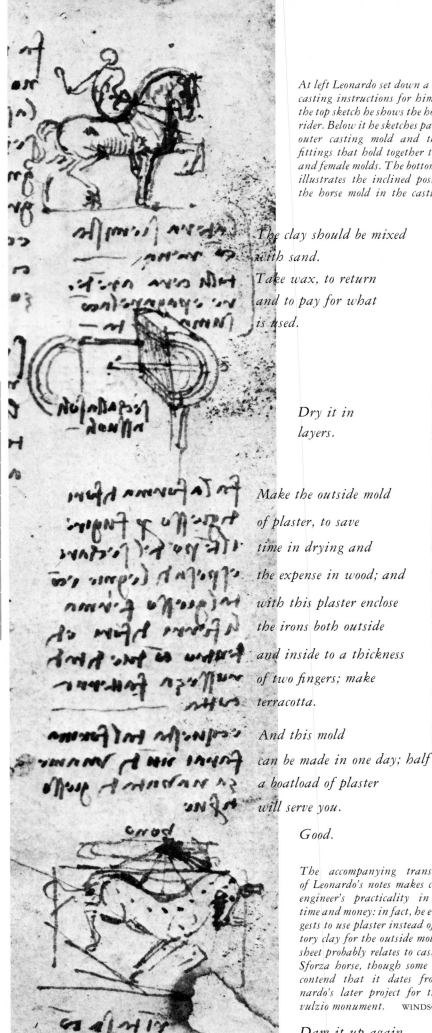

At left Leonardo set down a series of casting instructions for himself. In the top sketch he shows the horse and rider. Below it he sketches part of the outer casting mold and the iron fittings that hold together the male and female molds. The bottom sketch illustrates the inclined position of the horse mold in the casting pit.

The clay should be mixed with sand.
Take wax, to return and to pay for what is used.

Dry it in layers.

Make the outside mold of plaster, to save time in drying and the expense in wood; and with this plaster enclose the irons both outside and inside to a thickness of two fingers; make terracotta.

And this mold can be made in one day; half a boatload of plaster will serve you.

Good.

The accompanying transcription of Leonardo's notes makes clear his engineer's practicality in saving time and money: in fact, he even suggests to use plaster instead of refractory clay for the outside mold. This sheet probably relates to casting the Sforza horse, though some scholars contend that it dates from Leonardo's later project for the Trivulzio monument. WINDSOR 12347

Dam it up again with glue and clay, or white of egg, and bricks and rubbish.

At left Leonardo set down a series of

93/2

The accuracy with which Leonardo rendered horses and the play of their muscles indicates he probably dissected them. Contemporaries referred to his book on the anatomy of horses, which apparently was lost. The drawings shown here from the

93/3

Windsor Collection both date from the time of work on the equestrian monument commissioned by Marshal Gian Giacomo Trivulzio about 1508 in Milan. Trivulzio, who led the French invasion of Milan in 1499, had hoped to become governor of the city, but his chances were wrecked by intrigue. The sketch at top, No. 12344 recto, shows a horse with left foreleg bent high and without saddle or rider. In the bottom sketch, No. 12343, the rider wears armor and holds a baton in his right hand – a form influenced by antiquity as Donatello's mid-15th-century statue of Gattamelata.

In both his attempts to make equestrian monuments Leonardo, characteristically, kept on searching for a practical posture to cast and yet that did not compromise the free

lost-wax method and pointed out its drawbacks. Although the system Leonardo devised to cast the Sforza monument was aimed at eliminating the drawbacks of the lost-wax method, Gaurico seems unaware of Leonardo's system.[22]

The solder lines, or sutures, were ugly traces of the lost-wax casting method but the fact that the model was destroyed or lost was a worse aesthetic drawback, since it meant that the original could not be consulted to eliminate every imperfection when trimming the cast figure.

There were practical as well as aesthetic drawbacks to the lost-wax method. It was impossible to obtain a homogeneous thickness of the modeled wax and if the wax was not evenly thick, then the thickness of the bronze could not be controlled.

94/1

and spontaneous qualities of real horses. The sketch above, Windsor 12359, is another of his many studies for the Trivulzio monument. The horse below, Windsor 12345 recto, strongly suggests the ancient statue at Pavia known as the Regisole, since destroyed. Leonardo may have copied it in 1490 when he and Francesco di Giorgio Martini were in Pavia to study construction of the cathedral. Leonardo notes, in Codex Atlanticus 147 recto-b, "What is admired above all else in the Pavia horse is the movement. . . . The trot is almost of the same quality as the trot of a free horse."

94/2

The Marcus Aurelius in Rome (right) was very much like the Regisole that Leonardo saw in Pavia.

94/3

With no control over the thickness of the bronze, it is impossible to predict exactly the amount of bronze needed for casting. This constitutes an incredible technical problem, especially when it involves a figure of great proportions to be melted in a single casting, which is exactly what Leonardo had in mind.[23] For the Sforza project it was necessary to keep the weight of the mammoth statue as low as possible by reducing the thickness of the bronze. It was also necessary to calculate the quantity of metal precisely, for it would have been an irremediable drawback to find that the molten bronze in the ovens was insufficient to complete the casting. It was thus completely necessary for Leonardo to reject the lost-wax method, but it is also necessary for the modern reader to remain aware of the boldness of his proposal to cast an immense monument in a single operation using an entirely new and unproved method.

95/1

Donatello's monument in Padua to Condottiere Gattamelata (above) probably influenced some of Leonardo's sketches, though he had only secondhand knowledge of it.

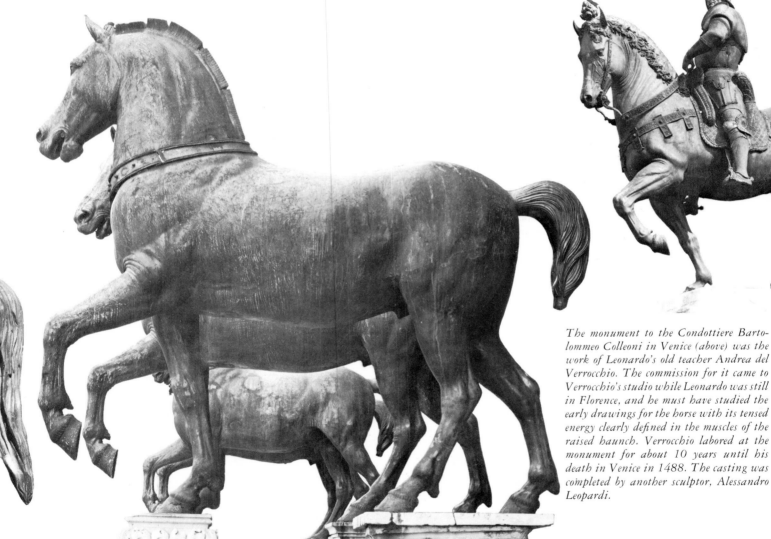

95/2

The monument to the Condottiere Bartolommeo Colleoni in Venice (above) was the work of Leonardo's old teacher Andrea del Verrocchio. The commission for it came to Verrocchio's studio while Leonardo was still in Florence, and he must have studied the early drawings for the horse with its tensed energy clearly defined in the muscles of the raised haunch. Verrocchio labored at the monument for about 10 years until his death in Venice in 1488. The casting was completed by another sculptor, Alessandro Leopardi.

95/3
The gilded bronze horses of San Marco in Venice (left) are the work of Hellenistic or perhaps Roman artists. Leonardo saw them in 1500 and perhaps before that.

Codex Madrid II is the link that, after years of loss, joins the modern reader to Leonardo's plans and experiments for this radical departure from casting traditions. Unfortunately, since Leonardo did not take notes in sequence, but rather wrote down what came to mind on whatever scrap of paper came to hand, the interpretation of his record of the casting process is not completely verifiable. In order to reach a clearer understanding of the casting process, it is helpful to refer to the notes in the Codex Atlanticus and the Windsor Collection, including notes for the monument planned for Gian Giacomo Trivulzio.[24]

Leonardo may have borrowed ideas from other equestrian monuments, but he ultimately referred to nature. In the ducal stables in Milan he studied horses, sketching their movements and structure and measuring the parts of their bodies to establish precise proportions. In the drawing below left, Windsor Collection 12319, he divides the horse into sections and jots down meas-

Leonardo's new plan for casting the enormous bronze horse began with the full-size earthen model in the old courtyard of the castle. Directly over the earthen model he made an impression in several pieces which would become the female section of the mold. The drawing on folio 157 recto of Codex Madrid II [101/1], of the head and neck of the horse, shows several pieces closed together over the model and held in position by iron rods. The pieces making up this mold, or form, would vary in number depending on whether they were placed on a flat or round part of the model. The codex reads, on 148 recto, paragraph 2, "You should prepare a form of three parts for each roundness of any of the limbs; it will be

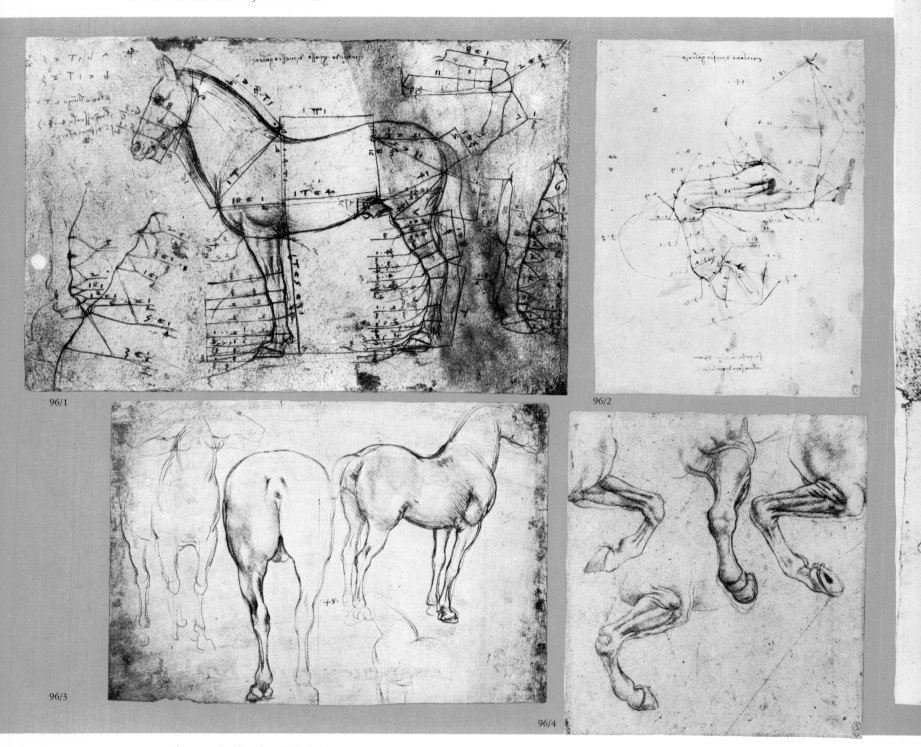

96/1

96/2

96/3

96/4

urements. At top right, Windsor 12294, he measures the foreleg of the Sicilian horse that belonged to Lodovico's son-in-law Galeazzo di Sanseverino. Above left, Windsor 12317, he sketches the hindquarters and two other views. Above right, Windsor 12299, are flexed forelegs – originally drawn by Leonardo but here in a copy, probably made by his pupil Francesco Melzi.

much easier to detach it from the earthen horse." The interfaces of the pieces were traced on the model appropriately greased; following this operation, the various pieces were strengthened by drying, detached, and then reassembled. There would thus be a hollow female mold in two halves, referred to as a "half and half mold." [25]

Within the hollow of this half and half mold, a homogeneous layer of a malleable substance was laid. This layer is referred to by Leonardo in Codex Madrid II as the

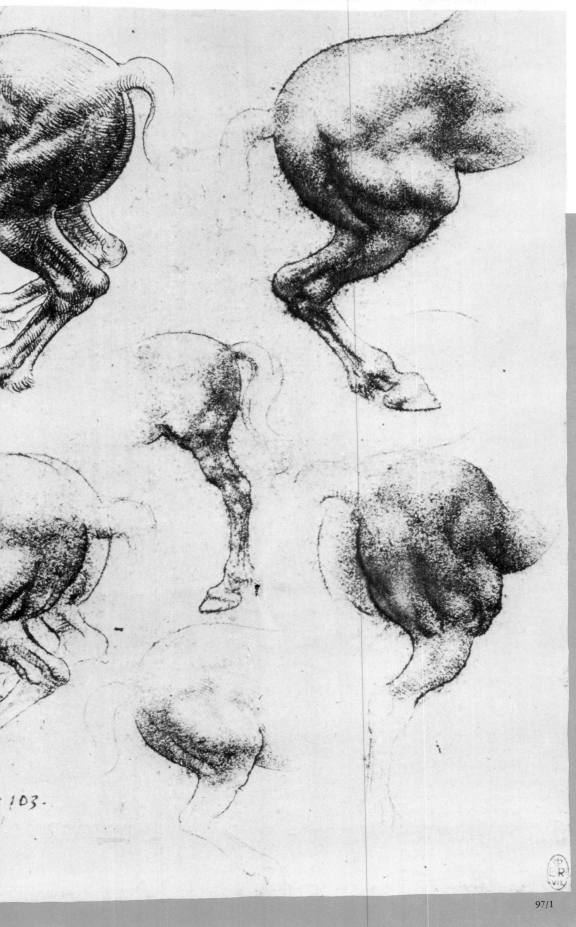

97/1

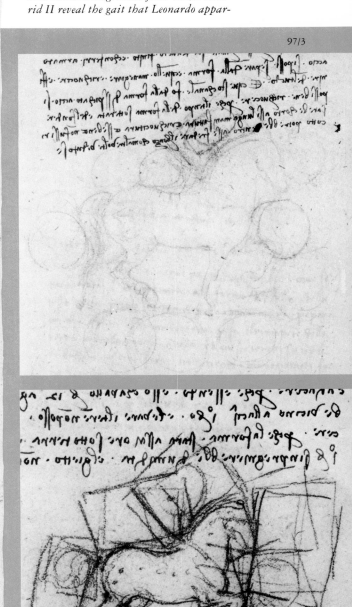

97/3

97/4

Leonardo's study of horses' hindquarters at left, Windsor 12333, seems to have faded about 15 years after he made it. Scholars discern in their outlines the hand of Francesco Melzi, who apparently traced over them. At bottom left, Windsor 12328 verso, Leonardo returns to prancing horses in a study from the period of the Battle of Anghiari.

The two drawings below from Codex Madrid II reveal the gait that Leonardo appar-

97/2

ently had settled upon for the Sforza horse – a brisk walk with left hind leg advancing and right foreleg bent almost at a right angle. On folio 147 recto (top) are notes for casting. On folio 151 verso (bottom) Leonardo notes the date, December 20, 1493, and announces, "I have decided to cast the horse without tail and lying on the side." He reconsidered later and chose to cast it upside down.

"thickness." The thickness (later referred to by Cellini as *lasagna*) was to have been made from an earthen material or wax. On folio 144 recto, paragraph 6, he mentions making the thickness of potter's clay and on folio 148 recto, paragraph 6, he refers to wax or potter's clay. The thickness was Leonardo's solution to the problem of calculating exactly the amount of bronze that would be needed. The ratio between the weight of the material used for the thickness and that of the bronze would make it possible for that calculation to be precise. Beneath it, in the hollow of the female, would be the male, made from refractory clay used by foundrymen and specially heat-resistant so that it could withstand baking and direct contact with the molten metal. This male mold would be constructed in relation to the iron gaggers that held it steady within the hollow.

There were two categories of gaggers positioned in the hollow of the mold: the first would remain in place after casting to give greater stability to the completed bronze monument; the second set of gaggers functioned to support the core and the outer casting layer in position and would be removed once casting was completed. Sketches and descriptions of these gaggers can be found in the Codex Atlanticus (datable to 1494)[26] and also in Windsor 12349 where the sketch of a mold for a rearing horse shows that Leonardo had been planning this new molding system during his first years in Milan working on the initial stages of *Il Cavallo*.

It was vital that the male mold be completely moisture-free. To ensure that, Leonardo planned to liberate it from the female mold and rebake it, in a process similar to that used by cannon founders. Leonardo could rely here on his previous experience as master of artillery in Florence, and from this he was well aware of the serious difficulties that might arise if the moisture were not completely eliminated from the male. To avoid this, he proposed another modification of the casting process.[27] He planned to make a layer of refractory clay, only 8 inches thick, to fit

The Trivulzio project was conceived as a much more elaborate funeral monument than the Sforza horse. Only one sketch datable from the years of the first drawings for the Sforza monument, from Codex Atlanticus, folio 148 recto-a, deals with a base for the life-size statue of Sforza, a high pedestal with arches underneath [98/2]. The illustration below, from a 1491 manuscript about Francesco Sforza, shows a walking horse much like Leonardo's, and suggests an elaborate setting most probably due to the miniaturist's fantasy. For the Trivulzio Leonardo planned a life-size horse and rider on a large ornate marble pedestal. In the sketch at far right, Windsor 12355, the base is a sort of triumphal arch. At right middle, Windsor 12353, the base is rounded and supported by many columns.

98/1

In the sketch below, Windsor 12353, the pedestal rests on Doric pillars at each corner, and nude athletic figures perch on the sides.

98/5

98/2   98/3   98/4

the hollow of the female mold. This would be the most superficial part of the male, forming an "envelope" which, after rebaking, would be filled with a mixture of brick dust, ash, gypsum, or lime mortar.[28] An "outlet" left on the inside would then ensure the discharging of any residual moisture still left at the moment of casting. Although Leonardo planned to use this process for the body of the horse, *Il Cavallo*'s mold of the head and neck was to be at once completely filled with the refractory clay of the male.

The layers of the mold at this stage are the female and its now joined interfaces, which could be closed around the male. This would essentially provide for a more elaborate version of the prevalent method of casting, but would still have many of the drawbacks of that method. There would be no way of checking the faithfulness of the impression made from the earthen model, and there would undoubtedly be many imperfections resulting from the elimination of the thickness, the repeated removals of the hollow pieces, and the many sutures between pieces.

The greatest achievement of Leonardo's new system of sectional molding was that a hollow plaster impression was obtained in which it would be possible to cast wax to obtain a countermodel of the original. The artist could check this countermodel

*Several studies for the Trivulzio monument
made use of an old sculptor's trick: resting
the forelegs of a rearing horse on some
objects. For Donatello's Gattamelata it was
a large ball. Tradition has it that even the
Marcus Aurelius originally was balanced
on a prostrate enemy warrior which long
ago disappeared. In these sketches Leonardo
opted for the fallen foe. The kneeling enemy
attempts to ward off the hoofs with his
right hand. The base has a cornice with the
marshal's trophies dangling from it and
a Tuscan column at each corner. Between*

99/2

*the columns is the plain rectangular sar-
cophagus for Trivulzio's body. At left the
sarcophagus underneath the pedestal has
an ornate curved form similar to one executed by Verrocchio. At the right of the
pedestal can be seen pillars where statues of
captives are chained.* WINDSOR 12355

*Overleaf: Two sheets from the 17 folios of
Codex Madrid II dealing with the horse.
On folio 156 verso, page 100, Leonardo
sketches (from top): "Irons of the side, legs,
and other slender pieces. Irons of the core
and its fastenings. Locking of the form with
the irons of the chest. Irons that sustain the
core and its support." The immense size of
the Sforza horse meant that the female outer
mold had to be formed in pieces. Folio 157
recto, page 101, shows the head and neck
sections of the female mold. The iron gridwork was intended to reinforce the plaster
or clay of the mold.*

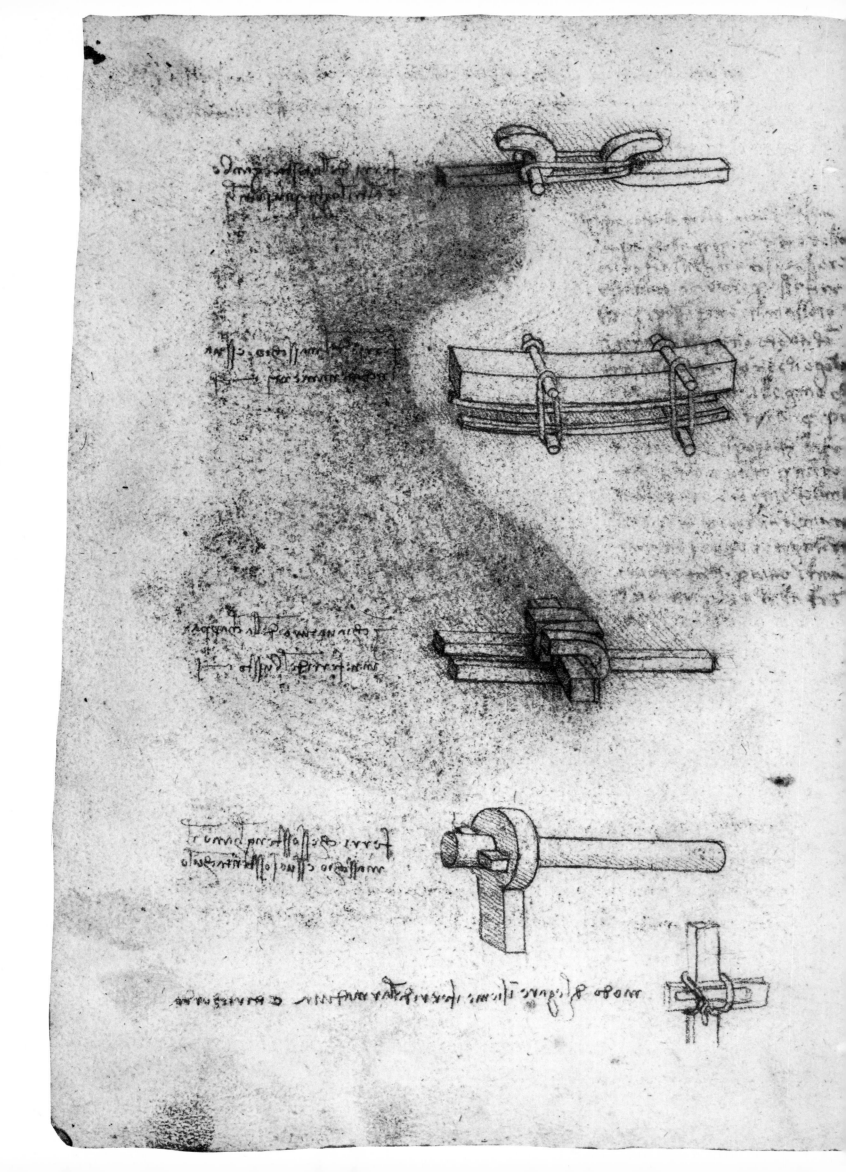

100/1

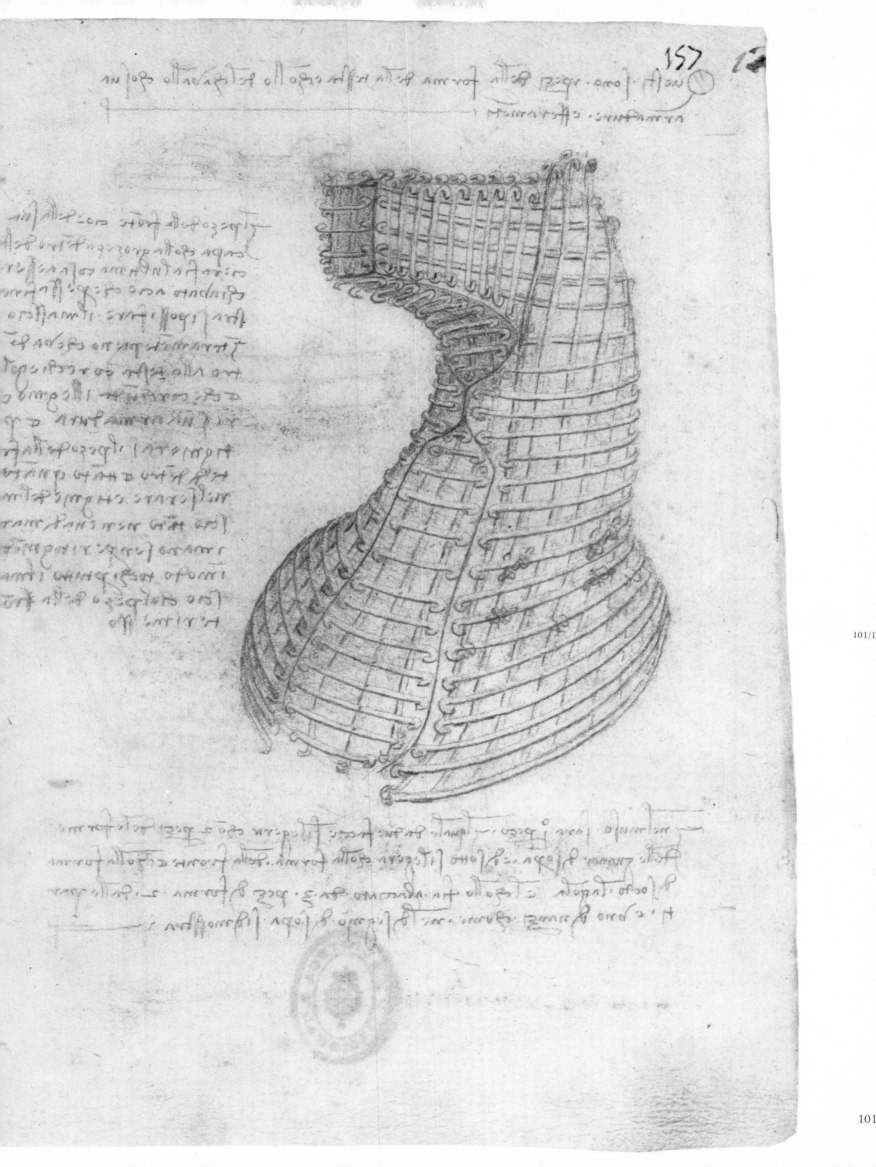

102/1

Leonardo's new casting system was put into practice for a large-scale monument 200 years later. This statue of Louis XIV is the first known example of a huge figure being made in a single casting. It was erected in Paris in 1699 while the great Sun King was still in the midst of a reign that lasted 72 years. In casting the statue the foundrymen followed the same procedure Leonardo had envisioned, preparing the mold and pouring the bronze in one casting. Even the figure of the horse itself – from a model created by François Girardon – bore a remarkable resemblance to the final drawings for the Sforza horse. The French must have heard of Leonardo's ideas through word of mouth or through handwritten copies of his notes. Cellini is supposed to

for deficiencies that might have occurred in the first impression, correct them, and trim the countermodel until maximum perfection in the image to be translated into bronze had been achieved. The molding process was thus no longer a matter of high-level manual labor, but rather a creative work that demanded the presence and intervention of the artist.

The folios of Codex Madrid II do not explicitly mention a wax countermodel, but it is hinted at, especially in the Codex Atlanticus: "... pour the rest [that is, of the wax] ... and then trim the wax as you require. ..."[29] Even though the wax countermodel here clearly described is for a figure of small proportions, it is extremely unlikely that Leonardo would not have tried to produce one for a project requiring such care as the Sforza horse, the more so as we know that he will include a wax countermodel in his estimate for the monument to Trivulzio.[30]

FIGURE EQUESTRE DE LOUIS XIV
que la Ville de Paris a elevée dans la Place de Louis le Grand en 1699
Avec Privilège du Roy

102/1

have bought in France a Leonardo book "on the three great arts: sculpture, painting, and architecture." The statue to Louis XIV survived less than 100 years: it was one of the great artworks destroyed during the French Revolution.

102/2

The illustration at right represents the mold in plaster which is the female mold of the original plaster model.

102/2

Other evidence from Codex Madrid II seems to allude to the probability of this wax model. Folios 142 verso, 148 verso, and 150 recto mention the necessity of calcination of the horse before covering it with the casting hood. Had this been an earthen model, it would have been covered with a greasy substance to avoid the adhesion of the soil of the hood. But when the casting hood is composed on a wax model, a calcination process is needed instead. Leonardo recommends, "Once you have applied 2 coats of ashes and wish to begin working on the form, rub the surface of the dried coat of ashes slightly with your hand, smoothing it out so that the form does not retain the imprints of the brush strokes."[31]

Considering all the information, it is clear that Leonardo must occupy an extremely important position in the history of the technique of casting: this piece-molding process with a wax countermodel asserted itself everywhere from the 16th century on, and was to remain in use until modern times.

The casting hood itself was fastened with large cross irons that immobilized the male within the hood. This is clearly illustrated by the drawing on folio 157 verso of Codex Madrid II which shows that the supporting gaggers were anchored to these iron bolts [104/1]. Folio 154 recto of Codex Madrid II has a drawing of the frame used for transporting the mold, which indicates that the casting hood was an "open" one, that is, one made in pieces which could be removed from the male after the liquefied wax of the countermodel had been melted away.

This open casting hood was not in general use, but indicates yet another measure designed by Leonardo to solve the challenge of *Il Cavallo.* In casting a monument of such enormous proportions, the casting pit itself posed problems. The pit would have to be fairly deep, and the subsoil in the area of Milan contains water-bearing strata close to the surface. This moisture would, of course, be a clear

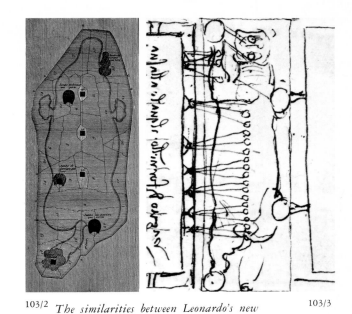

103/2

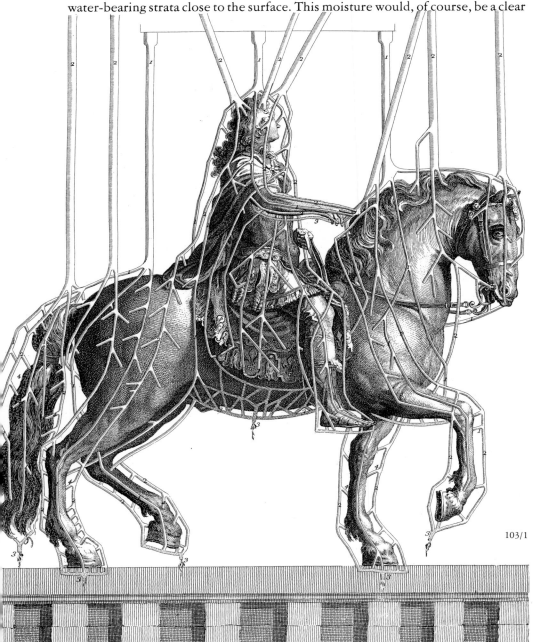

103/1

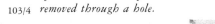

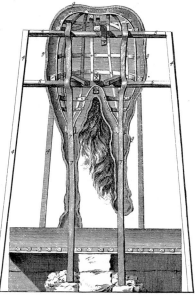

103/4

103/3

The similarities between Leonardo's new casting process and the method used 200 years later in making the monument to King Louis XIV can be documented by a comparison of manuscripts. The illustration at left, taken from an 18th-century report on the casting of Louis XIV, shows the wax countermodel of the horse and rider. The network of tubes served two main purposes. First, they allowed the wax that had been laid in the hollow space between the outer and inner molds to drain out when heated (drops of wax can be seen draining from the bottom openings of the lower tubes). Second, they permitted pouring of the molten bronze into the space vacated by the wax. The diagrams at top and bottom are comparable views, Leonardo and Louis XIV, of the casting process. At top is the view from above the casting pit. Leonardo's diagram (top right), a detail from Codex Madrid II, folio 149 recto, shows casting tubes leading to a rectangular furnace. At bottom is a comparison of the rear views. In Leonardo's sketch (bottom right), Windsor Collection 12351 verso, the shaded area represents the hollow space, which is occupied by the wax, then the bronze. The tail is missing because he had decided to cast it separately. In the drawing for the French statue (bottom left) the metal gridwork spanning the inner mold was designed to reinforce the cast horse after the materials of the inner mold were removed through a hole.

103/5

threat to the casting process. On folio 151 verso, dated December 20, 1493, Leonardo states that if the horse were to be cast upside down, "the water would be as close as one braccio." Thus the casting hood would have to be perfectly dried and waterproofed. The codex describes Leonardo's experiments to demoisturize the hood.[32]

It is clear that the hood was an open one, since it was taken off the male for the baking and tightening process necessary to dry it out fully. This solution is again similar to that which would be used in artillery making, and it would appear that Leonardo's knowledge of making firearms was once again extremely useful.[33]

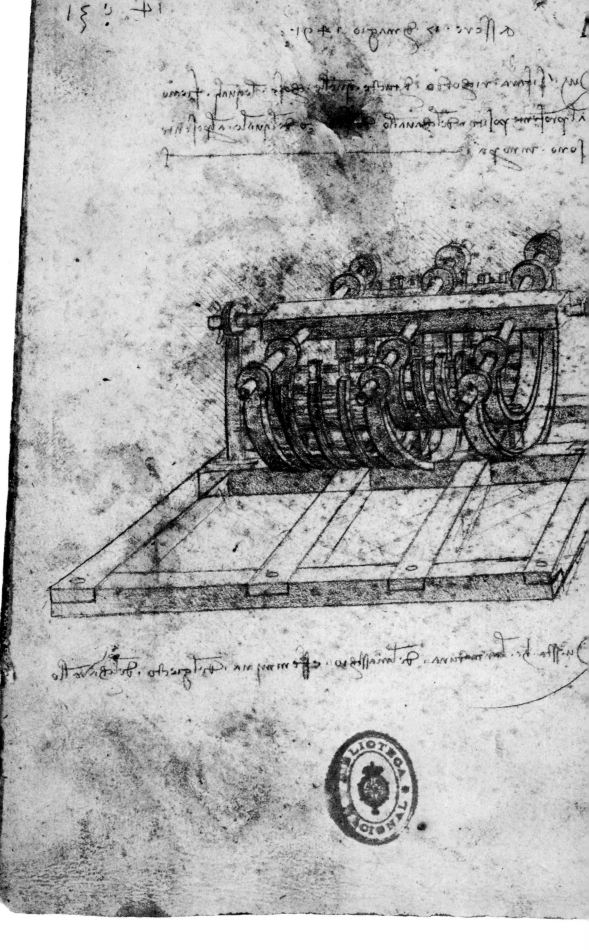

104/1

At the top of this page from Codex Madrid II – folio 157 verso – Leonardo writes: "In the evening, May 17, 1491. Here, a record shall be kept of everything related to the bronze horse presently under execution." Though it is the last page of the manuscript, this sheet actually is the first of 17 on which Leonardo describes the Sforza horse. He worked in his notebooks haphazardly, filling up whatever pages happened to be blank, and sometimes starting at the very end of a set of blank pages and working backward. Underneath the drawing on this sheet he writes, "This is the armature of the male and female of the cast of the horse." In the wooden frame can be seen the semicircular molds between which the bronze would be cast. The male molds are anchored inside the female molds with iron bolts – called gaggers by foundrymen – to keep them in precise register during casting.

For the Sforza horse Leonardo had to invent a new system of casting. He was a perfectionist and wanted to cast the giant horse in a single casting so it would have no unsightly seams. He also wanted to save the original model – as an art object, as a model against which to compare the finished casting, and as a precaution in case anything went wrong in his first try at casting. The method of casting prevalent among Renaissance sculptors – the lost-wax process – offered him none of these possibilities. With the common method one had to create a model in wax over a core of refractory clay, apply an outer mold over the wax, heat the figure to make the wax run out, and pour molten bronze into the cavity vacated by the wax. Leonardo's method, as it came into later use, was far more complex: create a model in clay; from the model make in sections an outer female mold of plaster; line the female mold with wax or potter's clay; inside the lined female mold make a male mold of refractory clay; take everything apart, rebake the male, reenclose it in the female mold after removing the thickness of wax or clay; in the empty space so created cast wax in order to obtain a countermodel of the original. Once freed from the pieces of the empty mold, finish the countermodel by eliminating all irregularities; over the wax make a new female mold of refractory clay that is resistant to the casting heat; heat to make the wax run out; remove and dry the outside mold and make it waterproof, then refit it on the male; pour bronze into the cavity vacated by the wax.

The hood was probably made of fewer pieces than the other mold pieces since, in contrast to the earlier stages, its removal was made easier by the fact that the pieces did not adhere to the model but, after the outflow of the wax of the countermodel, were isolated from the male by the cushion of air that was later to be occupied by the bronze. The codex discusses the removal of the casting hood "done evenly" [34] by pulling it horizontally and uniformly. Leonardo was concerned also with the weight of the hood[35] because of the pulling and shifting necessary for removing it from the male after the countermodel process and transporting it to the casting pit and reheating ovens. Since the hood was heavy, awkward, and rather fragile,[36] it was important to have the ovens and pit at the same site. Clearly, this site could not be at the palace, and for that reason Leonardo designed the frames exemplified by the drawings on folio 154 recto of Codex Madrid II and folio 216 verso-a of Codex Atlanticus.

The ovens were to be buried at the sides of the pit, and would first be used for rebaking and waterproofing the two halves of the hood. After this operation, the male would be lowered to the inside [106/1], fitted with the channels, or "mouths," necessary for casting the molten bronze.[37] To do this, Leonardo designed a special set of winches.[38] The hood would then be closed over the male, and the entire mold would be laid at the bottom of the pit.[39] This was the final stage of the most complex molding system ever elaborated, revolutionary in comparison with traditional techniques, and proving its superiority by its eventual general use.

Sadly, Leonardo was never to see his elaborate process completely tested. It is known, by a letter of Lodovico Sforza's brother-in-law Ercole I d'Este, the Duke of

This instrument is used to transport and to lower the form. And should you desire to lower it upside down, remove the cross-piece that is used for tying the instrument together and, reinforcing it on the side nearest the form, pull at the feet of the beams that support the half-form at points a and b. However, it would be preferable to detach the half-form; pull it out; and fasten it to the entire instrument, carrying it to the place where it shall be lowered. And in this way, you shall fasten it in an upright, perpendicular position. Then, carry the instrument to the opposite part and, with the frame facing the instrument, secure the form. Once it is lowered with the aid of ropes, turn the form over, face down. You shall proceed further, without any change in the instrument of the form.

MADRID II 154r

Ferrara, to his ambassador in Milan[40] that the mold for casting the horse was completed. That letter was requesting the mold for an equestrian monument to Ercole himself. Italian politics had turned again, and events beyond his control prevented Leonardo from further work on *Il Cavallo*.

From the notebooks, it is not difficult to imagine Leonardo, absorbed in his experiments, poring over designs, uninterested in court intrigues. Unfortunately, those intrigues ultimately threatened his magnificent project. Il Moro's position as Duke of Milan had never been satisfactorily secure. He was threatened by his nephew Gian Galeazzo, whose wife had powerful relatives in Naples. Neapolitan actions against Milan were discreetly followed by Florence, and Lodovico was confronted with the possibility of an Italian coalition directed against Milan. In 1494 Gian Galeazzo died, perhaps murdered at Il Moro's instigation, and in the same year, about the time that Leonardo was preparing the final molds, Lodovico persuaded King Charles VIII of France to prosecute an old French claim to Naples. This at first appeared to be a master stroke of political manipulation, but the results were disastrous to Il Moro. It is quite possible that he intended the French to remain a menacing threat only to the other Italian powers. In any case, it soon developed that France seriously intended to invade Italy, Milan included. Lodovico's brother-in-law in Ferrara was directly threatened. In November 1494 Il Moro was forced to use the 158,000 pounds of bronze designated for *Il Cavallo* for cannons.[41]

Leonardo did not abandon hope at this time. He was painting the *Last Supper* when he wrote to Il Moro, "Of the horse I shall say nothing because I know the times. . . ."[42] Leonardo in his final plans for the casting decided to cast the tail

Leonardo writes his own description for this device, which he would use to transport and to lower the form; see transcription below, at left.

105/1

This wooden "cage" – with a faint outline of the horse mold visible inside – was Leonardo's method for transporting the huge mold to the casting pit. His note – "all the heads of the bolts" – refers to the holes along the side of the horse into which he would anchor bolts to secure the inner and outer molds.

ATLANTICUS 216v-a

105/2

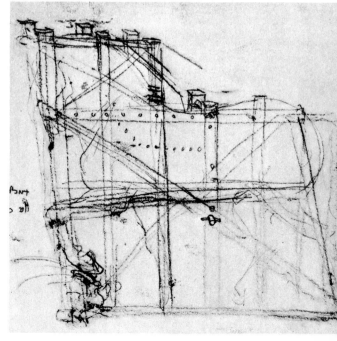

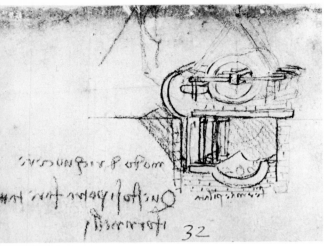

106/1

The precise position in which the Sforza horse would be cast gave Leonardo a great deal of trouble. He wanted to cast it upside down to allow proper distribution of the molten bronze. This would require digging a casting pit so deep it would strike water-bearing strata and create too much humidity in the molds. At one point in Codex Madrid II he decides to cast it "lying on the side." But he must have solved the humidity problem with a plan to rebake and water-proof the outer molds in an oven like the one above, Windsor 12348. His only complete drawing of the casting arrangements (opposite page) has the horse mold upside down. In a detail from this (below) can be seen the network of tubes that would carry the molten bronze to the space between the inner and outer molds where the wax had been.

106/2

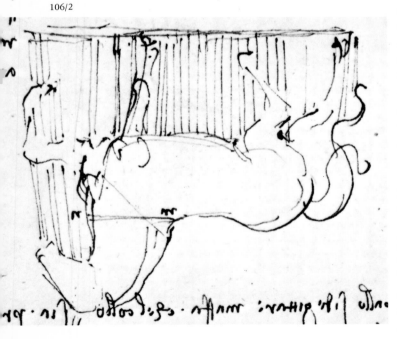

separately from the rest of the horse, because of the difficulty in making the bronze penetrate into the individual tufts.[43] Although he had decided earlier to cast the horse on its side to avoid the dampness near the bottom of the casting pit, he changed his mind and decided that he could cast the horse upside down as he had originally planned.[44] He also worked on the design of the ovens, and drew, on folio 149 recto of Codex Madrid II, a total of four – two circular and two rectangular [107/1]. Folios 142 and 148 discuss an intention to use even five or six ovenloads of bronze at a time, with one oven for each part of the horse. He was forced to stop, however, in 1499 when the troops of Louis XII were besieging Milan. Leonardo left with Luca Pacioli, his mathematician friend, for Venice and eventually for Florence. The enormous earthen model of *Il Cavallo* in the palace courtyard was used for target practice by Gascon archers after Lodovico's capture and incarceration in a French dungeon. The request by Ercole d'Este for the molds for his own monument was later vetoed by the King of France. Every trace of the casting mold was to disappear.

Leonardo occupied himself readily with other projects in Florence, and then in work for Cesare Borgia. Nearly a decade after he left Milan he was commissioned to create another equestrian statue by Gian Giacomo Trivulzio [88/2], the Italian-born commander of the French troops who had taken Milan from Il Moro. Here Leonardo worked on the problem of designing a life-size monument in bronze that would be practically possible to cast and at the same time reflect the liveliness of posture of an animated horse. Leonardo prepared a number of exquisite sketches [93/2; 98/3–5; 99/1–2] for the Trivulzio monument (especially in the Windsor Collection), but unfortunately, this horse too was never cast in bronze. Leonardo never saw his plans and designs realized.

It is more than likely, however, that some handwritten copy of Leonardo's writings on casting existed. Benvenuto Cellini was supposed to have bought in France a transcription "in pen" of a Leonardo book "on the three great arts: sculpture, painting, and architecture."[45] Whether from this book or some other source, Leonardo's exact casting system was put to use some 200 years later. Germain Boffrand[46] and others describe the system followed by Jean Baltazar Keller of Switzerland in molding and casting the huge equestrian monument of Louis XIV that was erected in Paris in 1699 from a model created by François Girardon. There are remarkable coincidences between Leonardo's procedures and those followed for the French statue. This monument is in fact the first historically documented example of a figure of exceptional proportions executed in a single casting, that is, just as Leonardo had planned for the Sforza horse. Besides this, we note in Boffrand some expedients elaborated by Leonardo and not mentioned either by Vasari or by Cellini, such as the "s" shaped irons worked out to support the earth of the male inside the female mold [91/2], or the precaution of striking the male mold with a piece of wood in order to make sure that no lesions exist. In addition, the sketch traced by Boffrand of the "upside down" horse enclosed in the plaster piece mold is remarkably close to Leonardo's drawing of the Sforza horse in its casting pit – even the figure of the horse itself is similar to the Sforza monument [103/1–5].

But this statue, although realized in bronze, was also destined for destruction: it was one of the great, but royalist, works of art torn down in the French Revolution.

Leonardo's work and designs for the Sforza horse then disappeared until 1967, when Codex Madrid II was rediscovered in the Biblioteca Nacional in Madrid. The importance of the section of the codex on *Il Cavallo* cannot be over-emphasized, for it clearly establishes Leonardo's great contribution to the history of casting sculpture. Additionally, it records the work of Leonardo, confirming our image of him as artist, scientist, and innovator struggling with the fluctuations of Italian Renaissance politics, creating works of art that endured longer than the reigning monarchs he worked for, and designs that were put into practice long after the powerful princes of his era had been forgotten.

And yet there is a sadness to this project that symbolizes a man trapped in times that do not permit him his fullest growth or award him his due recognition.

Void of the furnace, with straight barrel vault, in order to facilitate stirring.

The hole that is made for entrance into the cavity of the horse must be 7 ounces wide and one braccio long. And cast this small hatch, along with the horse, on a separate place, and with male and female hinges, in order to be able to close this door.

This is Leonardo's graphic vision of the casting pit for the Sforza horse. In the center, in a view from above, is the assembled outer mold of the horse. It is flanked on four sides by multiple furnaces — two rectangular and two circular — of the type he had designed for casting cannon to melt the bronze before it flowed into the mold. He could calculate how much bronze would be needed because he knew how much wax or potters' clay — which was used for the "thickness" — already had occupied the space between the outer and the inner molds. Tubes connecting one of the furnaces to holes in the mold carry the molten bronze. In a note transcribed here he refers to the fact that some of the tubes — "spouts" — would have to be vented. The sketch at the bottom shows "how the horse shall be cast" — upside down. The diagram and note at top right describe a hole about 12 by 23 inches for getting inside the finished horse. Through this hole would be removed the earthen materials that had formed the inner mold during casting. MADRID II 149r

Here you can make all the spouts for the body without vents, except at the uppermost part of the body. And the legs shall serve as the common exhalation of the enclosed air aside from the bronze which fills them up.

This is how the horse shall be cast, but provide that the neck first be filled up with its bronze by means of many spouts until line m n is reached. At this point, all the other spouts must be unplugged at once.

Perhaps this sense of disappointment, of isolation, is best expressed by Leonardo's own words on folio 141 recto of Codex Madrid II:

> *"Epitaph*
> *If I could not make*
> *If I"*

Again, the bronze horse may be taken in hand, which is to be to the immortal glory and eternal honor of the prince your father of happy memory, and of the illustrious house of Sforza.

These statements sum up in his words the tragic story of Leonardo and Il Cavallo. Above, in 1482, he writes to Lodovico Sforza offering his services.

Of the horse I shall say nothing because I know the times. . . .

A later letter to Lodovico refers to the "times" – the duke's regime is in trouble and the 158,000 pounds of bronze intended for casting the horse have been sent to Ferrara to be made into cannon barrels.

The Duke has lost his state and all of his possessions and his liberty and has seen none of his works finished.

Leonardo writes in his notebook a kind of epitaph.

Epitaph
If I could not make
If I

This "epitaph" ends Leonardo's notes about the horse in Codex Madrid II. He "could not make" the horse because of war – rather than because of his own restless striving to create technology that was new, better, and more difficult.

Today only Leonardo's notes and drawings for the horse survive. The molds were made. They disappeared. Even the wonderful earthen full-scale model of it was lost – to the arrows of the French invader. But in the illustration at right Leonardo's horse lives, if only in symbol. His drawing from Windsor 12347 has been enlarged and placed upon a schematic base, the size and placement of which, however, is merely a speculation. The monument is projected into the courtyard of the Sforza Castle, the proper proportions having been taken into consideration. Now, Il Cavallo looms majestically over the ducal courtyard, probably close to how Leonardo must have envisioned it.

108/1

HEIGHT OF THE HORSE: 24 FEET

HEIGHT OF THE BUILDING: 62 FEET

TO THE BUILDING: 144 FEET

TO THE VIEWER: 85 FEET

He accorded music the highest place among
the arts after painting . . .
calling it *figurazione delle cose invisibili*
('the shaping of the invisible').

Leonardo and Music

EMANUEL WINTERNITZ

He was an elegant speaker
and an outstanding performer on the lira,
and he was the teacher of Atalante Migliorotti,
whom he instructed on this instrument.
ANONIMO GADDIANO

111/1

The lira da braccio, *one of the ancestors of the violin, is, together with the lute, one of the foremost improvisation instruments of the Italian Renaissance. Singers, reciting poetry, accompanied themselves on the* lira da braccio *by providing additional strands of polyphony. The* lira da braccio *was a bowed instrument that had two sets of strings: five melody strings, which could be stopped – that is, pressed by the fingers against a finger board like the strings of a violin; and in addition, two open strings running through the air outside the finger board, each producing only one tone. It is because of these open strings, comparable to those of the ancient lyre of the Greeks, that the instrument was called* lira *(Italian for "lyre")* da braccio, *or simply* lira *in Leonardo's time.*

Although Leonardo has always been extolled as "the universal genius," his musical thought and his musical activities have received little serious attention and have never been treated systematically. It is characteristic that the standard works of Leonardo, even in our century, do not mention music at all,[1] or content themselves with quoting remarks by Vasari, the author of the famous *Lives of Painters*.

Leonardo was, in fact, profoundly occupied with music. He was a performer and teacher of music, he was deeply interested in acoustics and made many experiments in this field that had immediate bearing on music, he wrestled with the concept of musical time, and he invented a considerable number of ingenious musical instruments and made improvements on existing ones. He also had some highly original ideas about the philosophy of music that were intimately connected with his philosophy of painting. It is characteristic that in his *Paragone*, which forms an introduction to his *Treatise on Painting*, he accorded music the highest place among the arts after painting.[2] If we knew nothing of his classification of music other than his remark calling it *figurazione delle cose invisibili* ("the shaping of the invisible"), we would have a clear indication of the depth and originality of his musical thought.

There are several reasons why the musical merits of Leonardo have never been appropriately examined and evaluated. Art historians have concerned themselves little with the musical situation of Leonardo's time and environment, and have considered neither the properties and intricacies of musical instruments then in vogue nor the level reached by the musical technology of the time. Historians of music, on the other hand, would waste little time on a man who did not leave us any written compositions. Devoted to the collection and interpretation of the innumerable treasures of Renaissance polyphony that have come down to us, the historians of music have had, until recently, little time or love for the study of musical improvisation. Although it was not much discussed in musical treatises of the Renaissance, improvisation was in fact one of the most subtle and popular branches of musical performance, as revealed by countless paintings and other works of art showing the instruments of improvisation in the hands of angels, King David, and the great mythological figures of antiquity, such as Apollo, Orpheus, Amphion, and the Muses.[3]

The earliest source of biographical information on Leonardo, the Anonimo Gaddiano,[4]

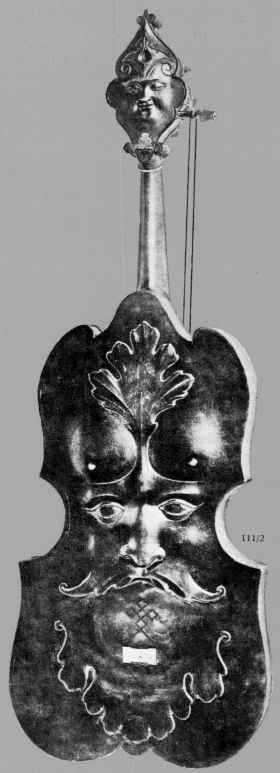

111/2

The lira da braccio *shown above and left, made by Giovanni d'Andrea in Verona in 1511, is the most beautiful of the few specimens that have survived. The belly is shaped like a male torso, and correspondingly the front of the pegbox shows a grotesque male face. The back, carved in strong relief, shows the form of a female torso with breasts and nipples strongly marked, with the back of the pegbox showing a woman's face. The middle region of the soundbox shows a large moustachioed* mascheróne *that overlaps the undulations of the female form. A little ivory plaque inserted into the back bears a Greek inscription quoting an ancient saying that can be freely translated as "The song of men is the remedy of pain."*
KUNSTHISTORISCHES MUSEUM, VIENNA

111

dating from the first half of the 16th century, twice mentions Leonardo's musical activities: "He was an elegant speaker and an outstanding performer on the lira, and he was the teacher of Atalante Migliorotti, whom he instructed on this instrument." "From Lorenzo the Magnificent, he was sent to the Duke of Milan to present to him, together with Atalante Migliorotti, a lira, since he was unique in playing this instrument."

Atalante Migliorotti was a Florentine born in 1466, and therefore still a boy of 16 when he accompanied Leonardo to the court of the Sforzas in 1482 or 1483. He too must have been an excellent performer on the *lira*, since in 1490 he was called to the court of Mantua by the Marchese Francesco Gonzaga to sing and play the title role in Poliziano's famous *Orfeo*.

About 1530 Paolo Giovio, in his short biography of Leonardo, called him a great genius of pleasant appearance, the inventor of many theatrical delights, and mentions his performance on the *lira*. The great mathematician, Luca Pacioli, who became a good friend of Leonardo in Milan and for whose treatise *De divina proportione* Leonardo designed geometric figures, refers to him as an outstanding painter, a master of perspective, an architect, and a musician.

Vasari reports that Leonardo "devoted much effort to music; above all, he determined to study playing the lira, since by nature he possessed a lofty and graceful mind; he sang divinely, improvising his own accompaniment on the lira." Vasari also records that "after Lodovico Sforza became the Duke of Milan, Leonardo, already famous, was brought to the duke to play for him, since the duke had a great liking for the sound of the lira; and Leonardo brought there the instrument which he had built with his own hands, made largely of silver but in the shape of a horse skull — a bizarre, new thing — so that the sound (*l'armonia*) would have greater sonority; with this, he surpassed all the musicians who met there to play. In addition, he was the best improviser of rhymes of his time." A number of later historians also extolled his musical ability, notably the Milanese painter Giovanni Paolo Lomazzo, who in his *Trattato dell'arte della pittura* of 1584, and *Idea del tempio della pittura* of 1590, names "Leonardo Vinci painter" as one of the outstanding masters of the *lira*.

The *lira* mentioned in these sources was the *lira da braccio*, the most noble and subtle polyphonic bowed instrument of Leonardo's day — a fiddle with seven strings. Five, as melody strings, could be stopped against the finger board, while two ran outside the finger board, providing a drone effect whenever plucked or touched by the bow. With the possible exception of the lute, it was the foremost improvisation instrument of the time, and it could be used by a singer to accompany himself.[5] One of the few extant specimens, and certainly the most beautiful one, made by Giovanni d'Andrea in Verona in 1511, is today one of the priceless treasures of the Kunsthistorisches Museum in Vienna [111/1 and 2].

Leonardo must have enjoyed musical instruction in his youth in Florence. According to Vasari, Verrocchio, in whose workshop Leonardo worked, was not only a sculptor and painter but also a musician.[6] It is hardly necessary to describe here the intense musical life at the court of the Medicis and in the churches of Florence. In Milan, Leonardo found himself in another active musical center; it was split between two camps — the Italian traditionalist, and the Flemish-German newcomers (Josquin, Compère, Jacotin, and Agricola). The guardian of the Italian tradition, Franchino Gafurio, a friend and exact contemporary of Leonardo, was the director of the cathedral choir in Milan from 1484 to 1522, and it is significant that his writings were characterized by emancipation from ancient philosophical tradition and by empirical analysis of musical phenomena as data of experience; his attitude is similar to Leonardo's.

In spite of his reputation as a musician, Leonardo probably did not come to Milan for musical purposes. His application for employment at the court of the Sforzas (page 7) did not mention music at all, but stressed his skill in constructing bridges, canals, fortifications, guns, tunnels, and armored cars — in short, all kinds of military engineering — and modestly said at the end that he

112/1

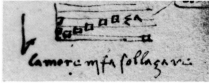

114/1

Love gives me pleasure

*Among the many rebuses invented by
Leonardo for amusement, some use musical
notation. These are the only examples of
musical script found in Leonardo's
notebooks. At his time, it was not customary
to commit improvisations to paper. Thus,
no scores of his improvisations, nor those of
the many other famous improvisers of his
time, exist.* WINDSOR 12692v

could execute sculpture and also paintings. But we know from many sources,
including Leonardo's own entries and sketches in his notebooks, that he took a
hand in luxurious entertainments arranged at the Milan court for such occasions
as weddings, receptions, and processions. Leonardo designed festival architecture, costumes [129/1], masks, and theatrical machines, and it would be absurd
to assume that a musician who as a performer was said to excel above all others at
the court would not have devoted himself also to the variegated musical activities
there.

Although we have no compositions from Leonardo's hand, this does not speak at
all against his technical knowledge of music. According to the fashion of the
time, he did not write down his improvisations, however subtle they were, but

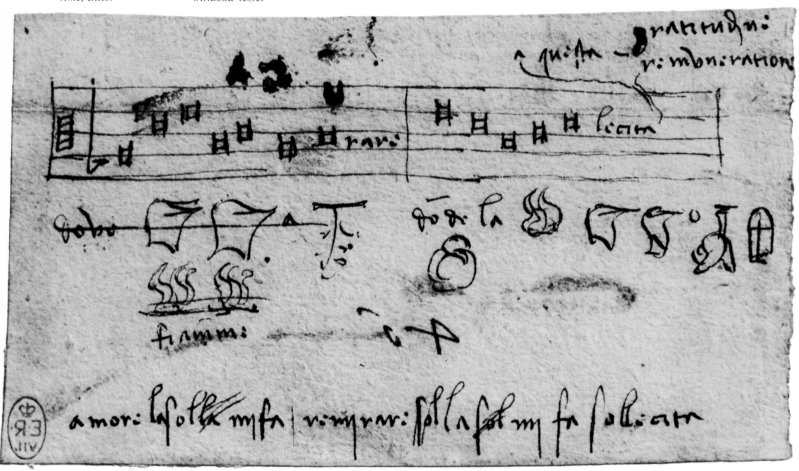

114/2

Love only makes me remember, it alone makes me alert

*One hundred and sixty rebuses made by
Leonardo have survived. Of these, 18
include musical notes, which demonstrate
his ability to write musical notation. In the
rebus illustrated above, he starts with a
fishhook, or* amo. *Next come the musical
syllables* re, sol, la, mi, fa, re, mi, *followed
by the word* rare. *The second group of musical notations,* la, sol, mi, fa, sol, *is followed
by* lecita. *The sentence reads,* Amore sol la
mi fa remirare, la sol mi fa sollecita
*("Love only makes me remember, it alone
makes me alert"). For the seven tones of the
scale, Leonardo used the Guidonian syllables, named for Guido d'Arezzo, who
invented the system about 1000* A.D.
WINDSOR 12697

there is no doubt that he could write music. Musical notation is used in no less
than 18 rebuses out of the more than 160 that are preserved in the folios of the
Royal Collection at Windsor Castle.

One of the more complex examples is a rebus presenting an aphorism dealing
with the nature of love [114/2]. The expression is for the most part in musical
notation.[7] First, after the clef, there appears a fishhook – in Italian, *amo* – then
the notes *re, sol, la, mi, fa, re, mi,* followed by *rare,* in normal handwriting. The
second group of musical notes is *la, sol, mi, fa, sol,* and is followed by *lecita* in
normal letters. Thus the whole sentence reads, *Amore sol la mi fa remirare, la sol
mi fa sollecita.* ("Love only makes me remember, it alone makes me alert.")[8]

Leonardo's thoughts about music were strewn apparently haphazardly throughout numerous notebooks, some as *aperçus* or marginal remarks, others explaina-
ble from the context if the reader is familiar with the natural sciences and the
technology of Leonardo's time. The systematic study of this substantial material
reveals an intense preoccupation with the phenomenon of music. Leonardo was
neither a humanist nor a philosopher in the strict sense in which his contem-

poraries understood this word. Among ancient theorists of music, only the thoughts of Pythagoras[9] and Boethius[10] are echoed in his writings. Had Leonardo decided − or had he found the time − to crystallize all his observations into a systematic treatise, it would have been a formidable compendium. Here we can only mention some of the most interesting points.

Leonardo inquired into the origin of sound ("What is sound produced by a blow?") and examined the sonorous impact of bodies upon bodies, expanding age-old Pythagorean notions.[11] He investigated the phenomenon of vibration and sympathetic vibration, of how the percussion of a body makes it oscillate and communicate its oscillation to the surrounding air or to liquid or solid matter. He studied the propagation of sound waves as differentiated from light waves,

Of the loss of voice because of distance

At distance a b, *the 2 voices* m n *are diminished by half; then although they are two half voices they are not powerful for [as] a full one, but only for a half one. And if infinite [an infinite number of] halves were at such [a] distance, they would be only for a half. And at the same distance, the voice* f, *which was double of* n *and* m, *has lost the fourth part of its power; then, it remains for one voice and a half and comes to be superior in treble power, that is in* g, f *will be powerful as much as* m *and* n *in* a b *distance [at distance* a b].

115/1

These diagrams are examples of Leonardo's research for acoustics. At left, he compares the fading of a loud sound with the fading of two sounds, of which each at its source is only half as loud as the first one. In the sketch below, seven equal sounds fade to nothing before they reach the ear. The design of seven flowers is probably a graphic reminder of a possible parallel between fading of sounds and fading of odor.

MS. L 79v and 80r

115/2

the reflection and refraction of sound waves and the phenomenon of echo, the speed of sound and the factors that determine degrees of loudness, investigating the laws that govern the fading of sound by varying the distance between its source and the ear. Especially characteristic of his approach in this context is his establishment of what can be called a perspective of sound, parallel to the laws of optical and pictorial perspective that were so important to him as a painter [115/1−2]. Also, as a musician he was naturally occupied with the factors that determine musical pitch and experimented with vases of different shapes and varying apertures. Of musical importance, though Leonardo could not foresee its implication, was another of his observations: when he struck a table with a hammer, small heaps of dust formed on its surface; here Leonardo anticipated by three centuries E. F. F. Chladni's discovery of the geometric sand figures produced by setting the edge of a plate in vibration with a fiddle bow. Leonardo's discovery must have had special significance for him, since it constituted an easily observable correspondence between the visual and the auditory realms.

Leonardo's characteristic approach to acoustical problems by analogy to other fields of physical research is exemplified by a neat juxtaposition of nine diagrams he did showing in a synoptic manner the various ways in which light, the force of a blow, sound, magnetism, and odor travel [116/1].

Leonardo was also deeply interested in the construction of musical instruments.[12] He invented new ones and improved existing ones. His ideas have never been systematically studied and their investigation is not easy, since it requires a thorough knowledge of the contemporary instruments and a familiarity with not only the status of technology in Leonardo's time (clockworks, the use of coiled springs, etc.) but also his own achievements in technology.

Leonardo deals with instruments in many brief references in several notebooks

This enlargement from a page in the Codex Atlanticus shows a comparison of the behavior of light, the force of a blow, sound, magnetism, and odor.

ATLANTICUS 126r-a   116/1

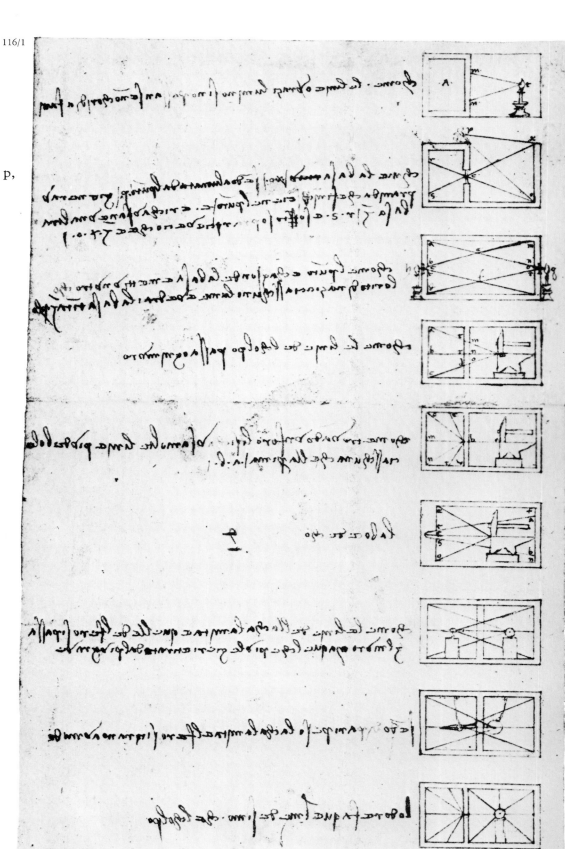

How the lines, or rather the rays of light, go only through transparent bodies.

How the basis XO, *when illuminated from point* p, *generates a pyramid that ends at point* c, *and results in another base at* r S, *and receives what is in* x o *upside down.*

How the point produces the base; place a colored glass before each light and you will see the base colored by it.

How the lines of the blow penetrate every wall.

How, when it finds a hole, it causes many lines, each weaker than the first a b.

The voice of the echo.

How the lines of a magnet and those of the iron go through the wall, but the lighter of the two is attracted by the heavier.

If of equal weight, the magnet and the iron attract each other equally.

Smell behaves like blow.

116

and in a great number of drawings, some elaborate and others only quick embodiments of passing ideas. Some have explanations in words; most have not. And even where explanations are given, they usually appear to be only notes of reminder and accordingly are difficult to understand.

Leonardo's notes and designs dealing with musical instruments are scattered among many pages in the Codex Atlanticus, Manuscript H, Manuscript B, the Codex Arundel, and the Madrid Codices. Cryptic as many of these notes and drawings appear to be if studied in isolation, methodical comparison reveals that they are not merely diverting devices for performing magic tricks, but that they serve systematic efforts by Leonardo to realize some basic aims, of which the

This sketch is for a mechanized military drum that could automatically play complicated rhythms as the carriage traveled. The axle of the carriage wheel drives a central cogwheel, which then turns other cogwheels activating five beaters on each side of the cylindrical drum. ATLANTICUS 306v-a

117/1

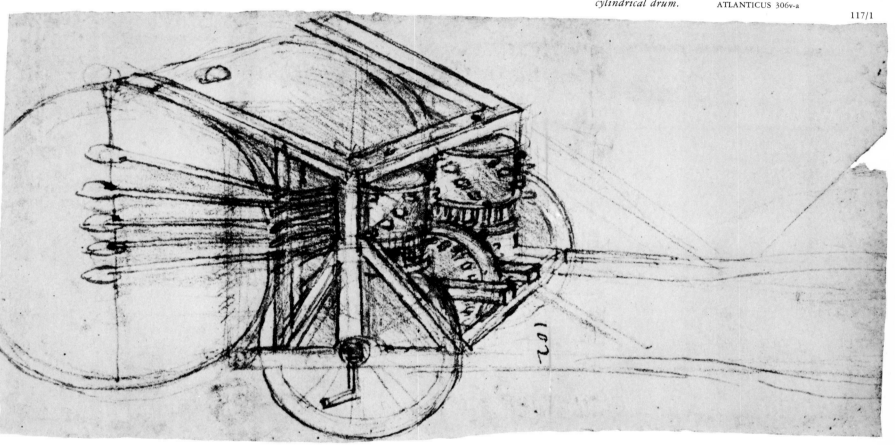

most important are the following: automation of certain instruments and facilitation of playing technique through new kinds of keyboards; increasing the speed of playing; extension of tonal range to make it possible, for instance, to play melodies on drums; overcoming the quick fading of the sound of plucked strings, by giving the instruments an endless bow; enriching comparatively simple instruments to make them capable of polyphony or a wide range of successive tones; and even having a polyphony of the sounds of bowed strings at the control of a keyboard.

Leonardo was greatly interested in the construction of drums. He not only tried to make them easier to play but also expanded their musical possibilities, such as tonal range, far beyond the limitations of the conventional instruments of his time. He also gave some thought to the mechanization of military drums, which is not strange if one recalls his interest in devising tools of war, from small daggers to gigantic war machines and fortifications.

The Codex Atlanticus contains no less than eight sketches of military drums — some cylindrical, some kettle drums. They show various methods of automation: in some models, the axle of the carriage wheels drives a central cogwheel, and this in turn, through other cogwheels or pinion cages, activates the beaters. As many as five beaters may be used on each side of one cylindrical drum, to perform complicated rhythms automatically while the carriage travels [117/1].

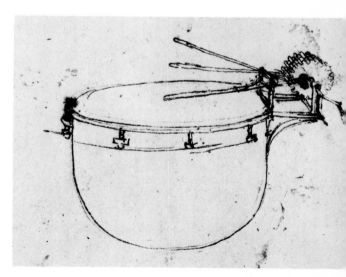

117/2

Here three beaters are turned by a cogwheel that is operated by a crank.

ATLANTICUS 355r-c

117

Other drums have eight beaters, evidently four for each of the two drum heads, and employ cogwheels and pinion cages in a variety of forms to connect the carriage wheels and the beaters.[13]

In the Codex Atlanticus a kettle drum is shown with three beaters operated by a cogwheel that is turned by a crank [117/2]. Thus here we have only a simplification of the action of the drummer. Whole sets of small kettle drums, graduated in size and arranged in a row, appear in the Codex Atlanticus and the Codex Arundel.[14] To employ even drums for playing a scale or chord is characteristic of Leonardo's turn of mind.

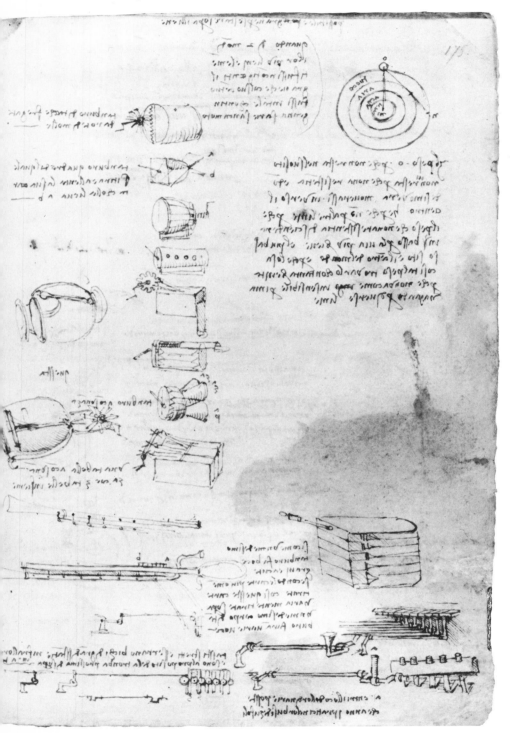

This page from the Codex Arundel reveals Leonardo's ideas for the construction of new types of drums. At the top and upper right he presents some observations on theoretical mechanics and a sketch concerning gravitation and the behavior of weights. The lower part of the page shows designs for wind-instrument keyboards. The rest of the page deals with drums, which are discussed in detail at right. ARUNDEL 175r

118/2

The body of the drum is clearly a cylindrical snare drum. The problem begins with the indented vertical line crossing the skin and the concentric cluster of black lines from which a crank protrudes on the left. Leonardo's explanation says, tamburo di tacche fregate da rote di molle *("a drum with notches scraped by a wheel of springs"). With the word* tacche, *Leonardo probably indicates a small board with many little saw-like indentations. The* rote di molle *is probably not a wheel in the strict sense of this word, but a number of flexible metal rods arranged like the spokes of a wheel. However, it is possible to read* roti *instead of* rote *and to translate it "fragments" (or little pieces) of springs. The protruding crank is unmistakable; but the way in which the cluster of springs is attached to the drum is not clear from the drawing. What, then, is the meaning of the whole? Leonardo's explanation gives the technical ingredients of the mechanism, not its purpose. Apparently the flexible rods carried along the notched edge by the turning crank would produce a continuous drumroll, perhaps with an unusual tone color.*

118/3

This sketch is of incomparably greater importance and novelty than 118/2. Leonardo says that it is a "square drum whose skin is tightened and slackened by means of the lever a b". The body of the drum is not, of course, square, but its head is. The function of the tightening mechanism becomes clear if the reader's eye separates, as it were, the outer shape of the drum from the levers, which have this form: ⋈ *If the player pushes apart the ends at the right, perhaps wedging his fist in between, the opposite ends open, scissor-like, thus tightening the skin, while the other hand is beating it. The result is that of a drum whose pitch can be changed during performance, something which the Occident did not know until the invention of the pedal machine drum, towards the end of the 19th century.*[16]

118/4

Here the shape of the drum is that of a kettle drum. This kind of drum was well known to Leonardo. Small kettle drums, always used in pairs (naqqârâ, nacchere, nacaires,

118/2

118/3

118/4

118/5

118/6

118/7

The most important source revealing Leonardo's ingenious ideas for the construction of new types of drums is a large page in the Codex Arundel [118/1]. It contains three groups of sketches and observations. One, concerned with theoretical mechanics — specifically, gravitation and the behavior of weights[15] — fills the top and the upper right of the page. The lower part of the page shows sketches for the construction of keyboards for wind instruments; these will be discussed later. The rest of the page — that is, the left upper half and center portion — deals with drums, and to this section belongs also the large chordal drum in the right lower section.

The 11 drum sketches represent an astonishing variety in purpose and construction. We should observe, too, that the sequence from top to bottom is not haphazard; the drawings are not isolated flights of fancy, but rather seem to follow a methodical order progressing from group to group, each group dealing with a different problem.

Sketches like these are interesting not only because of the originality of

nakers) entered the Occident from the Middle East during the Crusades, if not earlier. Large kettle drums (tympana) were known in Eastern Europe, especially Hungary and Poland, as early as the 15th century. Leonardo's sketch shows an extraordinary feature: the cords running from the circular frame of the drum are not fastened to its round bottom, but clearly go beyond it toward a sort of disc or ring to which we must suppose they are attached. From this contraption protrudes a screw and a crank, drawn in Leonardo's inimitable shorthand technique. The only interpretation that explains these unusual features is to consider them as a device that can when the crank is turned change the tension of all the cords simultaneously and thereby change the pitch in a minimum of time. On such a drum, any melody could be played by appropriate manipulation of the crank. The drum apparently is supported by a stand; the player could not hold the drum since both his hands would be engaged – one in turning the crank and the other in beating the drum. Thus, the presence of a stand tends to support the assumption that the crank serves to tighten the laces rather than to activate a beating mechanism.

118/5
This is one of the most original solutions to the problem of obtaining a series of different tones from a drum while beating it. Here a snare drum with a long, nearly cylindrical body has several side holes like those of a flute. Before finally convincing myself that the little circles indicate holes, I decided to experiment, and built a small wooden tube with a skin over one opening and with several side holes. The closing of the various holes while beating the skin results in clear pitch differences.

118/6
This sketch shows a square box with a ratchet wheel worked by a crank. The several slightly curved lines on top of the upper side of the box seem to indicate springy tongues attached at one end to the surface of the box, while the free ends are lifted by the teeth of the wheel and allowed to snap back against the surface. The way in which the wheel is attached to the box is not shown – unless one of the curved lines just

mentioned indicates such a connection. The unusual feature of this instrument is the flat oblong board on its right side; the board is softly shaded, while the square above it is strongly shaded. In my belief the board is a slide and the square above it a hole that can be opened or closed by moving the slide. The purpose would again be to obtain a change of pitch during playing. To verify my interpretation, I again built a model, whose performance fully corroborated my assumption. Notice also the little projections on the bottom end of the slider, which can hardly be anything other than loops or handles for moving the slide. There is still the question of whether this instrument has a membrane. We must rather assume that its upper surface is of wood, since only this would provide the right basis for the springy tongues of the ratchet mechanism.

118/7
The drum here is evidently based on the same principle as 118/6 – the slide action. Here the body is that of a conventional cylindrical drum with laces. The side hole and slide are on top, and the right end of the slide again has some sort of handle for pulling. This drum has an ordinary hand beater instead of a mechanical beater.

119/1
The next sketch introduces a group of three drums that are based on another method of expanding the function of drums: the production of simultaneous tones, or chords, by combining several drums into one compound instrument. 119/1 shows a side drum with snare and with several cones inserted into its base. At the right of the cones Leonardo noted, p^a, 3^a, 5^a, signifying the three tones of a triad. There cannot be any doubt that we have here a drum intended to produce a chord. It is a pity, however, that the drawing does not give the faintest idea about the connection between the body of the drum and the cones, or whether the cones are open or closed at their wide end or perhaps at their small end, or how deep they reach into the drum itself.

119/2
This is another "consonance" instrument. Leonardo's text says, "A drum for a chord (consonanza), that is, three drums together." The body consists of three shallow

boxes with a ratchet mechanism attached at the left. A spindle turned by a crank is furnished with three sets of spokes that simultaneously operate springy tongues beating on the top of the three boxes. Thus, this instrument was intended to produce a chord of three tones. We do not see from the drawing whether this instrument has membranes.

119/3
Still simpler in construction is this drum sketch. At first glance there may seem to be six "compartments" on the right side as opposed to five on the left. Actually, there are five skin trips at the left, which bend around the edge of the whole box and are tied with cords around it. The text says, "Since one and the same drum produces high or low tones according to the tighter or looser stretching of the skin, so the present skins stretched at various degrees over the same body of a drum produce different tones." The instrument clearly permits playing a scale or the tones of a chord.

119/4 and 5
The last two drawings of drums present greater difficulties in interpretation than all the others. Both are evidently pot drums with detachable drum heads and a mechanism inside the pot to make them sound. No separate beater is visible. In the first, what appears to be a lid or cover at the left (or upper end of the pot) is detached. Whether this left end of the pot is simply open, or covered by skin, cannot easily be decided. Since Leonardo uses shading for open holes, such as in sketches 118/6 and 118/7, we are inclined to interpret the round shape at this end as a head affixed to the drum, in addition to the one which is removed. Also difficult to explain are the curved lines at the right of the upper drum. They are likely to indicate a base or handle for holding the pot, or perhaps a device for activating the inner machinery. Since no outside beater or drum stick is illustrated, we must assume that it is the inner mechanism that beats the drum from inside. The last drum [119/5] has a different and longer shape, and also has a detachable cover and an inner mechanism. The latter, in this case, is activated by a spoked wheel outside, which is turned by a crank. The

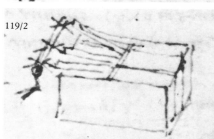
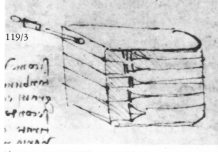

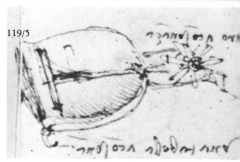

119/1

119/2

119/3

119/4

119/5

ends of the wheel spokes beat against two nearly parallel sticks or wires protruding from the pot. This dual number makes one think that it is a device employed to turn the object inside the pot, which may be a friction wheel. Problematic also is the line curving on the lower side of the drum, clearly outside it, extending from the frame of the spoked wheel towards a hook on the rim of the pot.[17]

Leonardo's inventions and the superb economy of his drawing technique; they also permit a glimpse at his habits of thinking. He begins his series of drums with what was probably a passing idea: an unusual tone color — or rather, noise color — for a drum and a mechanical contraption for playing it. But then a whole flood of novel ideas is let loose, all going beyond existing devices. Leonardo endeavors to enrich the traditional function of drums by making them capable of producing chords and scales. For this he tries two different methods. One is the combina-

The most complicated musical instrument invented by Leonardo was a mechanism that he called the viola organista. *In the Codex Atlanticus, folio 218 recto-c, there are several sketches of different contrivances for bowing a great number of strings at the same time utilizing a keyboard or a set of push buttons. The sketch at the top uses a bow moving back and forth across the strings. The three other sketches use a friction wheel. A technically more elaborate and practical drawing is shown in the illustration at right from Ms. H, folio 45 verso, using a belt of horsehair passing across the*

120/1

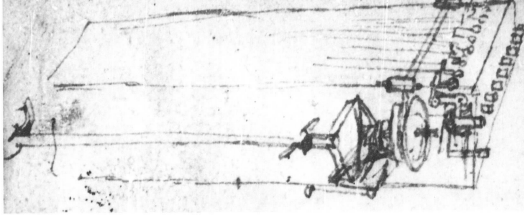

tion of several drums or skins of different pitch into one single instrument. The other consists of devices to make one skin produce tones of different pitch in rapid succession. This aim is realized in various ways: either through the introduction of side holes, or through the use of scissor levers or screw devices to change the tension of the skin while it is beaten, or through slides that open and close a large hole in the resonating body, or, finally, through mechanisms that detach the skin cover from the body of a pot drum. Hardly an opportunity offered by nature is overlooked in this series of quick though methodical sketches, jotted down on a page which began with quite a different subject — theoretical mechanics — and is going to wind up with new ideas for wind instruments.

These many ingenious sketches suggest the question of whether or not Leonardo used them for building actual instruments or at least working models. We do not know. Always pressed for time, he may have been satisfied with a brief record of his ideas. I have made models of most of them, and they work well.

Among the many musical instruments contrived by Leonardo, the *viola organista* is by far the most complicated. No less than six different pages in the notebooks contain sketches for it.[18] None of them are precise drawings intended for an instrument builder, and some are not even completely thought through, since several details would probably have been found impracticable in actual construction. However, to anticipate the outcome of our analysis, the drawings are all concerned with the idea of a stringed instrument with keyboard, in which the strings are set into vibration by a mechanical device — a wheel, a bow with a back-and-forth motion, or a belt of hair moving across the strings as a sort of endless bow. Such an instrument would fill a big gap in the multitudinous array of instruments, not only in Leonardo's time but also in our own. It would combine the polyphonic possibilities of the keyboard with the tone color of bowed strings and thus would be something like an organ with string timbre

120/2

instead of wind timbre, and in addition it would provide the possibility of producing crescendos and decrescendos by finger pressure.

Although it is not known in what order Leonardo made his sketches, it is possible to arrange the drawings in a logical sequence if we assume that Leonardo progressed from less workable solutions to more practical ones. In fact, he proceeds from an instrument with a bow moving back and forth across the strings, to one with a friction wheel, and finally to several versions of a revolving band of hair that sets the many strings into vibration.[19] One page of the Codex Atlanticus shows, on top, a drawing utilizing a bow, and beneath it, three different sketches exploring the possibility of a friction wheel [120/1].

The most workable, and apparently ultimate, solution is in Manuscript H, where we find a sketch of a perfectly consistent, workable keyboard instrument with an endless bow *(archetto)*, a belt of hair moved by a motor attached to the side of the sound box and passed across the strings by means of two small rollers [120/2]. Leonardo also designed a mechanism permitting the player, by pushing the small

strings and functioning as an endless bow, or archetto.

121/1

projecting buttons, to select the desired strings and draw them against the *archetto*.

We do not know, however, how near Leonardo came to the actual construction of the *viola organista* or whether he ever made working models. Today, with an electric motor in place of one using weights or springs, the construction would be greatly facilitated.

We must finally consider two instruments which have special interest because their invention seems directly inspired by Leonardo's anatomical studies; in fact, they are applications of mechanisms Leonardo found in the human body.

The first is in Codex Atlanticus, where we find, among numerous small sketches for various machinery, drawings of two pipes, evidently one of those countless passing ideas that were crying to Leonardo to be recorded just here and now, so as not to be forgotten in the perpetual flow of images, whims, and new ideas [122/1].

Leonardo's invention of the viola organista *fulfilled the old dream of having a great number of strings under the control of the ten fingers. The other existing keyboard instruments did not fulfill this ideal: the harpsichord, while having many strings operated by a keyboard, produced only rapidly fading sound; the organ, while producing a lasting sound, did not provide crescendos and decrescendos by variation of finger pressure. Independently of Leonardo, Fray Raymundo Truchado in 1625 constructed an instrument (above) which was actually a keyboard instrument with four friction wheels. It was a free imitation of the* Nurnbergisch Geigenwerck *invented half a century earlier by Hans Hayden in Nuremberg and described in great detail by the famous musical theorist and composer Michael Praetorius in his* Syntagma Musicum *of 1618.*

Every connoisseur of musical instruments will recognize immediately two recorders by their characteristic heads and mouth holes. Their basic structure has not changed substantially since Leonardo's time. Beneath the upper end held by the player's lips is a hole with a sharp edge which is struck by the air-stream emanating from his mouth. Ordinarily recorders have on their sides six finger holes which are closed and opened by the fingertips of the player to produce the distinct tones of the scale. But Leonardo's recorders look strange. The one on the left has two broad slits on the side of the tube, and the other has one long, thin slit. Fortunately we have an explanatory text in Leonardo's most beautiful calligraphy, running from right to left: "These two flutes do not change their tone by leaps as most wind instruments do, but in the manner of the human voice; and one does it by moving the hand up and down just as with the coiled trumpet and more so in the pipe *a*; and you can obtain one eighth or sixteenth of the tone and just as much as you want." Obtaining an eighth or a sixteenth obviously means — in acoustical language — to reach the upper octaves; and "moving the hand up and down" evidently means not to stop prearranged finger holes, but to move along the slits to change pitch gradually, or as we say today, to produce glissandos, or gliding tones.

Such a glissando instrument would not have fitted into the orchestra of Leonardo's days. Could he have foreseen, in one dreamy corner of his incredible brain, glissando instruments such as the one invented in 1924 by the Russian scientist Lev Theremin and called by the inventor's name and later also by the name Aetherophone? Did Leonardo perhaps want to imitate bird calls? Or did he just think of inventing another of his tricky toys to baffle or amuse the

These two flutes do not change

their tone by leaps as most wind

instruments do, but in the manner of

the human voice; and one does it by

moving the hand up and down just as

with the coiled trumpet and more so

in the pipe a; *and you can obtain*

one eighth or sixteenth of the

tone and just as much as you want.

cavaliers and ladies at the court of Lodovico Sforza, an occupation to which he devoted much of his time?

Where could he have found the idea or a model for his glissando pipes? The clue lies in the words "the human voice," though I must confess that I found the solution by chance and then had it confirmed by Leonardo's own words. The model for our glissando pipes is found in the larynx, and it is significant that Leonardo calls the larynx "the human voice," applying this term to the machinery that produces the voice as well.

Leonardo made designs of the larynx and the trachea, now in Windsor Castle, in which we recognize immediately that the upper opening resembles that of a recorder [123/1 and 2]. Furthermore, in accompanying texts in the anatomy manuscripts the trachea is called *fistola*, which is also the name of a vertical flute such as the recorder.

There is, though, one flaw in our analogy: Leonardo wrongly attributed the change of pitch of the human voice to the narrowing or widening of the cartilage rings of the trachea and failed to observe the function of the vocal cords in the

122/1

These two musical pipes, which resemble the recorder, apparently were inspired by Leonardo's profound knowledge of anatomy (opposite page). Moving the hand along the slits in the instruments would produce the gradual changes in pitch known today as glissandos. ATLANTICUS 397r-b

larynx. This failure was probably caused by the technical difficulty of dissecting the small and fragile larynx. (By the way, Leonardo's drawings are thought to have been based on the anatomy of an ox.)

Still, we have in Leonardo's glissando recorder a new musical instrument which opened, or could have opened, a new musical horizon; which works well (some reconstructions that I have made function perfectly); and which was patterned after an anatomical analogy, that of the larynx, even though Leonardo misunderstood its actual function. Hence we have here a positive result built upon wrong premises.

In the Codex Arundel, on the large page with the 11 drum sketches discussed earlier, we encounter an entirely different kind of analogy – and more than analogy – in the invention of finger boards for musical wind instruments, finger

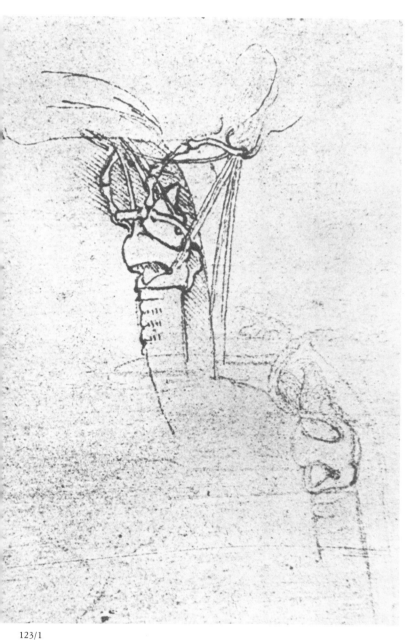

123/1

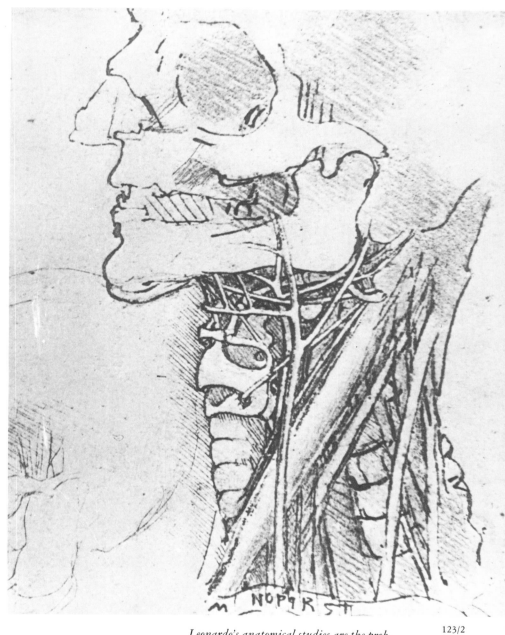

123/2

boards designed as an imitation of the muscles and tendons of thhe human hand, especially those of the fingers [124/1]. We notice two straight tubed instruments on the left, the lower with the mouth cup of a trumpet. Both instruments have a second, auxiliary tube. Here we must recall that the wind instruments of Leonardo's time did not possess the many keys that we find in our modern orchestral instruments. It was the fingertips of the players that closed and opened the six or seven finger holes spaced along the tube according to acoustical ratios. Now when *lower*, and therefore *longer*, instruments were

Leonardo's anatomical studies are the probable source for the recorder-like pipes depicted on the previous page. Here, two drawings show the larynx and trachea; the upper ending of the larynx is strikingly similar to that of a recorder.

WINDSOR 12608r and 12609r

needed, a problem arose. The stern laws of acoustics demanded finger holes spaced at certain mathematically determined intervals, but these holes would have been too far from each other to be controlled by the short 10 fingers of the player. Leonardo found a solution — actually several, though we will deal here only with one.

Leonardo draws the main tube of the lower instrument perforated by seven holes; seven little double lines, evidently levers for closing pads, reach over to the main tube from the auxiliary tube, which also possesses a compact keyboard of seven keys comfortably close to each other. But where is the connection between this central keyboard and the distant closing pads where motion is required? My suggestion is that Leonardo thought of wires; he indicated them at the right of the open end of the auxiliary tube. Leonardo knew that the mechanism of the human hand and fingers contained a solution for a problem of this kind. In Anatomy Manuscript A he draws the tendons of the hand as they transfer motion from a central point to the point where motion is needed, the fingertips [125/1 and 2]. He also illustrates there the similar situation that exists in the fingers themselves. There remains only to say that Leonardo's idea stayed buried in his notebooks; we do not even know whether he himself ever built an instrument embodying his invention. Still, the significance and novelty of his invention is indisputable. Three hundred and fifty years later the wind instru-

In this detail from his page of sketches shown on page 118, Leonardo develops designs for wind instruments with a keyboard. Again he finds clues in anatomy, this time in the structure and workings of the human hand (opposite page). In the top

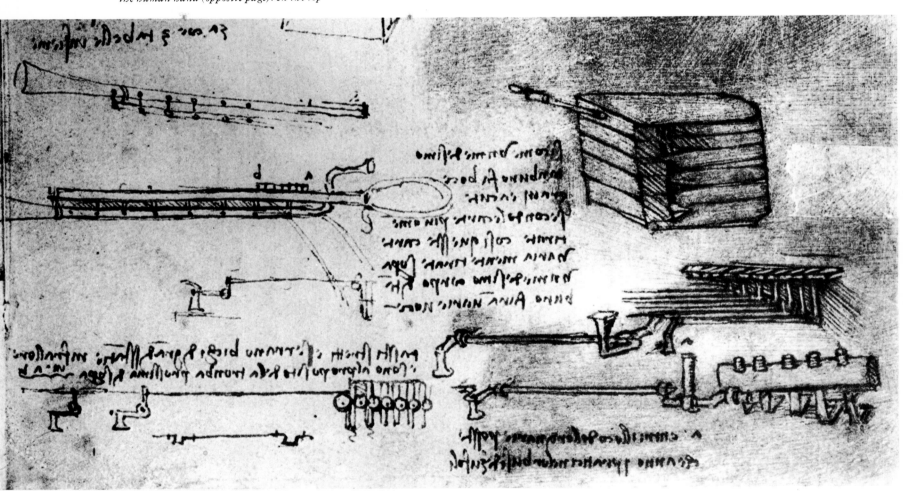

124/1

two drawings at left, the instrument's main tube has finger holes spaced according to acoustical laws. In the lower of these drawings, seven double lines, probably indicating wires or levers, connect the main tube to an auxiliary tube which has an easily played, compact keyboard. ARUNDEL 175r

ment with a complete keyboard was invented in Munich by Theobald Boehm [125/3]. Boehm — not without significance for our theme — was a flutist, a connoisseur of theoretical acoustics, and a silversmith.

Leonardo's philosophy of music is neither consistent nor systematic, at least on the surface. His thoughts are scattered over many notebooks and pages, and most of them occur in little clusters of phrases among different topics. But again, putting them together not only is rewarding but reveals, if not a systematic philosophy of music, at least his perpetual and ever-renewed wrestling with musical problems, which are conceived in a radically original light and

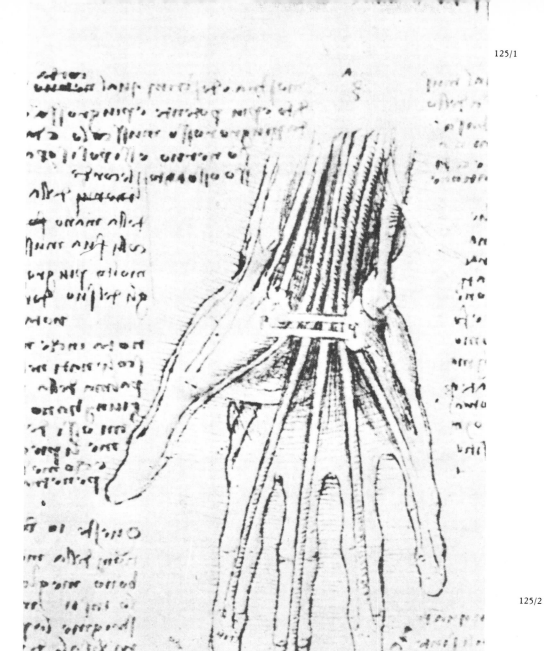

125/2

These drawings from Leonardo's anatomy manuscripts illustrate how he may have been inspired to solve the problem of opening and closing the holes of wind instruments. In the tendons of the hand he found the analogy for a system of wires with which he could link the keyboard and the closing pads.

125/3

Three hundred and fifty years after Leonardo, Theobald Boehm invented a complete keyboard for the flute shown above.
METROPOLITAN MUSEUM OF ART, NEW YORK

are notably independent of the traditional philosophy of music of his time.

This remarkable fact has been somewhat blurred by the many interpretations of the *Paragone* — the introduction to the *Treatise on Painting* — which is a compilation of parts of Leonardo's manuscripts made after his death under the supervision of his pupil Francesco Melzi and preserved in the Vatican Library as the Codex Urbinas. The choice of the material from Leonardo's manuscripts is incomplete, and the organization of the material is not his. In fact the *Paragone*, a comparison of the values of painting, sculpture, poetry, and music, in its present form is a mixture of traditional ideas and even common clichés with important and highly original thoughts of Leonardo. On a superficial reading of the dialogues between the painter, the poet, and the musician, music appears to have regrettable flaws: different from painting, it quickly fades ("it passes away as soon as it is born . . . it is afflicted with the disease of mortality"); furthermore, it requires repetition and can become tedious. But these somewhat banal statements must be taken with some reservation, for Leonardo had a strong interest in exalting painting and rating it, at least officially, higher than music. The musician — that is, the learned musician — had enjoyed high social status ever since the time of Boethius, the great philosopher, statesman, and musician, who lived about 500 A.D. For music was a philosophical discipline, one of the sisters in the quadrivium, together with mathematics, geometry, and astronomy, while the painter was still an *artigiano*, an artisan excluded from the *artes liberales*. It was the new art of *prospettiva*, the linear perspective based on mathematical ratios, that in Leonardo's time helped to bring about a radical change in the official status of the painter. Therefore we must not take too seriously Leonardo's arguments for the precedence of painting over music; what he had at heart was the elevation of the social status of the painter.

Indeed, if we closely examine the descriptions of the single arts one by one and regroup them into a systematic order, it appears that music ranks higher than poetry and painting. It is regarded as more noble than poetry because "within its harmonious flow it produces the sweet melodies generated by its various voices, while the poet is deprived of their specific harmonic action, and although poetry operates through the sense of hearing, it cannot create musical harmony since it is not able to say different things at the same time, as painting can do by the harmonious proportionality created between the various parts of the whole." And as for the comparison of music with painting, it was music that always had its firm mathematical foundations in its theory of harmony, and it is painting that only now borrowed this theoretical basis for its new theory and technique of linear perspective. Thus, in Leonardo's estimation, music is not inferior to any other art.[20]

The Madrid Codices contain only a few pages devoted to musical matters, but they add considerably to our knowledge of Leonardo's interest in music and musical instruments and to our comprehension of his indefatigable mind, so overwhelmed by new ideas, associations, and technological imagination that he could cope with this onslaught only by jotting down passing thoughts, often so sketchily that important details, which he evidently took for granted, are neither delineated nor explained in his comments.

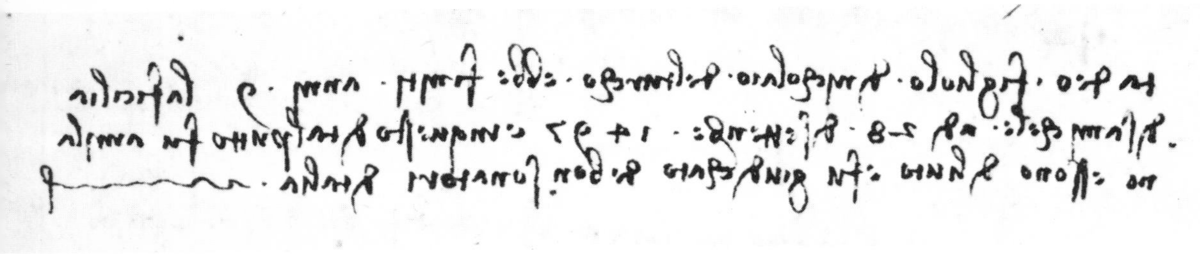

Tadeo, son of Nicolaio del Turco, was 9 years old on the eve of St. Michael, the 28th of September, 1497. And on this day the boy was in Milan and played the lute, and was judged one of the best players in Italy.

126/1

In Codex Madrid I Leonardo jotted down the note shown above in the transcription. This item of news about a child prodigy is symptomatic of his interest in music.

One of Leonardo's drawings of musical instruments in the Madrid Codices is of a bell with a wide rim [128/1]. Instead of a clapper inside two hammers strike the rim from opposite sides. To the left of the bell there is a mechanism including what seems to be a set of four keys operating on a tracker action that in its turn controls four levers ending in oval heads. In my opinion, these heads must be dampers. The accompanying text says, "The same bell will appear to be 4 bells. Organ keys with a fixed bell. And when struck by 2 hammers, there will be a change of tones as in an organ."

Acoustically important in this explanation are the indication that the bell is firm, neither swinging nor equipped with a clapper in the manner of a church bell, and the statement that it produces "a change of tones," which is in all probability one of pitch, not of timbre.[21] Thus Leonardo must have believed that the upper

The partition of bellows a *shall be secured at the belt and it functions as a bagpipe.* b *is fixed to the arm, which arm moving afterwards in and out, will open and shut the bellows according to need. That is, when bellows* n *opens, bellows* m *closes. And when* m *opens,* n *closes, and thus the blast will be continuous.*

Organs with flattened pipes, made out of boards or paper.

Or a viola, where the bow is drawn with the elbow, like the bellows.

The bow will move according to the motion of the right arm, from key to key. And in this way, it will diminish together with the notes.

viola with keys

Here, when the elbow moves two fingers, the teeth n *will also move 2 fingers. And the teeth will turn pinion* m *one entire revolution. Likewise, the major wheel will also turn one entire revolution, which will be ⅓ braccio. And so it will collect and release one braccio of bow upon the strings of the viola.*

elbow

127/1

Folio 76 recto of Codex Madrid II includes a series of novel musical mechanisms for bellows and for the viola organista, *and some comments. At the top is a bellows from which three trumpet-like tubes emerge. Beneath, he applies bellows to a small portable organ and then to a chamber organ. The two sketches at the bottom are studies related to the* viola organista. *At the center of the page is a youthful musician in fancy garb, possibly an idea for one of the colorful masquerades whose artistic preparations were among the duties of the courtier Leonardo.*

section of the bell has ring-shaped areas that produce tones of different pitch if they are slightly muted when the rim is set into vibration by the hammers.[22] It is interesting that Leonardo, here as in many other of his musical inventions, tried to obtain from one instrument what could normally be produced only by several instruments or by an entire set of instruments.

The first of the sketches in Illustration 127/1 represents a wind instrument; two pipes point into the air, a third one points downwards. They all emerge from a contraption that is, beyond doubt, a bellows. The three pipes give the instrument a superficial similarity to a bagpipe in that they resemble its chanter (the melody pipe) and its drones. And indeed, Leonardo begins his verbal description with the explanation that the new bellows here is made *per piva.* The word *piva* means, or at least can mean, "bagpipe." Leonardo was, of course, very familiar

128/1

Regarding this bell Leonardo says, "The same bell will appear to be 4 bells. Organ keys with a fixed bell. And when struck by 2 hammers, there will be a change of tones as in an organ."   MADRID II 75v

128/3

This evidently allegorical sketch shows a bagpipe squeezed by a vise.   MS. M 4v

128/2

In this detail from the previous page, the three pipes make the instrument look like a bagpipe.

with that popular instrument the bagpipe. In one of his drawings he shows a bagpipe squeezed by a vise [128/3].

The bellows shown in Illustration 128/2 is indeed ingenious.[23] It consists of two sections arranged to the left and right of an immovable dividing wall. If the right section is pushed against the wall, the air enclosed is compressed and pushed towards the pipes; at the same time, the left section is automatically expanded, inhaling air. This kind of automatically synchronized, alternating breathing is an improvement over, or at least a simplification of, the conventional two alternating bellows, which were ordinarily used in Leonardo's time and long thereafter for organs and of course for many extramusical purposes, such as the blacksmith's forge and metal-smelting furnaces, and which had to be pumped by two people or two motor impulses.

Leonardo's accompanying explanation reads as if his contraption had occurred to him as a new invention; and in fact I do not know of earlier examples of this type of bellows in texts or illustrations. Perhaps it worked best in small sizes, while for industrial purposes the arrangement of two alternating, large, separate bellows proved more practical.

At the end of his explanatory text, Leonardo claims that his new bellows produces continuous wind. This claim, of course, has to be taken with a certain reserve. There is, first, the inevitable dead point when, one of the bellows sections having reached its maximum volume and the other its minimum expansion, the pumping action goes into reverse. This imparts to the pipes a moment of silence which, however short, is just as noticeable as the pause between the upstroke and the downstroke of a fiddle bow, or when the player of a concertina turns from the expanding phase to the compressing phase or vice versa.[24]

And quite apart from this dead moment of silence, we have to bear in mind the fact that the wind stops immediately when the bellows action stops. This is not the case with the bagpipe. The sounding pipes of a bagpipe are supplied with wind by a bag, made of the skin of an animal. This flexible wind reservoir is filled with air either from the player's mouth by means of a blowpipe or, in later specimens, such as the musette of the 18th century, from a pair of bellows.[25] A

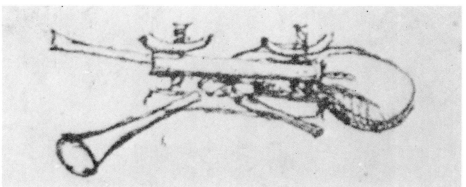

128/3

bag of this type supplies wind for some time, even after the player has ceased to breathe into the blowpipe or to pump the bellows. In this way, a real continuity of sound is achieved.[26] Such a bag is missing in Leonardo's contraption.

Furthermore, another essential feature of the bagpipe is missing: the chanter, or melody pipe, which is a reed pipe equipped with finger holes. These are stopped by the fingers of the player to produce the melody, while the larger drone pipes supply the continuous humming bass. Normally, the chanter has a shape different from that of the drones. In Leonardo's sketch, only the pipe on the left pointing down is approximately in the position of a bagpipe chanter, but it has the same shape as the other two pipes and, more important, does not show the faintest trace of finger holes. Therefore, Leonardo's contraption is certainly not a bagpipe, and if he calls it *piva*, he uses this word not as an equivalent for *cornamusa* or *zampogna*, both common names for bagpipes, but in its original sense, that is, *pipa*, meaning "pipe" or "pipe instrument."

What then is our instrument? Since there are only three tubes — not enough for a scale or melody — and since there is not even machinery for selecting or alternating single tones, we can only assume that three simultaneous tones of different pitch formed a chord, in all probability a triad. The tubes would then be reed pipes with a trumpet sound, and the whole machine would be not an instrument designed to play actual music, but possibly a gadget created to sound

129/1

a three-voice signal as a kind of fanfare. One recalls the manifold activities of Leonardo as an organizer of fetes, processions, and stage entertainments. Perhaps our musical gadget served as a hidden machine that produced fanfares easily to accompany the appearance of allegorical figures, such as Fama or Gloria, who, by long iconological tradition, had trumpets or even multiple trumpets. One example is the beautiful quadruple trumpet in the hands of Fama in one of the early-16th-century tapestries at the Metropolitan Museum of Art in New York, representing the Triumph of Fame over Death, one of the numerous illustrations of Petrarch's *Trionfi* in Leonardo's time [131/1].

Leonardo must have been more impressed with his new bellows than with the

Among the drawings at Windsor Castle there is a sketch showing a fantastic man resembling a bagpipe on horseback. This drawing has often been misinterpreted. Actually the rider masquerades as a bagpipe, his belly, or rather his whole upper body, forming the bag, and the continuance of his nose, the chanter. A large drone pipe appears over his head. Probably this amusing disguise was drawn for a procession or similar entertainment. WINDSOR 12585r

whole triple-trumpet machine, for in two other drawings he applied it to a small portable organ and even to a large chamber organ.

The sketch of the portable organ bears two inscriptions: on the left, *tasti dell'organo* ("organ keys"); and on the upper right, *canne schiacciate* ("flattened pipes") [132/2]. Leonardo describes the pipes as being made either of wood or of cardboard. Six pipes can be distinguished – a strange number, too many for a chord and too few for a scale, though the sketch may be only a hasty suggestion.

An indispensable element of an organ, the one by which the single keys open up and shut off the access of the wind to the single pipes, is not indicated at all. Here again Leonardo may not have taken the trouble, as so often happened in his quick embodiments of passing ideas, to include technical details that he took for granted.

The combination of organ pipes and bellows recalls immediately the construction of an *organetto*, an immensely popular and practical instrument used in Leonardo's time and for centuries before. We may therefore cast a quick glance at various types of *organetti*, concentrating on the question of bellows. If we disregard the larger instruments, which were played on a table and which required the use of both hands on the keyboard and therefore an extra person to operate the alternating bellows at the back, we find the following arrangements used in *organetti*: in one arrangement, one small bellows beneath the wind-chest was operated by the player's left hand [132/1]. In another, a single large bellows at the back of the wind-chest was operated by the player's left hand, while his right hand pressed the keys with the fingers in a position that would strike a later musician as very awkward [133/1]. In still another, two small alternating bellows at the back of the wind-chest were operated by the player's left hand [134/3].

In all these small instruments, where the single or alternating bellows had to be worked by one hand, there was an inevitable pause in the wind supply, and therefore in the music, between the movements of the bellows. However, as the fingers on the keys could only play melodic lines without substantial chords, the pause caused by the bellows mechanism was not more noticeable than that of an experienced singer breathing in the middle of a phrase; and the wind-chest, essential to every *organetto*, must have helped somewhat to bridge these pauses, although it did not have the flexibility of the bag in the bagpipe as a wind reservoir.

Leonardo's sketch of the portable organ does not include any visible wind-chest. Thus the wind supply depended exclusively on the action of his special bellows, which, as already pointed out, immediately stops providing air when pumping ceases. One possibility that would justify the new bellows remains. The sketch shows a little curve at the lower left corner of the bellows. If this indicates a handle, it was perhaps worked with the elbow *(con gomito)*, thus leaving both hands free for the keyboard, an achievement that would indeed have meant notable progress if we assume that this instrument was supposed to have many more pipes than the six delineated.

131/1
The early-16th-century North French tapestry on the opposite page shows the "Triumph of Fame over Death." The allegorical figure of Fama sounds a fantastic trumpet with four bells. Fantastic instruments such as this may be related to the workable triple-tubed instrument in Illustration 128/2.
METROPOLITAN MUSEUM OF ART, NEW YORK

Even more problematic is the small sketch of a chamber organ [134/1] flanked by two bellows evidently of the same construction as those in Illustrations 128/2 and 132/2. The big box from which the pipes arise contains, of course, the inevitable wind-chest that in every pipe organ guarantees an even wind pressure and continuous sound just as the bag does in the bagpipe. Therefore the application of Leonardo's special bellows to this organ makes little sense. Any simple conventional bellows would do just as well.

Operation *con gomito* may have captured Leonardo's mind to such a degree that he proceeded to extend this playing technique to string instruments. In two sketches in Illustration 127/1 he delineated schematically string instruments, of which at least one is operated by an elbow action, again possibly in order to free both hands for the keyboard [134/2]. Enigmatic as these instruments appear at first glance, their interpretation is easy if one recalls Leonardo's profound

131/1

interest in the *viola organista* [120/2], described earlier. Anyone looking at Illustration 120/2 will easily realize the link with the sketches in the Madrid manuscript [134/2] if he recognizes that the 16 dots marked in a horizontal line in the upper sketch of Illustration 134/2 are nothing other than cross sections of

This detail of the organ panels from Nájera by Hans Memling (c. 1465) shows an angel playing an organetto *with a large single bellows on the back of the instrument.*

ART MUSEUM, ANTWERP

In this 14th-century Florentine example of an organetto, *the angel is operating with the left hand the small bellows beneath the wind-chest.*

MUSEO DELL'OPERA DEL DUOMO, FLORENCE

132/1

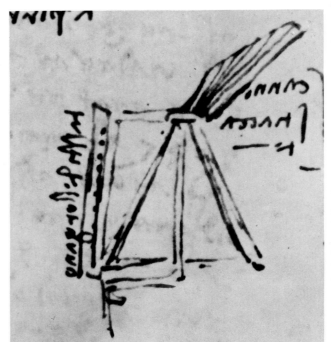

flattened pipes

Keys of the organ

This detail from Leonardo's sketches on page 127 shows six organ pipes emerging from bellows of the type illustrated in 128/2. Left of the bellows, small dots indicate "keys of the organ," and are so described by Leonardo in the vertically written words.

132/2

133/

the strings shown in the prior illustration. Over these strings moves the endless bow supported on the left and right by two rotating wheels. In other words, the upper sketch of Illustration 134/2 is a schematic front view of the instrument shown from the side in Illustration 120/2. Illustration 120/2 also shows clearly a keyboard, or rather a set of frontal push buttons which by means of a tracker action move little circular loops that grasp the strings in order to draw them against the moving *archetto*, which sets them vibrating; and this illustration shows a motor for driving the *archetto*.

In the upper sketch of Illustration 134/2 we see two interacting cogwheels moving the right wheel of the two that support the *archetto*. The cogwheels in turn must receive their impulse from a motor or from the player or an assistant.

The lower sketch differs from the upper one in several respects. It indicates only 11 dots for strings; below the dots is written *viola a tasti* ("viola with keys"). The left wheel is much smaller, and above all, the device for driving the right wheel is different: instead of two cogwheels, here only a segment of one is visible; it is operated by a lever with a handle inscribed *gomito*. The use of this wheel segment does not permit a continuous movement of the *archetto* in one direction, but only facilitates a forward and backward movement comparable to that of the actual bow of a viol or any other bowed instrument. All these features point to a smaller and simpler version of the *viola organista*, and possibly to a portable version. If *gomito*[27] here means not a movable part of the mechanism but the human elbow, then both hands would be free to operate the keys or push buttons, and this would constitute a substantial advantage over the hurdy-gurdy, in which the keys — a very small number for that matter — are operated by one hand while the other works the crank to turn the friction wheel.

It remains to comment on the charming little figure jotted down with a few rapid strokes in the center of Illustration 127/1. Unfortunately the instrument played by this youth is not recognizable, but in any case he is a musician in fancy garb; his three-tiered hat,[28] short pleated tunic with square neck, and shepherd buskins characterize him as a participant in a masquerade or stage entertainment.

His exotic appearance may provide the clue for the interpretation of all the instruments shown in Illustration 127/1, except for the chamber organ with the flanking bellows. Evidently these instruments are conceived not for the performance of serious music, but as contraptions for fetes,[29] stage entertainments, or one of the colorful masquerades whose organization and artistic preparation were among the duties of the courtier Leonardo. There are in Leonardo's other

notebooks many more sketches of instruments that must have served similar purposes.

The results of our interpretation, then, are comparatively meager as far as the musical importance of these machines is concerned. However, they are interesting in another way; they show Leonardo's restless, quick imagination at work, leaping by rapid association from one idea to the next. The triple trumpet begets

134/3

At right is a mid-15th-century relief by Agostini di Duccio from Rimini Cathedral. One of the angels plays an organetto *with two alternating bellows.*

In this hasty sketch, Leonardo applies his special bellows (see 128/2 and 132/2) to a

134/1

chamber organ (detail from page 127). The bellows flank the wind-chest from which the pipes arise.

These sketches, details from page 127, represent two different methods for moving the belt of hair, as an "endless bow," across the

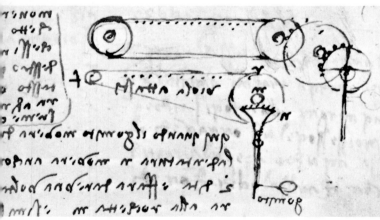

134/2

strings of a portable viola organista. *The wheel moving the* archetto *(endless bow) is turned by a cogwheel — or section of it — operated by the elbow of the player.*

135/1
Enlarged detail of the costumed youth from page 127.

the idea of a new kind of simplified bellows with automatic synchronization; these bellows are applied to a small set of organ pipes, and even to a massive, positive organ. Then fantasy takes another turn: just as the bellows can be operated by the elbow in wind instruments, an equivalent simple playing method *con gomito* may be applied to string instruments, and so a smaller, portable version of the *viola organista* is born. The number and variety of Leonardo's inventions of instruments permit a clear reconstruction of his leading ideas, which are admirably systematic.

135/1

THE MILITARY ARCHITECT

LUDWIG H. HEYDENREICH

From the numerous notes and drawings that Leonardo scattered through his manuscripts, it is well known that he extended his intensive studies of theoretical and practical architecture to the broad field of defensive engineering and military fortification. In a whole range of contemporary documents it is shown still further that in this very specialized field, too, he was held in high esteem, and that his advice and experience were being sought after constantly for important projects by high officials. But it is only with Codex Madrid II that we are given our first opportunity to grasp his effectiveness as a military engineer in the light of two large-scale tasks that we can follow closely in the notebook – and to judge relatively clearly the individuality and merit of his achievement in this field.

136/1

The incessant wars and campaigns waged in Italy around the beginning of the 1500s in the course of the political conflicts between the great powers of France, Naples, Milan, Venice, and the Papal States – mainly concerning the upper and central parts of the country – brought with them a situation that gave rapidly increasing importance to the technical means of warfare, defense constructions, and military engineering. All involved parties, even the smaller powers, whether they were town republics or princely estates, had directives of the same sort: they were to maintain in the best possible condition their systems of defense as well as their means of attack. As new firearms, explosives, and artillery were developing quickly, basic alterations in the system of fortifications and technical warfare had become all the more imperative.

136/1
The map on the opposite page reflects the concentration of powers in Italy at the beginning of the 16th century: The States of the Church, (French) Lombardy, Venice, Florence, and Naples were the main powers. Across these lines ranged Leonardo, military architect and engineer in the service of many masters. War – its art and its fortunes – was the cause for much of his wandering: from Florence to Milan and back, to Venice, Piombino, Imola, and Pisa, back to Florence and Milan, to Rome, and finally west to an honored retirement in France.

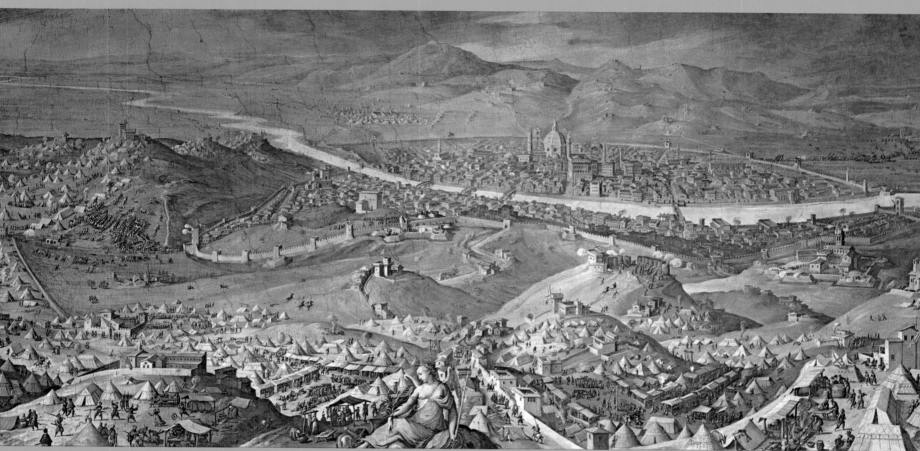

137/1

Thus new tasks of great import fell to the contemporary military architect and engineer, tasks that above all required an extended and specialized technical knowledge. In the early and middle decades of the 1400s Brunelleschi and Laurana had certainly been experienced fortress builders, yet towards the end of the century the professional position of the military architect came to be endowed with a very special character and increased esteem. The most important representative of this is Francesco di Giorgio Martini (1439-1501). Although respected as a painter, sculptor, and architect, he received the highest tributes during his lifetime as an ingenious master of fortification and as a strategic engineer. He occupied the position of chief director of building and waterworks in his native town of Siena, so that the entire architectural defense and hydraulic engineering of the city came under his control. The fortresses he built for Federigo da Montefeltro, Duke of Urbino, are impressive signs of princely power. Sassocorvaro (1470-1478), Rocca San Leo (1479) [139/1], Cagli (1481), and the fortress constructed in 1501 for Francesco della Rovere at Mongavio still bear witness to this today. Francesco's *Treatise on Architecture, Engineering, and Military Art,* which he wrote between 1480 and 1490 as the first comprehensive and systematically applied treatment of the subject, reached far beyond the works of his predecessors Taccola and Valturio, and it gained significant eminence in his time. In fact, in the declining years of the century, most of the architects of station were

Leonardo's own Florence was a focus of many of the wars that raged up and down the Italian peninsula. In the painting above, by Giorgio Vasari, troops of the Holy Roman Empire and the Papal States besiege the lovely city of towers to help the Medicis put down an attempt to restore the Republic of Florence in 1527. In such times of rapidly shifting alliances, when the existence of the state seemed constantly in peril, the most important of all the arts was war. Painters, sculptors, and architects were much in demand because many of them had the practical knowledge of engineering needed for the design of weapons and fortifications. Not surprisingly, Leonardo's letter of self-recommendation to the Duke of Milan (page 7) emphasized what was marketable: his skills as a military engineer and architect. Leonardo served several rulers and often switched sides after a war, apparently having little trouble rationalizing his military role.

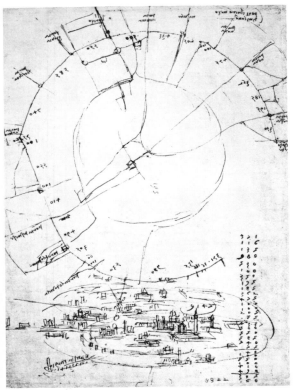

138/1

Leonardo's longest service was the 17 years he spent in Milan as architect, military engineer, painter, and master of ceremonies at the court of Lodovico Sforza. On this map of Milan, Leonardo drew the circular ground plan of the town and named the gates on its circumference. Below this he sketched a perspective view of the city, showing the main buildings, the cathedral in the middle and the Sforza Castle at the left.

ATLANTICUS 73b

138/2–6
During the six years after the downfall of his patron Lodovico Sforza (below, left) in 1499, Leonardo served several masters as

defense builders of experience. These names may be mentioned here as examples: Baccio Pontelli (1450-1492), who built the Rocca di Ostia; Luca Fancelli (1430-1495), Gonzaga's architect in Mantua, famous as engineer and canal builder in the Florence of the Medici; and the brothers Giuliano (1445-1516) and Antonio (1455-1534) da Sangallo.

So it seems only natural that Leonardo da Vinci, who was intensely occupied with the theory and practice of architecture throughout his life, should also from the very beginning have included the field of defense architecture and strategic engineering in his studies. Between 1490 and 1505, he served no less than five different masters as military architect and engineer. Until the fall of Lodovico Sforza in summer 1499, he was "ducal painter and engineer" at the court of Milan and functioned as expert for the installation of the duke's fortifications at Pavia, Vigevano, and Milan itself – although we have no more exact description of the nature of his work than that.

When Leonardo left Milan a few weeks after the triumphal entry of the French, he stopped off at Venice on his way to Florence. The government of the Serenissima, hard hit by the struggle at Lepanto on August 26, 1499, and worried by the possibility of a Turkish attack by land, seems to have taken the opportunity of Leonardo's presence to seek his counsel. A fragment of the draft of a letter to the governing council[1] attests that the master, evidently commissioned by the republic, traveled through the area that the Turks presumably intended to invade, the Isonzo valley in the Friuli, and considered artificial inundation of the area as an effective means of defense against the attacker. A small sketch map with the details "Ponte di Gorizia" and "Vilpago" is evidence for his presence there, but it is unknown how far his suggestions, which we can only infer from these outlines, were seriously considered.

This trip occurred in March 1500. By Easter, Leonardo was already in Florence, principally to exercise his function as a painter. But after only one and a half years he took the surprising step of entering the service of Cesare Borgia as "architect and general engineer." Cesare Borgia, the son of Pope Alexander VI, marshal of the papal troops, Duke of Valentinois by the grace of Louis XII of France, was then indeed at the zenith of his short rise to fame. The Pope had just appointed him Duke of Romagna, thereby ousting the existing and legitimate rulers of the territory in the name of the church. Cautious Florence had "bought," so to speak, the good will of the dangerous and powerful neighbor through a treaty that made

  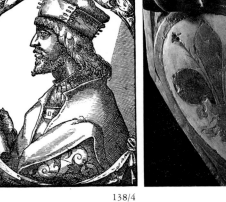  

138/2   138/3   138/4   138/5   138/6

military adviser: From left to right, Agostino Barbarigo, Doge of Venice; Cesare Borgia, Duke of Romagna; the Republic of Florence (arms); Jacopo IV Appiani, ruler of Piombino (arms).

139/1
The fortress at San Leo shown on the opposite page was built in 1479 by Francesco di Giorgio Martini, whose systematic treatment of military architecture and engineering greatly influenced Leonardo.

Cesare a condottiere of the republic, with an annual income of 30,000 gold ducats. No less a person than Machiavelli was delegated repeatedly and over long periods as chargé d'affaires at his court, and he had no other assignment than that of political observer. His task was to report on the favorableness or the unfavorableness of the general situation. The "Duke of Valentinois," therefore, was certainly the most salient figure of the times. In this light even Leonardo's strange decision to enter the service of such a man seems to find a certain justification. For several months starting in summer 1502, Leonardo exercised his office as chief inspector of military building and accompanied Cesare on his conquering expeditions through Emilia and the Marches. Leonardo's diary of this journey is in the small

139/

The contemporary who most resembled Leonardo in range of interests and talents was Francesco di Giorgio Martini (1439–1501). He was a painter, sculptor, and superintendent of buildings in his native Siena before becoming chief architect and military engineer for the Duke of Urbino. In 1495, during his service for Duke Alfonso of Calabria, Francesco successfully exploded a mine to cut a breach into the walls of the Castelnuovo in Naples, permitting the recapture of the important fortress from the French. He was one of the first to improve his fortifications with adequate means of defense against cannon fire and is known to have built well over 100 fortresses. Four of his designs from his Treatise (see below) are shown on these two pages. The plan on this page [140/2]

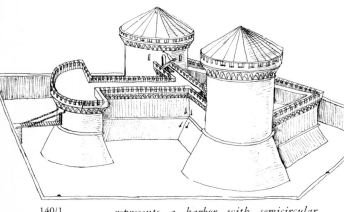

140/1

represents a harbor with semicircular breakwater. On the opposite page the breakwater is fortified by towers at the entrance and exit to make certain that only friendly ships sail in and out. In Milan Francesco advised on the construction of the dome of the cathedral, and together with Leonardo, he went to Pavia in 1490 to consult on the construction of the cathedral there. Francesco gave Leonardo a copy of his famous Treatise on Architecture, Engineering, and Military Art, with designs of weapons and fortifications, that anticipated Leonardo's own manuscripts.

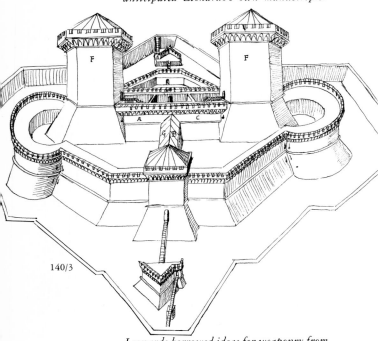

140/3

Leonardo borrowed ideas for weaponry from it and in Codex Madrid II made intelligent excerpts of Francesco's plans for fortifications.

140

Manuscript L in Paris, a notebook in which we can follow his exact itinerary in the company of Cesare. He records his halts in the region between Imola, Cesena, Rimini, Urbino, and Pesaro. However, apart from hasty jottings on an improvement of the docks at Porto Cesenatico, we gain no clearer insight into his official activity. Yet he had drawn up exact measurements of Borgia's area of operations. A part of the map he compiled of Tuscany and Romagna was indeed executed for this employer, as was Leonardo's magnificent plan of Imola [154/1].

Imola, under the rulership of Cesare Borgia after November 27, 1499, represented an important strategic base within the fighting terrain of the usurper. Leonardo must have drawn the town map during the autumn of 1502, at the time when Cesare armed his troops there for a new campaign against the condottieri and some members of the nobility who had allied against him. Around that period Machiavelli also was in Imola; he certainly must have met with Leonardo there.

The map is executed in color. Leonardo rendered the area of the city with great accuracy, as proved by a study sheet in the Windsor Collection[2] on which the individual sections have been surveyed properly and the fortifications as well as the town gates are sketched in. Similar preliminary studies of the towns of Cesena and Urbino in Manuscript L lead to the assumption that Leonardo designed a number of town plans similar in execution to the one of Imola, which, however, is the only one of its kind that has come down to us: a masterpiece of the "rationalizing fantasy" of the artist.

During the 1490s Leonardo sketched a map of the city of Milan [138/1] which mostly remains within the tradition of the Middle Ages of sketching circular town plans, as is shown by comparison with a Milan map from the 13th century at the Biblioteca Ambrosiana and a version from a Ptolemy manuscript of around 1450.

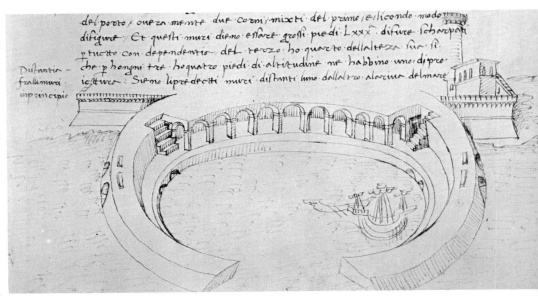

140/2

In his beautiful drawing Leonardo draws the ground plan and a perspective view of the city. He was also familiar with the simple land-register plans, which were located at the municipal council.

From these established norms Leonardo arrived at his particular principle of representation, as can be noted for the first time in the map of Imola, truly an incunabulum of modern cartography.

From the remarks in Manuscript L, the fact clearly emerges that during this time Leonardo also visited the area of Piombino, another estate of Cesare's at the northern end of the Tyrrhenian Sea. This fortified harbor city, opposite the island of Elba, was important economically as a market for iron ore coming from Elba, and politically as a focal point between the bordering territories of the Papal States to the south, of Lombardy and Genoa to the north, and of Florence to the east. Borgia had already taken it, after a long siege in 1501, from its ruler Jacopo IV

Presso alla terra honero principio dimuei sifacci due portoni
con lesaracinesche da chiudere et aprere acciocche plo Fluxo
et refluxo delmare neli tempi fortunosi aprendo aprosto quelli possino
Li detti porti da hongni spurcitia et arema benacuare sicho
me interuiene nel porto danchona che p spario di tempo leparti
utili delporto siriempino & con spendio bisongnia quelle euacuare
ilche essendo tale hordine daro intale spesa non sincorririo la
forma e loco di queste lafigura ilmonifesto

Porti p nesta ze uporto

Dpiu perfectione et forteza del porto sipuo fare inmare
distante dala intrata obocca sua p piedi dugento Cinquanta
uno muro grosso piedi Lxxx come appare limuei medicti
Longho piedi trecento scarepato achalice informa di angulo obtuso
presistere honeramente peuitare licholpi dellonde delmare Questi
porti et ingressi indue modi possano essare difesi ilpreimo facendo in
hongni extremita demuei una grossa torre tirando dalluno
allaltra chatene sicondo ilbisongnio ple quali non siposti ne intrare
ne uscire senza uolonta del principe come appare disengnato

Guisa della intrata

Primo modo Da difendere ilporto

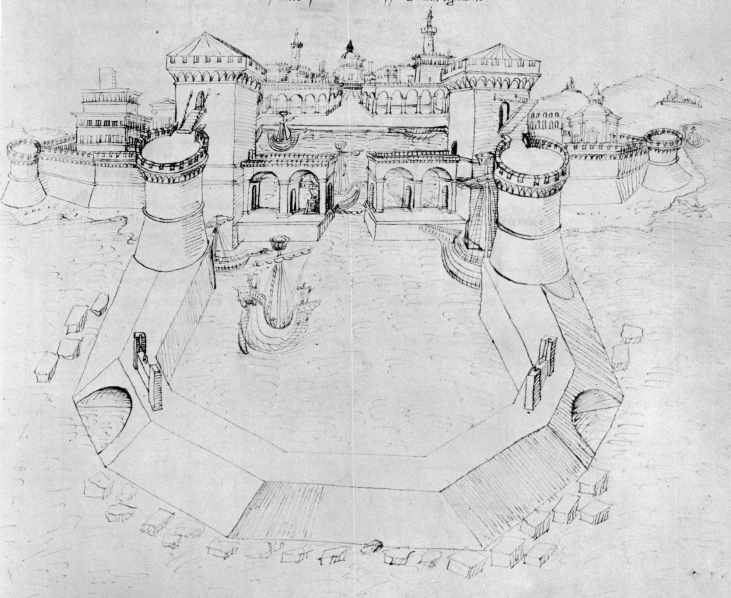

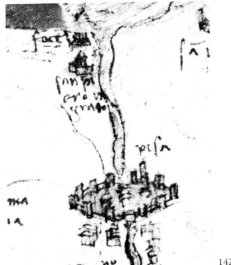

142/1

The city of Pisa – shown in the map above – figured in a bold Florentine scheme that involved Leonardo. The Pisans, under Florentine rule since 1406, had renounced their subordination in 1494, and successfully defended their independence thereafter. In 1503, when Leonardo returned to Florence to serve as military engineer, his native town had the daring plan to divert the course of the Arno River and deprive the besieged Pisans of their supply lines to the Ligurian Sea.   WINDSOR 12683

142/2

142/3

142/2–4

One of the chief promoters of the scheme to divert the Arno was the Florentine statesman and writer Niccolo Machiavelli [142/2]. He was then war minister for Florence, and he won support for the plan from the leader of the republic, Piero Soderini [142/3]. Machiavelli knew Leonardo personally from their meeting the previous year in the camp of Cesare Borgia. In the summer of 1503 Leonardo was sent at least twice by the republic to the Pisa area for the control of fortifications and also apparently to study preparations for the Arno plan. Beside a sketch of the Arno in Codex Madrid II, folio 1 verso, he noted the date: "The day of the Magdalene, 1503" – July 22. Across a double-page spread, folios 52 verso and 53 recto, he drew the map at right showing the Arno and the area of military operations around Pisa. The map, which shows Pisa just to the left of its centerfold, appears to lack any plan for the diversion.

Appiani; and Pope Alexander had made over the ruling rights to Cesare. He included among his many titles that of "Signore di Piombino"; and it must have been an important preoccupation of his to strengthen this territory against enemies from without and from within.

In Manuscript L Leonardo made geographic sketches of the spit of Piombino[3] and the whole Piombino coastline from the bay of the ancient harbor (Porto Vecchio or Porto Falesia) to the Gulf of Baratta, with its fortified site Populonia, of Etruscan origin.[4] In sketches on nearby pages, although it is unidentifiable in detail, one can conjecture the recording of a portion of the Maremma marshland bordering on Piombino.[5] These pages may be connected with a note in the Codex Atlanticus, "way to drain the marsh of Piombino," which dates from around 1503-1505.[6] That Leonardo must have been in Piombino during the period of his employment for Cesare Borgia is proved by a small sketch he made of wave movements accompanied by the text, "made at the sea of Piombino."[7] This fact, in the light of Leonardo's second stay in 1504, which has only become known to us through Codex Madrid II, will be seen to be of great importance later on.

In the spring of 1503 Leonardo was again in Florence, having given up his post with Cesare Borgia probably during the course of the winter. His native town took him forthwith into its service as military engineer. Florence was then engaged in a troublesome and protracted war with Pisa. In 1406 Pisa had been sold infamously to the Florentines. In 1494, under the protection of Charles VIII of France, it had renounced its enforced subordination, and thereafter defended its

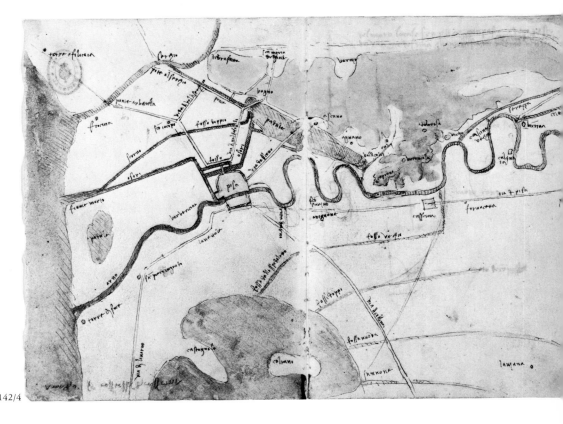

142/4

regained independence with passion and skill. In 1503 the Florentine Republic opened a new campaign against Pisa, and here emerged the daring plan to divert the course of the Arno River in order to cut off the Pisans from access to the sea, since from this the besieged town was constantly able to obtain supplies. Historical sources and documents reveal that the forceful project was especially promoted by Machiavelli, the secretary of state for war in the Florentine governing council, and that it won the support of Piero Soderini, the chief official of the Republic of Florence. Unquestionably Leonardo had knowledge of it; but whether he had any part in drawing it up, as some older scholars believe, must be left undecided.

In any case, Leonardo was sent off in July 1503 by order of the council, to the Florentine camp to examine the work of trench digging which had been undertaken. For over a year the plan to divert the river was worked upon. It made provision for one canal, in the area of the estuary, that was to lead the water of the Arno off into the river Serchio, and for another canal from Vico Pisano to the Stagno di Livorno. The instructions of the Florentine council issued through the letters of Machiavelli to headquarters reveal quite clearly that the project had been planned in detail. Two thousand workmen in 150 to 200 days were to accomplish the enormous shift of earth necessary to dig canals approximately 40 to 60 feet wide, and 16 to 21 feet deep. The calculation proved to be erroneous. Five times as much manpower would have been necessary, according to the more realistic calculations of other experts, to complete the affair. Besides that, the work suffered considerable difficulties. It proved to be impossible to muster the thousands of workers required, or rather to keep them at work, especially since wages were frequently overdue. A completed section of canal did not withstand the mass of water fed into it and collapsed. Because of such setbacks, opinion was split among the commanders. Machiavelli defended his idea in entreating letters and reports to the council until autumn 1504, but in vain. In October the enterprise was definitely broken off – much to the triumph of the Pisans. The Florentines had to fight another five years for Pisa, for only in 1509 did the exhausted city give itself up.

To us, judging the affair today, it seems almost inexplicable that men of such realistic disposition as Machiavelli and Piero Soderini could have succumbed to such an idea, which to every reasonable thinker must have appeared utopian from the beginning. To divert a river of the volume and current of the Arno, and over

I found that the complete excavation of the moat, which is, on average, 17 braccia wide, and 16 braccia deep, and 640 braccia long, reduced to square braccia, amounts to 174,080 braccia. Which reduced to square canne, amounts to 2720 canne. Of which, those at the mountain, due to the difficulty offered by the rock, deserve 5 lire the canna, an amount paid on other occasions to the diggers.
MADRID II 10r

143/1 and 2
Scholars now doubt that the Florentine scheme to divert the Arno was originated by Leonardo. The plan called for digging canals nearly 60 feet wide and 21 feet deep to carry the river as much as 7 miles off its normal course. He must have known from the beginning that such a feat would be difficult in peacetime and virtually impossible under wartime conditions. He also had the practical knowledge of a time-and-motion expert and could figure out how much digging men could do, how they ought to do it, and what it would cost. The diagram at left – part of his plans for an excavation at Piombino in Codex Madrid II, folio 10 verso – and the transcription above make clear his closely detailed approach to

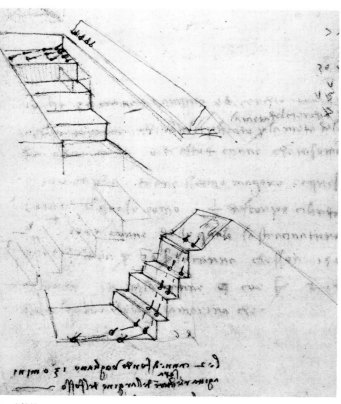

143/1

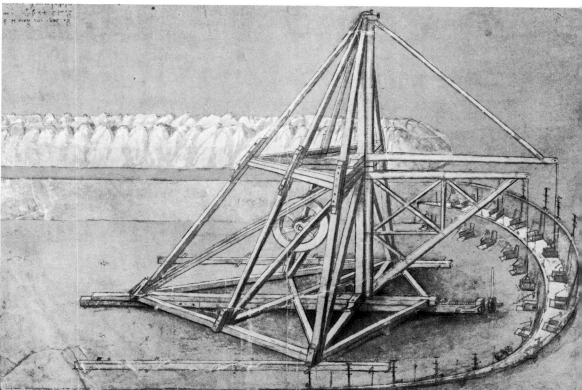

143/2

such a long distance – a diversion of 7 miles in one place was talked of – was certainly an undertaking that could never be carried out in such a restricted period of time as was actually and strategically provided during the siege of Pisa. In spite of that, the contemporary engineers, experienced hydraulic experts from Florence and Ferrara who had been sent to the site, must have considered the task to be feasible at first. Critical voices got very loud very soon, however, and when the enterprise collapsed, there was no lack whatever of bitter comment.

Leonardo's exact position in this scheme is very difficult to determine. The facts that he was appointed adviser by the government and that he accepted the task lead us to conclude that he must have been entrusted with the plan. But his own judgment is unknown; and from the new material that has come to light in the Madrid notebooks we must deduce that he was not as some have believed, the

such projects. His tiny figures on the top set of stairs indicate that getting the dirt out of the trench handily would require more workers near the edge of the excavation. He also was aware of the inefficiency of men equipped only with hand shovels, and he designed the big treadmill-powered digging machine shown here from Codex Atlanticus, folio 1 verso-b. For the Arno plan Leonardo's Florentine superiors had calculated it would take 2,000 workers about six months to dig the necessary canals. They miscalculated by a multiple of 5. One section of the excavation collapsed, and though Machiavelli tried to push the scheme, the project was abandoned.

originator of the idea, but rather that he remained undecided and certainly very critical.

In Codex Madrid II there is to be found only one reference to Leonardo's presence in the camp at Pisa [142/4]. This is something like an ordnance map, drawn over a double page, of the area of military operations around Pisa, extending to the sea. The topographic names inserted – for example, Serchio, Arno, Torre di Foce, Verrucola, Vico [Pisano], Cascina, Calci – correspond exactly to the places named as centers of operation in the letters between Machiavelli and the leaders of the camp. In this way, the canal courses (*fossi*) plotted in the estuary area of the Serchio (*fiume morto*) north of Pisa, as well as those between the Arno and the Stagno di Livorno to the south, provide an exact survey of the canal network in this sector of the coast. Leonardo's place names are written in a normal hand and not in mirror writing, so that this map was certainly destined to be

Leonardo had an abiding interest in changing the course of the Arno – but not to cut Pisa off from the sea. He wanted to create a great waterway to open Florence to the sea and bring agricultural and economic benefits to all Tuscany. The Arno was not navigable from Florence to Pisa because of its tortuous bends and sudden variations in level. The idea of diverting a long section of it into a man-made canal dated back more than a century before Leonardo's birth. From about 1490 on, Leonardo made it his own and drew a number of maps and studies. Below, in Codex Madrid II, folio 2 recto, he traces the serpentine course of the Arno from Pisa at the bottom to Empoli, which is near Florence. Between the towns along the river he notes the distances.

144/1

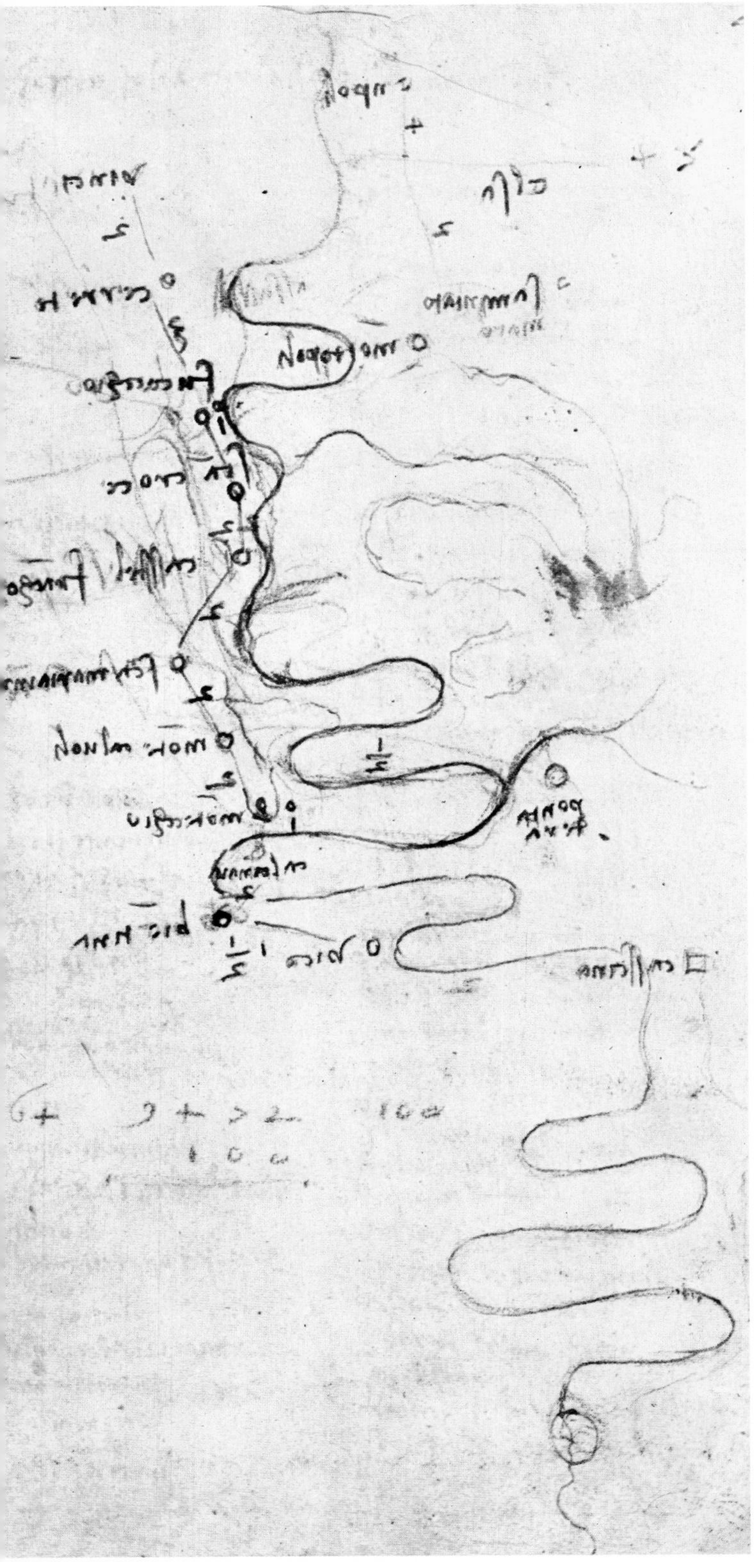

144/2

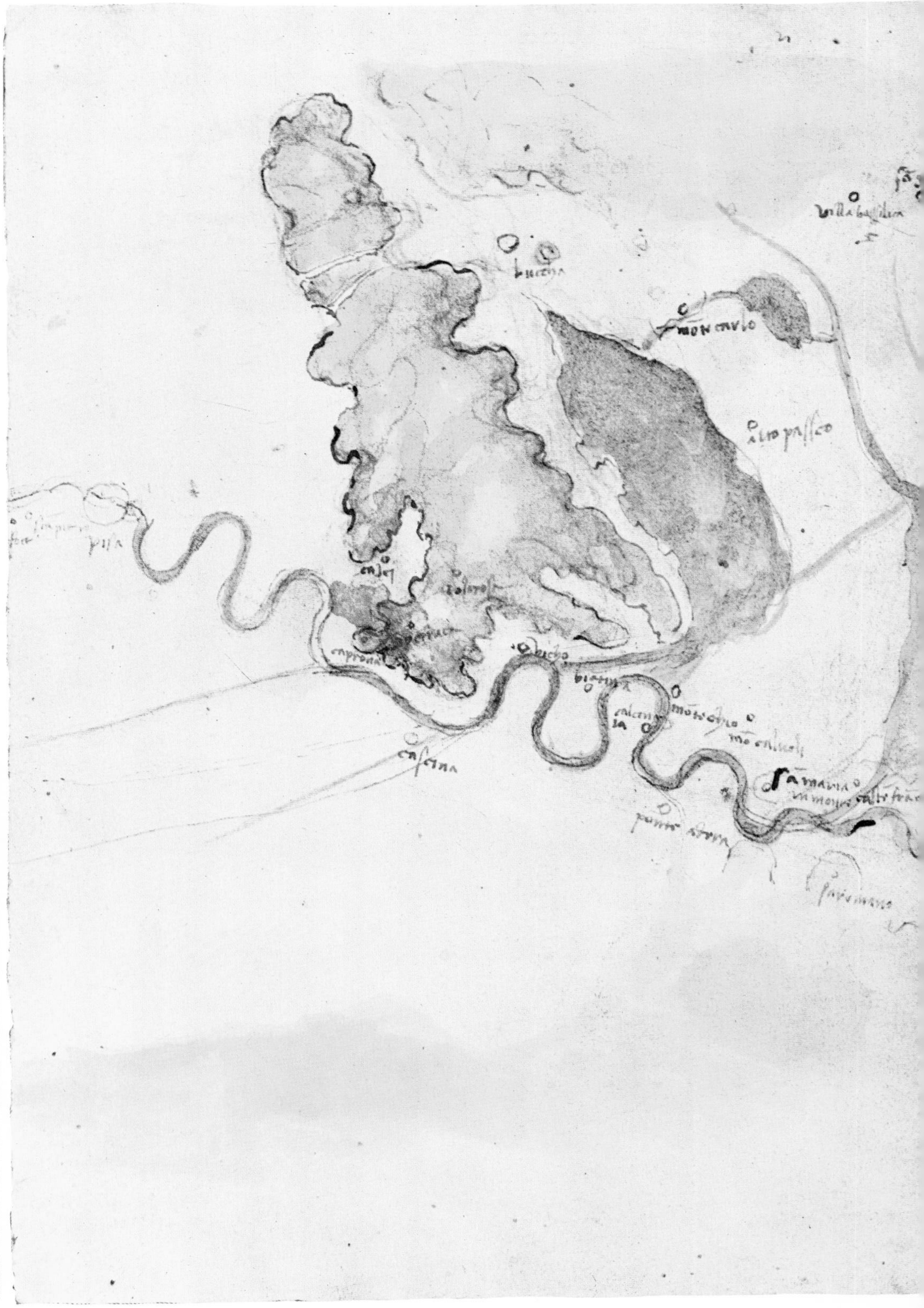

submitted to his employers. But we cannot infer from the map any proposal or plan of execution. Nor elsewhere in Codex Madrid II is there any more information on this project. From an entry on one sheet in the Windsor Collection we can much rather infer Leonardo's doubt over the undertaking. This inference gains more weight in that a large number of additional drawings have been preserved in the Madrid Codex which are indeed concerned with the course of the Arno River, but which have quite a different, pacific theme as their subject.

To amplify, on one double page of the codex is a colored map of the course of the Arno from Florence to the estuary behind Pisa and out to the sea [144/2]. The two groups of mountains north of the river – Monte Albano with its foothills from Serravalle to Signa, the Pisan mountains from Lucca to Vico Pisano – are set down against the wide plain. A large number of place names have been entered by Leonardo, again in normal script. On the Windsor sheet there is a preliminary

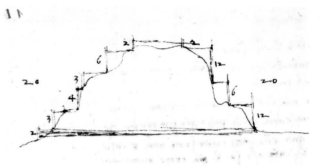

144/2 and 145/1   145/1

The mammoth scope of Leonardo's plan to open Florence to the sea is shown in the map at left from Codex Madrid II, folios 22 verso and 23 recto. The Arno can be seen snaking across the double-page spread from Florence at the lower right through Pisa at the extreme left. The two lines curving north from Florence indicate the alternate routes Leonardo studied between Florence and Pistoia: one to the east through Prato, the other via Poggio a Caiano. From Pistoia the proposed canal skirts Monte Albano, cuts through the pass at Serravalle, and runs south to link up with the Arno at Vico Pisano. This, in part, is the route followed more than 450 years later by the builders of the autostrada – superhighway – *from Florence to the sea. In the diagram at top, from Codex Madrid I, folio 111 recto, Leonardo shows an intention to tunnel through Serravalle – the same place chosen by the* autostrada *engineers for their tunnel. The transcription (below) from the map at left shows Leonardo's practical bent: he reflects on the law that landowners, enriched by the canal's water, must pay double the price of the land:*

The law which establishes that those who want to make mills can conduct water through any land, paying twice its value.

This map, Windsor No. 12279, is another study for the Arno canal. Leonardo is precise about distances – he says the canal will

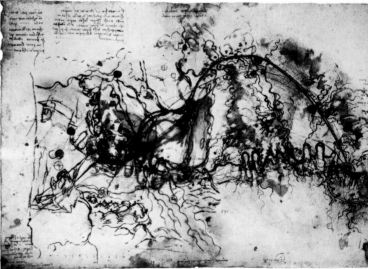

145/2

make the waterway 12 miles shorter – and benefits: "Prato, Pistoia, and Pisa, as well as Florence, will gain 200,000 ducats a year, and will lend a hand and money to this useful work."

146/1

146/1–4

As part of his own Arno project, Leonardo must have spent many days traveling up and down the river to observe the difficult terrain the canal would have to traverse. Characteristically, he recorded what he saw in a few words and many masterful drawings. The top sketch at right, from Codex Madrid II, folio 7 verso, presents the moun-

146/3

146/2

146/4

tainous panorama of the so-called Pisan Alps on the sides of the Arno. At right center, from Madrid II, folio 4 recto, he sketches Monte Veruca with the fortress that crowns its craggy summit, and fills up the space below with engineering calculations. The citadel atop Veruca, which had been recaptured by the Florentines in their war with Pisa in 1503 and inspected by Leonardo on June 21, was the outermost bastion in the much disputed border area. It still stands today (see photograph). At bottom right, in Madrid II, folio 17 recto, he draws the mountain range of Incontro above Florence, shading in the heavy shrubbery on the slopes. Leonardo's ideas for the Arno included a plan to straighten out its course above Florence.

study of the map in the Codex Madrid [145/2]. The nature or purpose of this topographic diagram becomes evident: Leonardo inserts the course of a large canal, which, by forming a detour of the unnavigable part of the Arno with its sharp bends, was intended to create a waterway between Florence and Vico Pisano. What Leonardo tries out with various attempts on the Windsor sheet is brought to a final solution in the map of the Codex Madrid. We recognize the great sweep of the canal leading from Florence to Prato to Pistoia (with an alternative route via Poggio a Caiano), and from there through the valley of Serravalle back again into the plain to return finally to the Arno at Vico Pisano. The idea of rendering the Arno navigable from Florence to the sea by means of a canal was old. As early as 1347 the Florentine governing council determined to set its hand to such a task, and it did so again in 1458. In 1487 the architect Luca Fancelli of Milan reminded Lorenzo de'Medici of such a project which he had discussed with the latter's father Piero. Thus Leonardo was taking up a long existing suggestion, the two economic aims of which he made his own: the creation of a waterway to the

147/2

147/3

147/1–3

In his rendering of mountainous land-scapes, Leonardo's roles as artist, engineer, and geologist fuse, and visual magic results. The haunting landscape details at top are from St. Anne and the Virgin *(left) and the* Mona Lisa. *The drawing, Windsor No. 12410, follows his own advice: "O painter, when you represent mountains, see that . . . the bases are always paler than the summits . . . and the loftier they are the more they should reveal their true shape and color."*

147/1

sea, with the compensation arising from the hydraulic works, and the provision of further territory for agriculture. And it seems that he concerned himself with the project as early as his Milanese years. Many of his relevant drawings and studies must date, for stylistic reasons, from the 1490s.

Leonardo developed this great project on several pages of the Codex Atlanticus.[8] Experienced scholars have examined it and investigated its practicability. The sensible calculations given of the daily working capacity of a digger, which serve as a basis for calculating the whole enterprise, are hardly consistent with an overly utopian conception. Because of the difference in level to be overcome (some 263 feet), the canal through Serravalle would have necessitated either the construction of a flight of locks of great dimensions or the building of a tunnel through the mountain. Leonardo indicated in Codex Atlanticus an intention to tunnel through Serravalle – exactly where the builders of the modern *autostrada* from Florence to

the sea did. Years earlier he had studied the problem of perforating a mountain. In Codex Madrid I there is a description of how to pierce a mountain [145/1] with a measuring device designed to guarantee that two tunnels started on the opposite sides of the mountain would meet each other at the right point.[9] Codex Madrid I belongs to Leonardo's years in Milan, and so would correspond approximately with the time when he met Luca Fancelli there. It is a somewhat bold but nice hypothesis that the two Florentines may have discussed together that great prob-

On these two pages Leonardo asserts his vivid imagination to create new perspectives made from viewpoints that then existed only in his mind. The drawing on the opposite page, Windsor No. 12409, looks down at a town in an Alpine valley where a storm is breaking and up to the sun-lit peaks above the storm.

149/1 and 2

The maps at right seem at first glance to have been drawn from the air, as if Leonardo had been able to construct and pilot aloft his flying machine. His imaginary perspective brings together previous views and fragmentary studies that he had made at first hand. Both maps, Windsor Nos. 12682 and 12278 recto, show Arezzo and the valley of the Chiana, or Val di Chiana, and probably were made in 1502 when Leonardo was in the service of the notorious Cesare Borgia. In the bottom map the place and river names are entered in careful left-to-right lettering, an indication that this was most likely a military map for Borgia's use. In the center is the Val di Chiana, at that time a swamp, with the Arno streaming out to the left towards Florence. The Val di Chiana and the Tiber River, at top, figured in Leonardo's plans for the Arno project — as a means of maintaining the river at an even level for navigation.

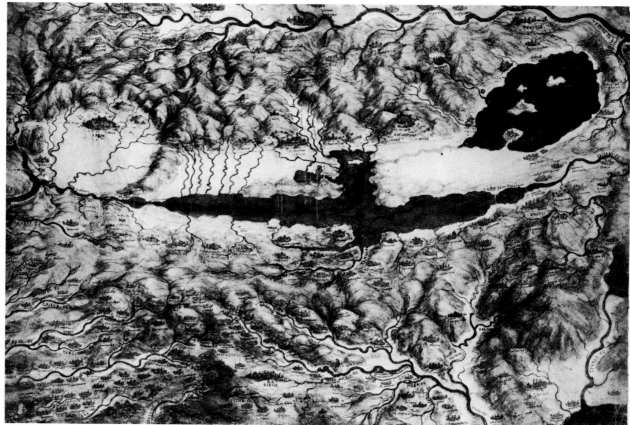

lem of their home country, the Arno canal. Whatever the case may be, when in 1503 Leonardo was sent in his capacity as strategic engineer to the camp at Pisa to inspect the efforts to divert the Arno from the city, he certainly discharged his duty conscientiously, as is shown by his "ordnance map" of the operational area in Codex Madrid II [142/4]. But it is comforting to note that the master's main interest remained not the war objective, but the peaceful project of the Arno canal as a waterway.

The coast of the Ligurian sea can be seen
along the bottom of Leonardo's map of the
Arno watershed in northern Italy. The
swamps near Pisa have been drained since,
as can be seen in the map at right.

150/2   WINDSOR 12277

Serchio

Arno

Pisa

Livorno

Castiglioncello

Fine

Cecina

Cecina

LIGURIAN SEA

Leonardo was certainly aware of the extent of the latter venture and of the technical difficulties connected with effectuating it, as is attested by notes in his manuscripts of a warning character.[10] His planning should, for this reason, be understood as a lengthy and systematic study of all factors; and the drawings in Codex Madrid II offer the best evidence of this. They complement studies in the Codex Atlanticus and the Windsor Collection in an enlightening fashion and show Leonardo at work on a project of the highest economic importance. It appears that these studies were broken off following his departure from Florence in 1506.

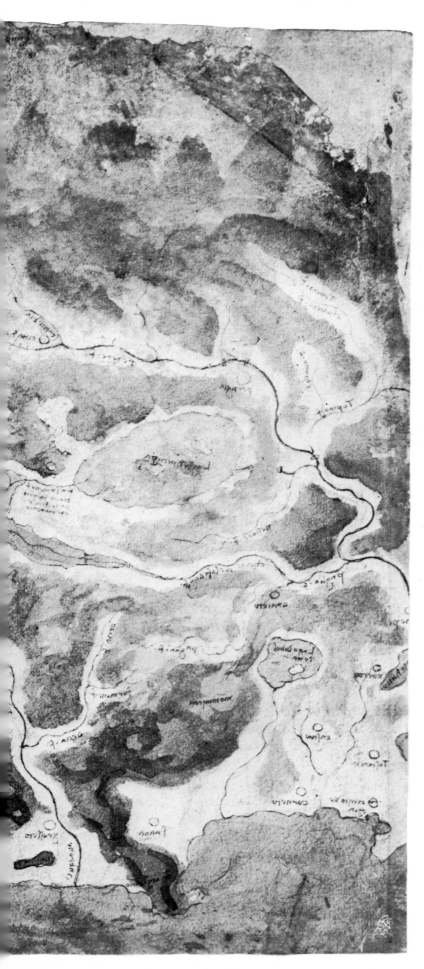

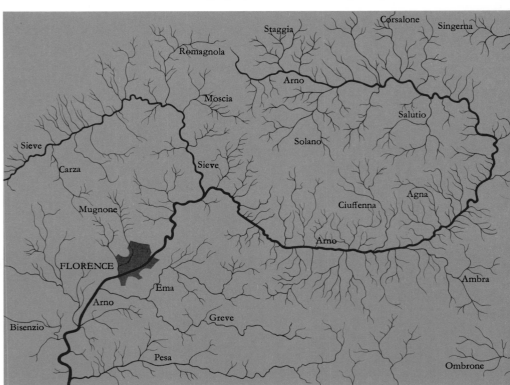

151/1

Leonardo drew the map at left during his service for Cesare Borgia, 1502–03, and it contains the borders of Cesare's ambitious "kingdom" as a ruler of central Italy. Even though the map was also drawn for strategic purposes, it is the masterpiece of

Leonardo's long-term studies of the Arno river and its tributaries – and perhaps the first modern map. It anticipates in execution as well as viewpoint the work of present-day map makers. Leonardo indicates by dark shadings the mountains of the Apennines and carefully shows and names the rivers, lakes, and towns. From the sea the Arno winds up through Pisa and Florence (near center); then, at the junction with the Sieve river, turns south towards Arezzo and back towards the north. The map above, of the Arno and its tributaries, rendering the central area of Leonardo's map, attests to his remarkably accuracy.

Cesare Borgia, the hero of the military and political power of the church under his father, Pope Alexander VI (above left), succeeded in occupying Imola in 1499 during the first of his Romagna campaigns. The following year, the Pope officially gave the town to his son, who commissioned

152/3

Leonardo to study possible modifications. After the death of the Pope in August 1503 and the subsequent fall of Borgia, the town was eventually subjected to the Vatican, then under Pope Julius II (top right).

152/3 and 4

In October 1502 Leonardo spent several weeks in the city of Imola with its leader Cesare Borgia, who had been detained by a revolt of his generals. During that period he studied the existing fortress there. The fortress, called the Rocca, is shown in a 17th-century drawing on the opposite page and in a photograph after its modern restoration. Leonardo's sketch (below) for a fortress with towers protected by semicircular moats in the Codex Atlanticus, folio 48 recto-b, may have been inspired by the Rocca. But he must have spent most of his time on the famous map of Imola (overleaf) in which his cartographer's skills reach their finest point.

152/4

The collapse of the plan to rob besieged Pisa of its access to the sea led to the temporary suspension of military action. The Florentine troops were recalled and all the more therefore did the governing council seek to isolate the enemy through political and diplomatic channels. In April of 1504 Machiavelli was sent to Piombino to treat with Jacopo IV Appiani – who had returned to his city after the fall of Cesare Borgia – and to resume friendly relations with him. The mission was delicate. Only a few years before, in 1499, Machiavelli had had an eye on winning Jacopo over to Florence with a highly paid post of condottiere. The negotiations had dragged out, but then, as Borgia's star was rising, were evidently broken off on the Florentine side, since it seemed to the Florentines more advisable to strike up good relations with the favorite of the Pope. Instead of Jacopo Appiani, they offered the position to Cesare Borgia and accorded him the title of "Signore di Piombino" before he had taken up possession of the territory. So in 1504 Machiavelli had a difficult diplomatic mission. He had first of all to win back again Jacopo Appiani's confidence in the governing council of Florence; second he had to ensure what we would call today the "benevolent neutrality" of the ruler of Piombino in the strained relations that Florence had with Siena and Pisa. With regard to Pisa, which the Appiani four generations previously had had to leave ignominiously, Jacopo's "benevolent neutrality" was not difficult to obtain. It was much more important to Florence to engage his neutrality towards Siena. Machiavelli's diplomatic task was exactly laid down by the council. In 1504, therefore, he betook himself to Piombino, and it is certainly no accident that in the late autumn of that same year Leonardo da Vinci also went to Piombino to advise Jacopo Appiani on the building of the fortifications of the city. This task, up to now unknown, is new information afforded to us by Codex Madrid II.

On one page of this codex we find Leonardo's entry, "The last day of November [he must have meant October], All Saints' Day 1504 [actually November 1], I made in Piombino for the Lord this demonstration."[11] The text is accompanied by a small drawing which envisages the leveling of a group of hills in the framework of the defense installations [158/3]. On the previous page there is a sketch of a tunnel [159/3]. The accompanying text says, "covered way; fortress [i.e., citadel] of Piombino the 20th of November 1504; the moat which I am straightening."[12]

The date November 1, 1504, is found once more in the codex in an entirely different context. Leonardo notes down an observation on green-colored shadows on a wall of a house; above the note is written, "1504 in Piombino, All Saints' Day."[13] At the end of December, presumably before Christmas, Leonardo is once more in Florence, as we know from other documents. Since he had withdrawn money there on October 31, 1504, he can only have traveled to Piombino from that day onward. On the very next day, after his arrival in the place, he explains his plan of construction to the "Signore," Jacopo Appiani. It is therefore obvious that he must have already had exact knowledge of the local situation and of his task. This causes us to reflect a little. He then spent 6 to 7 weeks in Piombino, which is an exceedingly limited period that must exclude the possibility of large building operations having been carried out under his supervision. From all these circumstances we must deduce that there in Piombino, in the same way as in Venice and in the siege camp at Pisa, Leonardo worked as expert and adviser rather than as practical architect.

There can be no doubt, in my opinion, that Leonardo da Vinci's task was connected with the political mission of Machiavelli. It seems only logical that the Florentine diplomat should offer to place at the re-enthroned ruler's disposal the most famous expert of Florence for advice in the most important task before Appiani: the fortification of the town he had won back again. Leonardo was the most suitable person, as he had already been fully entrusted with the same job during his period of activity for Cesare Borgia, that short-lived usurper of Piombino. So it was that in the irony of the game of historical circumstance, Jacopo Appiani came to profit by the very defense project that had originally been elaborated for his hated enemy.

Four different yet related construction projects concerning the fortification plans in Piombino can be singled out among Leonardo's sketches and notes scattered

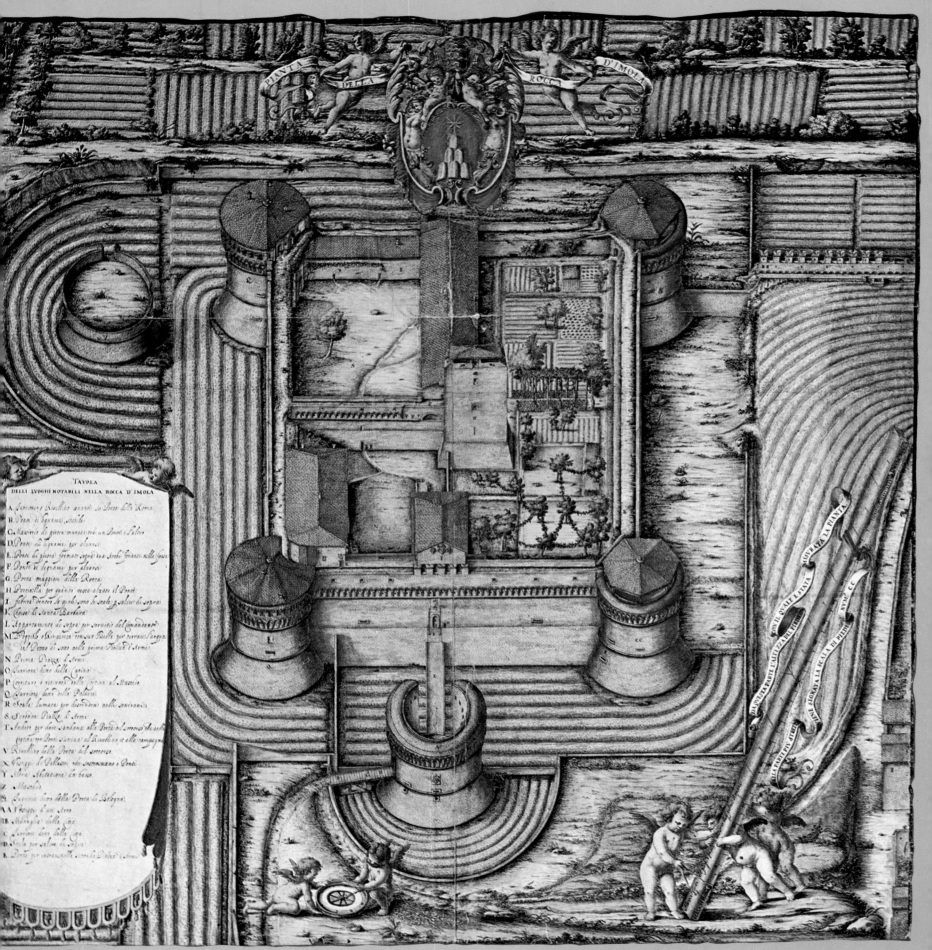

153/1

The Rocca, shown here in a 17th-century drawing, was the principal fortification of Imola when Leonardo visited there in 1502. His later ideas about fortress design may have been influenced by the semicircular moats that protect its outer towers.

Overleaf: In his map of Imola Leonardo, like an aerial photographer, pinpoints every physical detail. The houses are tinted pink, the public squares dark yellow, the streets white. The city and its fortress at lower left are surrounded by blue moats. Across the map Leonardo drew lines, and at the eight points where they intersect the circumference, he wrote the names of the winds. Notes on either side of the circle refer to the geography of Bologna and other cities in which Cesare Borgia had a military interest.

WINDSOR 12284

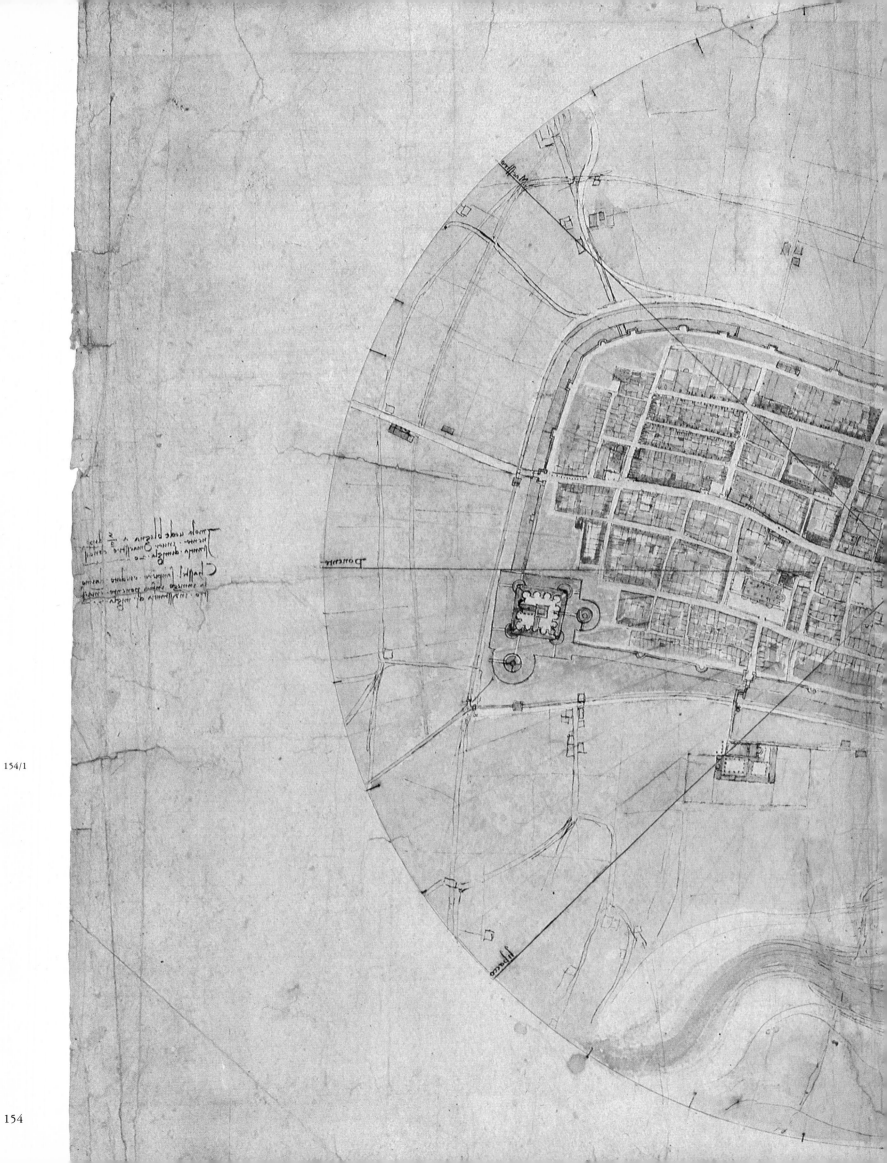

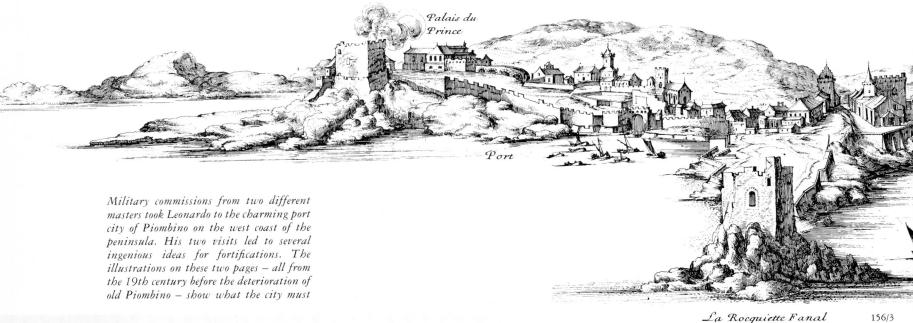

Palais du Prince

Port

throughout Codex Madrid II. Each individual project leads out from the citadel located at the east corner of the town.

The first of these projects was to dig a trench 640 braccia (about 1,260 feet) long, leading through rocky ground from the citadel to the spit of the land and the Rochetta.[14] According to modern maps of Piombino, the distance from the citadel to the spit is 1,312 feet, which corresponds closely to Leonardo's figure.

156/2

La Rocquiette Fanal 156/3

Military commissions from two different masters took Leonardo to the charming port city of Piombino on the west coast of the peninsula. His two visits led to several ingenious ideas for fortifications. The illustrations on these two pages – all from the 19th century before the deterioration of old Piombino – show what the city must

156/4

The old French maps of Piombino above and at the top of the page show the plan of the city. In the foreground above is the medieval Rochetta Castle, which guarded the waterway and made sure ships paid their tolls. At the left of the castle is the old fishing port – also seen in the photo at left. Near this port was a big fountain (photograph, top left). Piombino was protected by a seawall that joined another wall on the inland side. The main gate of the inland wall is shown on the opposite page in the photograph at top right. The keystone of the defense of the city was the citadel that can be seen rising from the right portion of the map above and in the middle of the 1894 painting shown at the bottom of the opposite page.

have looked like when Leonardo first went there in 1502 for Cesare Borgia. Porto Falesia, a harbor which was important ever since Roman times, bustled with ships bearing iron ore from the island of Elba a few miles away. Ships passing through the narrow waterway between or stopping for fresh water were charged a toll. The receipt for payment was a little lead coin. According to tradition, Piombino got its name from the Italian word for "little lead" – piombino.

The second project was to build a tunnel – a "covered way" which was also called "moat" (*fosso*) – the length of which was indicated by Leonardo to be 300 braccia (590 feet). This was to lead in a straight line from the citadel to the town gate of Piombino.[15] According to the modern city maps the distance from the citadel to the town gate actually corresponds very closely to the figure stated by Leonardo.

Third, it was intended to enlarge the citadel, essentially by constructing a massive tower with a height of 20 braccia (39 feet, which is not very much!) and a diameter of 25 braccia (49 feet).

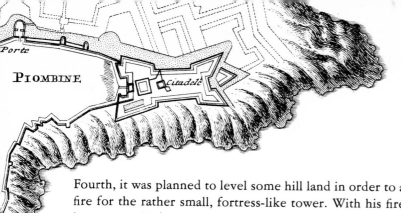

Fourth, it was planned to level some hill land in order to achieve an open line of fire for the rather small, fortress-like tower. With his firearms Leonardo would have controlled the open area in the east, around the port.

With relative accuracy only the tunnel between the citadel and the town gate may be located. As to the shape of the tower, Leonardo recorded various differentiating sketches and notes. There cannot, therefore, be singled out one final

The purpose of Leonardo's first visit to Piombino was to study draining the marshes there and to improve the fortifications. Piombino had great strategic interest for Florence, Siena, and the other powers around it. In 1499 Borgia had deposed the ruler of Piombino, Jacopo IV

plan concerning the tower's exact position within the entire complex of the fortification or concerning its construction. Neither can there be found further details of the plan for the 640-braccio-long trench. The repeated notes concerning the rocky terrain (causing the project to be more expensive) and the note *lungo la marina* ("along the coast"), however, lead with certainty to the assumption that this trench was to reach the spit of land.

During the weeks Leonardo spent in Piombino, work seems only to have commenced on the tunnel, or "moat," from the citadel to the town gate, as can be

Appiani. But by 1504 Borgia was expelled and Jacopo was back in power. Florence wanted to regain Jacopo's friendship, so Machiavelli was sent as an ambassador in the summer, and at the end of October 1504 Leonardo was dispatched to Piombino to help with the defenses. He obviously had a rather exact knowledge of the situation — drawn up for his erstwhile patron and Jacopo's enemy, Borgia. The evidence in Codex Madrid II indicates that Leonardo was in Piombino six to seven weeks. He

gathered from the note "the moat which I am straightening." The remaining projects apparently were left unexecuted.

The accompanying comprehensive texts, mostly calculations of cost, disclose that Leonardo was a well-versed engineer who differentiated exactly the daily capacity of a man according to the sandy or rocky nature of the ground. For the construction of the tunnel, or "moat," Leonardo also provides exact specifications for expedient distribution of labor, ranging from the deepest level of the tunnel to the uppermost edge of the rampart, so that the masses of earth can be disposed of freely and easily.[16]

drew detailed plans and made notes for a number of projects (see following pages). No one knows whether any actual construction was carried out, though the tower at the main gate (top photograph) is still known to inhabitants today as "the tower of Leonardo da Vinci."

158/2

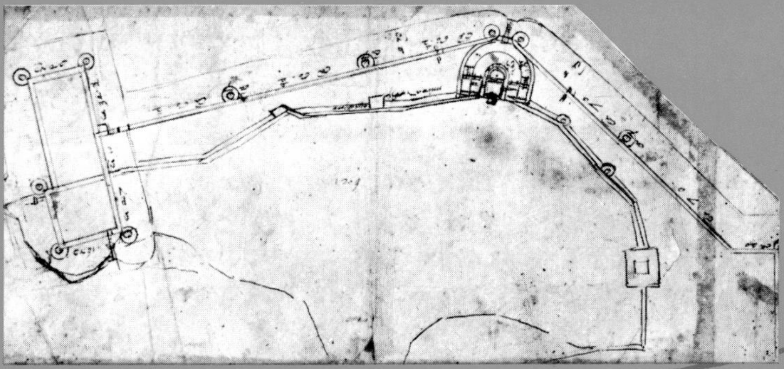

On this 16th-century map of Piombino are superimposed the four main tasks Leonardo meant to undertake for Jacopo IV Appiani. The biggest project was the digging of a trench from the citadel to the Rochetta at the spit of the land (I). This trench was to measure about 1,260 feet. Next he wanted to connect the citadel by means of a tunnel with the main gate of Piombino (II). Two sketches from Madrid II, folios 9 verso [159/1] and 24 verso [159/3], show the tunnel. This passageway was to be 590 feet long and was to serve as a means of communication and, if necessary, escape for the ruler of Piombino. To protect the ruler from betrayal by his own soldiers or townspeople, a common occurrence in those days, Leonardo planned to construct a drawbridge as the only means of reaching the tunnel. Next to the fortress and branching off the underground passageway, he designed a round tower (III) to help defend the fortress and the old wall. Sketches for this third project are shown at right, both details from Madrid II, folio 37 recto. The drawings below, from Madrid II, folio 25 recto, show the fourth project. In order to achieve an open line of fire from the round tower to the old harbor in the east, it was necessary to level some hill land (IV).

The small map of Piombino above plots a new wall outside the old one and builds up the defenses around the main gate. Though found in the Codex Atlanticus, folio 41 recto, it was drawn by someone other than Leonardo – perhaps Antonio da Sangallo the Elder, a noted Florentine architect and engineer, who was in the service of the republic at the same time.

158/3

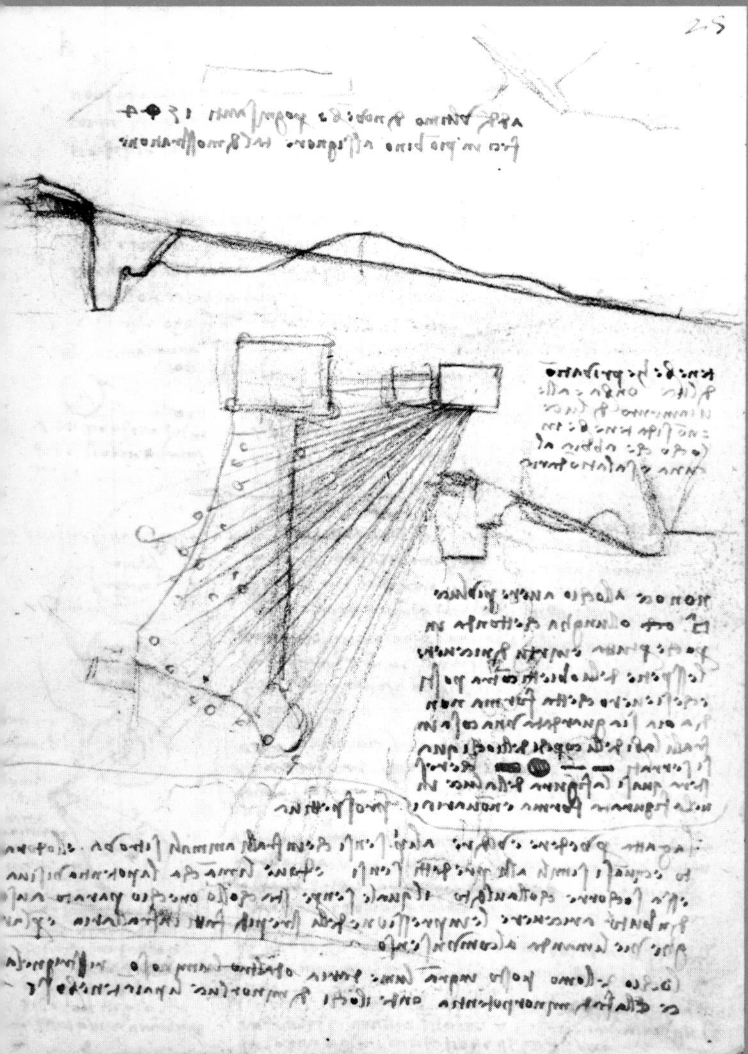

159/4

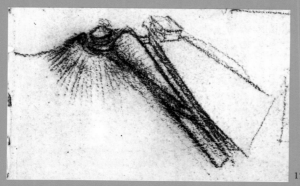

159/1

Only the moat between the citadel and the town gate may be located with relative accuracy. As to the shape of the tower, Leonardo has recorded various differentiating sketches and notes. There cannot, therefore, be singled out one final project concerning either the tower's exact position or its construc-

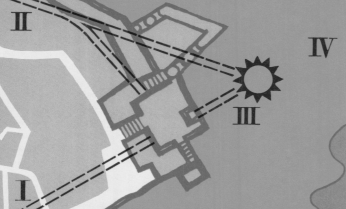

159/2

tion. Neither can there be found further details of the plan for the 1,260-foot-long trench (I). However, the repeated notes concerning the rocky terrain and the note lungo la marina ("along the coast") lead with certainty to the

assumption that this trench was to reach the spit of land. During the 6 weeks Leonardo spent in Piombino, work seems to have commenced only on the moat from the citadel to the town gate, as can be gathered from the note transcribed below. The remaining projects apparently were unexecuted.

159/3

Piombino's main shipping port was southeast of the city, the old Porto Falesia (map below, right). But in Manuscript L, which he used during his service with Borgia, Leonardo sketched a map (below, left) with a promontory jutting into the water next to Piombino – a hint that he may have considered building a new harbor.

159/5

159/4

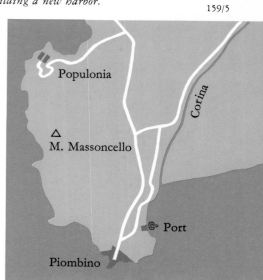

Populonia

Corina

M. Massoncello

Port

Piombino

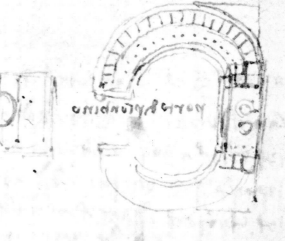

Harbor of Piombino

Above is a sketch from Codex Madrid II, folio 88 verso, in which Leonardo reconstructs the old harbor (Porto Falesia) with its breakwater that even then had fallen into ruin. At the left of the breakwater he designs a fortification to guard it.

159/6

covered way

fortress of
Piombino
the 20th
November 1504

the moat
which I am straightening

door

Though mathematically quite primitive, Leonardo's calculations of the masses of earth to be coped with in removing the hills are extremely interesting. His method of dealing with cubic mass is somewhat empirical, and one would not like to guarantee the exactitude of the calculations. However, the transposing of a hill massif into a geometric cone diagram and the evaluation of the volume of the cone show that he resorted to a certain mathematical principle in order to formulate the real dimensions of a practical task.[17]

Most enlightening indeed, as far as the political conditions of his times are concerned, is the precaution Leonardo took of safeguarding the covered connecting passage between fortress and town gate against not only the external but also the internal enemy. In case *il popolo* – i.e., the townsmen of Piombino – were to rebel against their lord and master and attempt to cut off the passage to the town

160/1–7 and 161/1
At the end of the 15th century, the rapid development and increasing power of firearms changed the principles of fortress building. Until the seventies, fortifications preferably had square turreted towers and high walls – as in the typical fortress shown

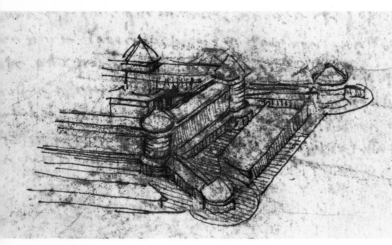

160/1

on the opposite page, the Castello di Tor-rechiara, which is still standing near Parma. Then architects began building fortifications with rounded towers and

160/2

"Tower of bosses."

MADRID II 93v

160/3

thick inclined walls geared to the effect of heavy artillery, both offensive and defensive. Francesco di Giorgio Martini was one of the most renowned specialists in military architecture and engineering of his time. Leonardo – 13 years younger – had certainly learned a lot from him by exchanging views and experiences when they met and by studying Francesco's Treatise, *a copy of which Leonardo owned. He borrowed from Martini the idea for the sketch of a fortress shown at the top of the page (Codex Madrid II, folio 79 recto) – a citadel that represented the transition to the low rounded bastion of later times.*

"The secondary towers must be low and wide, covered by a vaulted and beveled roof, at a very obtuse angle, in order to deflect the transversal shots."

MADRID II 93v

160/4

160/5

"If a square tower is provided with pyramids at the corners, with varied shelters, like stairs, ports, double bridges, devious entrances, ravelins and ditches, it will have, by itself, great resistance."

MADRID II 89r

MADRID II 93v

160/6

160/7

"If the fortress can be attacked only from a single side, make that side in the form of a massive acute angle, of 25 to 30 feet, with its lateral defenses. At this same side the doors should be located, with towers behind and shelters convenient to them."

MADRID II 93r

"Here the embrasures of one ravelin overlook and protect the sides of the other ravelin. And so do reciprocally all the others. And here no scaling ladders can be planted."

MADRID II 93r

gate, Leonardo provides a countermeasure and safety device. It is an eloquent illustration of the mistrust under which a ruler of those days exercised his position.[18] Again, in the construction of the great round tower of the citadel, the kernel of the fortifications, a system of preventive measures is provided to control the functions of the commander of the fortifications so as to exclude every possibility of betrayal to the enemy as well as surprise attack. The disgraceful surrender of the mighty citadel of Milan – which the commander abandoned in 1499 to the French after they had penetrated the city, thereby setting the seal to Lodovico Sforza's defeat – may well have been in Leonardo's mind. He may have been thinking, too, of the surprise attack on the fortress of Fossombrone in October 1502, when Cesare Borgia's troops succeeded in penetrating the secret accesses to the citadel during the night through the use of the enemy password *Feltre*. It is evident that Leonardo considered every military aspect in carrying out these tasks. He examined traditional fighting and tactical methods of medieval

"The lord of the manor must be able to go through the entire fortress, including the upper, the middle and the lower parts, using tunnels and underground

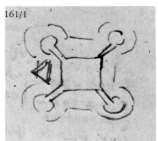

"At the strongest corners, towers should be placed, with lateral defenses, which defend the walls

passages, which shall be disposed in such a way that none of them

which contain the massive corners." MADRID II 92v

could be used to reach the dwelling of the lord, without his agreement. And through these ways using portcullis and other devices he must be able to imprison in their residence all those of his retinue, who may plot against him, and may close or open the door of the main entrance and the relief route. And this danger is even greater than the enemy itself because those on the inside have greater opportunity to do harm than the enemy who is shut out."

MADRID II 89v

"For defense against mortar-fire the tower should be built in such a way that the escarpment continues in straight lines that join at the summit of the tower."

MADRID II 92v

161/1–4
Leonardo's top two sketches above deal with the placement of towers within the fortress. The bottom two relate to the shapes of the towers themselves. In the notes for these designs and the ones on the opposite page – some of them variations on the ideas of Francesco di Giorgio Martini – Leonardo provides precise specifications for moats, construction of towers, and the organization of firepower against the enemy outside the gates. But he is also at pains to contain the potential enemies within – see the transcription from Codex Madrid II, folio 89 verso, above.

The plans for Piombino paid particular attention to a relatively new art – efficient organization of the firepower that was revolutionizing warfare. One of the chief functions of the soldiers in the old fortress towers had been to dump hot tar on assailants who tried to scale the towers with ladders. Leonardo was one of the first military architects to place a cannon in a tower, as in the sketch below from Codex Madrid II, folio 36 recto. In another sketch, from Codex

warfare, as well as innovations in fortification technique that had resulted from the increasing use of firearms.

Thus, as we have been able to follow from his short stay in Piombino, Leonardo developed for Appiani a project of fortification which must have demanded a considerable length of time to execute. Only the remark "the moat which I am straightening" allows us to conjecture that the digging of the tunnel started during Leonardo's presence there. It would be important to ascertain, through a trial excavation of the citadel, if any traces of this secret connecting passage still exist.

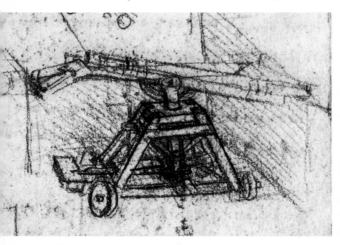

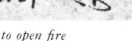

162/1

Atlanticus, folio 48 recto-b (above, right), he plots the lines of fire from tower-mounted cannon.

162/2

to open fire

Out of his labors at Piombino Leonardo evolved a design for a fortress so different its like would not be seen for centuries. In his sketches at right and below from the Codex Atlanticus, folio 48 recto-b, the first modern bastion begins to take form. Outposts on the four corners furnish flanking fire. Concentric fortified rings provide firing positions for the defenders of the citadel. Between the rings are trench-like areas that could be flooded if the enemy breached the outer walls, enabling the defenders to retreat to strongpoints in the innermost rings.

Along as many lines as the defender can strike at the offender, the offender will be able to strike at the defender.

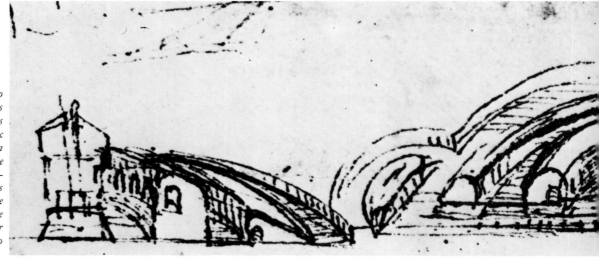

162/3

162/4

A drawing in the Codex Atlanticus which is not by Leonardo's hand reproduces the fortification system of Piombino with relative precision [158/2]. Whether the artist was Antonio da Sangallo the Elder, as has been suggested, must be left undecided. Antonio had met Leonardo in the camp at Pisa, and it is therefore quite possible that Antonio, an equally respected military engineer of the city of Florence, had knowledge of the Piombino project. Only further research can now throw light on the defense installations of Piombino. Nevertheless, the extent to which Leonardo was engaged in this task – first in the service of Cesare Borgia, then later in that of Jacopo Appiani – is corroborated by further evidence in Codex Madrid II. A series of pages are crammed with extracts taken by Leonardo from the treatise on architecture by Francesco di Giorgio Martini. A detailed examination of these extracts shows that the choice of texts was determined by direct reference to the fortifications of Piombino. Most of the texts selected are connected with this specific task, and they may have served Leonardo for his "demonstration" before Jacopo Appiani, which we have to envisage as a complete exposition of his project. Of equal importance, the majority of the remaining extracts concern the construction of a tower of fortification, just as the tower takes up most room in Leonardo's draft of his plans for Piombino.

Considering the aspect of the selection of Francesco's texts, it is of some consequence that two pages among them deal with the layout of a port. On one of these two pages is a small sketch of Leonardo's, accompanied by the note, "port of Piombino" [159/6]. It would seem that at the outset Leonardo sketched an ideal reconstruction of the ancient harbor of Piombino, even though it is a hasty jotting. Remains of the ancient mole, or foundation, can still be observed under water today, but it appears very probable that Leonardo had the intention of modifying the existing installation of his time, or that at least he toyed with the idea. The illustrations of certain appliances for construction under water assigned to

163/1 and 2
To open free fields of fire from his round tower, which would protect the citadel at Piombino, Leonardo had to level a cluster of hills. His sketch below at left, from Codex Madrid II, folio 25 recto, shows the line of fire through one of the hills. Below, in Madrid II, folio 32 verso, he uses a diagram to try to calculate the exact amount of dirt that would have to be dug out and then figures to the exact lira the cost of such an excavation.

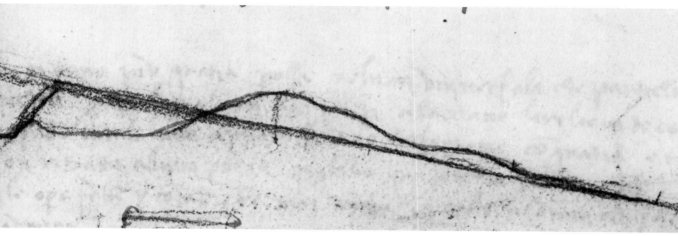

163/1

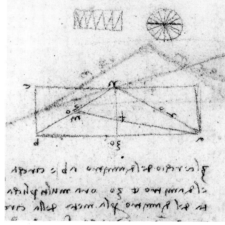

163/2

163/3

Francesco's extracts differ substantially from Francesco's drawings, and they justify the conjecture that Leonardo sketched in here his own modifications. More than 10 years later he was again to take up a similar theme, when, during his sojourn in Rome between 1513 and 1516, he studied and reconstructed the ancient port of Civitavecchia.

163/3 and 4
The cross-section model above of Leonardo's new fortress was built for the National Museum of Science and Technology in Milan from his designs in the Codex Atlanticus. His sketch below, in Atlanticus, folio 48 recto-a, shows a cross section of one of the tunnel-like fortification rings with portals for setting up fields of fire.

163/4

All this collected material, written and drawn, which Codex Madrid II has to offer us on Leonardo's brief stay in Piombino provides a rare, living glimpse into the uncommonly versatile and quick powers of perception of Leonardo's eye and mind. When on the day of his arrival, November 1, 1504, he presents his plan of construction to the ruler of the city, when on the same day he stands down at the harbor and while contemplating the rigging of the fishing boats observes the interplay of colored shadows on the pale wall of a house – an image that charms his painter's eye and provokes reflections on the optical phenomenon – we can sense, as if we were standing beside him, the complete open-mindedness and vitality of his intellect.

164/1

Leonardo's idea for a low rounded fortress represents a radical leap forward. Here the concept is contrasted with a typical design of his day. The model on this page has the turreted and slightly angled walls that characterized fortifications during the advent of heavy firepower. On the opposite page a composite photograph – making whole the semicircular model shown on the previous page – shows Leonardo's concentric fortifications each protected by a moat. Most dramatic of all is the side view of his fortress at the top of the opposite page, whose ominous streamlined profile truly foreshadows fortifications of later centuries.

164/2

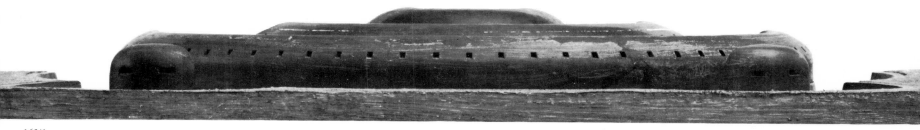

165/1

165/2

Nearly five centuries have passed since Leonardo recorded his thoughts and designs for machines intended to simplify the routine tasks that he saw being performed around him. His purpose was to have the work done more quickly and easily, while maintaining standards of uniformity and precision. As adviser to heads of state, military commanders, nobles, and estate managers, he acted as designer, engineer, architect, geologist,

MACHINES AND WEAPONRY

anatomist, master of ordnance, and seer, which must not have left much time for him to paint some of the most eminent masterpieces in secular and religious art.

Leonardo lived in a restless period in the history of Europe, an age much like our own. His birth coincided with the Gutenberg invention, one of the most revolutionary developments in all human history. During his life, furthermore, Vasco da Gama sailed around Africa, connecting Europe with India by ship, and Columbus and Leonardo's fellow Florentine, Amerigo Vespucci, opened vast new continents to the adventurous sailors and soldiers of Europe. This was an appropriate time and place for the innovative mechanical genius of this master of technology to be exercised, and his drawings record the creations of a most fertile mind and help define the status of the mechanical arts of the last quarter of the 1400s.

The large gathering of the Codex Atlanticus and Codex Madrid I contains most of the investigations that Leonardo made in machines and in military matters.

BERN DIBNER

"The muscle power of the peasant, horse,
and ox were replaced,
under Leonardo's pen,
by wind and water, gunpowder and steam,
and as he matured,
the machine and its parts became
the language
of his involvement in the world."

Leonardo was about 30 years old when he prepared the letter to Lodovico Sforza (page 7) in which he offered his services and listed his many talents. His recital of some 36 abilities which were put at the disposal of the duke can be used as a measure of the interests of Leonardo at that time. Thirty of the claims are of a technical nature and six are in the field of art. The studio of Verrocchio, where Leonardo had worked, was decidedly non-military. One therefore concludes that Leonardo was drawn by the mechanical and engineering challenge that military devices offered – the challenge to extend the power of firearms and to develop new combinations of machines and weapons. One sees this interest in increased effectiveness of the machine in his note, "Instrumental and mechanical science is the noblest and above all others the

The flowering of the Renaissance had little direct influence on the people whose bread had to be earned by their own hands. The aristocracy scorned manual labor and those who practiced it. Even the artists ignored working people, preferring to depict the lives of saints, angels, madonnas, and dukes.

167/1

most useful, seeing that by means of it all animated bodies which have movement perform all their action; and the origin of these movements is at the center of their gravity. . . ." [1]

Leonardo's dedication to the devices created by the mechanical arts can only be explained as his natural response to the benefits that come with their use, the constancy of the natural laws that control their operation, and the invariable honesty of their behavior. Unlike the men and women about him, they performed their work free of emotion, vanity, or influence. He was intent upon discovering universal laws by experimenting with basic machine elements and assigning quantitative values wherever he could.

Having visualized a mechanical solution to a problem, he sketched the parts and the assembly, noted the working directions, assigned to himself further tasks for study, and moved on to other problems. Yet no solution was ever adequate, for he would return later to some similar device to accomplish the same task by using different parts or a different assembly of parts. Consider, for instance, his concern with ways of converting reciprocating to rotary motion, a basic need in all machinery design. Leonardo sketched dozens of devices to accomplish this, never satisfied that he had attained *the* solution.

It was as a designer of machines and weapons for use on land that Leonardo prepared his widest variety of novel devices and left a heritage of drawings on military subjects unmatched in the rich history of this destructive profession. He lived in the age of transition when massed armies of crossbowmen and mounted, armored troops were giving way to fusiliers and cannoneers. With this change in Western society came social and political changes the impress

One significant exception was Leonardo, who sketched a number of scenes, like the ones shown here, of farmers and laborers at work. His painting and studies in anatomy had led him to close observation of the human figure in all its forms. But as an engineer he had to study the particulars of manual labor like a modern time-and-motion expert: his notebooks show him calculating in precise detail the man-hours and labor costs for such complex projects as the diversion of the Arno. Increasingly, he focused his imagination, technical know-how, and passion for invention on what was to become the principal task of the modern era: designing machines that would multiply manyfold the frail physical efforts of man. WINDSOR 12643, 12644v

167/2

of which has reached into the 20th century. The simpler tools and implements of Leonardo's day evolved into the myriad inventions that had germinated in his mind. The muscle power of the peasant, horse, and ox were replaced, under Leonardo's pen, by wind and water, gunpowder and steam. And as he matured, the machine and its parts became the language of his involvement in the world. Yet the transition of Leonardo the artist to Leonardo the technologist was not fully accepted even by some historians in our own time. It required the rediscovery of Leonardo's two codices in Madrid in 1967 to confirm that the prime interest of his mature years was engines, devices, and things of the material world of man the maker.

Nine-tenths of the Madrid Codices are devoted to technological subjects; they supplement Leonardo's other mechanical studies and provide the scholar of today with the most comprehensive corpus of Renaissance technology. It was the technicians who gleaned most from the new material, because Madrid I is almost solidly mechanics- and technology-oriented, while Madrid II contains much in geometry, mechanics, navigation, and topology.

On examining the hundreds of Leonardo's mechanical designs,[2] one sees in them attempts to combine motions and incorporate them into a machine to attain automated action. This was definitely an order of attainment above the results obtained from the classic mechanisms. The concept of automation is not related to complexity but to feedback. There is a dependence of one mechanical operation on another, which eliminates the need for a decision to perform the second operation after the first is completed; the sequence of actions is designed into the mechanism. Leonardo derived obvious satisfaction from creating such multiple designs, and a representative selection of them

In his famous letter to Lodovico Sforza, Leonardo had promised new and secret instruments of war. He sketched the technique shown in the drawing below – a warrior's hand-borne lance is augmented by

168/1

two others affixed to his horse's saddle – only a year or so after his arrival at the Sforza court in Milan. The tripling of the rider's lance power must have appealed to Leonardo's penchant for designs that multiplied a simple force, but he probably borrowed the basic idea from accounts of ancient warfare. He had a magpie mind that picked up ideas everywhere – from the books of others, from the tales of travelers to distant lands – ideas he then improved and made his own. WINDSOR 12653

Leonardo's drawing of a foundry courtyard (opposite page) depicts the enormous difficulty of mounting a cannon with the crude mechanisms then available for increasing muscle power. In the center nude men push the huge gun carriage under the cannon while others strain at the levers of the crane to raise the cannon. In the foreground is the cradle on rollers by which the cannon was brought in. When this drawing was made, about 1487, Leonardo was engaged in the founding of bronze cannon for Lodovico Sforza. He haunted the forges and foundries of Milan, but cannon were not his consuming interest. He was looking for better ways to cast his great horse monument. A few years later, of course, all the bronze earmarked for that epic project – Leonardo's grandiose dream – was to be poured into the casting of more gun barrels. WINDSOR 12647

has been made here to illustrate his genius in conceiving them and then drawing them vividly in perspective. Those selected indicate Leonardo's advanced acquaintance with the language of gears, pulleys, ratchets, cams, wedges, linkages, cranks, and racks and pinions. To them he brought a background of contact with field and shop and a grasp of fundamental physics and chemistry.

To interpret Leonardo's drawings, one usually begins with the point of application of the motive power – the crank. Though power in Leonardo's day was muscle power, derived from man or animal, where great power was required he resorted to the energy of falling water or to wind power. He also knew about the storing of power in springs and raised water and the inertia of flywheels. To speculate on what Leonardo might have accomplished with the availability of other energy sources is pointless.

Leonardo's machines were intended to be applied to general use in industry – hammering, shaping wood, stone, and metal, raising great weights, casting

169/1

metal, drawing strip and wire, weaving textiles, coining, grinding, digging canals, turning, winding, lifting, moving – the basic needs of any urban society. As intriguing as the machines were to Leonardo, one sees among his drawings his concern with multiple solutions to the problem of transfer of forces – concern, that is, with the spirit of the mechanism rather than its specific parts. What was its purpose? How might it best operate? How else might it be structured? Could it be made simpler, faster, more useful? Could steps be combined?

An inventory of Leonardo's machines divides them into the major categories of those for improving mechanical work (and therefore productive) and those for military application (and therefore destructive). The cities of Florence, Milan, and Venice were then among the most active in establishing patterns for mills, pumps, winches, wagons, tools, and the weapons of war, and the design of these intrigued Leonardo. He haunted the wrights and masters of forge and mill to observe design change and progress and to record them in his notebooks.

Beyond the general categories of civilian and military application, Leonardo's designs do not lend themselves readily to rational subdivision, since he usually followed the sketch for one device with another unrelated one. Let us therefore choose some readily distinguishable device, focusing on its ingenuity of design, and then move on to others.

170/1 and 2

One of Leonardo's earliest machine designs, the elegantly rendered file maker below from Codex Atlanticus, folio 6 recto, reflects his intuitive grasp of the modern concept of automation. He builds into the mechanism a sequence of co-ordinated and interdependent actions that, once started, do not require further human decision. Turning the crank in the foreground of this design sets off a series of co-ordinated motions: the rope wound around the crankshaft unwinds; the far end of the crankshaft strikes a lug attached to the pivoted axle which holds the long hammer handle; the prongs of the sprocket wheel strike the lugs of the hammer axle, raising the hammer; the hammer then falls to strike the blank file and leave a series of furrows on its surface. The design thus provides for increased production of files and, with the chance for

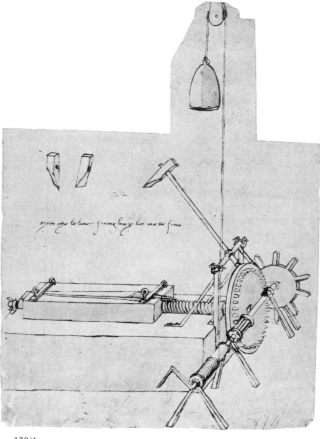

170/1

human error reduced, greater uniformity of product. About 1495, in Atlanticus, folio 21 recto-a, Leonardo incorporated the same advantages into the mechanism at right, which automatically stamps gold foil used for decorative purposes. The assembly view, at the top left of the drawing, shows the six stamping units that are activated by a master crown gear, which is turned by a power source such as an animal or water mill. The sketch at top right demonstrates how the foil is drawn into the machine. At the bottom are seven ways of loading the hammer for greater impact.

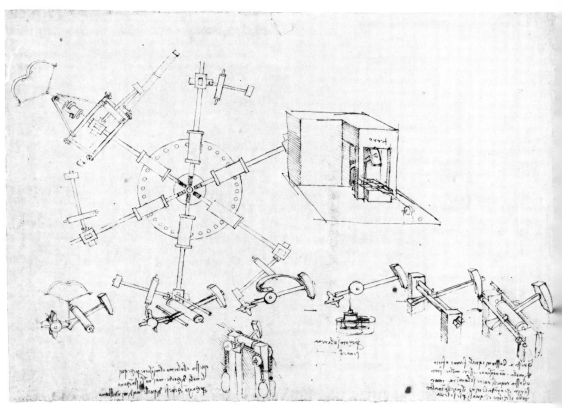

170/2

Let us examine a machine for making a tool almost as common as the hammer and used for shaping wood, metal, or stone – the rasp, or file. It is very easy to use but difficult to fashion. As with so many other efficient tools, higher skills go into their fabrication than are required for their use. Leonardo approached the solution to the file-making problem by designing a machine to strike file teeth evenly on the face of a metal blank, which could afterwards be hardened by the tempering methods then known to craftsmen [170/1].

The result of the automated and interlocked operation of this machine is a quickly executed file face of uniform grooves. When the weight's descent is completed, the hammer is raised to disjoin lug and sprocket, the crank again raises the weight, and the indenting of the grooves on the file's face is continued. At the left of his drawing of the machine – one of Leonardo's very early drawings, dated by G. Calvi at about 1480 – Leonardo sketched two different hammer heads with which to cut grooves with other angles or to produce cross-cut grooves. In its simplicity and elegance the line and wash rendering of the drawing makes it as ready a guide to the construction of the machine as to its understanding.

With the same need for transferring individual skills into devices that would provide greater uniformity of product and higher output per operator (at lower cost per unit produced), Leonardo designed a machine for the automatic stamping of gold foil. The assembly indicates a plan for six units motivated by a master crown gear turned by some prime mover, such as a water mill or an animal [170/2].

Leonardo sketched dozens of devices aimed at translating movement back and forth between rotary motion and piston-like reciprocating action. The drawing below of a windlass to be used for hoisting heavy loads is so exacting and finely detailed as to be the envy of a 20th-century engineering draftsman. The assembly view is at left, the exploded view at right. The weight to be lifted can be seen hanging from the lantern

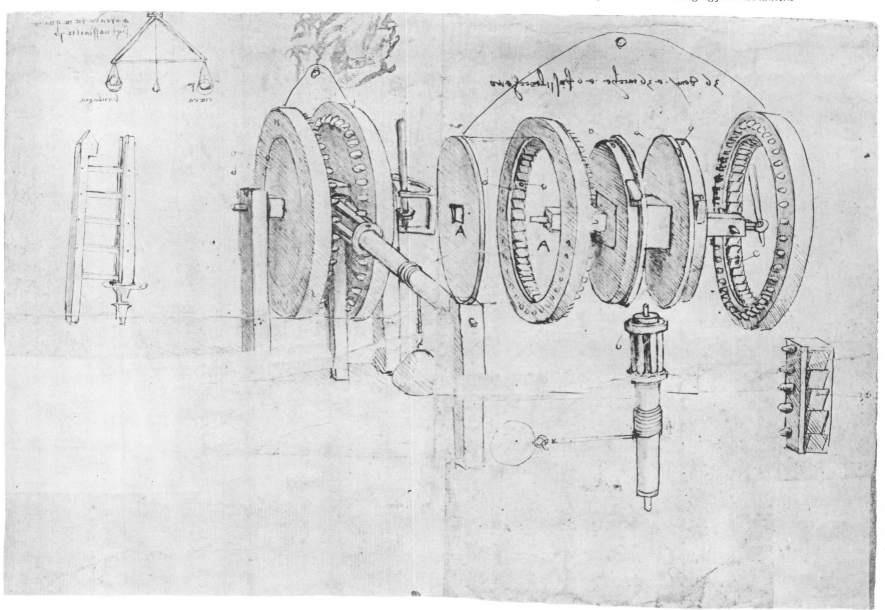

171/1

Turning from utilitarian designs to the more abstract, Leonardo sketched a brilliant resolution to the problem of translating rotary to reciprocating motion, or vice versa. The illustration is so clear and instructive that it hardly requires explanation [171/1].

This ingenious mechanism can be used as a windlass or a hoist or in several schemes Leonardo had for automotive vehicles. One application of the mechanism that was sketched by Leonardo is for the propulsion of a boat [172/1]. Another application is suggested by Leonardo in a Codex Madrid I drawing of a foot-operated grain mill [172/2].

Yet another of the many studies of the reciprocating-to-rotary-motion problem that occupied Leonardo's mind has a solution drawn in about 1495, in Codex Madrid I [172/4].[3]

gear. Motion begins when the operator manipulates back and forth the vertical lever which is set into a square shaft at the right of the assembly view. His reciprocating motion activates the system built into the wheels and shown in the exploded view. Pawls on the two inner discs engage ratchets that line the two outer rings. Gear teeth on the same outer rings engage the common lantern gear at the end of the shaft holding the weight. When the vertical lever is moved forward, one pawl moves one gear. When the lever is moved back, the other pawl grips the gear and turns the shaft. No matter which gear is activated, the lantern gear is moved constantly counterclockwise and the weight is lifted.   ATLANTICUS 8v-b

Below, a boat with vertical paddles is propelled by the same system used to operate
the windlass on the preceding page. The
paddles are turned by treadles which are
moved up and down by a mechanism similar to that of the windlass.

ATLANTICUS 344r-b

172/1

A foot-operated grain mill (below) is
another version of the windlass proposal.
Pumping the treadles seen in the assembly
view at center sets the levers into alternate
motion, making the central shaft revolve
and, through the crown gear, turn the mill-
stone.

MADRID I 70v

172/2

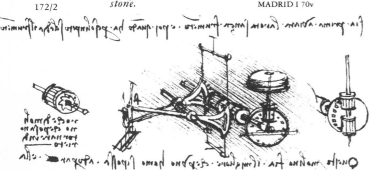

The mechanism at right was designed to
grind and polish the insides of cylinders.

ATLANTICUS 291r

172/3

The two sketches below, intended as studies
on the reciprocating-to-rotary motion problem, propose another solution. The lever in
the right-hand design is pumped up and
down while the pawls on the vertical rods
engage the ratchets on the cylinder. On the
downbeat, the pawls slide past the ratchets;
on the upbeat, they engage the ratchets and
turn the cylinder.

MADRID I 123v

172/4

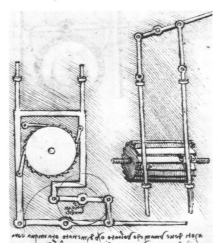

Some of the elements of the preceding machines are contained in an advanced
mechanism for grinding an internal cylindrical bore such as might be required
for a bearing – a grinding and lapping device [172/3]. Leonardo sketched
the rough cylinder clamped by two hollow vise jaws held firm by adjusting
wing nuts (which, to produce pressure, should have been on the inside of
the studs). The reamer, or lapper, extends partway into the bore. Grooves
are cut into the outer surface of the reamer to hold the polishing, or lapping,
compound of oil and emery. The top of the reamer rises through a complex
and ingenious mechanism consisting of a spur gear, as seen, having an internal
thread of high pitch. Into this thread is fitted a bolt having the matching
outer pitch and a rectangular inner bore. The gear is confined by the two
horizontal plates so it can revolve but not move vertically. The threaded bolt

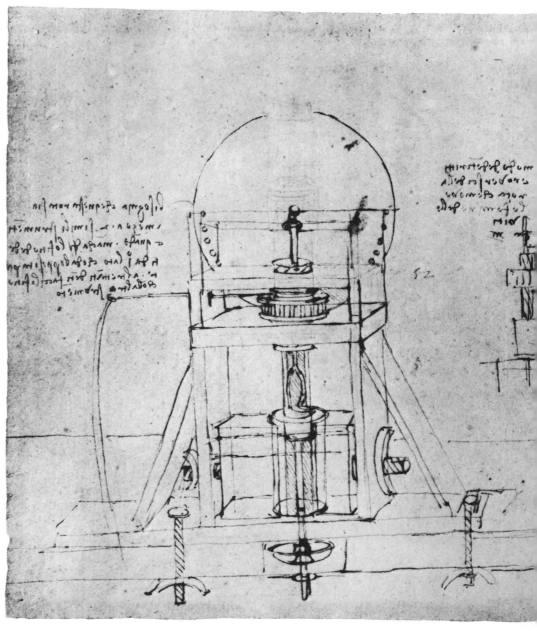

rides up and down within the gear as it turns, because it is confined by the
rectangular inner shank. The circular plate has a semicircle of gear teeth that
engage the horizontal gear. At the extreme left is a vertical spring rod. From
the top of this rod a string passes through the stud and is wound upon a
collar extending above the gear. The device is now ready to lap the cylinder
bore. The large disc is turned, the teeth engage the gear, it revolves and
so causes the bolt to turn and descend into the bore. But the disc teeth
and the gear become disengaged at the half-revolution. The spring takes over
and the taut string unwinds, causing the gear motion to reverse and the bolt
to ascend, thereby reversing the polishing motion. The top is reached, the
disc teeth engage once more, and the cycle is repeated as long as the disc

is revolved. The reamer thus turns and reverses as it moves up and down.[4] Excess lapping compound drips into the small dish beneath the bore.

The bent of Leonardo's mind and his efforts to automate as many coacting motions as possible are evident in this assembly. That there existed a practical application of such a device is evident from the growing number and variety of machines then being used. Boring devices were required for pumps and cylinders, for mills, locks, ships' gear, hydraulic fittings, valves for liquors and for cannon and other armaments. Close tolerances were required for the meshing of gears and for accurate bearings, and Leonardo was aware that a mechanized means of bearing fabrication was superior to a manual one.

That Leonardo was a journeyman's engineer and not an impractical dreamer is evident from his concern with the basic materials from which tools and engines were wrought. To build machines, a wright must have metal bands and plates, facilities for casting odd shapes, and tools for cutting, bending, twisting, and turning coarse and fine metal sections. Leonardo knew that after rough fashioning surfaces had to be prepared, ground, fitted, or polished. With increased industrialization an increase in standardization became mandatory, as well as a higher availability of cutting and shaping materials and tools and their greater mechanization. We shall therefore examine some of the devices that Leonardo designed to fashion metal sections by employing advance machines for converting simple motion and limited energy into uniform and required basic shapes of metal and wood.

One among a large family of metal-fashioning machines is an assembly of rollers for producing flat tin sheets that Leonardo drew [173/1]. The assembly is indicated in a bottom sketch that shows a crank-operated gear of small diameter acting on a large gear so as to provide a high mechanical advantage, since metal rolling is a very difficult task. The arrangement is elementary but Leonardo has added a significant touch, in an upper sketch. Realizing that the enormous stresses of this method of moving metal would cause a roller of any sturdiness to bow at its center (resulting in a convex section of rolled plate), he has added two pressure idlers, one at the center of the top roller and a corresponding one on the lower roller. These secondary rollers would reduce the diverging thrust at the main rollers' centers and give a more uniform cross section to the rolled plate. Simple as the rollers appear, they are considered by Feldhaus[5] to be the earliest known to historians of technology. They were drawn about 1497.

Leonardo revealed more of the thoughts he contributed to the rolling of metals in illustrating an assembly for drawing bands of copper [173/2]. Designed rather late (about 1515) it consists of a bench with a crank and worm gear slowly turning a horizontal spur gear having iron teeth. The gear's shaft has a second worm on it and this meshes with a vertical gear. Integral to the shaft of this gear is a cylinder on which the drawn coil of copper strip is wound. The drawing dies are shown at the right in Leonardo's plan view; a driven wedge controls the pressure of the upper die. The drawing of the plan view (from above the assembly) should have been placed above, not below, the elevation view (from the side).

For many people today all aspects of war arouse a negative feeling, a revulsion brought on by the excesses of four major wars in a century still only two-thirds over. A document such as the Madrid manuscripts therefore provides a measure of historical change and of the relationship of an unusual mind to its times. Leonardo hated war as strongly as any rational person has ever hated it, calling it "beastly madness"; but living in the unsettled condition of northern Italy at the end of the 1400s, he was exposed to the demands of incessant war and the sweep of invading armies against his people in Tuscany and Lombardy.

Leonardo served three lords in some military advisory capacity, displaying a continual interest in the design and technology of military structures and weapons rather than battlefield tactics and maneuvers.

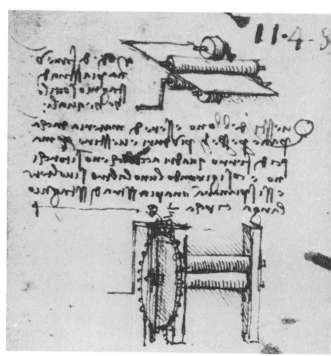

173/1

173/2

The machine below looks remarkably like a modern lathe and is often mistaken for one. Actually, its function is to bore holes in the centers of logs, which were used as water mains until cast-iron pipes took their place late in the 17th century. The drilling mechanism is in the foreground, but the novel aspect is the set of automatically adjustable chucks shown clamping the log in the four radial positions. The chucks ensure that the axis of the log always

In the wood planer sketched below, Leonardo makes use of a set of adjustable clamps similar in concept to that employed in the boring device at left. The main sketch shows the facing jaws that open or close according to the size of the log being planed. Their simultaneous action is regulated by a cord wrapped around the capstan in the foreground. A set of threaded nuts raises the timber to permit the plane to trim the top surface. ATLANTICUS 38v-b

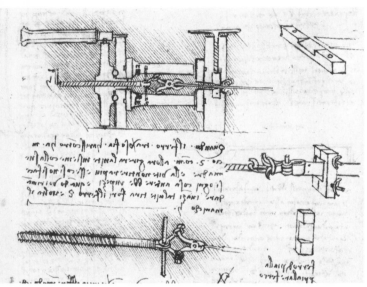

174/1

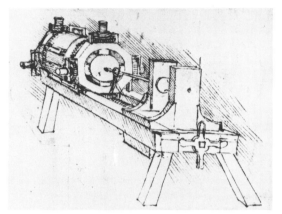

174/2

remains in the center of the machine regardless of the log's diameter. ATLANTICUS 393r-b

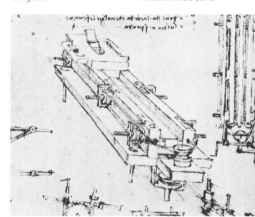

174/3

Leonardo's notebooks often read like a modern mail-order catalogue that offers an ingenious tool or gadget for every conceivable purpose. The device above mechanizes the primitive techniques then used for forming wire by pulling it through dies. The main view, a cross section, shows the large crank-operated bolt which ends in a hook-and-eye fitted over the handles of tongs. The tongs clasp the strip of wire (sketches below and at right of main view) so that the stronger the pull, the tighter the grip on the wire. The crank, at top left, is encased in a loose sleeve to afford the operator a more effective grip. The vertical threaded bolt in the right part of the main view adjusts the dies to proper spacing. Additional dies in horizontal and vertical positions are at the right of the drawing. Ball bearings reduce the friction between the two discs, top left.

MADRID I 84r

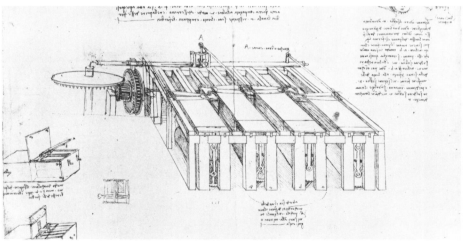

174/4

About 1495 Leonardo invented the shearing machine above to cut the nap off woolen cloth – a process then carried out by shearmen with enormous scissors who had to crop the nap like a barber. In Leonardo's design the cloth was stretched on a traveling frame which was pulled through the machine. The gearwork activated the second blades of scissor-like devices. Leonardo also devised a machine, called a gig mill, for raising the nap on woolen cloth. His gig mill and its successors were so efficient that they put manual laborers out of work; early in the

Industrial Revolution widespread use of the gig mill caused riots in England.

ATLANTICUS 397r-a

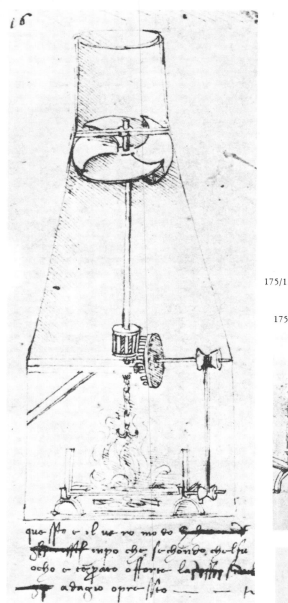

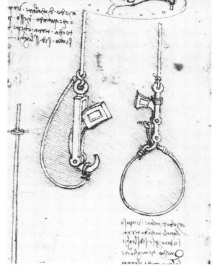

175/1

175/2

175/3

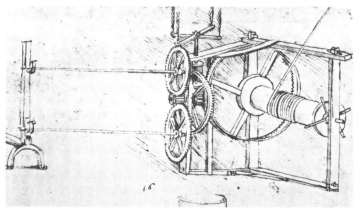

The devices above, from Codex Madrid I, are release mechanisms for automatically releasing a load when it reaches the bottom of its descent. The hooked weight on each device is kept in position by the tension of the load. When the cargo reaches bottom and tension eases, the weight pivots downwards, uncoupling the hook.   MADRID I 9v

Leonardo, who was born about the same time Gutenberg invented the printing press, proposed the device below for repositioning the press mechanically after an impression had been made. He also anticipated modern engraving methods with a process using copper plates etched in relief, which would have allowed much finer reproduction of his intricate drawings than the woodcuts then in use. In fact, though Italy was the printing center of Europe, none of the treatises that Leonardo intended to publish was printed until 132 years after his death. In 1651 an abstract of his notes on painting was published in Paris.   ATLANTICUS 358r-b

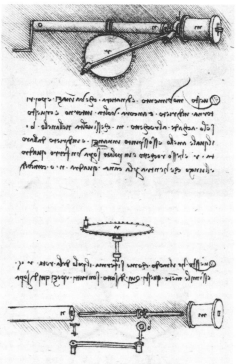

175/4

175/1 and 2

Leonardo became aware very early of the power inherent in the harnessing of heated air. Like an ingenious home handyman, he put his discovery to practical use in the kitchen. The roasting device above, which was drawn about 1480 in one of his earliest technical studies, utilizes the heat of the fire to turn the meat automatically. At a time when nearly all cooking was done over an open fire, Leonardo's design not only promised to liberate the cook but provided evidence of the first known use of a true airscrew. The upwards draft of hot air turns the vaned turbine set in the chimney. The turbine is geared to a pulley arrangement which turns the spit. "The roast will turn slow or fast depending on whether the fire is small or strong," noted Leonardo. He sketched on the same page of the Codex Atlanticus, folio 5 verso-a, another mechanical spit (above, right) powered in less imaginative fashion – by a descending weight attached to a pulley-and-gear drive.

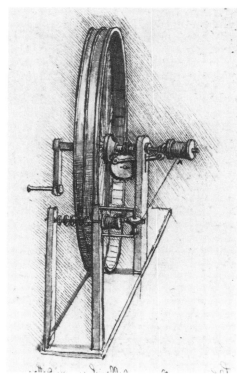

175/5 and 6

As a young man Leonardo learned the textile craft in Florence, then a mecca for those seeking fine cloth, and he later sketched scores of improvements. The design above ensures the even winding of thread onto a bobbin. The intricate winding mechanism is shown in detail in another illustration (above, right). The top sketch is an assembly view; below it is an exploded view. As the crank

turns the main shaft of the mechanism, the connecting rod moves the bobbin axially in and out of the hollow shaft, enabling the thread to be wound uniformly on the bobbin's cylindrical face. Leonardo also designed a number of mechanical looms and a needle-sharpening machine that he calculated in the Codex Atlanticus would earn him 60,000 ducats a year – a princely income that apparently never materialized.

MADRID I 65v, 29v

175/6

The design of Leonardo's weapons falls into three general categories: ballista (catapult), cannon, and arquebus (musket). The ballista was of classical origin. Leonardo derived much of his mechanical and military information from reading the references in technological texts in contemporary military literature and from his contact with military men who, like himself, were in the employ of the Duke of Milan. Through his father, Ser Piero da Vinci, notary to the governing council of Florence, he had contact with the military men of that strong city-state. From reading the works of Archimedes, Pliny, and especially

Leonardo's concept of a big ballista was classically drawn and so enormous that it dwarfed the bowman who had to trigger it. The huge bow is built with laminated sections for greater flexibility and firepower. The canted wheels on the carriage furnish a

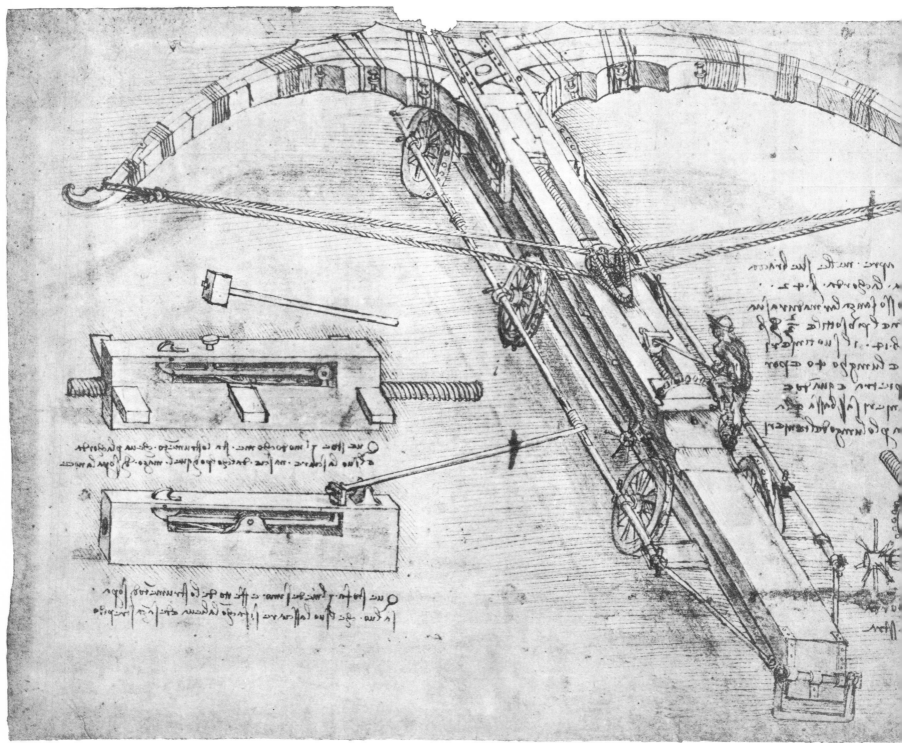

176/1

more stable firing base, a feature later incorporated in the wheels of artillery pieces. Two versions of tripping mechanisms are shown at left. ATLANTICUS 53v-ab

Vitruvius, he learned the military methods and technology of the Roman period. Among his contemporaries, he was influenced by Francesco di Giorgio Martini [6] and by Roberto Valturio, whose book *De re militari* was published first in 1472 and again in 1483. An older variation on his work is that of Flavius Vegetius, a Roman writer whose treatise on military tactics was reissued through the centuries and constantly modernized. Both books were illustrated by crude, naive, anachronistic woodcuts, in contrast to the clear, striking draftsmanship of Leonardo.

One of Leonardo's most famous drawings is that of a huge ballista shown with some advanced features of design; the drawing is so skillful as to make it a classic of graphic representation in engineering [176/1]. Leonardo indicated the great bow in laminated sections for maximum flexibility. The bowstring is drawn back by the worm and the gear shown in the lower right corner. Two releasing trips are shown, at lower left. The upper is spring-pivoted and released by a hammer blow; the lower is tripped by lever action. The bowman, as shown in the main view, bears down on the bar and, by lifting the encased lever, releases the string. The wheels are canted to give them a wider, more stable base and also to reduce road shock. A similar means was later used in canting the spokes of most artillery wheels.

A rapid-fire crossbow mechanism is as impressive in design as it is in its illustration by Leonardo [178/1]. Tension is given to the strings of each of four bows mounted on the inner periphery of a large treadwheel. The treadwheel

This crossbow spans 42 ells in its arms;
that is, where the rope is attached;
and without its armor it is 1 ell and
⅔ in the thickest point, and ⅔ of an
ell in the thinnest one. Its mounting is 14 ells.
Its stem is 2 ells large and 40 long; and
it charges 100 pounds of stone;
and when it is on the way, the stem is
lowered and the crossbow is aligned along the stem.

177/1

Until the refinement of the cannon, the principal artillery weapon was the catapult or ballista — as the larger models, such as Leonardo's on the opposite page, were called. The print above showing a ballista and the explosive shot that the weapon's multiple bows could fling at the enemy is from a copper engraving made in 1588. Similar devices, capable of hurling oversized lances and huge stones, were used 15 centuries earlier by the Roman legions, who called their deadly ballista "scorpion."

is rotated on a horizontal axle by a team of men who walk on a circumference of outer treads and thereby provide continuous rotation for rapid fire. An archer hangs suspended in the mechanism's center; his task is to trigger each crossbow as it descends the quadrant before him, shooting through the slot in the structure at left. The main axle is not rotative and could therefore be fitted with lines and hooks for drawing each bowstring back as the bow is rotated into firing position. A board is shown protruding into the firing line, indicating Leonardo's intention to hold the wheel for a proper aiming interval. Also noteworthy is the heavy, pivoted baffle of planks to protect the treaders. Leonardo places the treaders on the outer periphery of the rim (rather than on the inner rim, as was then customary) for greater leverage and efficiency. The drawing combines signs of hasty overdrawing of lines and circles with precise mortising of joists and braces, exact planking of the treads, and the long and precise shading lines of a left-hander, applied not to the object but to the background so as to accentuate the machine. To the right of the main design is a preliminary sketch showing the operators in dynamic activity.

Many other of Leonardo's sketches show ballistas and catapults using the energy stored in bent and twisted wooden arms, in metal springs, and in the torque of ropes twisted by the use of worms and gears or racks and pinions. Many of these designs appear in older sources, for Leonardo transferred to his notebooks any that were of interest to him.

The firepower of guns and artillery continually engaged Leonardo, and some of his finest studies concerned them. It was 150 years after that fateful day at Crécy in 1346 when two cannons attended by 12 English cannoneers first

This delightful contraption is a kind of crossbow, a machine gun that enables Leonardo's archer—suspended inside the big treadwheel—to keep the arrows flying at a

rapid pace. The archer's comrades furnish the foot power to turn the wheel under the protection of a planked shield Leonardo has provided for them. At right, a preliminary sketch shows wheel and bowmen in whirling action.   ATLANTICUS 387r-ab

fired a shot propelled by gunpowder at an enemy in battle. Yet a casual examination of some of Leonardo's sketches would indicate that his techniques were those of an artillerist of the mid-1800s. In some respects he was ahead of even those days. He was, for instance, concerned with good shrapnel[7] design, with breech instead of muzzle loading, with ease and speed of fire, with multiple fire, and with advanced gun-construction methods, including water cooling of gun barrels. Leonardo proposed setting the barrel of one breech-loading gun into a sealed copper casing filled with water "in order that once fired, the copper soon abandons its heat." This water-cooled gun fired iron-tipped bolts, and Leonardo called it *fulminaria* because of its lightning fury [179/2].

In Codex Madrid I there are more than a dozen notes and diagrams related to matters of arms and ordnance. These are essentially probes into the theoretical action of stressed crossbows and the behavior of discharged bolts; but, more interesting, two of the notes pertain to the coupling of rockets with balls fired from cannon. In the crossbow series [8] Leonardo attempted to relate bow

Make the stem, which gathers the rope charging the crossbow, ⅓ thick, so that a turn gathers one ell of rope. So, since the above-named stem is one third, its half will be one sixth, and the lever is five ells, that is, 30 sixths; and one sixth is the counter lever, so that you have here 30 against 1. Therefore it appears clear that if you place over the head of the lever 20 men weighing 4,000 pounds, they will exert against the counter lever a force of 120,000 pounds, enough to charge the 4 crossbows.

179/1
The deadly looking, dart-like missile below is an early form of the high-explosive artillery shell. Leonardo meant for this, and a similar projectile that he designed for Lodovico Sforza, to be fired from a catapult. The two fins jutting back from the pointed nose – Leonardo calls them horns – contain powder which ignites upon impact.
WINDSOR 12651

179/2
In a day when the use of long-range firearms was still relatively new, Leonardo advanced

179/1

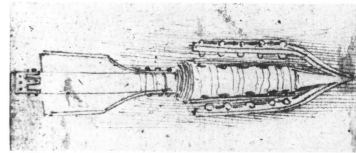

179/2

tension to the range of the arrow, reminding the reader to allow for air resistance. On folio 59 he described an elaborate series of tests of crossbow effectiveness carried out by gauging the vertical rise of a weighted, graduated, and iron-pointed arrow and enabling it to register its penetration into the test-range soil [180/1]. He concluded that the indicated depth of penetration was in direct proportion to the arrow's vertical rise and to the order of tension given the bowstring, as measured by increasing weights. Leonardo used weights as the measure

such modern notions as a water-cooled gun barrel. The barrel of the gun above is breech-loading – itself a novelty. In the bottom sketch it is set in a copper casing filled with water "in order that once fired," writes Leonardo, "the copper soon abandons its heat."
ATLANTICUS 361r-c

of the input force and held gravity and the vertical trajectory as constant. It was Leonardo who confirmed the notion that an arrow shot vertically into the air will fall vertically downwards.[9] He followed the precepts of Albert of Saxony in describing the trajectory of a missile and was the earliest to draw the trajectory as a continuous curve.

The more revealing concern of Leonardo with ballistics is shown on folio 58 verso, where he proposed the vertical firing of two balls (separated by equal gunpowder charges between the breech, the lower ball, and the upper ball) from the bore of the same cannon. He described the simultaneous discharge, the top ball clearing the muzzle for the second ball, but he held that the first (top) ball would rise higher, having been assisted by the second ball's charge in addition to its own charge. He then introduced the factors of help or hindrance of distance, sound, flash, and impact due to the direction of the wind on a projectile. Firing in foggy air will result in a louder burst, as also will firing against a water surface or against a wall. In vertical firing, Leonardo said, "the cannonball moving upwards – be it because of the assistance of the upwards-moving flame or because the air becomes thinner and less resistant as the height increases – the ball will have the greatest accidental motion among all other possible directions."[10]

In a note on folio 59 verso Leonardo revealed his design for the simultaneous firing of a shaft and a rocket in order to attain a great height – a mile or more. The project involved pointing an arquebus vertically, with shaft and

180/1–4
Leonardo made these sketches of crossbows in Codex Madrid I as he recorded a series of ballistics tests that are remarkable as examples of his experimental method. "Test it first and state the rule afterward," he cautions in a note over one sketch (above, right). In the margin of the page above, he states one of his "rules": "The length of the arrows' descent will be proportional to the weights used in the spanning of the crossbow."   MADRID 1 59r, 51r, 57r

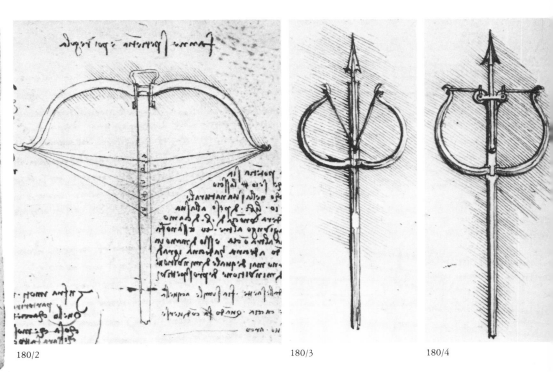

180/2   180/3   180/4

rocket of equal weight. Leonardo proposed that the rocket be ignited first, or that the rocket fire ignite the powder in the gun.

An expansion of this project is indicated by Leonardo on folio 81 verso [181/1]. He wrote, "To fire a rocket to great altitude, proceed this way: Set your cannon upright, as you see; load the cannon with a ball connected to a rocket by a chain, leaving the rocket on the outside, as shown by the figure. Then secure a small board, with gunpowder, level with the touchhole of the cannon. Having done this, fire the rocket, and the rocket's fire, falling on the board and the touchhole, will fire the cannon. The cannonball will drive the rocket more than 3 miles high and a flame half a mile long will be seen trailing the rocket." Here again, the coupling of rocket to cannonball is intended to reach unusually high altitudes.

Obviously Leonardo speculated about (or experimented with) these projects for no direct military purposes, since no target existed in vertical space. It can therefore be taken that these were exercises in novel ballistic combinations, with methods already provided to measure range by soil penetration. For the heading on one folio showing some of this investigation, 51 recto, Leonardo wrote, "Test it first and state the rule afterward."

He explained dynamic phenomena on the theory of "impetus," which meant to him that a moving body continued motion in a straight line. But he did not adhere to the view of Albert of Saxony that the trajectory of a projectile was divided into three periods: the initial violent impetus; the secondary period, in which gravity begins to act; and the tertiary, in which gravity and air resistance dominate over the impressed impetus.[11] The Italian mathematician Niccolò Tartaglia still followed this traditional belief in his first book (1537);[12] in a second book, written almost 10 years later,[13] he took up the subject again, arriving at the timid conclusion that no part of a trajectory can be perfectly rectilinear. But we are still far from the parabolic trajectories traced by Galileo and calculated mathematically by Newton (1687).

The fact is that up to the late 17th century all military treatises dealing with artillery still depict the trajectory of a cannonball in the form of two straight lines, the second perfectly vertical, united by a short curved section [181/2].

Leonardo could not develop mathematical ballistics. But his unerring eye saw the truth, and his precise pen put the correct curve, a parabola deformed

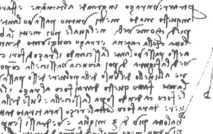

181/1
Some of Leonardo's proposals for ballistics tests seem to foreshadow the multistage rocket launchings of today. Below, he suggests a piggyback probe that combines the firepower of a cannonball and a rocket. The rocket ignites the cannonball, which would then drive the rocket (left) higher than anyone dreamed possible – "more than 3 miles high" and trailing flame, exults the inventor, "half a mile long." MADRID I 81v

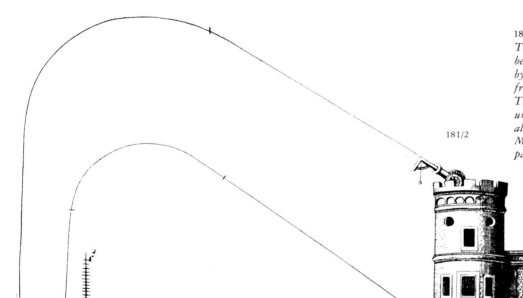

181/2

181/2 and 3
The trajectory of a cannonball, it was believed, formed two straight lines connected by a short curve – as in the drawing at left from a military treatise published in 1613. Though this erroneous notion prevailed until the late 17th century, Leonardo already had correctly drawn in Codex Madrid I, folio 147 recto (below), the proper parabolic curve deformed by air resistance.

181/3

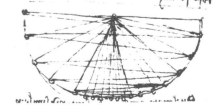

by air resistance, into many illustrations – in Codex Madrid I, for instance, when he was developing his theory about accidental and natural movements, comparing pendular motion with that of a projectile [181/3]. The same reasoning was done by Galileo in 1632.

Leonardo sensed the increase of air resistance to a projectile with the increase of the projectile's velocity, without determining the exact ratio of this increase. "The air becomes denser before bodies that penetrate it swiftly, acquiring so more or less density as the speed is of greater or lesser fury."[14] In spite of the inadequacy of his experimental equipment, Leonardo perceived the parabolic nature (without naming it as such) of ballistic trajectories. He recognized the important role of air influencing the curve, whereas Galileo considered air resistance negligible.[15] The marvelous ogive-headed projectiles provided with directional fins that were drawn by Leonardo several times illustrate a practical application of this recognition [182/1]. Leonardo studied also the more manageable curves of jets of water issuing from an orifice under varying heads of pressure and related these to projectile curves [182/2]. Torricelli, who followed the steps of Galileo, still neglected air resistance when tracing his ballistic curves.[16] But experimenting with water jets, Torricelli, like Leonardo 150 years before, observes that even if they describe a parabola, their descending part is *magis prona,* that is, deformed by the resistance of the medium.[17] The mathematical solution of the ballistic curve involving air resistance was provided by Newton in 1687.

A contribution was made by Leonardo to the then still novel mechanism for firing handguns, the matchlock. In a set of drawings of about 1495 are shown three matchlock mechanisms for uncovering the pan that holds the priming gunpowder at the barrel touchhole and applying simultaneously the lighted match in the form of a slow-burning wick soaked in nitre, not shown in the drawings [183/1]. Leonardo wrote, "The purpose of this mechanism is to get fire to the touchhole at the pan *g* and simultaneously to open the powder charge to be ignited." Action on the trigger, right, causes the complex of levers, springs, and bearings to lift the protective plate over the pan and apply the match held in the jaws of the "serpent" shown on the right of the coacting mechanism.

182/1 and 2
Leonardo was unable to arrive at a mathematical solution to the trajectory problem – that had to wait for Isaac Newton in 1687. Nor did he have the experimental equipment necessary for close

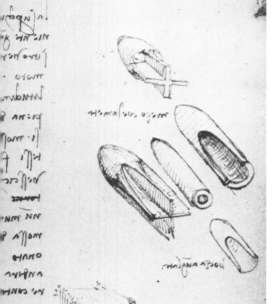

182/1

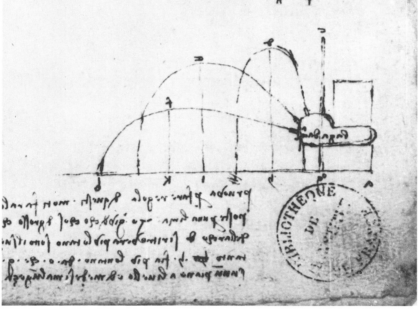

Test in order to make a rule of these motions. You must make it with a leather bag full of water with many small pipes of the same inside diameter, disposed on one line.

182/2

monitoring of actual cannonball trajectories. Instead, the resourceful engineer resorted to observation and analysis of jets of water in Manuscript C, folio 7 recto (right), and related their trajectories to those of projectiles. Unlike Galileo more than a century later, Leonardo recognized the role played by air resistance. To lessen that resistance, he proposed far ahead of his time the streamlining of missiles and providing them with directional fins (above) in Codex Arundel, folio 54 recto.

The effectiveness of the hand-held gun was recognized in the century 1470–1570. The arquebus with its clumsy matchlock evolved into the musket with its various types of firing mechanisms, including the flintlock. To Leonardo goes the credit for the earliest representation of a functioning wheel lock.[18] This can be seen from the several alternative forms in the sketches in the Codex Atlanticus [19] where a connecting chain from the mainspring to the wheel spindle is shown [183/2–3]. Leonardo sketched, in section, the main heavy coil spring, the tripping mechanism, right, and the sparking pyrites holder, left. This design, however, drew the attention of historians of technology more for its clear showing of a chain-and-sprocket linkage than as a gunpowder-ignition mechanism. Leonardo's sketch is believed to have been made by 1500, but the earliest wheel-lock mechanism is credited to a Nuremberg watchmaker 15 years later. The complex wheel lock continued in use for two centuries. Although it was more efficient than the flintlock, complexity and efficiency lost out to the simpler and cheaper flintlock until it also was replaced by the percussion musket with the fulminating cap in the mid-1830s and by the magazine rifle of 1890. The wheel-lock principle carries over into the modern flint-and-wheel cigarette lighter.

A favorite design theme for Leonardo was the multiple-barrel light cannon that approached the structure of the Gatling gun. By this means he tried to attain rapid fire, simpler manipulation, and more accurate aim (or widescattering of the shot) on the target [184/2]. The designs also permit the reloading of the powder and shot to proceed while the artillerist fires one set of guns and while the second set cools before being loaded [185/1]. These drawings of multiple-barreled guns illustrate both Leonardo's artistry and advanced designs. The traction wheels are represented by simple circles.

An unusual piece of artillery was designed and termed *architronito* by Leonardo. This consisted of a cannon that depended on the sudden generation of steam to drive the shot out of the barrel. The breech was built into a basket-like brazier containing the burning coals. With the shot rammed back and the breech section sufficiently heated, a small amount of water was injected into what would normally be the powder chamber. "And when consequently the water has fallen out it will descend onto the heated part of the machine, and there it will instantly become changed into so much steam that it will seem marvelous, and especially when one sees its fury and hears its roar. This machine has driven a ball weighing 1 talent 6 stadia" [186/1]. This would indicate that such a gun had actually been made. Evidently the rate of fire was a lesser consideration. Putting steam's expansive power to work was novel

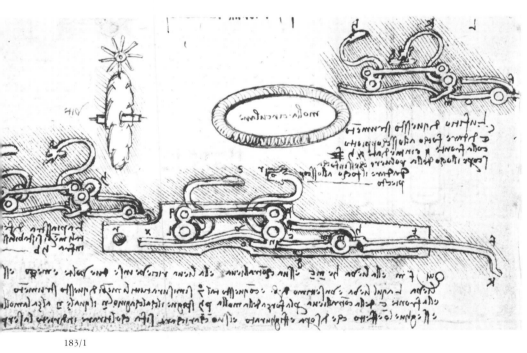

183/1

indeed, in Leonardo's time. The idea was by no means impractical. Steam cannons were used during the American Civil War and even in the Second World War (Holman projectors).[20]

A journey into future mechanization and use of hydraulic power (to wit, Pelton-type turbine blades) is made by Leonardo in a remarkable design for an assembly of elements to draw sections to form the barrel of a cannon. Large cannon were built up by combining forged tapered segmental sections to form the barrel, then binding the segments together by driving metal rings upon the barrel segments, much like driving hoops upon barrel staves, or by winding multiple layers of steel wires. Leonardo's scheme for drawing gun-barrel segments is one of several such proposed methods [186/2]. Starting with the prime mover, a horizontal water-driven reaction turbine shown at the lower left of the assembly as illustrated by Leonardo, the vertical power shaft drives the two geared wheels through a common worm. This causes the shaft attached to the left wheel to turn and give power to its own worm. The gear set

The matchlock – which fired a handgun by igniting powder with a slow match – was still a novelty about 1495, but Leonardo already was at work improving it. In the wonderfully sinuous drawing at left, Codex

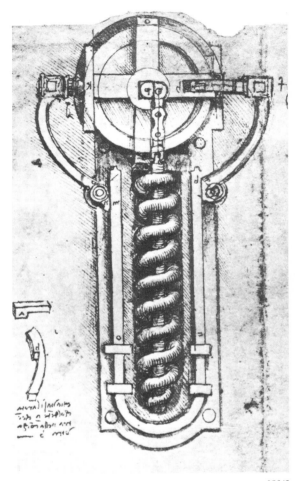

183/2

Madrid I, folio 18 verso, he sketches three mechanisms for simultaneously opening the powder charge and getting fire to the touch-hole. The match is gripped by the jaws of the "serpent" (top right of the drawing) and struck when the trigger is pulled. Nonetheless, the matchlock was a clumsy way to fire a gun and about five years later Leonardo came up with a clearly better method. The drawings shown above, Codex Atlanticus, folio 56 verso-b, are the earliest known rep-

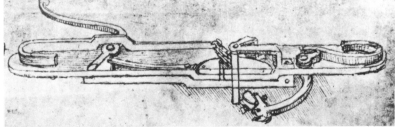

183/3

resentation of the wheel lock, which historians ascribe to a Nuremberg watchmaker 15 years later. The top sketch shows the steel wheel and helical mainspring. Next to them is the holder for the pyrite material used as the flint. The bottom sketch shows the trigger mechanism, which forces the wheel to rub against the flint and produce a spark, as in the modern cigarette lighter.

horizontally is caused to turn, thereby powering another vertical shaft and yet another worm. The engaged large vertical gear in the back is thereby rotated, and its power, now greatly multiplied (at a slower turning speed), is passed through the square shaft to the wheel on the right. This wheel is sturdily built and heavily armored by a helicoidal cam shown in the upper left sketch. Its purpose can be seen by following the sequence of operations passing from the prime mover through the gear wheel engaged on the right of its worm. This gear wheel has fastened to it an internally threaded shaft, through which rides a long threaded rod.

184/1–4 and 185/1 and 2

Leonardo's obsession with multiple effects in his weaponry led him to ingenious designs that were the forerunners of modern rapid-firing arms like the machine gun. His concepts called for a single artillery piece with a number of barrels, like the Gatling gun (below), which would not be invented

184/1

until 1862 during the American Civil War. A relatively simple Leonardo design with several barrels is shown at top right, Codex Atlanticus, folio 340 recto-b. A more complex version (center) from Atlanticus, folio 3 verso-a, has revolving racks of barrels, shown in enlarged detail at lower right, that enable the cannoneers to load one rack while a salvo is being fired from another set of barrels. The famous drawing on the opposite page, Codex Atlanticus, folio 56 verso-a, brings together two designs. In the center Leonardo cants the barrels to allow widescattering of the shot and provides a jack handle for raising or lowering the trajectory. At top and bottom the designs have rotating racks of barrels. The inset shows an actual model reconstructed from the drawing of the battery at top, consisting of three racks of 11 cannons each mounted on a triangular frame. Researchers have reconstructed models of a number of Leonardo's designs for weapons and machines. In building some machines they have found obvious mistakes in the drawings — a redundant wheel or extra gear — possibly put there deliberately by Leonardo to prevent others from stealing his designs and calling them their own.

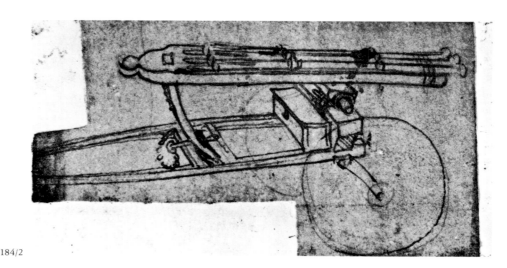

184/2

184/3

184/4

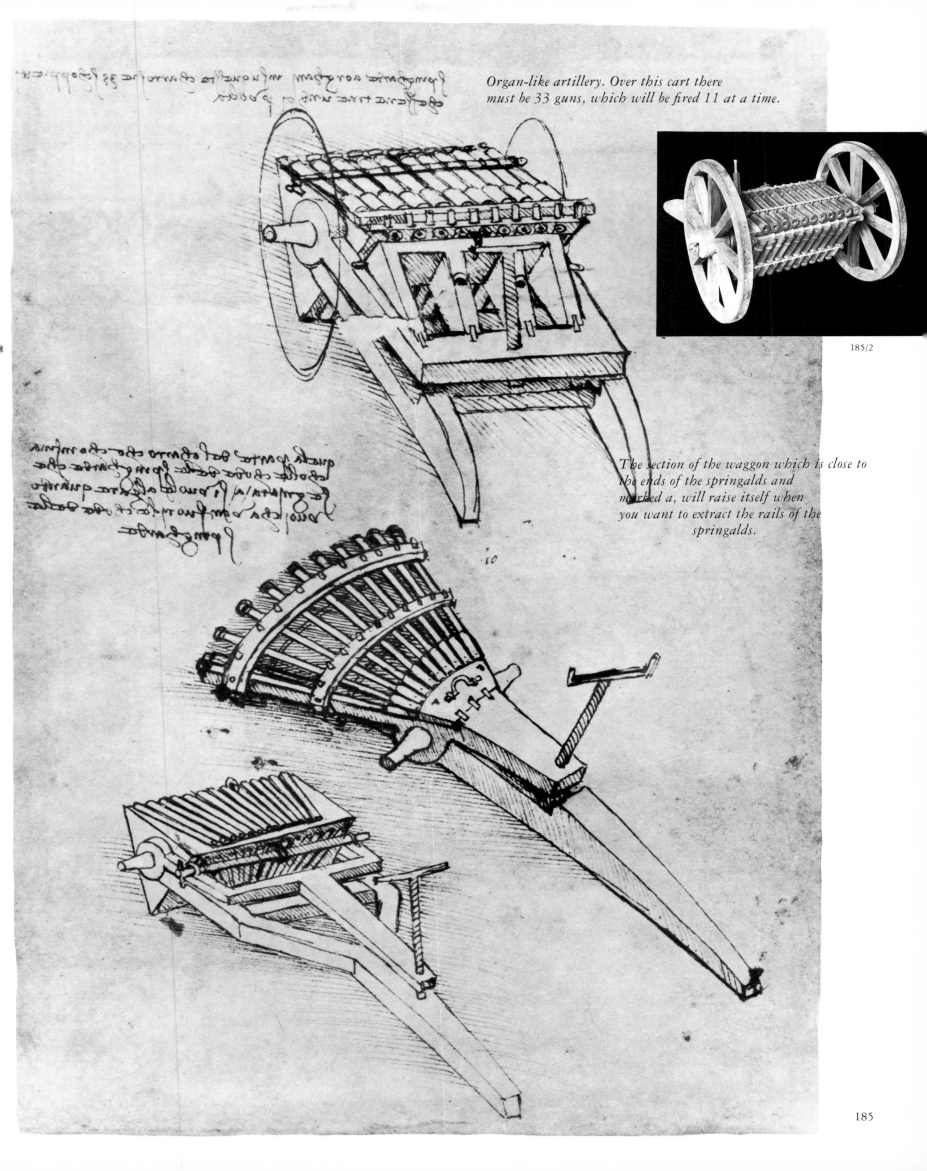

Organ-like artillery. Over this cart there
must be 33 guns, which will be fired 11 at a time.

185/2

The section of the waggon which is close to
the ends of the springalds and
marked a, will raise itself when
you want to extract the rails of the
springalds.

As the right gear wheel is turned, the threaded rod is drawn forward, thereby pulling a blank rod after it. This blank rod is forced into a segmental shape shown above the column of writing at the right. In addition, by means of the heavy cam pressure the breech end is drawn heavy, the muzzle end light, their inner-arc radii remaining the same. In the diagram below the drawing

Leonardo's ideas for putting the power of steam to work predated the designs of scientists who lived centuries later. The design below for the cannon he calls architronito — *a word he coined — depends upon steam*

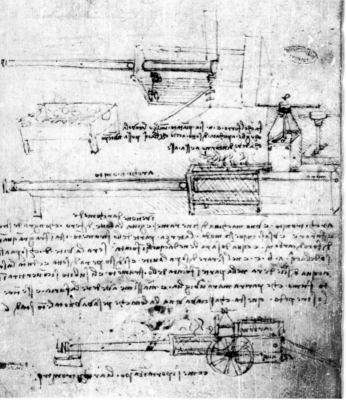

186/1

instead of gunpowder to fire the projectile. A brazier of burning coals heats the breech of the cannon. When water is poured into the powder chamber, writes Leonardo, "it will instantly become changed into so much steam that it will seem marvelous, and especially when one sees its fury and hears its roar."

MS. B 33r

186/2

At right, Leonardo designs a new machine tool for war. A hydraulically driven turbine powers the mill, which forms cannon barrels too large for traditional forging methods. In a remarkable complex sequence of co-ordinated actions, the mill fashions smooth, even segments for the barrel. The segments are then welded and banded together.

ATLANTICUS 2r-a

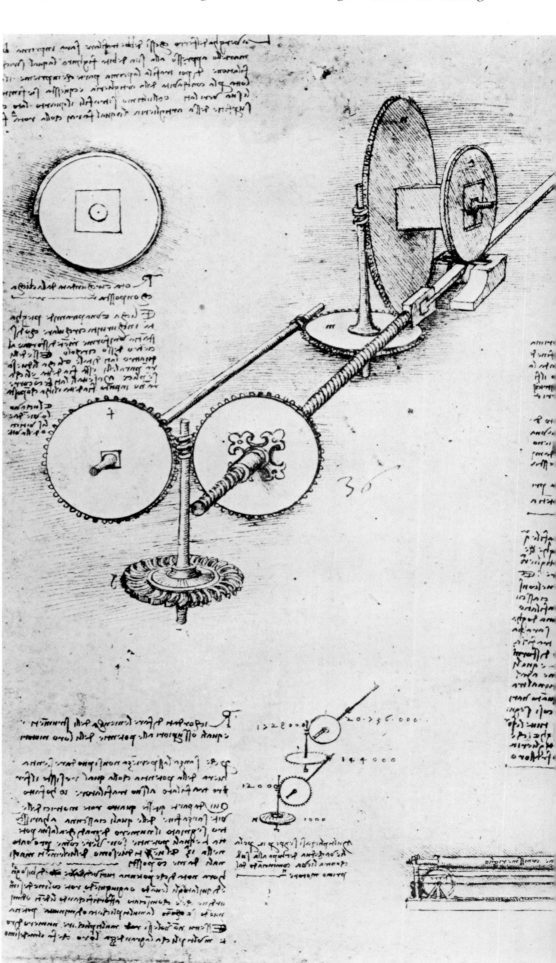

appears the schematic power ratio due to the gearing. Starting with the figure 1,000 at the turbine, there appears 12,000 at the first gear, 144,000 at the horizontal gear, 1,728,000 at the top big gear, and 20,736,000 at its shaft. A mechanical-advantage ratio of 1:12 is created at each step. Leonardo certainly knew the reduction of forces by friction, even though he does not seem to apply it here. Roller and ball bearings for friction reduction are one of his frequently used design elements.[21]

Some elaborate applications of ball and roller bearings are shown in several devices in the rediscovered Madrid material, where also the general subject of friction and friction-bearing materials is discussed. One also observes in these new notes Leonardo's striving for optimum mechanical advantage with

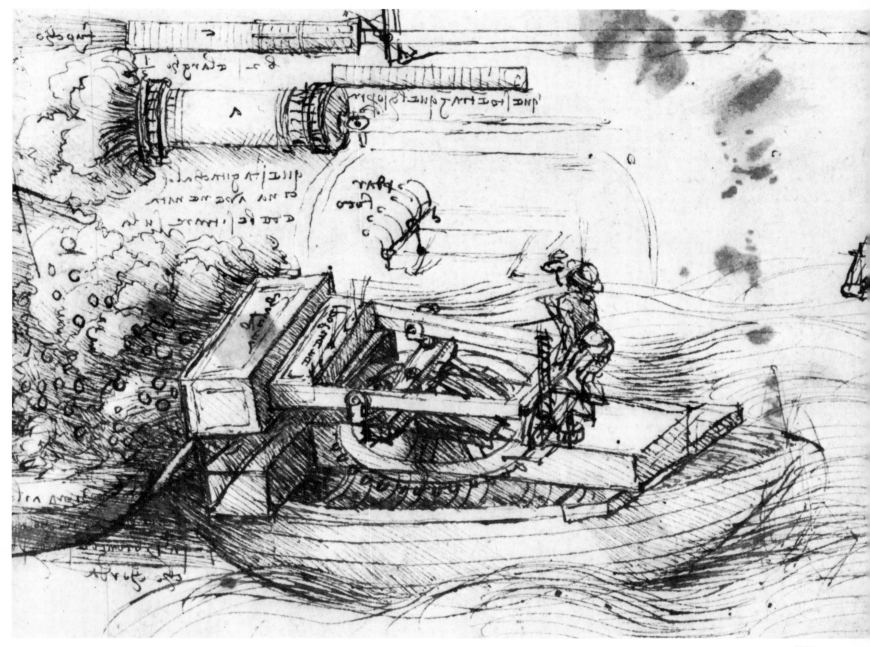

The fanciful artist and the practical military engineer join forces for a naval battle. At the top are two guns with barrels mounted on long shafts. The first one is to be fired by a tinder on a lever worked by a long string. The tube below this contains powder for the second gun. Below these sketches is a set of tinders for a six-barrel gun. But clearly it is the one-man battleship that captures Leonardo's fancy. A boxlike mortar

187/1

a minimum of friction. The Madrid Codices feature quite a number of mechanisms depending on ball and roller bearings and, to the surprise of many modern designers, on conical bearings. Leonardo experimentally determined an average coefficient of friction of one-quarter the weight of a flat-surfaced object.[22] He scoffed at perpetual motion and moved towards the elements of automation that one expects of modern mechanisms. In military affairs he aimed at replacing the vulnerable horse in battle by protected muscle-propelled vehicles. He was conscious of the lack of a motive prime mover (which came in our time with steam, the gas engine, and the electric motor).

is mounted on a revolving cradle manned by the lone sailor. From its side the mortar pours out awful salvos of a kind of Greek fire – incendiary shells – that ravages the enemy ships with flame. Ordinary cannonballs seemed old-fashioned to Leonardo. His idea for an incendiary bomb was one studded with spikes, and he proposed catapulting poison shells at the enemy so that "all those, who, as they breathe, inhale the said powder with their breath will become asphyxiated." WINDSOR 12652

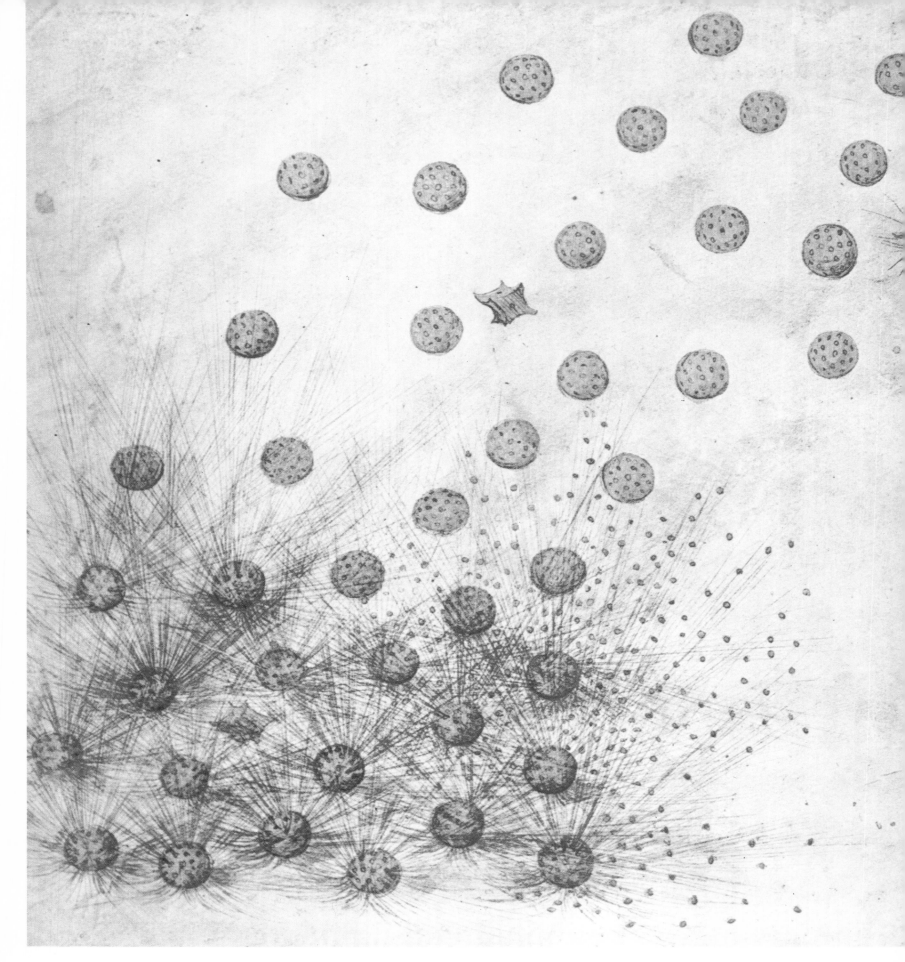

The Madrid Codices are replete with designs and problems in technology, optics, structures, topography, statics, and dynamics. These weigh heavily when one is considering the question, was Leonardo essentially an artist, scientist, or engineer? The conversion of those many pages of fine notes and diagrams into man-days would indicate a deep involvement on Leonardo's part with the structure and behavior of the physical world. The satisfactions that feed the spirit in the artist seem equally nurtured by the problems in matter and force that Leonardo posed and by the delight he took in solving them.

This huge mortar looks much like the powerful new cannon used in the American Civil War (right). The shrapnel are filled with powder and pocked with holes so that upon impact they will explode and scatter deadly fragments. Leonardo describes the shrapnel shell, in his Manuscript B, as "the most deadly machine that exists . . . the ball in the center bursts and scatters the others which fire in such time as is needed to say an Ave Maria." Leonardo hated war, calling it "beastly madness." Even in this, he seems to anticipate many scientists of the 20th century — abhorring war and yet putting his great genius into its employ.   ATLANTICUS 9v-a

We have reason to believe that Leonardo was not interested in hydraulics before he moved to Lombardy. For centuries, ever since the disappearance of the Etruscans as the ruling class of central Italy, significant hydraulic works had not even been attempted in the large valley of the Arno where Leonardo grew up to become a man of artistic and intellectual stature. And even the great Etruscan works – sewers, like the Cloaca Maxima in Rome, and

"All sciences are vain and full of errors that are not born of experience, mother of all certainty, and that are not tested by experience . . ."

THE MECHANICS OF WATER AND STONE

CARLO ZAMMATTIO

artificial cuts to carry away tidal waters, like the Tagliata della Regina, or Queen's Cut, at Ansedonia – were only aimed at the solution of limited problems, rather than at the hydraulic systematization of large areas. The orography and hydrography of central Italy were not conducive to such initiatives, not even to the drainage of swampy areas, the kind of project the Etruscans hardly ever considered anyway. In the Po valley, however, long before the Romans entered it at the end of the third century B.C., the flow of water was directed and controlled according to rules handed down from generation to generation since the time when the inhabitants of the lake settlements known as the Terramare built artificial ponds on which to erect their traditional houses on piles.

The practice of flooding the land to obtain grain harvests throughout the year was certainly very old, as confirmed by Vergil. In the areas below the foothills of the Alps the flood waters could only be obtained from the large Alpine rivers, although in these areas their beds were already meandering through the alluvial strata of the Po valley. Even during the barbarian domination of the valley the irrigation network was not neglected, as proved by present-day nomenclature which can be traced back to their languages. But these works, although based on a tradition thousands of years old, were not the result of theoretical research. Research in hydrodynamics was not even started by the Greeks or their Hellenistic followers: except for the discovery of the simplest laws of hydrostatics (such as the law of communicating vases or the buoyancy law, due to the genial intuition of Archimedes), the ancient world limited itself to conceiving wonderful and sometimes spectacular water contrivances, like those which have survived in writings attributed to Heron of Alexandria. Hydrodynamics remained a mystery for the Greeks probably because the nature of fluids, bodies that are unidentifiable by a well-defined shape, makes it particularly difficult to formulate their problems. The

As a student of hydraulics and structures Leonardo was heir to a rich legacy of practical experience. The Romans had built in Italy, France, and Spain vast networks of aqueducts to carry water to the cities of their

191/1

conceptual difficulty of formulating quantitative relationships for a continuum may have contributed to this neglect. Greek mathematical science was entirely based on visualizable geometric quantities, such as straight or curved lines, which were inherently representable by magnitudes, that is, by numbers; and relations between numbers were only conceived by the Greeks as ratios. The concept of magnitudes varying continuously was never considered by the Greeks; hence, for example, their difficulties in formulating laws of the free fall of bodies. The only phenomenon of continuum mechanics mathematically solved in classical antiquity was that of the vibrating string, which can be quantified and expressed by the numbers of the harmonic progression.

empire. These ruins rise above the Campania plains near the Via Appia leading to Rome. The oldest of the aqueducts, the Acqua Claudia, built in 312 B.C., is still in service. It was restored, along with the remains of the Acqua Marcia, by Pope Sixtus V, and even today supplies Rome with 5 million gallons of water daily.

The works of practical hydraulics in the Po valley, the irrigation network extending from the western Alps to the Adriatic, and, above all, the canals for inland navigation which at Leonardo's time were already two centuries old must have opened to his eyes new and unexpected horizons. They must have aroused in him a curiosity as to the very nature of the liquid element and the mechanical laws governing its behavior. Herein lie the absolute originality of the man in comparison with his predecessors and the mark of the new times, which aspired to understand intuitively a mechanical phenomenon before trying to find its scientific explanation.

We are thus led to identify two separate fields in Leonardo's studies in hydraulics: his research on hydrostatics and hydrodynamics, on the one hand, and his projects for large hydraulic works, on the other. We may safely assume that his speculations in the two fields proceeded simultaneously, one stimulated by the other, since a realization of the factual validity of empirical rules always prodded Leonardo into trying to understand them scientifically. To understand: this was the main goal of the man and of the new times he announces. To understand through rational thinking, since, in all physical phenomena, "if you understand the reason, you don't need experiments." Only when it is difficult to understand a priori the single theoretical cause of a variety of phenomena are experiments needed to find among many possible hypotheses the one that is capable of explaining them all. This philosophy is particularly essential in hydraulics because of the changing shape of fluids. While the mechanics of rigid bodies had been studied with notable success in ancient and medieval times, before Leonardo nobody had even tried a similar theoretical approach in the field of fluid dynamics, although hydraulic works, of great significance even to us, had been realized in the past – among them the aqueducts, from that of Eupalinos in the seventh century B.C. to those built by the Romans in Italy, France, and Spain in the first and second centuries A.D.

It is typical of Leonardo's mind to have tackled problems in these unexplored theoretical fields. He may also have been motivated to study hydraulics by the custom of the duchy of Milan to sell water for irrigation to the lands adjoining the network of canals: the corresponding dues were in proportion to the water drawn. The big canals, built in northern Italy between the 12th and 15th centuries, had not only navigational purposes but also the specific aim of furnishing water for the irrigation of vast areas at the foot of the Alps. These regions, situated above the level of the surface wells, next to the morainic hills of the Alpine glaciers, are arid because of the nature of the terrain. The land continues to be arid as it slopes towards the Po, until the upper water-bearing strata come to the surface and give to the plains of Lombardy and Piedmont their heathlike appearance. The practice of water measurement was unknown in Tuscany, on the other hand, where the water of the Apennine torrents was utilized almost exclusively to generate power for the local grain and textile mills, and this only in limited areas.

In the Po valley, where the rivers never go completely dry, the relatively minor changes in flow allowed the regular distribution of water in the areas crossed by the canals. This water was measured in "ounces," a unit related to the area of the outflow opening in the side of the canal. Leonardo's curiosity was immediately aroused by the following question: is this a correct way of measuring water flow? As the sale of water by the "ounce" was a substantial source of ducal income and as litigation about water measurements was common, it is not unlikely that Leonardo heard of it and may even have been consulted on this matter. The problem must have certainly fascinated him because it involved the whole question of the behavior of fluids in motion.

The sight of the great canals of Lombardy excited his imagination at the thought of what could be achieved in his own Arno valley, to the great financial benefit of Florence, but it also suggested to Leonardo the importance of theoretical studies on the flow of water. The Codex Atlanticus contains his first schemes and ideas on how to regulate and divert the flow of the Arno.[1] This was a grandiose project which went far beyond what had been done till then even by the enterprising people of the Po valley. Immediately upon leaving Florence, the river was to be diverted towards the plains of Prato and Pistoia (these towns, in return for the water and the power supplied to their wool industries, would provide "labor for the works"), crossing on canal bridges the Apennine torrents. The river would have provided water for the irrigation of those plains, which are dry to this day. The Arno was then to go under the mountain pass of Serravalle in a trench or a tunnel (the choice of solution is not clear – Leonardo merely says "cut across Serravalle") and via the marshes of Fucecchio, now drained, was to flow into the "Sesto" marshes, which correspond to the present zone of Coltano, south of Bocca d'Arno, thus avoiding Pisa, the hated enemy of Florence. Although Leonardo's thoughts are never even vaguely chauvinistic, it is not unlikely that a historical

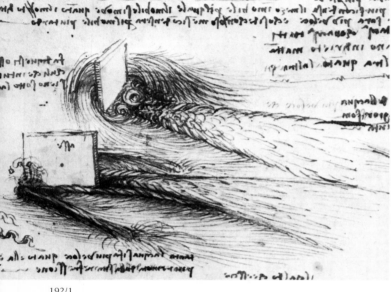

The movement and the behavior of liquid particles impelled by a motion different from that of the mass in which they are immersed, and the formation of fluid threads, for a long time formed one of the main subjects of the hydraulic case histories studied by Leonardo. He had realized that the behavior of true fluids was controlled by the effects of viscosity and by the reciprocal forces of the particles: these last were

192/1

still obscure quantities in his vision of the phenomena but whose determining presence he confusedly guessed. For their bearing on the movement of water in canals, the stationary deformations of the surface, due to the effect of wake produced by obstacles of unevenness of the walls, particularly excited his curiosity because of their apparent permanence while the fluid particles which form them continually change. WINDSOR 12660r

background of town fights may have influenced his decision not to end the course of the Arno in the harbor of Pisa, which in any case, although well equipped, was already in full decadence because silted up by the river.

Drawn up along these lines, the project would certainly have found support throughout the Florentine zone of influence. This support was all the more necessary because in order to regulate the flow of the Arno, particularly during the

193/1

summer months, Leonardo had foreseen two gigantic operations: the transformation of the huge valley of the Chiana, then marshy, into a large artificial lake to act as a retention basin; and the emission into this basin, through a tunnel under the hills between Mugnano and San Savino, of the waters of the Tiber, tapped below Perugia, south of Lake Trasimeno. Lake Trasimeno, moreover, was to become part of the large new artificial lake, whose level was to be stabilized by gates placed below Arezzo, thus regulating the Tiber waters destined to integrate the Arno's flow [194/195].

The details of the individual works for this project, scattered particularly through the pages of the Codex Atlanticus, show the evident derivation of Leonardo's

Leonardo's scientific drawings of water in motion endure today as works of art. Here he sees a shaft of water pouring from a square hole into a pool forming a chrysanthemum-like image of bubbles and swirling lines. This drawing probably was made about 1507 in connection with a hydraulic project in Milan. WINDSOR 12660v

Leonardo studied the possibility of building a waterway from Florence to the sea. The idea of diverting a long section of the Arno River into a man-made canal, to irrigate arid plains and make possible large-scale navigation from Florence, was more than 100 years old. But Leonardo made the idea his own and evolved the complex series of engineering challenges charted here.

plans from the works of the Po valley, as is to be expected, since these incorporated the results of centuries of practical experience. It is sufficient to remember here how two years after the Battle of Ugnano, which gave to the towns of northern Italy a large amount of independence from the German empire, work was started on the canal later to be called the Naviglio Grande. The waters for this canal were tapped from the Ticino River (hence its first name, Ticinello) below Sesto Calende, and remnants of its excavation and construction of dams may still

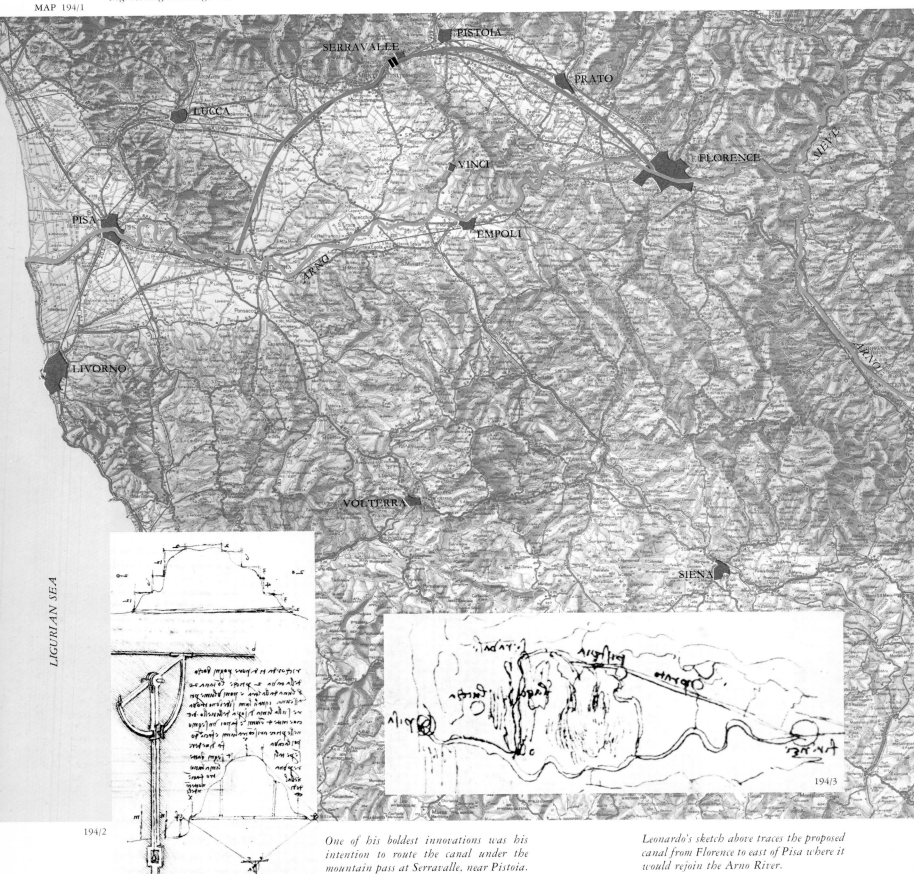

One of his boldest innovations was his intention to route the canal under the mountain pass at Serravalle, near Pistoia. His sketch at left demonstrates how excavations could be carried out accurately.

MADRID I 111r

Leonardo's sketch above traces the proposed canal from Florence to east of Pisa where it would rejoin the Arno River.

ATLANTICUS 46r-b

194/2

194/3

be seen today at the river bank. These waters at first were channeled only up to Abbiate Grasso, but under the *podesteria* ("mayoralty") of Martino della Torre in 1256 the canal was prolonged to Milan, where its waters entered the exterior moats of the city. The canal banks were equipped with wharves for barges, and in 1271 under Beno de' Gozzadini a large trench – Redifossi – was built which collected and discharged the waters of the canal and of the small torrents which passed through the city. This extraordinary work allowed the merchandise of the

The color map at left reveals the grand scope of Leonardo's Arno projects. The main section of the waterway begins at Florence, where the Arno, winding west to Pisa and the sea, becomes impossible to navigate. His canal (in green) cuts northwest past Prato and Pistoia, then turns southwest through a tunnel or trench at Serravalle and again meets the Arno east of Pisa. To maintain the Arno and its canal at a navigable level, Leonardo suggested creating a large artificial lake (in green) by flooding the marshes of the Val di Chiana (in blue), near Arezzo, and linking them with Lake Trasimeno. His sketch below, Windsor Collection No. 12682 recto, is an imaginary perspective of the upper part of the Val di Chiana, where gates with a regulating device were to be placed. The map also shows Arezzo and below it the junction of the canal and the Arno. To get water for the reservoir, he suggested tapping the Tiber River near Perugia, southeast of Lake

195/1

Trasimeno, by digging a tunnel (drawings below).

But a problem exists with this key element: at the point where the Tiber was to be tapped, it is lower in altitude than Lake Trasimeno. Perhaps Leonardo considered the solution of tapping the river north of Perugia?

The map below is a detail from Leonardo's map of Northern Italy, focusing chiefly on the watersheds of the Arno River. It shows

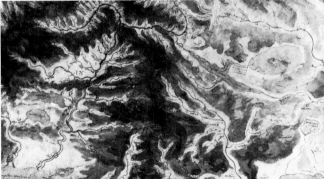

195/3

The detail from Leonardo's map at right clearly shows the tunnel linking the Tiber with Lake Trasimeno. WINDSOR 12278r

195/2

the west coast and Pisa at lower left and includes the entire course of the Arno, the marshlands of the Chiana valley, the upper part of the Tiber, and the junction with Lake Trasimeno. Leonardo drew this map during his service for Cesare Borgia, around 1502. WINDSOR 12277

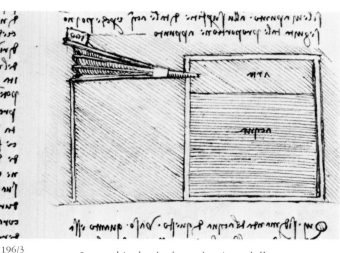

196/1

One of the few early researchers in hydraulics was the Greek Heron of Alexandria, who lived in the first century before Christ. He devised fountains which Leonardo copied (above and at right). In the drawing above, water squirts from a pipe held by the nude figure into the basket on his back. In the sketch at right, water rises to the top by means of a siphon, which Heron invented.

WINDSOR 12690

196/3

Leonardo's sketch above, showing a bellows pumping air into a vessel of water, is one of many aimed at calculating how the weight of a fluid is transmitted through that fluid.

MADRID I 114v

196/2

Milan market to travel by water to the foot of the Alps, a journey it had made by road since neolithic times by following the upper part of the Ticino valley up to the passes of San Bernardino, Lucomagno, and Gotthard, which had recently been opened to traffic. At the same time other waterways were being built at the initiative of other towns: one between the river Adda and the southern area around Lodi; another between the northern area around Novara and the middle valley of the Ticino, on its right bank; and a third between the rivers Dora and Sesia, which ran at the foot of Ivrea (the "Navilio d'Invrea," notes Leonardo). These canals, wide enough to allow the simultaneous passage of two large barges, had required the solution of many complex problems in construction and hydraulics, because their waters were drawn from rivers which were periodically flooded by the sudden melting of the Alpine snows in the spring and by the fall rains. To obtain such results a good knowledge of water flow, based at least on sound experience, if not on theoretical studies, was necessary; and this is the ancient empirical legacy Leonardo found in the Po valley.

It is here that his individuality and novelty contrasts with the thought of the preceding centuries: his scientific curiosity needed to know the reasons behind the empirical rules and could not be contented with their passive acceptance. Leonardo was the first man to realize that any physical phenomenon must be reduced to its mechanical essentials, and to him hydraulics was a totally unknown field which had to be thus explored. He was particularly attracted to it by the fact that a fluid, in adjusting itself continually to the shape of its boundary, realizes ideally continuity of mass motion, a concept studied today in continuum mechanics. What strikes most the careful observer of such fluid motions is that under certain conditions they appear to be stationary, i.e., that while the fluid mass flows, at any point along the flow path all the (invisible) fluid particles behave identically. The surfaces which define the shape of the fluid mass, such as the banks of a river or a canal, are subjected instead to permanent changes due to the local accelerations (impacts and suctions) of the water, which erode and tear the material of these surfaces. Leonardo realized that to understand the great works built along the rivers of the Po valley, one had to grasp the laws of fluid flow. To be able to think about the realization of the great projects he dreamed of for his own Tuscany, one had to establish first the mechanical behavior of fluids.

This behavior is of a very particular kind. The individual particles of a fluid, although bound by their common volume, seem to behave independently of each other and yet to feel the impulses of the other particles, both near and far. This is not the case for solid bodies, each one of which can be considered as separate and with given finite dimensions. (Because of these characteristics, mechanisms made of wheels, gears, and ropes are easier to study, to understand, and even to invent.) The field of fluid flow, besides being mechanically different, was entirely new: there was nothing Leonardo could have learned from classical science about either liquid or gases.

Here we come to appreciate the qualities of Leonardo's mind. He started from the drawings of the water contrivances invented by Hellenistic technologists, contained in the work of Heron; by analyzing and co-ordinating the results of this technology, he was able to invent new contrivances, which show him to be the first man in history to have tackled hydraulic theory. (Some pages of Codex Madrid I throw light on devices of Leonardo which were already known to us, but not as clearly, from two folios of the Codex Atlanticus.) How is the weight of water transmitted through water? This is the basic problem of hydrostatics and was also the first studied by Leonardo on the basis of his reading of Heron. We do not know whether its solution came to him in a flash of intuition or as the result of studying the analogy between the equilibrium of fluid particles and that of transparent spheres (such as glass marbles), but the fact is that he categorically asserts in Codex Madrid I that "every part of the skin feels equally the pressure of the weight."[2] Of course, the question to be asked is not only qualitative but also quantitative: in what measure does each part of the bag containing the fluid feel the weight acting on it? All the devices used by Leonardo to answer this question in Madrid I[3] are derived, relying on the principle that water in communicating containers seeks its own level, from a scheme in the codex[4] which is very similar to a scheme in Heron, reproduced in the Latin translation of Commandino and the Italian translation of Giorgi.

It must be pointed out that Leonardo, in studying connected containers, takes into account both the liquid and the air in the containers, thus showing that he considers the behavior of these two fluids as equivalent. Here, however, begin Leonardo's difficulties: he failed to notice that the pressure inside a container depends not only on the weight of the liquid but also on the surface on which the weight acts, so that it is the force per unit of area at a given level which is equal to any unit area of the bag in contact with the fluid. When he drew the drawings in Madrid I,[5] Leonardo believed that the pressure due to the weight would spread to the whole of its "vacuum," that is, over the entire remaining surface of the container [196/3 and 197/3]. This seems to us the only plausible interpretation in which Leonardo's speculations on this subject are presented in a detailed and

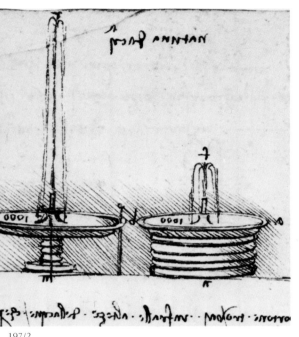

197/2

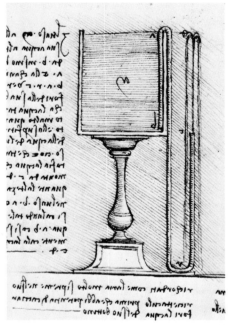

197/3

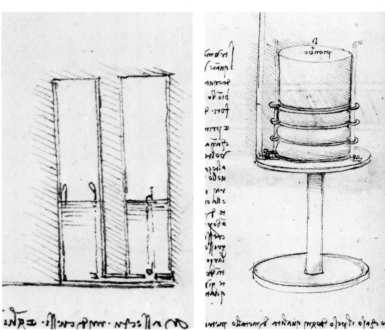

197/4

197/5

197/6

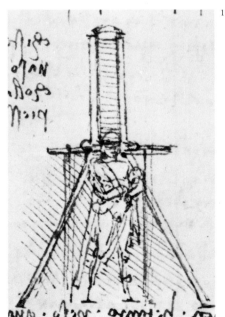

precise manner. (What was known about it before Madrid I was quite vague and undetermined.) It probably seemed absurd to him that the sum of the outward fluid pressures could be much greater than the resultant of the entire weight, since to him this was tantamount to saying that power could be generated from nothing. At the time he was not in a position to consider the equilibrium of an element of fluid in contact with the surface of the container and to realize that this element must be equally pressed on all sides if it is not to move away from the container's surface, since this kind of consideration was only developed 300 years later. His error, which seems to have become firmly established in his mind in two successive stages, is understandable. In fact, previously, in a "Definition" in Madrid I under the heading "Nature of Water,"[6] the pressure in a cylindrical container with an accordion-like expandable bottom, full of water and burdened by an additional weight, is equivalent from the height reached by a jet of water issuing from a pipe connected to the container [197/2]. This height is assumed to vary inversely as the ratio of the "magnitude" (diameter) of the pipe to that of the container and hence is not referred to its entire bottom surface.

Nevertheless, Leonardo obtained results at least qualitatively correct, so much so that in his drawings of cylindrical containers loaded by the same weight (1,000 pounds), the jet of water spouting out of the smaller-diameter container m is higher than that spouting out of the large-diameter container n. We say that this happens because the loaded surface of the container m is one-tenth of that of the container n and hence the pressure in m is 10 times that in n. Leonardo instead reasoned that since the jet pipes of both containers had the same dimensions, the pipe in n had a diameter equal to one-hundredth of its container's diameter, while the diameter of the pipe in m was one-thousandth of its container's diameter, i.e., 10 times smaller. Leonardo noted that the top of the water jet reached the level of

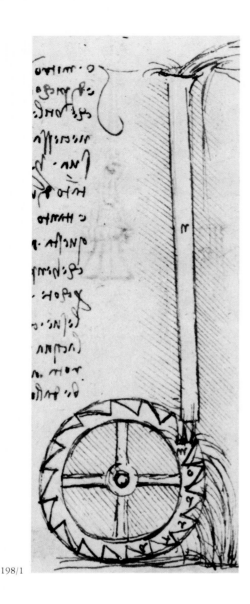

198/1

Here the question is asked: which of these four waterfalls has more percussion and power in order to turn a wheel: fall a or b, c or d? I have not yet experimented, but it seems to me that they must have the same power, considering that a, even if it descends from a great height, has no other water chasing it, as has d, which bears upon itself the whole height of the thrusting water. Now, if fall d has a great percussion, it has not the weight of fall a. And the same is true for b and c. Consequently, where the force of percussion is lacking, it is compensated by the weight of the waterfall.

198/1 and 2 and 199/1 and 2
The motion of fluids had everyday significance in the Po region, where canals were used to generate power. Here, perhaps because of his role as ducal engineer, Leonardo studies the work done by three types of waterfalls. Above, in the case of a small flow from a high fall, he suggests in Codex Madrid I, folio 22 verso, the use of a narrow vertical pipe to concentrate the force of the water as it strikes the vaned wheel. On the opposite page, in two sketches from folio 151 verso, he considers the problem of splitting a strong flow from a small fall into four equal flows. Most important is his study in 134 verso (right) of water falling at four different heights from a container. He concludes that the "power," or energy, is the same for each waterfall, a basic theorem of modern hydrodynamics.

the water in the container, as shown by one of his Codex Madrid I sketches [197/3].[7] Equally correct were his experiments with collapsible-walls containers to determine the specific weights of solids by using different liquids in the container [197/5].[8] In this case Leonardo saw to it that the weight was cylindrical and of the same diameter as the upper surface of the cylindrical container, so that the pressure in the fluid equaled the weight of a column of unit area of the solid. In this situation, to explain the role of the fluid pressure, Leonardo imagines the cylindrical weight subdivided into many elementary vertical cylinders, under each of which is a liquid vertical cylinder of equal diameter. While for all the other liquid cylinders the pressure due to the weight is balanced by the reaction of the container's bottom, for the elementary cylinder located over the bottom's opening (which has the same diameter as the elementary cylinder) the pressure due to the weight is balanced by the weight of the column of water which rises in an external U-pipe connected to the bottom opening. The water in the pipe rises a multiple of the weight's height which represents the ratio of the specific weight of the solid to that of the liquid. The same device is used by Leonardo for schemes of hydrostatic scales in equilibrium in Codex Madrid I[9] and in other contexts in the Codex Atlanticus and the Codex Leicester.[10]

While Leonardo was thus trying to establish the laws of hydrostatics, he did not lose sight of the importance of studying fluid motion, since it was common knowledge that when the flow of water is deviated or prevented, a pressure is created which, if devastating at times, may also be put to profitable use. This knowledge was particularly important in the Po region, where the water of the large canals was utilized to generate power and was a rich source of government income. The high cost of the damming and banking works, on one hand, and the value of the concession of hydraulic power, on the other, gave high priority to a problem, probably submitted to Leonardo by the fiscal authorities, which involved the role of two essential variables: how did the work done by the distributed water depend on its mass and on the height of the waterfall, measured from the distribution orifice to the collecting canal? We can consider in this context three situations studied by Leonardo in some notes of Codex Madrid I: (1) a small flow

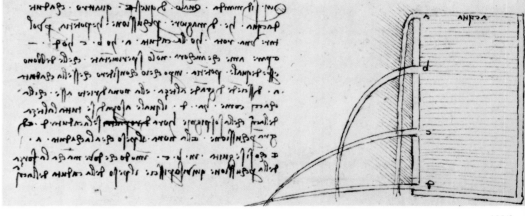

198/2

from a high fall [198/1]; (2) a flow from a small fall (about 5 feet high) of such magnitude as to require splitting into four equal flows, each producing the same amount of work [199/1 and 2]; and (3) the general case of tapping water at various heights from the wall of a container, in which the water level is presumably kept constant [198/2].

Let us only consider the last case, which is the most interesting because it contains elements of wider scientific scope than the other two.[11] Even though the individual jets start to leave the container under different conditions, with initial spouting speeds which increase as the tapping level is lowered, Leonardo concludes that the "power" (*potentia*) is the same for all the spouts, because "where the force of percussion is lacking, it is compensated by the weight of the waterfall." Leonardo's argument, which is written as if he were debating it with himself and were in need of later experimental verification, seems to run as follows: Each water particle, while falling freely, obeys the action of its own weight only; it moves because it has weight. In so doing it acquires an impetus [what we call momentum] which leads to percussion [what we call impact] if it finds an obstacle. A particle at the bottom of the container, however, feels not only its own but also the weight of all the particles above it up to the free level of the water, which weigh down on it. The weight of the particles all the way down to the container's bottom is all that determines the power of a particle at the point where it leaves the container through the bottom orifice. But for a particle initially above the bottom of the container the power upon reaching the level of the bottom consists of two parts: one due to the weight of the column of water initially above it and another due to the momentum deriving from the speed acquired during the fall. As the part due to one cause increases, the part due to the other decreases. At the free upper surface of the water the power due to the superimposed weight vanishes, at the bottom of the container the power due to speed vanishes. Hence at any other level the power remains constant.

Naturally, in his reasoning, Leonardo did not and could not use our precise terminology. In particular, the concept "energy" had to wait more than three and a half centuries before its precise definition allowed it to become a fundamental concept in our understanding of the physical world. Nevertheless, the conclusion reached by Leonardo is of the greatest importance because it constitutes nothing less than the basic theorem of hydrodynamics. In its wording as well as in its substance it is the law announced in 1738 by Daniel Bernoulli [200/1]: all we have to do is to substitute our term "energy" for the word "power" (potentia), our "potential energy" for "weight," and our "kinetic energy" – what Leibnitz improperly called "live force" – for "percussion."

The great importance of Leonardo's conclusion, particularly in his time, becomes clearer if we notice that it is not at all self-evident that "where the force of percussion is lacking, it is compensated by the weight." For this assertion to be true, one must assume that at the beginning of its free fall the initial speed of a particular jet is equal to that reached at the same level by the jets tapped higher up, so that, from the level of this particular jet on, the water in all the jets moves under

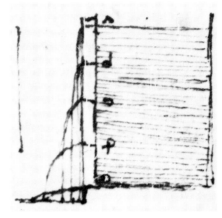

199/3

Probably entrusted by the French governor of Lombardy with the job of solving once and for all the problem of water measurement. Leonardo proposed a method for measurement of water by the "ounce." In his sketch above, the quantity of water issuing from the opening is directly proportional to the water head above it. The accompanying text states that "the quantity of water that pours through a given opening in a given time will be the same as that from the given height of the opening," meaning by "height" the vertical distance from the upper surface. Not knowing the law of falling bodies, Leonardo could only think of a linear proportionality between rate of flow and the hydrostatic head, instead of its square root. MS. F 53r

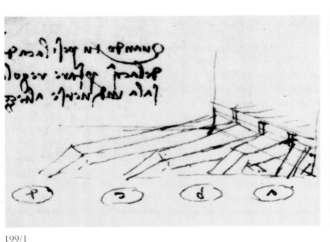

199/1

199/2

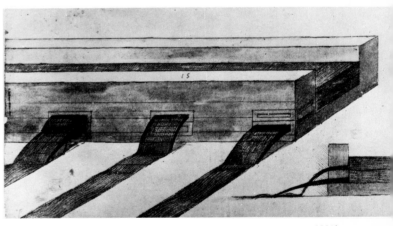

199/4

identical conditions. But this implies the validity of the law governing the speed of falling bodies, a law deduced from the experiments of Galileo [200/2] and clearly enunciated by Torricelli [200/3] in 1642.

Of course, what has been said so far is only valid while the flow in all the taps is identical. Leonardo does not say so explicitly, but this premise must have been in the back of his mind, because it is obvious that comparisons can only be made between identical quantities of water flowing in identical time intervals. It would be absurd to consider equivalent the "power" of a trickle of water and that of a river. But since Leonardo had already recognized that the flow from an orifice depends on its area and on the exit velocity and since this last increases from top to bottom, to obtain the same amount of flow from all the taps one would have had to vary the orifice cross sections with the depth. Since the orifices in Leonardo's drawing for the water-tapping case have all the same height and since Leonardo only considered rectangular orifices (like those used in his time in Lombardy for

Leonardo's observations on water measurement and distribution for irrigation purposes found their practical application one year following the study at top. The precise execution of this drawing leaves hardly any doubt that it was meant to be shown to the French authorities. Leonardo became convinced that the outlets for irrigation should have a prevalently horizontal development, of small height, so as to reduce the dragging influence of the faster lower strata. ATLANTICUS 395r-a

the water outlets of the irrigation canals), their widths would have had to vary inversely as the square root of their vertical distances from the free level of the water to be in accordance with Torricelli's law.

At that time the law governing the fall of heavy bodies was not known, and Leonardo seems to have felt a need to prove the correctness of his intuitions about "power" by giving a more specific definition of fluid flow. That he was turning this thought over in his mind seems to be proved by the fact that when, some years later, he proposed a method of measurement for water by the "ounce," he returned in Manuscripts F and I to the same scheme, drawn in the same manner, noting on the side "Quantity of a true ounce of water." [12] (The French governor of Lombardy probably entrusted him with the job of solving once and for all the problem of water measurement during his second stay in Milan.) [199/3 and 4]

It is likely that as ducal engineer Leonardo was given charge of the hydraulic sector, one of the most important for the economy of the duchy. In any case, his interest in the hydraulic works of Lombardy was permanent and went even beyond his fantastic plan of making Florence a center of water traffic. But Leonardo's notes consider, besides questions on hydraulic works, problems of water power, and it is doubtful that he would have tried the solutions of problems like those mentioned above had he not been requested to do so. Among the water-power problems we find that of the full utilization of the flow from a large canal, which he subdivides into four channels activating four separate waterwheels, since, for purely mechanical reasons, it was then impossible to absorb the entire power of the canal by means of a single wheel. And here his thought goes to the water mills of the Certosa 4 miles above Pavia (still in existence on the Pavese Canal and with a head of about 15 feet), which might well be identified with a drawing in the Codex Atlanticus.[13]

It is certain that Leonardo had made a name for himself in the field of hydraulics since, after the fall of Il Moro, he was requested by the Venetian senate to work out a plan for the flooding of the lower Isonzo plains below Gorizia (Friuli) in the event of potential incursions on the part of the Turks, at that time the major threat at the eastern frontiers of the Venetian domains. The folios of the Codex Atlanticus contain the outline of part of the report Leonardo gathered at the time of his mission to Friuli. In it he suggests an adjustable dam on the Isonzo, mounted on trestles and equipped with gates pivoted along their upper horizontal edge, which would allow the rapid raising of the water level as well as the free flow of sudden floods. Leonardo remembered this device again 15 years later in France when he studied the flood control of the Loire and Cher rivers and, especially, the draining of the Romorantin marshes.

In the field of river-flow regulation Leonardo was helped by his prolonged studies on flow perturbation in canals and rivers, started at the beginning of his stay in Milan. It would seem that for him the key problem consisted in understanding and explaining why the current abandons a rectilinear course and tends to become tortuous, and why perturbations in the shape of waves appear on the surface. These waves seem to be stable, so that the motion of the water particles follows their profile and makes a constant angle with the axis of the current similar to that made with the ship wake by the waves at the bow of a ship moving in calm waters.

Leonardo called this phenomenon "columnar waves" and put together a large documentation on them [202/2-4]. Realizing at once that its causes were many and were complicated by their interaction, he thought it wise to collect information on many different aspects of the phenomenon so as to give himself the chance of establishing, through studying them, a common law. Codex Madrid I contains some of his studies on this, but most of them appear in Manuscripts B, C, and G.

The sight of the sea was most suggestive to Leonardo. His fleeting visits to Genoa in the retinue of Il Moro were followed by his stay in Venice, by his visits to the Adriatic during the Romagna campaigns with Borgia, and, finally, by his stay in Piombino. His attention was held particularly by the motion of the sea waves breaking on the shore and by the sight of those reflected by the beach, which move

200/1

200/2

200/3

Leonardo's conclusions about the power of falling water were so farseeing that they brought him to the brink of theories formulated by three famous scientists much later. In his consideration on page 198 of waterfalls from four different heights, he correctly saw that the energy of the falls depended upon the relationship between their velocity and the height of the water inside the container. In everything but precise terminology he had arrived at the basic theorem of hydrodynamics developed in 1738 by Daniel Bernoulli (top left), one of a Swiss family of distinguished mathematicians. Even more astonishing, his conclusion involved an intuitive understanding of the law governing the speed of falling bodies. This law was not deduced until the experiments of the Italian physicist and astronomer Galileo Galilei (above right) were performed and not clearly enunciated until 1642 by his countryman Evangelista Torricelli (above).

seaward and are superimposed on the incoming waves. This phenomenon suggested to him the laws of the independence of wave motions and of the specularity of their reflections. According to these laws, which constitute Huygens' principle (1673), each point struck by a wave becomes the origin of a new concentric disturbance, and the interference and superposition of all these perturbations determine the configuration of the advancing wave front [203/2].

This and many other observations are collected in the Codex Leicester, which can be considered a huge index of queries and arguments on practical hydraulics in canals and rivers, on wave motion, and on problems of fluid flow and its measurement. We find repeated here the measurements of the speed of flowing water by means of floating shafts kept upright by appropriate floats and ballasted at their lower end so as to keep them in an almost vertical position, shafts that were to be called "reitrometric" (flow-measuring) by Bonati, an 18th-century scholar. These shafts, still in use today, were later attributed variously to more recent scholars than Leonardo, as Benedetto Castelli and Father Cabeo of Ferrara, but perhaps they had already been used for some time by the hydraulicians of the Po valley, from whom Leonardo may have borrowed the idea, which he found wise and practical. He himself does not take any credit for their invention.

But he had also conceived other devices to measure directly, besides the speed, the "power" of both air and water flows. This is proved by an interesting device consisting of a fan-type wheel with many blades, braked by a counterweight hanging from a rope wrapped around its axle [202/1].[14] How and how much this device may have been of use to him is hard to say. On the other hand, it is almost certain that Leonardo was the first hydraulician to busy himself with flow measurements based on discharge cross sections and exit velocities. The crowning piece of his research in hydraulics belongs to his second Milanese period, during the French occupation (the time of his notes about the "true ounce of water" in Manuscripts F and I), to which also belong his last grandiose projects, culminating in the study to provide Milan with a waterway connecting it

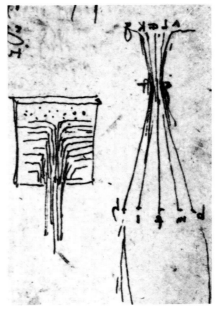

201/1

In order to observe the motion and paths of liquid particles issuing from a container, built of glass plates set up closely to one another, Leonardo suggests adding some small seeds to the liquid. He now sees that the particles do not all issue forth parallel to the axis of the outlet, that they also move from the side towards the opening (sketch at left), and that the outflowing stream is first contracted and then expanded (sketch at right). This latter sketch is accompanied by letters for which an explanatory text is lacking – perhaps it was on an opposite folio now missing. ATLANTICUS 81r-a

201/2

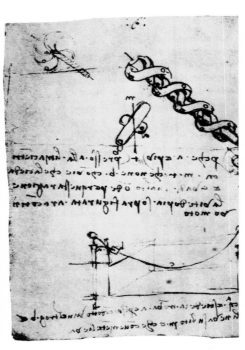

201/3

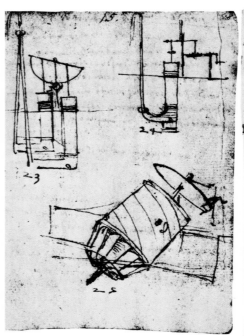

201/4

201/2–5

201/5

Leonardo must have observed that a liquid in curvilinear motion, led by the wall of a groove or a pipe, exerts a pressure back onto the same wall: he must have inferred that this pressure can furnish torque and, accordingly, he conceived conical spiral tubes (with rising lever arm) as a substitute for the usual waterwheels, in order to activate snail tube machinery for raising water. FORSTER I₁ 42v, 43v, 48r, 52v

with Lake Como and the Alpine passes of Spluga and the Engadine (something which could not be achieved through the Martesana Canal because it came out of the Adda River too far downstream and at too low a point) [206/1]. Leonardo first thought of using for this purpose the lakes of the Brianza [204/1], but then his attention became focused on the idea of a dam on the Adda at a point about 2.5 miles above Trezzo, immediately below the bridge at Paderno [204/2–205/3]. Here lay a natural gorge – the Tre Corni under the Rocchetta a Santa Maria – created by a massive formation of conglomerate rock, resistant to water erosion, which made navigation impossible for large barges [207/1].

The course of the river could be dammed by a stone dike about 90 feet high, set against the rocks of the Tre Corni. A large lock would be built on the hillside of the valley, in the conglomerates, which would allow the navigational surface to be lowered (by means of a tunnel passing under the Tre Corni) to such a level that Milan could be reached without any further locks. This was the final solution of a problem under discussion for decades – from the time of the Sforza, when the Martesana Canal was proved insufficient for the purpose.

The project as envisaged by Leonardo was too grandiose for his time: even the discharge via a tunnel closed by a sluice gate presented a number of problems not easy to overcome, whose confrontation was bound to stop dead the available technology. But the project, perhaps on account of its boldness, remained in the minds and hearts of the leaders of government in Lombardy through different successive regimes, and was never completely abandoned. It was taken up again after the reoccupation of Milan by the French after the Battle of Melegnano: Leonardo himself, who was already in France, recommended to the king the names of technicians capable of realizing this project. On a much smaller scale the project was finally completed towards the end of the 16th century, but because of the limited sections adopted and the reduction of the necessary works for the main lock, it never had the economic importance envisaged by its original planners.

In Milan the government sold water by the "ounce," a crude measurement related to the size of the outflow opening. The imprecision often led to arguments and litigation, and Leonardo may have been called upon to settle the issue of how to measure an exact "ounce." Below, in the Codex Arundel, folio 241 recto, he sets up an experiment for gauging the increased flow in openings with areas reduced by the use of cones. He rigs an anemometer with vanes to make the first known flowmeter.

202/1

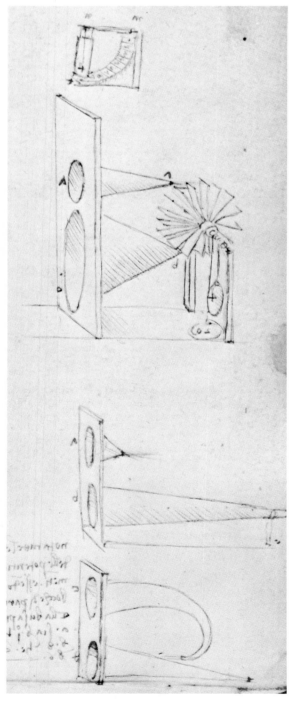

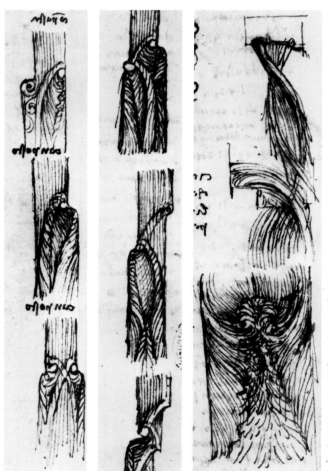

202/2, 3, and 4
The windups of currents in rivers and canals were another of Leonardo's preoccupations. He tried to explain why the current would abandon its straight course and form waves that made a constant angle with the current similar to the waves at the bow of a ship. He called them "columnar waves" and made many drawings such as these, which appear in Manuscript F, folios 90 verso, 90 recto, and 47 verso.

202/2   202/3   202/4

This was the last of Leonardo's great hydraulic projects. However, his well-established fame caused him to be consulted also on great problems of swamp clearance. He was entrusted by Giuliano de' Medici, brother of Pope Leo X, with the clearance of the Pontine Marshes, and he illustrated his proposed solution in a beautifully colored drawing. Even though his proposal could not lead to a final solution, it was realizable even from an economic viewpoint. Finally, Leonardo studied for the King of France the systematization of the plain of Romorantin by regulating the Cher through the use of a dam with movable gates, "like those that I recommended in Frigholi," notes Leonardo.

While he was busy with the conception of the dam on the Adda, Leonardo became steadily more interested in the rotational motion of cages made of thin spiral pipes

The power of ocean waves crashing upon the shore also interested Leonardo. During a visit to Piombino, where he designed new fortifications in late 1504, he made the sketches of waves below in Codex Madrid II, folio 126 recto, and wrote: "Nothing is carried away from the shores by the waves of the

203/3

sea. The sea cast back to the shore all things left free out at sea. The surface of the water keeps the imprint of the waves for some time." He went on to describe the way the waves broke on the shore and bounced back atop the incoming waves. His description correctly guessed the laws of wave motion. These laws constitute Huygens' principle – each point struck by a wave becomes the origin of new disturbances and all these perturbations determine the shape of the advancing wave front. They were not formulated until 1673 by the Dutch physicist and astronomer Christian Huygens (top).

and loaded by water from above, the *cichognole*. Probably he was pushed in this direction by the increasing use by industry of water power. Leonardo had previously designed waterwheels with radial blades for low heads. Now he adopted the principle of reaction, clear to his mind even in its aerodynamic implications, in numerous applications involving *cichognole*. The arrangement of these spiral tubes – which repeat in many ways the Archimedean screw, even in the uses to which they were put – may seem strange. It is repeated in many versions, usually in couples of spirals, one on the outside which is the driving element, the other on the inside (of smaller diameter) which is the driven element. The first utilizes the fall of water, while the second lifts the water to a greater height. It is not clear what

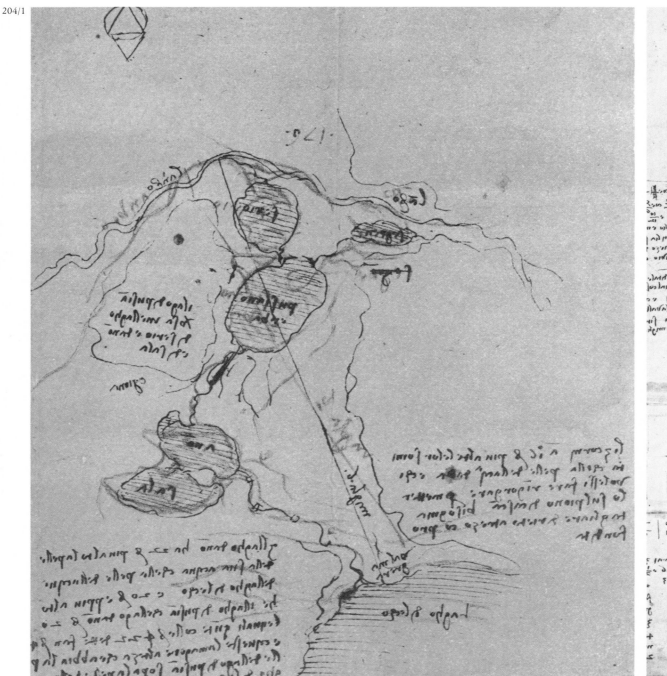

204/1

204/1

The last great hydraulic project undertaken in Milan by Leonardo was a plan to provide a waterway from the city north to Lake Como and the Alpine passes of Spluga and the Engadine. The existing Martesana Canal could not be used because it left the Adda River too far downstream and at too low a level for navigation. Leonardo, now in

204/2

the employ of the French who had deposed Lodovico Sforza, first proposed the route for the waterway shown here in the Codex Atlanticus, folio 275 recto-a. This plan utilizes the course of the Lambro River (top of the map) and the lakes of the Brianza to reach the Lake of Lecco and then Como. But Leonardo soon discovered that considerable differences in level would necessitate construction of a number of locks. Typically, he turned to the more innovative and intriguing plan shown on the opposite page.

was the purpose of Leonardo's research, since his related sketches have no captions. In any case, one should not infer from them that Leonardo ever gave up his conviction that perpetual motion was an impossibility. These thoughts of his may rather be related to the determination of power of waterfalls on which he had been working for a long time and, in addition, to the couple of the reaction forces due to the outflow which created driving and resisting moments with respect to their common rotational axis.

These studies are particularly interesting because they show us that Leonardo understood and applied the jet reactive thrust more completely than was done in the windmill of Heron. In Leonardo's driving *cichognola* the liquid accelerates while falling, with a motion analogous to that of the water particles in a modern, highly reactive turbine; moreover, as the water accelerates and increases its thrust on the lateral walls of the spirals, the radius of curvature of these increases, thus increasing the lever arm of the reactive couple. Newton's third law (1663) appears here to be thoroughly understood and applied. On the other hand, from the surviving sketches it would not seem that Leonardo ever proceeded from these graphic schemes to scale models: the technology of the time was not yet sufficiently advanced to allow effective and conclusive experiments.

204/2 and 205/1–3

The key to the route Leonardo finally chose for the Milan-Lake Como waterway was a stretch of the Adda River that offered a seemingly insurmountable challenge. The map at left [204/2], in the Codex Atlanticus, folio 335 recto-a, traces this part of the Adda from Trezzo at the bottom to the lake port of Brivio. At the center of the map is the Tre Corni, a natural gorge created by

In order to construct the foundation of the stone dike below water level, Leonardo proposed the stake frame shown below. Usually such stakes are rammed into the sandy river bed. Leonardo, however, had to somehow attach them on the rocky ground; therefore, the log frame connecting the stakes had to be stable.

The stone dike is open in the middle: it is possible that Leonardo planned to insert a sluice gate in order to allow the passage of strong waves.

To clearly render his thought, Leonardo combined two perspectives in the sketch below.

navigable tunnel
sluice gate for the tunnel

stone dike, damming the valley.

The line drawings above are taken from Leonardo's folio reproduced at right.

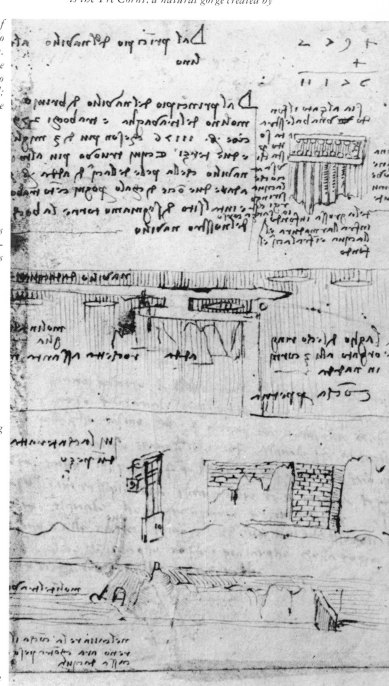

205/1   205/2   205/3

We may consider these to be the last theoretical studies of Leonardo in the field of hydraulics. The development of the wide series of case histories in the field of practical hydraulics contained in the Codex Leicester stopped at the enunciation of principles, which were already the fruit of a long and meditated harvest of observations. Even if these studies contain theoretical implications, which are of the greatest importance even to our eyes, it does not seem that Leonardo followed them up: he stopped at these schematic sketches and at the small notebooks called today the Codex Forster, which only contain ideas going back to his second Milanese period. They are not taken up or repeated anywhere else among the

a huge rock formation that made navigation impossible to all but the smallest barges [205/1]. To bypass the rock, Leonardo proposed the complex plan sketched above in the Atlanticus, folio 141 verso-b: a 90-foot-high stone dike to dam the river; a large lock on the hillside to adjust the surface of the water; diversion of the water into a navigable tunnel with a sluice gate under the Tre Corni. In this ingenious manner Milan could be reached without building additional locks.

abundant graphic material which can be dated to the last years of his life in Rome and in France. This seems to be also the fate of other lines of Leonardo's thought. Perhaps the search for the goal he had in mind seemed exhausted to him at a certain point, and, as was customary with him, he abandoned it because it no longer held his interest. This was a characteristic feature of Leonardo's personality which might explain why he left so much work unfinished in his legacy, something he has often been reproached for by posterity. The source of this attitude may be found in his permanent anxiety to do new research, an anxiety that was the sole

The map below shows the route of Leonardo's proposed waterway: from Milan along the Adda, tunneling under the Tre Corni (drawing at right, encircled on the map), and into the Lake of Lecco and Lake Como. The project as envisaged by Leonardo was too grandiose for his time, but the project, perhaps on account of its boldness, remained in the minds and hearts of the leaders of government in Lombardy through

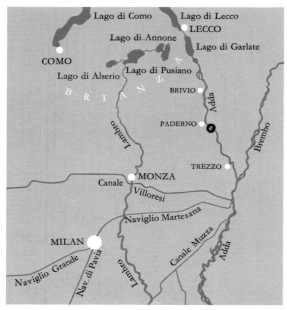

206/1

different successive regimes, and was never completely abandoned. It was taken up again after the reoccupation of Milan by the French after the Battle of Melegnano; Leonardo himself, who was already in France, recommended to the king the names of technicians capable of realizing this project. On a much smaller scale the project was finally completed towards the end of the 16th century, but because of the limited sections adopted and the reduction of the necessary works for the main lock, it never had the economic importance envisaged by its original planners.

motivation of his superhuman activity. Once his curiosity was satisfied, once the causes and the solutions were found, even if the device invented to conduct the research was incomplete, it became unimportant to build it in its final form. Time was too precious not to devote it to other goals: there was so much still to be brought to light. Leonardo always viewed subjects in the large, in their fullest scope, displaying the same universal vision that in the end had suffocated Greek scientific speculation. The fullness he sought could be encompassed neither by the knowledge of his time nor by the capacity of one man's life.

In the course of surveying the Adda for the Milan-Lake Como waterway, Leonardo made this drawing at the Tre Corni where he wanted to build a dam, lock, and tunnel. To the right rise the steep rocks of the Tre Corni, which prevented large-scale navigation. At the far left, next to a house, are the ruins of the old fortress Rochetta a Santa Maria. WINDSOR 12399

W hen Leonardo took the post of ducal engineer at Milan, even though this position was at first of secondary importance, he became sensitive to the appeal of the great construction problems which were essential to success in his new post. Until then Leonardo had lived on the fringe of that world of builders which had made of Tuscany a school of daring achievement in the field of large vaulted roofs. Brunelleschi's dome of Santa Maria del Fiore, the Duomo of Florence, completed just at the time of Leonardo's birth, was an example of constructive genius, hard to emulate and the likes of which were not to be found anywhere else [209/1]. But Brunelleschi's achievement had also raised problems of size. His solution could be considered optimal as far as structural stability under loads and thrusts and economy of masonry were concerned; but other similar attempts had failed. The nave of the enlarged Cathedral of Siena, although different in its proportions, repeated the failures of the first proto-Romanic vaults in the Po region of Italy immediately after the year 1000.

It may be proper to notice here that the building techniques, when they were revived in the West seven centuries after their disappearance in the East, took up again the general types of solutions based on the use of the three fundamental structural elements: the column, the beam, and the arch (which by translation give origin to the wall, the floor, and the vault). But the techniques used in building two of these elements had changed considerably. The beam was unchanged and made out of wood, as always, and the same was true of the floors. But the column and the arch were built in a completely different way. All clay elements had disappeared and above all the classical sesquipedal brick (1.5 feet long), which together with pozzolana mortar had deeply influenced Roman building technique in the first centuries A.D. when it became truly monumental. In their place came the hewn stone, taking advantage of the fact that in the region of the Lombard lakes at the foothills of the Alps the Liassic limestone and the gneiss appear in parallel strata, which are easy to split. So much so that the new building technique, so reminiscent of that developed in the Syriac Orient before the Arab invasion, was called *comacina* ("from Como") even in referring to structural solutions (unless this name refers to builders in the western Mediterranean who were refugees from the Commagene).

The column and the arch, when thus built without relying on a material with the high binding properties of pozzolana, presented many connection problems. But it was the arch that gave the builders most of their troubles, just as it had at the time of the great achievements of imperial Rome. The magnitude and direction of the arch thrust (which depend on the span-to-rise ratio of the arch and the loads on it) were the unknowns, which the ancient and the medieval builders estimated on the basis of traditional experience, of techniques handed down from generation to generation, and of their own intuition. Ignoring aesthetic considerations – which, if ever, came into play much later (for instance, the tendency to verticality) – the great builders' guilds beyond the Alps had adopted the ogive for both arches and cross vaults (vaulted with arches supported by ribs) for the specific purpose of reducing the magnitude of the horizontal thrust at the haunches, which jeopardized the stability of the roofing of the nave through its tendency to overturn the pier supports. Flying buttresses had been used to displace laterally and to lower the point of application of the thrust, and the weight of pinnacles and spires had been utilized to verticalize the arch reaction so that it would be contained within the base of the piers. As shown by the failure of the Cathedral of Siena, these developments were never thoroughly understood in Italy, nor did similar developments take place there which could be compared with those in northern France, from the Rhine to the Atlantic, and in the British Isles. These developments enhanced the knowledge of the builders beyond the Alps and ensured them a solid store of safe empirical rules, which were the secret of the individual guilds and a means of economic pressure on their customers. Yet though these rules were little, if at all, known in Italy, they were nevertheless empirical rules, and Leonardo must have heard them mentioned in the artistic circles of Florence, where the work of Brunelleschi was still the object of discussions and arguments.

Leonardo must have brought up these Florentine arguments with the ducal technicians at the court of Il Moro and compared them with the opinions of the

208/1 and 209/1
The great builder in Florence had been Filippo Brunelleschi (1377–1446), whose work in mathematical proportions and perspective influenced both the painting and architecture of Leonardo. Brunelleschi's magnificent dome for the cathedral in Florence is shown on the opposite page.

208/2

Another powerful influence on Leonardo was the architect Donato Bramante, portrayed above in a sketch by Raphael. Bramante settled in Milan about the time of Leonardo's move there and was working on the church of Santa Maria delle Grazie, while Leonardo was painting the Last Supper *in the refectory of the adjoining convent.*

209/1

most important architect of the Sforza court, Bramante [208/2]. Probably spurred on by the knowledge of the latter, Leonardo must have often wondered how to attack the arch and vault problems. Actually his attempts at solution were unsuccessful, but by mere intuition he got only one step away from an approximate geometric solution adopted four centuries later and obtained by the method of the funicular polygon [210/1].[15]

The idea of subdividing the arch into a number of blocks may have been suggested

Weight m *will exert upon counterweight* n

as many different exertions as its positions are varied when shifted along the beam. It is indeed evident that n *will suffer a different exertion when the weight is at* h *and when it is at* a.

carry out the experiment

Rope b c *will sustain as many different weights as the sites where the rope is tied to the beam are varied.*
If the rope is tied at i, *the weight of* X *will become very heavy for the rope, and if the rope is tied at* q, *the weight of* X *will diminish greatly.*

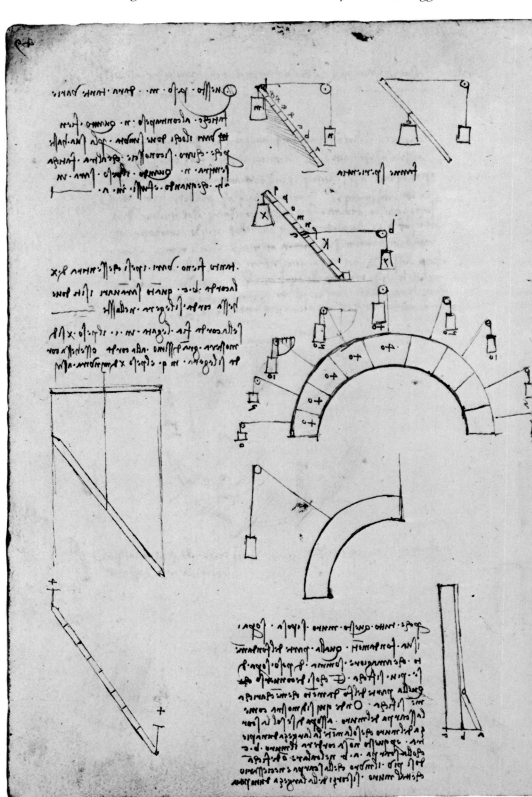

210/1

As the entire wall rests on its foundation, that part of the foundation which is loaded with more weight sinks more. And, conversely, that which receives a smaller load sinks less. Hence, it is here demonstrated that the batter of the wall supports only the outside of the wall, which has the thickness of only a single stone. For this reason, as the wall sinks, wall b c *will not correspond to batter* a b. *And as the wall will sink more than the batter, it is necessary to make the wall shorter by the width of one stone.*

to him by the very construction of arches in stone voussoirs. However, he used this idea by referring back to his research on the equilibrium of wedges[16] between two inclined struts [212/1]. He actually obtained the horizontal component of the reaction of each voussoir by means of a geometric construction based on the cosine of the angle between the corresponding radius and the horizontal, as if each voussoir behaved like half of one of the wedges he had considered previously. To establish equilibrium he considered the rotational tendency about a support point: the moment of the weight of a body must be balanced by the moment of a "counterweight," as in the case of some balanced triangles and rectangles considered in Codex Madrid I.[17] It is important to realize that these considerations are mistaken only because they are incomplete, since, besides the rotational equilibrium about a support point considered by Leonardo, one must also guarantee translational equilibrium [211/1].

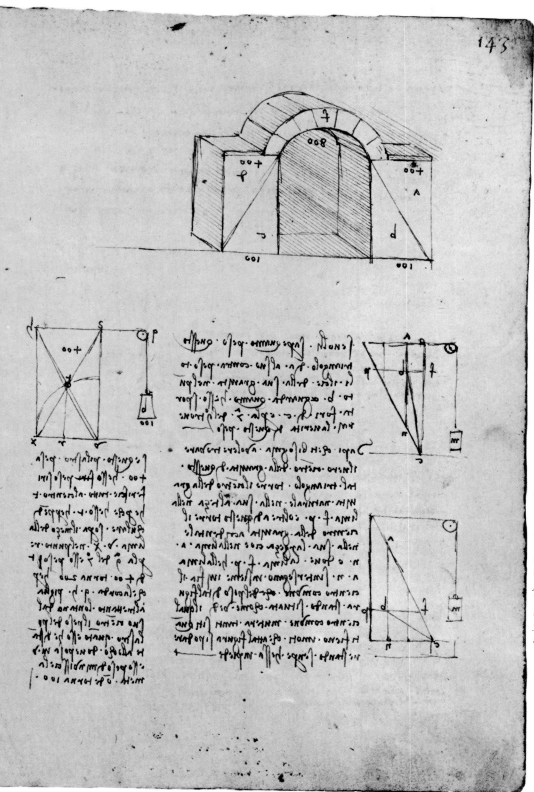

210/1 and 211/1
The Renaissance builders revived ancient construction techniques based on the three fundamental structural elements – the column, the beam, and the arch. Of these the arch, which was essential in constructing the huge vaulted domes such as the Duomo of Florence, presented the most difficult problems. Instead of the brick used by the old Roman builders, Lombardian architects worked with hewn stone found in abundance in the foothills of the Alps. The drawings on these two pages – Codex Madrid I, folios 142 verso (opposite page) and 143 recto – show Leonardo attempting to arrive at theoretical solutions to the problem of arch stability. He splits the arch into individual voussoirs – wedge-shaped stones – of equal weight. His calculations indicate that he came close to realizing the modern method of determining the horizontal thrust in the arch.

If you wish to know the weight which this triangle imposes upon its counterweight, take the center of its gravity at point b and see how great is its projection beyond c. According to the seventh of the ninth, you will find the true amount of this weight.

You must know, that in order to find the true center of gravity of this triangle, you have to take the center of the natural gravity at the height of line f p. Furthermore, you must take the center of the accidental gravity at its width, that is, line a n. And where line f p intersects line a n, there will be the common center of the weight of such a figure, placed as you see it. This center will change to as many places as are the motions which you can impart to such a figure, provided it remains always upright.

If this pilaster weighs 400, such a weight corresponds entirely to center t. And because t is perpendicular upon the center of line v X, at point r, according to the 9th of the 7th, weight t from 400 becomes 200. And because rope q h is attached at the same distance from its center – the weight of the pilaster – as this is distant from the place where it rests, at v, that weight is diminished by a half, becoming 100.

At this point it would seem easy to us, equipped as we are with a knowledge of graphic statics, to take the final step and reach the solution by (1) evaluating the component of the weight of each voussoir in the direction normal to one of its faces, (2) finding the resultant of this component and of the thrust coming from the keystone, (3) applying this resultant tentatively to the center of gravity of each voussoir, and thus (4) obtaining an approximate understanding of the direction and magnitude of the force transmitted by the arch to its haunches.

Leonardo may have been prevented from taking this final step by some conclusions he had reached in accordance with the rules and propositions of mechanics, and in particular of statics, which he had shaped into a systematic body of theoretical knowledge before his dedication to the physical interpretation of mechanical phenomena. It is impossible to establish whether this set of rules was carefully written down or merely jotted down in note form and then elaborated as time went on, given the present state of the Vincian manuscripts that have survived. However, various heading lists of the books on mechanics that Leonardo planned to write have been preserved; and it is certain that the references he makes in his discussions to numbers of chapters and propositions are as precise as if he were referring to an already definite compilation.

Among these propositions, one to which he refers in Codex Madrid I when discussing the stability of arches and vaults reads as follows: "That part of the disunited weight burdens more, which is nearest to its center of gravity."[18] In other words, that part of a distributed weight which is nearer to the vertical through its centroid exerts a greater pressure. Of course, this is not true when, in addition to

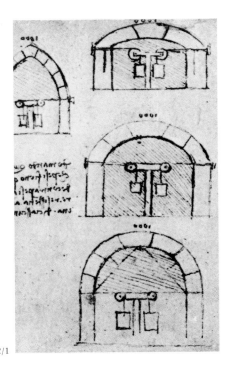

212/1

About the stretch of the arch.

The method of making the arch durable is to fill its angles with a good filling as far as its summit.

On loading up the round arch.

On well loading the ogive arch.

On the inconvenience derived from loading the ogive arch on its middle.

On the damage received by the ogive arch when it is loaded over its sides.

212/1–213/3
Arches used as structural elements often collapsed and no one, not even Leonardo, was quite sure why. In these drawings he attempts to establish rules for the stresses that cause failure in arches. The drawings are found in Codex Forster II, folio 92 recto (top), and, from left to right, in Manuscript A, folio 56 verso, the Codex Arundel, folio 158 recto and verso, Manuscript A, folios 50 recto and 49 verso, and Codex Madrid I, folio 139 recto. In the Arundel sketches, entitled "On the breaking of arches," he uses a chain as a tie rod to absorb the horizontal thrust acting upon the supports. Tuscan architects believed that such chains were the solution to the problem of arch stability. Actually, chains often failed because builders lacked the theoretical knowledge needed for proper sizing and anchoring. Though he failed to find another solution, Leonardo observes, "The arches which are held together by means of chains will not last." He was also able to prove that a masonry arch would fall under a concentrated load applied off the crown of the arch, while it would sustain a load at the crown.

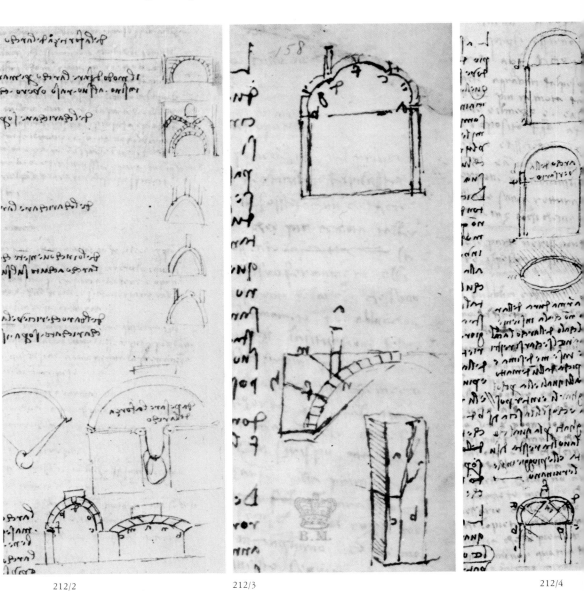

212/2   212/3   212/4

vertical forces, moments are present which shift the line of action of the forces. In fact, acknowledging the rule by means of an example on the same folio, Leonardo concluded erroneously that an arch representing the main section of the dome of the Grazie in Milan, weighs more on the inside edge of the center ring support (i.e., at the intrados of the arch) than on its outside edge (i.e., at the extrados of the arch). The partial double coaxial vault of this dome had in fact the sole purpose of widening its base support and of increasing the weight of the lower part of the dome only so as to bring nearer to the vertical the force resulting from the thrust and the weights of its upper part and of the lantern.

As also shown by this example, Leonardo seems to attach no importance to the horizontal thrust of the arch as a factor critical for its stability. His stand on this question may have been due to his awareness of the use of tie rods, first introduced in arch construction by Tuscan architects. Applying this tensile element to the arch, these master builders believed they had solved once and for all the problem of the horizontal thrust on the arch haunches and could therefore consider the arch as hinged to fixed supports. Actually this was often a mistaken assumption, because they lacked criteria for dimensioning the tie rod cross section and for anchoring it correctly to the masonry so that the supports would be practically fixed. In any case, the phenomenon of arch failure was always considered by Leonardo for the case of fixed supports [213/3],[19] and was assumed to consist of the splitting of the original arch line into separate sections corresponding to the various pieces into which the structure breaks up. From the geometric constructions he seems to use in trying to establish the nature of the stresses causing the arch failure, one would be led to think that he sees the failure as resulting from a bending moment which develops at the point of application of the loads. But there is no mention of this explanation in the text next to the figure. Perhaps Leonardo

213/5

213/4 and 5
Leonardo was far more successful in searching out the behavior of a bar or spring under stress. In Codex Madrid I, folio 84 verso (below), he describes the mechanism of a bending spring with uncanny accuracy: the fibers of the spring are lengthened at the outside of the curvature and shortened at the inside; the fibers in the middle are not deformed; lengthening and shortening occurs in proportion to the distance from

213/4

Of bending of the springs.

If a straight spring is bent, it is necessary that its convex part become thinner and its concave part, thicker. This modification is pyramidal, and consequently there will never be a change in the middle of the spring. You shall discover, if you consider all of the aforementioned modifications, that by taking part a b in the middle of its length and then bending the spring in a way that the two parallel lines, a and b, touch at the bottom, the distance between the parallel lines has grown as much at the top as it has diminished at the bottom. Therefore, the center of its height has become much like a balance for the sides. And the ends of those lines draw as close at the bottom as much as they draw away at the top. From this, you will understand why the center of the height of the parallels never increases in a b nor diminishes in the bent spring at c o.

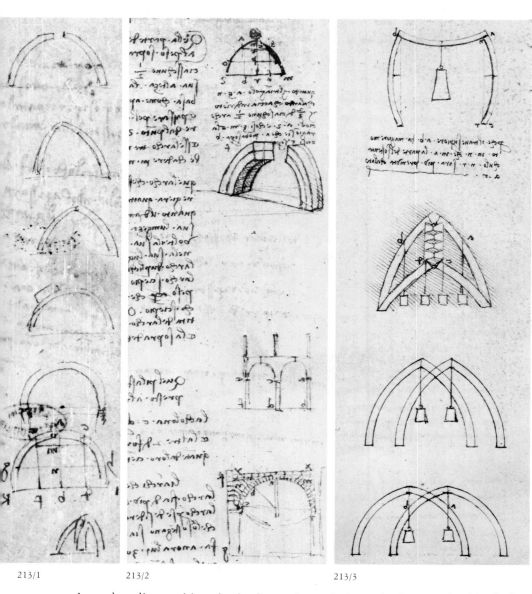

213/1   213/2   213/3

planned to discuss this point in the mathematical treatise he promised in Codex Madrid I to write.[20]

Perhaps he would have also explained in this same treatise why in a frame made of two posts and a beam the posts bend outward and the beam bends inward, i.e., downward, as stated in Madrid I;[21] but at the time Leonardo only made this statement without going into a quantitative analysis of it.

the undeformed middle fibers. When this hypothesis of internal stress distribution was stated more than two centuries later by Johann Bernoulli (top) – the father of Daniel Bernoulli – it became the basis for the modern theory of elasticity.

213

214/1 and 2 and 215/1
For years the unfinished central cupola of the Milan Cathedral was a source of great controversy. In 1488 Leonardo entered a

214/2

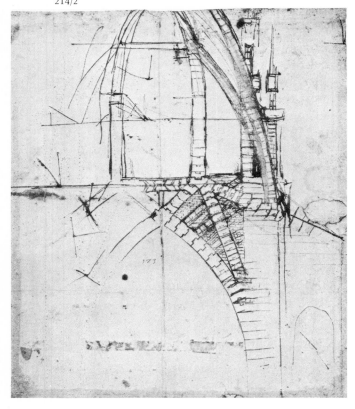

competition for its design with a plan based on these sketches in the Codex Atlanticus, folios 310 verso-b and 310 recto-b (opposite page). For unknown reasons he later withdrew from the contest.

On the other hand, in considering the deformation of a bent bar, Leonardo succeeded in this codex in describing exactly the phenomenon due to the stressing of its fibers under the heading "Of bending of the springs."[22] There he clearly realized that (1) the inner part of the bar (facing the center of curvature) shortens, i.e., the inner fibers are compressed, and (2) the outer part of the bar lengthens, i.e., the outer fibers are tensed, so that (3) the length of the middle axis of the bar remains unchanged, and (4) the lengthening or shortening of the fibers is proportional to their distance from the middle axis of the bar [213/4].

This is the exact scheme of longitudinal stress distribution along the depth of the cross section of a bent elastic body that was hypothesized, amid much controversy, 200 years later (in 1705) by Johann Bernoulli [213/5]. On the basis of his hypothesis and with the help of the calculus Bernoulli was able to synthesize the resistance of the cross section of a bar in its "moment of inertia" and to relate to it Hooke's law, "strain is proportional to stress," which is the basis of the modern theory of elasticity. (Let us note, in passing, that Galileo thought the entire cross section of a bent bar to be in tension, as stated in the *Trattato delle resistenze* gathered by Vincenzo Viviani and completed by the abbot Giulio Grandi of the University of Pisa in 1712.)

In this case, too, Leonardo stopped at the observation of the spring behavior; to obtain from it useful results, one needed to formulate Hooke's law and to extend the observation by induction to the general case of a body of arbitrary cross section bent along its longitudinal axis. However, at the time, the notion of an external bending moment acting at a section was lacking, as was that of a resisting internal moment of the fiber stresses capable of equilibrating the external moment.

As far as generalizations are concerned, we are here in a situation analogous to that created by Leonardo's statement on the *potentia* ("power" or energy) from the fall of water discussed earlier in this chapter. This statement is only a particular case of the basic law of hydrodynamics, which in turn represents but one aspect of a universal principle of dynamics: the energy of a system consists of two terms, one depending on the position and the other on the state of motion of the system in the field of forces, which influence its position (Hamilton's principle and the Hamilton-Jacoby equations, 1863). Nevertheless, it is precisely in the passage of Leonardo's Codex Madrid I containing this statement that we read for the first time in the history of human thought that energy is a function of position and motion. Before him "gravity" was simply either "natural" or "accidental." Not even Jakob Bernoulli, when he stated his law of hydrodynamics, realized that it was a particular case of a general law of immeasurable significance, since this law could only be formulated when theoretical mechanics and the differential calculus had become so developed as to allow the rational justification of such generalizations. Many similar cases of generalizations in the field of applied mechanics can be mentioned today which were implicit in the genial intuitions of its forerunners.

One cannot expect the appearance of conceptual analyses as complex as those just mentioned at a time when the basic concepts themselves were still quite nebulous. Nor must we forget that although the centuries-old dispute on the "universals" had been practically exhausted at the time Leonardo wrote, it had failed to show how to proceed towards the universalization of basic concepts and contented itself with comparisons and measurements of "greater" and "lesser universality." The process of universalization was accomplished many centuries later by means of a philosophical, critical approach under the impulse of the Kantian spirit. This must be emphasized for us to realize that, whenever he could, Leonardo tried to reach "general" statements in his discussions. In the majority of cases his generality cannot become a generalization, but only the extension to a whole class of phenomena of the observations he made on the concrete case he was analyzing. Generalizations can be ours now on the basis of the additional knowledge we have acquired in the five centuries since Leonardo.

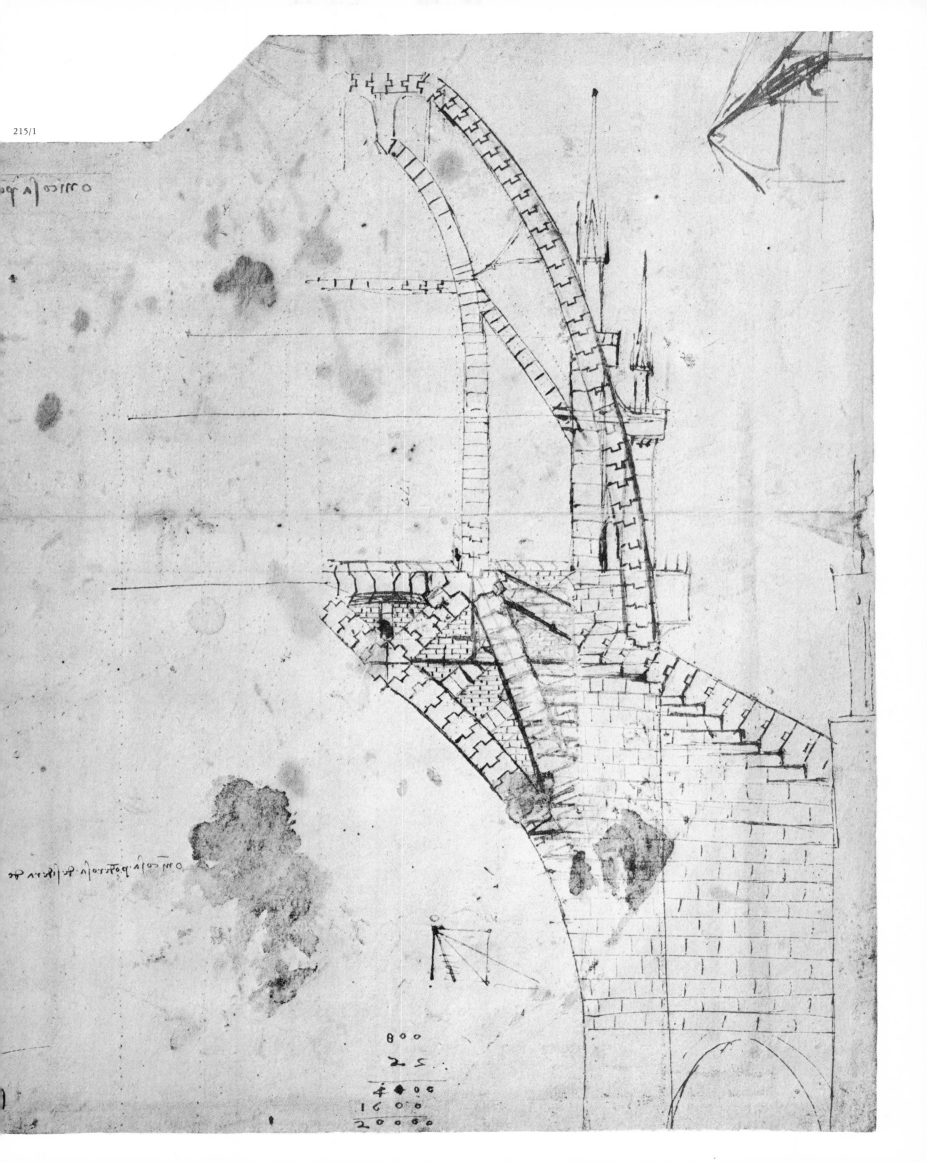

Leonardo's Treatise on Painting *was
published in Paris in 1651 – 132 years
after his death. He had begun noting
down his ideas on painting theory and
practice in the 1480s and continued
throughout most of his life. But it was
left to his heir Francesco Melzi to assem-
ble and copy the notes, which represent
the greatest quantity of writing on his
art to be handed down by a painter.*

216/1

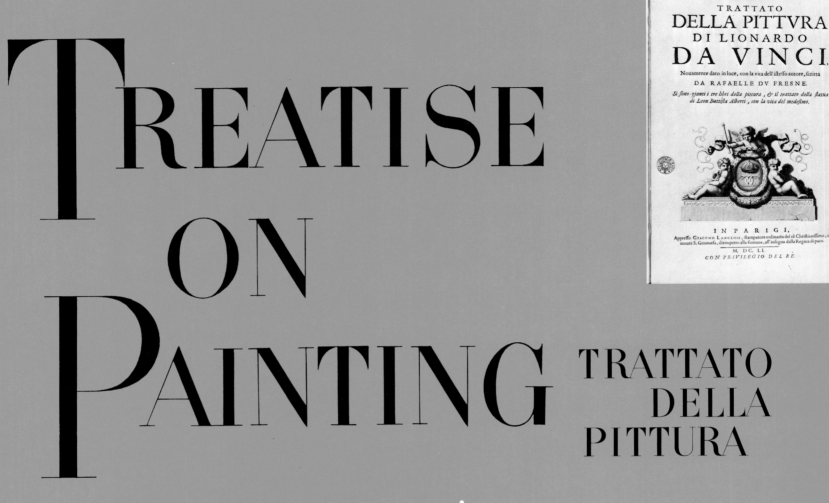

TREATISE ON PAINTING

TRATTATO DELLA PITTURA

ANDRÉ CHASTEL

As a theoretician of art Leonardo is
remarkable on two accounts. On the one
hand, there is no other artist in the whole
of history whose notes, observations, and
theoretical reflections have been preserved in such quantity.[1] On the other
hand, whereas some of his contemporaries
published treatises on art, Leonardo left
only annotations, sketches, and projects. If
his intention was indeed to produce a new
organon of art, nothing came of it in the
end. Yet even so, as Codex Madrid II helps
us to see, Leonardo remains a supremely
important theoretician.

217/1–6
*The ideas of the thinkers who wrote
these treatises were known to Leonardo –
though not all uncritically accepted –
when he was at work composing his
Treatise on Painting. From the left,
Alberti on architecture, 1550; Vitruvius on architecture, 1486; Pacioli
on geometric proportions, 1499; Alberti
on painting, 1547; above, Gauricus on
sculpture, 1504; below, Alberti again
on architecture, 1485.*

A t a certain point in his career, toward 1489–1490, Leonardo began to draw up his observations with a view to writing a didactic work.[2] The project developed, and according to Paolo Giovio,[3] some partial collections, such as the "book on anatomy," were ready to appear even with illustrations. Leonardo was convinced, like Alberti, that matters relating to art and especially to painting are subject to demonstration – that art can be explained. Alberti [219/1] died in 1472; the period of his reflection on the arts is that of the second quarter of the 15th century. The timing of his work enabled him to formulate new concepts and precise guidelines in matters not only of painting (*De pictura,* 1436), but also of sculpture (in *De statua,* a small opus drawn up towards 1464) and architecture (*De re aedificatoria,* partly drawn up in 1452 and printed in 1485). Nonetheless, as J. Schlosser has correctly observed, the effect of these writings on the artistic movement is difficult to grasp; and only in 1547 in Venice was an Italian version of Alberti's *Treatise on Painting,* so vivid and so clear, to be printed.[4] The same is true of the small opus on sculpture and the treatise on architecture: their diffusion

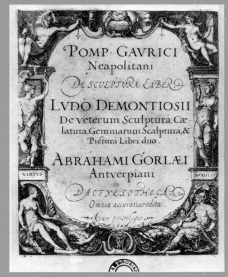

217/5

217/3

217/4

217/1

217/2

217/6

became general only toward the middle of the 16th century. In the meantime, other theoretical works had appeared, including, in 1504, the *De sculptura* of Gauricus and, beginning in 1486, many editions of Vitruvius.[5] This situation is quite revealing: it is as if Alberti's works were a century overdue in acquiring their authority. Until the mid-16th century they had been unevenly known and admired.

Thus during the 30 years from 1490 to 1519 Leonardo was able to undertake the same task as if nothing had happened. No codified and universally accepted rules existed. And in any case, Alberti's works belong to the productions of the humanist milieu and reflect its ideas on the arts. Only indirectly do they reflect those of artistic circles, and so they do not constitute a satisfactory expression of what can be termed "the culture of the workshops."[6] However close his links with artists may have been, Alberti always seems like a great amateur beside the professional men, the craftsmen and the artists trained in his *bottega.*

Leonardo's starting point is appreciably different from Alberti's and even entails a move in the opposite direction. He was 20 years old when Alberti died. Despite all his gifts, he did not have the intellectual and social standing that would have allowed him to compel recognition. He still had to make a success of his career as an artist and to complete his philosophical education.

218/1

In his writings on art Leonardo portrayed painting as "the sole means of reproducing all the known works of nature." The painter, in short, was a kind of god who could create – or at least recreate – the world. In the Treatise on Painting he describes some of the painter's powers:

The painter can call into being the essences of animals of all kinds, of plants, fruits, landscapes, rolling plains, crumbling mountains . . . places sweet and delightful with meadows of many-colored flowers bent by the gentle motion of the wind which turns back to look at them as it floats on . . . .

Leonardo rejected the practice of many Renaissance painters who looked at nature as if it were a mere backdrop for their human figures. In the Treatise he attacks

218/2

the "very bad landscapes" of Botticelli. The painter "is not well rounded," he writes, "who does not have an equally keen interest in all of things within the compass of painting."
In Leda and the Swan he captured a landscape and a woman bursting with new life. The painting was lost, but numerous copies have survived. The details shown here are from a copy at the Borghese Gallery.

218

218/3

The original situation of a workshop like Verrocchio's and the very climate of Florence at that time favored in an exceptional way what Panofsky calls the "decompartmentalization" of the disciplines.[7] Members of the Medici circle now intervened in artistic matters much more than they had during Alberti's youth, and they developed an impure Platonism, impregnated with aestheticism, which young Leonardo could neither adhere to fully nor withdraw from completely. The *botteghe* had become little centers of scientific study: anatomy and perspective were not taught at the *Studio* but at Verrocchio's and Pollaiuolo's. Empirical, technological knowledge needed to be systematized, but a conceptual framework and appropriate linguistic forms were required, and the scientific texts of antiquity and even of the Middle Ages only partly provided them.[8]

During the last quarter of the 15th century it can be observed that in all the centers of the peninsula the great heads of workshops – Piero della Francesca, Mantegna, Bramante, the Bellinis – endeavored to raise the professional status of artists by breaking the traditional distinction between the *artes mechanicae* and the *artes liberales.* The most enterprising, the most obstinate, the most brilliant of these Italian masters conscious of their force and of their responsibilities was Leonardo.

Leonardo's entry in 1482 into the court of the Sforzas coincides with an extraordinary program of activity in which the demands made on him as an engineer outweighed those made on him as a sculptor or painter [7/1]. It was in this milieu that Leonardo realized the necessity of composing new treatises, based on the analysis of the scholar and the praxis of the technician. And from 1489 on, scattered notes show the intellectual freshness with which Leonardo approached questions on painting.[9] In 1492 Manuscript A revealed the general lines of the future *Treatise on Painting.* The dedicatory letter placed by Luca Pacioli [70/1] at the head of his treatise *De divina proportione* and dated February 1498 mentions it

219/1

One of the inspirations for Leonardo's Treatise on Painting *was the work of the architect and scholar Leon Battista Alberti. Before Alberti's early treatise on art in 1435, apprentices had access only to some collections of technical recipes – the best known of them being the* Trattato *by Cen-*

nino Cennini of about 1390; there was no proper art theory in written form. Alberti elevated to scientific theory the principles of linear perspective that had been worked out by the architect Brunelleschi earlier in the 15th century. He urged artists to master geometry and optics and to learn the

219/2

In his first dated pen drawing (right) Leonardo revealed at age 21 the extraordinary feeling for landscape that would mark several of his greatest paintings. Perhaps sensing its importance, Leonardo noted the date in the upper left corner, "Day of St. Mary of the Snows, August 5, 1473." The German scholar Ludwig Heydenreich has termed the drawing "the first true landscape in art." The view is from a height down into the valley of the Arno near Florence, where Leonardo was undergoing his apprenticeship. Already he has begun to master the effects of light and the illusion of atmosphere. The quick broken strokes convey a strong sense of motion: trees, water, and mountains seem to swim together, unifying foreground and background.

UFFIZI, FLORENCE

as well, speaking of Leonardo as "having completed with all diligence his great treatise on painting and human movement."[10] Leonardo held up its publication, but continued to study ways to give the work the necessary illustration. This delay, which was fatal to the project, can be explained by the continuous expansion of the investigation and the difficulty of co-ordinating all its various aspects. Nor did Leonardo's return to Florence simplify matters.

We must imagine the favorable climate that surrounded Leonardo there just after

mechanisms of the human body. In the practice of art Leonardo did all this and more. He became a scientist and theoretician of painting, and in his own unfinished treatise he elaborated what Sir Kenneth Clark has called "the most precious document in the whole history of art."

Despite – or maybe because of – Leonardo's apparent lack of real fondness for women, he painted fascinating portraits of them. Isabella d'Este hounded him for five years and never did get a portrait. He had to do some portraits to earn a living and to satisfy his patron the Duke of Milan. He made the task less arduous by adding visual puns to

amuse himself. In his first portrait (bottom) he painted the melancholy Ginevra de' Benci against a tree of juniper – ginevra in an Italian dialect. The painting, purchased by the National Gallery in Washington for 5 million dollars, was the first Leonardo in an American museum. The Lady with an Ermine *(top), at the Czartoryski in Cracow, portrays Cecilia Gallerani, one of the duke's mistresses. The ermine, a symbol of the duke, represented purity.* Beatrice d'Este *(opposite page), at the Biblioteca*

Ambrosiana in Milan, is the portrait of the duke's young wife and Isabella's sister. On her dress Leonardo – or perhaps a pupil – added the lacework pattern used in his Sala delle Asse *decorations. The Italian word for the wicker pattern provided an oblique pun on the name Vinci.*

the turn of the century: "His fame had grown so great," wrote Vasari, "that all lovers of art, indeed the whole city, wanted him to leave them something to remember him by, and everywhere they spoke of nothing other than to have him carry out some great and wonderful work. . . ." Demands upon the artist were heavy during these years when Florence had regained an artistic and cultural importance not yet disputed by Rome. Everyone was beginning to realize – in Florence as elsewhere – that Leonardo, who was 50 in 1502, was adding to his talent as a painter and to his aptitudes as an engineer the role of a theoretician. At the end of 1504 a rather arid but at the same time informed and complex treatise on sculpture by a lesser-known Neapolitan humanist was published by Giunti in Florence. In the foreword to this work the editor invoked the patronage of Lorenzo Strozzi, who, along with Bernardo Rucellai (who had been Florence's ambassador in Milan from 1484 to 1486, during Leonardo's stay), was the life and soul of the city's most active intellectual circle. Leonardo, too, must have known about these men, and they must have known about Leonardo. In short, if there was a call for a great doctrine, it was in this period that it must have become urgent, when Leonardo was in the limelight.

The fragments found in Codex Madrid II [222/1–4] prove that during these years of frantic activity the undertaking of the *Treatise* again forced itself upon the artist. In 1504 the plan for the *Treatise* went back about 15 years; and Leonardo now had only 15 more years to live. So we are at the center of the 30 years during which Leonardo was obsessed by the idea of the *Treatise*. Never was he to find the leisure or, more important, the frame of mind that would have allowed him to arrange his mass of notes in order and bring the task to completion. The few pages *de pictura* of Codex Madrid II precede by little their elaboration in a collection, Libro A, whose organization is much more solid than all he had composed up until then; it has been brilliantly reconstituted by C. Pedretti, from paragraphs of the Codex Urbinas [223/1–4], where its 107 elements have been transcribed.[11] Each of the painterly themes evoked in Codex Madrid II finds a more advanced development in extremely similar notes in Libro A. This latter notebook dates from the years following 1505, with a certain concentration around 1508. But around 1508 Leonardo's plan for publication lost steam; the project for a treatise on anatomy seems to have broken away from the all-embracing enterprise of the *Treatise on Painting*. It is at this time that he wrote the famous and rather pathetic note excusing himself for being able to achieve only "a miscellany devoid of order," because he could not reread and confront everything. This would have been too complicated a task "especially in view of the great intervals of time separating one moment of writing from the next."[12] It remains true, however, that during the years 1505–1508 Leonardo returned to the theoretical problems of painting.[13]

Leonardo's manuscripts have accustomed us to an incredible diversity and to an often disconcerting intermingling of records. In Codex Madrid II calculations and rough sketches dealing with the deviation of the Arno (from 1503 to the end of summer 1504) or the fortification of Piombino (autumn 1504) alternate with studies for the conversion of volumes and observations on gliding and musical instruments. We also find here and there remarks on totally different subjects, some of which have proved to be of capital importance – such as the note that gives the date of an accident that befell the cartoon for the mural of the *Battle of Anghiari*. This little note [45/2] serves as a reminder that the period of 1503–1505 to which the manuscript belongs is also – and in a sense is especially – that of the *Battle of Anghiari,* commissioned in October 1503. Leonardo therefore had the notebook at hand during the two years when, in spite of his work as engineer, his mind was on this project of the governing council of Florence. One might have expected it to contain remarks concerning the elaboration of the work. In fact, however, the observations deal mainly with anatomy or how the eye sees – that is, with general problems. These may be connected with the council's complex project, but they only deal with it through Leonardo's customary problem-solving approach.

Apart from the record of the thunderstorm on folio 1, the notes appear on 18 leaves. One note, dealing with perspective, is found at the end of the first quire.[14] All the others are spread out over the internal quires and are distributed in three

areas quite distinctly towards the beginning, in the middle, and towards the end of the collection.[15] There are no special conclusions to be drawn from this, for the same subjects of reflection reappear from area to area: (1) observations on anatomy, (2) observations on the eye, its pupil, and the perception of light, and (3) indications on reflections and the range of color tones.

CODEX MADRID II

*Le figure aranno più gratia posste ne' lumi universali che particu-
lari e picoli, perchè li gran lumi non potenti abracciano li rilievi de' corpi, e ll' opere fatte in tali lumi apparisscano da lontano con gratia e cque-
le che sson ritratte a' llumi picoli, pigliano gran somma d' onbra,
e ssimile opere, fatte con tale onbre mai aparisscan da llochi lontani altro che tinte.*

MADRID II 25v

De pittura.

*Il colore che ssi trova infra lla parte onbrosa e alluminata
de' corpi onbrosi, fia di minor belleza che cquello che ffia integralmente alluminato. Adunque la prima belleza de' co-
lori fia ne' principali lumi.—*

MADRID II 26r

*Delle machie dell' onbre che apariscano
ne' corpi da llontano.—*

*Senpre la gola o altra perpendicular dirittura, che
sopra di sè abbia alcuno sporto, sarà più osscu-
ra che lla perpendiculare faccia d' esso sporto.—*

*Seguita che quel
corpo si dimos-
sterrà più allu-
minato, che da
maggior somma
d' um medesimo
lume sarà ve-
duto.—*

*Vedi in a, che non v' allumina parte alcuna del cielo
f K, e in b v' alumina il cielo i K e in c v' allumina il cielo h K, e in d il cielo g K, e in e
il cielo f K integralmente. Adunque il petto sarà
di pari chiareza della fronte, naso e mento. Ma cquel
che io t' ho a ricordare de' volti, che ttu consideri in
quelli come in diverse disstante si perde diverse
qualità d' onbre, ma ssol ressta quelle prime machie,
cioè della incassatura dell' ochio e altre simile.*

MADRID II 71r

*boca della strada, allumina insino, quasi insino, vici-
no al nasscimento delle onbre che stan sotto gli oget-
ti del volto, e così di mano in mano si va mutando in chiareza, insino che ttermina sopra del mento, con oscurità insen-
[si]bile per qualunche verso. Come se ttal lume fussi a e, vedi*

*la linia f e del lume che alumina insin sotto il
naso, e lla linia c f solo allumina insin sotto il labro.
E lla linia a h s' asstende insin sotto il mento, e cqui il naso
riman forte luminoso, perchè è venduto da ttutto il lume a b c d e.*

MADRID II 71v

222/1–4
*The rediscovery of the Madrid Codices
revealed a new manuscript source for the
statements appearing in the* Treatise on
Painting. *Above, from Codex Madrid II,
are four of Leonardo's notes that correspond
to passages in the Codex Urbinas (opposite
page). They confirm the accuracy with
which Francesco Melzi brought together
and copied into Urbinas his master's
thoughts about art – now known as the*
Treatise on Painting.

222/1

222/2

222/3

222/4

A recapitulation of the content of these brief notes scattered in Codex Madrid II is enough to reveal the link between them and the problems of the *Treatise*. Its tone, its questions, its turns of phrase are recognizable. What we have here are not unconnected notes or aphorisms, but elements of demonstration. The impression we get is of a scholarly monologue proceeding in the midst of other occupations.

These notes were not afterwards neglected: 14 passages were transcribed into the Codex Urbinas; and all the paragraphs taken from Leonardo's manuscript bear the little sign testifying that they were in fact picked out by Francesco Melzi in the arduous compilation of around the 1550s, which made the belated publication of the *Treatise* possible. Therefore, Codex Madrid II was certainly one of the group

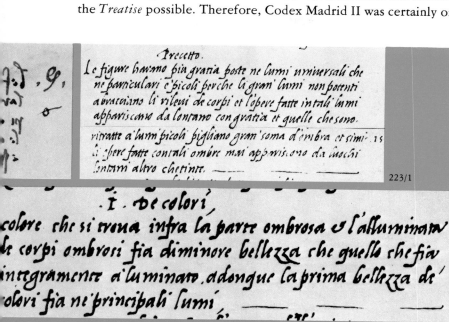

223/1

223/2

223/3

223/4

CODEX URBINAS

Precept. *Figures are more attractive when they are placed under the universal light of the sky than when they are lighted by small individual lights, because large lights that are not powerful bring out the relief of bodies, and works made with such lighting appear attractive from a distance. Those which are painted with individual lighting are greatly shadowed, and works made with so many shadows, viewed from distant positions, never look like anything but stains.*

Of colors. *Color found between the shadowed and the illuminated parts of shadowed bodies is less beautiful than that which is entirely illuminated, so that the prime beauty of colors is to be seen in the principal lights.*

Of spots of shadows that appear on distant bodies. *The throat or other straight perpendicular, which has some projection above it, will always be darker than the perpendicular face of that projection; this occurs because that body will appear most illuminated which is exposed to the greatest number of rays of the same light.*

You see that A is illuminated by no part of the sky F K, and B is illuminated by I K of the sky, and C is illuminated by H K of the sky, and D by G K, and E by the whole sky from F to K. Thus, the breast will be of the same brightness as the forehead, nose, and chin.

But what I should remind you of about faces is that you should consider how, at different distances, different kinds of shadow are lost, and there remain only the essential spots, that is, the pits of the eye and places of similar significance. Finally the face remains obscure

of faces, brightening them somewhat. The length of the above-mentioned light from the sky confined by the edges of roofs and their façades, illuminates almost as far as the beginning of the shadows which are below the projections of the face, gradually changing in brightness, until it terminates over the chin with imperceptible shading on every side.

It is as if the light were A E. The line F E of the light illuminates as far as beneath the nose, and the line C F only illuminates as far as beneath the lip. The line A H extends as far as beneath the chin. Here the nose remains very bright because it faces all the rays of light, A B C D E.

223/1-4
In all, Francesco Melzi copied 14 passages from Codex Madrid II and put them into the Codex Urbinas (above). Each note in Madrid II is marked with the sign Melzi placed on relevant passages in the 18 source manuscripts to indicate he had copied them. Leonardo is believed to have worked on several other treatises, including one on the horse and another on architecture, which were lost in his lifetime or when the dispersal of the manuscripts began after Melzi's death.

of notebooks to which Melzi strove – following Leonardo's instructions – to extract the substance and co-ordinate the passages.[16]

Comparison of the originals and the text recopied into the Codex Urbinas [223/1–4] confirms the faithfulness of Melzi's collating; only two paragraphs have been shortened. Those that were not retained were useless repetitions of notes to be taken from other manuscripts.[17] If 14 passages were taken from Codex Madrid II for the final compilation, it is because this notebook was considered, despite the relatively small number of these notes, as a valid contribution.

Of these 14 passages, 2 must be considered apart. They appear as warnings that the painter is supposed to be giving himself. The first concerns the effect of perspective in great compositions with a strong horizontal extension: "In itself, a perspective offered by a straight wall will be false unless it is corrected by presenting to the beholding eye a foreshortened view of the wall [225/1–3]."[18] Leonardo is talking about murals. In the case of a long horizontal span, the spectator placed at the center unconsciously discerns the most distant parts as though they were slightly deformed, for it would require a slightly concave wall to maintain all the elements equidistant from the visual focus. The spreading out of forms achieved by the

Leonardo's study for the Adoration of the Magi *below – drawn about 1481 – is a virtually perfect illustration of linear perspective as it was practiced in Florence. The illusion of three dimensions is created by the lines that recede from the very foreground and converge on a vanishing point to the right of center. Over this severe geometric base swarm a host of agitated figures, including the prancing horses that appear later in Leonardo's studies for the Sforza monument and the* Battle of Anghiari.

UFFIZI, FLORENCE

224/1

system of "artificial perspective" – which does not take into account this deformation – thus calls for an excessive enlarging of the lateral parts, judging by what one should perceive in nature. Leonardo resolves the difficulty by supposing that a kind of spontaneous correction takes place there; the deformation caused by the projective system of the painter is compensated by the very perception of the spectator placed in the axis.[19]

The reason for his statement in the codex being so laconic becomes clear when we observe that the little explanatory diagram had already appeared in Manuscript A of 1492, that the problem is taken up again in Manuscript D and in the Codex Arundel around 1508, and that it finds a more elaborated formulation in Manuscript E around 1513–1514. The fragment of Codex Madrid II is thus only one of the instances of a reflection that began some 12 years before and was to continue 10 years later. But the composition of the *Battle of Anghiari,* whose probable dimensions exceeded those of the *Last Supper,* gave the problem a strong current interest.

Below is another kind of perspective – the imaginary bird's-eye view that appears in many of Leonardo's maps and drawings of the Arno valley. WINDSOR 12683

224/2

The second passage takes on even more clearly the form of a principle: "In narrative paintings never put so many ornaments on your figures and other bodies that they hinder the perception of the form and attitude of such figures and the nature of the aforesaid other bodies."[20] This rule was to be copied into the Codex Urbinas,[21] and in fact bears the mark *de pictura* signifying that it belongs to the *Treatise*. It is not by chance that it appears in Codex Madrid II, for this warning would have little relevance to the *Last Supper,* but it has much for the *Battle of Anghiari.* The composition required a great variety of military armor and equipment [227/1]. What we know of it from Rubens's famous sketch reveals the fantasies that could carry away Leonardo's imagination: the armor decorated with ram's head and the shoulder plate in the form of a spiraling shell, the helmet shaped like a mask, and so on. It seems reasonable to suppose that the remark on ornaments corresponds, like the preceding one on perspective, to a current problem.[22]

The same may well be true of the Codex Madrid II notes relating to anatomy; but these nevertheless fit precisely into the general framework of the future *Treatise.*

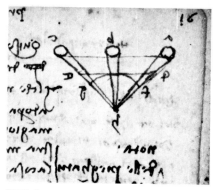

225/1–3

225/2

As he became increasingly intrigued by the science of art, Leonardo went beyond the earlier linear perspective (opposite page) to investigate how the eye sees. In the sketches

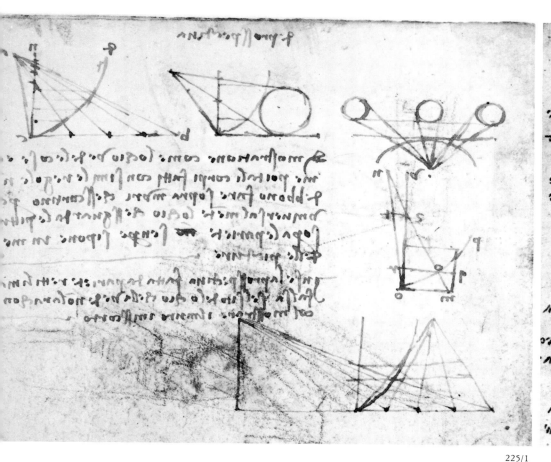

225/1

The one that clarifies the role of the muscles in operations of pushing and pulling defines their mechanism in relation to the seat of the shoulder: "Pushing and pulling are of one and the same nature. . . . Pushing and pulling can be done along diverse lines around the center of the power of the mover. As for the arms, the center is located at the place where the sinew of the shoulder, that of the breast, and that of the shoulder-blade opposite the breast meet with the bone of the upper shoulder."[23] This text is accompanied by rapid little sketches. The idea has been taken up again in the Codex Urbinas,[24] where it is united with other remarks of the same kind on scapular articulation. These notes must be studied on the one hand in connection with Windsor sheets 19003 recto and verso [229/2], and on the other with the famous drawing in red chalk [230/2] Windsor 12640, which it is difficult not to relate to the period of the *Battle of Anghiari.*[25] The section of the arm of the two warriors is reminiscent of some ancient marble,[26] and it is only more remarkable to come across the principle again later in the anatomical plates of Vesalius. The embryo of a complete style of presentation of the anatomical "complexes" appears in the drawings corresponding to the passage on pushing and pulling.

225/3

on this page he considers the problem of perspective in large wall paintings, such as the Battle of Anghiari. Like a scientist he works out the optics in the sketches from Manuscript E – at top from folio 16 recto, above from folio 16 verso. In the detail at left from Codex Madrid II, folio 15 verso, he notes, "As a rule, the eye looking at a painting on a wall places itself always at the center of the picture." The eye is able to take in a small painting without trouble. But in a wide fresco the figures at each end will be slightly distorted because they are at a greater distance from the eye than is the center of the picture. Either the wall has to be made concave to equalize the distances or, more practically, the figures at the ends must be painted larger, creating a kind of curved perspective.

Anatomical analysis, in Leonardo's view, made it possible to rediscover the mechanics that correspond to emotion: the exact image of muscular movements suggests the movements of the soul. Their presentation presupposes, however, an intuitive sense of perception and a feeling for proper balance, both of which Leonardo seems to value above all else. On one page of Codex Madrid II he calls to mind that every muscle varies in volume according to whether it is or is not in action,[27] and on another he says, "Do not make all the muscles of your figures apparent, because even if they are in their right places they do not show prominently unless the limbs in which they are located are exerting great force or are greatly strained. Limbs which are not in exercise must be drawn without showing the play of the muscles. And if you do otherwise, you will have imitated a bag of nuts rather than a human figure."[28] This comparison has a familiar ring about it; the passage has been taken up textually in the Codex Urbinas.[29] From 1490 on we find

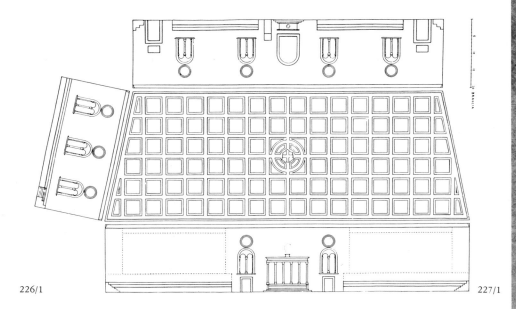

226/1 and 2 and 227/1

In the Treatise *Leonardo wrote a self-warning probably related to the epic fresco he was executing in 1504, the* Battle of Anghiari. *"In narrative paintings," he cautions, "never put so many ornaments on your figures and other bodies that they hinder the perception of the form and attitude of such figures and the nature of the aforesaid other bodies." Leonardo loved decoration, and a detail from Rubens's Louvre copy of* Anghiari *(opposite page) hints that Leonardo did not heed his own warning. The spiraling decorative motifs on the warrior's helmet and shoulder plate suggest the composition of the battle itself: a compact whirl of violence turning in on itself. Leonardo painted his fresco in the Sala del Gran Consiglio of the Palazzo Vecchio in Florence (diagram at right). Scholars believe the most likely location was the east wall (bottom of diagram) in the space indicated by the dotted rectangle at the left of center. Michelangelo's fresco the* Battle of Cascina *was to be on the other side of the wall. Leonardo never finished his painting. It was partially ruined by technical failures; later covered over with another painting. Copies of the* Battle of Anghiari

226/1   227/1

criticism of "barren and woody figures";[30] the formula of the "bag of nuts" and the phrase "bunch of radish" are applied to nudes that are "woody and without grace" in a passage of Manuscript L which must date from 1502.[31] Since Leonardo attacks numerous artists who were guilty of this abuse, we recognize here one of his polemic stings against a certain widespread Tuscan practice. But an insistent

226/2

show only a central group of fighting horsemen. But the vast size of the wall space — about 22 by 58 feet — and a number of Leonardo's studies lead to the belief that he intended a much more panoramic work. The reconstruction at bottom, which is based on his drawings, shows the central battle flanked on either side by groups of foot soldiers and horsemen.

tradition, passing from Dolce (1557) to Lomazzo (1584) and Armenini (1586), has identified Michelangelo as the chief culprit. This interpretation does have some foundation: the imprecation reappears in Manuscript E of the years 1513–1514,[32] which we may assume to be a criticism of the nudes of the Sistine Chapel [231/1]. And so the "bag of nuts" of Codex Madrid II may well refer to the *Battle of Cascina* [230/1], where the display of musculature had taken on incredible proportions. And as Leonardo is at grips with an analogous theme, this no doubt is also a reminder to himself to beware of falling into these excesses.

The graceful style that contrasts with the thoughtless anatomical display requires "sweet fleshiness, with simple folds and roundness of limbs," Leonardo says in Codex Madrid II.[33] A Windsor study dating from the same period[34] describes by means of a little diagram how the folds of the skin are formed in the case of knotty muscles and in the contrary case of beautiful rounded shapes. The first formation is called *antico,* the second *moderno.* The same appellations will reappear a few years later, around 1510, in Manuscript G.[35] This time the analysis has considerable extensions and reflects a determined reaction against the harsh style of certain

Leonardo studied the anatomy of men living and dead to learn the mechanics of the body. The drawings of a torso below probably were related to his studies for the Battle of Anghiari, *in which he portrayed the contorted bodies of men caught up in war. His*

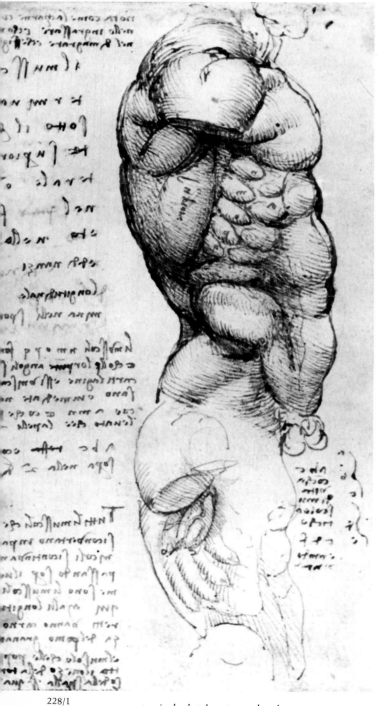

228/1

anatomical sketches properly show every muscle. But his painter's conclusion is a preference for "sweet fleshiness with simple folds and roundness of the limbs...." In a little diagram at the right of the lower drawing he contrasts this with the technique of showing bulging muscles. He calls the latter "antique" and his own method "modern." WINDSOR 19032v

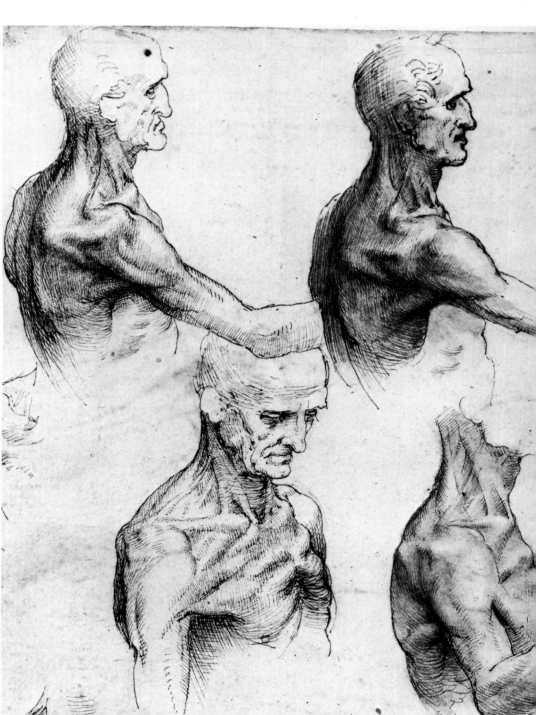

228/2

Tuscans. An echo of it is found in Gauricus's treatise *De sculptura* (1504), where the Colleoni horse is regarded as an "anatomical model." Leonardo's critical attitude had decisive consequences everywhere – in Venice, where it combined with Giorgione's trend, in Emilia, and everywhere else that the more relaxed style had paved the way. A sort of cleavage thus established itself between the old style and the modern; Leonardo's terms were taken up and developed by Vasari in the opposition to the "hard, barren, and harsh style" that contrasted with the new way indicated by Leonardo and Giorgione. Vasari's list of the artists of the 15th century who were surpassed by this process gives an account, in a way, of all these artists who "in order to appear great draftsmen, make their nudes woody and devoid of grace." Naturally this list does not include Michelangelo.[36] The transition has thus been made from scientific analysis to aesthetic recommendations: anatomy is the key to the exact representation of the "movements of the soul," that is, emotions. Its use, however, must be based on stylistic requirements, and these requirements are taken into account in the notes of Codex Madrid II, with regard to optics, the basis of the whole painting operation, and the proportions of shadow and light, the regulating of which depends on an essentially artistic choice. Leonardo starts from the analysis of the mechanisms of perception. But in the physiology and even in the anatomy that he adopts, he instinctively – and wrongly – gives the organs of sight a privileged place.[37] So the organ of the eye deserves all the attention: some notes deal with the way in which the pupil reacts to the intensity of light,[38] others with the effect of binocular perception.[39] The model of the *camera obscura,* of the optic box through which the rays travel to produce an image after crossing a narrow opening, seems indispensable to Leonardo. Towards 1508 he will make the analogy clear in Manuscript D, where he will take up all these indications again [233/5], resuming, through the rapid notes of Codex Madrid II, his previous general studies.[40]

Optics make it possible to analyze plays of light and shadow. In about 1490 a little collection, *De lume e ombra,* had outlined the laws and variations of the phenomenon. Codex Madrid II comes back to it strongly, underlining the importance of the bluing brought about by the density of interposed air, an effect more pronounced in dark colors than in bright ones,[41] the relative blending of dark and bright colors at a distance,[42] and the fullness of color under the prevailing light.[43] To these observations is added advice, in which Leonardo no longer speaks as a physicist who analyzes, but as a painter who chooses: natural light gives more gentle and more enveloping shades than special lighting;[44] there are "places which should be selected in order to give relief and grace to the subjects."[45]

The notes on the whole reveal a completely new attention to open-air effects, which appear to be the fresh stimulus in Leonardo's research. The evidence of Codex Madrid II thus confirms the conclusion reached from the study of the

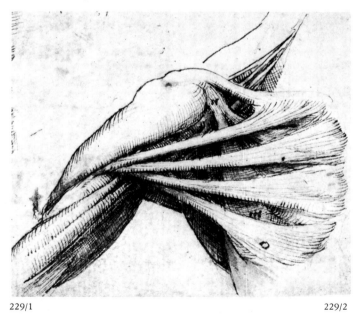

228/2 and 229/1 and 2
His anatomical drawings were so precise that many are still used to illustrate medical textbooks. The details at left and right are from the Windsor Collection, No. 19001 verso. The sheet at far right, Windsor 19003 verso, shows the shoulder muscles and, in the upper right portion, a wire model of how they work. Leonardo writes, "The painter who has acquired knowledge of the nature of the sinews, muscles, and tendons will know exactly in the movement of any limb how many and which of the sinews are the cause of it, and which muscle by its swelling is the cause of this sinew's contracting."

229/1   229/2

manuscripts already known: towards 1505 Leonardo modifies his approach to the problems of light and shadow and those of color: "he has shifted their study from the inside of the studio to the open air and the countryside."[46] But at the same time he continues as strongly as ever his polemic against violent lighting and oversharp outlines, insisting on the necessity of looking for the right moment and the right arrangement. The same preoccupation will reappear in the famous notes of the years 1508–1510 on "the kind of lighting to choose for painting portraits."[47] In these analyses of the delicate blend of the shades that fade towards a fringe of light and of the thousand hues of chiaroscuro that appropriate lighting makes possible, it is difficult not to think of the contemporary experiments of the *Mona Lisa,* the

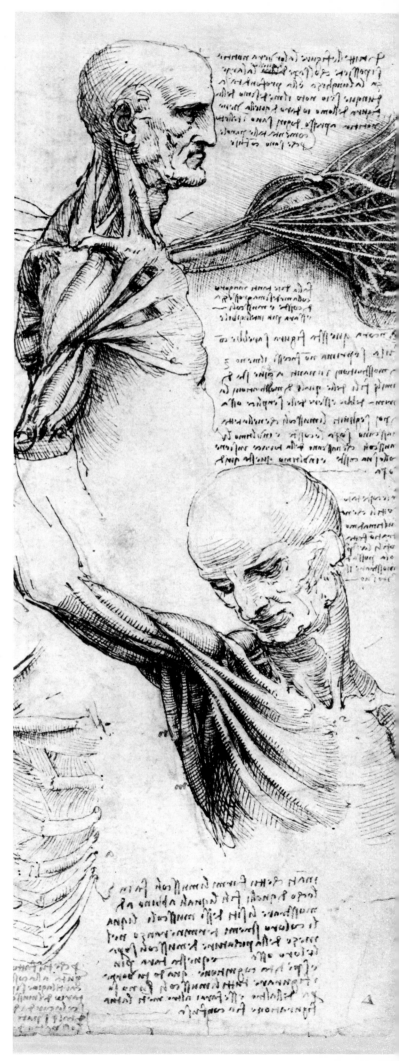

Leonardo and his rival Michelangelo were both masters of the nude. Michelangelo's figures were sculptural, revealing the play of every muscle – as in his studies for the Battle of Cascina *(below) and a sibyl (opposite page) for his epic painting on the ceiling of the Sistine Chapel. Leonardo at*

230/1

his best could match him in heroic nudes – his sketch at right for the Battle of Anghiari, Windsor Collection No. 12640, *resembles an ancient marble statue. But Leonardo, switching from anatomy to art, wanted his muscles to suggest the "movements of the soul." Perhaps with Michelangelo in mind, he writes in Codex Madrid II, "Do not make all the muscles of your figures apparent, because even if they are in their right places they do not show prominently unless the limbs in which they are located are exerting great force or are greatly strained. Limbs which are not in exercise must be drawn without showing the play of the muscles. And if you do otherwise, you will have imitated a bag of nuts rather than a human figure."*

230/2

lost *Leda,* and the *St. Anne* [234/1–3]. The scientific approach tends to establish the validity of the new painting technique.

The most remarkable passage in Codex Madrid II is probably that in which the phenomenon of *lustro,* the reflection of light, is studied: "Luster will take on much more the color of the light that illuminates the reflecting body than the color of that body. And this occurs in the case of opaque surfaces";[48] the hues depend on the nature of the reflecting body. Here Leonardo deals with the point or sheet of light that is reflected on smooth and polished surfaces. This is one aspect of what is called *riverberazione* in Manuscript A. Properly speaking, *lustro* is separate from reflection (*riflesso*) in which a specular image is produced. This is important insofar as it involves the transfer of a neighboring color on the local tint of a given object. The indirect reflections imbue the shadows with shimmering and accidents which, all things considered, are not desirable.

One of the last notes of Codex Madrid II concerns the harmony of the shadows with the lights that are associated with them and recommends that the artistic "compromise" be found and that, for example, "to the shadows of green bodies green things" must correspond.[49] This is to avoid disturbing contrasts caused by the repercussions of *lustro,* which emphasizes the relief but blurs the color. Leonardo's practice is in accordance with these principles. But the observations of Codex Madrid II bear witness to a new interest in these problems. Leonardo seeks not only to justify his own procedure; his insistence seems to imply the taking up

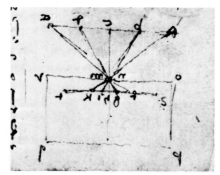

233/2

233/1–5
In his optical research Leonardo dismissed the then prevalent notion that the eye saw by sending out light rays. He dissected the eyes of animals and probably of humans. He drew a schematic diagram of the eye (below

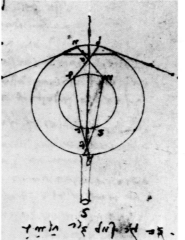

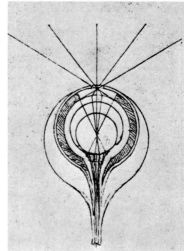

233/3 233/4

right) in the Codex Atlanticus, folio 337 recto-a, misplacing the spherical lens. He studied binocular perception – at left in Codex Madrid II, folio 25 verso. In Manuscript D, folio 3 verso, he created a model of sight (bottom) – analogous to the camera obscura, *a device that projects an image through a tiny hole – and made diagrams (above left and top) on folio 8 recto.*

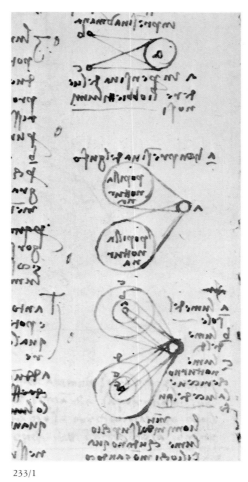

232/1
The detail at left from Signorelli's Resurrection *displays the "antique" bulging muscles that Leonardo deplored. Leonardo uses the phrases "bag of nuts" and "bunch of radishes" to describe such nudes. His biographer Vasari takes up the cudgel and attacks those who "in order to appear great draftsmen, make their nudes woody and devoid of grace."*

233/1

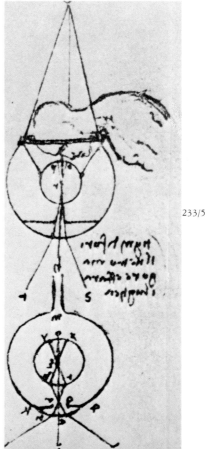

233/5

of a definite position with regard to the Flemish experiments. It was impossible for Leonardo to ignore the beauty of the pictorial material of the Northern artists and the originality of a style that paid particular attention to irradiations, to the accidents of *lustro,* and to the surprising plays of *riflessi.* The text of Codex Madrid II shows that he perfectly understood their mechanisms, but he was in no way anxious to adopt them. In this he is unquestionably faithful to the Southern attitude, which is more attentive to the fullness of forms in space than to the scintillation of light and the vividness of textures.[50]

We thus see how the relation of theory to its application becomes established for Leonardo. In the study of reflections and the dialectics of light and shade, the procedure is the same as in anatomy. By identifying unacceptable fading of the local tint and harsh contrasts of light as well as display of musculature, Leonardo was able to avoid the pitfalls.

The general policy of the *Treatise* is then clearly indicated by the notes of Codex Madrid II, where the tendency towards a didactic work becomes manifest: the analyses reveal the *possible* methods of painting, which were not all to be adopted by Leonardo in his own work. We note with pleasure the charming and previously unpublished note contained in the Madrid manuscript, "As the sun was declining, I saw the green shadows of the ropes, mast, and yard cast upon a white wall."[51] But this lingering observation does not make Leonardo a precursor of impressionism. For the phenomenon is not considered "pictorial," and if it were, it would not belong to Leonardo's painting.

Sfumato ("soft, shaded"), a term that had not yet appeared, was now Leonardo's

234/1

234/1–3 and 235/1
Leonardo's work in optics led naturally to studies of the interrelationships between light and shadow. He goes from his studio into the open air and develops new recommendations, which are then applied in his own practice. He cautions against harsh lighting and outlines that are too sharp. He seeks, in the paintings shown here, a transparency of shadow around the head that relates the figures to their environments. His chiaroscuro is a delicate contrast of light and dark that gives a rounded modeled effect of three-dimensional mystery. Above is a detail from a copy of his lost Leda and the Swan *(opposite page). At right are details from the Louvre* St. Anne *and the* Mona Lisa. *The subtlety of lighting relates all three women. So, too, in his eloquent and slightly "decadent" description of the* Mona Lisa *in the book* The Renaissance, *Walter Pater linked them:*

"All the thoughts and experience of the world have etched and molded there . . . and, as Leda, [she] was the mother of Helen of Troy, and, as St. Anne, the mother of Mary; and all this has been to her but as the sound of lyres and flutes."

234/2

234/3

reply to the whole of pictorial problems.[52] His method was opposed, in a way, to all existing practices. The effects of the irradiation of light, where the Flemish were past masters, were not lost, but the poetics of numerous reflections and brightened colors were to be put aside in favor of infinitely delicate ranges of colors. Relief as practiced by Masaccio, who defined the form from a constant order of light and dark colors, was maintained, but with a deliberate softening of contours, making new liaisons possible between the foreground and the background. A general toned-down key is at the same time the condition and the consequence of the new style. In order to enhance its possibilities in the realm of values, the painting must reduce the height of the tones.

The notes of Codex Madrid II do not then include any great doctrinal developments, but they show how Leonardo, like a chess player carrying on several games at the same time, advanced certain concrete problems and specified certain demonstrations within an important match he was playing. He was conscious of the fact that all these analyses of natural phenomena and these explorations of the living organism took him far away from the practical requirements of the *Treatise* and that it would be necessary to disassociate himself from the analyses. He realized that the development of his speculations led him to statements that would seem like theoretical detours away from the specific problems of the *Treatise.* He wrote, for example, on the subject of a demonstration of optics, "Although this case cannot be listed among the precepts of painting, I shall not omit it, because speculators may find it useful."[53] And again, "Although such speculations [on the

eye] are not needed by the practitioners, I deem it convenient to put them forward because they are often received with admiration by speculative men of talent." [54] In short, the preliminary study of the mechanism of sight seems to banish the positive conclusions that are expected of the theoretician, but it maintains the intellect and the imagination in a sort of exalted vigilance, which is also one of the purposes of the *Treatise*.

The proof and reason why among the illuminated parts certain portions are in higher light than others

When you compose a historical picture take two points, one the point of sight, and the other the source of light; and make this as distant as possible.

Shows how light from any side converges to one point.

I will make further mention of the reason of reflections.

Where the angles made by the lines of incidence are most equal there will be the highest light, and where they are most unequal it will be darkest.

Although the balls a b c are lighted from one window, nevertheless, if you follow the lines of their shadows you will see they intersect at a point forming the angle n.

Since it is proved that every definite light is, or seems to be, derived from one single point the side illuminated by it will have its highest light on the portion where the line of radiance falls perpendicularly; as is shown above in the lines a g, and also in a h and in l a; and that portion of the illuminated side will be less luminous, where the line of incidence strikes it between two more dissimilar angles, as is seen at b c d. And by this means you may also know which parts are deprived of light as is seen at m k.

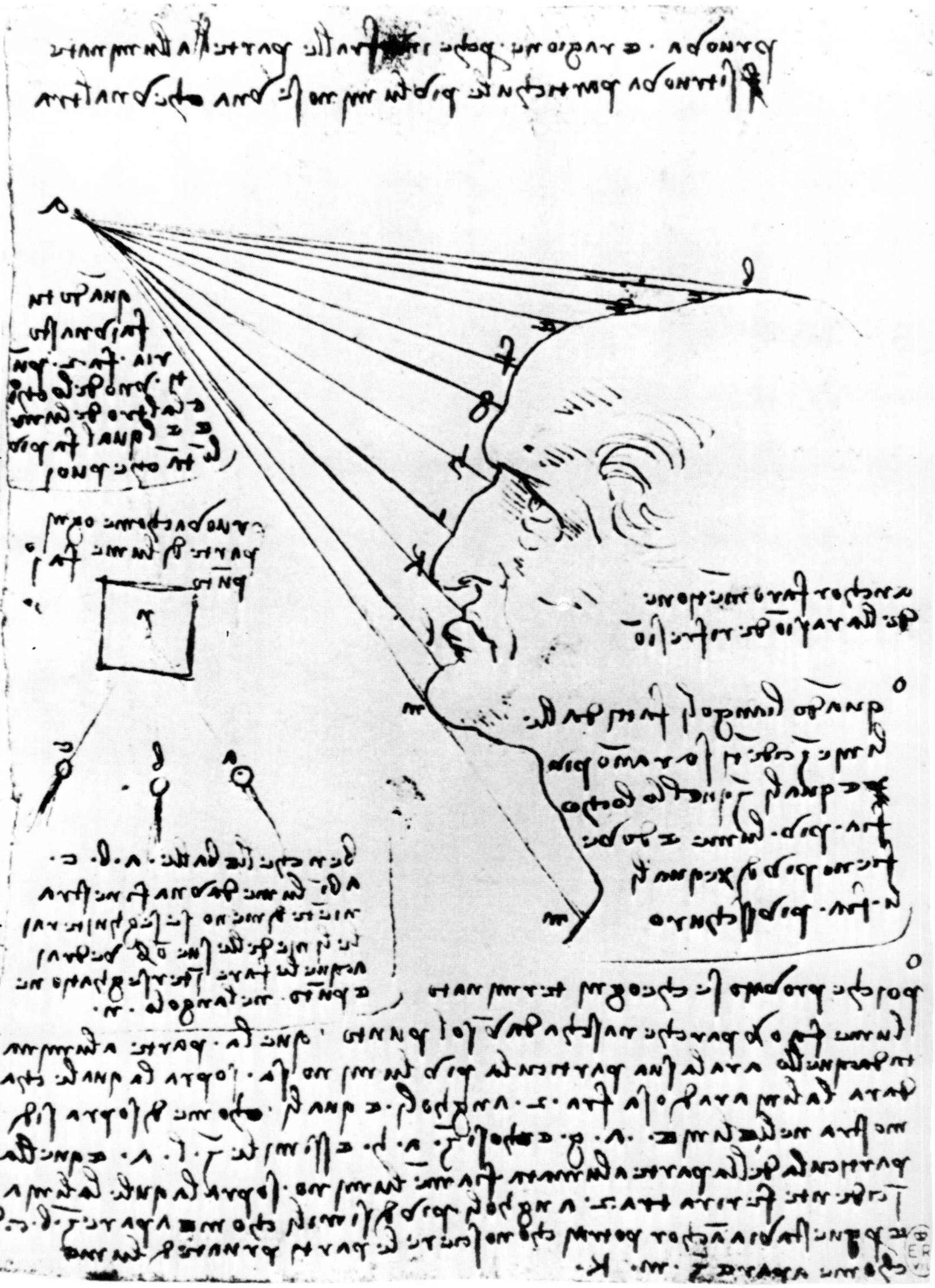

236/1

This study – treating the profile of a man as if it were a mountainous landscape – demonstrates the varying effects of light from a single source striking the face. The little diagram at left and the notes immediately above and below it relate to the action of light within a room. Above those is a note of advice on composing "a historical picture." WINDSOR 12604

We see in what way Leonardo has finally withdrawn from Alberti. The latter recommended to the painter a good education for the arrangement of the *storie* and a knowledge of geometry in order to give exact structure to the compositions. Leonardo reversed the terms: painting coincides ideally with the integral knowledge of nature; and without an all-embracing intuition, which analyses will never be able to detail completely, nothing valid can be achieved. Whence the new character of the discourse on art: it was no longer defined by the humanist framework; this would have subjected the *Treatise* too narrowly to the literary models whose pertinence had been rejected in the *Paragone,* the comparison of poetry and painting.

The *Treatise,* whose final contours were still not established and were to change again several times, is characterized by its form, which adopts the manner of mathematical demonstrations. Most of the notes *de pictura* of Codex Madrid II take on the aspect of theorems illustrated with little figures. The structure remains supple, and the presentation is rigorous. Such was the logic of the art-science that undertook the conquest, practically inexhaustible, of reality. The decisions necessary to the painter were to proceed from choice the consequences of which could be clearly explained, but the principle of which eluded demonstration precisely because, as we have seen, it was the artist who guided it. It was the moment of *sfumato* – of grace, of ambiguity – that for Leonardo tended more and more to

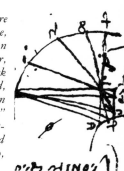

237/2

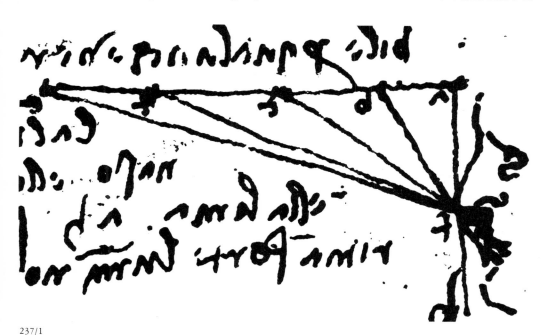

237/1

These studies from Codex Madrid II are demonstrations of the effects of light. Above, on folio 23 verso, Leonardo sketches an experiment, showing the sun, eyes, paper, and a board, to prove his point: "A dark object, seen against a luminous background, will appear much smaller than when seen against a background darker than itself." At left, on folio 71 verso, he diagrams outdoors light rebounding off the pavement and striking a face. At right, on folio 71 recto, he studies light striking the face.

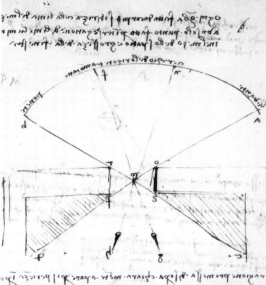

237/3

become integrated in the finality of the painting. This was all the more faithful to its vocation since it was capable of impressing upon the conscience the strangeness of the real that it had to explore. Practice completed theory, as it required a choice between the many possibilities displayed by scientific speculation on objective data. The specific capacity of the style is the other side and the indispensable complement of the doctrinal effort of the *Treatise.*

237/4–6
The drawings below are all studies by Leonardo of the effects of light falling in through a window.
At left, he observes particularly the gradations in shadow as the light hits a spherical body. MS. B.N. 2038 13v, 14r, 15r

237/4   237/5   237/6

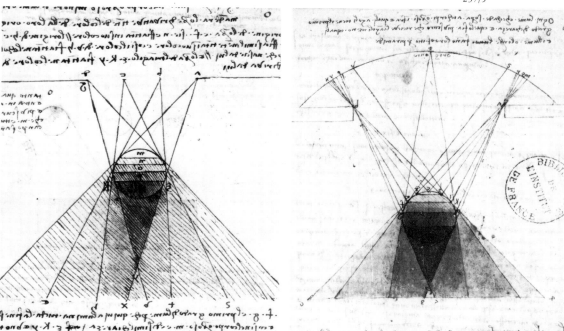

237

238/1

238/2

In Codex Madrid II Leonardo takes up the question of lustro – the reflection of light. On folio 26 recto he writes:

Luster will take on much more the color of the light that illuminates the reflecting body than the color of that body. And this occurs in the case of the opaque surfaces.

Renaissance painters differed on the use of reflections in their work. The angels shown here represent four approaches. The angel of Piero della Francesca (above) has no real reflections. The angel at right, by the Flemish painter Gerard David, illustrates the Flemish tendency towards strong reflections from eyes, lips, and jewels.

239/1

239/2

In his angel (above), Piero di Cosimo imitates the Flemish style but adds simple shadows on the face. Leonardo was intrigued by the Flemish use of reflection but wanted to avoid the harsh contrasts. His solution gives the illusions of indirect bounced light, such as that used by photographers today. The result – as shown at left in the angel from the **Virgin of the Rocks** of the National Gallery, London – is an intricate, complex play of shadow and light that restores to the angel her ethereal mystery. Leonardo's art builds upon science but transcends it to achieve grace, ambiguity, and beauty.

An ingenious concern
with the science of timekeeping
and new clues that he
may have conceived
the first pendulum-regulated
clockwork.

Time glasses such as this one were still a principal means of measuring the hours in Leonardo's day. The passage of sand from one vessel to the other could consume anywhere from four seconds to four hours.

240/2

HOROLOGY

SILVIO A. BEDINI
LADISLAO RETI

240/1

Sol per te le mie ore son generate

Sun
Only through you my hours are generated.

A long-standing myth about Leonardo stemmed from his fascination with clocks and other timekeeping instruments. His caption for the sketch of a sundial, above, constitutes a clever pun. Some 60 years ago a scholar's misreading of the Italian gave the caption a wholly different twist: "I have wasted my hours." Those who were aware of Leonardo's propensity for pursuing the new and leaving old projects assumed it to be a penitent's confession of misspent time.

WINDSOR 19106v

Leonardo's concern with time and its measurement is illustrated by numerous sketches in his notebooks relating to the mechanical clock and to other forms of timekeepers. For example, in the Windsor Collection is a sketch of a sundial [240/1] to illustrate the motto *sol per te le mie ore son generate* ("sun, through you my hours are generated").[1] Time glasses [241/2] appear on several pages, especially in connection with experiments he carried out in an attempt to determine the velocity of a ship.[2] And various drawings are concerned with water clocks [241/1].

Leonardo attempted to improve upon the favorite timekeeper of classical antiquity – the water clock. Leakage of water from one vessel into another kept time for the Romans, Greeks, and Chinese. Leonardo's design (left) depicts a float, moving up and down a screw-like guide, that controls the spigot delivering water to a series of containers. ATLANTICUS 343v-a

241/1

Some quicksilver must always remain in the ball as far as the mouth of the tap which pours it.

Quicksilver for an hour. And the hour must be divided in grades, minutes, and seconds. And the quicksilver must be distilled.

The rule of the course must be made in the sample.

241/2

The time glass above was part of Leonardo's attempt to design a mechanism for determining the velocity of a ship – of special significance during the great age of exploration. ARUNDEL 191v

The monastic alarm clock below, dating from Leonardo's era, is the earliest surviving domestic clock known. The toothed dial wheel makes one revolution every 24 hours.

241/3

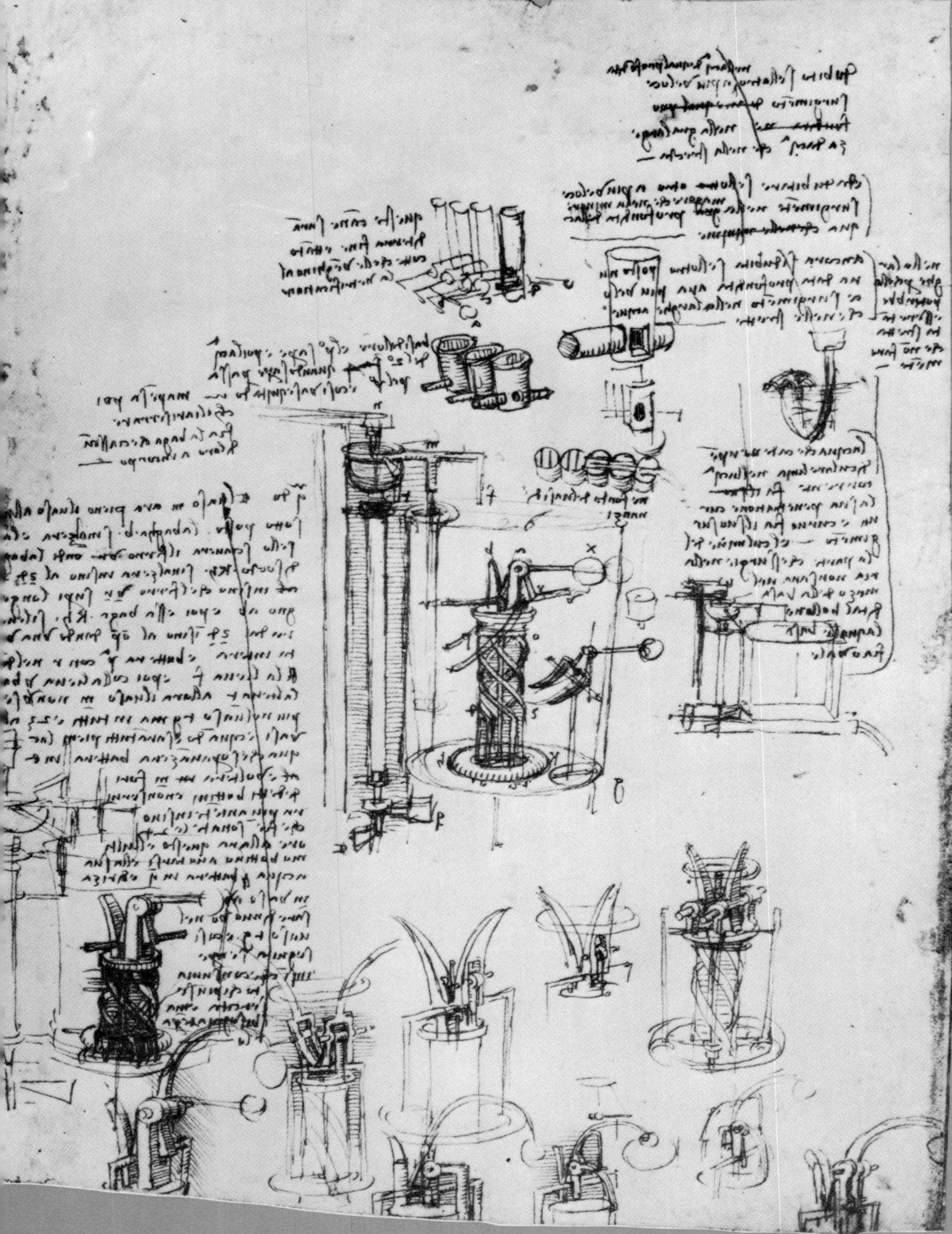

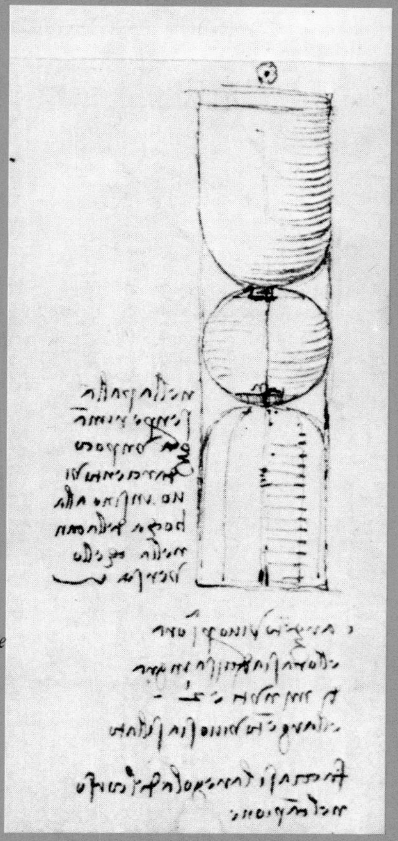

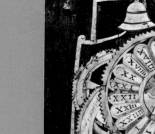

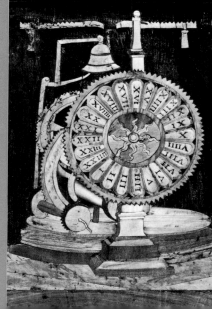

In the Codex Atlanticus a number of pages contain studies for a water clock of involved design. A float moving up and down along a screw-like guide was supposed to open and shut the faucet delivering the water to a number of containers placed in series. A striking mechanism was also provided for.[3]

As for Leonardo's consideration of the mechanical clock, a number of sketches in the Codex Atlanticus are illustrations of various aspects of clockworks and their components. And now the study of the Leonardo codices in Madrid has thrown new light on Leonardo's horological interests and activity – and in particular on the question of whether pendulums found in mechanisms projected by him had anything to do with timekeeping.

Timekeeping by means of water clocks, mercury clocks, sundials, and sand glasses has been extensively documented in epochs earlier than Leonardo's and the mechanical clock for domestic use had made its appearance in Europe by approximately the beginning of the 14th century. The mechanical clock may well have been the product of several independent devices which had a prior invention. First of all, there was the geared planetarium, or model representing the solar system, which was developed not for time telling, but for astronomical or astrological purposes. Second, there was the alarm for use in convents and

242/1

The first man-made indicator was possibly a stick that, through the length and direction of the shadow it cast, formed a primitive sundial some 4,000 years ago. A sundial is mentioned in the Old Testament in the Book of Isaiah:

Behold, I will make the shadow cast by the declining sun on the dial of Ahaz turn back ten steps. So the sun turned back on the dial the ten steps by which it had declined.

During the Renaissance large sundials were public timepieces and ornaments. The monumental sundial above was added to an earlier sculptural figure in front of Chartres Cathedral in France about 1578.

The old astrological chart at right, with its 12 signs of the zodiac, is an indicator of the close alliance that existed between astrology, astronomy, and horology. Belief in horoscopes was widespread. Even Leonardo, who mocked alchemists and soothsayers, is claimed to have consulted astrologers. Each of the heavenly bodies was believed to exert influence on particular hours of the day and week. Saturn was the ruling planet for the first hour of Saturday, the sun for the first hour of Sunday, the moon for the first hour of Monday. Astrology, astronomy, and horology also are historically related through the astrolabe, an Arabic instrument for determining the positions of the stars for a particular latitude at any time of the day or night. It was a predecessor of the mechanical clock.

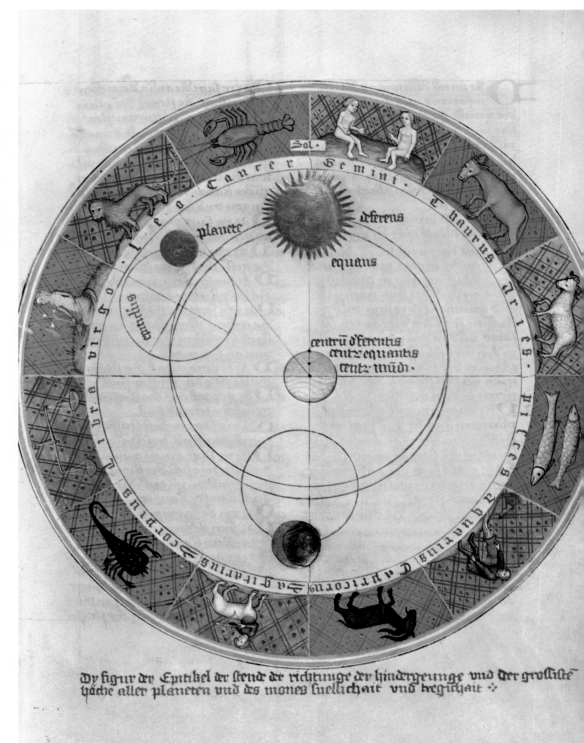

242/2

monasteries. To these may have been added the revolving clock dial borrowed from the Roman anaphoric water clock, of which fragments of three examples have survived. These individual units may well have been combined to produce the domestic timepiece, first for public use and then for the diversion of princes and prelates.

On a larger scale, public clocks existed in some abundance in Italy, France, Germany, and England during the period of Leonardo's career; and some of the most notable astronomical clocks and planetaria were in existence then also. It is generally agreed that the first public clock known was made of iron and erected in the campanile of the Church of Sant'Eustorgio in Milan, in 1309. Within the next quarter of a century at least two other clocks were installed in the same city. By the end of the 14th century there were seventeen more public clocks in the major cities of Europe, and another half-dozen were recorded before the end of the 15th

This illuminated manuscript from about 1450 presents examples of the timekeeper's art at Leonardo's birth. The huge clock at left is separate, as was often the case, from the tall bell-ringing mechanism that stands on the other side of the allegorical figure of Wisdom. An astrolabe is shown at far left. On the table at right are three types of sundials, a sector, and an octagonal table clock, which is of extraordinary historical interest. The table clock is depicted without its case, probably to display the then

243/1

century. Meanwhile, significant achievements had been made in the development and production of complicated astronomical clocks. Notable among these were the great clock designed and installed by Richard Wallingford at the Abbey of St. Albans in England [244/1], Giovanni de' Dondi's outstanding work called the *astrarium* at Pavia [247/1] and Lorenzo della Volpaia's astronomical clock in the

new conical device called a fusee, which contributed much to the timekeeping of spring-driven clocks. The discovery of this old manuscript verifies that both spring-powered clocks and the fusee had been invented by the mid-15th century. Previously, Leonardo's drawings of the fusee were believed to be the first depiction of that device.

*The earliest recorded astronomical clock –
an elaborate mechanism that showed, in
addition to time, the motions of the sun,
moon, and the five planets then known –
was built in England about 1330 by
Richard of Wallingford. Richard, depicted
here with his invention in a miniature
painting, was the abbot of St. Albans.*

map room of the famous Palazzo Vecchio in Florence, dating to 1480–1484.

There can be no doubt, therefore, that Leonardo, with his avid interest in all things mechanical, was aware of the intimate details of construction of many timepieces and related devices; and the possibility is suggested by his writings that other

244/1

*When King Edward III worshipped there,
he rebuked Richard for spending time on
such occupations instead of on the reconstruction of the old church.*

244/2–4

*The astrolabe, a direct forerunner of the
astronomical clock, enabled the user to
determine the time by the positions of the
stars in a given latitude. The ingenious
brass astrolabe shown here was made in
1221-1222 by a Persian, Muhammad b.
Abi Bakr. The rete, or pierced plate (above,*

244/3

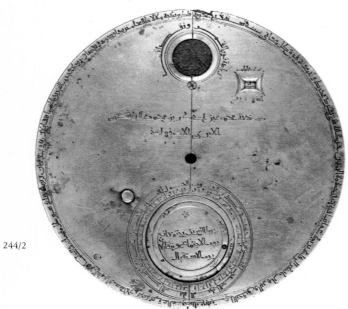

244/2

244/4

*right), indicates the positions of the stars.
On its reverse side (above) the upper circular
opening reveals the phases of the moon and
the lower concentric rings show the relative
positions of the sun (outer ring) and the
moon. The geared clocklike mechanism of
the astrolabe is shown at right.*

important examples of clockwork existed in his time, came to his notice, were subsequently lost, and have gone unnoted by historians. Leonardo unquestionably saw and examined the astrarium of de' Dondi, displayed in the ducal library of the Visconti castle at Pavia, around 1489 and 1490, while he visited that city in the service of Lodovico il Moro.[4] He visited the library frequently before he departed

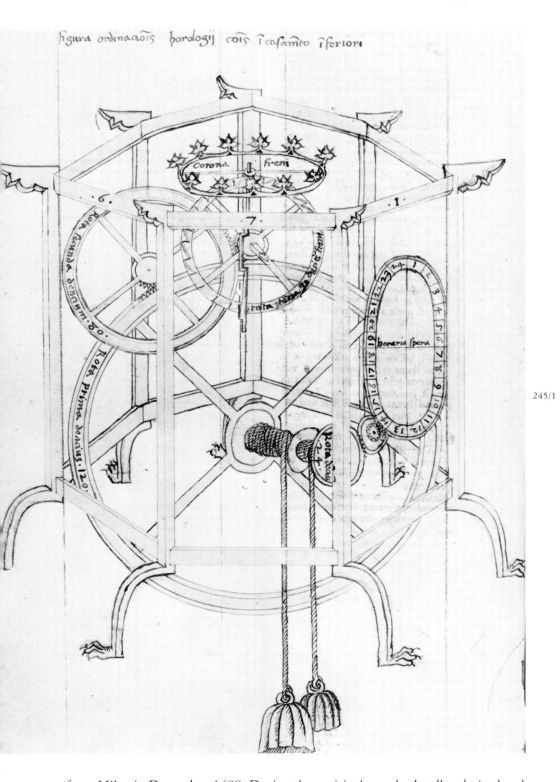

The finely cut rete below was part of a late Gothic astrolabe, perhaps made in Italy about 1400. But its design – 120 teeth divided into 12 sections named with the months of the year – indicates that it originally formed part of an early astronomical

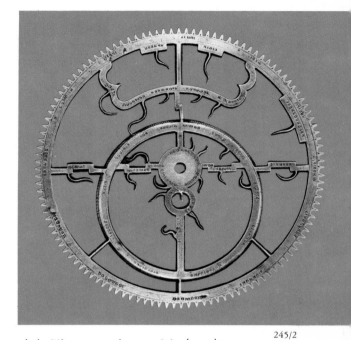

245/2

clock. The gear teeth are original to the piece, not a later addition.

245/1 and 3

During his visits to the ducal library of the Visconti castle in Pavia in about 1490 Leonardo saw a remarkable astronomical clock known as the astrarium. This 14th-century mechanized model of the universe was the work of Giovanni de' Dondi, a versatile professor of medicine at the University of Padua who later settled in Pavia. He was the son of a physician, Jacopo de' Dondi, who himself had constructed an astronomical clock on a palace tower in Padua. One of Giovanni's drawings for the astrarium is shown at left. It could perform an astonishing array of feats: in addition to telling mean time and sidereal – by the stars – time, the astrarium included a calendar of both fixed and movable feast days of the church, and individual dials illustrated the motions of the sun, moon, and five planets then known to man. Leonardo's sketch below, in Manuscript L, folio 92 verso, is of a dial of an astronomical clock and is believed to be a representation of the astrarium's dial of Venus.

245/1

245/3

from Milan in December 1499. During these visits he undoubtedly admired and studied the great clockwork, which was installed at the center of this room on the ground floor of the right-hand tower of the castle. There are indeed sketches in his notebooks that appear to represent dials and mechanisms of the astrarium. It has been said that one of these sketches, from Manuscript L [245/3], may be a drawing of the dial of Venus from the de' Dondi astrarium.[5] On a nearby page of the same manuscript is a faint sketch that resembles the astrarium's dial of Mars.[6]

Carlo Pedretti has indicated that these two sketches are similar to drawings on two pages of the Codex Atlanticus.[7] Furthermore, comparison with some of the pages of Codex Madrid I now shows that their first drafts are found precisely on these

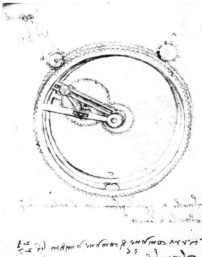

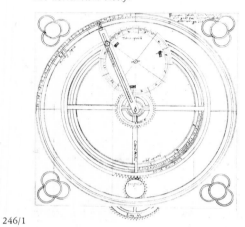

246/1

This drawing of the astrarium's dial of Venus is from one of the 11 known manuscripts detailing the mechanism. Differences between this sketch and Leonardo's rendering on the previous page may be due to Leonardo's having worked directly from the astrarium itself.

pages of the Atlanticus. But in the course of transfer the sketches undergo a substantial change in significance: they cease to be part of a horological complex and become isolated mechanisms, according to Leonardo's intention to compose a book on the elements of machines.

Leonardo's association with the astrarium of de' Dondi did not terminate with his visits to the ducal library at Pavia. Around 1490 Lodovico il Moro decided to develop the little village of Vigevano, which had been his birthplace, and part of the project was the reconstruction of the former Castello Visconteo [248/4] there. Bramante was appointed in 1492 to participate in this work, and among his tasks was the decoration of the ducal apartments. The astrarium was selected as one of the themes for the frescoes, so Bramante was sent to the library at Pavia in March 1495 to make sketches of the mechanism. During this period Leonardo was intimately involved with the works in progress in and around Vigevano, and was certainly aware of the selection of the astrarium as the theme of one of Bramante's frescoes.[8]

One of the best known and most frequently reproduced of Leonardo's horological drawings, found in the Codex Atlanticus, depicts the time train of a clock [248/5]. The drawing is no doubt related to the old tower clock of the Cistercian church at the monastery of Chiaravalle Milanese [248/1], about three miles from the Porta Romana of Milan on the road to Pavia. The church, made of brick and dedicated in 1221, stands on the site of the original monastery, founded by St. Bernard of Clairvaux. The interior is decorated with frescoes by important 15th-century Milanese artists including Bramante and Luini, and Leonardo undoubtedly visited there when he was working in Milan.

246/2 246/3 246/4

246/2–4

The photographs above depict three dials on the working model of the astrarium at the Smithsonian Institution: from left, those of the sun, Jupiter, and Mercury. The astrarium may not only have served as a technological stimulus for Leonardo; it also may have inspired the astronomical stage setting for his masque Il Paradiso, which provided the spectacular climax of the wedding of Lodovico Sforza's nephew to Isabella of Aragon in 1490.

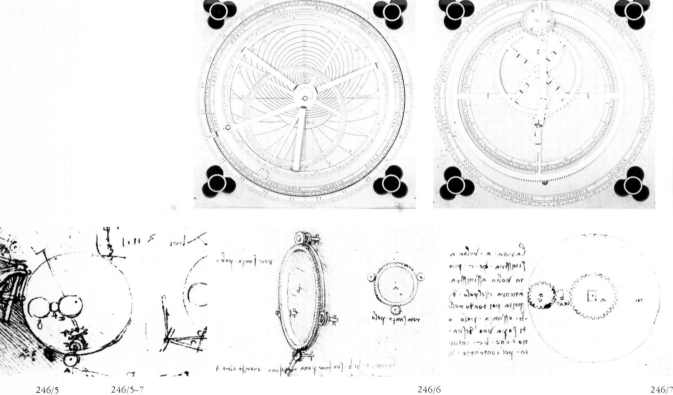

246/5

246/5–7

A drawing similar to Leonardo's sketch of the dial of Venus is found in his Codex Atlanticus, folio 366 recto-b (above, left). The annular gear of the Venus dial reappears in Codex Madrid I, folio 14 recto (above, middle), and it apparently inspired his sketch of a gear-train on Madrid I folio 112 recto (above, right). The inventions of others often evolved, under Leonardo's pen, into mechanisms wholly unrelated to the original inspiration.

246/6 246/7

Nor is the page of the Codex Atlanticus where this drawing appears the only one showing the profound impression made upon Leonardo by the clockwork of Chiaravalle. Two other pages of the Atlanticus are inspired by, if not directly derived from, his observations at Chiaravalle. Among more than 100 little sketches on these adjacent pages, sketches having to do with horological subjects prevail.

And again, as with many pages of the Atlanticus, there are correspondences in the

247/1

The astrarium was regarded as one of the wonders of the Renaissance world. A contemporary of de' Dondi called it "a work of divine speculation, a work unattainable by human genius and never produced in generations past." Giovanni had devoted 16 years of his leisure time to it, building the complicated mechanisms out of brass and bronze with his own hands. In Leonardo's time the astrarium belonged to Gian Galeazzo Sforza, Lodovico's nephew, who lived in the Visconti castle in Pavia. About the time of his death in 1494, the

247/2

clock was moved temporarily to the castle of Lodovico's astrologer near Milan for repair. After it was restored to Pavia, written references to the clock dwindle. Some 35 years later it disappears from historical accounts, and no known remnants survive. Two working models of the astrarium have been handed down. The model at left was produced for the Museum of History and Technology at the Smithsonian Institution in 1960 under the technical guidance of a noted British horologist, H. Alan Lloyd. A second model (above) was made in Italy in 1963 by Luigi Pippa and is now on exhibit at the National Museum of Science and Technology in Milan. The Smithsonian model is 4 feet, 4 inches high and 30 inches in diameter at the widest point. It consists of 297 parts, of which 107 are wheels and pinions. The Italian model is shorter and includes a calendar dial, which does not correspond to the surviving manuscript drawings.

247/3

Leonardo's sketch of a dial from an astronomical clock, believed to be the dial of Mars, probably the astrarium.   MS. L 93v

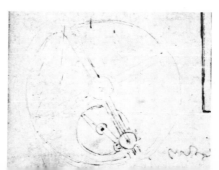

contemporary Codex Madrid I. In fact the clock of Chiaravalle is specifically mentioned in the latter, on a page where "axles within axles, as in Chiaravalle," are depicted. On two nearby pages variations on the lunar mechanism of Chiaravalle are shown. Finally, almost all of the 100-odd sketches of the Atlanticus are taken up again in Codex Madrid I. Unfortunately, nothing now remains in Chiaravalle of the tower and clock seen by Leonardo, which have been replaced. However, an important original document does exist there: a vellum-bound chronicle[9] of the abbey, written by a lay brother of the order, in which he describes the clock in

The astrarium was originally installed in
the Ducal Library of the Palazzo Visconteo
in Pavia (right). It was there that
Leonardo and Bramante saw it.

248/1

248/4

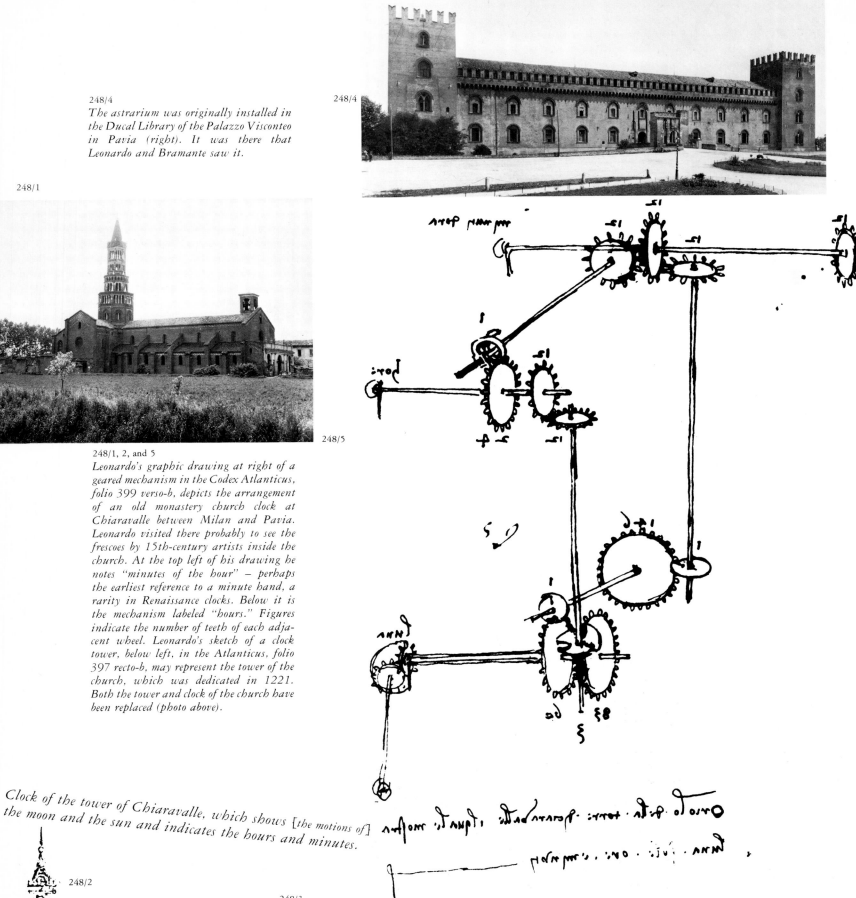

248/5

248/1, 2, and 5

Leonardo's graphic drawing at right of a
geared mechanism in the Codex Atlanticus,
folio 399 verso-b, depicts the arrangement
of an old monastery church clock at
Chiaravalle between Milan and Pavia.
Leonardo visited there probably to see the
frescoes by 15th-century artists inside the
church. At the top left of his drawing he
notes "minutes of the hour" – perhaps
the earliest reference to a minute hand, a
rarity in Renaissance clocks. Below it is
the mechanism labeled "hours." Figures
indicate the number of teeth of each adjacent wheel. Leonardo's sketch of a clock
tower, below left, in the Atlanticus, folio
397 recto-b, may represent the tower of the
church, which was dedicated in 1221.
Both the tower and clock of the church have
been replaced (photo above).

Clock of the tower of Chiaravalle, which shows [the motions of]
the moon and the sun and indicates the hours and minutes.

248/2

248/3

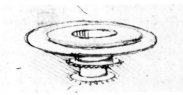

248/3

The clock of Chiaravalle is mentioned by
Leonardo again in the sketch above of "axles
in axles, as in Chiaravalle." MADRID I 11v

terms which correspond singularly to Leonardo's sketching in the Atlanticus.

Codex Madrid I, on which our study will be focusing more and more, is not an
ordinary notebook. It represents a close approach to a systematic treatise dealing
with the branch of mechanical engineering called today "Mechanisms" or "Elements of Machines." In other words, its subject is not complete machines, but the
isolated mechanisms which are part of the co-ordinated whole. Of the 191 folios of
the codex, more than half are devoted to practical applications, while the remain-
der take up the corresponding theoretical background.[10] And since he was dealing

with mechanisms in general, Leonardo did not state the specific horological implication of his drawings in many cases. However, in some cases there can be no doubt as to their purpose: there was simply no possible application for such devices outside this field. In his day, precision mechanisms could be used only in two widely separated and easily distinguishable groups of machines: clockworks,

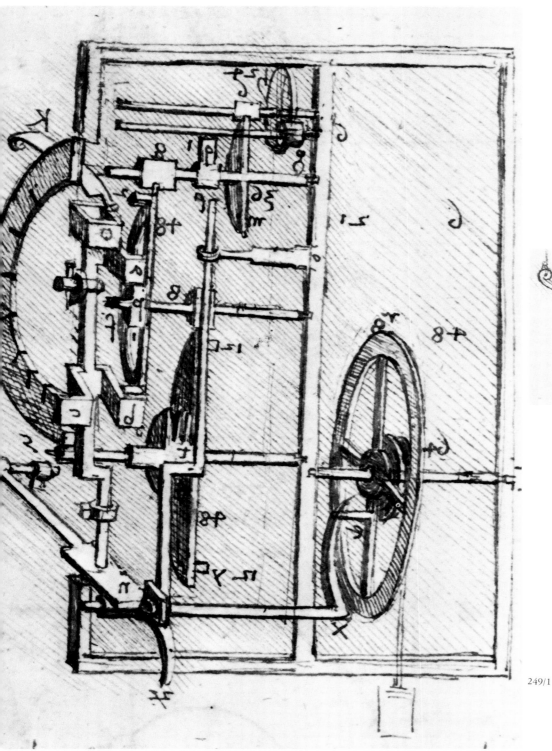

249/1

249/2

The complete wheelwork of a clock (below) was sketched by Leonardo in the Codex Atlanticus, folio 348 verso-d. The design has been reconstructed in modern times, and scholars believe that it is a copy, perhaps of plans developed around 1370 for a clock at the Royal Palace in Paris.

249/2

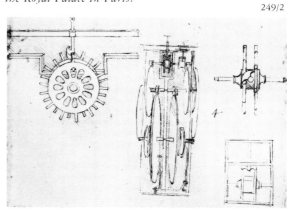

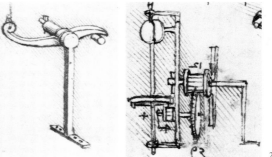

249/3

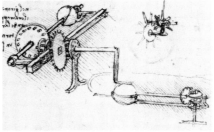

249/4

Leonardo recalled his earlier study of the clock at Chiaravalle when he designed clockwork mechanisms in Codex Madrid I.

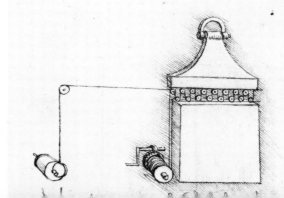

249/5

The elements [249/3] on folio 27 verso and [249/4], folio 10 verso, are parts of a striking mechanism. Above, also on folio 10 verso, is a variation on the Chiaravalle lunar mechanism.

An exception to the illustration of separate horological elements in Codex Madrid I is folio 27 verso (left), which shows a weight-driven clockwork complete with striking mechanism. Below, folio 27 recto displays a system of pulleys employed to regulate the descent of the weight and thus reduce the vertical space normally needed in a clock.

249/6

often complicated by astronomical integrations or by automata destined to amuse and astonish, and textile machines.

Devices related to horology seem to be concentrated in the first third of the book. The subject is spread out in widely separated pages. But a serious interest in it on the part of Leonardo is revealed not only by the loving care and magnificent draftsmanship lavished on many of the pages dealing with this theme but also by the fact that he took it up systematically, as far as this attribute can be applied to the work of Leonardo.

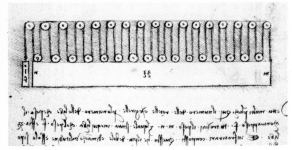

250/1

The reverse of the counterweight system for regulating a clock shown at the bottom of page 249 is illustrated above: in a tackle rigged with 33 pulleys, 1 pound will raise a 33-pound stone – disregarding friction, which will be considerable.   MADRID I 36v

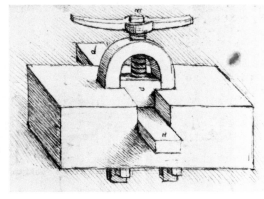

250/2

The spring as a power source for clocks was still only a few decades old when Leonardo designed the spring-making device above.   MADRID I 14v

250/3

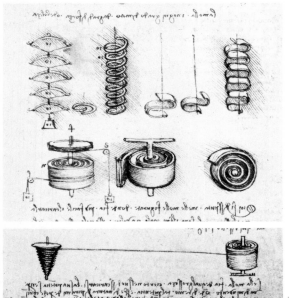

250/4

Leonardo illustrates several types of springs (above) and shows how a clock spring is wound under tension with a key. On the same folio (bottom sketch) he demonstrates his awareness of the fusee, the 15th-century invention that parceled out the force of the spring evenly as it ran down. Leonardo's fusee is a conical-shaped drum that slowly feeds catgut cord to the unwinding spring. The name probably came from the Latin fusata, *which appropriately meant a spindle filled with thread.*   MADRID I 85r

On the opposite page, a Renaissance sovereign explains the "clock of wisdom" to a court audience in this miniature painting from a 15th-century manuscript.

A mechanical timepiece consists essentially of the following parts: the framework; the drive, or motor; the power-transmitting and registering system (gear-trains, dials, and hands or pointers); the regulation system (escapement); and in some cases, the striking train (train of wheels causing the clock to strike). All these parts, except for the framework, are discussed and described by Leonardo in Codex Madrid I. In accordance with the special nature of the book, we cannot expect to find in it descriptions of complete clockworks. The only exception is found on one page where the general setup of a weight-driven clockwork provided with striking mechanism is presented. But even here many important parts are missing.

On the other hand, on an adjacent page Leonardo is revealed at work on a practical problem of the weight-driven clock. The motion of a mechanical timepiece is generally obtained by the running down of a weight or by the uncoiling of a spring, previously drawn or wound up. To maintain a regular motion a constant driving force is required. A slowly descending weight exerts a practically constant force. Weight-driven clocks certainly preceded clocks motivated by a spring. However, weight-driven clocks must be installed at a suitable height in order to ensure a running-down time of sufficient duration. Leonardo offers an interesting solution for reducing the vertical-space requirement of a clockwork [249/6].

Another of Leonardo's preoccupations, demonstrated in a number of pages of Codex Madrid I, was the production of springs and their application for various purposes, especially clockwork. He illustrated and described a device for making springs [250/2]. He examined how the power of springs depends on shape, dimensions, and position.[11] He hinted at the horological application of short S-shaped springs.[12] He took up the subject of springs at length on a page titled with the statement, "The spring will have different degrees of either power or weakness in each degree of its motion."

On this page he demonstrated his awareness of the necessity of equalizing the diminishing force of the spring as it unwinds, which became apparent as spring-driven clocks were introduced. Indeed, he described accurately the uneven performance of the spring and the remedy which should be applied: "If the spring is of uniform thickness, its power diminishes gradually as it is unwound. We shall say, therefore, that such power is in the nature of a pyramid, since its beginning is great and it ends in nothing. For this reason, it is necessary to contradict, or better to oppose, such pyramidal power with another pyramidal power that has an opposite diminution of resistance." Having said this, he suggested equalization by means of the fusee, neatly presented at the bottom of the same page [250/4]. The fusee is a conical-shaped drum that compensates for the decrease in spring force. With a fusee properly proportioned to the spring, the radius is exactly proportional to spring tension at every point so that torque output is constant.

The direct application of Leonardo's sketches and descriptions of the spring as part of the clockmaker's standard practice of his time is confirmed in documentation brought to light by a number of scholars, according to whom spring-driven clocks and the fusee (the invention of which has been wrongly attributed to Leonardo) were known in Europe at least by the second half of the 15th century.

The spring-driven clock may even date back to the first years of the 15th century. Such a device is described in the biography of the great Florentine architect and engineer Filippo Brunelleschi (1377–1446), claimed by his contemporary biographer Antonio Manetti to have become expert in clockmaking in his youth. Manetti's statement about Brunelleschi's clockwork may be translated as follows from the Italian original: "Being interested in the past, he made some clocks and alarms, in which various and diverse generations of springs multiplied by various and numerous mechanical devices, all or the major part of which he had seen and which provided considerable assistance to him in the creation of various machines for carrying, lifting, and pulling weights."[13]

The most significant and puzzling phrase in the statement of Manetti is *varie e diverse generationi di mole*, translated above as "various and diverse generations of

25

ue ama
ui et quisi
ui a uiuen
tute mea
et quesiui eam michi as
sumere sponsam. ce
sont les paroles que

salmon le sage dist en
son liure de sapience
ou viii.e chappitre. en
quoy il dist. iay amne
e sapience et si lay que
se les en ma ieunesse
pour de elle faire mon

A series of springs and fusees arranged to regulate one clock is illustrated. The device is a kind of "generation of springs" – a phrase used by a contemporary biographer in describing the clockmaking of Filippo Brunelleschi, the 15th-century architect whose theories had a great influence on Leonardo's painting and structural designs.

MS. B 50v

252/2–4

One shortcoming of the fusee was the tendency of the gut cord (later replaced by chain) to stretch or snap, and the three sketches below, in Codex Madrid I, show Leonardo searching for better ways to equalize the force of the clock spring. On folio 4 recto below he suggests a volute gear on the spring barrel and in mesh with a sliding pinion guided by the edge of the volute. On folio 16 recto (below, middle) a similar effect is sought by means of a tapered pinion. On folio 14 recto (far right) is a more complex device: the upper rim of the spring barrel has teeth that engage a spiral volute proportioned like a fusee. On the axis with this volute are two screws, one which has the same pitch as the spiral on the conical gear and another which actuates a worm wheel, pinion, and rack to vary the position of the spring barrel as necessary to accommodate the variable center distance required by the conical gear. Of the three devices this is most workable and would function as shown. Possibly it was sketched from an existing mechanism. In the sketch from folio 4 recto the straight guide on the

252/1

springs." Just what does "generations of springs" mean? In order to resolve the riddle presented by Manetti's reference, Frank D. Prager advanced the hypothesis that the spring may have been built up from shorter lengths of wire welded together. Such a built-up spring, according to Prager, could be said to comprise a generation of springs.[14] This would provide a rational explanation of what Manetti wrote and what Brunelleschi probably built.

Among Leonardo's papers, however, we can point out a device which may throw a new light on Manetti's mysterious statement. It is found in Manuscript B [252/1]. The device belongs explicitly to horology and represents a battery of spring and fusee units arranged for the purpose of prolonging the running time of a clockwork. The accompanying text reads, "Four springs for the clock, working in such a way that when one has completed its run, the other begins. During the revolution of the first, the second stands still, while the first works itself into the second by means of a screw. And when it has screwed itself quite firmly, the second spring takes up the same motion and so do all the others."

This device, even if the sketch is extremely rough, can be truly called a "generation of springs" in the figurative as well as the concrete sense of the phrase. The fact that this scheme is found in Manuscript B – of about 1489, the earliest of Leonardo's notebooks – strengthens the supposition that it is related to Brunelleschi's technological heritage, still very much alive in Leonardo's time, even if all pertinent original documents from Brunelleschi have disappeared.

It is quite interesting to follow Leonardo's indefatigable mechanical ingenuity in the search for spring equalizing devices superior to the fusee. The fusee has, among others, the drawback that the gut cord that moves it (later replaced by a chain) may stretch or even snap. Would it not be possible to construct conical equalizing devices connected with the mainspring by a more consistent transmission? In Codex Madrid I we can admire a number of such solutions [252/2–4, 253/6]. They may not all have been practicable, but they show great ingenuity

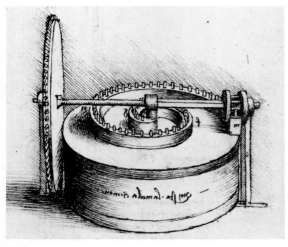

252/2

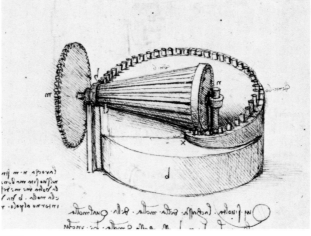

252/3

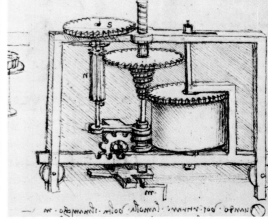

252/4

side of the pinion would interfere on the inside curve of the volute, increasingly so as the center of the volute were approached. The sketch from folio 16 recto may represent a constantly changing level for the volutes as it revolves in mesh with the tapered pinion, but certainly it is not very clear. The constant circular pitch of the volute teeth precludes their successful mesh with the varying circular pitch of the pinion teeth. It appears that the spring-barrel axis is represented by the vertical shaft supporting the large end of the pinion, making an awkwardly eccentric barrel. These considerations suggest that the figures from folios 4 recto and 16 recto represent tentative concepts rather than functioning mechanisms.

and their presentation offers significant examples of Leonardo's magnificent draftsmanship applied to technical subjects.

Another spring equalizing instrument – a checking spring called *stackfreed* [253/1], to be used on portable clocks – appeared in south Germany around 1520. An irregularly shaped cam is mounted on a wheel connected with the spring arbor (spindle). A stiff spring terminating generally in a roller acts against the edge of the cam. The spring has a braking and retarding action on the cam and consequently slows the uncoiling of the mainspring. When the shape of the cam is well chosen, the retarding action will decrease in proportion to the diminishing force of the mainspring.

It is quite surprising to find in Leonardo's sketches mechanisms which correspond to this description. On one page of Manuscript M, contemporary with Codex

Madrid I, two devices of this kind are depicted [253/2]. Unfortunately, Leonardo's accompanying description is left unfinished and a horological implication is not stated. But for what other purpose if not mainspring regulation could such a device have been suggested?

Fortunately, the idea is followed up in Codex Madrid I, and this time the purpose is unmistakable. On the center of a page which belongs to a section almost entirely dedicated to illustrating clockwork mechanisms, there is a beautiful sketch representing the spring barrel of a clock. The bottom of the housing is secured to a toothed wheel, while the top is shaped like a helix, forming a circular inclined plane [253/3].

To the arbor of the mainspring an arched spring is firmly secured. The outer end of this auxiliary spring holds a roller that, moving down along the helical path of the top, exerts a progressively decreasing braking action. The text underneath states, "Here the axle only turns in order to wind up the spring, which never returns." This interesting device, probably an original idea of Leonardo, fulfills the same purpose as the stackfreed [253/1]; the only difference consists in the fact that the follower of the stackfreed is moved by a disc cam, while in Leonardo's mechanism the cam is a translating one. In short, what we have here is a three-dimensional stackfreed.

A great many pages of Codex Madrid I deal with the transmission of motion and power by means of toothed wheels, screws, and levers. The subject is dealt with analytically; only seldom is there a direct reference to a specific application. The horological implication is manifest in many cases, however, even if it is not explicitly stated.

Leonardo labored persistently on designs to improve gearings and bearings in order to reduce frictional resistance.[15] He was apparently the first to suggest that pivots could be nested in bearings made of semiprecious stones[16] and even

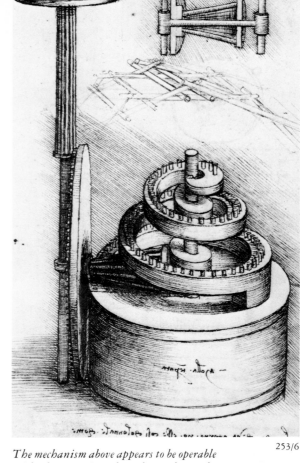

The mechanism above appears to be operable with the exception that the teeth on the volute are shown to be of a constant pitch, while in fact they must vary in accordance with the varying pitch between one end of the pinion and the other. MADRID I 45r

In seeking a substitute for the fusee Leonardo foreshadowed the stackfreed (far

253/6

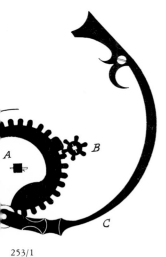

253/1

253/2

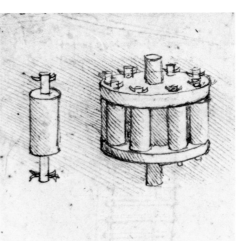

253/3

253/4

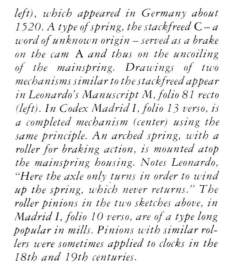

253/5

left), which appeared in Germany about 1520. A type of spring, the stackfreed C – a word of unknown origin – served as a brake on the cam A and thus on the uncoiling of the mainspring. Drawings of two mechanisms similar to the stackfreed appear in Leonardo's Manuscript M, folio 81 recto (left). In Codex Madrid I, folio 13 verso, is a completed mechanism (center) using the same principle. An arched spring, with a roller for braking action, is mounted atop the mainspring housing. Notes Leonardo, "Here the axle only turns in order to wind up the spring, which never returns." The roller pinions in the two sketches above, in Madrid I, folio 10 verso, are of a type long popular in mills. Pinions with similar rollers were sometimes applied to clocks in the 18th and 19th centuries.

diamonds.[17] His projects for improving the construction of gear wheels show great ingenuity, as do his studies on the mechanical effects that can be obtained by varying the position, the design, and the size of the wheels. Enormous effort and great ingenuity have been devoted since the dawn of the timekeeper's art to finding the ideal mechanism capable of ensuring the precision and reliability of a timepiece – that is, an efficient regulator. Several solutions had already been worked out before Leonardo became interested in clockwork. He seemed to know them all.

The earliest known practical device for the regulation of clockworks – that is, a mechanism to control and slow down the speed at which the driving weights descend – was the foliot and crown wheel, and verge escapement. This regulating mechanism consists of three parts: the crown wheel; a shaft, called verge, provided with two projections (pallets) placed at a right angle; and at the top of the verge a

253

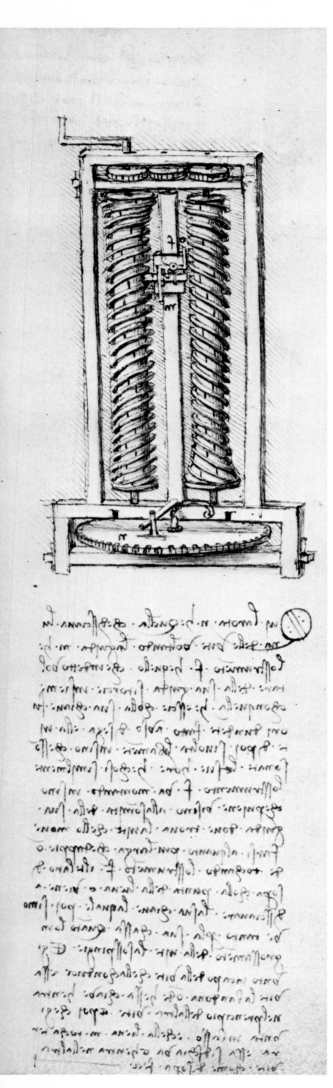

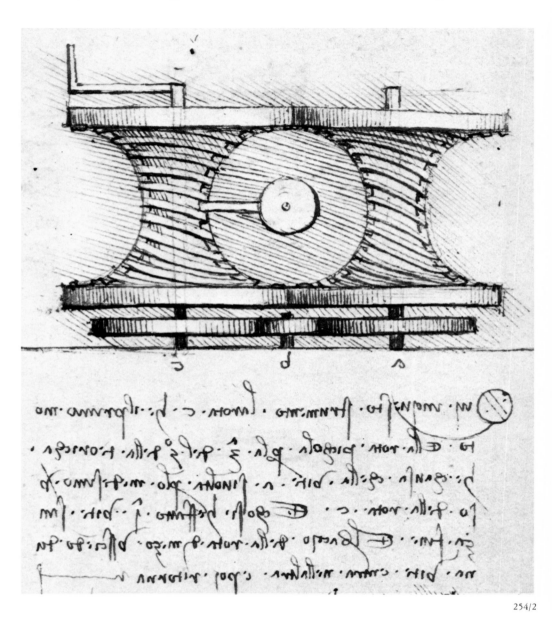

horizontal bar with adjustable sliding weights. This crossbar is called the balance or the foliot. Sometimes, especially in older timepieces, like that of de' Dondi, the foliot at the top of the verge was developed in the form of a ring or crown.

254/1

On folio 115 verso of Codex Madrid I Leonardo discusses this all-important element of a clockwork in detail:

"Some people are of the opinion that by making the shaft of the escapement in the shape of a circle there will be obtained an unvarying contact with the air, and that in this way the resistance against the air will be the same whether it is straight or in

254/2

another shape. But I believe that they are deluded, since by making the escapement round, a transverse piece to sustain the ring must be added, and as a consequence, the weight will increase. This additional weight makes the circle-shaped escapement equivalent to one which is straight."

Having made this explanation, he proceeds to comment on the escapement and describes its function:

"It is customary to oppose the violent motion of the wheels of the clock driven by their counterweights with certain devices called escapements, as they keep the timing of the wheels which move it. They regulate the motion according to the required slowness and the length of the hours. The purpose of the device is to lengthen the time, a most useful thing. They are made according to several different methods, but all have the same nature and value. Their variety is born out of the necessity of taking into account the space available for the collocation."

After making a detailed sketch of several forms of the verges which engage the teeth of the wheel, Leonardo provides specifications for their adjustment. These instructions are illustrated with simple but meaningful drawings of the spindle with its pallets, and of the relation of the pallets to the teeth of the crown wheel in the positions described. An interesting excursion into the shape of the balance regulator, in which the artist included sketches of four variations [256/1], occurs elsewhere in Codex Madrid I, on a page of apparently unrelated subjects.

Another form of the foliot, showing the weights attached to both arms, with the verge on a vertical crown wheel and a weight drive, is shown in Codex Forster I.[18]

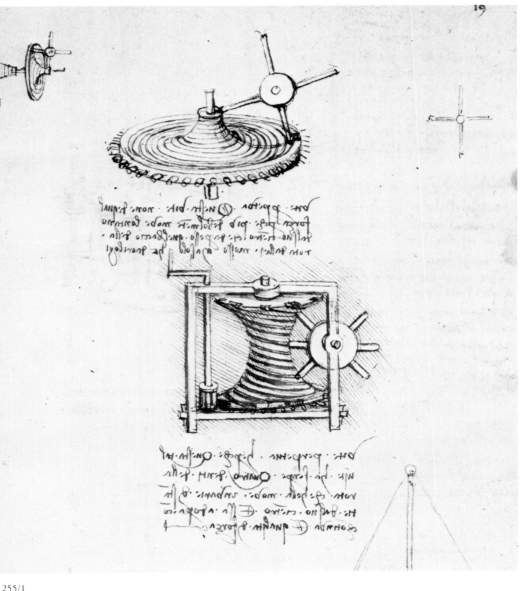

255/1

The drawing bears only the brief note *del tempo.* For Leonardo and his contemporaries, *tempo* meant not only time but also a regulator, or escapement. This sense of the term *tempo* remained in use in Italy until at least the 18th century.

Leonardo knew that precise time regulation and measurement were difficult because of unpredictable variations in the environment (temperature, atmospheric pressure, humidity) and in the timepiece itself (constructive imperfections, friction, wear). This awareness is documented on several pages of his writings. At one point in Codex Madrid I he ponders the question "Why the hours are sometimes long and other times short" in this fashion: "This [lengthening of the hours] happens as a result of the humidity inherent in bad weather; the air becomes thick and the escapements of the clocks find more resistance in such air. As a consequence, the clocks slow down and the hours become longer. But if you want to be sure of this, pay attention to the cords of the clock's counterweights, which swell in bad weather, and as a result their center is drawn away from the

254/1 and 2
255/1

Some of Leonardo's most exquisite drawings in Codex Madrid I trace the transmission of power and motion through the precisely rendered screws and wheels related to clockwork. Since his intention in the codex is to analyze the basic elements of machines, he seldom refers directly to timekeeping mechanisms. In the left sketch on the opposite page, from folio 15 recto, it is clear that the two screws, powered by a crank, move a mechanism along the central bar. But only Leonardo's notes – "the screw revolves freely until the corresponding hour is rung" – indicate that the device was probably associated with the alarm or striking mechanism of a clock. He does not define the purpose of the other mechanism on the opposite page, from folio 18 verso. The turning of the two screws moves an arm – somewhat akin to a clock hand – around

Endless screw. This screw is of unequal power because the arm of the wheel moved by the screw has less power when the contact is made from the screw's center than when it is made closer to it. But it is only for clockwork.

the circle formed by the concave screws. In notes for another instrument using screws of similar shape (left), on folio 19 recto, Leonardo points out that it "can be used only in clockwork." The concave screws, which side by side form a circle or globe, are an early version of today's globoidal gear.

Endless screw. This screw acts upon the wheel with equal and continuous force because it is always touched by four teeth, at varying distances from the center of the wheel it moves.

The toothlike devices below are pallets. By intermittently engaging the teeth in the

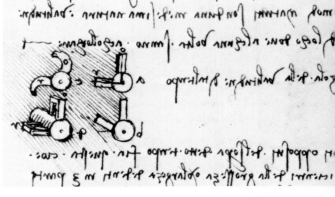

255/2

escape wheel of a weight-driven clock, they control the descent of the weight (see following page).   MADRID I 115v

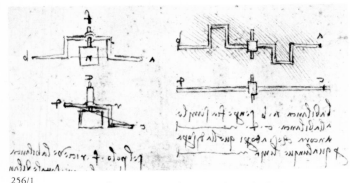

The key to precision timekeeping in weight-driven clocks is an efficient system of

regulators to control the speed at which the weights descend. In Leonardo's day the most widely known practical regulator was the foliot and verge escapement, and indeed it went unchallenged until about 1660. This escapement consists of three parts: the crown or escape wheel; a shaft called the verge – from the Latin virga, *meaning "rod" or "wand" – with two toothlike projections known as pallets, which alternately engage the teeth of the crown wheel, allowing it to advance intermittently; and at the top of the verge a crosspiece called the balance or foliot, equipped with adjustable sliding weights. In his sketch above, in Codex Madrid I, folio 98 verso, Leonardo experiments with four different shapes for the foliot crosspiece. He and his contemporaries referred to the clock regulator as* tempo, *which also means "beat" and "time." In a discussion of "why the hours are sometimes long and other times short" Leonardo described the effects of humidity on weight cords. He also experimented with a regulator for the clock strike, the fly. This was a revolving axle with vanes that used air resistance to slow the fall of the weight. His sketch at left, in Madrid I, folio 8 recto, used a two-vaned fly in a mechanism which he did not describe.*

"It is possible to make a clock which shows the hours, and it is both simple and good,

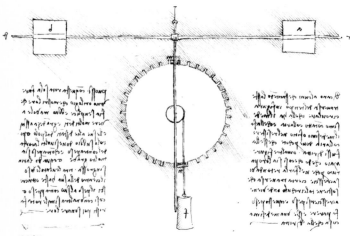

with a single wheel," writes Leonardo above. His one-wheeled clock – a form that long has intrigued clockmakers – is fitted with a foliot and verge escapement, but in place of a crown wheel has an escape wheel with radical teeth. The horizontal foliot across the top has, instead of counterweights, two large projections that Leonardo called alia *(wings) or* ventola *(vanes).* MADRID I 115v

drum, which should make the hours shorter. Actually, however, the hours become longer in humid weather. Therefore, the lengthening of the hours is caused solely by the clock escapements and has no other possible cause."[19]

The unequal resistance of the air seems to be the main cause of irregularity, but others were also considered, especially the very nature of gear transmission.[20]

In Leonardo's time a true understanding of the complex phenomena involved in the function of time regulators was not possible. He seemed to relate their action to air resistance. If he were correct in doing so, the clockmaker would still have another device at his disposal to slow down the speed of descent of the driving weight or the unwinding of the spring: the fly. And in fact Leonardo was aware of, and studied, the fly [256/2]. The fly was probably the first, though an imperfect, regulator applied in clockworks, appearing long before the foliot and verge. A fly is a revolving axle provided with vanes. The vanes, as the axle revolves, meet with a resistance that depends on their number, area, angle, and speed. By changing any of these conditions, the speed of the motion can be modified. The device is still used in the striking train of clockworks and in music boxes.

Regulators in the form of a fly appear often in Leonardo's horological projects. The principle of the fly is examined in Codex Madrid I, where, beneath the sketch of a four-vaned fly, the following observations are made:

"This is a fly that resists air. And the question is: which fly will, in its revolution, resist the percussion of the air more, a fly of 2 vanes or one of 4 or 8?

"I ask: which fly will turn faster or slower, a fly having many vanes or one that has only a few; flies with vanes long or short, with wide or thin, with light or heavy? And the difference of each variety shall be investigated. You may also have flies with vanes of diverse length but equal weight, or vanes that are perforated like a sifter, interwoven like a sieve, or fringed like a comb. You may also have framed vanes with stretched-out tissue, with the diaphragm being shaggy or smooth, slack or taut."[21]

This is not only an acute examination of the possibilities inherent in the use of the fly as a regulator; it is also illustrative of Leonardo's method when confronted with a scientific or practical problem. And this examination must have had an experimental follow-up, because on another page of Codex Madrid I, beneath a sketch of a four-vaned fly, Leonardo observes, "A fly of a clock having more vanes resists less against the wind, because the progress of its motion is continuously facilitated."[22]

A most original regulating device is found on the same page where the foliot and verge escapement is discussed. It belongs to a one-wheeled timepiece [256/3]. The one-wheeled clock was a curiosity that frequently preoccupied early-17th-century horologists, but the manuscript literature indicates beyond question that such simple clocks were successfully produced much earlier, and that the form probably had its origin in the 14th century.[23] Leonardo illustrated a single large wheel with 36 teeth fixed to a central arbor projecting from a drum around which the rope suspending the weight is wound. The clock is fitted with a foliot and verge escapement, but it differs from the conventional type on several accounts. There is no crown wheel; the pallets, probably of the curved shape shown at lower left, engage on pins or cogs placed radially. The very long foliot is provided not with the ordinary adjustable counterweights, but with two large vanes, called by Leonardo *alia* or *ventola*. The regulation is based, therefore, not on a natural period of vibration like that of the balance or the pendulum, but on the resistance of the air.

A fly or an oscillating fan can be used to slow down a mechanical motion or to move the air itself, and it is no surprise to find among Leonardo's papers a device in which this principle of aerodynamic reciprocity, always present in his mind, is applied. A well-known example is a drawing of around 1490 in the Codex Atlanticus; it represents a mechanical fan moved by a regulator as used in clocks, including a crown wheel and verge [257/1]. Leonardo notes that "the method for raising the counterweight is accomplished in the same manner as in a clock." The crown wheel and verge, instead of activating a balance or foliot, move a pendulum, which is the fan itself. This arrangement is closely related to an escapement found in the clock erected in the square of the Pitti Palace in Florence [257/3] between 1655 and 1658.[24]

Which leads us to the difficult question, when was the pendulum first used as a regulator of clockwork?

A fly fan can either rotate or oscillate to slow down the motion in clockwork and other machines – Leonardo's middle sketch on the opposite page shows an oscillator. But in about 1490 Leonardo made use of the fly in a mechanism in the Codex Atlanticus, folio 278 recto (far left), in such an intriguing way that to this day scholars have not been able to agree to his intention. In the sketch the weight at right drives a crown wheel and verge – as in clockwork – which move

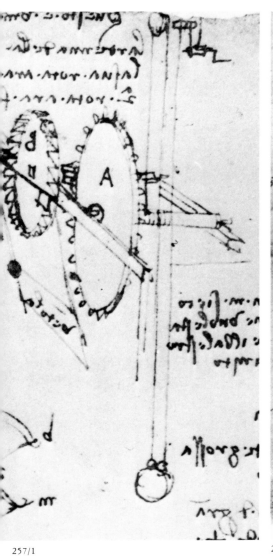

257/1

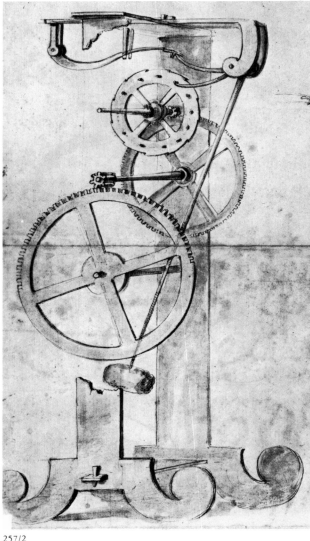

257/2

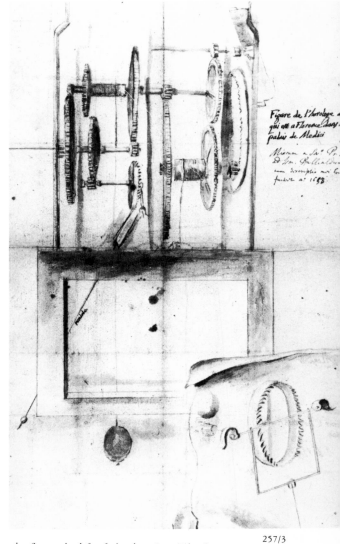

257/3

It is an established fact that the idea of pendulum regulation of clocks had been conceived long before the issuance of a patent for an invention achieving it by the States-General of the Netherlands to Christian Huygens in 1657.[25] Much earlier Galileo had enunciated his famous laws about the isochronism of pendular motion. As early as 1583 Galileo had recognized that natural law of pendular motion when observing the oscillation of a lamp in the Cathedral of Pisa. By 1637 he had also thought of its practical application [257/2]. However, either lack of mechanical aptitude or the fact that he became taken up with other interests prevented him from making practical use of the consequences implicit in his discovery. But recent research has brought to light the fact that the application of the pendulum regulator to clockwork had been anticipated by mechanicians of even earlier times than Galileo's. Thus in a manuscript of Benvenuto della Volpaia in the Biblioteca Nazionale di San Marco in Venice, written around 1525, a pendulum is shown in relation to a crown wheel and verge escapement. The manuscript illustrates and describes various machines and clocks made by members of the Volpaia (or Golpaia) family. It includes works of the author's father, Lorenzo della Volpaia, who was a friend of Leonardo.[26] We know that Leonardo himself on several occasions suggested the use of heavy pendulums as inertia

the fly at the left of the drawing. The fly serves as a kind of pendulum. It may be compared to the regulator added to the clock of the Pitti Palace in 1656 (above) by Johann Philipp Treffler. The controversy centers around whether Leonardo actually applied the pendulum as a regulator to clockwork, an accomplishment credited to others. Galileo Galilei is credited with having discovered the principle of isochronism of the pendulum – he established that because of gravity a pendulum swung in equal time intervals no matter how wide the arc – and subsequently he attempted to apply his discovery to clockwork. The drawing at left above shows a model constructed for Galileo's son Vincenzo, based upon his blind father's instructions. The pendulum is attached directly to the pallets at the top, which engage and release teeth on the pinwheel with each pendular swing.

257

accumulators in order to equalize the motion imparted to pumps and mills. Did he also attempt to apply the pendulum to timekeeping?

This is a question that has intrigued scholars since the revival of interest in Leonardo's manuscripts near the end of the last century. After studying a number of Leonardo's sketches, several scholars answered it in the affirmative. The claim did not, however, pass without opposition.[27] The numerous horological references found in Codex Madrid I permit the re-examination of claims and counterclaims advanced on the issue in the course of the past 70 years. Shortly after the rediscovery of the Madrid Codices their content was described and the important

As a result of the rediscovery of Codex Madrid I it seems that Leonardo clearly intended to apply pendular mechanisms to clockwork. Below, he sketches a silent escapement with pendulum – the verge escapement was noisy – and he notes that it "may be used for a clock escapement." The

Movement that proceeds
and returns like a fan and,
if heavy, may be used
for a clock escapement.
It is noiseless.

258/2

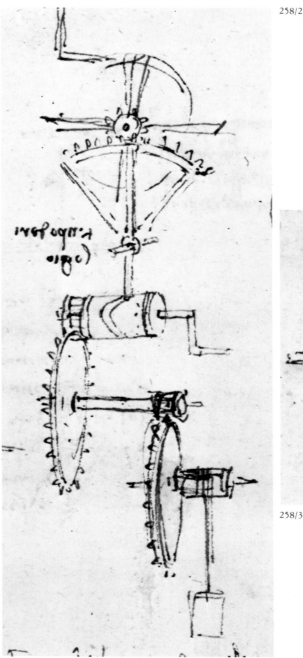

258/2–4
Variations on the sinusoidal-track arrangement depicted at far left appear in Codex Madrid I, folio 157 verso. On the drawing at left Leonardo notes that it is of a tempo d'orilogio, *that is, a clock escapement. The left sketch below apparently has a pen-*

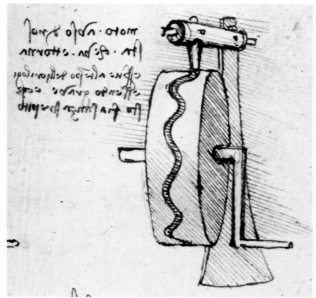

258/1

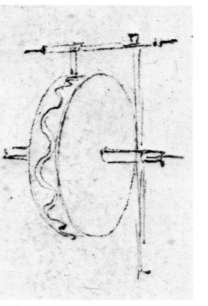

258/3

258/4

pendulum, in the back, is shaped like the sector of a circle – the shape of Besson's and of Galileo's more than a century later. It is attached to a follower that moves along a sinusoidal groove in the drumlike wheel. Leonardo adds a crank, which would be superfluous if the device were actually integrated with clockwork. The Dutch scientist Christian Huygens is credited with construction of the first practical pendulum clock in 1657, but recent research shows that earlier inventors besides Leonardo may have anticipated him. One 16th-century manuscript illustrates pendulum clockwork drawn by a member of the family of Lorenzo della Volpaia, a friend of Leonardo.   MADRID I 8r

dulum connected to the follower moving in the grooved track. The sinusoidal cam was adopted during the Second World War in a magnetic arrangement (above, right) for use in delayed-action fuses on explosive mines. Later, it served the use Leonardo had originally envisioned for the sinusoidal track – as a silent escapement in clocks.

information they contain on the history of horology was pointed out.[28] Now, after more careful study, a balanced assessment can be attempted.

One of the more curious horological devices that Leonardo illustrated in Codex Madrid I is a silent escapement [258/1]. The device consists of a drumlike wheel attached to a shaft. Along the edge of the drum wheel is a sinusoidal groove which is traced by a follower connected to a pendulum in the shape of a sector of a circle. In his own description Leonardo specifies a timekeeping purpose for this device: "Movement that proceeds and returns like a fan and, if heavy, may be used for a clock escapement. It is noiseless." It is noteworthy here that the idea for a pendulum regulator for clockwork suggested by Galileo in 1637 was based on a massive pendulum made of copper or bronze in the shape of a sector of a circle of 12 to 15 degrees. The presence of a crank connected to the drum should not prejudice our interpretation since in this book Leonardo did not intend to describe complete machines. Leonardo often provides an individual mechanism with a crank which would be superfluous when the mechanism was actually integrated with a working complex.

At the foot of the page where this device occurs is shown another sinusoidal-cam arrangement which motivates a two-vaned fly, but without description [256/2]. Presumably this was for the purpose of developing a back-and-forth action. On another page of Codex Madrid I, Leonardo sketched another version of the drum wheel with sinusoidal track [258/2, 3]. The follower is connected with the rod of what appears to be a pendulum. The drum wheel with sinusoidal groove and follower appears two times in the Codex Atlanticus, on pages contemporary with the sketches found in Codex Madrid I.[29]

Were Leonardo's cam escapements workable? At least in principle they were – and centuries later the sinusoidal cam received full appreciation when utilized in a pendulum-regulated electric clock to provide a silent magnetic escapement. This was developed by Horstmann-Clifford and employed for delayed-action fuses in mine work during the Second World War [258/4]. It was later adopted for clock and watch movements.[30]

Other sketches with a form of crown wheel and verge that occur in the previously known manuscripts of Leonardo are brought into new focus as depicting possible pendulum-regulated timing devices by the presence of similar and more detailed drawings in Codex Madrid I. Folio 257 recto-a of the Codex Atlanticus is especially interesting in this regard. Careful study of Madrid I has led to a surprising discovery: a great number of its neatly elaborated drawings originate from preliminary sketches found in the Codex Atlanticus. A single page of the Atlanticus may contain the drafts for a number of pages of the Madrid manuscript. Folio 257 recto-a of the Atlanticus definitely belongs to this group of preparatory studies. We can recognize in this single sheet no less than eight independent projects which found their final version on five different pages of Codex Madrid I.[31] And two of them, folios 61 verso and 9 recto, contain elements that may become decisive in the reassessment of the pendulum controversy.

On folio 61 verso two pendulum mechanisms are presented [259/1]. In the drawing at the left a horizontal crown wheel is shown; a similar device at the right is provided with a vertical one. In both cases the verge is connected with a heavy pendulum. Beneath the main drawings Leonardo sketched a detail belonging to the figure marked S. The purpose of the neatly drawn mechanisms is stated in the descriptive text beneath: "This is one of the teeth of the escapement [tempo] that moves the upper wheel S. Its two teeth must be articulated because this is necessary when the escapement moves the wheel. But should it be the wheel which moves the escapement, as shown in the clocks, then the teeth of the escapement must be firmly joined to its shaft. This tooth is now solid with its rings o and r, and shaft f n g is now also made from a single piece. On the opposite side, facing n, the shaft is provided with a spring which permanently forces tooth m against n."

We see here the development of Leonardo's ideas about the usefulness of the pendulum in the design of machines. It is very important to understand his reasoning and interpret correctly the linguistic subtleties.

Leonardo distinguishes two kinds of motions related to the oscillations of the pendulum. With one kind, the oscillator, or escapement, moves the wheel; that is, the pendulum is put into motion by an outside force. This would be the case with the often cited moving of a millwork by manually swinging a heavy pendulum, which acts to store and release power alternately. With the other kind, the wheel moves the oscillator. This may occur only in clockwork, and in case the pendulum

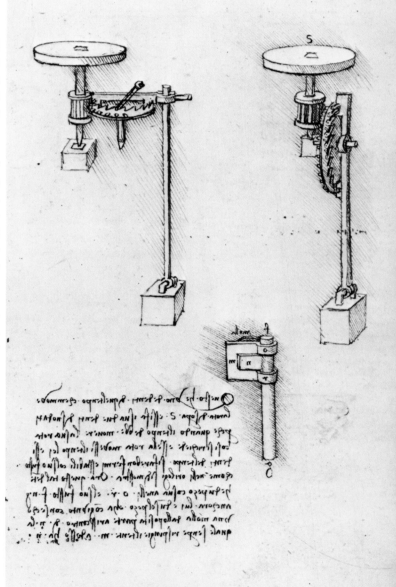

259/1

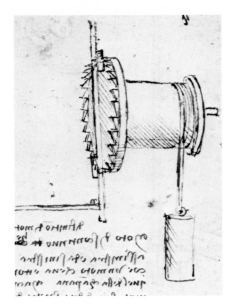

In Codex Madrid I, folio 9 recto (above), a driving drum and crown-wheel and verge escapement are connected to a horizontal rod of a type later used to transmit the oscillations of a pendulum.

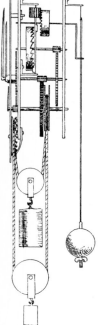

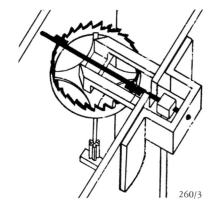

260/3

Christian Huygens patented the first pendulum-regulated clockwork, shown in the design at left, and illustrated it in his work Horologium Oscillatorium, *published in 1673. It is similar to Leonardo's pendulum-regulated horizontal crown wheel shown on the previous page. The early English clock above, with pendulum rigidly mounted on the staff of the verge, also bears resemblance to Leonardo's design.*

260/2

Below, Leonardo may have conceived of a metronome-like mechanism using an inverted pendulum to measure time by means of beats. ARUNDEL 191v

260/4

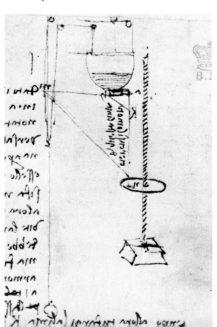

acts as a regulator. The horological application is clearly and explicitly stated: "But should it be the wheel which moves the verge, as shown in the clockwork, then the teeth of the escapement must be firmly joined to its shaft."

By completing Leonardo's drawing with a driving drum, we arrive necessarily at Huygens' pendulum-regulated horizontal crown-wheel arrangement of 1673 [260/2]. Or rather, because Huygens' clock already had an added improvement, the suspended pendulum, we arrive at the early English clock illustrated in Britten's book *Old Clocks and Watches and Their Makers*,[32] in which the pendulum is rigidly mounted on the staff of the verge [260/3].

The new evidence shows that both parties of the pendulum controversy were right: Leonardo made projects for machines, especially mills, in which the pendulum was to act as power accumulator (in the manner of a flywheel). For such applications Leonardo foresaw articulated pallets. Detailed drawings and descriptions of these are found in the Codex Atlanticus.[33] But when the pendulum was to be used as a regulator in clocks, the pallets of the verge had to be rigidly mounted on the staff of the verge.

A further piece of evidence in support of this interpretation, were it needed, is offered by folio 9 recto of Codex Madrid I, where the missing driving drum is depicted in combination with a verge escapement [260/1]. The staff of the verge is connected at right angles with an oscillating rod. Again we are confronted with the two types of pendular motion. The oscillations of a bell, if left without impulse, would slowly cease, as each oscillation would be progressively shorter than the preceding one. The pendulum of a clock always describes the same arc because the impulse conferred by the escapement, which in turn is moved by a weight or a spring, supplies the force required to overcome the frictional resistance of the system.[34]

Crown wheel and verge, combined with a pendulum, are found on several other pages of Codex Madrid I.[35] The weight of the pendulum is omitted, but the purpose is unmistakable. In his sketches Leonardo usually depicted the pendulum regulator as directly connected to the verge shaft. This form of pendulum is rarely encountered in the clocks of England, France, or Germany in any epoch (the figure of an English clock in Britten's book is an exception), but it was fairly common in Italy. Numerous clocks of 17th-century Italian production have survived in which it was employed in the original mechanism as well as when the conversion was made from balance-wheel to pendulum regulation.

Characteristically, Leonardo concerned himself with the measurement of time in various contexts. Thus he made frequent use of the word *tempo* as a unit of measure of time in his manuscripts. In a most interesting study Augusto Marinoni has discussed the several phrases in which Leonardo made use of it in this sense, including *tempo armonico* and *tempo di musica*. Although the metronome based on the inverted pendulum was an invention made in a much later period, Marinoni suggested that Leonardo may have conceived a device of similar nature for measuring elapsed time by means of beats as in music.[36] Notes on *tempo* appear especially in writings where the performance of men working on the excavation of earth is analyzed. Leonardo was engaged in earthworks while building canals in Lombardy and later in the Romagnas and Tuscany in 1502 and 1503. By 1508 the problem of establishing the velocity of flowing water and that of sailing ships progressing in still water had drawn Leonardo's interest to the measurement of small time intervals again.

As was his custom, Leonardo examined also the theoretical background of the interesting mechanical devices he was working on. He was trying to comprehend the natural laws that govern pendular motions. A general theory of the pendulum is discussed in Codex Madrid I, where its motion is assimilated to that described by a projectile. It is quite significant that this same juxtaposition reappears in the "Second Day" of Galileo's *Dialogò sopra i due massimi sistemi del mondo* (1632),[37] which includes the imaginary experiment of letting a body fall through a hole reaching beyond the center of the earth. Leonardo correctly recognized the conservation of motion which makes the bob of the pendulum ascend but not as much as it descended. He knew also that the fall of a body along a circular arc takes less time than the fall along the corresponding chord, and that if the arc is small, the oscillations of the pendulum will be more uniform. The first rule is an anticipation of the brachistochrone curve dealt with by Galileo; the second was fundamental for the improvement of pendulum-regulated clockworks.[38]

Leonardo did not notice the fundamental properties of the pendulum, that is, the isochronism of the oscillations and the rule that governs their period – a failure

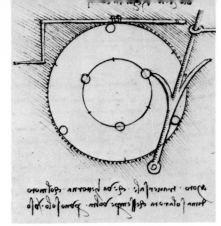

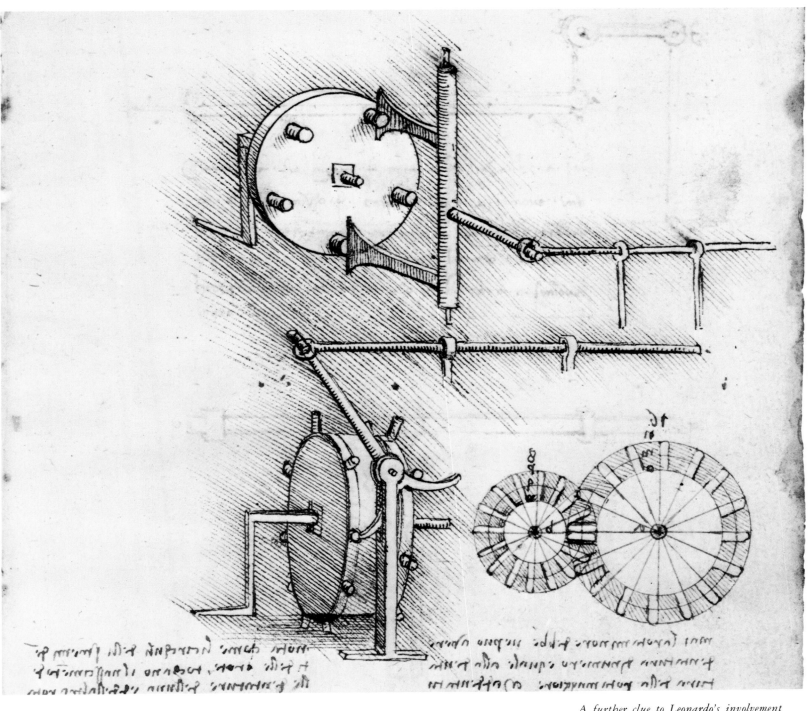

that prevented him from recognizing in the pendulum a better regulator than the balance or the fly, leading him to the already cited opinion, "They are made according to several different methods, but all have the same nature and value." However, he appears to have had at least an intuitive grasp of the relationship between length and period, although it was first formulated as a law by Galileo.

Even after Huygens presented his scientifically designed pendulum clocks, no substantial improvement on the precision of the timekeepers was achieved. No serious advance could be made as long as the motive power interfered with the

A further clue to Leonardo's involvement with clockwork is found in these two exquisite sketches from Codex Madrid I, folios 7 recto (above) and 27 recto (top). This is a form of pinwheel escapement in which the drums are controlled by verge-like pawls. Leonardo does not cite the purpose of his device, but Galileo later invented a pinwheel escapement with pendulum. In 1666, 24 years after his death, a clock with such an escapement was installed in the tower of the Palazzo Vecchio in Florence.

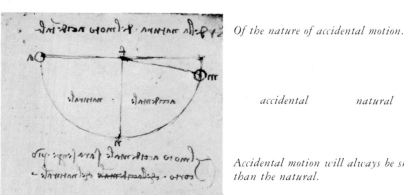

Of the nature of accidental motion.

accidental *natural*

Accidental motion will always be shorter than the natural.

In order to demonstrate the truth of this statement, we shall propose as example a round weight suspended from a cord, and let this weight be a. And it shall be lifted as high as the point of suspension of the cord. This point will be f and the cord will be f a, which should always be pulled along a straight line. I affirm thus, that if you let this weight fall, all the motion made from a to n will be called natural, because it moves in order to stop at n, that is, beneath its point of suspension f, seeking to approximate itself as near to the center of the world as possible. After reaching the desired site, that is, n, another motion takes place, which we will call accidental, because it goes against its desire. Such accidental motion will be from n to m and will always be less than the natural a n. Consequently, natural motion, the more it approaches its end, increases its velocity. Accidental motion does the contrary. However, the end of the accidental motion will be that much weaker than the beginning of the natural motion as the former is less than the latter. But if such motions are made towards the sky, as stones thrown in an arc, then the motion made by accident will be greater than the one we call natural. The reason for this is, that when the stone has completed the accidental motion, at whatever distance depending on the thrusting force, the stone will cease to follow in the air the shape of the arc it began, but due to the great desire to go back down, it describes a line of much greater curvature and shorter than when it went upwards.

If you join together the accidental and natural motions, that is, the natural and accidental courses of stones thrown through the air, you will observe a greater length of motion in stones thrown up perpendicularly towards the sky than in those directed nearer to the earth, provided that their primary motion is equal. In the first case, the motion, called natural, will be equal to the artificial. The greater the arc of their maximum height, the smaller will be the natural motion, and, conversely, a smaller arc will cause a greater natural motion.

262/1

The smaller is the natural motion of a suspended weight, the more the following accidental motion will equal it in length.

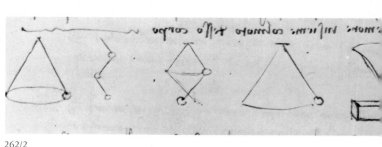

262/2

Leonardo also made drawings to describe and explain the laws that govern the motion of the pendulum. Above, in the Codex Arundel, folio 2 recto, he analyzes five types of moto ventilante – oscillating motion – including those of a conical and an inverted pendulum.

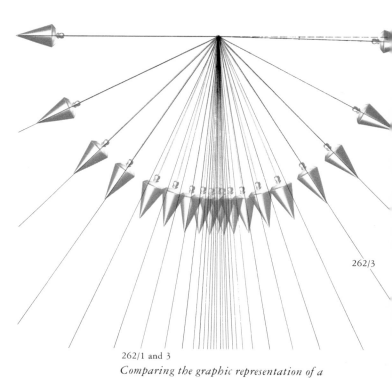

262/3

262/1 and 3

Comparing the graphic representation of a pendulum, above, with Leonardo's studies at left from Codex Madrid I, folio 147 recto, makes evident Leonardo's intuitive grasp of the phenomena, even though he did not notice its fundamental properties. His observation on the uniformity of pendular motion, depending on the size of the arc, clearly figures within the indicated acute angle in the graph above. On the folio at left, Leonardo also juxtaposes (a general theory of) the pendulum motion with that of a projectile. It is interesting to note that this very juxtaposition reappears in a book by Galileo Galilei, including the imaginary experiment of letting a body fall through a hole reaching beyond the center of the earth.

regulator, as is the case in the crown-wheel and verge arrangement. Pendulum clocks became reliable only after the introduction of the anchor escapement and the compensated pendulum rod, both invented by English mechanicians.[39]

These facts limit Leonardo's place in the history of horology but do not negate it. And now it has been reconfirmed for us by the magnificent legacy of Codex Madrid I. Some of the drawings there, such as those which appear to be of dials of

263/1

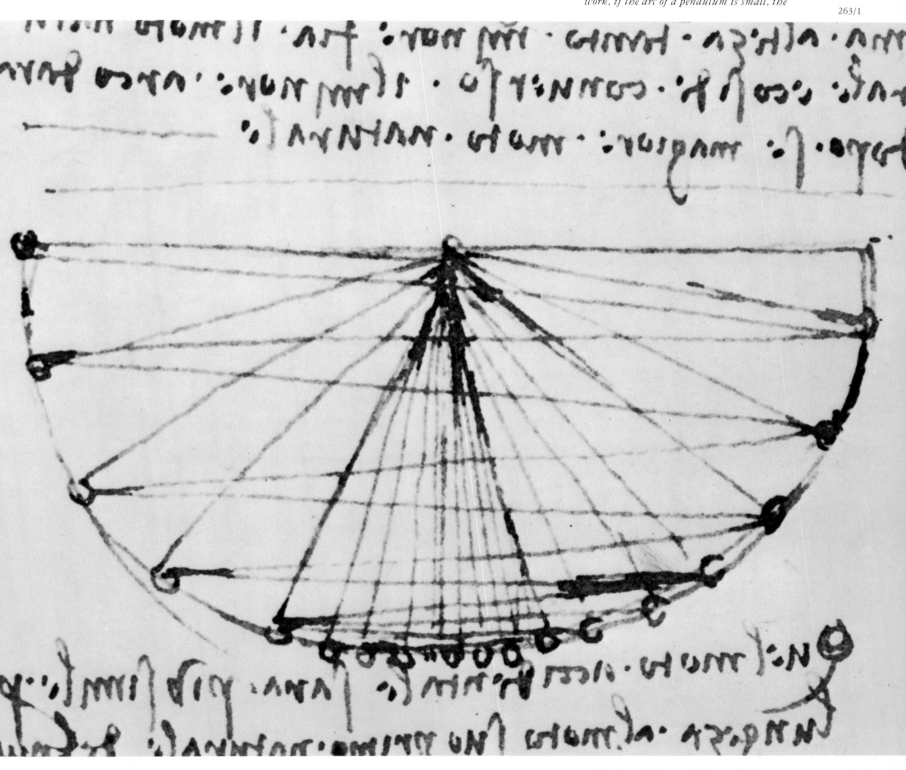

the astrarium of de' Dondi, confirm Leonardo's familiarity with such achievements in his time. Others, such as those related to the clock at Chiaravalle, have preserved details of important timepieces as they existed in Leonardo's time and the details and state of which have not otherwise survived in contemporary records. These and the many other materials related to horology in the Madrid notebook represent a new wealth which will be studied and analyzed for decades to come.

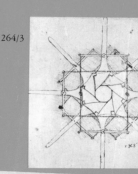

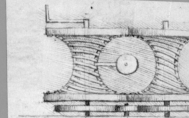

Elements of Machines

Ladislao Reti

Leonardo's restless intellect leaped yet-to-come centuries of scientific progress and yielded many solutions to complex mechani-

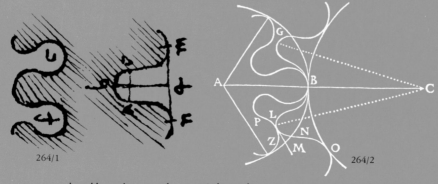

264/1   264/2

264/7

264/8

cal problems that were later copied or rediscovered. The drawings above offer graphic evidence of his intuitive grasp of the concept of rolling friction: his two sketches of gear profiles (left) in Codex Madrid I, folio 118 verso, closely resemble the design (right) arrived at nearly 200 years later by the 17th-century scientist Philippe de La Hire.

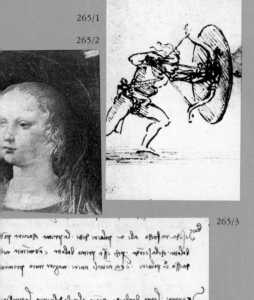

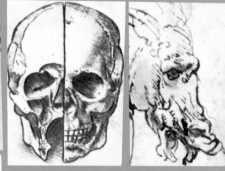

265/4

265/5

265/6

265/7

265/8   265/9

265/10

265/11

265/12

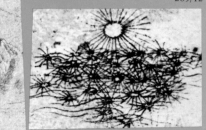

L eonardo's interests were extraordinarily diversified: his notes and sketches bear witness to an intellectual hunger that includes all human knowledge, from geometry to mechanics, from anatomy to botany, from geology to astronomy. And even accepting that the largest and perhaps the best part of Leonardo's legacy is lost – a conservative estimate points to the disappearance of about 75 percent of his work – it is reasonable to assume that the qualitative and quantitative distribution of the subjects treated by Leonardo is well represented in the material that has come down to us.

While no more than 10 paintings indisputably by the master's hand can be admired on the walls of the world's greatest art galleries (a disturbing aspect of the inventory of what remains of his works) and the drawings of a purely artistic nature are estimated to number a few hundred, thousands of studies and drawings dealing with geometry, mechanics, and engineering point to the predominant interests of Leonardo. The two manuscripts recently brought to light in Madrid add to the already impressive gathering almost 700 pages of technical drawings and notes only accidentally interrupted by unrelated subjects.

Every official appointment Leonardo received refers to him not only as an artist but as an engineer as well – at the court of Lodovico il Moro, for example, where he remained nearly 20 years, he was "engineer and painter"[1] – and correspondingly, his scientific and technological activities were well known to, even if not always approved by, his contemporaries and early biographers. They became more noticeable when he started to neglect his artistic activities as he became more and more involved in science and technology. In April 1501 Fra Pietro di Novellara, agent of Isabella d'Este, the Marchesa of Mantua, in the course of efforts to persuade Leonardo to accept an artistic commission from his mistress, wrote her describing some ongoing painting activity of the master and assuring her of the good will of Leonardo, but also pointed out that "he is so much distracted from painting by his mathematical experiments as to become intolerant of the brush."[2] Isabella pursued Leonardo for years with letters and intermediaries in order to obtain from him a painting; her admirable patience was in vain.

In technology Leonardo set his sight beyond the bounds of Italy and even Europe. Thus on a page of Manuscript L that is datable 1502–1503 there is a small sketch representing a bridge in plan and elevation, with its accompanying text: "Bridge from Pera to Constantinople 40 braccia wide, 70 braccia high above the water, and 600 braccia long; that is, 400 over the sea and 200 resting on the land, providing by itself its abutments."[3]

The varied illustrations at left – all from the hand of Leonardo – evoke the diversity of his works. His curiosity took him from art to science and increasingly, as he grew older, to mathematics, mechanics, and engineering. Thus when his works are juxtaposed, extraordinary contrasts emerge – such as those reflected here in the Madonna and bowman's shield, the military map and nature study, drawings of the tyrant Cesare Borgia and of the geometry of optics, and the precocious helicopter and lovely Alpine landscape.

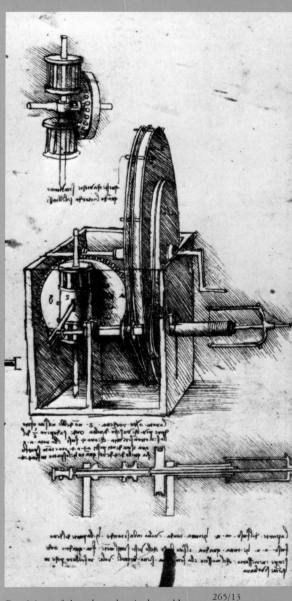

Precision of hand and mind enable Leonardo to communicate his ideas for mechanical contrivances in sketches more explicit than words. The drawings above, in Codex Atlanticus, folio 393 verso-a, depict the workings of an automated spool-winding machine. The crank turns the bobbin and flyer in opposite directions as the gear mechanism (shown in detail in the top sketch) moves the flyer back and forth to distribute the thread evenly on the bobbin.

One of Leonardo's engineering visions was of a colossal bridge over the Golden Horn at Istanbul, which he offered to undertake for the Sultan of the Ottoman Empire. Below, in Manuscript L, folio 66 recto, he sketches the bridge from overhead and in elevation and notes the dimensions of the 1,150-foot-long structure. The photographs at right show comparable views of a model of the bridge at the National Museum of Science and Technology in Milan.

266/1

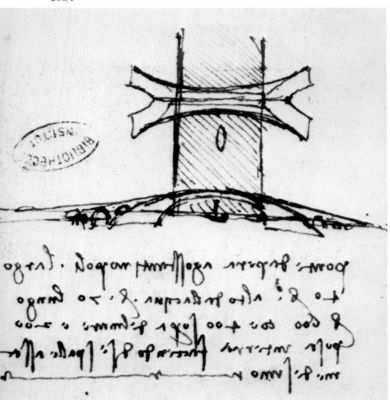

Bridge from Pera to Constantinople 40 braccia wide, 70 braccia high above the water, and 600 braccia long; that is, 400 over the sea and 200 resting on the land, providing by itself its abutments.

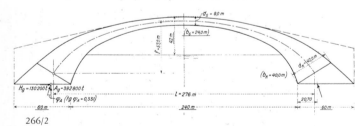

266/2

266/2 and 3

Leonardo's bridge would have arched so high above the water, he wrote Sultan Bajazet II, that a ship with sails up could pass under it. The diagram above shows the dimensioning of a modern Swiss scientist, D. F. Stüssi of Zurich, who concluded that the plans were technically feasible. Below, the model in the Milan museum.

266/3

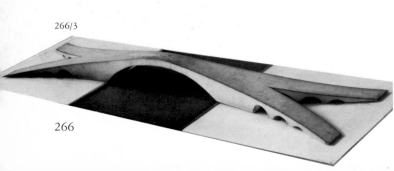

266

This grandiose project might appear to be just a flight of fancy were it not for some significant circumstances first pointed out by J. P. Richter.[4] Richter believed that the sketch must have been made about 1502, when ambassadors of Sultan Bajazet II of the Ottoman Empire were in Rome looking for Italian engineers to replace

266/4

266/5

the bridge of pontoons over the Golden Horn by a permanent structure. Vasari's life of Michelangelo, cited by Richter, relates the sultan's plans to Michelangelo, saying that "he thought of going to Constantinople to serve the Turk by means of some Franciscan friars, from whom he learned that the Turk wanted him to make a bridge between Constantinople and Pera."[5] But in 1952 a surprising piece of evidence involving Leonardo came to light. Franz Babinger, examining a document found in the archives of the Topkapi Serayi in Istanbul, recognized it as a Turkish translation of a letter by Leonardo da Vinci offering Sultan Bajazet II his services for the execution of four engineering projects.[6]

The projects were a special kind of windmill, an automatic device for pumping a ship's hull dry, the construction of a bridge between Galata and Istanbul, or Constantinople, and the erection of a drawbridge in order to reach the Anatolian coast. Babinger, assisted by Ludwig H. Heydenreich, dates this document around 1502–1503, which corresponds to the period of Manuscript L. And in Manuscript L we find not only the sketch and the description of the bridge between Pera or Galata and Constantinople but also constructive details for windmills[7] and a sketch for a pump for draining ship hulls.[8]

In Giorgio Vasari's biography of Leonardo[9] we find a reflection of the sentiments of contemporaries faced by such behavior in a man endowed by Providence with such great artistic gifts, as well as testimony about the variety of Leonardo's technological projects that is important in assessing the influence of Leonardo on the development of technology: "He would have made great profit in learning had he not been so capricious and fickle, for he began to learn many things and then gave them up . . . he not only worked in sculpture . . . but also prepared many architectural plans and elevations, and he was the first, though so young, to propose to canalise the Arno from Pisa to Florence. He made designs for mills, fulling machines and other engines to go by water.... By the grace of God he was endowed with a terrible gift of reasoning that, combined with intelligence and memory and a capacity of expressing himself by means of his drawings, enabled him to confound the boldest opponents. Every day he made models and designs for the removal of mountains with ease and to pierce them to pass from one place to another, and by means of levers, capstans and screws to raise and draw heavy weights; he devised methods for cleansing ports and to raise water from great depths, schemes which his brain never ceased to evolve. Of such ideas and efforts many designs are scattered about, and I have seen many of them...."

And after Leonardo's death, more seems to have remained than models and

A Leonardo method of bending beams into arches found expression more than 300 years later in Swiss wooden bridges. His drawing at left, in Codex Atlanticus, folio

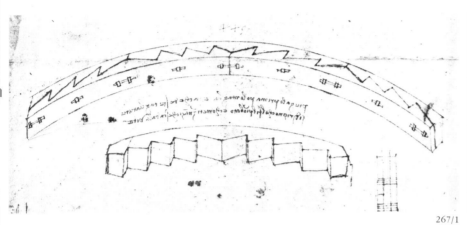

267/1

267/2

designs. For example, the distinguished Milanese cleric Giovanni Ambrogio Mazenta (1565–1635), who once had 13 of Leonardo's manuscripts, left in his memoirs testimony of Leonardo's technical activities in Lombardy.[10] The information contained is significant because it is based on widespread tradition still alive at the time and on the content of books by Leonardo that Mazenta had in his hands. He speaks of "Leonardo's invention of machines and gates to level, intercommunicate and make navigable" the waterways connecting the Lombard lakes. He also speaks of the "many machines depicted in the ... books, that have been put to use in the region of Milan, like weirs, locks and gates, mostly invented by Leonardo." And he speaks of other technical contributions by Leonardo: "In the *botteghe* of the arts, many machines invented by Leonardo are in use, for cutting

344 verso-a, demonstrates how the beams can be notched so that the fibers in the wood will not split. The wooden bridge at bottom, built in 1839 in Signau in the canton of Bern, has two bearing arches constructed precisely as in the Leonardo drawing. A detail of the bridge shows the interlocking of the bent and notched timbers in one of the bearing arches. About 155 feet long, the bridge spans the Emme River and has a load capacity of more than 40 tons. Another bridge of similar construction in the same canton spans nearly 200 feet. Bridges of this type, unknown before the 19th century, represent another modern application of Leonardo's thinking.

267/3

His surviving drawings and writings and the accounts of his contemporaries attest to Leonardo's interest in the design of water-powered gristmills. The sketch at right, in Codex Atlanticus, folio 304 verso-b, is for a large-scale mill. Below, again at the National Museum of Science and Technology in Milan, is a model of the mill. In the detail of the model shown on the opposite page can be seen the two front waterwheels and the connecting shafts that power the mills on the upper level. The 16th-century Italian painter and writer Giovanni Paolo Lomazzo recalled a collection of 30 sheets by Leonardo depicting mills "some of them moved by water and some not, all different from each other." In Atlanticus Leonardo lists 11 kinds of uses for such water mills, including silk spinning and the manufacture of gunpowder.

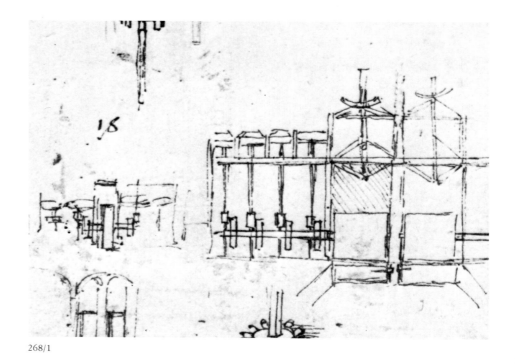

268/1

268/2

Mills powered by the wind were of little significance in Italy because of unfavorable meteorological conditions. The two sketches for a windmill at right were probably made in connection with Leonardo's offer of his services to Sultan Bajazet II of the Ottoman Empire. Leonardo's letter to the sultan, written about 1502, came to light in a Turkish translation that was found in 1952. Leonardo said that, in addition to a windmill and the bridge over the Golden Horn (page 266), he could build a drawbridge and an automatic device for pumping out the hull of a ship.

MS. L 35v, 34v

268/3

268/4

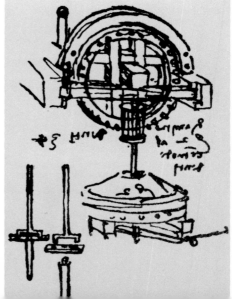

and polishing crystal, iron and stones; and there is one much used in the cellars of Milan, for grinding large amounts of meat to make *cervellato* – [a Milanese specialty, a sausage made with pork meat, and brain] with the help of a wheel turned by a boy without being troubled by flies or stench." "There are also many sawmills for marble and wood on the rivers and sand dredges on boats moved by the stream."

All this and much more historical evidence, pointing to Leonardo's double vocation and the actual fulfilment of important technical works, contradicts by itself the opinion of a number of contemporary scholars, who have questioned the possible influence of Leonardo upon the development of the mechanical arts and even the practicability of his technological projects. Yet even as recently as the 1950s and 1960s some have done so. To cite only two of many possible examples:

In a book by Leonardo Olschki, published in 1950, Leonardo da Vinci's technological work is assessed as follows: "Leonardo's technology still belongs to the traditional type of antiquity and the Middle Ages; it was highly developed craftsmanship, with no attempt to apply scientific principles. . . . His scientific and technological work is little more than a mass of eloquent literary fragments and

269/1

realistic drawings, of ingenious projects that would hardly have withstood a practical test."[11] There is no need to answer this except to say that were Olschki right, numerous distinguished scholars who have found to the contrary would have toiled in vain.

The second example is more specific. At a 1952 international congress in observance of the 500th anniversary of Leonardo's birth, Bertrand Gille, speaking of Leonardo's attempts to convert rotary to reciprocating motion, said that "when Leonardo tries to find the solution of the problem of the transformation of a continuous circular motion into an alternating reciprocal motion, he imagines the most unlikely solutions before ending simply with the rod-crank system known since the start of the 15th century."[12] Further, in the 1960s, Joseph Needham, in his monumental *Science and Civilisation in China*, accepted Gille's statement.[13] In fact a review of the Vincian corpus provides a count of 137 single-crank

269/2, 3, and 4
Leonardo's longtime fascination with the creation of a waterway from Florence to the sea resulted in a number of hydraulic contrivances. He devised the ingenious sluice gates below, in Codex Atlanticus, folio 240 recto-c, to control water levels. The key to

269/2

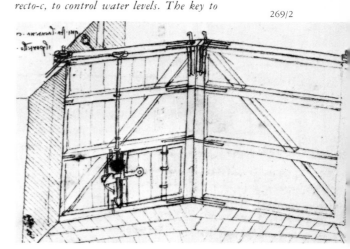

their operation is in the lower part of the left-hand gate – a simple trapdoor controlled by a latch from above. Opening the trapdoor permits water to flow in and equalize the pressure on both sides so that the main gates can be opened. The photograph below shows a model of the sluice gates, complete with trapdoor, built by A. De Rizzardi for the

269/3

269/4

National Museum of Science and Technology in Milan. Another model by De Rizzardi (bottom photo) is based on Atlanticus, folio 46 verso-a. It demonstrates one of Leonardo's ideas for the use of the sluice gates – to control the level of a canal that carries a boat across a bridge.

motions and 67 crank-and-rod motions, most of them connected with a piston rod, some transmitting the movement to a second crank or to swinging devices. Additionally, Codex Madrid I includes 104 simple and 24 compound crank motions.

On an admirable page of this codex[14] Leonardo not only discusses the theory underlying its use but also refers to it as a device generally known to practitioners. There is a legend that James Watt was obliged to resort to complicated transmission systems because the crank-and-rod transmission had been previously patented. The truth is that engineers were afraid of applying the simple crank-and-rod motion to the steam engine because it was imagined that the engine would stop or turn back or that something would give way as a consequence of the irregularity of the stroke of a steam piston. No one, not even Watt, could believe that the movements of a reciprocating engine could be controlled by means of a flywheel and a crank.[15] Had Watt seen Leonardo's illuminating page, where the theory of the crank-and-rod motion is discussed in connection with that of the flywheel, he would perhaps have been less reluctant to adopt it in his steam engine.

But I shall not discuss at any further length Leonardo's scientific and technological

and notes that even then – Vasari was first published in 1550 – much of Leonardo's work already was "scattered about."

Every day he made models and designs for the removal of mountains with ease and to pierce them to pass from one place to another, and by means of levers, capstans, and screws to raise and draw heavy weights; he devised methods for cleansing ports and to raise water from great depths, schemes which his brain never ceased to evolve. Of such ideas and efforts many designs are scattered about, and I have seen many of them.

An eminent contemporary who came under the influence of Leonardo's artistic and technological projects was the German artist Albrecht Dürer (right). The son of a goldsmith, Dürer was born in Nuremberg but traveled widely. He went to Italy at least twice, in 1494 and in 1505, for a long sojourn in Venice. His engravings, woodcuts, and paintings show the effects of his contact with the work of Leonardo and the other Italian masters. Though there is no evidence that Dürer met Leonardo, he must have seen some of his works, including manuscripts now considered lost. He borrowed the knotwork pattern that Leonardo wove through the decoration of the *Sala delle Asse*, adopted some of his ideas for drawing instruments [270/4], and was influenced by Leonardo's representation of horses [271/1].

270/2

work in order to affirm the validity of my positive point of view. Instead, I shall attempt to let Leonardo speak for himself and shall limit my comments to explaining the meaning of what he says when the distance in time of his language makes the interpretation difficult and to putting Leonardo's ideas in the place where they belong in the history of the technical arts. In the introduction to his book *The Kinematic of Machinery* (1876), which is a classic in its field, Franz Reuleaux, the founder of the modern theory of mechanisms, discusses the principles by which a

Two of Leonardo's devices for aiding the artist that were adopted by Albrecht Dürer are shown at right. The perspectograph, in *Codex Atlanticus*, folio 1bis recto-a, was a device that permitted the artist to see and draw from a fixed position in true perspective – a subject of great interest to the mathematically inclined Leonardo. The ellipsograph, shown at far right in a copy after Dürer (Albertina, Vienna) based on Leonardo's lost drawing, was known to medieval Arab mathematicians and may have existed in ancient times. In Leonardo's version, three legs of the compass formed a triangle and the tube holding the brush proved able – in a modern working model made from the sketch – to inscribe perfect ellipses.

270/3

270/4

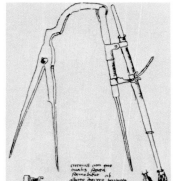

machine should be studied and defined. One of its passages runs as follows: "In earlier times men considered every machine as a separate whole, consisting of parts peculiar to it; they missed entirely or say but seldom the separate groups of parts which we call mechanisms. A mill was a mill, a stamp a stamp and nothing else, and thus we find the older books describing each machine separately from beginning to end. So for example Ramelli (1588), in speaking of various pumps

271/1

271/2

The most dramatic example of Leonardo's effect on Dürer is evident in the German's master engraving Knight, Death, and the Devil (far left). The knight is transplanted almost unchanged from Dürer's drawing of 15 years earlier Man in Armor on Horseback. But the horse, wooden and lifeless in the earlier work, has come alive – and looks remarkably like Leonardo's studies for his equestrian Sforza monument (left, Windsor 12347 recto). Scholars suspect that Dürer saw Leonardo's lost work on horse anatomy and his studies of human anatomy, which apparently also had a profound effect on the German.

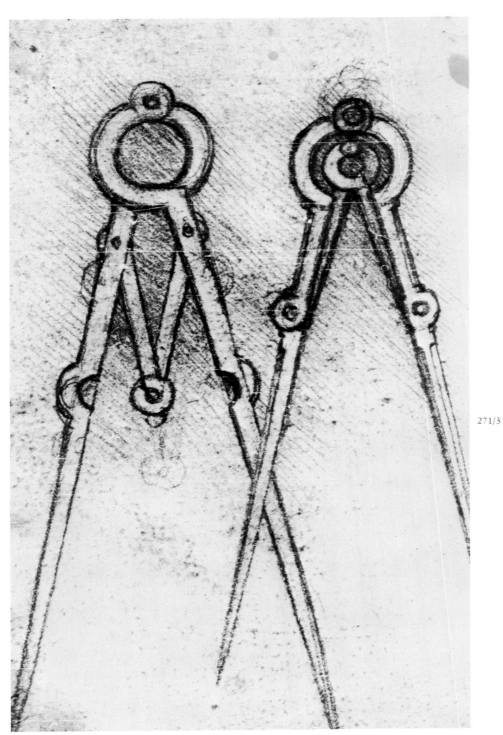

271/3

Leonardo's interest in mathematics led to the use and even invention of a wide variety of compasses. He drew devices for making parabolas and ellipses and a proportional compass that would form a figure similar to another and in given proportion to it. The pair of compasses shown here are from Manuscript H, folio 108 verso. The same compasses also appear in a book by Benvenuto Lorenzo della Golpaja, a collection of drawings based on inventions by his father and several contemporaries including Leonardo. The volume contains many references to Leonardo's technological accomplishments.

Despite the invention of printing with movable type about the time of Leonardo's birth, none of his works was published until 132 years after his death. This irony is compounded by a revelation in the rediscovered Madrid Codices: Leonardo had prescribed a method of printing that could have made his drawings and text widely available. Leonardo was aware that the woodcuts then in use could not adequately reproduce his finely detailed drawings and that the new metal engravings were too costly. His method produced a new kind of relief etching on metal. In Codex Madrid

driven by water-wheels, describes each afresh, from the wheel, or even from the water driving it, to the delivery pipe of the pump. The concept 'waterwheel' certainly seems tolerably familiar to him, such wheels were continually to be met with, only the idea 'pump' – and therefore also the word for it – seems to be absolutely wanting. Thought upon any subject has made considerable progress when general identity is seen through the special variety; – this is the first point of divergence between popular and scientific modes of thinking. Leupold (1724) seems to be the first writer who separates single mechanisms from machines, but he examines these for their own sakes, and only accidentally in reference to their manifold applications. The idea was certainly not yet very much developed. This is explained by the fact that so far machinery has not been formed into a separate subject of study, but was included, generally, under physics in its wider sense. So soon, however, as the first Polytechnic School was founded in Paris in 1794, we see the separation between the study of mechanisms and the study of machinery, for which the way had thus been prepared, systematically carried out."[16]

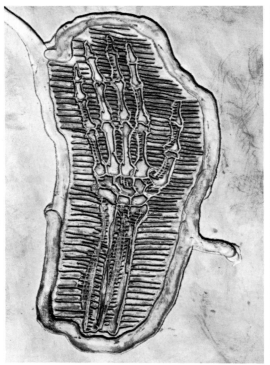

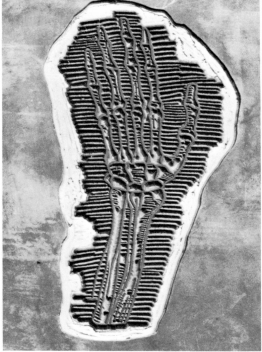

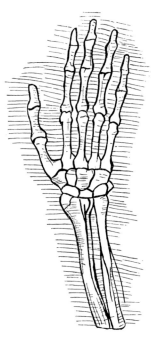

Leonardo's anatomical drawing was made into a relief etching by his own method (far left) and by modern means (center). At left is the hand as reproduced by Leonardo's etching method.

272/1

272/2

272/3

II, folio 119 recto, he set down precise details "Of casting this work in print. Coat the iron plate with white lead and eggs and then write on it lefthanded, scratching the ground. This done, you shall cover everything with a coat of varnish, that is, a varnish containing giallolino or minium. Once dry, leave the plate to soak, and the ground of the letters, written on the white lead and eggs, will be removed together with the minium. As the minium is frangible, it will break away leaving the letters adhering to the copper plate. After this, hollow out the ground in your own way and the letters will stay in relief on a low ground." Following these instructions, a modern Italian artist, Attilio Rossi, succeeded in reproducing a fine line block (above left) after one of Leonardo's drawings of a hand, Windsor Collection No. 19009 verso. Three centuries after Leonardo, the mystic poet and artist William Blake reinvented the same etching process. He too needed a simpler, less expensive method of reproducing his works. Appropriately, the means was revealed to the English mystic in a vision. The Blake method was improved in 1850 by the Frenchman Firmin Gillot, and became the basis for modern relief printing.

It has been pointed out that the notebooks of Leonardo afford ample evidence of the existence of this separation in his mind.[17] But whereas up to the rediscovery of the Leonardo manuscripts in Madrid this evidence was scattered and fragmentary, Codex Madrid I, datable around 1495, proves beyond doubt not only that Leonardo had adopted this outlook, characteristic of modern minds, but also that in this work he attempted to compose a true treatise on the composition and work of machines and mechanisms in general.

This recognition comes as a surprise to the historians of technology, who have traditionally seen in the work of early 19th century scholars of the Ecole Polytechnique the first systematic approach to the study of what were called elements of machines or mechanisms. According to Reuleaux, the constructive elements of machines can be listed as follows:

1. Screws
2. Keys
3. Rivets
4. Bearings and plummer blocks
5. Pins, axles, shafts
6. Couplings
7. Ropes, belts and chains
8. Friction wheels
9. Toothed wheels
10. Flywheels
11. Levers and connecting rods
12. Click wheels and gears
13. Ratchets
14. Brakes
15. Engaging and disengaging gears
16. Pipes
17. Pump cylinders and pistons
18. Valves
19. Springs[18]

The following important elements, which Reuleaux handles in another section, must be added:

      20. Cranks and rods
      21. Cams
      22. Pulleys[19]

Of the elements listed by Reuleaux, only the rivets are apparently missing in Leonardo's manuscripts. This is not because rivets were unknown in Leonardo's

The chart below compares the mechanisms known by Leonardo with the 22 elements of machines listed by the 19th-century German Franz Reuleaux in The Kinematic of Machinery. *In Codex Madrid I, nearly 400 years before, Leonardo described and drew all but two of the elements – pump cylinders and pistons, which are found in Codex Atlanticus, and rivets, which he had purposely excluded.*

273/1

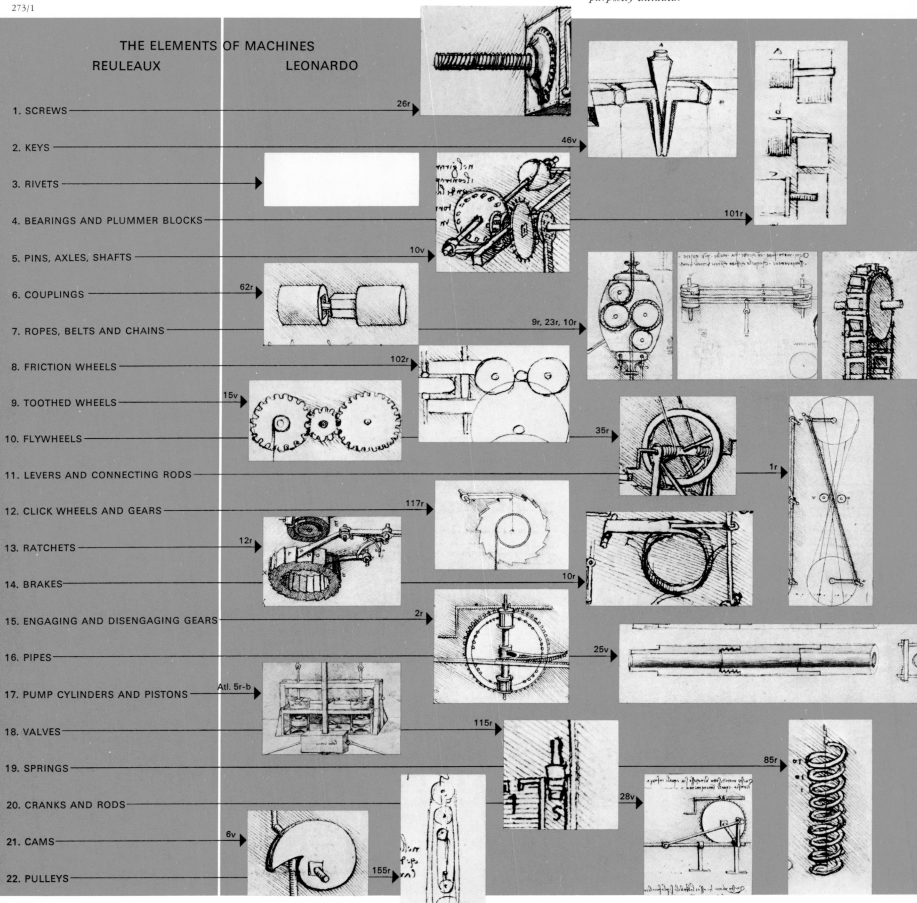

THE ELEMENTS OF MACHINES
REULEAUX   LEONARDO

1. SCREWS
2. KEYS
3. RIVETS
4. BEARINGS AND PLUMMER BLOCKS
5. PINS, AXLES, SHAFTS
6. COUPLINGS
7. ROPES, BELTS AND CHAINS
8. FRICTION WHEELS
9. TOOTHED WHEELS
10. FLYWHEELS
11. LEVERS AND CONNECTING RODS
12. CLICK WHEELS AND GEARS
13. RATCHETS
14. BRAKES
15. ENGAGING AND DISENGAGING GEARS
16. PIPES
17. PUMP CYLINDERS AND PISTONS
18. VALVES
19. SPRINGS
20. CRANKS AND RODS
21. CAMS
22. PULLEYS

time, but because he deliberately desired to present "instruments . . . without their armatures or other structures that might hinder the view of those who will study them."

That Leonardo wanted to compose a book of mechanisms and not just of machines is manifested by the extremely interesting page containing the phrase above – a page that was evidently intended to serve as an introduction:

"We shall discuss here the nature of the screw and of its lever, and how it [the screw] shall be used for lifting rather than for thrusting; and how it has more power when it is simple and not double, and thin rather than thick, when moved by a lever of the same length and force. We shall briefly discuss the many ways there are to use screws, the various types of endless screws, and the many motions that are performed without screws, but which serve the same purpose; how the endless screw shall be combined with toothed wheels, and how to use many screws together. We shall examine the nature of their nuts, and if they are more useful having many threads or less. We shall also speak of inverted screws and screws that by a single motion thrust and pull a weight, and screws which, by turning them only once, will rotate the nuts more than once. And likewise, we shall discuss a great many of their effects and the variety of their labors and strengths, and slowness, and swiftness. Account, too, will be given of their nature and their uses, their composition, levers, and utility. Their method of construction will also be discussed, how to put them to work, and how some people were deceived because they ignored the true nature of the screw."

"All such instruments will generally be presented without their armatures or other structures that might hinder the view of those who will study them. These same armatures shall then be described with the aid of lines, after which we shall discuss the levers by themselves, the strength of supports, and their durability and upkeep. We shall also deal with the differences existing between a lever operating with constant force, that is, the wheel, and the lever of unequal power, that is, the straight beam, and why the former is better than the latter and the latter more compact and convenient than the former. We shall also discuss the ratchet wheel and its pawl, the flywheel and the impetus of the motion, the axles and their wear; ropes and pulleys, capstans and rollers, will also be described. We shall describe how air can be forced under water to lift very heavy weights, that is, how to fill skins with air once they are secured to weights at the bottom of the water. And there will be descriptions of how to lift weights by tying them to submerged ships full of sand and then how to remove the sand from the ships."[20]

The intention to compose a book on the elements of machines is set forth in Codex Madrid I, folio 82 recto. The page, with accompanying transcription at right, makes clear a trait that set Leonardo apart from technologists of his time and long after: an understanding of individual mechanical elements as distinct from whole machines.

The notes of the last sentences must refer to a subject dealt with on one of the missing pages, because there is no trace of it in the book. It is very important and shows once again the plunder to which Leonardo's ideas fell victim. The text hints at a method of salvaging sunken ships or cargoes by pumping air into skins secured to the object to be raised. This invention is credited to Bakker of Amsterdam, about 1688, and the vessels were called camels or caissons. They were used to lift the largest men-of-war over the shoals of the Zuider Zee. An improved version of the same system is still in use today.

Leonardo's summing up presented above is incomplete, but becomes quite comprehensive when integrated with a similar list found in a note in the Codex

Atlanticus.[21] This note is important because the available evidence shows it to be contemporary with Codex Madrid I. More machine elements – 18 – are listed in the Atlanticus note, which it would appear was meant to complement the summary given in the Madrid manuscript.

It is noteworthy that Arturo Uccelli, in his book reconstructing the mechanical work of Leonardo,[22] included as an important part a section called Elementi

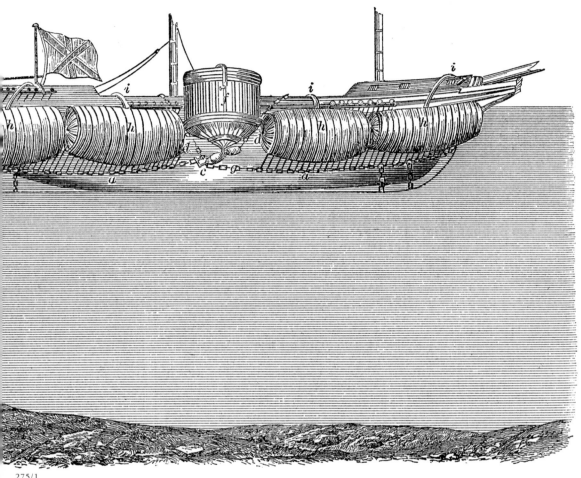

A new method for salvaging sunken ships is hinted at in the last item on Leonardo's list of intentions for a book of mechanisms shown on the opposite page. The Dutch developed an idea apparently very similar to Leonardo's. By pumping air into containers called camels or caissons, which were attached to ships, they raised large men-of-war over the shoals of the Zuider Zee. An inventor known as Bakker of Amsterdam got credit for the device about 1688. In the 19th century a British sea captain named Austin evolved a similar method (left) for raising sunken ships by means of inflated bags. An improved version of the system is still in use today, as are several other of Leonardo's ideas for seagoing devices – including the life preserver and oversized buoyant shoes that enable men to walk on water.

275/1

macchinali ("Elements of machines"), observing at the beginning that very likely a work bearing this title had actually been written by Leonardo. A work on the "elements of machines" is often mentioned by Leonardo in his writings. We know now that it is not Codex Madrid I, but another work, divided into four books, or volumes, in which the theory of mechanical motions was discussed. On one page of Codex Madrid I Leonardo states, "Once the instrument is created, its operational requirements shape the form of its members. They may be of infinite variety but will still be subject to the rules of the four volumes."[23] In the Codex Atlanticus, on a page that is datable 1502 because it deals with the excavation of canals for Cesare Borgia, he mentions "the fifteenth conclusion of the fourth book composed by me on the elements of machines."[24] Apparently the same books are referred to on a great number of pages of Codex Madrid I itself, as proof of mechanical demonstrations, with numbers indicating similar subdivisions – e.g., ". . . and its toothing will be very durable, according to the seventh of the fourth, dealing with power and resistance."[25]

As Codex Madrid I is not so divided, it cannot be identified with the work Elementi macchinali, which unfortunately must be considered lost. What exactly Leonardo meant by this designation is difficult to ascertain; what is sure is that the term does not correspond to its modern meaning. The true book of the elements of machines is the first part of Codex Madrid I, devoted to practical mechanics. Possibly its second part, on theory, without being the original, may resemble in some respects the four lost books of Leonardo.

Be this as it may, it would be materially impossible even to recapitulate here all that Leonardo depicted and discussed in Codex Madrid I relating to the construc-

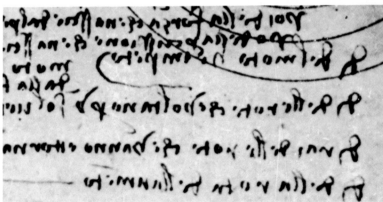

275/2

Another list enumerating Leonardo's plans for a discussion of mechanisms appears in Codex Atlanticus, folio 155 verso-b (above). This was written about the same time as the Madrid I folio on the opposite page, and its list of 18 elements apparently was meant to complement the Madrid summary. Leonardo's writings often refer to a work on the "elements of machines" which was divided into four volumes and discussed the theory of mechanical motions. This work is part of the estimated 75 percent of his writings and drawings that have been lost.

tive elements of machinery. I shall have to limit myself to showing some of the most important cases.

A screw is an inclined plane wrapped around a cylinder. A wedge is also an inclined plane, but whereas an inclined plane per se is stationary, the wedge moves in order to lift, split, or separate some material. In Leonardo's analytic mind these three simple machines are intimately related and mechanically equivalent. Magnificent diagrams illustrate the points he wants to make; only a few can be presented here.

276/1

In his studies of mechanisms Leonardo clearly perceived how different elements were interrelated and mechanically equivalent. Below, in Codex Madrid I, folio 64 verso, he shows that pulling a weight up an inclined plane and pushing an equivalent wedge beneath the same weight require equal amounts of force. Folio 86 verso (below, center) compares the work of an

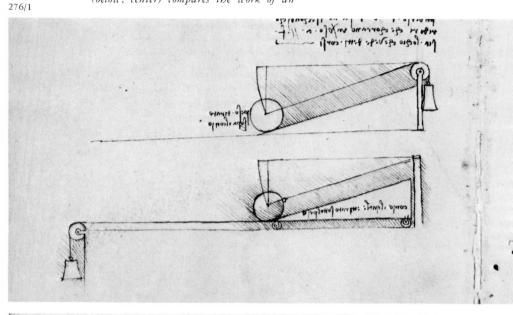

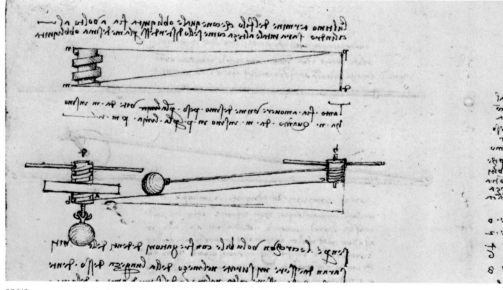

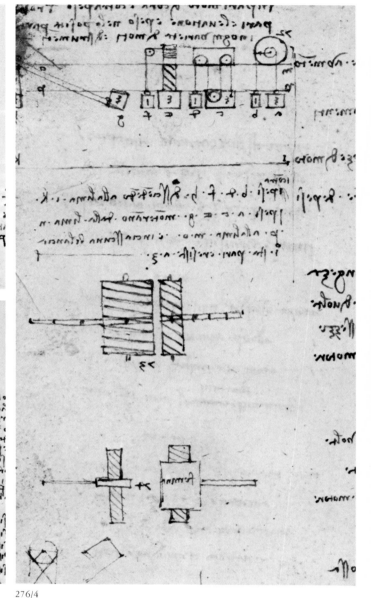

276/2

276/4

inclined plane and a screw (a rolled-up inclined plane). Folio 94 recto (bottom) gives geometric evidence of Leonardo's finding that a screw acts like a lever. Folio 175 verso (right) demonstrates, in the sketch at top, the mechanical equivalence of four mechanisms – inclined plane, screw, block and tackle, and differential hoist.

276/3

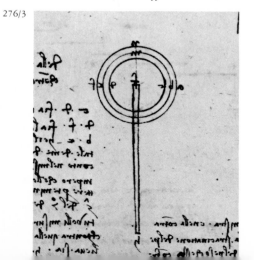

The screw has an important place in Leonardo's mechanical studies, as indicated by the extent to which it is dealt with in his summary quoted above. The geometry of the screw is examined on many pages of Leonardo's works, and in Codex Madrid I as well as in other writings by Leonardo, we find a great variety of screws and their applications.

For special purposes screws can undergo various modifications. The form of the thread varies with the use to which the screw will be put. Leonardo knew V-shaped and square-threaded screws, as well as right- and left-handed screws. A favorite device of his was the combination of right- and left-handed screws on a single spindle in order to obtain special mechanical effects. Screws can also be compounded in order to augment quickly the distance of the elements connected with them. But Leonardo notes that "even if this motion is highly speculative and very fancy, it is nonetheless too intricate and difficult. It is therefore preferable to use screws having multiple threads." Such "fast" thread screws are well known and used today.

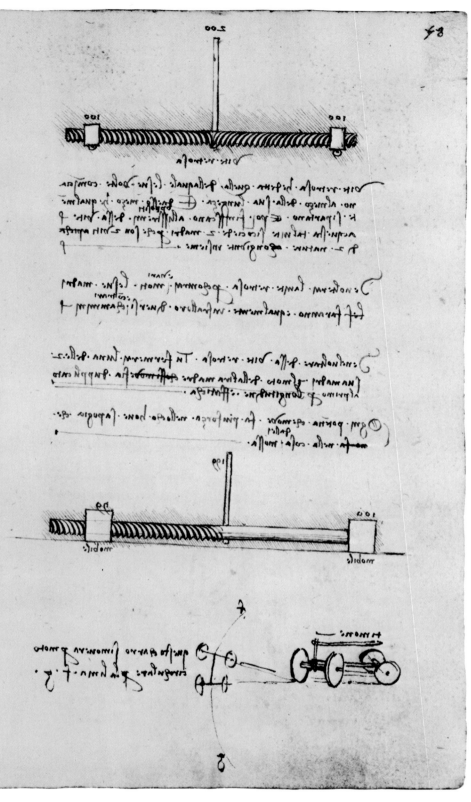

The inverted screw is a screw in which the threads begin in the middle of its length, and departing from the middle, terminate at the opposite ends of the screw. Such a screw must have 2 nuts, since 2 different types of screws are actually being joined together here.

If you turn the inverted screw by both contrary and varied motions, their nuts will also have contrary and varied motions between them.

If in turning the inverted screw, you keep one of its nuts steady, the motion of the other nut will double that of the first one in both length and effort.

Every moving force exerts more strain on the point upon which it rests than on the thing which is moved.

277/1   *Scores of Leonardo's mechanical sketches depict the screw in its many varieties and applications. At left, in Codex Madrid I, folio 58 recto, he demonstrates the mechanical effects that can be obtained by combining right- and left-handed threads on a single shaft. Turning the lever in the top diagram tightens or loosens both nuts at the same time, thus doubling the efficiency of the effort.*

The effect of combining right- and left-handed screws can be compound through the use of multiple threads on a single shaft — as shown at left in Codex Madrid I, folio 57 verso, and below in Codex Atlanticus, folio 379 verso-a. Known as "fast" threads, such screws are used in many modern mechanisms.

277/2

277/3

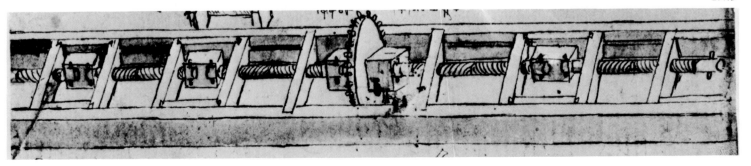

In Leonardo's papers we also find the drawing and the neat description of the first differential screw, that is, a spindle provided with two screw threads of different pitch. Leonardo unfortunately does not tell us about the use of this device. The invention of the differential screw, so important for the construction of scientific instruments, has been attributed to Hunter (1781).

History's first record of a differential screw – a shaft equipped with two screw threads of different pitch – appears in Codex Madrid I, folio 33 verso (right). Next to Leonardo's sketch is a modern diagram of the device, which has been attributed to Hunter in 1781 and which is essential in scientific instruments such as astronomical telescopes.

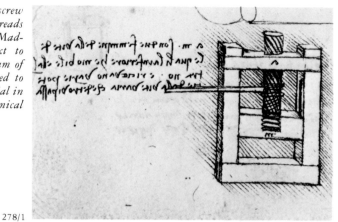

278/1

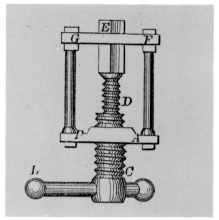

278/2

278/3–7
To test the power of screws, Leonardo developed in Codex Madrid I the five devices shown below, which indicate the use of weights to measure performance. From left: folios 121 recto, 121 verso (two illustrations from this folio), 4 verso, and 81 verso.

The thoroughness of Leonardo's method is revealed by his concern to examine not only the shape but also the work or function of the mechanical elements investigated. He seems to apply here the same kind of reasoning that led him to the study of the human body, both as anatomist and as physiologist. Or was it the other way around?

278/3

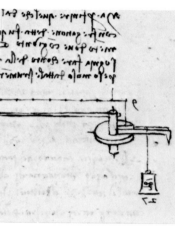

278/4

278/5

278/6

278/7

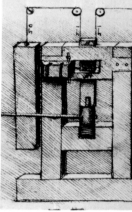

278/8 and 9
He also drew and described precision means for machining screws. The screw-cutting device below is in Codex Madrid I, folio 91 verso. A more elegant model (below, right) in Manuscript B, folio 70 verso, is a forerunner of modern machine-shop practices.

Screws must be tested before using them in order to establish the correctness of their shape and the limits of their performance and resistance. In Codex Madrid I we find explanations of the theory of screw action, and screw-testing machines are presented. But it is useless to discuss screws unless precise tools and processes for their making have been developed. A handy screw-cutting instrument is described

278/8

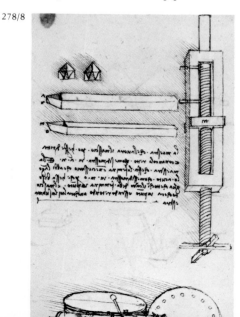

278/9

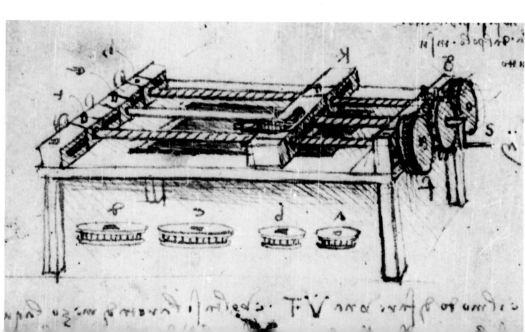

in our codex, but more striking is the well-known one presented in Manuscript B. This screw cutter is a true forerunner of modern machine-shop practices, with its interchangeable operating wheels and double screw rods, which ensure stability and precision.

Up to this point screws have been discussed as independent entities. In combination with other machine elements, screws can be used for the most diverse functions. Leonardo projected hundreds of instruments in which the screw is the principal element. As a general rule he advises, "Dealing with heavy weights, do not commit yourself to iron teeth, because one of the teeth may easily break off;

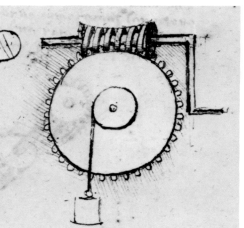

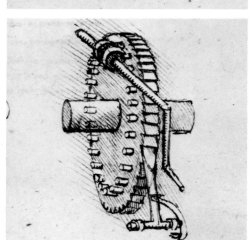

Leonardo's worm gear (left), in Codex Madrid I, folio 17 verso, is the same as the Hindley worm gear (below), named for the 18th-century English clockmaker Henry Hindley, who got the credit for inventing it.

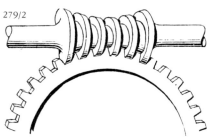

On the same folio, 17 verso, Leonardo drew the traditional type of worm gear and noted its drawback:"When you make a screw that engages only a single tooth on the wheel, it will be necessary to add a pawl in order to avoid the reversal of the wheel's motion should that tooth break." Such a screw, he says, "could cause great damage and destruction."

Leonardo worked with a simple efficient mechanism familiar to machine builders today as a worm gear (photo below). It meshes a gear or toothed wheel with a worm screw, which because of its infinitely spiraling thread Leonardo called an "endless screw." Engineers apply the worm gear with its low turning speed and relatively high amplification of power to rack-railways.

you will use therefore the screw, where one tooth is bound to the other." But a screw "shall be employed pulling, not thrusting, because thrusting bends the shaft of the screw, while pulling straightens the bent one."[26]

Worm gears, that is, the combination of screw and toothed wheel, . . . are among the favorite mechanisms of the machine constructor for two main reasons: their motion is irreversible and they ensure a high mechanical advantage. On one page of Codex Madrid I Leonardo considers two kinds of worm gear. One follows the traditional design. However, Leonardo observes, "When you make a screw that engages only a single tooth on the wheel, it will be necessary to add a pawl in order to avoid the reversal of the wheel's motion should that tooth break." The other design is Leonardo's own idea of how a worm gear should be constructed. He explains, "This lifting device has an endless screw which engages many teeth on the wheel. For this reason the device is very reliable. Endless screws that engage only one of the teeth on the working wheel could cause great damage and destruction if the tooth breaks." This device depicted by Leonardo is well known to modern machine constructors. It is called a Hindley worm gear, named after the English clockmaker Henry Hindley, who was very proud of having invented it. He died in 1770.

In another original combination of screws and gears depicted in Codex Madrid I, two long screws are turned at the same speed by a single shaft provided with two identical worms. The shaft is turned by another worm connected to a hand crank. The device is a double screw-jack, of slow motion but enormous power.

Interesting examples of keys, in the sense of joining devices, are also provided in Codex Madrid I. The keying together of wooden pipes is demonstrated, and joints for the legs of pieces of furniture and the pivots of compasses are illustrated.

Through variations on the worm-gear idea, Leonardo could design machines to multiply manyfold the lifting power of men. This double screw-jack is powered by the crank at left. One worm gear turns the horizontal

280/1

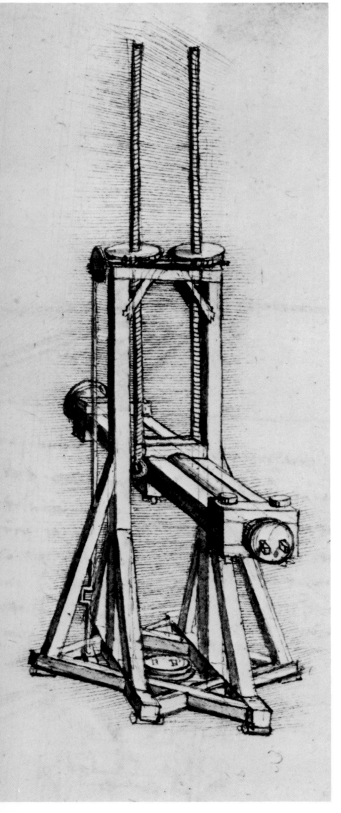

shaft, which is equipped with two identical worm gears. These turn the two long vertical screws at the same speed. Slow but powerful, the device probably was intended for lifting into place such tall heavy objects as stone columns or even cannon barrels.

MADRID I 34r

Lessons in joinery are provided by Leonardo in Codex Madrid I. Folio 25 verso (right) illustrates a method of making water pipes from logs with the boring device at far right. If the logs are not long enough, he suggests constructing the pipes in foot-long sections. The sections are then keyed together by metal couplings buried in each joint.

280/2

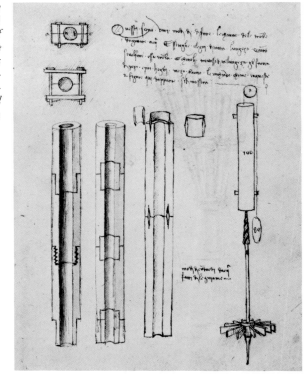

280/3

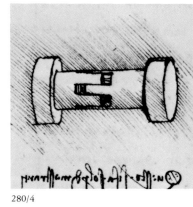

280/3-6

Leonardo also offered tips, in Codex Madrid I, folio 62 recto, for joining the pivots of compasses and the legs on furniture – at left and below. "This is a method for inserting one piece of wood into another," he writes, "and you shall never be able to pull it from its cavity." He adds a practical note: "It could be used for the legs of a bench."

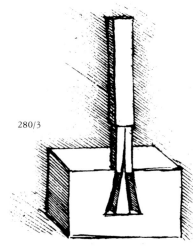

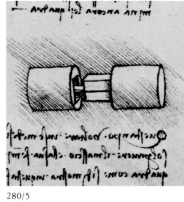

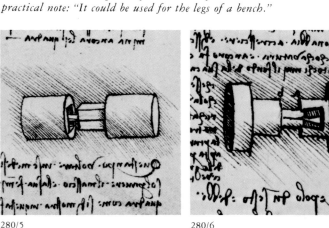

280/4

280/5

280/6

In Leonardo's time and later, the bearings in which shafts and pivots rotated were generally little more than holes in the wooden or metallic frame of the machine. Efforts at lubrication were made by trying to pour oil or spread tallow between the moving surfaces in contact. Searching through the Spanish archives in the ancient town of Simancas for records of the forgotten waterworks constructed by Juanelo

Turriano in Toledo, which were in use from about 1569 to 1620, I found only two items of heavy expense for maintenance: tallow for lubrication and charcoal for the forges that had to be operated constantly to repair the machine elements that broke down or wore out.

Leonardo investigated and described the wear on axles and bearings, searching for its cause and suggesting means for its relief. In Codex Madrid I he shows that the amount of wear in a bearing supporting a horizontal axle is related to the load and that the direction of the wear is not necessarily vertically downwards, but follows the main vector or direction of the load.

On another page of the codex the wear of axles and bearings is reexamined in relation to the length and thickness of the shafts. The central sketch represents two horizontal spindles, one of them provided with a modern-looking self-oiling device. But Leonardo observes that such a system would not work well because filings from the wear, dust, and oil would soon clog the outlets.

An interesting demonstration is given in the lower drawing: the result of reciprocal wear of shaft and bearing in a horizontal axle. The shaft is slowly consumed by the bearing but so is the bearing itself, leading to the tapering groove depicted. The problem of the shape of axles resulting from wear is discussed on many pages. Realizing that lubrication alone could not prevent the rapid wear of an axle and its bearing, Leonardo began to explore new ways, such as the use of materials that would minimize friction and the development of designs that would compensate the inevitable wear. In the same Madrid Codex we find a surprisingly modern concept along these lines. Leonardo devised a bearing in the form of a two-piece block that would prevent an axle from jumping out of the bearing "in spite of any strain." As he described this system, the cheeks of the block, in which the axle rotated, would be made of a smooth "mirror metal" consisting of "three parts of copper and seven of tin melted together." This "mother," as Leonardo called it, would be closed at the top with a wedge for tightening or with a cover that could be adjusted by a screw. Thus the cheeks, or bushings, could be tightened around the axle as wear progressed. We have here, in Leonardo's detailed description, the first suggestion of a bearing block, with split, adjustable bushing of antifriction metal, almost two centuries before Robert Hooke proposed the use of such metal to the Royal Society of London and more than two centuries before the split-bushing idea was embodied in hardware.[27]

Leonardo went on to study the possibilities of minimizing friction by means of rolling elements, as his experiments had shown that rolling friction was always preferable to sliding friction. The use of rollers and balls to facilitate movement in machines is by no means original to Leonardo. Such devices had been employed in machines as early as the ancient Greek period. As next earliest, credit must go to the bearings of the rotating platforms of the Roman ship built between A.D. 44 and 54 that was recovered from Lake Nemi, near Rome.[28] Those were not true ball bearings, however, because the balls did not rotate freely in their holds: each ball was prolonged at two poles into short shafts or trunnions, kept in place by clamps.

Disc bearings – that is, axles rotating between two crossed or almost touching discs – must have been known before Leonardo. He depicts such devices in his early Manuscript B (of about 1489)[29] and in other manuscripts. They also appear in Georgius Agricola's De re metallica,[30] showing that they were well known in the praxis of the first half of the 16th century. However, in an interesting note on folio 12 verso of Codex Madrid I, beneath the drawing of a disc bearing, Leonardo notes, "Giulio says that he has seen two such wheels in Germany and that they became worn down at axle *m*" (the spindle). Giulio was a German mechanic who entered the service of Leonardo in 1493.[31] The note is important not only for dating the Madrid manuscript; it also proves that the inadequacy of disc bearings was a problem common to builders of machines.

Folio 12 verso of the Madrid Codex is a remarkable document. It shows how Leonardo's mind works, starting from what is known and experimenting with solutions that seem to him to be improvements on existing practices.

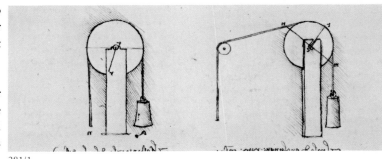

281/1

Leonardo's investigations of friction and the use of bearings to ease it are of special interest to modern engineers. Above, in Codex Madrid I, folio 132 verso, he studies the direction of the wear on axles and bearings and concludes that it follows the direction of the load.

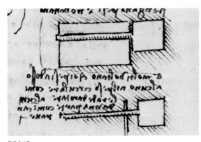
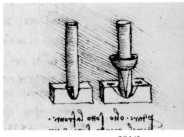

281/2   281/3

Folio 118 recto (above) examines wear in relation to the length and thickness of axles. The sketch at right equips one of the shafts with a modern-looking self-oiling device, but Leonardo rejects this because it would soon become clogged with grit.

281/4   281/5   281/6

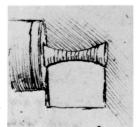

Folio 119 recto (above) presents the problem of shapes of axles resulting from wear. At left are shown an axle and bearing shaped to prevent lateral motion as the axle wears. At right are cone-shaped axles and a bearing for taking up the wear.

On folio 100 verso (below) Leonardo arrived

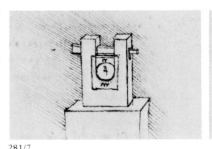
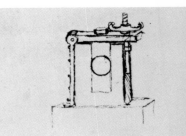

281/7   281/8

at a modern concept for minimizing friction. He suggests a two-piece bearing block with bushings made of an alloy of copper and tin – a smooth "mirror metal." As the axle wears down, the bushing can be tightened on the axle – at left by means of a wedge, at right by a thumbscrew.

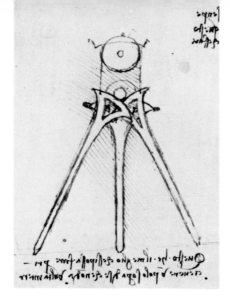

Roller bearings, wrote Leonardo, are "marvels of mechanical genius." With them he engineered the system shown on these two pages for supporting a bell with relatively little friction. Below, in Codex Madrid I, folio 12 verso, he sketched ordinary disc bearings – an axle rotating between two

discs. But he knew the discs wore down the axle and already had rejected them in Manuscript B, folio 33 verso (bottom), striking a line through the sketch and writ-

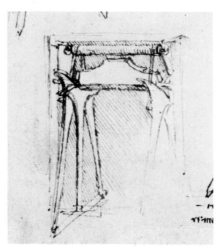

ing falsa. On the same Madrid folio, 12 verso, he places the shaft holding the bell upon a single roller bearing – actually a cam-like sector – and adds two additional rollers to stop lateral thrusts (above and top). His final solution (right), in Codex Atlanticus, folio 392 recto-b, puts the side rollers at right angles to the vertical roller.

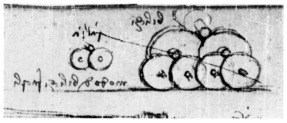

The problem to be discussed is the best possible arrangement for a horizontal bearing. In the first sketch at upper right Leonardo returns to the compound disc bearings that he has already rejected – in Manuscript B the same drawing is invalidated by a pen stroke and the word *falsa* added. At the upper center of the Madrid page the wear of a horizontal bearing is sketched again. Under the sketch are three studies on the disc bearing with the information given by Giulio. Then a new idea strikes Leonardo: instead of placing an axle *between* two rollers that inevitably exert a shearing action on the shaft, which in turn permanently forces them apart, why not try to place the axle *upon* a roller?

The answer is given in the scheme sketched to the right of the disc-bearing series.

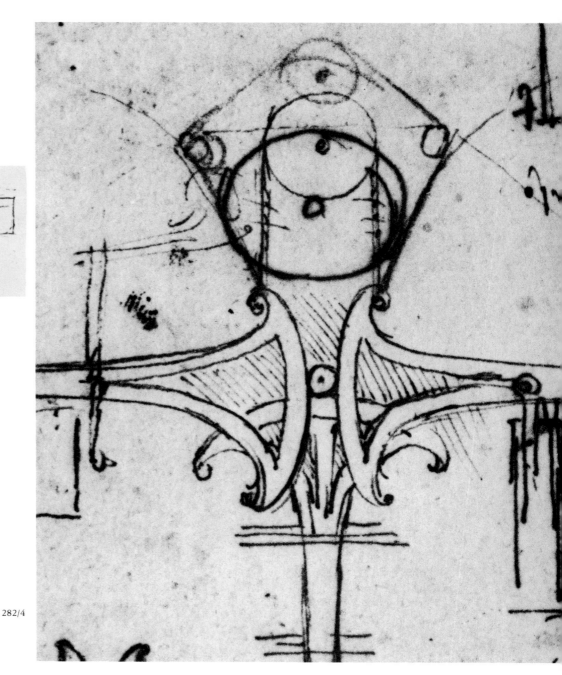

An unexpected difficulty immediately arises: as the axle turns, a lateral pressure is exerted, which cannot be taken up by a roller placed under the axle. So two additional rollers are added to the system in order to compensate lateral thrusts. The three-roller system is drawn beneath the sketch of the axle on one roller. Under the drawing, Leonardo proudly adds, "This is the best possible solution if the axle makes complete revolutions."

This is a good solution for a continuously revolving shaft. But what if the axle makes only partial to and fro revolutions, as in the case of a bell shaft? Evidently sectors could substitute for a complete roller. Leonardo first tries two inclined

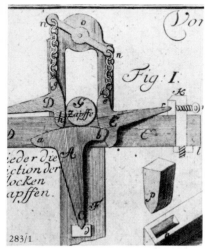

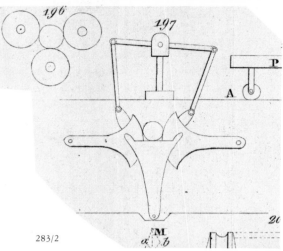

More than 200 years after Leonardo made the sketches for the bell support shown on the opposite page, an identical system appeared in Jacob Leupold's Theatrum Machinarum Generale (far left). Then, another century later, J. V. Poncelet in his Traité de Mécanique Industrielle described the method used in supporting the Mutte bell in the Cathedral of Metz (left) – an exact copy of Leonardo's solution. A working model (photo below) based on Leonardo's drawings was commissioned by the author of this chapter and carried out by Sinibaldo Parrini of Florence.

sectors, but finds that the shearing action has returned. The final solution appears in the two diagrams at the bottom of the page; the shaft is supported by a single sector, and the lateral thrust is taken up by two additional inclined sectors. Under this drawing, Leonardo declares, "This is the best solution to support an axle that does not make complete revolutions."

The presence of bell yokes in the drawings points to the main application Leonardo had in mind. The solution found needs, however, to be improved: the lateral segments can be made more efficient by placing them horizontally. This Leonardo does in other sketches that appear in the Codex Atlanticus – on folios 351 recto-a and 392 recto-b. All this would seem to be interesting play with kinematic problems, were it not that the same device appears more than 200 years later in Leupold's renowned *Theatrum Machinarum*,[32] where a bell support identical to Leonardo's is called "the oldest and most common system." Apparently, the first solution in Codex Madrid I was sketched around 1495; other solutions were elaborated by Leonardo later, becoming identical to the model described by Leupold.[33]

Was this system invented by Leonardo? Apparently it was. It was unknown to him a few years before Codex Madrid I, when dealing with the same problem in Manuscript B. It was unknown to Francesco di Giorgio Martini, who was well acquainted with bells and their making. In a treatise which precedes these writings of Leonardo, Francesco discusses several solutions, none of them good because the center of gravity of the bell is irrationally placed. He seems to know about axles resting *between* rollers, but not *on* rollers. But our surprise increases when looking at the solutions proposed by Biringuccio in 1540 in his treatise dealing with metallurgy called *Pirotechnia*.[34] He was an expert founder of bells, and he dedicated four chapters of his book to the subject; but when the problem of their hanging arises, he finds no better solution than to copy Francesco di Giorgio. The figures are redrawn, but the source is evident.

So when do these solutions of Leonardo enter in the stream of technological developments, solutions that according to Leupold were "most common" in the first half of the 18th century?

Leupold does not tell us about the origin of this interesting device. But about 120 years after him, when better ways of avoiding friction were beginning timidly to be suggested, the great French engineer J. V. Poncelet, in his *Traité de mécanique industrielle* published at Liège in 1845, tells us how the problem was resolved in the case of the famous *Mutte* bell of the Cathedral of Metz, which has an exact copy of Leonardo's bell supports. A sector sustains the axle, which, instead of sliding, rolls on it, while two lateral sectors take up side displacements. To sustain turning axles, Poncelet proposed to have them surrounded by three complete rollers – another correspondence to Leonardo's proposal.[35]

The original *Mutte* bell is supposed to have been installed in the Cathedral of Metz in 1381. But this bell was not successful. In the same year work was begun again; the new bell lasted for a very short time. In 1427 a fresh attempt was made, but with no success, for on March 21, 1442, the bell cracked and it was decided to recast it. The work of taking it down caused two deaths and a number of injuries. In 1443 a new bell was completed, but it did not last long; in 1459 it was out of use. A new bell was cast in 1479, this time by expert founders, and installed in 1482. It lasted almost a century – until 1569. The *Mutte* was recast for the last time in 1605.[36] The fact that it has lasted since then indicates that better techniques had by then been developed.

But how can the same problem be resolved when the rolling axle moves vertically instead of horizontally? Jacks operated by the turning of a screw for lifting heavy loads were in wide use in Leonardo's day; their usefulness was limited, however, because under strong pressure severe friction developed between the turning nut and the plate on which it weighed.

So Leonardo decided to introduce what we today call a thrust bearing. In Codex

Although Leonardo's bell-support system using roller bearings was put to practical application in the Mutte *bell at the Cathedral of Metz (below), precisely how the idea found its way to the cathedral is a mystery, as with so many applications of Leonardo's work. The cathedral's original bell is believed to have been installed in 1381. It was not a success, and over the next two centuries several new bells were cast.*

The bell was recast for the final time in 1605. Leonardo's preliminary solution to the bell-support problem was drawn in Codex Madrid I about 1495. Then no trace of the idea appeared in the literature – not even in a 1540 treatise by Biringuccio, who devoted four chapters to bells – until 1724, when it suddenly showed up in Jacob Leupold's book, which calls it "the oldest and most common system" but says nothing of Leonardo's role. In 1845 J. V. Poncelet's treatise made clear the same method was used at Metz – again without reference to its apparent inventor, Leonardo.

Madrid I the use of ball and roller bearings is presented, and there is a sketch which can be compared with a modern ball thrust bearing. Leonardo's extremely interesting text shows his awareness of the problems of friction in roller bearings.

The idea is further developed on other pages of Codex Madrid I. On one page we can admire a surprising array of roller and ball bearings sustaining the thrust of a vertical axle. Commenting on the ball bearing Leonardo declares that "three balls under the spindle are better than four, because three balls are of necessity certainly always touched, while by the use of four there would be the danger that one of them is left untouched."

Leonardo is in favor of design *a*, incorporating three conical rollers supporting a pivot provided with a conical head of the same size and shape as the rollers. He says, "This way we shall have three equal cones that are identical to the cone of the spindle, and by each turn of the spindle, the supporting cones will have each made a complete revolution."

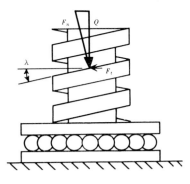

285/2

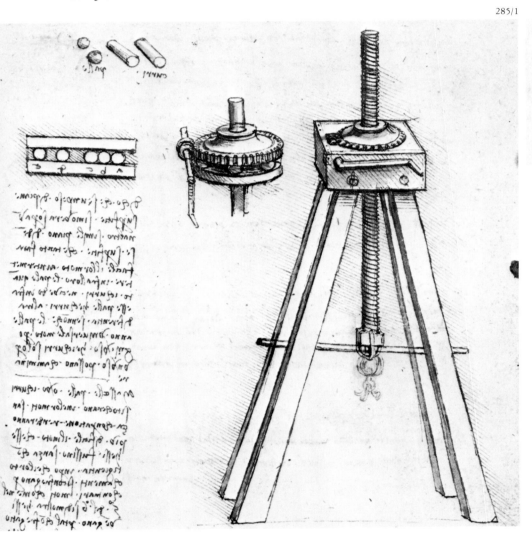

285/1

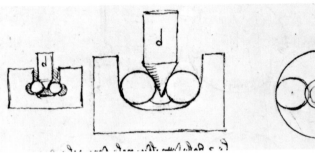

285/3

An array of bearing shapes intended to support a vertical axle is presented on folio 101 verso (above and below). In the sketch above a conical-shaped pivot rests in a nest of three ball bearings – a concept that had to be reinvented during the 1920s for blind-flying instrumentation on airplanes.

285/4

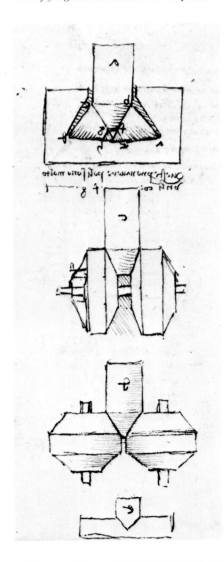

I am indebted to Preston Bassett, former president of the Sperry Gyroscope Company, and to Bern Dibner, founder of the Burndy Library of Norwalk, Connecticut, for permission to quote from a letter that Dr. Bassett wrote to Dr. Dibner on March 8, 1967, after seeing this Leonardo drawing reproduced in *Life*. "I must tell you my greatest shock in looking over the Da Vinci sketches was the balls nested around a conical pivot. When we were developing our blind-flying gyro instruments in the 1920's we had the problem of designing a ball-bearing that would have absolutely no end play. We thought we had an innovation with our conical pivot ball bearing, but it is a dead-ringer of Da Vinci's sketch!"

Leonardo very soon recognized that a bearing would work satisfactorily only if the balls or rollers did not touch each other during operation. In Codex Madrid I a ring-shaped race for a ball bearing is devised, to eliminate the friction that would result if the individual balls in a bearing came in contact with one another. The

Leonardo drawing has become quite well known to today's public thanks to its use for publicity by a large American pen company.

Since Leonardo's principal language was graphic representation, his experimental investigations of friction can be best understood by examining his drawings. One shows a bank device for the measurement of sliding friction (identical with a friction bank that Charles Augustin de Coulomb devised 300 years later) and also illustrates an apparatus for measuring rolling friction. Other drawings picture

286/1

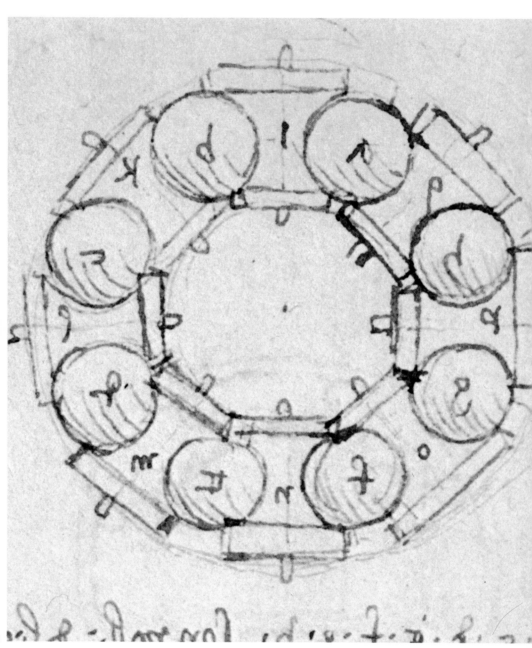

286/2

experiments in which Leonardo measured frictional resistance on an inclined plane, looked into the question of whether or not frictional resistance depended on the area of contact between surfaces, and examined how the ease of rolling motion of a shaft might be affected by the shaft's diameter.

From his measurements Leonardo derived several general principles, namely that frictional resistance differs according to the nature of the surfaces in contact, that it depends on the degree of smoothness of those surfaces, that it is independent of the area of the surfaces in contact, that it increases in direct proportion to the load, and that it can be reduced by interposing rollers or a lubricating fluid between the sliding surfaces. These laws sound obvious today, but one should bear in mind that Leonardo demonstrated them quantitatively two centuries before scientists initiated the modern study of friction and three centuries before the study of this subject was elaborated by Coulomb.

For better or for worse, our times are dominated by technology. So were all times past, even if this appears less evident to us today. And there is no reason to suppose that the future will be different unless we are willing to reduce drastically our numbers and accept a civilization based on serfdom, or reduce humanity to a condition of general misery. Technology, however, should be the servant, not the master of man; its faults can be remedied, its values enhanced. One thinks, in this context, of a world where all the money and effort used up by armaments are dedicated to solving the ecological problems forced upon us by political and economic mismanagement.

This ambivalence in the impact of technology on human affairs was keenly understood by Leonardo, in an epoch when the ecological problems that afflict us today were just beginning to take shape.

Nothing characterizes better Leonardo's inner feelings before these problems than some of his "prophecies," a literary genre that seems original to him. The "prophecies" are in fact riddles that were recited at court gatherings or in gay companies, and were to be solved by the participants. In them, under the subtle veil of play, Leonardo succeeded not only in pointing out the vices and abuses of his time ... without incurring disgrace, but also in expressing his despair about the wickedness of humanity in general.

An appropriate example is this "prophecy" found in the Codex Atlanticus: "There shall come forth out of dark and gloomy caves that which shall put the whole human race into great afflictions, dangers, and deaths. To many of its followers, after great troubles, it will offer delight; but whoever is not its supporter shall perish in want and misery. This shall commit an infinity of treacheries, prompting wretched men to assassinations, larcenies, and enslavement; this shall hold its own followers in suspicion, this shall deprive free cities of their liberty, this shall take away the lives of many people, this shall make men afflict upon each other many kinds of frauds, deceits, and treacheries. O monstrous animal, how much better were it for men that thou shouldst go back to hell! Because of this the great forests will be deprived of their trees and an infinity of animals will lose their lives."

The solution of the riddle is given in the title: "Of metals." [37]

Nearby there is another even more ominous "prophecy" entitled "Cruelty of man." It is a remarkable document in which Leonardo makes mankind responsible for the evils of society and for the destruction of nature's gifts and beauty: "Creatures shall be seen upon the earth who will always be fighting one with another, with very great losses and frequent deaths on either side. These shall set no bounds to their malice; by their fierce limbs a great number of the trees in the immense forests of the world shall be laid level with the ground; and when they have crammed themselves with food it shall gratify their desire to deal out death, affliction, labors, terrors, and banishment to every living thing. And by reason of their boundless pride they shall wish to rise towards heaven, but the excessive weight of their limbs shall hold them down. There shall be nothing remaining on the earth or under the earth or in the waters that shall not be pursued, carried away, or destroyed, and that which is in one country shall be taken away to another; and their own bodies shall be made the tomb and the means of transit of all the living bodies which they have slain. O Earth! what delays thee to open and hurl them headlong into the deep fissures of thy huge abysses and caverns, and no longer to display in the sight of heaven so savage and ruthless a monster?"

All the animals languish, filling the air with lamentations.
The woods fall in ruin. The mountains are torn open, in
order to carry away the metals which are produced
there. But how can I speak of anything more
wicked than (the actions) of those
who raise hymns of praise to
heaven for those who
with greater zeal have injured their country and the human race?

ATLANTICUS 382v-a

287/1

THE BICYCLE

AUGUSTO MARINONI

It is well known that in the 16th century Pompeo Leoni, in order to prevent the dispersion of many loose folios of Leonardo's, glued them onto the large pages of an album which subsequently became known as the Codex Atlanticus. When writing appeared on both sides of a page, Leoni made a window opening in the supporting sheet and glued onto its margins those of Leonardo's sheet. However, when the reverse side did not bear Leonardo's writing, Leoni did not make the opening, and that side remained hidden until a few years ago, when restoration of the codex brought to light every sheet contained within it. Of the present pages 132 and 133, only the rectos, previously numbered 48 recto-a and 48 recto-b, were known to scholars. Today we have access to the respective versos, which offer us the most extraordinary revelation of the codex.

Let us examine folio 133 verso. We immediately note at the upper right what can only be defined as a bicycle, drawn by a youthful hand. The two wheels were drawn with a compass which opened slightly while completing its rotation. The rims of the wheels with eight spokes are colored brown to imitate wood. The chassis is entirely horizontal, with two gears to hold the wheels, but only one is well defined. Against the back hub are propped the braces supporting the large saddle, which has a third point of support at the center of the chassis. The rather strange handlebar is in the form of a T, from which a bolt projects, and is connected to the front hub by two arched and probably flexible rods. To prevent these parts from

288/1

288/1–4 and 289/2 and 3
The recent restoration of Leonardo's Codex Atlanticus revealed for the first time the reverse side of numerous pages which have been pasted to mountings for the past 400 years. Folios 48 recto-a and 48 recto-b are shown above as originally mounted and the previously hidden reverse sides are shown in the first illustration at right. Obviously the two sheets were originally one and were apparently cut apart and rotated 90 degrees before Leonardo used them for his drawings of the fortress discussed previously in detail on pages 162 and 163. On the reverse side are various drawings: a caricature of a boy in Renaissance costume, several pornographic sketches, and an amazing depiction of a bicycle. These drawings are apparently by and about students in Leonardo's studio. One student, Salai, is referred to by name with the inscription "salaj," as shown below.

288/2

288/3

288/4

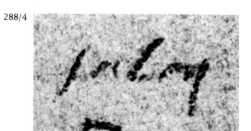

rubbing it, the wheel is provided with a guard. To the center of the chassis is fixed a gear wheel with large wooden teeth, of cubic rather than pointed shape, in order to withstand traction. It is not clear how the front wheel can be steered. We do not know if the youth copying from another drawing is responsible for some omission or if the problem had not been solved even in the original drawing. But we must surely attribute to the inexperience of the draftsman the disproportionate length of the pedals and the transparency of the wooden-toothed wheel, which looks like a rim without supporting spokes.

While they recognize the unmistakable nature of this machine, the few scholars who have examined the drawing are decidedly reluctant to admit its antiquity. Since the application of the chain-drive to the bicycle goes back only to the end of the 19th century, they propose a dating of the drawing within the early years of the present century. Such a hypothesis, however, collides with insurmountable difficulties: (1) The page in question remained hidden for almost four centuries, and it is unimaginable that 70 or 80 years ago a boy would have obtained from the directorship of the Biblioteca Ambrosiana the permission to view the codex, detach one or two pages, and then draw upon them and glue them back again. (2) Even in that case, he would have drawn a bicycle of a type then existent, not one of wood with wheelbarrow wheels, no means of steering, and the teeth of the central gear so squared off that they could not be fitted to the chain. (3) The odd toothed wheels and the chain coincide exactly with those drawn by Leonardo in Codex Madrid I, folio 10 recto. (4) We cannot separate the bicycle from the other drawings visible on folios 132 verso and 133 verso of the Codex Atlanticus. Actually they were drawn when the pages were united as the two halves of one page. Reuniting them, we see that another hand has drawn, also in pencil and from left to right, two pornographic drawings obviously meant as a joke, over which, on the right-hand side, is written clearly *salaj*, that is, Salai, the name of Leonardo's pupil, model, and servant. Further up, to the left of the bicycle, we see the caricatured bust of a Renaissance boy with thin, long hair, his suit tied with elegant fastening cords, his face terribly deformed. The receding chin, missing cheeks, and pointed eyes under hawk-like brows accord with the hooked nose transformed into a beak. It is more than believable that the caricature represents the same Salai already mocked in the obscene drawings. Besides, other more or less obscene drawings appear on the verso of folios 73 and 154b, as well as 24 recto-b and 55 verso-b.

These drawings bring us within the intimacy of Leonardo's studio, where paper for writing and drawing was always readily available and where many young pupils lived and worked: Salai, the somewhat older Marco d'Oggiono, Gian Antonio Boltraffio, and others. One of them (Salai?) copied on one sheet of this paper his master's drawing – we say he copied it, because we cannot attribute to a mere boy the formidable foresight that anticipated today's bicycle by three or four centuries.

289/1
The incredible drawing above recently found on the reverse side of folio 48 recto-b (now numbered 133 verso) in Codex Atlanticus was obviously drawn by a youthful hand. However, the extraordinary vision displayed by the creation of a vehicle that must be balanced on two wheels while in motion, and the advanced mechanical concepts primitively rendered force us to the conclusion that this is actually a copy of someone else's work, presumably Leonardo's.

289/2

289/3

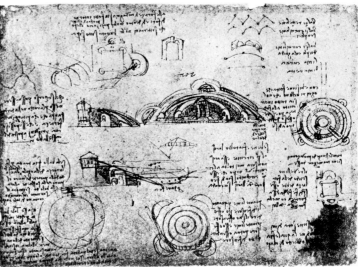

The dream of Icarus, which long preoccupied Leonardo, is less original than the subtle and brilliant idea of traveling while balanced on only two wheels. And then a fellow student and worker, perhaps a bit older and cleverer, drew his ribald satire on the same sheet. The beautiful face of Salai, which to the master would suggest faces of men and women full of sweetness, is fiercely distorted and likened to some kind of bird. The joke probably vented resentment against the possessor of the privileged beauty, destroying the very part of him that was most splendid, the face. But it also could represent the vendetta of Marco or Gian Antonio against the little "stubborn one, thief, liar, glutton," who robbed indifferently strangers, companions, and the very master, who was like a father to him. Further down on the page, the satire continues with the obscenity of the larger, more complicated drawing. The more heavily covered parts of the obscene drawings have left their imprint upon the opposite half of the original sheet, and measuring the respective distances of drawing and imprint from the margins of the two current folios, we note that folio 132 has lost 5 to 7 millimeters. We do not know for how many days, months, or years afterwards Leonardo, then occupied with military problems, used the divided sheet for notes and drawings of powerful fortifications. We do not even know whether the sheet was cut by himself or by someone else. The Codex Atlanticus contains many other examples of large sheets folded and worn out along the fold to a degree that might have suggested cutting them. However, it is certain that Leonardo wrote upon the already cut sheet without giving importance to what the pupils had drawn there. It was his custom to utilize for economy's sake the reverse or the blank spaces of sheets already used by others. He rotated the two half sheets by 90 degrees, and where the vertical fold had been there appeared the upper horizontal margin of the two new pages, as indicated by the succession of lines of writing. If the sheet had still been uncut, Leonardo, as in many other instances, would have begun to write from what is now the right-hand margin and continued in lines parallel to it.

Not even Pompeo Leoni paid attention either to the obscene drawings or to that of the bicycle, which represented not a physically existing object, but an idea still gestating. To become a reality, the idea required the final solution of some challenging problems, such as the matter of steering and the adaptation of the large squared-off teeth with their jutting corners to the links of the chain, not to mention weight and friction – but the idea in itself and the solutions were of so impressive a genius that the sculptor Pompeo Leoni could not grasp it. To him does go the credit for having saved this sheet from destruction by gluing it in his great album, removing it for nearly four centuries from the eyes of others but guaranteeing thereby the antiquity and authenticity of a stunning discovery.

290/1

ca. 1493   290/1–9
The bicycle depicted in Codex Atlanticus is apparently made of wood, with equal-sized wheels and with a rear-wheel chain drive. In the series of drawings below showing the development of the modern bicycle from its beginning around 1817, the same elements are found again, but never in the same

290/2–5

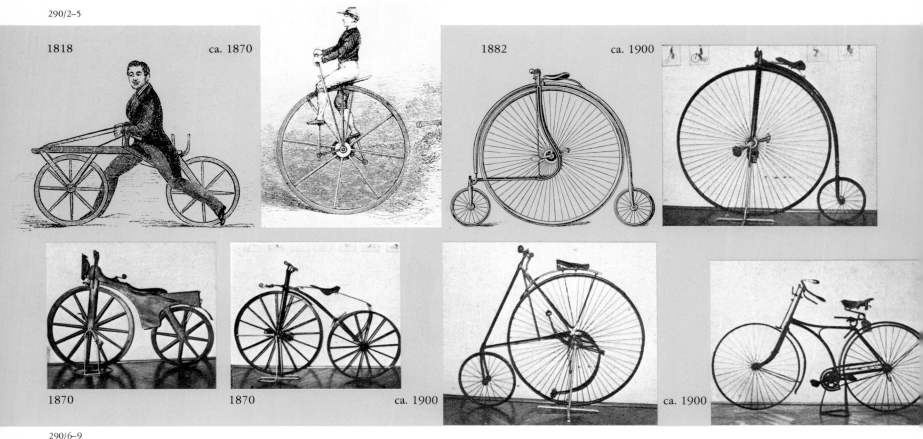

290/6–9

vehicle. The earliest versions were made of wood, but they lacked the chain-drive mechanism. By the time they had a rear-wheel chain drive, they were made of metal.

It remains, if possible, to fix the date of the drawing. The hypothesis that the caricature as well as the other drawings concern Salai encounters a not insurmountable obstacle: Salai entered Leonardo's house in 1490, aged 10 and was a beautiful boy with "curly hair in ringlets," a feature that does not appear in this intentionally distorted portrait. But even the elimination of the charming curls could be intentional. A straight line above the head suggests the idea of an unfinished hat. It would be useless to claim for a deforming and carelessly tossed-off drawing a true resemblance to the much-maligned boy. From all indications, however, we can

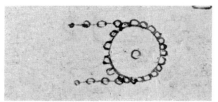

291/1–6
Below, left is an axonometric projection by Antonio Calegari of the drawing from Codex Atlanticus, folio 133 verso. This reconstruction corrects the disproportions and contradictions which can be noted in the distances between the spokes, in the steering bar supports, and in the length of the pedals. The reconstruction further contains the addition of a second support for the rear wheel, and completes the driving gear, which has been made solid, as Leonardo drew it in Codex Madrid I, folio 10 recto (291/3 and 5). Of course, it is

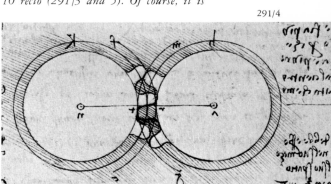

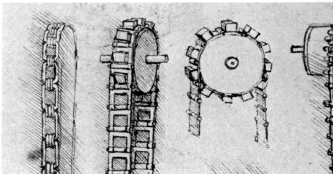

impossible to know how many omissions from the original were made when this copy was drawn. However, the depiction of the gears and the chain agree completely with

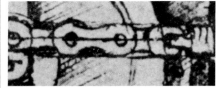

Leonardo's drawings in Codex Madrid I and Codex Atlanticus. Notice the square shape of the teeth which make the design impractical. Leonardo worked on this problem in depth, and in Codex Madrid I, folio 5 recto (291/4), he draws gears with rounded teeth, which would facilitate the functioning of a chain. In Codex Atlanticus, folio 56 verso-b (see detail above), he arrives at a remarkably modern design for a chain link.

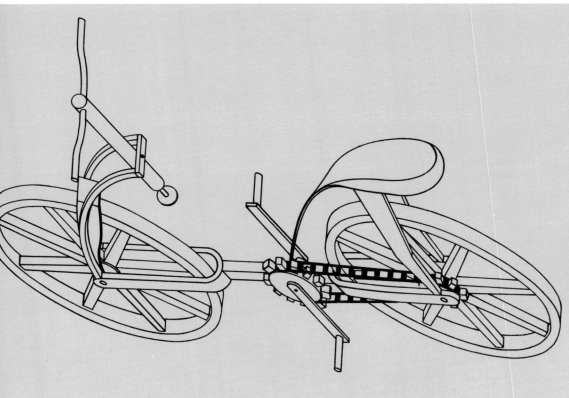

speculate that Salai must have been 12 or 13 years old when drawn, which brings us to approximately 1493, and to a coincidence that is scarcely negligible: Leonardo was at that time sketching Codex Madrid I, on whose tenth folio he drew the same toothed gear and chain which we now view with astonishment – on "his" bicycle.

The concluding pages of the book offer the reader a sampling of Leonardo's own words in their own language and style.

THE WORDS OF LEONARDO

ANNA MARIA BRIZIO

When I undertook to edit the brief anthology which follows, I hesitated for some time over the question of what criteria would determine my choice. Obviously it would be insufficient to compile a pleasant group of pretty passages chosen according to aesthetic norms, just for their suggestive beauty. I needed a thread that would bind the passages into a discursive continuum, and nothing seemed to me as responsive to Leonardo's aims themselves, or as illustrative of his personality, as the theme of knowledge.

The sequence opens with a lively and highly descriptive early passage, taken from the Codex Arundel, in which a youthful Leonardo symbolically stands poised at the mouth of a great cavern, bending to discover "whether it contained some marvelous thing." It ends with several excerpts drawn from his last years. They encompass a world view of extraordinary profundity; here Leonardo's evident awareness of the universal values he expressed creates a tone we can only call solemn. In a consecutive

reading, the striking contrast of viewpoint and manner between the passages gives us the measure of the immense distance he had traveled.

The intervening passages, arranged in generally chronological order, demonstrate beyond doubt that Leonardo's point of departure was painting, "which alone imitates all the visible works of nature." In Renaissance language imitation has a meaning clearly distinct from that of portrayal, reproduction, or copy: it means the creations of forms analogous to those of nature by following nature's own laws. Hence the definitions of painting as "subtle science" and "true daughter of nature" and the statement that "the painter contends with and rivals nature" must be understood not rhetorically, but literally. Leonardo begins with painting and with the sharpness of optical perception, and draws from painting his means of exploring nature: perspective. While other Florentine painters continued to consider perspective only as an instrument of figurative representation, Leonardo discovered how perspective can become an outstanding instrument for measuring and knowing the physical world.

The optical pyramid, with its sheaf of rays converging on or diverging from a point, and the proportionality of its bases at whatever distance they are drawn to intersect with the sheaf of rays provide him with the means of demonstration. The pyramid further avails him of the ability to quantify the entity of forces that strike a point or a surface. Single rays determine for him the course of forces in motion, as well as the angles of incidence and

reflection between the blow of a motor force and the flight of the moved object.

Leonardo has a dynamic and mechanistic concept of the physical world, including the human body and the animal kingdom. According to his theory, four powers move the world and determine the continual transformations that occur within it: gravity, force, accidental motion, and percussion – and the last exceeds in great abundance any of the others. The phenomenon of percussion is created not only macroscopically – by the blow of a heavy body in motion against another body ("mover" and "moved object") – but also by optical rays that strike the eye, thus conveying to it images of things, by sound that strikes the ear, and by all the stimuli that strike the terminal nerves of the senses, awakening sensation. All are phenomena of percussion: water that strikes other water or an intervening obstacle, the motion of air against air, the beating of a bird's wings in the air or the impact of air upon the wings, and the darting of fish in water. "Describe underwater swimming and you will have described the flight of birds."

Leonardo's investigation branches out ceaselessly in every direction. The crossing and recrossing of his thought over myriads of cases and propositions may often seem to meander tortuously and turn in upon itself. But as we progress in reading and understanding his manuscripts, the apparent knot of intricacy dissolves, and we discover that the innumerable variety of subjects addressed by his mind actually constitutes the infinite aspects of one sole power which he tirelessly pursues in all its forms. Descending from a general principle to the interpretation of a particular phenomenon, and from the penetrating analysis of particulars rising again to first principles, he discovers the unbounded variety of their manifestations in nature.

There is no antagonism in Leonardo's mind between art and science. They flow perpetually from one another, each increasing by experience of the other. Only by admitting the participation of every aspect of his work in this ever-growing continuum of mental processes may we understand all its significance, its deep and prolonged resonances. This guides our approach to his prose, where a precise description of a phenomenon, analyzed in its diverse phases by a tightly linked use and reuse of certain key terms, unfolds at last and dilates into splendid images of nature; in his words from Codex Arundel, 94 verso: "The countless images refracted from the countless waves of the sea by solar rays where they strike them produce an immense and continuous splendor over the surface of the sea."

Etirato dalla mia bramosa voglia,
vago di vedere la gran copia delle varie e strane
forme fatte dalla artifiziosa natura, raggiratomi
alquanto infra gli ombrosi scogli, pervenni all'entrata di
una gran caverna, dinanzi alla quale restato
alquanto stupefatto e ignorante di tal cosa, piegato le mie reni
in arco e ferma la stanca mano sopra il ginocchio,
e colla destra mi feci tenebra
alle abbassate ... ciglia.
E spesso piegandomi in qua e in là per vedere
se dentro vi discernessi alcuna cosa e questo vietatomi
la grande oscurità che là entro era,
stato alquanto, subito salse in me 2 cose, paura
e desidèro: paura per la minacciante e scura spilonca;
desidèro per vedere se là entro fusse
alcuna miracolosa cosa.

And drawn by my ardent desire,
impatient to see the great abundance of strange forms
created by that artificer, Nature, I wandered for some time
among the shadowed rocks.
I came to the mouth of a huge cave before which I stopped
for a moment, stupefied
by such an unknown thing. I arched my back,
rested my left hand on my knee, and with my right shaded
my lowered eyes;
several times I leaned to one side, then the other,
to see if I could distinguish anything,
but the great darkness within made this impossible.
After a time there arose in me both fear and desire—
fear of the dark and menacing cave;
desire to see whether it contained
some marvelous thing.

ARUNDEL 155r

Proemio: So bene che per non essere io litterato,
che alcuno prosuntuoso gli parrà ragionevolmente
potermi biasimare coll'allegare io essere omo sanza lettere –
gente stolta!
Non sanno questi tali ch'io potrei,
sì come Mario rispose contro a' patrizi romani,
io sì rispondere dicendo: quelli che dell'altrui fatiche
sè medesimi fanno ornati le mie a me medesimo
non vogliano concedere.
Diranno che per non avere io lettere,
non potere ben dire quello di che voglio trattare.
Or non sanno questi che le mie cose son più da essere
tratte dalla sperienzia che d'altrui parola;
la quale fu maestra di chi ben scrisse, e così per maestra
la piglio e quella in tutti i casi allegherò.

Since I am not a man of letters,
I know that certain presumptuous persons will feel
justified in censuring me,
alleging that I am ignorant of writing–fools!
They do not know that I could reply, as did Marius
to the Roman nobles,
"They who adorn themselves with the labors of others will not
concede me my own."
They will hold that because of my lack of literary training
I cannot properly set forth the subjects I wish to treat.
They do not know that my subjects require for their expression
not the words of others
but experience, the mistress of all who write well.
I have taken her as my mistress
and will not cease to state it.

ATLANTICUS 119v-a

Fuggi i precetti di quelli speculatori
che le loro ragioni non sono confermate dalla isperienza.

Avoid the teachings of speculators
whose judgments are not confirmed by experience.

MS. B 4v

Se tu isplezzerai la pittura,
la quale è sola imitatrice di tutte l'opere evidenti di natura,
per certo tu sprezzerai una sottile invenzione,
la quale con filosofica e sottile speculazione
considera tutte le qualità delle forme:
aire e siti, piante, animali, erbe e fiori,
le quali son cinte d'ombra e lume;
e veramente questa è scienzia legittima figliola di natura...

If you disparage painting,
which alone imitates all the visible works of nature,
you disparage a most subtle science which by philosophical
reasoning examines all kinds of forms:
on land and in the air, plants, animals, grass, and flowers,
which are all bathed in shadow and light.
Doubtless this science
is the true daughter of nature....

MS. A 100r

Il dipintore disputa e gareggia colla natura.

The painter contends with and rivals nature.

FORSTER III 44v

Intra li studi delle naturali
considerazioni, la luce diletta più i contemplanti;
intra le cose grandi delle matematiche la certezza
della dimostrazione innalza più plecarmente

Of all studies of natural causes,
light gives greatest joy to those who consider it;
among the glories of mathematics the certainty of its
proofs most elevates the investigator's mind.

l'ingegni delli investiganti.
La prospettiva adunque è da esser preposta a tutte
le traduzioni e discipline umane, nel campo della quale la linia
radiosa complicata dà i modi delle dimostrazioni,
nella quale si truova la gloria
non tanto della matematica quanto della fisica...

Perspective, which shows how linear rays differ according
to demonstrable conditions,
should therefore be placed first among all the sciences
and disciplines of man,
for it crowns not mathematics
so much as the natural sciences....

Prospettiva è ragione dimostrativa,
per la quale la sperienzia conferma tutte le cose mandare
all'occhio per linee piramidali la lor similitudine;
e quelli corpi d'equali grandezze faranno maggiore
o minore angolo a la lor piramide secondo la varietà
della distanzia che fia da l'una a l'altra.
Linie piramidali intendo esser quelle,
le quali si partano da' superfiziali stremi de' corpi
e per distante concorso si conducano in un sol punto.
Punto dicono essere quello il quale in nessuna parte
si pò dividere,
e questo punto è quello il quale, stando ne l'occhio,
riceve in sè tutte le punte della piramide.

Perspective is the rational law by which experience
confirms that all objects transmit their image
to the eye in a pyramid of lines.
Bodies of equal size produce angles that are
more or less acute
depending on their respective distances.
I call "pyramid of lines" the lines
that emanate from the surfaces and outlines of the bodies
and, as they converge from a distance, end
in a common point.
We call a point that which cannot be divided in any way,
and that point, situated in the eye,
receives in itself the apexes of all the pyramids.

Ogni corpo empie
la circustante aria della sua similitudine,
la quale similitudine è tutta per tutto e tutta nella parte.
L'aria è piena d'infinite linie rette e radiose
insieme intersegate e intessute sanza occupazione
l'una dell'altra, [che] rappresentano a qualunque obbietto
la vera forma della lor cagione.

Every body fills the surrounding air
with images of itself, and every image appears
in its entirety and in all its parts.
The air is full of an infinity of straight lines and rays
which cut across each other without displacing each other and
which reproduce on whatever they encounter
the true form of their cause.

Perchè in tutti i casi
del moto l'acqua ha gran conformità con l'aria,
io l'allegherò per esempio alla sopraddetta proposizione.
Io dico: se tu gitterai in un medesimo tempo
2 picciole pietre alquanto distanti l'una dall'altra
sopra un pelago d'acqua sanza moto,
tu vederai causare intorno alle due predette percussioni
2 separate quantità di circuli, le quali quantità, accrescendo,
vengano a scontrarsi insieme e poi a 'ncorporarsi
intersegandosi l'un circulo coll'altro,
sempre mantenendosi per cientro i lochi
percossi dalle pietre.
E la ragion si è che benchè lì apparisca qualche
dimostrazione di movimento,
l'acqua non si parte del suo sito...
E che quel ch'io dico ti si facci più manifesto,
poni mente a quelle festuche che per lor leggerezza
stanno sopra l'acqua,
che per l'onda fatta sotto loro dall'avvenimento
de' circuli non si partan però del lor primo sito, essendo
adunque questo tal risentimento d'acqua più tosto
tremore che movimento...

I will demonstrate the proposition
that in all cases the motion of water conforms
to that of air.
If you simultaneously throw two small stones
at some distance from each other
onto a motionless body of water,
you will notice around the places of impact
two groups of widening circles
which finally meet and merge,
one circle intersecting with the other,
each having as its
center the point of impact.
The reason is
that despite some evidence of movement,
water does not leave its location....
And to ascertain the truth of what I say,
consider the reeds which by virtue of their lightness
remain above water
without being displaced by the waves
thus created under them,
for the stirring of the water is a tremor,
rather than a movement....

L'acqua percossa dall'acqua fa circuli

Water struck by water forms circles

dintorno al loco percosso;
per lunga distanzia la voce infra l'aria;
più lunga infra il foco;
più la mente infra l'universo;
ma perchè ell'è finita
non si astende infra lo infinito.

around the point of impact;
the voice in the air creates the same
along a greater distance; fire goes still farther,
and still farther the mind in the universe; but since
the universe is finite,
the mind does not reach infinity.

MS. H 67r

La gravità, la forza e 'l moto
accidentale insieme con la percussione son le quattro
accidentali potenzie colle quali tutte l'evidenti opere
de' mortali hanno loro essere e loro morte.

Gravity, force, and accidental motion,
together with percussion, are the four accidental
powers in which all the visible
works of mortals find their existence and their death.

FORSTER II2 116v

Ogni cosa mossa con furia seguiterà per l'aria
la linia del movimento del suo motore.
Se quello move la cosa in circulo,
s'ella fia lasciata in quel moto, il moto suo fia curvo;
e se il moto fia principiato in circulo
e finito in dirittura, in dirittura fia il suo corso;
e così sendo cominciata diritta e finita torta,
torto fia il suo cammino.
Ogni cosa mossa dal colpo si parte infra angoli uguali
del suo motore.

Every object that is hurled furiously
through the air follows its mover's line of motion.
If the object is moved and released in a circular motion,
its own motion will be curvilinear,
and if the motion began as a circle and ended as a straight
line, its course will follow a straight line, and if
its beginning was straight and its completion crooked,
its path will be tortuous.
Every object that is moved
travels at equal angles from its mover.

MS. A 81v

Ogni corpo sperico di densa e resistente superfizie,
mosso dai pari potenzia, farà tanto movimento
con sua balzi causato da duro e solio smalto quanto
a gittarlo libero per l'aria.
O mirabile giustizia di te, primo motore.
Tu non hai voluto mancare a nessuna potenzia l'ordini
e qualità de' sua necessari effetti,
con ciò sia che una potenzia debe cacciare 100 braccia
una cosa vinta da lei e quella nel suo obbedire
trova intoppo, hai ordinato che la potenzia del colpo
ricausi novo movimento, il quale per diversi balzi
recuperi la intera somma del suo debito viaggio.
E se tu misurerai la via fatta da detti balzi,
tu troverai essere di tal lunghezza qual sarebbe a trarre
con la medesima forza
una simil cosa libera per l'aria.

Every spherical body
with a dense and resistant surface,
if moved by bodies of equal force, will perform
as much movement in leaps caused by hard, solid impact
as by throwing it freely into the air.
O how wondrous is your justice, Prime Mover!
You have willed that no power lack the orders and qualities
of the acts necessary to it. Since a power must hurl
at a distance of one hundred braccia an object that
it controls, and that object obey its drive, you
ordered that the power of the blow must cause new movement,
which by diverse leaps recuperates the whole total
of its rightful journey. And if the trajectory of
those leaps is measured, it is found to be of such length
as it would take to draw a similar thing through the air
with the same force.

MS. A 24r

Ogni grave che libero discende,
al centro del mondo si dirizza; e quel che più pesa,
più presto discende;
e quanto più discende, più si fa veloce.
Tanto pesa l'acqua che si parte del suo sito per causa
della nave, quanto il peso di essa nave appunto.

Every weight that falls freely
falls toward the center of the earth;
those of greater weight fall more quickly,
and as they descend their velocity increases.
The water displaced by a ship has a weight equal
to that of the ship.

FORSTER II2 65v

Ogni moto attende al suo mantenimento
ovvero ogni corpo mosso sempre si move,
in mentre che la impressione della potenzia del suo motore
in lui si riserva.

The continuity of every motion
and the motion of every moving body
depend upon the maintenance of
power of the mover.

VOLO DEGLI UCCELLI 13 (12)r

Ogni piccol moto fatto dal mobile circundato dall'aria, si va mantenendo con l'impeto.

Every slightest motion performed by an object in space is maintained by its impetus. MS. K3 111 (31)r

Perchè si sostiene l'uccello sopra dell'aria. L'aria che con più velocità di mobile è percossa, con maggior somma di sè medesima si condensa. ...essendo l'aria corpo atto a condensarsi in sè medesima quando essa è percossa da moto di maggior velocità che non è quel della sua fuga, essa si prieme in sè medesima e si fa infra l'altra aria a similitudine del nuvolo... Ma quando l'uccello si trova infra 'l vento, egli pò sostenersi sopra di quello sanza battere l'alie, perchè quello offizio che fa l'alia mossa contro all'aria stando l'aria sanza moto, tal fa l'aria contro all'alia essendo quella sanza moto.

Why birds are supported in the air. Air that is struck with greatest velocity of motion condenses the most. Since air is a body capable of condensation when struck with a motion of greater velocity than its own, it then becomes as dense as a cloud.... But when the bird is in the wind, he can support himself upon it without beating his wings, for the function of wings that move against the air when it is motionless is performed by the air moving against the wings when they are motionless. ATLANTICUS 77r-b

Scrivi del notare sotto l'acqua, e arai il volare dell'uccello per l'aria.

Describe underwater swimming and you will have described the flight of birds. ATLANTICUS 214r-d

La scienzia strumentale over machinale è nobilissima e sopra tutte l'altre utilissima, con ciò sia che mediante quella tutti li corpi animati che hanno moto fanno le loro operazioni.

Mechanical science is most noble and useful above all others, for by means of it all animated bodies in motion perform their operations. VOLO DEGLI UCCELLI 3r

...mia intenzione è allegare prima la sperienza e poi colla ragione dimostrare perchè tale esperienza è costretta in tal modo ad operare.

...it is my intention first to cite experience, then to demonstrate through reasoning why experience must operate in a given way. MS. E 55r

Convertansi li elementi l'uno nell'altro, e quando l'aria si converte in acqua pel contatto ch'ell'ha colla sua fredda regione, allora essa attrae a sè con furia tutta la circunstante aria, la quale con furia si move a riempiere il loco evacuato della fuggita d'aria ...e questo è il vento.

The elements are converted into one another, and when air is converted to water by contact with its cold regions, it then furiously attracts to itself the surrounding air, which rushes to fill the vacated place... and this is the wind. ATLANTICUS 169r-a

L'onda percossa nel lito per forza di vento fa il tomolo, mettendo la sua superior parte sul fondo; e per quel torna indirieto insino al loco dove di novo ripercote nella succedente onda che le viene di sotto e la rovescia indirieto con rivescio tomolo e di novo la fa ripercotere nel predetto lito; e così successivamente seguita; ora col moto superiore torna al lito e ora collo inferiore si fugge da quello.

The wave struck on its side by the wind makes a leap, moving its upper part to the bottom, and is deflected to where it beats once again upon the successive wave arising from underneath it, and reversing it, again strikes its side, and continues thus, now with motion of its upper part turning back to shore, now with inferior part turning away. LEICESTER 26v

Ogni figura
creata dal moto, col moto si mantiene.
Quando tira vento spiana la rena, e vedi in che modo essa
crea le sue onde, e nota quanto essa si move più tarda
che 'l vento; e 'l simile fa dell'acqua
e nota le differenzie ch'è dall'acqua alla rena.

Every configuration of dust, smoke, and water
that is created by motion is maintained by it.
When the wind blows the sands are leveled, and you see
how it forms waves, and note how they move more slowly than
the wind; consider the waters,
and what differences exist between water and wind.

ATLANTICUS 37v-c

Nota il moto del livello dell'acqua,
il quale fa a uso de' capelli, che hanno due moti,
de' quali l'uno attende al peso del vello
l'altro al liniamento delle volte.
Così l'acqua ha le sue volte revertiginose,
delle quali una parte attende a l'impeto
del corso principale, l'altra attende
al moto incidente e refresso.

Observe how the movement of the surface of the water
resembles that of hair,
which has two movements,
one of which stems from the weight of the hair
and the other from its waves and curls.
In the same way, water has its turbulent curls, a part of
which follows the force of the main current, the other
obeying the movement of incidence and reflection.

WINDSOR 12579r

Scrivi come li nugoli si compongano
e come si risolvano, e che causa leva li vapori
dell'acqua dalla terra infra l'aria,
e la causa delle nebbie e dell'aria ingrossata,
e perchè si mostra più azzurra e meno azzurra una volta
che un'altra; e così scrivi le regioni dell'aria
e la causa delle nevi e delle grandini, e del ristrignersi
l'acqua e farsi dura in diaccio,
e del creare per l'aria nuove figure di neve e alli alberi
nuove figure di foglie ne' paesi freddi,
e per li sassi diacciuoli...

Show how clouds form and dissolve,
how water vapor rises from the earth into the air,
how mists form and air thickens,
and why one wave seems more blue than another;
describe the aerial regions
and the causes of snow and hail,
how water condenses
and hardens into ice,
and how new figures form in the air,
and new leaves on the trees,
and icicles on the stones of cold places....

MS. F 35r

E già sopra a Milano, inverso Lago Maggiore,
vidi una nuvola in forma di grandissima montagna,
piena di scòli infocati, perchè li razzi del sole,
che già era all'orizzonte che rosseggiava,
la tignea del suo colore.
E questa tal nugola grande ... non si movea di suo loco;
anzi riservò nella sua sommità il lume del sole insino
a una ora e mezza di notte, tant'era la sua immensa grandezza.
E infra due ore di notte generò sì gran vento, che fu
cosa stupente, inaudita; e questo fece nel riserrarsi,
che l'aria che infra quella si rinchiudeva,
essendo premuta dalla condensazione del nugolo,
rompea e fuggia per le parte più debole, scorrendo
per l'aria con ispesso tomulto, facendo a similitudine
della spugna premuta dalla mano sotto l'acqua,
della quale l'acqua di che era imbeverata fugge infra
le dita della man che la preme,
fuggendo con impeto infra l'altr'acqua.

And recently above Milan toward Lake Maggiore,
I saw a cloud in the shape of an immense mountain
covered with fiery stones,
for it was tinged with red
by the sun on the horizon.
This huge cloud... stood motionless;
such was its immensity that its summit contained
the sun's light for one hour and a half into night.
And within two hours of night
it produced so great a wind,
it was a stupefying, unheard-of thing;
the air contained in it, compressed by condensation,
erupted and escaped through the cloud's weakest part,
rushing tumultuously, as happens
when a sponge is pressed under water by a hand
and the water it had absorbed
escapes between the fingers of the hand
and through the surrounding water.

LEICESTER 28r

Come la chiarezza dell'aria nasce dall'acqua
che in quella s'è resoluta e fattasi in insensibili
graniculi, li quali, preso il lume del sole
dall'apposita parte, rendan la chiarezza che in essa aria
si dimostra; e l'azzurro che in quella apparisce nasce
dalle tenebre che dopo essa aria si nascondano.

The clarity of air derives from water
dissolved into imperceptible drops
which take the sunlight from the opposite direction,
thereby rendering the air clear;
and the blue that appears in the air is caused
by the shadows concealed in it.

LEICESTER 20r

Movesi l'aria come fiume e tira con seco di nuvoli,
sì come l'acqua corrente
tira tutte le cose che sopra di lei si sostengano.

The air moves like a river
and draws clouds in its wake, just as rushing water
draws with it all things that are above its surface. MS. G 10r

La fiamma fa moto infra l'aria
quale fa l'aria infra l'acqua cioè moto fressuoso;
e massime dov'è gran fiamma.

Flame moves in the air as air moves in water,
in a flexible motion,
especially from where the flame is great. ARUNDEL 139v

Quando il sole s'innalza e caccia le nebbie
e si comincia a rischiarare e colli,
da quella parte donde esse si partano e' fansi azzurri
e fumano inverso le nebbie fuggenti...

When the sun rises
and drives away the mist,
the hills become blue where the mist is departing
and smoke in the direction of the escaping mist.... ARUNDEL 169r

Noterai nel tuo ritrarre come infra le ombre
sono ombre insensibili d'oscurità e di figura...
Le cose vedute infra 'l lume e l'ombre si dimosterranno
di maggiore rilievo che quelle che son
nel lume o nell'ombre.

You will observe in your painting
that shadows among shadows
are imperceptible in density and outline....
Things seen between light and shadow will display
much more relief than those seen in light or in shadow. MS. E 17r

Poni mente per le strade, sul fare della sera,
i volti d'omini e donne, quando è cattivo tempo,
quanta grazia e dolcezza si vede in loro.

Observe how much grace and sweetness
are to be seen in the faces of men and women on the streets,
with the approach of evening in bad weather. MS. A 100v

Questi libri
contengano in ne' primi della natura
dell'acqua in sé e ne' sua moti;
li altri contengano delle cose fatte da e sua corsi,
che mutano il mondo di centro e di figura.

These books contain
the nature of water and its motion;
the others contain the things produced by its flow
which have changed the face
and the center of the world. LEICESTER 5r

Io truovo il sito della terra
essere ab antico nelle sue pianure tutto occupato
e coperto dall'acque salse; e i monti, ossa della terra,
con le loro larghe base, penetrare e elevarsi infra l'aria,
coperti e vestiti di molta e alta terra.
Di poi le molte piogge, accrescimento de' fiumi,
con ispessi lavamenti ha dispogliato in parte l'alte cime
d'essi monti, lasciando in loco della terra il sasso...
E la terra delle spiagge e dell'alte cime
delle montagne è già discesa alle sue base e ha alzato
i fondi de' mari ch'esse basi circavano
e fatta discoperta pianura, e di lì in alcun loco,
per lontano spazio, ha cacciato i mari.

I conclude that in oldest times
salt waters entirely occupied and covered the earth,
and the mountains,
skeleton of the earth with their wide bases,
penetrated and arose into the air,
covered and decked with abundant, deep soil.
Since then great rains, enlarging the streams,
despoiled with their frequent lavings the high peaks
of those mountains, leaving stone in place of soil....
And the earth of the beaches and of high mountain peaks
has already descended to their bases and raised the
sea bottom which they had surrounded, and uncovered a plain,
from which in some places it has driven the seas.

ATLANTICUS 126v-b

Nessuna parte della terra
si scopre dalla consumazione del corso dell'acqua,
che già non fussi superfizie di terra
veduta dal sole.

No part of the earth exposes itself
by the depredations of the course of the waters
which was not once a land surface
seen by the sun. ATLANTICUS 45v-A

L'acqua disfa li monti e riempie le valle
e vorrebbe ridurre la terra in perfetta spericità,
s'ella potessi.

The waters destroy the mountains, fill the valleys,
and would reduce the world to perfect sphericalness
if they could.

ATLANTICUS 185v-c

Perpetui son li bassi lochi
del fondo del mare e il contrario son le cime dei monti;
seguita che la terra si farà sperica e tutta coperta
dall'acque e sarà inabitabile.

The depths of the sea bottom are perpetual,
and the peaks of the mountains are not;
it follows that the earth will become spherical,
covered with water, and uninhabitable.

MS. F 52r

Farai regola e misura di ciascun muscolo
e renderai ragione di tutti li loro uffizi e in che modo
s'adoprano e chi li move.

You will take the measure of all the muscles
and learn their functions,
who moves them, and how they are implemented.

ANAT. B 27r

E questo vecchio, di poche ore inanzi la sua morte,
mi disse lui passare cento anni
e che non si sentiva alcun mancamento nella persona,
altro che debolezza;
e così standosi a sedere sopra uno letto
nello spedale di Santa Maria Nova di Firenze,
senza altro movimento o segno d'alcuno accidente,
passò di questa vita.
E io ne feci notomia,
per vedere la causa di sì dolce morte:
la quale trovai venire meno per mancamento di
sangue e arteria, che notria il core
e li altri membri inferiori,
li quali trovai molti aridi, stenuati e secchi.
La qual notomia discrissi assai diligentemente
e con gran facilità, per essere privato
di grasso e di omore,
che assai impedisce la cognizione delle parte...

And an old man,
only a few hours before he died,
told me that he had lived for one hundred years
without experiencing any
physical failure other than weakness;
and sitting on the bed in the hospital
of Santa Maria Nova in Florence,
he passed from this life,
giving no sign of any accident.
And I dissected his body,
in order to understand the cause of so easy a death.
I discovered that it came to him
through a lack of blood
in the arteries that fed the heart and the lower parts,
which were used up and dried out.
I performed this dissection
minutely and easily, as there were neither fat nor humors
to impede recognition of anatomical parts....

ANAT. B10v

Tu non farai mai se non confusione
nella dimostrazione dei muscoli e lor siti,
nascimenti e fini, se prima non fai una dimostrazione
di muscoli sottili a uso di fila di refe;
e così li potrai figurare l'un sopra dell'altro
come li ha situati la natura...

You will only confuse
your representation of the muscles and their location,
derivation, and purpose if you first
do not show the network of the small muscles;
depict them one above the other
as nature has placed them....

ANAT. A 18r

E tu che di' esser meglio
il vedere fare la notomia che vedere tali disegni,
diresti bene se fussi possibile
veder tutte queste cose,
che in tali disegni si dimostrano, in una sola figura;
nella quale, con tutto il tuo ingegno,
non vedrai e non arai notizia se non d'alquante
poche vene; delle quali io,
per averne vera e piena notizia,
ho disfatti più di dieci corpi umani,
destruggendo ogni altri membri,
consumando con minutissime particule tutta la carne

You who claim that it is better
to watch an anatomical demonstration
than to look at these drawings—you would be right,
if you could see in a single form
all the details shown in the drawings;
with all your ability,
you would not see or get to know in one form
more than a few veins.
To obtain an exact and complete knowledge,
I have dissected more than ten human bodies,
destroying all the other parts
and removing to the last particle

che dintorno a esse vene si trovava,
sanza insanguinarle,
se non d'insensibile insanguinamento delle vene capillare.
E un sol corpo non bastava a tanto tempo;
che bisognava procedere di mano in mano
in tanti corpi, che si finissi la intera cognizione;
la qual ripricai due volte per vedere le differenzie.
E se tu arai l'amore di tal cosa,
tu sarai forse impedito dallo stomaco;
e se questo non ti impedisce, tu sarai forse impedito
dalla paura coll'abitare nelli tempi notturni
in compagnia di tali morti,
squartati e scorticati e spaventevoli a vederli;
e se questo non t'impedisce,
forse ti mancherà il disegno bono,
il qual s'appartiene a tal figurazione.
E se tu arai il disegno,
e' non sarà accompagnato dalla prospettiva;
e se sarà accompagnato, e' ti mancherà l'ordine delle
dimostrazion geometriche e l'ordine delle calculazion
delle forze e valimento de'muscoli;
o forse ti mancherà la pazienzia, se tu non sarai diligente.
Delle quali, se in me tutte queste cose sono state o no,
centoventi libri da me composti
ne daran sentenzia del si o del no,
nelli quali non sono stato impedito nè d'avarizia
o negligenzia, ma sol dal tempo. Vale.

Se guarderai le stelle sanza razzi
(come si fa vederle per un piccolo foro
fatto colla strema punta de la sottile acucchia,
e quel posto quasi a toccare l'occhio), tu vedrai esse
stelle essere tanto minime,
che nulla cosa pare essere minore.
E veramente la lunga distanzia dà loro ragionevole
diminuizione, ancora che molte vi sono,
che son moltissime volte maggiore che la stella
ch'è la terra coll'acqua.
Ora pensa quel che parrebbe quessa nostra stella
in tanta distanzia, e considera poi quante stelle
si metterebbe' e per longitudine e latitudine infra
esse stelle, le quali sono
seminate per esso spazio tenebroso.

Alli ambiziosi,
che non si contentano del benefizio della vita
nè della bellezza del mondo,
è dato per penitenzia che lor medesimi strazino essa vita,
e che non possegghino la utilità e bellezza del mondo.

O speculatore delle cose,
non ti laldare di conoscere le cose che ordinariamente
per sè medesima la natura conduce,
ma rallegrati di conoscere il fine di quelle cose
che son disegnate dalla mente tua.

all the flesh surrounding these veins,
without any bleeding other than that,
nearly imperceptible, of the capillary veins.
A single body did not suffice for so long a time;
I had to proceed by stages with many bodies
to achieve complete knowledge.
I did this twice in order to understand the differences.
In spite of your love of such investigations,
you may be deterred by repugnance;
if not, then by the fear of spending the nights
in the company of corpses that are cut up
and flayed and horrible to look upon.
And if this does not deter you,
then perhaps you lack the skill in drawing
necessary for such representations;
and if you can draw,
you may have no knowledge of perspective;
and if you have it,
you may not be versed in geometrical exposition
or in the method of calculating
the forces and energy of the muscles;
or perhaps you are lacking in patience,
so that you will not be diligent.
Whether or not I possess all these qualities
will be attested in one hundred twenty books,
whose composition was delayed not by avarice or negligence,
but by time alone. Farewell.   ANAT. C 13v

If you scrutinize the stars without rays
(as is done through a little hole
in the end of a small lens, placed
so as almost to touch the eye),
you will perceive these stars
as so tiny that nothing could be smaller.
And indeed,
the great distance confers upon them a certain diminution,
though many of them are several times larger
than that star which is our earth and its waters.
Now consider
what our star would seem at such a distance,
and how many stars could be longitudinally
and latitudinally interposed
between those which are scattered through dark space.   MS. F 5r

The ambitious, who are not content
with the gifts of life and the beauty of the world,
are given the penitence of ruining
their own lives and never possessing the utility
and beauty of the world.   ATLANTICUS 91v-a

O investigator,
do not flatter yourself that you know
the things nature performs for herself,
but rejoice in knowing the purpose
of those things designed by your own mind.   MS. G 47r

FOOTNOTES
LIST OF ILLUSTRATIONS
INDEX
ACKNOWLEDGMENTS

FOOTNOTES

INTRODUCTION

NOTE: In his quotation, Freud [*Leonardo da Vinci, a Study in Psychosexuality* (New York, 1947)] repeats a simile taken from Dimitri Merezhkovsky's *The Romance of Leonardo da Vinci* (London, 1903).

THE PAINTER

[1] W. M. Ivins, Jr., *On the Rationalization of Sight*, The Metropolitan Museum of Art, Paper no. 8, New York, 1938.

[2] *Leonardos Visionen von der Sintflut und vom Untergang der Welt* (Bern, 1958).

[3] Leonardo da Vinci, *Treatise on Painting* (Codex Urbinas Latinus 1270), translated and annotated by A. Philip McMahon (Princeton, 1956), pp. 9, 30–31.

[4] Fols. 101v and 102r and v.

[5] For instance, in the three lower figures of fol. 63v.

[6] Fols. 30r, 49r, 54r.

[7] Codex Urbinas Latinus 1270.

THE WRITER

[1] Fols. 2v-3r.

[2] On fol. 3v.

[3] It may be assumed that the "small" books are in sextodecimo (in Melzi's list they are called "booklets") and the "still larger" books in octavo or in quarto. For the 2 "larger" books we should be tempted to think of Manuscript C and Codex Leicester, the only 2 "in folio" in all subsequent lists. Manuscripts D, E, F, and G, Codex Forster I1 (i.e., the first part of Forster I), and the Codex on the Flight of Birds, written either in 1505 or in the following years, could not be among the 16 in quarto or in octavo; those that could be are Manuscripts A and B, Codex Forster I2, the Codex Trivulzianus, both parts of Codex Madrid I, at least the 17 folios on the "horse" of Codex Madrid II which were afterwards bound there together with the rest of it, a notebook on anatomy. Among the 25 "small" books in sextodecimo could be Manuscripts L and M, the 2 I manuscripts (I1 and I2), the 3 H manuscripts, perhaps the first of the 3 K manuscripts, the 2 Forster II codices, and Forster III.

[4] Codex Madrid II included.

[5] In the manuscripts that exist today we can in fact read the following alphabetical marks made by Leoni: A, B, C, D, G, L, O, T, W, Y, W, and perhaps Z, then BB, II, KK, LL, NN, OO, SS.

Evidently the letters of the alphabet were not enough to mark all of them and therefore Leoni recommenced the alphabetical series using double letters. We deduce from this the loss of the manuscripts marked E, F, H, I, M, N, P, Q, R, S, U, AA, CC, DD, EE, FF, GG, HH, MM, PP, QQ, RR; we cannot say with certainty whether any manuscripts existed beyond SS or how many there may have been. Let us say that, adding to the 19 surviving manuscripts the 22 that have disappeared, 5 are still needed to make up the number 46 – without by this affirming that 46 was the last number of the list. We consider 50 to be an acceptable approximate figure.

[6] There remains a little problem as yet unsolved. The symbols for a single letter of the alphabet are almost invariably followed by an *e* (for which an *a* is substituted only once) in tiny characters, while the symbols for double letters are not: Be 100, Da 114, Le 17, Ge 55, Xe 64, Ye 46, Te 91, Oe 38, We 93. The simplest explanation would be that the writing reflects the pronunciation of the consonants: Be, Ge, Te, etc.; but it does not apply to Le, Da, Oe, C, and Ye, and perhaps not to Xe and We. On the whole, the anomalies seem excessive.

[7] On the other hand, Codex Madrid II was still divided into two distinct parts to which Leoni applied the marks C and L. In fact C 140 can be read on fol. 140, and Le 17 can be read on fol. 157. Even from its unusual composition and from the presence of various half sheets, this second part of only 17 folios would seem to be what remains of a larger unit that had already been reduced to its present dimensions at the time of Leoni. Later the two parts of Codex Madrid II were bound together and someone took care to unify the numeration, changing the numbers 1 to 17 of the L codex into the numbers 141 to 157 by placing the figure 14 in front of the first numbers which went from 1 to 9 (but whoever was responsible inadvertently wrote a 12 which he then corrected to 14). The numbers that followed, on the other hand, were written beneath the old numbers 10, 11, etc., which were partly crossed.

[8] With a certain approximation we could put the series of manuscripts into the following order: between 1485 and 1490 B, Trivulzianus, Forster I2, part of Forster III and some folios of Anatomy B; 1490 C; 1492 A and also Madrid II1 that reaches 1493. Madrid I carries the date of January 1, 1493 in a note added later; therefore it was started in 1492 and was perhaps continued until 1497. Around 1494 the 3 manuscripts H were written, between 1493 and 1496 part of Forster III, between 1495 and 1497 the 2 Forster II. Between 1497 and 1499 M and I (but M precedes I). In the same years the manuscript L was started and it was continued also up to 1503, when Madrid II, which stretches to 1505, was started. Contemporarily were written K1 (1504) and part of K2 which was still being written for some years. In 1505 the Codex on the Flight of Birds and Forster I1 are followed by Leicester, D, and F (about 1508). During these years the study of anatomy was intensified: in fact the greatest part of the folios gathered in the "Quaderni di Anatomia" was written between 1506 and 1513. The last manuscripts spread over a certain number of years: K3 between 1509 and 1512, G between 1510 and 1516, E between 1513 and 1514. The great number of sheets gathered in the Codex Atlanticus, the Codex Arundel and the Windsor Collection cover a long period of time. It is not easy to date every single folio. Important contributions on matters related to chronology have been made by scholars such as Calvi and Giacomelli and, more recently, Pedretti and Clark; but it is a difficult problem, and much remains to be done.

[9] Examples of this type are Forster I1, Forster II2, C, Madrid I, On the Flight of Birds, Leicester, and the notebooks on anatomy. In actual fact, however, not one of these manuscripts corresponds to an organic, completely unitary treatment.

[10] Madrid II was originally made up of 9 quires, each containing 8 small sheets folded so as to form 16 folios (later numbered on the recto only by Leoni), or 32 pages. They should make a total of 144 folios, but the present numeration goes only as far as 140, because of the loss of 1 sheet (or 2 folios, between 133 and 134) in the ninth quire, of half a sheet (a folio between the first and the second) in the first quire and because of the repetition, through oversight, of number 62. We know that the "correct number" for making up a volume was normally 6 quires with a total of 96 sheets. Perhaps the volume grew during the course of its composition.

[11] Still blank today are fols. 7v, 12r-14v, 20r, 30v, 40v, 51v, 52r, 54r, 57v-60r, 83r, 103r-104r, and 128v-130r. In many cases Leonardo goes back, even after several years, to the pages already written on and fills up the unoccupied spaces with new notes. He sometimes uses his black or red pencil to write, sometimes a pen; he sometimes traces over with the pen what he has written in red chalk.

[12] Perhaps the first five if we count the two lost ones, and on fols. 3r, 15r, and 16r.

[13] Fols. 16v, 17r and -v, 18v, 19r and -v, 20r and -v, 21r.

[14] Fols. 22v-23r, 52v-53r.

[15] Fols. 64r and 126r.

[16] To fol. 140v.

[17] Here he proceeds in the opposite direction from that of the numeration of the pages up to 138v – in other words, from the definition of "point, line, area" to the first proposition.

[18] Placed at the top of 112r.

[19] Some of the pages involved were grouped as follows: 64v-75v, 80v-82v, 105r-120v, 130v to the end.

[20] The list of clothes is on fol. 4v.

[21] An example occurs at the end of Manuscript B on the verso of the cover, where Leonardo wrote a series of separate notes. The first three read *Trova Lodovico M° – Della carabe inelle Pandette – Il Vicario* (the capital letters are mine apart from M°). They are three independent memoranda, the second of which refers to the fact learned by Leonardo that Justinian's Digest of the Roman civil law (*Pandette*) speaks of yellow amber (*carabe*). But the existing transcriptions of Manuscript B read *della carne nel panetto*. Accordingly, Ravaisson-Mollien, making a single note of the first and second memoranda, translated thus: *Trouve, M. Ludovic, de la chair dans le petit pain* ("Find, M. Ludovic, some meat in the small loaf"). At this point Calvi intervened, objecting that in Milanese dialect *panetto* meant *fazzoletto* ("handkerchief"). So someone was hiding meat in his handkerchief. Searching through the archives of Milan, Calvi discovered edicts that the *Vicario* of Milan of Leonardo's period had issued against black marketeers in times of famine.

[22] The majority of readers have seen only anthologies, such as those of Richter, McCurdy, Solmi, Fumagalli, and Brizio.

[23] Manuscript B, the Trivulzianus, and part of Anatomy B.

[24] *De re militari, De ponderibus.*

[25] Including the *Rudimenta grammatices* of Perotto and Pulci's *Vocabolista*.

[26] The list in Codex Madrid II of the books in Leonardo's possession in 1504 records grammars of Priscian and Donatus (*Maior* and *Minor*, Latin and Latin-Italian), Perotto's *Rudimenta*, two *vocabolisti*, the *Synonima* of Flisco, the *Doctrinale* of Alexander de Villa Dei, and two books on rhetoric.

[27] It seemed strange to him that dividing two-thirds by three-quarters would give eight-ninths, a quantity greater than the dividend (Codex Atlanticus, fol. 279r-c). He proposed a very simple but absurd rule for finding the square and cube roots of any number, defining the root as a fraction of which the *numerator alone* is multiplied by itself and supplies the square or cubic number required. This method would give the cube root of three, for example, as three-ninths, because three-ninths by three-ninths would give twenty-seven ninths, or three (Codex Atlanticus, fol. 245r-b; Codex Arundel 200r). It probably did not take him long to notice that this method was not very safe, and he noted in the Codex Atlanticus (fol. 120r-d), "Learn the multiplication of the roots from Master Luca," and ended by transcribing from Pacioli's *Summa de arithmetica* into the Atlanticus all the rules for doing operations with fractional numbers.

[28] Manuscript M, fol. 19r.

[29] Codex Madrid II contains a copy of a version in the vernacular of the first pages of that classic book. We also know from the list of books that Leonardo had in his possession that year a Latin edition of Euclid and an Italian version of the first three books of the same author.

[30] Fols. 72v, 75v.

[31] In *De expetendis et fugiendis rebus*. Leonardo refers to one of the fundamental passages by Valla on this subject in the Codex Arundel (fols. 178v-179v) and translates it into Italian. The translation is correct, but the little alphabetical letters that refer to the geometric drawings are often so incorrectly transcribed as to render the text incomprehensible. The handwriting, too, is rather unusual: not close and compact as when Leonardo makes a fair copy, and not abounding in changes of mind and cancellations as when he writes the first draft. A probable explanation that would resolve our doubts would be that Leonardo was writing the translation of that extract from dictation.

[32] Codex Atlanticus, fol. 218v-b.

[33] *De ludo geometrico.*

[34] Codex Atlanticus, fol. 139r-a.

[35] Codex Madrid I, fol. 87v.

[36] *Treatise on Painting*, chap. 31.

[37] Ibid., chap. 10.

38 Ibid., chap. 9.

39 Ibid., chap. 19.

40 Ibid., chap. 7.

41 Ibid., chap. 1.

42 Manuscript G, fol. 96v.

43 *Treatise on Painting,* chap. 33.

44 Codex Atlanticus, fol. 11r-b.

45 Quaderni d'Anatomia, vol. II, fol. 1r. This is valid for the descriptive disciplines such as anatomy, machines, and the like. The folios on anatomy at Windsor and in Codex Madrid I can be considered a collection of illustrations accompanied by captions like the pages of an atlas.

46 Codex Atlanticus, fol. 108v-b.

47 Added at the top of Codex Madrid I, fol. 6r.

48 Codex Atlanticus, fol. 119v-a.

49 Quaderni d'Anatomia, vol. II, fol. 14r.

IL CAVALLO

1 Vannoccio Biringucci, *Li dieci libri della Pirotechnia* (ed. 1550), p. 82r; Giorgio Vasari, *Le Vite* (ed. Milanesi), vol. I, p. 158 ff.; Benvenuto Cellini, *I trattati della oreficeria e della scultura* (ed. Firenze, 1857), p. 164 ff.; Germain Boffrand, *Descriptio omnium Operarum Quibus ad Fundendam ex Aere Una Emissione Metalli Ludovici Decimiquarti Statuam Equestrem . . .* (Paris, 1743), p. 29 ff.

I am indebted to the late Dr. Ladislao Reti for bringing Boffrand's work to my attention.

2 The letter was published by Luca Beltrami in *Il Castello di Milano* (1894), p. 314. It was therefore known to Leonardo scholars; nevertheless, it is G. Castelfranco, *Storia di Milano,* vol. VIII, p. 511, that we must thank for not having overlooked the important reference to a life-size monument.

3 Codex Atlanticus, fol. 391r-a.

4 For instance Windsor 12357 and 12358r.

5 Windsor 12349r.

6 Codex Atlanticus fol. 148r-a is dated 1487 by C. Pedretti, *A Chronology of L. da Vinci's Architectural Studies after 1500* (Geneva, 1962), p. 61; it is dated ca. 1490 by L. Beltrami, *L. da Vinci negli studi per il tiburio . . .* (Milan, 1903), and by L. Firpo, *Leonardo architetto e urbaniste* (Turin, 1963), p. 136. It may be added that the base and pedestal sketched on fol. 148r-a find analogies with some of the studies for the Trivulzio equestrian group; see Windsor 12353.

7 The letter was published by G. Poggi in *Leonardo da Vinci: Vita di G. Vasari commentata . . .* (Florence, 1919), p. 23 ff.; on the same subject, see Castelfranco, op. cit.

8 Manuscript C, fol. 15v.

9 Windsor 12345. This drawing is a fragment of fol. 147r-b of the Codex Atlanticus. Leonardo's presence in Pavia with Francesco di Giorgio Martini is recorded in 1490; see G. Calvi, *Archivio storico lombardo,* vol. XLIII, 1916, p. 468.

10 On the Regisole of Pavia, see especially L. Heydenreich's study "Marc Aurel u. Regisole" in *Festschrift fur Erich Meyer* (Hamburg, 1959), p. 146 ff.

11 Paolo Giovio, *Leonardio Vincii vita*; see recent anthology by R. Cianchi in *Raccolta Vinciana,* fasc. XX, 1964, pp. 288–289.

12 See Windsor 12294 and 12319.

13 In his painting "The Hunt of Meleagro" kept in the Prado Poussin exemplified the various types of horses studied by Leonardo. We are thankful to Xavier da Salas for drawing our attention to this interesting document confirming Poussin's deep knowledge of Leonardo's drawings. About this see J. Bialostocki, "Poussin et Léonard," in *Colloque Nicolas Poussin,* vol. I (Paris, 1960), p. 133 ff.

14 The horse of Marcus Aurelius can be compared here: originally the forehoof was resting on the figure of a barbarian in subjection. See K. Kluge – K. Lehmann Hartleben, *Die antiken Grossbronzen* (1927), vol. II, p. 85; P. Ducati, *L'Arte classica* (ed. of 1956), p. 671.

15 Ph. Argelati, Bibliotecha scriptorum mediolanensium . . . premittitur Joseph Antonii Saxii Historia Literaria – Typographica Mediolanensis, ab anno MCDLXV ad annum MD . . . ed. Mediolani 1745, vol. I, col. 356.

16 Paris, Bibliothèque Nationale 3141, Manuscript Italien 372. This manuscript, which deals with the history of the Sforza family, was first mentioned by Rio, *L. da Vinci e la sua scuola* (ed. of 1856), p. 30, in relation to the monument of Francesco Sforza, and most recently by K. Clark, *The Drawings of Leonardo da Vinci at Windsor Castle,* 2d ed. revised with the assistance of C. Pedretti, vol. I (London, 1968), p. xxxvii, note 1.

17 Fol. 148r, par. 2.

18 *De divina proportione,* 1497 (Vienna ed. of 1896), dedicatory page to Lodovico Sforza.

19 Paolo Cortese, *De cardinalatu* (1510), line 1, p. 50 (published in G. Tiraboschi, *St. d. lett. italiana,* t. VI, part V, p. 1599); Paolo Giovio, op. cit. (published in G. Tiraboschi, t. VII, p. 1718 ff.); Matteo Bandello, *Le Novelle* (ed. of 1910), vol. II, *Proemio alla novella,* n. 58.

20 Fol. 320r-a.

21 Theophilus, *Diversarum artium schedula,* edited by W. Theobald (Berlin, 1933); on casting see especially 1, III, chaps. XXX and LX. This work contains the first written description of the lost-wax casting system still in existence.

22 Pomponio Gaurico, *De sculptura* (ed. 1542), p. 37 ff. See also Pomponius Gauricus, *De sculptura,* annotated by A. Chastel and R. Klein (Geneva-Paris, 1969), chap. VI, p. 209.

23 Codex Madrid II, fol. 151v, where Leonardo declared, "I have decided to cast the horse without tail," thereby confirming his intention to cast the horse in one piece.

24 Folios 12350 and 12347r from the Windsor Collection contain short notes about the casting procedure described in Codex Madrid II: cf. M. V. Brugnoli, Documenti, notizie e ipotesi sulla scultura di Leonardo in *Leonardo saggi e ricerche* (ed. Roma, 1954), p. 368 ff. Not all scholars agree that Windsor 12347r is datable from the period of the Sforza monument: nevertheless such a date really seems to be confirmed by Codex Madrid II (type of pacing horse from folio 149r; note concerning "the mold of the horse" nearly identical in Codex Madrid and on Windsor 12347r).

25 In Windsor 12347r.

26 Fol. 396v-c.

27 Fol. 142r, par. 3. It is interesting to note that neither Vasari nor Cellini mention this process, while Germain Boffrand describes it in connection with the casting method applied for the colossal equestrian monument to Louis XIV.

28 Fol. 144v, par. 3.

29 Fol. 352r-c, datable to 1490.

30 Codex Atlanticus, fol. 179v-a: "to make the mold of clay and then of wax."

31 Codex Madrid II, fol. 148v, par. 3.

32 Codex Madrid II, fols. 145r, par. 1, and 143r, par. 2. Cf. also Windsor 12350.

33 Vannoccio Biringucci, op. cit., p. 90r. See also Codex Trivulzianus (ed. Milano, 1939), fol. 16r.

34 Codex Madrid II, fol. 144v, par. 2.

35 Codex Madrid II, fol. 147v, par. 2.

36 See Biringucci, op. cit., p. 90v: "Re-baked earth breaks easily and is difficult to repair once it has broken."

37 Codex Madrid II, fol. 147r, par. 1.

38 See the drawing on Windsor 12348.

39 Codex Madrid II, fol. 147v, par. 1.

40 An accurate transcription of the duke's letter was given by C. Pedretti, *Leonardo da Vinci a Bologna e in Emilia* (Bologna, 1953), pp. 151–152. Clark, op. cit., 1968, p. 23, note to 12321, underlines that in this letter it is not the model, but the mold of the horse that is requested.

41 In November 1494 Il Moro handed over the metal intended for the casting of the Sforza horse to Ercole d'Este, who sent it to Ferrara. See Marino Sanudo, "Spedizione di Carlo VIII in Italia," op. cit. in *Raccolta Vinciana,* fasc. XIII, p. 83.

42 Codex Atlanticus, fol. 335v-a datable about 1497.

43 Codex Madrid II, fols. 145r, par. 3 and 151v.

44 Codex Madrid II, fols. 149r and 141v, par. 2.

45 Cellini, op. cit., p. 225. This work was first published in 1568.

46 Boffrand, op. cit.

LEONARDO AND MUSIC

I am very much indebted to the American Philosophical Society for supporting my research on Leonardo da Vinci. My sincere thanks go to my assistant at the Metropolitan Museum, Miss Mary McClane, who with untiring devotion helped me with the preparation of my manuscript.

1 Thus Ludwig Heydenreich, *Leonardo* (Berlin, 1943), one of the classical treatises on Leonardo's life and work. Kenneth Clark, *Leonardo da Vinci: An Account of His Development as an Artist* (Cambridge, 1939; rev. ed. 1958), one of the most perceptive books written about Leonardo the artist, is hardly an exception. Although it mentions the silver instrument that Leonardo brought to Milan, Leonardo's *lira* is translated as "lyre," which would indicate the totally different Greek or Roman instrument with two arms and one crossbar, and the horse skull (*teschio*) is mistranslated – as in many other books on Leonardo – as "horse's head," a shape that would lack the eyeholes corresponding to the sound holes in a *lira da braccio.*

The excellent book by Roberto Marcolongo, *Leonardo da Vinci, artista, scienziato* (Milan, 1950), containing a fundamental analysis of Leonardo's scientific achievements, has nothing to say about Leonardo's musical thoughts and activities except for mentioning that Leonardo was an excellent player of the "cetra" – a term meaning either the ancient Greek kithara or the Renaissance cittern – and that he "constructed various musical instruments and the monochord" – an obvious misunderstanding, since the monochord goes back to antiquity.

The admirable survey of publications about Leonardo by Anna Maria Brizio, "Rassegne," in *L'Arte,* 1968, part I, includes the statement, "Properly speaking, the studies on Leonardo and music do not belong in the category of his scientific studies." Then would music, and Leonardo's concern with this art and its acoustical foundations, have no place among his multifarious interests and activities?

J. P. Richter, *The Literary Works of Leonardo da Vinci,* 2d ed. (London, 1939), pp. 69–81, a formidable contribution when it appeared and still indispensable, includes remarks about Leonardo's "lyra," his other instruments, his statements on sound and voice, and his comparison of painting and music. Inevitably, the practice of improvisation was not fully understood in Richter's time, and most of the instruments mentioned, such as the *"viola organista"* and the "zither," were not recognized for what they actually were.

2 See E. Winternitz, "The Role of Music in Leonardo's Paragone," in *Phenomenology and Social Reality: Essays in Memory of Alfred Schutz,* edited by Maurice Natanson (The Hague, 1970), pp. 270–296.

3 See E. Winternitz, "Lira da braccio," in *Die Musik in Geschichte und Gegenwart,* vol. 8 (Kassel, 1960), col. 952–953.

4 Florence, Codice Magliabecchiano 17.

5 See E. Winternitz, "Lira da braccio" col. 935, 948; "Archeologia musicale del Rinascimento nel Parnaso de Raffaello," in *Rendiconti della Pontificia Accademia Romana di Archeologia,* vol. XXVII, 1952–1954; *Gaudenzio Ferrari, His School, and the Early History of*

the *Violin* (Milan, 1967); and *Musical Instruments and Their Symbolism in Western Art* (New York and London, 1967).

6   It is not without significance in our context that Benvenuto Cellini, in his treatise on the arts of the goldsmith and of the sculptor, when mentioning Verrocchio as an outstanding goldsmith, says, "He was the master of the great Leonardo da Vinci, who was a painter, sculptor, architect, philosopher, and musician." By the way, Cellini himself was not only a sculptor but also a skilled musician.

7   This notation is on the customary five- or six-line staff, but one has to keep in mind that the notes are named not by letters, such as A, B, C, and D, but by syllables from among *do, re, mi, fa, sol, la,* and *si*, for the seven tones of the scale – also called Guidonian syllables, since the system was invented by Guido d'Arezzo, about 1000 A.D.

8   A detailed interpretation of this and all other rebuses of Leonardo is found in A. Marinoni's *I Rebus di Leonardo da Vinci, raccolti e interpretati* (Florence, 1951).

9   Pythagoras is mentioned by name in one of Leonardo's "jests." Manuscript M 586.

10   Boethius was still the accepted ancient authority on music in Leonardo's time; the first printed edition of his *De institutione musica* appeared in Venice in 1492.

11   How little Leonardo, even recently, has been credited with a deep interest in acoustics can be learned from *Die Musik in Geschichte und Gegenwart*, vol. 1, p. 213, where the "Acoustics" article contains the sentence, "Not even Leonardo da Vinci, though otherwise rich in ideas, has profoundly occupied himself with acoustical problems."

12   A detailed description of Leonardo's sketches and notes on musical instruments can be found in E. Winternitz, "Leonardo's Invention of the Viola Organista," "Melodic, Chordal, and Other Drums Invented by Leonardo da Vinci," and "Leonardo's Invention of Key-Mechanisms for Wind Instruments," all in *Raccolta Vinciana*, fasc. XX, pp. 1–82, 1964.

13   Codex Atlanticus, fol. 319r-b.

14   Codex Atlanticus, fol. 355r-c; Codex Arundel, fol. 137v.

15   See the transcription of these passages in Arturo Uccelli, *Leonardo da Vinci: I Libri di meccanica* (Milan, 1940), p. 20.

16   West Africa and the Far East know the "hourglass drum," whose two skins are connected by external ropes which can be pressed by the player's arm or elbow to increase or decrease the tension of the skins and thereby to change the pitch during performance. It is improbable, however, that Leonardo knew this type of drum.

17   While this attempt at interpreting the drawings themselves remains guesswork, we may find relevant information in contemporary instruments of Leonardo's time, and recall certain folk instruments that show similarities to Leonardo's pot drum. There is one folk instrument that combines pot and membrane, and is so widely disseminated that it must have a very long history. It is the *rommelpot*, to use its Dutch name mentioned already in Mersenne's *Harmonie Universelle*, Paris 1636. In Provence it was known as the *pignato*; in Naples, *caccarella*; in Apulia, *cupacupa*. Lombard forms are not known to me – neither as existing specimens nor in paintings, not even in Saronno. But the similarity between this and Leonardo's instruments is so striking that it is not unlikely that Leonardo may have known these folk instruments in one form or another.

18   Manuscript H, fols. 28r, 28v, 45v, 46r; Manuscript B, fol. 50v; and Codex Atlanticus, fol. 218r-c.

19   For a detailed account and interpretation of the *viola organista* and a survey of more simple mechanical string instruments known in Leonardo's time, see E. Winternitz, "Leonardo's Invention of the Viola Organista."

20   See the detailed analysis in E. Winternitz, "The Role of Music in Leonardo's Paragone."

21   Theoretically the change could also be one of timbre; but this is not likely, since a difference between the four kinds of timbre would be small, and also since

Leonardo insists that his invention enables the bell to do the job of four bells, implying the effect of a carillon.

22   Hermann von Helmholtz, in his famous book *On the Sensations of Tone as a Physiological Basis for the Theory of Music* (Dover: New York, 1954), p. 72, did not rule out at least the possibility of areas of a bell producing tones of different pitch: "The deepest tone is not the strongest. The body of the bell when struck gives a deeper tone than the 'sound bow,' but the latter gives the loudest tone. Probably other vibrational forms of bells are also possible in which nodal circles are formed parallel to the margin. But these seems to be produced with difficulty and have not yet been examined." My own experiments with smaller and medium-sized bells in the collection of the Metropolitan Museum of Art in New York brought no conclusive results.

23   Another apparently original form of bellows is described in Manuscript B, fol. 81r. This bellows is made of wood, not using any leather – in the words of Leonardo, "like a sugar loaf with partition."

24   How much Leonardo was aware of the mechanical limitations of bellows is clear from an observation he made in quite a different realm: "If flies produced with their mouths the sound that can be heard when they fly, they would need a great pair of bellows for lungs in order to produce a wind so strong and long, and then there would be a long silence in order to draw into themselves an equal volume of air; therefore; where there was a long duration there would be a long intermission." Codex Arundel, fol. 257r.

25   The blowpipe, unbecoming to a lady's cheeks, was replaced by a dainty little bellows attached to her wrists. This was the case in the elegant and lavishly decorated musette, the fashionable bagpipe of the perfumed pseudo-shepherdesses in the *fêtes champêtres* of Versailles and Fontainebleau.

26   For the evolution and mechanism of bagpipes, including those of Leonardo's time, see E. Winternitz, "Bagpipes and Hurdy-Gurdies in their Social Setting," *The Metropolitan Museum of Art Bulletin* 2, 1943, pp. 56–83.

27   The text to the left and beneath the upper and lower sketch is largely cryptic, partly because of the use of this ambiguous term, which can mean the human elbow or certain parts of machines.

28   My colleague at the Metropolitan Museum, Dr. Olga Raggio, Chairman of Western European Arts, has kindly led my attention to the fact that similar hats occur in the embroideries after designs by Pollaiuolo in the Museo dell'Opera del Duomo in Florence. See Sascha Schwabacher, *Die Stickereien nach Entwürfen des Antonio Pollaiuolo in der Opera di S. Maria del Fiore zu Florenz* (Strassburg, 1911), especially pls. XIX, XXXI. The designs for the biblical scenes depicted there may also have been used for, or inspired by, the performances of sacred plays.

29   See E. Winternitz, "Instruments de musique étranges chez Filippino Lippi, Piero di Cosimo et Lorenzo Costa," *Les Fêtes de la Renaissance*, I (Paris, 1956), pp. 379–395.

THE MILITARY ARCHITECT

1   Codex Atlanticus, fol. 234v-b.

2   Windsor 12686r.

3   Manuscript L, fol. 80v.

4   Ibid., fols. 81v and 81r.

5   Ibid., fols. 82v, 83r, 83v, 84r.

6   Codex Atlanticus, fol. 130r-c.

7   Manuscript L, fol. 6v.

8   For example, fol. 46r.

9   Codex Madrid I, fols. 110v and 111r.

10   Codex Atlanticus, fols. 289 and 398r.

11   Codex Madrid II, fol. 25r.

12   Ibid., fol. 24v.

13   Ibid., fol. 125r.

14   Ibid., fols. 1v, 6r, 10r, 37v.

15   Ibid., fols. 9r, 15r, 21v, 24r, 25r, 32r (?), 36v, 38r, 38v, 62v bis, 64v.

16   Ibid., fols. 9r, 10r.

17   Ibid., fol. 32v.

18   Ibid., fol. 38r.

MACHINES AND WEAPONRY

1   Codex on the Flight of Birds, fol. 3r.

2   Theodor Beck in his *Beiträge zur Geschichte des Maschinenbaues* (Berlin, 1899) lists over 400 machines and devices. The Madrid Codices added hundreds more.

3   Cf. L. Reti, "The Double-acting Principle in East and West," *Technology of Culture*, vol. 11, pp. 178–200, 1970

4   Leonardo's intent is quite clear, but the mechanism as he sketched it is not fully functional.

5   F. M. Feldhaus, *Leonardo der Techniker und Erfinder* (Jena, 1913).

6   Chief engineer to the Duke of Urbino. He served with Leonardo on commissions to erect the *tiburio*, or central tower, of the Cathedral of Milan and to construct a cathedral at Pavia. A treatise on civil and military architecture, that he wrote and illustrated himself, now in the Laurenziana in Florence, has manuscript notes by Leonardo.

7   After the British artillery officer Henry Shrapnel, who lived from 1761 to 1842.

8   On fols. 51r, 53r, 54v, 59r, 59v, 131r, and 143r.

9   A. R. Hall, *Ballistics in the Seventeenth Century* (London, 1952), pp. 42, 83.

10   The term "accidental motion" is used in contradistinction to "natural motion."

11   See A. C. Crombie, *Augustine to Galileo* (London, 1952), pp. 254, 280, and Hall, op. cit. L. Reti deals with Leonardo's ballistics in "Il moto dei projetti e del pendolo secondo Leonardo e Galileo," *Le Macchine*, Milan, December 1968.

12   Tartaglia, *La nova scientia* (Venice, 1537).

13   Tartaglia, *Quesiti et inventioni diverse* (Venice, 1546).

14   Manuscript E, fol. 70v.

15   Galileo Galilei, *Dialogo . . . sopra i due massimi sistemi del mondo . . .* (Florence, 1632), in *Opere*, vol. VII, pp. 47, 177 ff.

16   E. Torricelli, *De motu gravium et proiectorum*, in *Opere* (Faenza, 1919), p. 157.

17   Ibid., p. 188.

18   See H. L. Peterson, *Pageant of the Gun* (New York, 1967), p. 18, and T. Lenk, *The Flintlock* (New York, 1965), p. 13, where Lenk says, "Most recent research accepts the Leonardo drawings as the earliest record of the wheel-lock and certain Italian combined crossbows and wheel-lock guns in the Palazzo Ducale, Venice, as the earliest surviving examples of the construction." This note appeared two years before the re-exposure of the Madrid Codices.

19   Codex Atlanticus, fols. 56v-b, 217r-a, 353r-c.

20   Cf. L. Reti, "Il Mistero dell'architronito," *Raccolta Vinciana*, fasc. XIX, pp. 171–183, 1962.

21   Codex Madrid I, fols. 26r, 84v.

22   Codex Atlanticus, fol. 198v.

THE MECHANICS OF WATER AND STONE

1   Codex Atlanticus, fol. 46r-b.

2   Codex Madrid I, fol. 169r.

3 Ibid., fols. 114v, 115r, 124v.

4 Ibid., fol. 125r.

5 In particular, fols. 114v and 115r.

6 Codex Madrid I, fol. 124v.

7 Ibid., fol. 115r.

8 Ibid., fol. 33r.

9 Ibid., fol. 150v.

10 Codex Atlanticus, fols. 20r, 206r-a, 351r-a. Codex Leicester, fol. 11r.

11 It is illustrated in Codex Madrid I, fol. 134v.

12 Manuscript F, fol. 53v. See also Manuscript F, fol. 0r, and Manuscript I, fol. 73v.

13 Codex Atlanticus, fol. 7r-b.

14 Codex Arundel, fol. 241r.

15 See Codex Madrid I, fol. 142v.

16 Ibid., fol. 140v; Codex Forster II₂, fol. 92r.

17 Codex Madrid I, fol. 143r.

18 Ibid., fol. 113v.

19 For example, ibid., fols. 139r, 139v, 140v.

20 Ibid., fol. 139r.

21 Ibid.

22 Ibid., fol. 84v.

TREATISE ON PAINTING

NOTE: The author of this chapter discussed the relation between Codex Madrid II and the *Treatise on Painting* also in "Les Notes de Leonardo de Vinci sur la peinture d'après le nouveau manuscrit de Madrid," *Revue de l'art*, no. 15, 1972.

1 In order to place the enterprise of the *Treatise on Painting* into the frame of the epoch, it is always necessary to consult J. Schlosser, *La Letteratura artistica* (first published in 1924, Italian ed. 1935, re-ed. Florence, 1956) and A. Blunt, *Artistic Theory in Italy 1450–1600* (Oxford, 1940; re-ed. 1956).

2 The chronological classification presented by A. M. Brizio, *Scritti scelti di Leonardo da Vinci* (Turin, 1952) reveals the technical nature of Leonardo's first writings (ballistics), and his philological (studies on vocabulary) and literary (fables) exercises.

3 He then tabulated all the different parts down to the smallest veins and the composition of the bones with extreme accuracy in order that this work on which he had spent so many years should be published from copper engravings for the benefit of art. Text in J. P. Richter, *The Literary Works of Leonardo da Vinci*, 2d ed. (London, 1939), vol. I, p. 3.

4 Edition procured by Domenichi at the publisher Giolito's. The work is dedicated to Salviati, a fact which is not without interest. His friend Doni calls his attention to it in a letter of June 3: "I have also seen Leon Battista Alberti's book on painting, translated by Domenichi and dedicated to you." Letter quoted in A. F. Doni's edition of Mario Pepe *Disegno* (Milan, 1970), p. 109.

5 J. Schlosser, *La Letteratura artistica*, Italian translation, 2d ed. (Florence, 1956), p. 126 ff. (the editions of Alberti), p. 251 ff. (the Vitruvian studies).

6 See A. Chastel, "Léonard et la culture," in *Léonard de Vinci et l'expérience scientifique* (Paris, 1963).

7 See E. Panofsky, "Artist, Scientist, Genius," in *The Renaissance: A Symposium* (New York, 1952).

8 L. Olschki, *Geschichte der neusprachlichen wissenschaftlichen Literatur*, vol. I, *Die Literatur der Technik* (Leipzig, 1919).

9 On the 2d of April 1489, book entitled "Of the human figure" Windsor 19059, and all the passages in A. M. Brizio, op. cit., p. 153.

10 Edition of C. Winterberg (Vienna, 1889), p. 33.

11 C. Pedretti, *Leonardo da Vinci on Painting: A Lost Book (Libro A)* (Berkeley, 1964). On the long elaboration of the *Treatise*, see the introduction to the Pedretti work, the introduction to Richter, op. cit., L. H. Heydenreich's introduction to the Princeton edition of the Codex Urbinas (1956).

12 Br.M.Ia, in Richter, op. cit., p. 112, no. 4.

13 "The years 1505–1508 represent a crucial point in the development of Leonardo as a theorist of art." Pedretti, op. cit., p. 20, note 32.

14 Fol. 15v.

15 Fols. 23v-28v, 70v-78v, and 125r-128r.

16 It is, however, difficult to specify the recording of the Madrid manuscript in the list carefully established and presented by Melzi; see Pedretti, op. cit., app. I, p. 229 ff.

17 These connections with the Codex Urbinas have been closely examined in Pedretti, *Le Note di pittura di Leonardo da Vinci nei manoscritti inediti a Madrid*, Lettura Vinciana VIII (Florence, 1968).

18 Fol. 15v.

19 J. White, *The Birth and Rebirth of Pictorial Space* (London, 1957), p. 207 ff. D. Gioseffi, *Perspectiva artificialis* (Trieste, 1957). C. Pedretti, "Leonardo on Curvilinear Perspective," in *Bibl. Humanisme et Renaissance*, vol. XXV, p. 584 ff., 1963. Final text of Manuscript E, fol. 16v, in Richter, op. cit., nos. 107 and 108.

20 Fol. 25v.

21 Fol. 60v.

22 C. Pedretti, "La Battaglia d'Anghiari," *L'Arte*, 1968, pp. 62–73.

23 Fol. 78v.

24 Fol. 128.

25 A. E. Popham, *The Drawings of Leonardo* (London, 1946), pl. 237. K. Clark, *The Drawings of Leonardo da Vinci at Windsor Castle*, 2d ed. revised with the assistance of C. Pedretti, vol. I (London, 1968–1969), p. 135, suggests for Windsor 12640 possible dating after *Anghiari*, which is difficult to accept.

26 K. Clark, "Leonardo and the Antique," in *Leonardo's Legacy: An International Symposium* (Berkeley and Los Angeles, 1969).

27 Fol. 70v.

28 Fol. 128r.

29 Fols. 116v-117v.

30 B.N. 2038, fol. 33v.

31 Manuscript L, fol. 79r, taken up again in the Codex Urbinas, fol. 118v. See C. Pedretti, *Leonardo da Vinci on Painting*, p. 135.

32 Fol. 20.

33 Fol. 71r.

34 Windsor 19032v.

35 Fol. 26r. The subject is taken up again in the Codex Urbinas, fol. 117.

36 Vasari, *Proemio* of the third part. See A. Chastel, *Le grand atelier d'Italie* (Paris, 1965), p. 321 ff.

37 M. Kemp, "Il Concetto dell'anima in Leonardo's Early Skull Studies," *Journal of the Warburg and Courtauld Institutes*, vol. XXIV, pp. 115–136, 1971. On the subject of the cranial sections of 1489, see Windsor 19057r.

38 Fol. 26r.

39 Fols. 24-25.

40 R. Marcolongo, *Leonardo da Vinci, artista, scienziato* (Milan, 1930), p. 169 ff.

41 Fol. 71r.

42 Fol. 70v.

43 Fol. 26r.

44 Fol. 25v.

45 Fol. 71v.

46 M. Rzepinska, "Light and Shadow in the Late Writings of Leonardo da Vinci," *Raccolta Vinciana*, fasc. XIV, pp. 250–266, 1962.

47 Codex Urbinas, fol. 40 ff.

48 Fol. 26r.

49 Fol. 127v.

50 E. H. Gombrich, "Light Form and Texture in XVth Century Painting," *Journal of the Royal Society of Arts*, 1964, pp. 826–849. The connections of Leonardo's art with that of the Flemish artists remain to be investigated, bearing in mind the familiarity of the Italian word with Northern painting at the end of the 15th century and the opposition of the two mentalities. Some indications are given in A. Chastel, *Le grand atelier*, p. 275 ff.

51 Fol. 125r.

52 J. Sherman, "Leonardo's Colour and Chiaroscuro," *Zeitschrift für Kunstgeschichte*, vol. XXV, pp. 13–47, 1962.

53 Fol. 26v.

54 Fol. 127v.

HOROLOGY

1 Windsor 19106. The first part of the phrase was read by the editors of vol. III of the Quaderni d'Anatomia (Christiania: Dybwad, 1913), fol. 12v, as *Ho sparto le mie ore*, and translated accordingly as "I have wasted my hours." There is no need to recollect all the drivel that followed such a stupendous confession. The apparently canceled line which follows – *son generate* – was not related to the previous one until Carlo Pedretti recognized as a sundial the sketch near the writing and read the sentence correctly, revealing a beautiful pun on *sol* meaning "sun" and *sol*, or *solo*, meaning "only." For the line can also be read as referring to the lover who lives only for his beloved. See Carlo Pedretti, *Studi Vinciani* (Geneva: Droz, 1957), p. 6.

2 Ladislao Reti, "Il Moto dei proietti e del pendolo secondo Leonardo e Galilei," *Le Machine*, vol. I, no. 2–3, pp. 28–29, 1968.

3 See Ladislao Reti, "Non si volta chi a stella è fisso," *Bibl. d'Humanisme et Renaissance*, tome XXI, pp. 26–32, 1959.

4 Silvio A. Bedini and Francis R. Maddison, "Mechanical Universe" (the astrarium of Giovanni de' Dondi), *Transactions of the American Philosophical Society*, new ser., vol. 56, part 5, pp. 29–37, 1966.

5 Manuscript L, fol. 92v. Derek J. De Solla Price, "Leonardo da Vinci and the Clock of Giovanni de Dondi," *Antiquarian Horology*, vol. 2, no. 7, pp. 127–128, 1958; H. Alan Lloyd, "Letter to the Editor," *Antiquarian Horology*, vol. 2, no. 10, p. 199, 1959; and Price, "Letter to the Editor," *Antiquarian Horology*, vol. 2, no. 11, p. 222, 1959. See also Bedini and Maddison, op. cit., pp. 31–33.

6 Manuscript L, fol. 93v.

7 Codex Atlanticus, fols. 27v-a and 366r-b. *Leonardo da Vinci: Fragments at Windsor Castle from the Codex Atlanticus*, edited by Carlo Pedretti (London: Phaidon, 1957), pp. 39–40.

8 Francesco Malaguzzi Valeri, *La Corte di Lodovico Il Moro* (Milan: Hoepli, 1915), vol. I, *La Vita privata e l'arte*, p. 657, and vol. II, *Bramante e Leonardo da Vinci*, p. 162. Bedini and Maddison, op. cit., pp. 33–36.

9 The abbot of Chiaravalle, Reverendo Padre Giovanni Maria Rosavini, kindly arranged the search in which the chronicle was found. The part of the chronicle dealing with the Chiaravalle clock was presented by Jean-Baptiste De Toni, in "Léonard et l'horloge de Chiaravalle," in *Léonard de Vinci* (Rome: Nouvelle Revue d'Italie, 1919), pp. 230–235. However, he

ignored the existence of the original chronicle and used a transcription he found in the Biblioteca Brera in Milan. Apparently Antonio Simoni used the same Brera document in his reconstruction of the Chiaravalle clock. Simoni, "Le Sfere italiane e la trasmissione ad angolo retto," *La Clessidra*, May, 1968.

10 Leonardo da Vinci, *The Manuscripts of Leonardo da Vinci Codex I (8937) at the Biblioteca Nacional of Madrid*, transcribed, translated, and annotated by Ladislao Reti (New York: McGraw-Hill, 1974).

11 Codex Madrid I, fols. 4v, 11r, 79v.

12 Ibid., fol. 9v.

13 Antonio di Tuccio di Marabottino Manetti, *Vita di Filippo di Ser Brunellescho* (Florence: E. Toesca, 1927), p. 19. The original is in Florence, Biblioteca Nazionale Centrale, Manuscript II II.325. See also C. von Fabriczy, *Filippo Brunelleschi* (Stuttgart, 1892).

14 Frank D. Prager, "Brunelleschi's Clock?," *Physis*, vol. X, fasc. 3, pp. 203–216, 1968.

15 Ladislao Reti, "Leonardo on Bearings and Gears," *Scientific American*, vol. 224, no. 2, pp. 100–110, February 1971.

16 Codex Atlanticus, fols. 296r-a and 371v-b.

17 Ibid., fol. 30v-a.

18 Codex Forster I, fol. 13r.

19 Codex Madrid I, fol. 48v.

20 Ibid., fol. 1v.

21 Ibid., fol. 32r.

22 Ibid., fol. 145v.

23 Silvio A. Bedini, "The One-wheeled Clock, and Clocks Having Two and Three Wheels," *La Suisse Horlogère*, vol. 77, no. 4, pp. 23–34, December 1962, and vol. 78, no. 1, pp. 27–40, April 1963.

24 For a detailed discussion of the clock for the Pitti Palace, see Silvio A. Bedini, *Johann Philipp Treffler, Clockmaker of Augsburg*, separate publication of the National Association of Watch and Clock Collectors (1956), pp. 9–10; and Silvio A. Bedini, "Galileo Galilei and the Measure of Time," in *Saggi su Galileo Galilei* (Florence: Barbera, 1967), pp. 27–28. The original drawing of the Pitti Palace clockwork is preserved at Leiden, Bibliothek der Rijksuniversiteit, Huy. 45", Bouilliau ad Christiaan Huygens (Jan. 15, 1660).

25 Dutch patent, June 16, 1657, described in C. Huygens, *Horologium* (Hag. Com., 1658).

26 Manuscript It. IV. 41-5363. Particularly significant is the analysis of the manuscript by Carlo Pedretti, who found in it a number of references to Leonardo and to machines and devices originally constructed by him. Pedretti, *Studi Vinciani*, pp. 23–33.

27 Those on the affirmative side included M. A. Ronna, *Léonard de Vinci: Peintre, ingénieur, hydraulicien* (Paris, 1902), p. 71; F. M. Feldhaus, "Das Pendel in Maschinenbau und Erfindung der Penduluhr," *Deutsche Uhrmacher Zeitung*, n. 13, Stuttgart, 1908, and "Das Pendel bei Leonardo da Vinci," *Deutsche Uhrmacher Zeitung*, n. 15, 1909; and L. Reverchon, "Le Pendule de Léonard de Vinci," *Revue chronométrique*, vol. 59, no. 678, p. 41, 1913. Even a future Pope entered the discussion: Achille Ratti, "L'Apolicazione del pendolo al meccanismo degli orologi," *Raccolta Vinciana*, fasc. VI, pp. 131–133, 1910. A. Favaro was one who approached the problem with measured criticism, in his "Adversaria Galilaeana," *Atti e memori della R. Accademia di Scienze, Lettere ed Arti di Padova*, vol. XXXII, p. 123, 1916. The fact that Feldhaus finally withdrew his claim – in *Deutsche Uhrmacher Zeitung*, Stuttgart, 1952 – apparently ended the controversy. But Enrico Morpurgo later brought up the problem again in a book and several articles published in 1958. Morpurgo, *L'Orologio e il pendolo* (Rome: Ed. La Clessidra, 1957), and "The Clock and the Pendulum," *Antiquarian Horology*, vol. 2, no. 8, p. 138, London, 1958.

28 Ladislao Reti, "The Leonardo da Vinci Codices in the Biblioteca Nacional of Madrid," *Technology and Culture*, vol. 8, p. 437, Chicago, 1967; "Die wiedergefundenen Leonardo Manuskripts der Biblioteca Nacional in Madrid," *Technikgeschichte*, vol. 34, p. 193, Düsseldorf, 1967; and "The Two Unpublished Manuscripts of Leonardo da Vinci in the Biblioteca Nacional of Madrid," *Burlington Magazine*, vol. CX, pp. 10–22 and 81–89, London, 1968. See also note 2.

29 Codex Atlanticus, fols. 216v-b and 388v-a.

30 We personally are indebted to Dr. Klaus Maurice for the beautiful working model of the stackfreed-like cam device Leonardo depicted in Codex Madrid I, which Dr. Maurice kindly made for Dr. Reti.

The evolution of the Horstmann–Clifford silent magnetic escapement to modern clocks is presented in detail in H. Alan Lloyd, *Some Outstanding Clocks over Seven Hundred Years 1250-1950* (London: Leonardo Hill Books, 1958), pp. 145–150.

31 Codex Madrid I, fols. 9r, 60v, 61v, 132v, 133r. See introduction to Leonardo da Vinci, *The Manuscripts of Leonardo da Vinci, Codex Madrid I (8937)*.

32 Britten's *Old Clocks and Watches and Their Makers*, 7th ed. (New York: Bonanza Books, 1956), p. 71.

33 Codex Atlanticus, fol. 385r-b.

34 See Ladislao Reti, "Il Moto dei Proietti e del pendolo," p. 19.

35 For instance, fols. 11v and 157v.

36 Augusto Marinoni, "Tempo armonico o musicale di Leonardo da Vinci," *Lingua nostra*, vol. XVI, p. 45, Florence, 1955.

37 G. Galilei, *Opere*, vol. VII, p. 177.

38 Piero Ariotti, "Galileo on the Isochrony of the Pendulum," *Isis*, vol. 59, part 4, no. 199, pp. 414–436, 1968.

39 Harrison invented the gridiron pendulum, while the priority of the anchor escapement is attributed by some scholars to Clement and by others to Hooke. Cf. Britten's op. cit., p. 72.

ELEMENTS OF MACHINES

1 Gerolamo Calvi, *Notizie dei principali professori di belle arti che fiorirono in Milano durante il governo de' Visconti e degli Sforza*, part III: Leonardo da Vinci (Milan, 1869).

2 Luca Beltrami, *Documenti e memorie riguardanti la vita e le opere di Leonardo da Vinci* (Milan, 1919), no. 108. See also no. 107.

3 Manuscript L, fol. 66r.

4 J. P. Richter, *The Literary Works of Leonardo da Vinci*. 2d ed. (London, 1939), vol. II, p. 215, no. 1109.

5 *Le Vite de' piu eccellenti architetti, pittori et scultori* (1st ed. Florence, 1550; 2d ed. 1568). English translation by A. B. Hinds, edited with an introduction by William Gaunt (London: Everyman's Library, 1927; last reprint 1963), Giorgio Vasari, vol. 4, p. 122.

6 Franz Babinger, "Vier Bauvorschläge Leonardo da Vinci's an Sultan Bajezid II. (1502/3) mit einem Beitrag von Ludwig H. Heydenreich," *Nachrichten der Akad. der Wissensch. in Göttingen*, Philologisch – Hist. Klasse, Jahrg. 1952, no. 1, pp. 1–20.

7 Manuscript L, fols. 34v, 35r, 35v, 36r.

8 Ibid., fol. 25v.

9 In *Le Vite de' piu eccellenti architetti, pittori et scultori* (1st ed. Florence, 1550; 2d ed. 1568). English translation by A. B. Hinds, edited with an introduction by William Gaunt (London: Everyman's Library, 1927; last reprint, 1963), vol. 2, pp. 156–168. In the following excerpts Hinds's generally excellent translation has been slightly modified.

10 The memoirs, part of Codex H227 inf. of the Biblioteca Ambrosiana of Milan, have been transcribed by Luigi Gramatica as *Le Memorie su Leonardo da Vinci di Don Ambrogio Mazenta* (Milan: Alfieri & Lacroix, 1919).

11 Leo Olschki, *The Genius of Italy* (London, Gollancz, 1950), p. 308.

12 Translated from "Leonard de Vinci et la technique de son temps," in *Léonard de Vinci & l'expérience scientifique au seizième siècle* (Paris: Centre National de la Recherche Scientifique – Presses Universitaries, 1952), p. 146.

13 Joseph Needham, *Science and Civilisation in China*, vol. IV: 2 (London: Cambridge, 1965), p. 383: "When Leonardo faces the problem of interconversion in the late 15th century, nearly two hundred years after Wang Chen, he shows, as Gille has acutely pointed out, that most curious disinclination to use the eccentric (or crank), connecting-rod and piston-rod combination. In fact he does so only for a mechanical saw. In order to avoid it he has recourse time after time to the most complicated and improbable devices."

14 Fol. 86r.

15 H. W. Dickinson, *James Watt* (London: Cambridge, 1936), p. 124.

16 Franz Reuleaux, *The Kinematics of Machinery*, new ed., with an introduction by Eugene Ferguson (New York: Dover, 1963), p. 9. 1st German ed. 1875; English translation by A. B. W. Kennedy 1876.

17 See Theodor Beck, *Beiträge zur Geschichte des Maschinenbaues* (Berlin, 1899), and Abbot Payson Usher, *A History of Mechanical Inventions*, rev. ed. (Cambridge: Harvard, 1954).

18 Reuleaux, op. cit., p. 437.

19 Ibid., p. 580.

20 Codex Madrid I, fol. 82r.

21 Codex Atlanticus, fol. 155v-b.

22 Leonardo da Vinci, *I Libri di meccanica*, nella recostruzione ordinata di Arturo Uccelli (Milan: Hoepli, 1940).

23 Codex Madrid I, fol. 96v.

24 Codex Atlanticus, fol. 164r-a.

25 Codex Madrid I, fol. 97v.

26 Codex Atlanticus, fol. 207v-b.

27 Charles Plumier, *L'Art de tourner* (Paris, 1701).

28 Guido Ucelli, *Le Navi di Nemi* (Rome: Libr. dello Stato, 1955), pp. 191–195.

29 Manuscript B, fol. 33v.

30 Georgius Agricola, *De re metallica*, translated from the first Latin ed. of 1556 by H. H. Hoover and L. H. Hoover (London, 1912), p. 173.

31 Codex Forster III, fol. 89v.

32 Jacob Leupold, *Theatrum Machinarum Generale* (Leipzig: C. Zuntel, 1724).

33 I had a reconstruction made according to Leonardo's drawings on Codex Atlanticus fol. 351r-a, dated probably around 1500. The work was carried out by Dr. Sinibaldo Parrini, the well-known scientific instrument rebuilder of Florence, using a 14th-century bell. The result could not have been more satisfactory.

34 English translation by Maria Teach Gnudi and Cyril Stanley Smith.

35 I went to Metz to see the bell arrangement, but I was not allowed to go up to the tower because of the dangers. Dr. Ludolf von Mackensen of the Deutsches Museum in Munich was more fortunate, and I am very grateful to him for the helpful photographs he was able to take.

36 Marcel Aubert, *La Cathédrale de Metz* (Paris: Picard, 1931), pp. 251–263.

37 Codex Atlanticus, fol. 370r, datable around 1495.

NOTE: Phaidon Press Limited, London, has kindly given permission to reprint the various excerpts of translations from Jean Paul Richter, *The Literary Works of Leonardo da Vinci*, 2d ed. (London, 1939).

LIST OF ILLUSTRATIONS

The folios from the following manuscripts by Leonardo da Vinci are reproduced with the kind permission of the institutions listed below:

Codex Arundel: The Trustees of the British Museum, London.
Codex Atlanticus: Biblioteca Ambrosiana, Milan (page numbering of Pompeo Leoni).
Codex on the Flight of Birds: Biblioteca Reale, Turin.
Codex Forster I, II, III: Crown Copyright, Victoria & Albert Museum, London.
Codex Madrid I and Codex Madrid II: Biblioteca Nacional, Madrid, and McGraw-Hill Book Company, New York.
Manuscripts A, B, C, D, E, F, G, H, I, L, M, B.N. 2037, 2038: Institut de France, Paris.
Codex Urbinas: Vatican Library, Rome.
Windsor Collection: Royal Library, Windsor. By Gracious Permission of Her Majesty Queen Elizabeth II.

THE PAINTER

THE WRITER

213/2 Arches. Ms. A 53r.

213/3 Arches. Madrid I 139r.

213/4 Study on the bending of springs. Madrid I 84v.

213/5 Portrait of Johann Bernoulli, engraving from M.–M. Bousquet dated 1743. Schweizerisches Landesmuseum, Zurich.

214/1 Dome of Milan Cathedral. Photo Anderson. American Heritage Photographic Service.

214/2 Study for the cupola of Milan Cathedral. Atlanticus 310v-b.

215/1 Study for the cupola of Milan Cathedral. Atlanticus 310r-b.

TREATISE ON PAINTING

216/1 Frontispiece of *Trattato della pittura di Lionardo da Vinci* by Rafaelle du Fresne. Bibliothèque Nationale, Paris.

217/1 Frontispiece of *L'Architettura di Leonbatista Alberti*. Bibliothèque Nationale, Paris.

217/2 First folio of *L. Vitruvii Pollionis ad Caesarem Agustum de architectura: Liber primus*. Ambrosiana, Milan.

217/3 *De divina proportione* by Luca Pacioli. Ambrosiana, Milan.

217/4 Frontispiece of *La Pittura di Leonbatista Alberti*. Ambrosiana, Milan.

217/5 Frontispiece of *Ludo Demontiosii* by Pompeius Gauricus. Ambrosiana, Milan.

217/6 First folio of *De re aedificatoria* by Leonbatista Alberti. Ambrosiana, Milan.

218/1–3 Details from *Leda and the Swan* by unknown artist. Galleria Borghese, Rome. Scala.

219/1 Portrait of Leobaptista Alberti, coin. British Museum, London.

219/2 Arno landscape by Leonardo. Uffizi, Florence. Scala.

220/1 Detail of *Lady with an Ermine* by Leonardo. Czartoryski Gallery, Cracow. Scala.

220/2 Detail of the portrait of Ginevra de'Benci by Leonardo. National Gallery, Washington, D.C. Scala.

221/1 Portrait of Beatrice d'Este by Leonardo. Ambrosiana, Milan.

222/1 Detail from text on Madrid II 25v.

222/2 Detail from text on Madrid II 26r.

222/3 Detail from text on Madrid II 71r.

222/4 Detail from text on Madrid II 71v.

223/1 Extract from Codex Urbinas No. 444.

223/2 Extract from Codex Urbinas No. 189.

223/3 Extract from Codex Urbinas No. 523.

223/4 Extract from Codex Urbinas No. 452.

224/1 Perspective study for the *Adoration of the Magi* by Leonardo. Uffizi, Florence. Alinari.

224/2 Detail from a map. Windsor 12683.

225/1 Study of perspective in a painting. Madrid II 15v.

225/2 Study of perspective. Ms. E 16v.

225/3 Study of perspective. Ms. E 16v.

226/1 Diagram of Sala del Gran Consiglio, Palazzo Vecchio, Florence, reconstructing the location of the *Battle of Anghiari*. The Warburg Institute, London.

226/2 Reconstruction of the *Battle of Anghiari* by Carlo Pedretti.

227/1 Detail from the copy of the *Battle of Anghiari* by Rubens. Louvre, Paris.

228/1 Anatomical sketch. Windsor 19032v.

228/2 Anatomical sketches. Windsor 19001v.

229/1 Anatomical sketch. Windsor 19001v.

229/2 Anatomical sketches. Windsor 19003v.

230/1 Study for the *Battle of Cascina* by Michelangelo. British Museum, London.

230/2 Drawing of a nude man. Windsor 12640.

231/1 Study for a Libyan sibyl by Michelangelo. The Metropolitan Museum of Art, New York, Joseph Pulitzer Bequest, 1924.

232/1 *Resurrection* by Signorelli. Duomo, Orvieto. Scala.

233/1 Sketches for optical research. Madrid II 25v.

233/2–3 Sketches for optical research. Ms. D 8r.

233/4 Schematic diagram of the eye. Atlanticus 377r-a.

233/5 Model of sight. Ms. D 3v.

234/1 Head of Leda from *Leda and the Swan* by unknown artist. Galleria Borghese, Rome. Scala.

234/2 Head of St. Anne from *St. Anne and the Virgin* by Leonardo. Louvre, Paris.

234/3 Head of *Mona Lisa* by Leonardo. Louvre, Paris.

235/1 *Leda and the Swan* by unknown artist. Galleria Borghese, Rome. Scala.

236/1 Study on the effects of light. Windsor 12604r.

237/1 Study on the effects of light. Madrid II 71v.

237/2 Study on the effects of light. Madrid II 23v.

237/3 Study on the effects of light. Madrid II 71r.

237/4 Study on the effects of light. Ms. B.N. 2038 13v.

237/5 Study on the effects of light. Ms. B.N. 2038 14r.

237/6 Study on the effects of light. Ms. B.N. 2038 15r.

238/1 Angel. Detail from the *Madonna di Senigallia* by Piero della Francesca. Palazzo Ducale, Urbino. Scala.

238/2 Detail from the triptych of Jean de Sédano by Gérard David. Louvre, Paris. Service de Documentation de la Réunion des Musées Nationaux.

239/1 Angel. Detail from the *Virgin of the Rocks* by Leonardo. National Gallery, London.

239/2 Angel. Detail from the *Nativity with the Infant St. John* by Piero di Cosimo. National Gallery of Art, Washington, D.C.

HOROLOGY

240/1 Sketch of a sundial. Windsor 19106v.

240/2 Time glass from the 16th century. Collection R. Gest, Beauvais.

241/1 Studies for a water clock. Atlanticus 343v-a.

241/2 Drawing of a time glass. Arundel 191v.

241/3 Alarm clock built by Frà Damiano Zambelli. Basilica di San Domenico, Bologna. Photo Villani.

242/1 Sundial in front of Chartres Cathedral. Giraudon.

242/2 Astrological chart with 12 signs of the zodiac. Ms. 722 fol. 18. Pierpont Morgan Library, New York.

243/1 Spring-powered clocks and fusee. Ms. IV 111 fol. 13v. Bibliothèque Royale Albert 1er, Bruxelles.

244/1 Miniature representing Richard of Wellingford with astronomical clock. Ms. Cotton Nero D. vii fol. 20r. British Museum.

244/2–4 Three views of the Persian astrolabe made by Muhammad b. Abi Bakr in 1221–1222. Museum of the History of Science, Oxford.

245/1 Drawing for the astrarium by Giovanni de'Dondi. Ms. Laud Misc. 620 fol. 10v. Bodleian Library, Oxford.

245/2 Part of a late Gothic astrolabe. Museum of the History of Science, Oxford.

245/3 Sketch of an astronomical clock dial. Ms. L 92v.

246/1 Drawing of the astrarium's dial of Venus by Giovanni de'Dondi. Ms. Laud Misc. 620 fol. 44r. Bodleian Library, Oxford.

246/2–4 Three dials on the working model of the astrarium. Smithsonian Institution, Washington D.C.

246/5 Study for an astronomical clock. Atlanticus 366r-b.

246/6 Annular gear of the Venus dial. Madrid I 14r.

246/7 Sketch of a gear-train. Madrid I 112r.

247/1 Model of de Dondi's astrarium by H. Alan Lloyd, 1960. Museum of History and Technology, Smithsonian Institution, Washington, D.C.

247/2 Model of de Dondi's astrarium by Luigi Pippa, 1963. National Museum of Science and Technology, Milan.

247/3 Sketch of a dial from an astronomical clock. Ms. L 93v.

248/1 Monastery of Chiaravalle. Photo Enit.

248/2 Sketch of a clock tower. Atlanticus 397r-b.

248/3 Sketch of axles within axles. Madrid I 11v.

248/4 Palazzo Visconteo in Pavia. Alinari.

248/5 Drawing of a geared mechanism. Atlanticus 399v-b.

249/1 Drawing of a weight-driven clockwork. Madrid I 27v.

249/2 Sketch of a wheelwork of a clock. Atlanticus 348v-d.

249/3 Study for a striking mechanism. Madrid I 27v.

249/4 Study for a striking mechanism. Madrid I 10v.

249/5 Sketch of a lunar mechanism. Madrid I 10v.

249/6 Drawing of pulleys. Madrid I 27r.

250/1 Sketch of a counterweight system. Madrid I 36v.

250/2 Sketch of a spring-making device. Madrid I 14v.

250/3 Sketches of springs. Madrid I 85r.

250/4 Sketch of a fusee. Madrid I 85r.

251/1 *Clock of Wisdom*. Ms. 43657, Fr. 455 fol. 9. Bibliothèque Nationale, Paris.

252/1 Sketch of a series of springs and fusees. Ms. B 50v.

252/2 Drawing of a volute gear on the spring barrel. Madrid I 4r.

252/3 Drawing of a volute gear. Madrid I 16r.

252/4 Drawing of a volute gear. Madrid I 14r.

253/1 Drawing of a stackfreed. Author's collection.

253/2 Sketches of two mechanisms similar to the stackfreed. Ms. M 81r.

253/3 Drawing of a completed stackfreed mechanism. Madrid I 13v.

253/4–5 Sketches of roller pinions. Madrid I 10v.

253/6 Drawing of a tempered spring. Madrid I 45r.

254/1 Drawing of an alarm or striking mechanism of a clock. Madrid I 15r.

254/2 Drawing of a screw mechanism. Madrid I 18v.

255/1 Drawing of a screw instrument. Madrid I 19r.

255/2 Sketches of pallets. Madrid I 115v.

256/1 Sketch of four shapes for the foliot crosspiece. Madrid I 98v.

256/2 Sketch of a two-vaned fly. Madrid I 8r.

256/3 Sketch of a one-wheeled clock. Madrid I 115v.

257/1 Sketch of a mechanism with fly. Atlanticus 278r-b.

257/2 Drawing of model of Galileo Galilei's pendulum. Biblioteca Nazionale Centrale, Florence. Photo Sansoni.

257/3 Drawing of clock at the Palazzo Pitti. Ms. Hug. 45. Royal University Library, Leiden.

258/1 Sketch of a silent escapement with pendulum. Madrid I 8r.

258/2–3 Variations on the sinusoidal-track arrangement. Madrid I 157v.

258/4 Sinusoidal cam in magnetic arrangement. Published in *Horological Journal*, 1948.

259/1 Sketches of two pendulum mechanisms. Madrid I 61v.

260/1 Sketch of a driving drum. Madrid I 9r.

260/2 Early English clock. Drawing in *Old Clocks and Watches and Their Makers* by Britten, 1956.

260/3 Pendulum-regulated clockwork by Christian Huygens. Museum of the History of Science, Leiden.

260/4 Sketch of a metronome-like mechanism. Arundel 191v.

261/1 Sketch of pinwheel escapement. Madrid I 27r.

INDEX

Note: Page numbers in *italics* refer to illustrations.

PUBLISHER'S ACKNOWLEDGMENTS

Professor Ladislao Reti
conceived of this book and was its Editor.
His untimely death on October 25, 1973,
at a time when the book
started to go to press,
ended a distinguished career in Vincian scholarship.
We deeply regret that he did not see
the final fruits of his labor.

Undoubtedly, there are many people
whom Dr. Reti would have wished to thank
for their contributions to the book,
most particularly the authors
whose essays appear here
for their generous cooperation
and outstanding scholarship.
Assisting Dr. Reti throughout his work
on the book, in translating various essays
into English and in preparing his own essay,
was Alan Morgan.

There are certainly many other people
who aided Dr. Reti in his research
and in his role as Editor
whose names unfortunately
are not known to us
but to whom the publisher is most grateful.

Assisting in the editing
and production processes of the book
were the following individuals:
Managing Editor: Floyd Yearout
Copy Editor: Hunt Cole
Proofreader: Antonia Stires
Production Supervisor: Francine Peeters
Layout Assistant: Robert Tobler
Introduction: Aline Wolff
Index: Delight Ansley
Translator of "The Words of Leonardo":
Marianne Shapiro
Maps and charts: Franz Coray
Reconstruction of the bicycle: Antonio Calegari